# PLAYFAIR
## FOOTBALL ANNUAL
## 2001–2002

54th edition

Editors: Glenda Rollin and
Jack Rollin

D1341070

**HEADLINE**

Copyright © 2001 HEADLINE BOOK PUBLISHING

First published in 2001
by HEADLINE BOOK PUBLISHING

10 9 8 7 6 5 4 3 2 1

**Cover photographs** Front and spine: David Beckham (Manchester United);
back: Marcus Stewart (Ipswich Town) – both *Actionimages*.

ISBN 0 7472 6621 2

Typeset by Wearset, Boldon, Tyne and Wear

Printed and bound in Great Britain by
Clays Ltd, St Ives plc

HEADLINE BOOK PUBLISHING
A division of Hodder Headline
338 Euston Road
London NW1 3BH

www.headline.co.uk
www.hodderheadline.com

# CONTENTS

## European and International Football

## Other Football

## Information and Records

# EDITORIAL

An apparently improving England squad under the direction of new Swedish born coach Sven-Goran Eriksson and a buoyant Premier League which returned a further increase in overall attendances during 2000–01, might lead everyone to believe the game to be in such a healthy state that it needs no investigation to the contrary.

When Eriksson was appointed, there was criticism in many quarters that it was a retrograde step to give the job to a foreigner. In the short term he has won respect and given respectability to the national team. There is still a long way to go in the actual matter of qualifying for the 2002 World Cup finals, but it is a start.

In the Premier League, which is to have a new sponsor in Barclaycard, the final crowd figures for the season showed an increase of 6.89 percent on 1999–2000. The aggregate attendances were 12,472,094 compared with 11,668,497. The weekend of 5 May 2001 produced 362,784, a record for the competition. It beat the previous total of 359,168 established over the weekend of 20 January 2001.

While events at the top seem to be running along in a satisfactory manner there are problems lower down which need to be addressed. Continuing disappointment at intermediate levels for the national set-up represent a worry for the future. To be comprehensively beaten 4-0 at home by the Spanish Under-21 team and losing 3-1 to Greece at the same level indicates a serious deficiency, even allowing for the changes of personnel which this type of match produces.

Moreover the call on the services of international players at all levels is increasing and to seemingly little good effect. The staging of the European Under-16 Championship finals in this country was a further disappointment in that the players selected attached to Premier and Football League clubs could only manage to figure in fourth place. The calls on young players also continues to escalate. The Under-16's completed a staggering 24 fixtures during the season!

With a winter which saw water levels rising alarmingly to disrupt fixture lists, the necessity for non-league clubs to pay more and more money for players leaving less to be spent on pitches, the Football Association's decision in 1974 to abandon amateur status and by the same token to encourage the growth of semi-professional football, has presented the grass roots game with a dilemma. In addition, the FA's banning of artificial pitches was another retrograde step, given the advances in preparing surfaces which would have withstood overplaying and the ravages of the elements. Happily, FIFA have now decided that plastic has a future after all.

Naturally heavy downpours of rain on artificial surfaces can present a different situation, but there is technology available to remove excess water quickly and efficiently. In many non-league circles there is a lack of imagination when fixture lists are produced. Not enough advantage is taken of the early season months when the grounds are hard and can withstand any premature adversity. FIFA still insists that it wants a calendar season to apply one day, meaning the game should be played universally from February to December!

Then there is the need for this welter of semi-professionalism to be afforded more opportunities of progressing into full-time through the Football League. This body is now being squeezed to some extent from both sides; the Premier and the Conference. Having rejected the latter's plea for two instead of one club to be accommodated in a two-up, two-down scheme, the League want more financial guarantees before they entertain the idea. Last season the League co-opted Conference clubs into its Associate Members Cup, known as the LDV Vans Trophy, so there is some common ground between the two bodies. Also the Conference has gone ahead by announcing plans for a shake-up of its own structure with the introduction of play-offs. This would see the winners of the League season having to meet the winners of play-offs between clubs finishing second to fourth respectively, a revolutionary move indeed.

Fiscal requirements remain a dominating factor all round. The bench mark for players at the highest level is now around £50,000 a week. The expectations lower down grow accordingly. While money continues to flow in from TV and other communications it will be seen to be manageable, but the majority of clubs are living beyond their means.

# STOP PRESS

**Top Transfers:** The world transfer record was broken on 9 July 2001 when Real Madrid signed Zinedine Zidane from Juventus for £47.7 million. There were other high priced deals pending during the summer months, including Gianluigi Buffon from Parma to Juventus for £34m; Rui Costa, Fiorentina to AC Milan £25.9m; Lilian Thuram, Parma to Juventus £25.9m; Filippo Inzaghi, Juventus to AC Milan £25.9m and Pavel Nedved, Lazio to Juventus £25.9m. Manchester United broke the British record by signing Juan Sebastien Veron from Lazio for £28.1m and this, after £19m for Ruud Van Nistelrooy from PSV Eindhoven. Aston Villa replaced David James, a £3.5m transfer to West Ham United, by securing Peter Schmeichel from Sporting Lisbon.

**Arsenal:** Francis Jeffers (Everton) £10m; Giovanni Van Bronckhorst (Rangers) £8.5m; Richard Wright (Ipswich T) £6m; Sol Campbell (Tottenham H) Free. **Aston Villa:** Hassan Kachloul (Southampton) Free; Giovanni Sperenza (Eintracht Frankfurt) Free; Mustapha Hadji (Coventry C) – deal includes Julian Joachim + £2m. **Blackburn R:** Corrado Grabbi (Ternana) £6.75m; Gordon Greer (Clyde) £200,000. **Bolton W:** Henrik Pedersen (Silkeborg) £650,000; Nicky Southall (Gillingham) Free; Djibril Diawara (Torino) Loan. **Charlton Ath:** Jason Euell (Wimbledon) £4.75m; Shaun Bartlett (Zurich) £2m. **Chelsea:** Frank Lampard (West Ham U) £11m; Emmanuel Petit (Barcelona) £7.5m; William Gallas (Marseille) £6.2m. **Everton:** Alan Stubbs (Celtic) Free. **Fulham:** Luis Boa Morte (Southampton) £1.7m; Matt Clarke (Bradford C) Loan. **Ipswich T:** Pablo Counago (Celta Vigo) Free; Andy Marshall (Norwich C) Free. **Leicester C:** Dennis Wise (Chelsea) £1.6m; Ian Walker (Tottenham H) £2.5m. **Liverpool:** John Arne Riise (Monaco) £4.6m. **Manchester U:** Ruud Van Nistelrooy (PSV Eindhoven) £19m. **Middlesbrough:** Gareth Southgate (Aston Villa) £6.5m Szilard Nemeth (Inter Bratislava) Free. **Newcastle U:** Craig Bellamy (Coventry C) £6.5m; Robbie Elliott (Bolton W) Free. **Southampton:** Rory Delap (Derby Co) £4m; Anders Svensson (Elfsborg) £500,000. **Sunderland:** Lilian Laslandes (Bordeaux) £3.6m; Nicolas Medina (Argentinos Juniors) £3.5m; David Bellion (Cannes) Free; Baki Mercimek (Haarlem) Free. **Tottenham H:** Goran Bunjevcevic (Red Star Belgrade) £4m; Gustavo Poyet (Chelsea) £1.5m; Teddy Sheringham (Manchester U) Free; Shwan Jalal (Hastings T) Free. **West Ham U:** Sebastian Schemmel (Metz) £465,000.

*Other moves completed and pending:* Jorg Albertz, Rangers to Hamburg £3m; Peter Crouch, QPR to Portsmouth £1.5m; Maikel Aerts, Den Bosch to Wolverhampton W £700,000; Ulises De la Cruz, La Coruna to Hibernian £700,000; Carsten Fredgaard, Sunderland to FC Copenhagen £500,000; Bernard Lambourde, Chelsea to Bastia £300,000; Lawrie Dudfield, Leicester C to Hull C £250,000; Neil Alexander, Livingston to Cardiff C £200,000; Stuart Campbell, Leicester C to Grimsby T £200,000; Jermaine Darlington, QPR to Wimbledon £200,000; Paul Crichton, Burnley to Norwich C £150,000; Gary Fletcher, Northwich Vic to Leyton Orient £150,000; Phillip Jevons, Everton to Grimsby T £150,000; Paul Peschisolido, Fulham to Sheffield U £150,000; Ryan Williams, Chesterfield to Hull C £150,000; Alen Orman, Antwerp to Hibernian £100,000; Carl Griffiths, Leyton Orient to Luton £65,000; Matthew Glennon, Bolton W to Hull C £50,000; Mark Freeman, Cheltenham T to Boston U £15,000; Mike Marsh, Southport to Boston U £15,000; Colin Alcide, York C to Cambridge C; Gary Alexander, Swindon T to Hull C; Derek Allan, Kingstonian to Q of S; Mark Angel, Darlington to Boston U; Stuart Balmer, Wigan Ath to Oldham Ath; Michael Bingham, Blackburn R to Mansfield T; Matthew Bloomer, Grimsby T to Hull C; Ian Cambridge, Cambridge C to Chelmsford C; Billy Clark, Forest Green R to Newport Co; Dave Clarke, Dover Ath to Kingstonian; Jamie Clarke, Ilkeston T to Kings Lynn; Michael Davis, Bath C to Basingstoke T; Clint Easton, Watford to Norwich C; Ian Ferguson, Forfar Ath to Stenhousemuir; Alan Gray, Workington to Q of S; Peter Handyside, Grimsby T to Stoke C; Warren Haughton, Tamworth to Woking; Andrew Holt, Oldham Ath to Hull C; Scott Kerr, Bradford C to Hull C; Dominic Ludden, Preston NE to Halifax T; Stuart MacKenzie, Farnborough T to Hampton & Richmond B; Ross Matheson, Morton to Raith R; Mark McGregor, Wrexham to Burnley; Paul McGregor, Plymouth Arg to Northampton T; Steve McKimm, Hayes to Kingstonian; Paul McLaren, Luton T to Sheffield W; Stephen McPhee, Coventry C to Port Vale; Craig Midgley, Hartlepool U to Halifax T; Nicky Mohan, Stoke C to Hull C; Mark Monington, Rochdale to Boston U; Tommy Mooney, Watford to Birmingham C; Paul Morgan, Preston NE to Lincoln C; John O'Kane, Bolton W to Blackpool; Gary Patterson, Kingstonian to Farnborough T; Tony Pennock, Yeovil T to Rushden & D; Paul Pettinger, Rotherham U to Lincoln C; Ben Petty, Stoke C to Hull C; Geoffrey Pitcher, Kingstonian to Brighton & HA; Michael Pollitt, Chesterfield to Rotherham U; David Pratt, St Albans C to Chesham U; Ben Smith, Yeovil T to Southend U; Grant Smith, Clydebank to Sheffield U; Nico Vaesen, Huddersfield T to Birmingham C; Philip Warner, Southampton to Cambridge U.

# LEAGUE REVIEW AND CLUB SECTION

The record books will show that Manchester United won their seventh Premier League title in the nine years of the competition by a ten-point margin. Alas the passage of time will give an entirely wrong impression of the actual events as outlined by the bare facts. For United won the title with five games to spare in slightly bizarre circumstances on 14 April.

With a morning kick-off against Coventry City, United emerged as 4-2 winners after a hard fought encounter with a team struggling to avoid relegation. Arsenal, with a later start at home to Middlesbrough, were at least expected to prolong the inevitable. Arsenal were the only Premiership team not to have lost at home. Instead the Gunners were beaten 3-0, the visitors benefiting from two own goals by Brazilians! This handed the trophy back to Manchester United who thus became the first Premier League team to win three such trophies in succession.

At the time of this 33rd League game, Manchester United had lost only three times. From their remaining five fixtures, they were beaten on a further three occasions.

Despite the lapses of the last five encounters, Manchester United had a strength in defence which was often dismissed by critics. The ebullient French international goalkeeper Fabien Barthez, the club's only signing for the season, was often outstanding but amazingly no player managed more than 32 appearances and only Gary Neville reached that figure. The squad system was never better used by Alex Ferguson. Teddy Sheringham, top scorer with 15 goals from less than twice the number of appearances, was not only the Football Writers' Player of the Season, but made it a personal double with the PFA version.

Ole Gunnar Solksjaer was the only other United player to reach double figures and his ten goals came from 31 appearances, a dozen of which were as a substitute. For the second season in a row United called upon 29 players in League games. Increased capacity at Old Trafford saw gates total 1,283,329 for an average of 67,544.

For a third year in succession Arsenal finished runners-up and such are the standards by which Premier League teams are judged, finishing runners-up for a club of the calibre of Arsenal is hugely disappointing. But in contrast, third place for Liverpool was considered a fine achievement, coupled as it was with their three cup successes: League, FA and UEFA. It would be hard not to avoid giving team of the season to the Anfield club, especially as they beat Manchester United home and away.

There would be many who would have voted for Ipswich Town in this particular category. Promoted teams invariably struggle in the Premiership and Ipswich were firm favourites to go back down again before the season started. They confounded their critics and manager George Burley was rightly given the manager of the year award.

At one time they were on course for finishing third, but eventually Leeds United, who also did well in Europe, edged them out of even fourth place. Chelsea, as inconsistent as ever, managed sixth place.

Bradford City, who had avoided relegation the previous season at the last gasp, failed this time and Coventry after many such struggles accompanied them along with Manchester City.

Up from the First Division are Fulham, the only Football League club to reach a century of points, Blackburn Rovers ten points behind them and Bolton Wanderers through the play-offs. At the foot of the First Division Huddersfield Town, Queens Park Rangers and Tranmere Rovers went down to be replaced by Millwall, Rotherham United and Walsall.

Controversy reigned in the Third Division where runaway leaders Chesterfield were docked nine points for financial irregularities, but still scraped into the third automatic promotion place along with champions Brighton & Hove Albion and Cardiff City. Blackpool though finishing seventh were the successful team from the play-offs. This quartet replaced Bristol Rovers, Luton Town, Swansea City and Oxford United relegated from the Second Division.

Out of the League went Barnet, their fate sealed on the last day of the season when they were beaten 3-2 at home by Torquay United, who would have gone out had they themselves lost the match. This despite a record League win for Barnet earlier in the season against Blackpool of all teams. Up from the Conference have come Rushden & Diamonds.

# FA Carling Premiership

| | | | Home | | Goals | | Away | | | Goals | | | |
|---|---|---|---|---|---|---|---|---|---|---|---|---|---|
| | | P | W | D | L | F | A | W | D | L | F | A | GD | Pts |
| 1 | Manchester U | 38 | 15 | 2 | 2 | 49 | 12 | 9 | 6 | 4 | 30 | 19 | 48 | 80 |
| 2 | Arsenal | 38 | 15 | 3 | 1 | 45 | 13 | 5 | 7 | 7 | 18 | 25 | 25 | 70 |
| 3 | Liverpool | 38 | 13 | 4 | 2 | 40 | 14 | 7 | 5 | 7 | 31 | 25 | 32 | 69 |
| 4 | Leeds U | 38 | 11 | 3 | 5 | 36 | 21 | 9 | 5 | 5 | 28 | 22 | 21 | 68 |
| 5 | Ipswich T | 38 | 11 | 5 | 3 | 31 | 15 | 9 | 1 | 9 | 26 | 27 | 15 | 66 |
| 6 | Chelsea | 38 | 13 | 3 | 3 | 44 | 20 | 4 | 7 | 8 | 24 | 25 | 23 | 61 |
| 7 | Sunderland | 38 | 9 | 7 | 3 | 24 | 16 | 6 | 5 | 8 | 22 | 25 | 5 | 57 |
| 8 | Aston Villa | 38 | 8 | 8 | 3 | 27 | 20 | 5 | 7 | 7 | 19 | 23 | 3 | 54 |
| 9 | Charlton Ath | 38 | 11 | 5 | 3 | 31 | 19 | 3 | 5 | 11 | 19 | 38 | -7 | 52 |
| 10 | Southampton | 38 | 11 | 2 | 6 | 27 | 22 | 3 | 8 | 8 | 13 | 26 | -8 | 52 |
| 11 | Newcastle U | 38 | 10 | 4 | 5 | 26 | 17 | 4 | 5 | 10 | 18 | 33 | -6 | 51 |
| 12 | Tottenham H | 38 | 11 | 6 | 2 | 31 | 16 | 2 | 4 | 13 | 16 | 38 | -7 | 49 |
| 13 | Leicester C | 38 | 10 | 4 | 5 | 28 | 23 | 4 | 2 | 13 | 11 | 28 | -12 | 48 |
| 14 | Middlesbrough | 38 | 4 | 7 | 8 | 18 | 23 | 5 | 8 | 6 | 26 | 21 | 0 | 42 |
| 15 | West Ham U | 38 | 6 | 6 | 7 | 24 | 20 | 4 | 6 | 9 | 21 | 30 | -5 | 42 |
| 16 | Everton | 38 | 6 | 8 | 5 | 29 | 27 | 5 | 1 | 13 | 16 | 32 | -14 | 42 |
| 17 | Derby Co | 38 | 8 | 7 | 4 | 23 | 24 | 2 | 5 | 12 | 14 | 35 | -22 | 42 |
| 18 | Manchester C | 38 | 4 | 3 | 12 | 20 | 31 | 4 | 7 | 8 | 21 | 34 | -24 | 34 |
| 19 | Coventry C | 38 | 4 | 7 | 8 | 14 | 23 | 4 | 3 | 12 | 22 | 40 | -27 | 34 |
| 20 | Bradford C | 38 | 4 | 7 | 8 | 20 | 29 | 1 | 4 | 14 | 10 | 41 | -40 | 26 |

# LEADING GOALSCORERS 2000-2001

**FA CARLING PREMIERSHIP**

| | League | FA Cup | Worthington Cup | Other | Total |
|---|---|---|---|---|---|
| Jimmy Floyd Hasselbaink (Chelsea) | 23 | 2 | 0 | 0 | 25 |
| Marcus Stewart (Ipswich T) | 19 | 1 | 1 | 0 | 21 |
| Thierry Henry (Arsenal) | 17 | 1 | 0 | 4 | 22 |
| Mark Viduka (Leeds U) | 17 | 1 | 0 | 4 | 22 |
| Michael Owen (Liverpool) | 16 | 3 | 1 | 4 | 24 |
| Teddy Sheringham (Manchester U) | 15 | 1 | 0 | 5 | 21 |
| Emile Heskey (Liverpool) | 14 | 5 | 0 | 3 | 22 |
| Kevin Phillips (Sunderland) | 14 | 2 | 2 | 0 | 18 |
| Alen Boksic (Middlesbrough) | 12 | 0 | 0 | 0 | 12 |
| Alan Smith (Leeds U) | 11 | 0 | 0 | 7 | 18 |
| Jonatan Johansson (Charlton Ath) | 11 | 0 | 3 | 0 | 14 |
| Frederic Kanoute (West Ham U) | 11 | 3 | 0 | 0 | 14 |
| James Beattie (Southampton) | 11 | 1 | 0 | 0 | 12 |
| Gustavo Poyet (Chelsea) | 11 | 1 | 0 | 0 | 12 |
| Ole Gunnar Solskjaer (Manchester U) | 10 | 1 | 2 | 0 | 13 |
| Eidur Gudjohnsen (Chelsea) | 10 | 3 | 0 | 0 | 13 |
| Les Ferdinand (Tottenham H) | 10 | 0 | 0 | 0 | 10 |

*Other matches consist of European games, LDV Vans Trophy, Charity Shield and Football League play-offs.*

# Nationwide Football League Division 1

| | | P | Home W | D | L | Goals F | A | Away W | D | L | Goals F | A | GD | Pts |
|---|---|---|---|---|---|---|---|---|---|---|---|---|---|---|
| 1 | Fulham | 46 | 16 | 5 | 2 | 49 | 14 | 14 | 6 | 3 | 41 | 18 | 58 | 101 |
| 2 | Blackburn R | 46 | 15 | 5 | 3 | 43 | 20 | 11 | 8 | 4 | 33 | 19 | 37 | 91 |
| 3 | Bolton W | 46 | 10 | 10 | 3 | 40 | 28 | 14 | 5 | 4 | 36 | 17 | 31 | 87 |
| 4 | Preston NE | 46 | 12 | 6 | 5 | 32 | 18 | 11 | 3 | 9 | 32 | 34 | 12 | 78 |
| 5 | Birmingham C | 46 | 14 | 3 | 6 | 34 | 22 | 9 | 6 | 8 | 25 | 26 | 11 | 78 |
| 6 | WBA | 46 | 13 | 5 | 5 | 37 | 23 | 8 | 6 | 9 | 23 | 29 | 8 | 74 |
| 7 | Burnley | 46 | 14 | 5 | 4 | 30 | 17 | 7 | 4 | 12 | 20 | 37 | −4 | 72 |
| 8 | Wimbledon | 46 | 7 | 11 | 5 | 33 | 26 | 10 | 7 | 6 | 38 | 24 | 21 | 69 |
| 9 | Watford | 46 | 11 | 6 | 6 | 46 | 29 | 9 | 3 | 11 | 30 | 38 | 9 | 69 |
| 10 | Sheffield U | 46 | 14 | 4 | 5 | 34 | 18 | 5 | 7 | 11 | 18 | 31 | 3 | 68 |
| 11 | Nottingham F | 46 | 11 | 3 | 9 | 28 | 24 | 9 | 5 | 9 | 27 | 29 | 2 | 68 |
| 12 | Wolverhampton W | 46 | 7 | 9 | 7 | 25 | 20 | 7 | 4 | 12 | 20 | 28 | −3 | 55 |
| 13 | Gillingham | 46 | 9 | 6 | 8 | 32 | 28 | 4 | 10 | 9 | 29 | 38 | −5 | 55 |
| 14 | Crewe Alex | 46 | 12 | 5 | 6 | 30 | 24 | 3 | 5 | 15 | 17 | 38 | −15 | 55 |
| 15 | Norwich C | 46 | 10 | 7 | 6 | 25 | 18 | 4 | 5 | 14 | 21 | 40 | −12 | 54 |
| 16 | Barnsley | 46 | 11 | 3 | 9 | 32 | 26 | 4 | 6 | 13 | 17 | 36 | −13 | 54 |
| 17 | Sheffield W | 46 | 9 | 4 | 10 | 34 | 38 | 6 | 4 | 13 | 18 | 33 | −19 | 53 |
| 18 | Grimsby T | 46 | 10 | 4 | 9 | 26 | 27 | 4 | 6 | 13 | 17 | 35 | −19 | 52 |
| 19 | Stockport Co | 46 | 6 | 11 | 6 | 29 | 26 | 5 | 7 | 11 | 29 | 39 | −7 | 51 |
| 20 | Portsmouth | 46 | 9 | 8 | 6 | 31 | 25 | 1 | 11 | 11 | 16 | 34 | −12 | 49 |
| 21 | Crystal Palace | 46 | 6 | 6 | 11 | 28 | 34 | 6 | 7 | 10 | 29 | 36 | −13 | 49 |
| 22 | Huddersfield T | 46 | 7 | 6 | 10 | 29 | 26 | 4 | 9 | 10 | 19 | 31 | −9 | 48 |
| 23 | QPR | 46 | 6 | 9 | 8 | 24 | 28 | 1 | 10 | 12 | 21 | 47 | −30 | 40 |
| 24 | Tranmere R | 46 | 8 | 7 | 8 | 30 | 33 | 1 | 4 | 18 | 16 | 44 | −31 | 38 |

**NATIONWIDE DIVISION 1**

| | League | FA Cup | Worthington Cup | Other | Total |
|---|---|---|---|---|---|
| Louis Saha (Fulham) | 27 | 0 | 5 | 0 | 32 |
| Matt Jansen (Blackburn R) | 23 | 1 | 0 | 0 | 24 |
| Lee Hughes (WBA) | 21 | 1 | 0 | 1 | 23 |
| Michael Ricketts (Bolton W) | 19 | 2 | 1 | 2 | 24 |
| Tommy Mooney (Watford) | 19 | 1 | 2 | 0 | 22 |
| Jon Macken (Preston NE) | 19 | 0 | 3 | 0 | 22 |
| Jason Euell (Wimbledon) | 19 | 1 | 0 | 0 | 20 |
| Luis Boa Morte (Fulham) | 18 | 0 | 3 | 0 | 21 |
| Barry Hayles (Fulham) | 18 | 0 | 1 | 0 | 19 |
| Iwan Roberts (Norwich C) | 15 | 1 | 3 | 0 | 19 |
| Bruce Dyer (Barnsley) | 15 | 0 | 1 | 0 | 16 |
| Marlon King (Gillingham) | 15 | 0 | 0 | 0 | 15 |
| Clint Morrison (Crystal Palace) | 14 | 1 | 4 | 0 | 19 |
| Jason Roberts (WBA) | 14 | 0 | 2 | 1 | 17 |
| Chris Bart-Williams (Nottingham F) | 14 | 0 | 1 | 0 | 15 |
| Neil Shipperley (Barnsley) | 14 | 0 | 0 | 0 | 14 |
| Gerald Sibon (Sheffield W) | 13 | 1 | 1 | 0 | 15 |
| Mikael Forssell (Crystal Palace) | 13 | 0 | 2 | 0 | 15 |

# Nationwide Football League Division 2

|    |               | P  | W (Home) | D (Home) | L (Home) | F (Goals) | A (Goals) | W (Away) | D (Away) | L (Away) | F (Goals) | A (Goals) | GD  | Pts |
|----|---------------|----|----|----|----|----|----|----|----|----|----|----|-----|-----|
| 1  | Millwall      | 46 | 17 | 2  | 4  | 49 | 11 | 11 | 7  | 5  | 40 | 27 | 51  | 93  |
| 2  | Rotherham U   | 46 | 16 | 4  | 3  | 50 | 26 | 11 | 6  | 6  | 29 | 29 | 24  | 91  |
| 3  | Reading       | 46 | 15 | 5  | 3  | 58 | 26 | 10 | 6  | 7  | 28 | 26 | 34  | 86  |
| 4  | Walsall       | 46 | 15 | 5  | 3  | 51 | 23 | 8  | 7  | 8  | 28 | 27 | 29  | 81  |
| 5  | Stoke C       | 46 | 12 | 6  | 5  | 39 | 21 | 9  | 8  | 6  | 35 | 28 | 25  | 77  |
| 6  | Wigan Ath     | 46 | 12 | 9  | 2  | 29 | 18 | 7  | 9  | 7  | 24 | 24 | 11  | 75  |
| 7  | AFC Bournemouth | 46 | 11 | 6  | 6  | 37 | 23 | 9  | 7  | 7  | 42 | 32 | 24  | 73  |
| 8  | Notts Co      | 46 | 10 | 6  | 7  | 37 | 33 | 9  | 6  | 8  | 25 | 33 | -4  | 69  |
| 9  | Bristol C     | 46 | 11 | 6  | 6  | 47 | 29 | 7  | 8  | 8  | 23 | 27 | 14  | 68  |
| 10 | Wrexham       | 46 | 10 | 6  | 7  | 33 | 28 | 7  | 6  | 10 | 32 | 43 | -6  | 63  |
| 11 | Port Vale     | 46 | 9  | 8  | 6  | 35 | 22 | 7  | 6  | 10 | 20 | 27 | 6   | 62  |
| 12 | Peterborough U | 46 | 12 | 6  | 5  | 38 | 27 | 3  | 8  | 12 | 23 | 39 | -5  | 59  |
| 13 | Wycombe W     | 46 | 8  | 7  | 8  | 24 | 23 | 7  | 7  | 9  | 22 | 30 | -7  | 59  |
| 14 | Brentford     | 46 | 9  | 10 | 4  | 34 | 30 | 5  | 7  | 11 | 22 | 40 | -14 | 59  |
| 15 | Oldham Ath    | 46 | 11 | 5  | 7  | 35 | 26 | 4  | 8  | 11 | 18 | 39 | -12 | 58  |
| 16 | Bury          | 46 | 10 | 6  | 7  | 25 | 22 | 6  | 4  | 13 | 20 | 37 | -14 | 58  |
| 17 | Colchester U  | 46 | 10 | 5  | 8  | 32 | 23 | 5  | 7  | 11 | 23 | 36 | -4  | 57  |
| 18 | Northampton T | 46 | 9  | 6  | 8  | 26 | 28 | 6  | 6  | 11 | 20 | 31 | -13 | 57  |
| 19 | Cambridge U   | 46 | 8  | 6  | 9  | 32 | 31 | 6  | 5  | 12 | 29 | 46 | -16 | 53  |
| 20 | Swindon T     | 46 | 6  | 8  | 9  | 30 | 35 | 7  | 5  | 11 | 17 | 30 | -18 | 52  |
| 21 | Bristol R     | 46 | 6  | 10 | 7  | 28 | 26 | 6  | 5  | 12 | 25 | 31 | -4  | 51  |
| 22 | Luton T       | 46 | 5  | 6  | 12 | 24 | 35 | 4  | 7  | 12 | 28 | 45 | -28 | 40  |
| 23 | Swansea C     | 46 | 5  | 9  | 9  | 26 | 24 | 3  | 4  | 16 | 21 | 49 | -26 | 37  |
| 24 | Oxford U      | 46 | 5  | 4  | 14 | 23 | 34 | 2  | 2  | 19 | 30 | 66 | -47 | 27  |

**NATIONWIDE DIVISION 2**

|                                   | League | FA Cup | Worthington Cup | Other | Total |
|-----------------------------------|--------|--------|-----------------|-------|-------|
| Jamie Cureton (Reading)           | 27     | 1      | 1               | 2     | 31    |
| (Including 1 League goal for Bristol R) | | | | | |
| Neil Harris (Millwall)            | 27     | 1      | 0               | 0     | 28    |
| Martin Butler (Reading)           | 24     | 2      | 0               | 2     | 28    |
| Mark Robins (Rotherham U)         | 24     | 0      | 1               | 1     | 26    |
| Tony Thorpe (Bristol C)           | 19     | 3      | 1               | 0     | 23    |
| Jorge Leitao (Walsall)            | 18     | 1      | 2               | 0     | 21    |
| Andy Scott (Oxford U)             | 18     | 0      | 2               | 0     | 20    |
| (Including 13 League goals for Brentford) | | | | | |
| Jemaine Defoe (Bournemouth)       | 18     | 1      | 0               | 0     | 19    |
| Mark Stallard (Notts Co)          | 17     | 3      | 3               | 0     | 23    |
| Jamie Forrester (Northampton T)   | 17     | 2      | 0               | 0     | 19    |
| Peter Thorne (Stoke C)            | 16     | 0      | 0               | 0     | 16    |
| Nathan Ellington (Bristol R)      | 15     | 0      | 2               | 1     | 18    |
| Tony Naylor (Port Vale)           | 14     | 1      | 0               | 5     | 20    |
| Tom Youngs (Cambridge U)          | 14     | 1      | 0               | 0     | 15    |
| Lee Peacock (Bristol C)           | 13     | 1      | 1               | 0     | 15    |
| Alan Lee (Rotherham U)            | 13     | 1      | 0               | 1     | 15    |
| Brett Angell (Notts Co)           | 13     | 1      | 0               | 0     | 14    |
| Paul Moody (Millwall)             | 13     | 1      | 0               | 0     | 14    |
| Danny Allsopp (Notts Co)          | 13     | 0      | 0               | 0     | 13    |
| Leon McKenzie (Peterborough U)    | 13     | 0      | 0               | 0     | 13    |

# Nationwide Football League Division 3

|   |   | P | W | D | L | F | A | W | D | L | F | A | GD | Pts |
|---|---|---|---|---|---|---|---|---|---|---|---|---|----|-----|
|   |   |   | **Home** | | | **Goals** | | | **Away** | | | **Goals** | | | |
| 1 | Brighton & HA | 46 | 19 | 2 | 2 | 52 | 14 | 9 | 6 | 8 | 21 | 21 | 38 | 92 |
| 2 | Cardiff C | 46 | 16 | 7 | 0 | 56 | 20 | 7 | 6 | 10 | 39 | 38 | 37 | 82 |
| 3 | Chesterfield | 46 | 16 | 5 | 2 | 46 | 14 | 9 | 9 | 5 | 33 | 28 | 37 | 80* |
| 4 | Hartlepool U | 46 | 12 | 8 | 3 | 40 | 23 | 9 | 6 | 8 | 31 | 31 | 17 | 77 |
| 5 | Leyton Orient | 46 | 13 | 7 | 3 | 31 | 18 | 7 | 8 | 8 | 28 | 33 | 8 | 75 |
| 6 | Hull C | 46 | 12 | 7 | 4 | 27 | 18 | 7 | 10 | 6 | 20 | 21 | 8 | 74 |
| 7 | Blackpool | 46 | 14 | 4 | 5 | 50 | 26 | 8 | 2 | 13 | 24 | 32 | 16 | 72 |
| 8 | Rochdale | 46 | 11 | 8 | 4 | 36 | 25 | 7 | 9 | 7 | 23 | 23 | 11 | 71 |
| 9 | Cheltenham T | 46 | 12 | 5 | 6 | 37 | 27 | 6 | 9 | 8 | 22 | 25 | 7 | 68 |
| 10 | Scunthorpe U | 46 | 13 | 7 | 3 | 42 | 16 | 5 | 4 | 14 | 20 | 36 | 10 | 65 |
| 11 | Southend U | 46 | 10 | 8 | 5 | 29 | 23 | 5 | 10 | 8 | 26 | 30 | 2 | 63 |
| 12 | Plymouth Arg | 46 | 13 | 5 | 5 | 33 | 17 | 2 | 8 | 13 | 21 | 44 | −7 | 58 |
| 13 | Mansfield T | 46 | 12 | 7 | 4 | 40 | 26 | 3 | 6 | 14 | 24 | 46 | −8 | 58 |
| 14 | Macclesfield T | 46 | 10 | 5 | 8 | 23 | 21 | 4 | 9 | 10 | 28 | 41 | −11 | 56 |
| 15 | Shrewsbury T | 46 | 12 | 5 | 6 | 30 | 26 | 3 | 5 | 15 | 19 | 39 | −16 | 55 |
| 16 | Kidderminster H | 46 | 10 | 6 | 7 | 29 | 27 | 3 | 8 | 12 | 18 | 34 | −14 | 53 |
| 17 | York C | 46 | 9 | 6 | 8 | 23 | 26 | 4 | 7 | 12 | 19 | 37 | −21 | 52 |
| 18 | Lincoln C | 46 | 9 | 9 | 5 | 36 | 28 | 3 | 6 | 14 | 22 | 38 | −8 | 51 |
| 19 | Exeter C | 46 | 8 | 9 | 6 | 22 | 20 | 4 | 5 | 14 | 18 | 38 | −18 | 50 |
| 20 | Darlington | 46 | 10 | 6 | 7 | 28 | 23 | 2 | 7 | 14 | 16 | 33 | −12 | 49 |
| 21 | Torquay U | 46 | 9 | 9 | 6 | 30 | 29 | 4 | 4 | 15 | 22 | 48 | −25 | 49 |
| 22 | Carlisle U | 46 | 8 | 8 | 7 | 26 | 26 | 3 | 7 | 13 | 16 | 39 | −23 | 48 |
| 23 | Halifax T | 46 | 7 | 6 | 10 | 33 | 32 | 5 | 5 | 13 | 21 | 36 | −14 | 47 |
| 24 | Barnet | 46 | 9 | 8 | 6 | 44 | 29 | 3 | 1 | 19 | 23 | 52 | −14 | 45 |

* 9pts deducted for breach of rules.

## NATIONWIDE DIVISION 3

| | League | FA Cup | Worthington Cup | Other | Total |
|---|---|---|---|---|---|
| Bobby Zamora (*Brighton & HA*) | 28 | 2 | 0 | 1 | 31 |
| Robert Earnshaw (*Cardiff C*) | 19 | 6 | 0 | 0 | 25 |
| Chris Greenacre (*Mansfield T*) | 19 | 1 | 1 | 0 | 21 |
| Steve Kerrigan (*Halifax T*) | 19 | 0 | 0 | 1 | 20 |
| John Murphy (*Blackpool*) | 18 | 1 | 5 | 0 | 24 |
| Brett Ormerod (*Blackpool*) | 17 | 2 | 1 | 6 | 26 |
| Kevin Henderson (*Hartlepool U*) | 17 | 0 | 0 | 2 | 19 |
| Tommy Miller (*Hartlepool U*) | 16 | 0 | 2 | 2 | 20 |
| Luke Beckett (*Chesterfield*) | 16 | 0 | 2 | 0 | 18 |
| Paul Brayson (*Cardiff C*) | 15 | 0 | 0 | 0 | 15 |
| Nigel Jemson (*Shrewsbury T*) | 15 | 0 | 0 | 0 | 15 |
| Carl Griffiths (*Leyton Orient*) | 14 | 4 | 0 | 0 | 18 |
| Guy Ipoua (*Scunthorpe U*) | 14 | 4 | 0 | 0 | 18 |
| David Reeves (*Chesterfield*) | 13 | 0 | 1 | 2 | 16 |
| Neil Grayson (*Cheltenham T*) | 13 | 2 | 0 | 0 | 15 |
| Steve Flack (*Exeter C*) | 13 | 0 | 0 | 0 | 13 |

# FA CARLING PREMIERSHIP

| HOME TEAM | Arsenal | Aston Villa | Bradford C | Charlton Ath | Chelsea | Coventry C | Derby Co | Everton | Ipswich T | Leeds U |
|---|---|---|---|---|---|---|---|---|---|---|
| Arsenal | — | 1-0 | 2-0 | 5-3 | 1-1 | 2-1 | 0-0 | 4-1 | 1-0 | 2-1 |
| Aston Villa | 0-0 | — | 2-0 | 2-1 | 1-1 | 3-2 | 4-1 | 2-1 | 2-1 | 1-2 |
| Bradford C | 1-1 | 0-3 | — | 2-0 | 2-0 | 2-1 | 2-0 | 0-1 | 0-2 | 1-1 |
| Charlton Ath | 1-0 | 3-3 | 2-0 | — | 2-0 | 2-2 | 2-1 | 1-0 | 2-1 | 1-2 |
| Chelsea | 2-2 | 1-0 | 3-0 | 0-1 | — | 6-1 | 4-1 | 2-1 | 4-1 | 1-1 |
| Coventry C | 0-1 | 1-1 | 0-0 | 2-2 | 0-0 | — | 2-0 | 1-3 | 0-1 | 0-0 |
| Derby Co | 1-2 | 1-0 | 2-0 | 2-2 | 0-4 | 1-0 | — | 1-0 | 1-1 | 1-1 |
| Everton | 2-0 | 0-1 | 2-1 | 3-0 | 2-1 | 1-2 | 2-2 | — | 0-3 | 2-2 |
| Ipswich T | 1-1 | 1-2 | 3-1 | 2-0 | 2-2 | 2-0 | 0-1 | 2-0 | — | 1-2 |
| Leeds U | 1-0 | 1-2 | 6-1 | 3-1 | 2-0 | 1-0 | 0-0 | 2-0 | 1-2 | — |
| Leicester C | 0-0 | 0-0 | 1-2 | 3-1 | 2-1 | 1-3 | 2-1 | 1-1 | 2-1 | 3-1 |
| Liverpool | 4-0 | 3-1 | 1-0 | 3-0 | 2-2 | 4-1 | 1-1 | 3-1 | 0-1 | 1-2 |
| Manchester C | 0-4 | 1-3 | 2-0 | 1-4 | 1-2 | 1-2 | 0-0 | 5-0 | 2-3 | 0-4 |
| Manchester U | 6-1 | 2-0 | 6-0 | 2-1 | 3-3 | 4-2 | 0-1 | 1-0 | 2-0 | 3-0 |
| Middlesbrough | 0-1 | 1-1 | 2-2 | 0-0 | 1-0 | 1-1 | 4-0 | 1-2 | 1-2 | 1-2 |
| Newcastle U | 0-0 | 3-0 | 2-1 | 0-1 | 0-0 | 3-1 | 3-2 | 0-1 | 2-1 | 2-1 |
| Southampton | 3-2 | 2-0 | 2-0 | 0-0 | 3-2 | 1-2 | 1-0 | 1-0 | 0-3 | 1-0 |
| Sunderland | 1-0 | 1-1 | 0-0 | 3-2 | 1-0 | 1-0 | 2-1 | 2-0 | 4-1 | 0-2 |
| Tottenham H | 1-1 | 0-0 | 2-1 | 0-0 | 0-3 | 3-0 | 3-1 | 3-2 | 3-1 | 1-2 |
| West Ham U | 1-2 | 1-1 | 1-1 | 5-0 | 0-2 | 1-1 | 3-1 | 0-2 | 0-1 | 0-2 |

# 2000–2001 RESULTS

| Leicester C | Liverpool | Manchester C | Manchester U | Middlesbrough | Newcastle U | Southampton | Sunderland | Tottenham H | West Ham U |
|---|---|---|---|---|---|---|---|---|---|
| 6-1 | 2-0 | 5-0 | 1-0 | 0-3 | 5-0 | 1-0 | 2-2 | 2-0 | 3-0 |
| 2-1 | 0-3 | 2-2 | 0-1 | 1-1 | 1-1 | 0-0 | 0-0 | 2-0 | 2-2 |
| 0-0 | 0-2 | 2-2 | 0-3 | 1-1 | 2-2 | 0-1 | 1-4 | 3-3 | 1-2 |
| 2-0 | 0-4 | 4-0 | 3-3 | 1-0 | 2-0 | 1-1 | 0-1 | 1-0 | 1-1 |
| 0-2 | 3-0 | 2-1 | 1-1 | 2-1 | 3-1 | 1-0 | 2-4 | 3-0 | 4-2 |
| 1-0 | 0-2 | 1-1 | 1-2 | 1-3 | 0-2 | 1-1 | 1-0 | 2-1 | 0-3 |
| 2-0 | 0-4 | 1-1 | 0-3 | 3-3 | 2-0 | 2-2 | 1-0 | 2-1 | 0-0 |
| 2-1 | 2-3 | 3-1 | 1-3 | 2-2 | 1-1 | 1-1 | 2-2 | 0-0 | 1-1 |
| 2-0 | 1-1 | 2-1 | 1-1 | 2-1 | 1-0 | 3-1 | 1-0 | 3-0 | 1-1 |
| 3-1 | 4-3 | 1-2 | 1-1 | 1-1 | 1-3 | 2-0 | 2-0 | 4-3 | 0-1 |
| — | 2-0 | 1-2 | 0-3 | 0-3 | 1-1 | 1-0 | 2-0 | 4-2 | 2-1 |
| 1-0 | — | 3-2 | 2-0 | 0-0 | 3-0 | 2-1 | 1-1 | 3-1 | 3-0 |
| 0-1 | 1-1 | — | 0-1 | 1-1 | 0-1 | 0-1 | 4-2 | 0-1 | 1-0 |
| 2-0 | 0-1 | 1-1 | — | 2-1 | 2-0 | 5-0 | 3-0 | 2-0 | 3-1 |
| 0-3 | 1-0 | 1-1 | 0-2 | — | 1-3 | 0-1 | 0-0 | 1-1 | 2-1 |
| 1-0 | 2-1 | 0-1 | 1-1 | 1-2 | — | 1-1 | 1-2 | 2-0 | 2-1 |
| 1-0 | 3-3 | 0-2 | 2-1 | 1-3 | 2-0 | — | 0-1 | 2-0 | 2-3 |
| 0-0 | 1-1 | 1-0 | 0-1 | 1-0 | 1-1 | 2-2 | — | 2-3 | 1-1 |
| 3-0 | 2-1 | 0-0 | 3-1 | 0-0 | 4-2 | 0-0 | 2-1 | — | 1-0 |
| 0-1 | 1-1 | 4-1 | 2-2 | 1-0 | 1-0 | 3-0 | 0-2 | 0-0 | — |

| HOME TEAM | Barnsley | Birmingham C | Blackburn R | Bolton W | Burnley | Crewe Alex | Crystal Palace | Fulham | Gillingham | Grimsby T |
|---|---|---|---|---|---|---|---|---|---|---|
| Barnsley | — | 2-3 | 1-2 | 0-1 | 1-0 | 3-0 | 1-0 | 0-0 | 3-1 | 2-0 |
| Birmingham C | 4-1 | — | 0-2 | 1-1 | 3-2 | 2-0 | 2-1 | 1-3 | 1-0 | 1-0 |
| Blackburn R | 0-0 | 2-1 | — | 1-1 | 5-0 | 1-0 | 2-0 | 1-2 | 1-2 | 2-0 |
| Bolton W | 2-0 | 2-2 | 1-4 | — | 1-1 | 4-1 | 3-3 | 0-2 | 3-3 | 2-2 |
| Burnley | 2-1 | 0-0 | 0-2 | 0-2 | — | 1-0 | 1-2 | 2-1 | 1-1 | 1-1 |
| Crewe Alex | 2-2 | 0-2 | 0-0 | 2-1 | 4-2 | — | 1-1 | 1-2 | 2-1 | 2-0 |
| Crystal Palace | 1-0 | 1-2 | 2-3 | 0-2 | 0-1 | 1-0 | — | 0-2 | 2-2 | 0-1 |
| Fulham | 5-1 | 0-1 | 2-1 | 1-1 | 3-1 | 2-0 | 3-1 | — | 3-0 | 2-1 |
| Gillingham | 0-0 | 1-2 | 1-1 | 2-2 | 0-0 | 0-1 | 4-1 | 0-2 | — | 1-0 |
| Grimsby T | 0-2 | 1-1 | 1-4 | 0-1 | 1-0 | 1-3 | 2-2 | 1-0 | 1-0 | — |
| Huddersfield T | 1-1 | 1-2 | 0-1 | 2-3 | 0-1 | 3-1 | 1-2 | 1-2 | 2-3 | 0-0 |
| Norwich C | 0-0 | 1-0 | 1-1 | 0-2 | 2-3 | 1-1 | 0-0 | 0-1 | 1-0 | 2-1 |
| Nottingham F | 1-0 | 1-2 | 2-1 | 0-2 | 5-0 | 1-0 | 0-3 | 0-3 | 0-1 | 3-1 |
| Portsmouth | 3-0 | 1-1 | 2-2 | 1-2 | 2-0 | 2-1 | 2-4 | 1-1 | 0-0 | 1-1 |
| Preston NE | 1-2 | 0-2 | 0-1 | 0-2 | 2-1 | 2-1 | 2-0 | 1-1 | 0-0 | 1-2 |
| QPR | 2-0 | 0-0 | 1-3 | 1-1 | 0-1 | 1-0 | 1-1 | 0-2 | 2-2 | 0-1 |
| Sheffield U | 1-2 | 3-1 | 2-0 | 1-0 | 2-0 | 1-0 | 1-0 | 1-1 | 1-2 | 3-2 |
| Sheffield W | 2-1 | 1-0 | 1-1 | 0-3 | 2-0 | 0-0 | 4-1 | 3-3 | 2-1 | 1-0 |
| Stockport Co | 2-0 | 2-0 | 0-0 | 4-3 | 0-0 | 3-0 | 0-1 | 2-0 | 2-2 | 1-1 |
| Tranmere R | 2-3 | 1-0 | 1-1 | 0-1 | 2-3 | 1-3 | 1-1 | 1-4 | 3-2 | 2-0 |
| Watford | 1-0 | 2-0 | 0-1 | 1-0 | 0-1 | 3-0 | 2-2 | 1-3 | 0-0 | 4-0 |
| WBA | 1-0 | 1-1 | 1-0 | 0-2 | 1-1 | 2-2 | 1-0 | 1-3 | 3-1 | 0-1 |
| Wimbledon | 1-1 | 3-1 | 0-2 | 0-1 | 0-2 | 3-3 | 1-0 | 0-3 | 4-4 | 2-2 |
| Wolverhampton W | 2-0 | 0-1 | 0-0 | 0-2 | 1-0 | 0-0 | 1-3 | 0-0 | 1-1 | 2-0 |

# DIVISION 1 2000–2001 RESULTS

| Huddersfield T | Norwich C | Nottingham F | Portsmouth | Preston NE | QPR | Sheffield U | Sheffield W | Stockport Co | Tranmere R | Watford | WBA | Wimbledon | Wolverhampton W |
|---|---|---|---|---|---|---|---|---|---|---|---|---|---|
| 3-1 | 1-0 | 3-4 | 1-0 | 0-4 | 4-2 | 0-0 | 1-0 | 0-2 | 1-1 | 0-1 | 4-1 | 0-1 | 1-2 |
| 2-1 | 2-1 | 0-2 | 0-0 | 3-1 | 0-0 | 1-0 | 1-2 | 4-0 | 2-0 | 2-0 | 2-1 | 0-3 | 0-1 |
| 2-0 | 3-2 | 3-0 | 3-1 | 3-2 | 0-0 | 1-1 | 2-0 | 2-1 | 3-2 | 3-4 | 1-0 | 1-1 | 1-0 |
| 2-2 | 1-0 | 0-0 | 2-0 | 2-0 | 3-1 | 1-1 | 2-0 | 1-1 | 2-0 | 2-1 | 0-1 | 2-2 | 2-1 |
| 1-0 | 2-0 | 1-0 | 1-1 | 3-0 | 2-1 | 2-0 | 1-0 | 2-1 | 2-1 | 2-0 | 1-1 | 1-0 | 1-2 |
| 1-0 | 0-0 | 1-0 | 1-0 | 1-3 | 2-2 | 1-0 | 1-0 | 1-2 | 3-1 | 2-0 | 0-1 | 0-4 | 2-0 |
| 0-0 | 1-1 | 2-3 | 2-3 | 0-2 | 1-1 | 0-1 | 4-1 | 2-2 | 3-2 | 1-0 | 2-2 | 3-1 | 0-2 |
| 3-0 | 2-0 | 1-0 | 3-1 | 0-1 | 2-0 | 1-1 | 1-1 | 4-1 | 3-1 | 5-0 | 0-0 | 1-1 | 2-0 |
| 2-1 | 4-3 | 1-3 | 1-1 | 4-0 | 0-1 | 4-1 | 2-0 | 1-3 | 2-1 | 0-3 | 1-2 | 0-0 | 1-0 |
| 1-0 | 2-0 | 0-2 | 2-1 | 1-2 | 3-1 | 0-1 | 0-1 | 1-1 | 3-1 | 2-1 | 2-0 | 1-1 | 0-2 |
| — | 2-0 | 1-1 | 4-1 | 0-0 | 2-1 | 2-1 | 0-0 | 0-0 | 3-0 | 1-2 | 0-2 | 0-2 | 3-0 |
| 1-1 | — | 0-0 | 0-0 | 1-2 | 1-0 | 4-2 | 1-0 | 4-0 | 1-0 | 2-1 | 0-1 | 1-2 | 1-0 |
| 1-3 | 0-0 | — | 2-0 | 3-1 | 1-1 | 2-0 | 0-1 | 1-0 | 3-1 | 0-2 | 1-0 | 1-2 | 0-0 |
| 1-1 | 2-0 | 0-2 | — | 0-1 | 1-1 | 0-0 | 2-1 | 2-1 | 2-0 | 1-3 | 0-1 | 2-1 | 3-1 |
| 0-0 | 1-0 | 1-1 | 1-0 | — | 5-0 | 3-0 | 2-0 | 1-1 | 1-0 | 3-2 | 2-1 | 1-1 | 2-0 |
| 1-1 | 2-3 | 1-0 | 1-1 | 0-0 | — | 1-3 | 1-2 | 0-3 | 2-0 | 1-1 | 2-0 | 2-1 | 2-2 |
| 3-0 | 1-1 | 1-3 | 2-0 | 3-2 | 1-1 | — | 1-1 | 1-0 | 2-0 | 0-1 | 2-0 | 0-1 | 1-0 |
| 2-3 | 3-2 | 0-1 | 0-0 | 1-3 | 5-2 | 1-2 | — | 2-4 | 1-0 | 2-3 | 1-2 | 0-5 | 0-1 |
| 0-0 | 1-3 | 1-2 | 1-1 | 0-1 | 2-2 | 0-2 | 2-1 | — | 1-1 | 2-3 | 0-0 | 2-2 | 1-1 |
| 2-0 | 0-1 | 2-2 | 1-1 | 1-1 | 1-1 | 1-0 | 2-0 | 2-1 | — | 2-0 | 2-2 | 0-4 | 0-2 |
| 1-2 | 4-1 | 3-0 | 2-2 | 2-3 | 3-1 | 4-1 | 1-3 | 2-2 | 1-1 | — | 3-3 | 3-1 | 3-2 |
| 1-1 | 2-3 | 3-0 | 2-0 | 3-1 | 2-1 | 2-1 | 1-2 | 1-1 | 2-1 | 3-0 | — | 3-1 | 1-0 |
| 1-1 | 0-0 | 2-1 | 1-1 | 3-1 | 5-0 | 0-0 | 4-1 | 2-0 | 0-0 | 0-0 | 0-1 | — | 1-1 |
| 0-1 | 4-0 | 2-0 | 1-1 | 0-1 | 1-1 | 0-0 | 1-1 | 3-2 | 1-2 | 2-2 | 3-1 | 0-1 | — |

# NATIONWIDE FOOTBALL LEAGUE

| HOME TEAM | AFC Bournemouth | Brentford | Bristol C | Bristol R | Bury | Cambridge U | Colchester U | Luton T | Millwall | Northampton T |
|---|---|---|---|---|---|---|---|---|---|---|
| AFC Bournemouth | — | 2-0 | 4-0 | 1-2 | 1-0 | 1-1 | 2-2 | 3-2 | 1-2 | 2-0 |
| Brentford | 3-2 | — | 2-1 | 2-5 | 3-1 | 2-2 | 1-0 | 2-2 | 1-1 | 1-1 |
| Bristol C | 3-3 | 1-2 | — | 3-2 | 4-1 | 6-2 | 1-1 | 3-1 | 2-1 | 2-0 |
| Bristol R | 1-1 | 0-0 | 1-1 | — | 2-0 | 2-1 | 2-0 | 3-3 | 1-2 | 0-1 |
| Bury | 2-5 | 0-1 | 0-1 | 1-0 | — | 0-1 | 0-0 | 1-1 | 2-1 | 1-0 |
| Cambridge U | 0-2 | 1-1 | 1-0 | 0-3 | 0-1 | — | 2-1 | 2-1 | 1-5 | 1-2 |
| Colchester U | 3-1 | 3-1 | 4-0 | 2-1 | 1-1 | 2-0 | — | 3-1 | 0-1 | 0-2 |
| Luton T | 1-0 | 3-1 | 0-3 | 0-0 | 1-2 | 1-0 | 0-3 | — | 0-1 | 0-2 |
| Millwall | 0-1 | 1-0 | 1-1 | 3-0 | 4-0 | 3-1 | 6-1 | 1-0 | — | 0-1 |
| Northampton T | 0-3 | 1-1 | 2-0 | 2-1 | 2-1 | 0-2 | 2-0 | 0-1 | 3-3 | — |
| Notts Co | 0-2 | 2-2 | 2-1 | 1-1 | 1-0 | 0-1 | 2-2 | 1-3 | 3-4 | 2-0 |
| Oldham Ath | 2-1 | 3-0 | 0-0 | 1-0 | 1-1 | 1-3 | 1-1 | 2-0 | 0-1 | 2-1 |
| Oxford U | 1-2 | 0-1 | 0-1 | 0-1 | 1-0 | 1-1 | 0-1 | 0-0 | 0-2 | 3-1 |
| Peterborough U | 1-2 | 1-1 | 2-1 | 2-2 | 1-1 | 4-1 | 3-1 | 1-1 | 1-4 | 1-2 |
| Port Vale | 2-1 | 1-1 | 1-2 | 1-0 | 1-1 | 4-2 | 3-1 | 3-0 | 1-1 | 2-2 |
| Reading | 3-3 | 4-0 | 1-3 | 1-0 | 4-1 | 3-0 | 0-1 | 4-1 | 3-4 | 1-1 |
| Rotherham U | 3-1 | 2-1 | 1-1 | 3-0 | 1-2 | 3-0 | 3-2 | 1-1 | 3-2 | 1-0 |
| Stoke C | 2-1 | 1-0 | 1-0 | 4-1 | 2-1 | 2-3 | 3-1 | 1-3 | 3-2 | 1-1 |
| Swansea C | 0-3 | 6-0 | 2-2 | 0-0 | 0-2 | 1-1 | 0-2 | 4-0 | 0-0 | 1-1 |
| Swindon T | 1-1 | 2-3 | 1-1 | 1-3 | 3-0 | 3-1 | 0-0 | 1-3 | 0-2 | 1-1 |
| Walsall | 1-1 | 3-2 | 0-0 | 2-1 | 1-2 | 3-1 | 0-1 | 3-1 | 0-0 | 3-0 |
| Wigan Ath | 1-1 | 1-3 | 0-0 | 0-0 | 1-0 | 2-1 | 3-1 | 2-1 | 1-0 | 2-1 |
| Wrexham | 2-2 | 2-1 | 0-2 | 1-0 | 0-1 | 2-2 | 1-0 | 3-1 | 1-1 | 3-0 |
| Wycombe W | 0-3 | 0-0 | 1-2 | 0-1 | 2-1 | 0-2 | 1-1 | 1-1 | 0-0 | 1-0 |

## DIVISION 2 2000–2001 RESULTS

| | Notts Co | Oldham Ath | Oxford U | Peterborough U | Port Vale | Reading | Rotherham U | Stoke C | Swansea C | Swindon T | Walsall | Wigan Ath | Wrexham | Wycombe W |
|---|---|---|---|---|---|---|---|---|---|---|---|---|---|---|
| | 0-1 | 1-1 | 4-3 | 2-1 | 1-1 | 1-2 | 0-1 | 1-0 | 2-0 | 3-0 | 2-2 | 0-0 | 1-2 | 2-0 |
| | 3-1 | 1-1 | 3-0 | 1-0 | 1-1 | 1-2 | 0-3 | 2-2 | 0-0 | 0-1 | 2-1 | 2-2 | 1-0 | 0-0 |
| | 4-0 | 2-2 | 0-0 | 2-1 | 1-1 | 4-0 | 0-1 | 1-2 | 3-1 | 0-1 | 1-3 | 1-1 | 2-1 | 1-2 |
| | 0-0 | 0-2 | 6-2 | 1-2 | 0-3 | 2-2 | 1-1 | 0-3 | 1-0 | 0-0 | 0-0 | 0-0 | 4-0 | 1-2 |
| | 1-1 | 1-1 | 3-1 | 2-1 | 2-0 | 0-2 | 0-0 | 1-0 | 3-0 | 1-0 | 2-0 | 0-1 | 1-4 | 1-1 |
| | 2-2 | 2-0 | 1-0 | 0-0 | 4-0 | 1-1 | 6-1 | 1-1 | 3-3 | 0-1 | 0-1 | 1-2 | 2-3 | 1-0 |
| | 2-0 | 1-1 | 3-2 | 2-2 | 0-1 | 2-1 | 0-1 | 0-1 | 3-0 | 0-1 | 0-2 | 0-2 | 1-1 | 0-0 |
| | 0-1 | 0-0 | 1-1 | 3-2 | 1-1 | 1-1 | 0-1 | 1-2 | 5-3 | 2-3 | 0-0 | 0-2 | 3-4 | 1-2 |
| | 2-3 | 5-0 | 5-0 | 0-0 | 1-0 | 2-0 | 4-0 | 2-0 | 1-0 | 1-0 | 2-0 | 3-1 | 1-0 | 1-2 |
| | 1-0 | 2-1 | 0-1 | 0-0 | 0-2 | 2-0 | 0-1 | 2-2 | 2-1 | 0-1 | 0-3 | 1-0 | 2-2 | 2-2 |
| | — | 1-0 | 2-1 | 3-3 | 0-1 | 3-2 | 4-1 | 2-2 | 0-1 | 3-2 | 2-0 | 2-2 | 1-0 | 0-2 |
| | 0-1 | — | 3-2 | 1-4 | 4-1 | 0-2 | 2-3 | 1-2 | 1-1 | 1-0 | 0-0 | 2-1 | 5-1 | 2-0 |
| | 2-3 | 0-1 | — | 0-1 | 1-1 | 0-2 | 4-3 | 1-1 | 3-1 | 0-2 | 2-1 | 0-2 | 3-4 | 1-2 |
| | 1-0 | 0-0 | 4-2 | — | 2-0 | 1-0 | 1-1 | 0-4 | 0-2 | 4-0 | 2-0 | 2-0 | 1-0 | 3-2 |
| | 2-3 | 0-0 | 3-0 | 5-0 | — | 0-1 | 0-2 | 1-1 | 1-0 | 3-0 | 0-2 | 0-0 | 1-1 | 0-1 |
| | 2-1 | 5-0 | 4-3 | 1-1 | 1-0 | — | 2-0 | 3-3 | 5-1 | 2-0 | 2-2 | 1-0 | 4-1 | 2-0 |
| | 0-0 | 3-0 | 3-1 | 3-0 | 3-2 | 1-3 | — | 2-1 | 4-2 | 4-3 | 2-3 | 1-1 | 2-0 | 1-0 |
| | 0-1 | 0-1 | 4-0 | 3-0 | 1-1 | 0-0 | 1-1 | — | 1-2 | 4-1 | 0-0 | 2-0 | 3-1 | 0-0 |
| | 0-1 | 1-2 | 1-2 | 2-2 | 0-1 | 0-1 | 0-0 | 2-1 | — | 0-0 | 3-1 | 0-0 | 0-1 | 3-1 |
| | 1-2 | 3-0 | 2-1 | 2-1 | 0-1 | 0-1 | 2-1 | 0-3 | 1-1 | — | 1-4 | 2-2 | 2-2 | 1-1 |
| | 5-1 | 3-2 | 3-2 | 1-1 | 2-1 | 2-1 | 1-1 | 3-0 | 5-1 | 1-0 | — | 2-0 | 2-3 | 5-1 |
| | 1-1 | 3-1 | 3-2 | 1-0 | 1-0 | 1-1 | 0-2 | 1-1 | 2-0 | 0-0 | 1-1 | — | 0-0 | 2-1 |
| | 1-1 | 3-1 | 5-3 | 2-1 | 1-0 | 1-2 | 1-3 | 1-2 | 1-0 | 1-1 | 0-1 | 1-3 | — | 0-0 |
| | 3-1 | 2-1 | 3-1 | 2-0 | 0-1 | 1-1 | 0-1 | 0-1 | 2-1 | 0-0 | 3-1 | 1-2 | 1-1 | — |

# NATIONWIDE FOOTBALL LEAGUE

| HOME TEAM | Barnet | Blackpool | Brighton & HA | Cardiff C | Carlisle U | Cheltenham T | Chesterfield | Darlington | Exeter C | Halifax T |
|---|---|---|---|---|---|---|---|---|---|---|
| Barnet | — | 7-0 | 0-1 | 2-2 | 0-1 | 2-2 | 1-1 | 3-0 | 1-1 | 1-0 |
| Blackpool | 3-2 | — | 0-2 | 1-0 | 3-2 | 2-2 | 1-3 | 2-1 | 3-0 | 0-1 |
| Brighton & HA | 4-1 | 1-0 | — | 1-0 | 4-1 | 3-0 | 1-0 | 2-0 | 2-0 | 2-1 |
| Cardiff C | 1-0 | 1-1 | 1-1 | — | 4-1 | 3-1 | 3-3 | 2-0 | 6-1 | 4-2 |
| Carlisle U | 0-2 | 1-0 | 0-0 | 2-2 | — | 1-1 | 2-4 | 0-2 | 0-1 | 2-2 |
| Cheltenham T | 4-3 | 0-1 | 3-1 | 3-1 | 1-0 | — | 0-1 | 1-0 | 1-0 | 4-2 |
| Chesterfield | 1-2 | 2-1 | 1-0 | 2-2 | 1-1 | 2-0 | — | 2-0 | 2-0 | 3-0 |
| Darlington | 1-0 | 1-3 | 1-2 | 2-0 | 1-0 | 1-0 | 0-3 | — | 1-1 | 0-1 |
| Exeter C | 1-0 | 2-0 | 1-0 | 1-2 | 1-0 | 0-2 | 1-1 | 1-1 | — | 0-0 |
| Halifax T | 3-0 | 1-2 | 0-0 | 1-2 | 0-0 | 1-2 | 2-2 | 1-0 | 3-1 | — |
| Hartlepool U | 6-1 | 3-1 | 2-2 | 3-1 | 2-2 | 0-0 | 1-2 | 2-1 | 2-0 | 1-1 |
| Hull C | 2-1 | 0-1 | 0-2 | 2-0 | 2-1 | 0-2 | 3-1 | 2-0 | 2-1 | 1-0 |
| Kidderminster H | 2-1 | 1-4 | 0-2 | 2-4 | 0-1 | 1-1 | 0-2 | 0-0 | 0-0 | 2-1 |
| Leyton O | 3-1 | 1-0 | 0-2 | 2-1 | 1-0 | 0-0 | 2-0 | 1-0 | 2-1 | 3-0 |
| Lincoln C | 2-1 | 1-1 | 2-0 | 2-0 | 1-1 | 1-0 | 1-1 | 2-2 | 3-1 | 1-1 |
| Macclesfield T | 3-0 | 2-1 | 0-0 | 2-5 | 1-0 | 2-1 | 1-2 | 1-1 | 0-2 | 0-0 |
| Mansfield T | 4-1 | 0-1 | 2-0 | 2-1 | 1-1 | 2-1 | 0-1 | 3-2 | 1-1 | 5-1 |
| Plymouth Arg | 2-3 | 2-0 | 0-2 | 2-1 | 2-0 | 0-0 | 3-0 | 1-1 | 1-0 | 1-0 |
| Rochdale | 0-0 | 1-0 | 1-1 | 1-1 | 6-0 | 1-1 | 2-2 | 1-1 | 3-0 | 0-1 |
| Scunthorpe U | 2-1 | 1-0 | 2-1 | 0-2 | 3-0 | 1-1 | 1-1 | 1-1 | 0-2 | 1-0 |
| Shrewsbury T | 3-2 | 1-0 | 3-0 | 0-4 | 0-1 | 1-0 | 0-0 | 1-0 | 2-0 | 2-1 |
| Southend U | 2-0 | 0-3 | 2-0 | 1-1 | 1-1 | 0-1 | 3-2 | 0-2 | 1-1 | 0-3 |
| Torquay U | 2-1 | 3-2 | 0-1 | 1-4 | 4-2 | 1-2 | 0-0 | 2-1 | 2-1 | 1-2 |
| York C | 1-0 | 0-2 | 0-1 | 3-3 | 0-0 | 0-2 | 0-1 | 2-0 | 0-3 | 2-1 |

# DIVISION 3 2000–2001 RESULTS

| Hartlepool U | Hull C | Kidderminster H | Leyton O | Lincoln C | Macclesfield T | Mansfield T | Plymouth Arg | Rochdale | Scunthorpe U | Shrewsbury T | Southend U | Torquay U | York C |
|---|---|---|---|---|---|---|---|---|---|---|---|---|---|
| 1-3 | 1-1 | 0-0 | 1-2 | 4-3 | 0-2 | 3-3 | 1-1 | 3-0 | 4-2 | 3-0 | 2-1 | 2-3 | 2-0 |
| 1-2 | 3-1 | 5-1 | 2-2 | 2-0 | 2-1 | 2-2 | 1-0 | 3-1 | 6-0 | 0-1 | 2-2 | 5-0 | 1-0 |
| 4-2 | 3-0 | 0-2 | 2-0 | 2-0 | 4-1 | 2-0 | 2-0 | 2-1 | 0-0 | 4-0 | 0-2 | 6-2 | 1-1 |
| 3-2 | 2-0 | 0-0 | 1-1 | 3-2 | 2-0 | 2-0 | 4-1 | 0-0 | 3-0 | 3-1 | 2-2 | 2-1 | 4-0 |
| 2-3 | 0-0 | 2-0 | 1-0 | 1-1 | 1-0 | 2-1 | 1-1 | 1-2 | 1-2 | 1-0 | 3-1 | 1-0 | 1-1 |
| 1-2 | 0-1 | 1-3 | 1-1 | 2-1 | 1-1 | 2-2 | 5-2 | 0-2 | 1-0 | 1-1 | 2-1 | 2-0 | 1-1 |
| 0-0 | 1-0 | 1-0 | 4-1 | 1-2 | 4-1 | 4-0 | 2-1 | 1-1 | 1-0 | 3-0 | 1-1 | 3-0 | 4-1 |
| 1-1 | 0-2 | 1-2 | 1-1 | 3-0 | 1-1 | 2-1 | 1-0 | 1-2 | 2-1 | 3-0 | 1-1 | 2-0 | 1-1 |
| 1-1 | 0-1 | 2-1 | 2-3 | 0-0 | 0-0 | 0-0 | 0-2 | 0-1 | 2-1 | 1-0 | 2-2 | 1-1 | 3-1 |
| 0-1 | 0-2 | 3-2 | 2-2 | 1-1 | 3-0 | 3-4 | 2-0 | 1-2 | 3-4 | 0-0 | 0-1 | 2-1 | 1-3 |
| — | 0-1 | 3-1 | 2-1 | 1-0 | 2-2 | 1-1 | 1-1 | 1-1 | 1-0 | 1-3 | 1-0 | 3-1 | 1-0 |
| 0-0 | — | 0-0 | 1-0 | 1-1 | 0-0 | 2-1 | 1-1 | 3-2 | 2-1 | 1-0 | 1-1 | 1-2 | 0-0 |
| 0-1 | 2-2 | — | 2-1 | 1-3 | 2-1 | 1-0 | 3-0 | 0-0 | 0-0 | 3-1 | 2-1 | 2-0 | 3-1 |
| 3-1 | 2-2 | 0-0 | — | 1-0 | 2-1 | 2-1 | 1-1 | 1-1 | 1-1 | 2-0 | 0-2 | 0-2 | 1-1 |
| 0-2 | 2-0 | 3-3 | 2-3 | — | 1-2 | 0-2 | 2-1 | 1-1 | 1-1 | 2-2 | 3-0 | 1-2 | 2-1 |
| 0-1 | 0-0 | 1-0 | 0-2 | 2-0 | — | 0-1 | 3-1 | 0-0 | 0-1 | 2-1 | 1-0 | 2-1 | 0-1 |
| 4-3 | 1-1 | 2-1 | 2-0 | 2-3 | 4-4 | — | 0-0 | 1-0 | 1-0 | 1-0 | 1-1 | 0-0 | 1-3 |
| 0-2 | 1-1 | 4-0 | 0-1 | 1-0 | 0-1 | 2-0 | — | 0-0 | 1-0 | 3-1 | 3-3 | 3-1 | 1-0 |
| 2-1 | 1-0 | 0-0 | 3-1 | 3-1 | 2-2 | 1-0 | 2-1 | — | 3-2 | 1-7 | 0-1 | 2-1 | 0-1 |
| 3-0 | 0-1 | 2-0 | 1-1 | 2-1 | 2-2 | 6-0 | 4-1 | 0-0 | — | 2-0 | 1-1 | 3-0 | 4-0 |
| 1-1 | 0-2 | 1-0 | 1-1 | 3-2 | 2-2 | 2-1 | 4-1 | 0-4 | 0-2 | — | 0-1 | 1-1 | 2-0 |
| 2-1 | 1-1 | 1-1 | 0-1 | 1-0 | 3-1 | 3-1 | 2-2 | 3-0 | 1-0 | 0-0 | — | 1-1 | 1-0 |
| 1-0 | 1-1 | 1-1 | 1-2 | 1-1 | 2-0 | 2-2 | 1-1 | 1-0 | 0-2 | 0-0 | 1-1 | — | 2-2 |
| 1-1 | 0-0 | 1-0 | 1-1 | 0-0 | 1-3 | 2-1 | 1-2 | 0-2 | 2-0 | 2-1 | 1-0 | 3-2 | — |

| Player | Ht | Wt | Birthplace | D.O.B. | Source |
|---|---|---|---|---|---|
| Adams Tony (D) | 6 3 | 13 02 | Romford | 10 10 66 | Apprentice |
| Aliadiere Jeremie (F) | 6 0 | 11 00 | Rambouillet | 30 3 83 | Scholar |
| Barrett Graham (F) | 5 10 | 11 07 | Dublin | 6 10 81 | Trainee |
| Bergkamp Dennis (F) | 6 0 | 12 05 | Amsterdam | 18 5 69 | Internazionale |
| Chilvers Liam (D) | 6 0 | 12 04 | Chelmsford | 6 10 81 | |
| Cole Ashley (D) | 5 8 | 10 10 | Stepney | 20 12 80 | Trainee |
| Danilevicius Tomas (F) | 6 2 | 12 06 | Lithuania | 18 7 78 | Lausanne |
| Demel Guy (M) | 6 1 | 13 07 | Orsay | 13 6 81 | Nimes |
| Dixon Lee (D) | 5 9 | 10 12 | Manchester | 17 3 64 | Stoke C |
| Edu (M) | 6 1 | 12 04 | Sao Paulo | 15 5 78 | Corinthians |
| Grimandi Gilles (D) | 5 10 | 11 08 | Gap | 11 11 70 | Monaco |
| Grondin David (D) | 5 9 | 11 11 | Paris | 8 5 80 | St Etienne |
| Halls John (D) | 6 0 | 11 00 | Islington | 14 2 82 | Scholar |
| Henry Thierry (F) | 6 2 | 13 01 | Paris | 17 8 77 | Juventus |
| Israel (D) | 5 9 | 10 03 | Sao Paulo | 9 7 83 | Scholar |
| Kanu Nwankwo (F) | 6 5 | 12 01 | Owerri | 1 8 76 | Internazionale |
| Keown Martin (D) | 6 1 | 12 04 | Oxford | 24 7 66 | Everton |
| Lauren Etame-Mayer (M) | 5 11 | 11 03 | Londi Keisi | 19 1 77 | Mallorca |
| Ljungberg Frederik (M) | 5 9 | 10 13 | Halmstad | 16 4 77 | Halmstad |
| Luzhny Oleg (D) | 5 10 | 12 01 | Ukraine | 5 8 68 | Dynamo Kiev |
| Malz Stefan (M) | 5 10 | 12 01 | Ludwigshafen | 15 6 72 | Munich 1860 |
| Manninger Alex (G) | 6 2 | 13 03 | Salzburg | 4 6 77 | Graz |
| Mendez Alberto (M) | 5 11 | 11 04 | Nuremberg | 24 10 74 | FC Feucht |
| Noble David (M) | 6 0 | 12 04 | Hitchin | 2 2 82 | Scholar |
| Oates Greg (D) | 6 0 | 12 04 | Maldon | 3 10 81 | Scholar |
| Osei-Kuffour Jo (F) | 5 7 | 10 03 | Edmonton | 17 11 81 | Scholar |
| Parlour Ray (M) | 5 10 | 11 12 | Romford | 7 3 73 | Trainee |
| Pennant Jermaine (M) | 5 8 | 10 01 | Nottingham | 15 1 83 | |
| Pires Robert (M) | 6 1 | 11 09 | Reims | 29 10 73 | Marseille |
| Seaman David (G) | 6 3 | 13 00 | Rotherham | 19 9 63 | QPR |
| Silvinho (D) | 5 7 | 10 06 | Sao Paulo | 12 4 74 | Corinthians |
| Stack Graham (G) | 6 2 | 12 06 | Hampstead | 26 9 81 | Scholar |
| Stepanovs Igor (D) | 6 4 | 13 05 | Ogre | 21 1 76 | Skonto Riga |
| Svard Sebastian (D) | | | Hvidovre | 15 1 82 | |
| Taylor Stuart (G) | 6 4 | 13 06 | Romford | 28 11 80 | Trainee |
| Upson Matthew (D) | 6 1 | 11 04 | Hartismere | 18 4 79 | Luton T |
| Vieira Patrick (M) | 6 4 | 13 00 | Dakar | 23 6 76 | AC Milan |
| Volz Moritz (D) | 5 10 | 12 06 | Germany | 21 1 83 | |
| Wiltord Sylvain (F) | 5 9 | 12 04 | Neuilly-sur-Mame | 10 5 74 | Bordeaux |

**League Appearances:** Adams, T. 26; Bergkamp, D. 19(6); Cole, A. 15(2); Danilevicius, T. (2); Dixon, L. 26(3); Edu, 2(3); Grimandi, G. 28(2); Henry, T. 27(8); Kanu, N. 13(14); Keown, M. 28; Lauren, E. 15(3); Ljungberg, F. 25(5); Lukic, J. 3; Luzhny, O. 16(3); Malz, S. (1); Manninger, A. 11; Parlour, R. 28(5); Pires, R. 29(4); Seaman, D. 24; Silvinho, 23(1); Stepanovs, I. 9; Upson, M. (2); Vernazza, P. (2); Vieira, P. 28(2); Vivas, N. 3(9); Wiltord, S. 20(7).

**Goals – League** (63): Henry 17 (1 pen), Wiltord 8, Ljungberg 6, Vieira 5, Parlour 4, Pires 4, Bergkamp 3, Cole 3, Kanu 3, Lauren 2, Silvinho 2, Adams 1, Dixon 1, Grimandi 1, Vernazza 1, own goals 2.

**Worthington Cup** (1): Stepanovs 1.

**FA Cup** (16): Wiltord 6, Pires 3, Adams 1, Bergkamp 1, Henry 1 (pen), Ljungberg 1, Vieira 1, own goals 2.

**Ground:** Arsenal Stadium, Highbury, London N5 1BU. Telephone (020) 7704 4000.

**Record attendance:** 73,295 v Sunderland, Div 1, 9 March 1935. **Capacity:** 38,500.
**Manager:** Arsène Wenger.
**Secretary:** David Miles.
**Most League Goals:** 127, Division 1, 1930–31.
**Highest League Scorer in Season:** Ted Drake, 42, 1934–35.
**Most League Goals in Total Aggregate:** Cliff Bastin, 150, 1930–47.
**Most Capped Player:** Kenny Sansom, 77 (86), England, 1981–1988.
**Most League Appearances:** David O'Leary, 558, 1975–93.
**Honours – FA Premier League:** Champions – 1997–98. **Football League:** Division 1
Champions –1930–31, 1932–33, 1933–34, 1934–35, 1937–38, 1947–48, 1952–53, 1970–71,
1988–89, 1990–91. **FA Cup winners** 1929–30, 1935–36, 1949–50, 1970–71, 1978–79,
1992–93, 1997–98. **Football League Cup winners** 1986–87, 1992–93. **European
Competitions: European Cup-Winners' Cup winners:** 1993–94. **Fairs Cup winners:**
1969–70.
**Colours:** Red shirts with white sleeves, white shorts, red and white stockings.

## ASTON VILLA                          FA PREMIERSHIP

| Name | | | Birthplace | | | Previous club |
|---|---|---|---|---|---|---|
| Alpay Ozalan (D) | 6 2 | 14 00 | Izmir | 29 | 5 73 | Fenerbahce |
| Angel Juan Pablo (F) | 6 0 | 12 10 | Medellin | 24 | 10 75 | River Plate |
| Barry Gareth (D) | 5 11 | 12 06 | Hastings | 23 | 2 81 | Trainee |
| Berks David (M) | 5 8 | 10 07 | Stoke | 23 | 12 81 | Scholar |
| Bewers Jonathan (D) | 5 8 | 9 13 | Kettering | 10 | 9 82 | Trainee |
| Boateng George (M) | 5 9 | 10 12 | Nkawkaw | 5 | 9 75 | Coventry C |
| Cooke Stephen (M) | 5 7 | 9 00 | Walsall | 15 | 2 83 | |
| Cutler Neil (G) | 6 1 | 12 00 | Birmingham | 3 | 9 76 | Chester C |
| Delaney Mark (D) | 6 1 | 11 07 | Haverfordwest | 13 | 5 76 | Carmarthen T |
| Dillon Sean (D) | 6 0 | 12 06 | Dublin | 30 | 7 83 | Scholar |
| Dublin Dion (F) | 6 2 | 12 04 | Leicester | 22 | 4 69 | Coventry C |
| Edwards Rob (D) | 6 1 | 11 10 | Telford | 25 | 12 82 | Trainee |
| Enckelman Peter (G) | 6 2 | 12 05 | Turku | 10 | 3 77 | TPS Turku |
| Ennis Pierre (D) | 5 10 | 12 03 | Dublin | 25 | 2 84 | Scholar |
| Fahey Keith (M) | 5 10 | 12 07 | Dublin | 15 | 1 83 | |
| Folds Liam (D) | 5 11 | 12 01 | Bedford | 21 | 1 82 | Scholar |
| Ginola David (F) | 5 10 | 12 07 | Gassin | 25 | 1 67 | Tottenham H |
| Haynes Danny (D) | 6 2 | 12 02 | Nuneaton | 24 | 8 82 | Scholar |
| Henderson Wayne (G) | 5 11 | 12 02 | Dublin | 16 | 9 83 | Scholar |
| Hendrie Lee (M) | 5 10 | 11 00 | Birmingham | 18 | 5 77 | Trainee |
| Hitzlsperger Thomas (D) | 6 0 | 11 12 | Germany | 5 | 4 82 | Bayern Munich |
| Hylton Leon (D) | 5 9 | 11 00 | Birmingham | 27 | 1 83 | |
| Hynes Peter (F) | 5 9 | 11 12 | Dublin | 28 | 11 83 | |
| Jackman Daniel (D) | 5 4 | 9 08 | Worcester | 3 | 1 83 | Scholar |
| James David (G) | 6 5 | 14 02 | Welwyn | 1 | 8 70 | Liverpool |
| Joachim Julian (F) | 5 6 | 12 00 | Boston | 20 | 9 74 | Leicester C |
| Marfell Andrew (F) | 6 1 | 12 07 | Gloucester | 20 | 2 82 | Scholar |
| McGrath John (F) | 5 10 | 10 04 | Limerick | 27 | 3 80 | Belvedere |
| Melaugh Gavin (M) | 5 7 | 9 07 | Derry | 9 | 7 81 | Trainee |
| Merson Paul (F) | 6 0 | 13 02 | Northolt | 20 | 3 68 | Middlesbrough |
| Moore Stefan (F) | 5 10 | 10 12 | Birmingham | 28 | 9 83 | Scholar |
| Myhill Boaz (G) | 6 3 | 14 06 | California | 9 | 11 82 | Scholar |
| Nicholas Alexis (M) | | | London | 13 | 2 83 | Scholar |
| Samuel J Lloyd (D) | 5 11 | 11 04 | Trinidad | 29 | 3 81 | Charlton Ath |
| Smith Jay (M) | 5 7 | 10 00 | London | 24 | 9 81 | Scholar |
| Southgate Gareth (D) | 6 0 | 12 06 | Watford | 3 | 9 70 | Crystal Palace |
| Standing Michael (M) | 5 10 | 10 05 | Shoreham | 20 | 3 81 | Trainee |
| Staunton Steve (D) | 6 0 | 12 12 | Drogheda | 19 | 1 69 | Crystal Palace |

| Stone Steve (M) | 5 8 | 12 07 | Gateshead | 20 8 71 | Nottingham F |
| Tarrant Neil (F) | 6 1 | 11 05 | Darlington | 24 6 79 | Ross Co |
| Taylor Ian (M) | 6 1 | 12 00 | Birmingham | 4 6 68 | Sheffield W |
| Vassell Darius (F) | 5 7 | 12 00 | Birmingham | 13 6 80 | Trainee |
| Walker Richard (F) | 6 0 | 12 04 | Sutton Coldfield | 8 11 77 | Trainee |
| Willetts Ben (D) | 5 9 | 11 05 | West Bromwich | 10 2 83 | |
| Wright Alan (D) | 5 4 | 9 09 | Ashton-under-Lyme | 28 9 71 | Blackburn R |

**League Appearances:** Alpay, O. 33; Angel, J. 7(2); Barry, G. 29(1); Boateng, G. 29(4); De Bilde, G. 4; Delaney, M. 12(7); Dublin, D. 29(4); Ehiogu, U. 1(1); Ginola, D. 14(13); Hendrie, L. 27(5); Hitzisperger, T. (1); James, D. 38; Joachim, J. 11(9); McGrath, J. (3); Merson, P. 38; Nilis, L. 3; Samuel, J. 1(2); Southgate, G. 31; Staunton, S. 13(1); Stone, S. 33(1); Taylor, I. 25(4); Vassell, D. 5(18); Wright, A. 35(1).
**Goals – League (46):** Dublin 8 (1 pen), Joachim 7, Hendrie 6, Merson 6, Taylor 4, Vassell 4, Ginola 3, Southgate 2, Stone 2, Angel 1, Boateng 1, Nilis 1, Wright 1.
**Worthington Cup (0).**
**FA Cup (3):** Joachim 1, Stone 1, Vassell 1.
**Ground:** Villa Park, Trinity Rd, Birmingham B6 6HE. Telephone (0121) 327 2299.
**Record attendance:** 76,588 v Derby Co, FA Cup 6th rd, 2 March 1946.
**Capacity:** 42,584.
**Manager:** John Gregory.
**Secretary:** Steven Stride.
**Most League Goals:** 128, Division 1, 1930–31.
**Highest League Scorer in Season:** 'Pongo' Waring, 49, Division 1, 1930–31.
**Most League Goals in Total Aggregate:** Harry Hampton, 215, 1904–15.
**Most Capped Player:** Paul McGrath, 51 (83), Republic of Ireland.
**Most League Appearances:** Charlie Aitken, 561, 1961–76.
**Honours – Football League:** Division 1 Champions – 1893–94, 1895–96, 1896–97, 1898–99, 1899–1900, 1909–10, 1980–81. Division 2 Champions – 1937–38, 1959–60. Division 3 Champions – 1971–72. **FA Cup:** Winners 1887, 1895, 1897, 1905, 1913, 1920, 1957. **Football League Cup:** Winners 1961, 1975, 1977, 1994, 1996. **European Competitions:** European Cup winners 1981–82, **European Super Cup winners:** 1982–83.
**Colours:** Claret shirts with blue and yellow trim, white shorts with claret and blue trim, sky blue stockings with claret and white trim.

# BARNET     NATIONWIDE FOOTBALL CONFERENCE

| Arber Mark (D) | 6 1 | 12 11 | Johannesburg | 8 10 77 | Tottenham H |
| Bell Leon (M) | 5 7 | 9 07 | Hitchin | 19 12 80 | Trainee |
| Berkley Austin (M) | 5 9 | 10 10 | Gravesend | 28 1 73 | Shrewsbury T |
| Bossu Bertrand (G) | 6 7 | 14 00 | Calais | 14 10 80 | |
| Brown Daniel (M) | 6 0 | 12 06 | Bethnal Green | 12 9 80 | Leyton Orient |
| Currie Darren (M) | 5 10 | 12 07 | Hampstead | 29 11 74 | Plymouth Arg |
| Darcy Ross (D) | 6 0 | 12 02 | Balbriggan | 21 3 78 | Tottenham H |
| Doolan John (M) | 6 1 | 13 00 | Liverpool | 7 5 74 | Mansfield T |
| Flynn Lee (D) | | | Hampstead | 4 9 73 | Hayes |
| Gledhill Lee (D) | 5 10 | 11 02 | Bury | 7 11 80 | Trainee |
| Goodhind Warren (D) | 5 11 | 11 02 | Johannesburg | 16 8 77 | Trainee |
| Gower Mark (M) | 5 11 | 11 12 | Edmonton | 5 10 78 | Tottenham H |
| Harrison Lee (G) | 6 2 | 12 07 | Billericay | 12 9 71 | Fulham |
| Heald Greg (D) | 6 1 | 13 01 | Enfield | 26 9 71 | Peterborough U |
| Midgley Neil (F) | 5 11 | 11 02 | Cambridge | 21 10 78 | Ipswich T |
| Naisbitt Danny (G) | 6 1 | 11 12 | Bishop Auckland | 25 11 78 | Walsall |
| Niven Stuart (M) | 5 11 | 12 08 | Glasgow | 24 12 78 | Ipswich T |
| Pluck Lee (D) | | | Enfield | 25 3 82 | Scholar |

| Purser Wayne (F) | 5 9 | 11 13 | Basildon | 13 4 80 | QPR |
| Richards Tony (F) | 6 0 | 13 06 | Newham | 17 9 73 | Leyton Orient |
| Sawyers Robert (D) | 5 10 | 11 03 | Dudley | 20 11 78 | Wolverhampton W |
| Searle Stevie (M) | 5 10 | 11 08 | Lambeth | 7 3 77 | Sittingbourne |
| Stockley Sam (D) | 6 0 | 12 00 | Tiverton | 5 9 77 | Trainee |
| Strevens Ben (F) | 6 1 | 11 00 | Islington | 24 5 80 | Wingate & Finchley |
| Taylor Mark (D) | 5 10 | 12 00 | Hertfordshire | 14 7 82 | Trainee |
| Toms Frazer (M) | 6 1 | 11 00 | Ealing | 13 9 79 | Trainee |

**League Appearances:** Arber, M. 45; Basham, M. 8; Bell, L. 7(4); Brown, D. 22(7); Charlery, K. 6(1); Collis, D. 1(1); Cottee, T. 16; Currie, D. 43(2); Darcy, R. (3); Dawson, K. 5; Doolan, J. 31; Flynn, L. 17; Gedhill, L. 1(4); Goodhind, W. 30(1); Gower, M. 10(4); Harrison, L. 30; Heald, G. 39; McGleish, S. 14(5); Midgley, N. 3(1); Naisbitt, D. 16(3); Newton, E. 2(2); Niven, S. 20(4); Pluck, L. (1); Purser, W. 4(14); Richards, T. 27(6); Riza, O. 7(3); Sawyers, R. 25(4); Stockley, S. 45; Strevens, B. 13(15); Toms, F. 19(7).
**Goals – League** (67): Currie 10 (2 pens), Cottee 9, Richards 8, Arber 7, McGleish 5, Riza 4, Strevens 4, Charlery 3, Doolan 3 (2 pens), Heald 3, Purser 3, Niven 2, Goodhind 1, Gower 1, Sawyers 1, Stockley 1, own goals 2.
**Worthington Cup** (3): Doolan 1, McGleish 1, Richards 1.
**FA Cup** (3): Cottee 1, Currie 1, Richards 1.
**Ground:** Underhill Stadium, Barnet Lane, Barnet, Herts EN5 2BE. Telephone (020) 8441 6932.
**Record attendance:** 11,026 v Wycombe Wanderers. FA Amateur Cup 4th Round 1951–52.
**Capacity:** 5560.
**Manager:** John Still.
**Most League Goals:** 81, Division 4, 1991–92.
**Highest League Scorer in Season:** Dougie Freedman, 24, Division 3, 1994–95.
**Most League Goals in Total Aggregate:** Sean Devine, 47, 1995–99.
**Most Capped Player:** Ken Charlery, 4, St Lucia.
**Most League Appearances:** Paul Wilson, 263, 1991–2000.
**Honours – FA Amateur Cup winners** 1945–46. **GM Vauxhall Conference winners** 1990–91.
**Colours:** Amber and black shirts, amber shorts, amber stockings.

---

# BARNSLEY                                               DIV. 1

| Appleby Matty (D) | 5 10 | 11 08 | Middlesbrough | 16 4 72 | Darlington |
| Austin Kevin (D) | 6 1 | 15 00 | Hackney | 12 2 73 | Lincoln C |
| Austin Neil (D) | 5 10 | 11 00 | Barnsley | 26 4 83 | Trainee |
| Barker Christopher (D) | 6 0 | 11 08 | Sheffield | 2 3 80 | Alfreton |
| Barnard Darren (D) | 5 9 | 12 03 | Rinteln | 30 11 71 | Bristol C |
| Barrowclough Carl (M) | | | Doncaster | 25 9 81 | Scholar |
| Bertos Leo (F) | 6 0 | 12 00 | Wellington | 20 12 81 | |
| Brown Keith (D) | 5 11 | 11 02 | Edinburgh | 24 12 79 | Blackburn R |
| Chettle Steve (D) | 6 1 | 13 07 | Nottingham | 27 9 68 | Nottingham F |
| Corbo Mateo (D) | 5 11 | 12 08 | Montevideo | 21 4 76 | Oviedo |
| Crooks Lee (D) | 6 2 | 13 13 | Wakefield | 14 1 78 | Manchester C |
| Dudgeon James (D) | 6 2 | 12 04 | Newcastle | 19 3 81 | Trainee |
| Dyer Bruce (F) | 5 11 | 12 06 | Ilford | 13 4 75 | Crystal Palace |
| Evans Andy (F) | 6 2 | 12 02 | Aberystwyth | 25 11 75 | Cardiff C |
| Fallon Rory (F) | 6 2 | 11 09 | Gisbourne | 20 3 82 | North Shore U |
| Gartland Graham (M) | | | Dublin | 13 7 83 | |
| Hayward Steve (M) | 5 11 | 13 00 | Walsall | 8 9 71 | Fulham |
| Jackson Paul (F) | 5 8 | 11 04 | Rochdale | 14 5 81 | Trainee |

| | | | | | |
|---|---|---|---|---|---|
| Jones Lee (F) | 5 8 | 10 06 | Wrexham | 29 5 73 | Tranmere R |
| Kay Antony (M) | 5 11 | 11 08 | Barnsley | 21 10 82 | Trainee |
| Marriott Andy (G) | 6 2 | 13 04 | Sutton-in-Ashfield | 11 10 70 | Sunderland |
| McClare Sean (M) | 5 11 | 11 08 | Rotherham | 12 1 78 | Trainee |
| Miller Christopher (M) | | | Paisley | 19 11 82 | Scholar |
| Miller Kevin (G) | 6 1 | 16 00 | Falmouth | 15 3 69 | Crystal Palace |
| Morgan Chris (D) | 6 1 | 12 09 | Barnsley | 9 11 77 | Trainee |
| Mulligan David (M) | | | Fazakerley | 24 3 82 | Scholar |
| Neil Alex (M) | 5 9 | 11 00 | Coatbridge | 9 6 81 | Dunfermline Ath |
| O'Callaghan Brian (D) | 6 1 | 12 01 | Limerick | 24 2 81 | Pike Rovers |
| Parkin Jonathan (F) | 6 4 | 13 07 | Barnsley | 30 12 81 | Scholar |
| Parry Craig (M) | | | Barnsley | 10 3 84 | Scholar |
| Rankin Isiah (F) | 5 10 | 11 00 | London | 22 5 78 | Bradford C |
| Ravenhill Richard (M) | 5 10 | 11 01 | Doncaster | 16 1 81 | Trainee |
| Regan Carl (D) | 6 0 | 11 05 | Liverpool | 9 9 80 | Everton |
| Salli Janne (D) | 6 2 | 11 13 | Finland | 14 12 77 | |
| Savic Sinisa (M) | | | Starnberg | 8 11 80 | |
| Sheron Mike (F) | 5 10 | 12 07 | Liverpool | 11 1 72 | QPR |
| Shipperley Neil (F) | 6 0 | 14 01 | Chatham | 30 10 74 | Nottingham F |
| Tinkler Eric (M) | 6 2 | 13 08 | Roodepoort | 30 7 70 | Cagliari |
| Ward Mitch (D) | 5 8 | 11 13 | Sheffield | 19 6 71 | Everton |

**League Appearances:** Appleby, M. 17(2); Barker, C. 39(1); Barnard, D. 26(4); Barrowclough, C. 2(5); Bertos, L. (2); Brown, K. 1; Bullock, M. 15(3); Chettle, S. 35; Corbo, M. 10(7); Dyer, B. 27(11); Fallon, R. 1; Hayward, S. 10; Jones, L. 15(12); Kay, A. 3(4); Maddison, N. 3; McClare, S. 5(5); Miller, K. 46; Morgan, C. 40; Moses, A. 11(3); Neil, A. 19(13); O'Callaghan, B. 20(6); Parkin, J. 4; Rankin, I. 6(3); Regan, C. 25(2); Ripley, S. 8(2); Salli, J. 6(1); Sheron, M. 21(13); Shipperley, N. 38(1); Thomas, G. 1(10); Van der Laan, R. 16(2); Ward, M. 34(2); Woan, I. 2(1).
**Goals – League** (49): Dyer 15, Shipperley 14 (1 pen), Jones 5, Appleby 2, Barnard 2 (2 pens), Bullock 1, Hayward 1, McClare 1, Morgan 1, Rankin 1, Ripley 1, Sheron 1, Van der Laan 1, own goals 3.
**Worthington Cup** (13): Sheron 5, Barnard 2, Shipperley 2, Corbo 1, Dyer 1, Jones 1, Van der Laan 1.
**FA Cup** (0).
**Ground:** Oakwell Ground, Grove St, Barnsley S71 1ET. Telephone (01226) 211211.
**Record attendance:** 40,255 v Stoke C, FA Cup 5th rd, 15 February 1936. **Capacity:** 23,186.
**Manager:** Nigel Spackman.
**Secretary:** Michael Spinks.
**Most League Goals:** 118, Division 3 (N), 1933–34.
**Highest League Scorer in Season:** Cecil McCormack, 33, Division 2, 1950–51.
**Most League Goals in Total Aggregate:** Ernest Hine, 123, 1921–26 and 1934–38.
**Most Capped Player:** Gerry Taggart, 35 (50), Northern Ireland.
**Most League Appearances:** Barry Murphy, 514, 1962–78.
**Honours – Football League:** Division 3 (N) Champions – 1933–34, 1938–39, 1954–55. **FA Cup:** Winners 1912.
**Colours:** Red shirts, white shorts, red stockings.

# BIRMINGHAM CITY                                    DIV. 1

| | | | | | |
|---|---|---|---|---|---|
| Adebola Dele (F) | 6 3 | 12 08 | Lagos | 23 6 75 | Crewe Alex |
| Bennett Ian (G) | 6 0 | 12 10 | Worksop | 10 10 71 | Peterborough U |
| Burrows David (D) | 5 8 | 11 08 | Dudley | 25 10 68 | Coventry C |
| Capaldi Tony (D) | 6 0 | 12 00 | Porsgrunn | 12 8 81 | Trainee |
| Eaden Nicky (D) | 5 9 | 12 02 | Sheffield | 12 12 72 | Barnsley |

| | | | | | |
|---|---|---|---|---|---|
| Furlong Paul (F) | 6 0 | 11 00 | London | 1 10 68 | Chelsea |
| Gill Jeremy (D) | 5 11 | 11 00 | Clevedon | 8 9 70 | Yeovil T |
| Grainger Martin (D) | 5 10 | 11 07 | Enfield | 23 8 72 | Brentford |
| Grondin Christophe (M) | | | Toulouse | 2 9 83 | Toulouse |
| Holdsworth David (D) | 6 1 | 12 10 | Walthamstow | 8 11 68 | Sheffield U |
| Horsfield Geoff (F) | 6 1 | 13 07 | Barnsley | 1 11 73 | Fulham |
| Hughes Bryan (M) | 5 9 | 10 00 | Liverpool | 19 6 76 | Wrexham |
| Hutchinson Jonathan (M) | | | Middlesbrough | 2 4 82 | Scholar |
| Hyde Graham (M) | 5 7 | 12 04 | Doncaster | 10 11 70 | Sheffield W |
| Johnson Andrew (F) | 5 7 | 10 00 | Bedford | 10 2 81 | Trainee |
| Johnson Michael (D) | 5 11 | 11 00 | Nottingham | 4 7 73 | Notts Co |
| Lazaridis Stan (M) | 5 9 | 12 00 | Perth | 16 8 72 | West Ham U |
| Luntala Tresor (M) | 5 9 | 11 00 | Dreux | 31 5 82 | |
| Marcelo (F) | 6 0 | 13 04 | Niteroi | 11 10 69 | Sheffield U |
| McCarthy Jon (M) | 5 9 | 11 05 | Middlesbrough | 18 8 70 | Port Vale |
| O'Connor Martin (M) | 5 8 | 10 08 | Walsall | 10 12 67 | Peterborough U |
| Parker Sonny (M) | | | Middlesbrough | 28 2 83 | Trainee |
| Purse Darren (D) | 6 2 | 13 08 | Stepney | 14 2 76 | Oxford U |
| Randrianantoanina Marco (M) | | | Bourg La Reine | 24 8 83 | |
| Sabathier Mickael (M) | | | Auch | 14 4 82 | Toulouse |
| Sonner Danny (M) | 5 11 | 12 08 | Wigan | 9 1 72 | Sheffield W |
| Ward Christopher (M) | | | Preston | 28 4 81 | Lancaster C |
| Williams Jacques (M) | 5 9 | 11 00 | Wallasey | 25 4 81 | |
| Woodhouse Curtis (M) | 5 8 | 11 06 | Driffield | 17 4 80 | Sheffield U |

**League Appearances:** Adebola, D. 16(15); Atherton, P. 10; Bass, J. (1); Bennett, I. 45; Burchill, M. 4(9); Burrows, D. 8(5); Charles, G. 3; Eaden, N. 44(1); Edghill, R. 3; Furlong, P. (4); Gill, J. 21(8); Grainger, M. 35; Holdsworth, D. 24(5); Horsfield, G. 25(9); Hughes, B. 38(7); Hyde, G. 1(2); Jenkins, S. 3; Johnson, A. 20(14); Johnson, M. 39; Lazaridis, S. 26(5); Marcelo, 16(15); McCarthy, J. 7(8); Ndlovu, P. 10(2); O'Connor, M. 28(2); Pollock, J. 4(1); Poole, K. 1; Purse, D. 34(3); Robinson, S. (4); Sonner, D. 22(4); Tiler, C. 1; Williams, J. 1(2); Woodhouse, C. 17.

**Goals – League** (59): Horsfield 7, Marcelo 7, Adebola 6, Grainger 6 (3 pens), O'Connor 5 (2 pens), Burchill 4, Hughes 4, Johnson A 4, Purse 3 (2 pens), Eaden 2, Johnson M 2, Lazaridis 2, Ndlovu 2, Woodhouse 2, Holdsworth 1, Sonner 1, own goal 1.

**Worthington Cup** (22): Adebola 5, Horsfield 3, Johnson A 3, Johnson M 2, Burchill 1, Eaden 1, Grainger 1, Hughes 1, Marcelo 1, Ndlovu 1, Purse 1 (pen), Sonner 1, 1 own goal.

**FA Cup** (2): Adebola 1, Grainger 1.

**Ground:** St Andrews, Birmingham B9 4NH. Telephone 0709 111 25837.

**Record attendance:** 66,844 v Everton, FA Cup 5th rd,11 February 1939. **Capacity:** 30,009.

**Manager:** Trevor Francis.

**Secretary:** Alan Jones BA, MBA

**Most League Goals:** 103, Division 2, 1893–94 (only 28 games).

**Highest League Scorer in Season:** Joe Bradford, 29, Division 1, 1927–28.

**Most League Goals in Total Aggregate:** Joe Bradford, 249, 1920–35.

**Most Capped Player:** Malcolm Page, 28, Wales.

**Most League Appearances:** Frank Womack, 491, 1908–28.

**Honours – Football League:** Division 2 Champions – 1892–93, 1920–21, 1947–48, 1954–55, 1994–95. **Football League Cup:** Winners 1963. **Leyland Daf Cup:** Winners 1991. **Auto Windscreens Shield:** Winners 1995.

**Colours:** Blue shirts, white shorts, blue/white stockings.

| Name | Ht | Wt | Birthplace | Birthdate | Source |
|---|---|---|---|---|---|
| Bell Andrew (F) | | | Blackburn | 12 2 84 | Scholar |
| Bent Marcus (F) | 6 2 | 12 04 | Hammersmith | 19 5 78 | Sheffield U |
| Berg Henning (D) | 6 0 | 12 04 | Eidsvoll | 1 9 69 | Manchester U |
| Bjornebye Stig Inge (D) | 5 10 | 11 09 | Elverum | 11 12 69 | Brondby |
| Blake Nathan (F) | 5 11 | 13 12 | Cardiff | 27 1 72 | Bolton W |
| Blakeman Liam (M) | | | Southport | 6 9 82 | Scholar |
| Broomes Marlon (D) | 6 1 | 13 00 | Meriden | 28 11 77 | Trainee |
| Burgess Ben (F) | 6 3 | 14 04 | Buxton | 9 11 81 | Trainee |
| Corbett Jimmy (F) | 5 10 | 12 00 | Hackney | 6 7 80 | Trainee |
| Curtis John (D) | 5 10 | 11 13 | Nuneaton | 3 9 78 | Manchester U |
| Danns Neil (F) | | | Liverpool | 23 11 82 | Scholar |
| Douglas Jonathan (M) | | | Monaghan | 22 11 81 | Trainee |
| Doyle Robert (M) | | | Dublin | 15 4 82 | Trainee |
| Duff Damien (F) | 5 9 | 11 07 | Ballyboden | 2 3 79 | Lourdes Celtic |
| Dunn David (M) | 5 10 | 12 06 | Gt Harwood | 27 12 79 | Trainee |
| Dunning Darren (M) | 5 6 | 11 12 | Scarborough | 8 1 81 | Trainee |
| Filan John (G) | 6 2 | 12 12 | Sydney | 8 2 70 | Coventry C |
| Fitzgerald John (M) | | | Dublin | 10 2 84 | Scholar |
| Flitcroft Garry (M) | 6 0 | 11 08 | Bolton | 6 11 72 | Manchester C |
| Friedel Brad (G) | 6 3 | 14 00 | Lakewood | 18 5 71 | Liverpool |
| Gillespie Keith (F) | 5 10 | 11 03 | Bangor | 18 2 75 | Newcastle U |
| Grayson Simon (D) | 6 0 | 13 07 | Ripon | 16 12 69 | Aston Villa |
| Hignett Craig (M) | 5 9 | 11 03 | Whiston | 12 1 70 | Barnsley |
| Howson Stuart (M) | | | Chorley | 30 9 81 | Trainee |
| Hughes Mark (F) | 5 11 | 13 00 | Wrexham | 1 11 63 | Everton |
| Jansen Matt (F) | 5 11 | 12 06 | Carlisle | 20 10 77 | Crystal Palace |
| Johnson Damien (M) | 5 9 | 11 07 | Lisburn | 18 11 78 | Trainee |
| Kelly Alan (G) | 6 3 | 14 02 | Preston | 11 8 68 | Sheffield U |
| Kenna Jeff (D) | 5 11 | 12 03 | Dublin | 28 8 70 | Southampton |
| Martin Anthony (M) | | | Dublin | 20 9 83 | Scholar |
| McAteer Jason (M) | 5 11 | 12 04 | Birkenhead | 18 6 71 | Liverpool |
| McLean Matthew (M) | | | Brighton | 3 12 83 | School |
| McNamee David (D) | 5 11 | 11 02 | Glasgow | 10 10 80 | St Mirren BC |
| Miller Alan (G) | 6 3 | 14 06 | Epping | 29 3 70 | WBA |
| Morgan Alan (M) | | | Edinburgh | 27 11 83 | Scholar |
| Murray Frederick (M) | | | Clonmel | 22 5 82 | Trainee |
| O'Brien Burton (M) | 5 10 | 10 12 | South Africa | 10 6 81 | S Form |
| Ostenstad Egil (F) | 5 11 | 13 00 | Haugesund | 2 1 72 | Southampton |
| Richards Marc (M) | | | Wolverhampton | 8 7 82 | Trainee |
| Short Craig (D) | 6 1 | 11 10 | Bridlington | 25 6 68 | Everton |
| Taylor Martin (D) | 6 4 | 14 00 | Ashington | 9 11 79 | Trainee |
| Taylor Michael (M) | | | Liverpool | 21 11 82 | Scholar |
| Thomas James (F) | 6 1 | 13 04 | Swansea | 16 1 79 | Trainee |

**League Appearances:** Bent, M. 21(7); Berg, H. 41; Berkovic, E. 4(7); Bjornebye, S. 30(3); Blake, N. 11(1); Broomes, M. 1; Carsley, L. 3(5); Curtis, J. 46; Dailly, C. 3(7); Diawara, K. 1(4); Duff, D. 31(1); Dunn, D. 41(1); Dunning, D. 1; Filan, J. 12(1); Flitcroft, G. 41; Friedel, B. 27; Gillespie, K. 12(6); Hignett, C. 15(15); Hughes, M. 21(8); Jansen, M. 31(9); Johnson, D. 12(4); Keller, M. (2); Kelly, A. 7; Kenna, J. 5(1); Mahon, A. 14(4); McAteer, J. 20(7); Ostenstad, E. 7(6); Short, C. 35; Taylor, M. 12(4); Thomas, J. 1(3).

**Goals – League** (76): Jansen 23, Dunn 12 (4 pens), Bent 8, Blake 6, Hughes 5, Flitcroft 3, Hignett 3, Ostenstad 3, Taylor 3, Berkovic 2, Berg 1, Bjornebye 1, Duff 1, McAteer 1, Short 1, Thomas 1, own goals 2.

**Worthington Cup** (12): Dunn 4 (3 pens), Duff 2, Thomas 2, Blake 1, Carsley 1, Diawara 1, Ostenstad 1.
**FA Cup** (11): Bent 3, Dunn 2 (1 pen), Flitcroft 2, Hignett 2 (1 pen), Jansen 1, Taylor 1.
**Ground:** Ewood Park, Blackburn BB2 4JF. Telephone (01254) 698888.
**Record attendance:** 61,783 v Bolton W, FA Cup 6th rd, 2 March, 1929. **Capacity:** 31,367.
**Manager:** Graeme Souness.
**Secretary:** Tom Finn.
**Most League Goals:** 114, Division 2, 1954–55.
**Highest League Scorer in Season:** Ted Harper, 43, Division 1, 1925–26.
**Most League Goals in Total Aggregate:** Simon Garner, 168, 1978–92.
**Most Capped Player:** Bob Crompton, 41, England.
**Most League Appearances:** Derek Fazackerley, 596, 1970–86.
**Honours – FA Premier League: Champions – 1994–95. Football League:** Division 1 Champions – 1911–12, 1913–14. Division 2 Champions – 1938–39. Division 3 Champions – 1974–75. **FA Cup:** Winners 1884, 1885, 1886, 1890, 1891, 1928. **Full Members' Cup:** Winners 1986–87.
**Colours:** Blue and white halved shirts, white shorts, white stockings, blue trim.

---

# BLACKPOOL                                           DIV. 2

| Name | | | Birthplace | | | From |
|---|---|---|---|---|---|---|
| Barnes Phil (G) | 6 1 | 11 01 | Rotherham | 2 | 3 79 | Trainee |
| Clarkson Phil (M) | 5 10 | 12 05 | Garstang | 13 11 68 | | Scunthorpe U |
| Coid Danny (M) | 5 11 | 11 07 | Liverpool | 3 10 81 | | Trainee |
| Collins Lee (M) | 5 8 | 10 08 | Bellshill | 3 | 2 74 | Swindon T |
| Hills John (D) | 5 8 | 10 08 | St Annes-on-Sea | 21 | 4 78 | Everton |
| Hughes Ian (M) | 5 10 | 12 08 | Bangor | 2 | 8 74 | Bury |
| Jaszczun Tommy (D) | 5 11 | 11 02 | Kettering | 16 | 9 77 | Aston Villa |
| Jones Eifion (D) | 6 3 | 13 00 | Llanrug | 28 | 9 80 | Liverpool |
| Milligan Jamie (M) | 5 7 | 9 12 | Blackpool | 3 | 1 80 | Everton |
| Milligan Mike (M) | 5 10 | 11 06 | Manchester | 20 | 2 67 | Norwich C |
| Murphy John (F) | 6 2 | 14 00 | Whiston | 18 10 76 | | Chester C |
| Murphy Neil (D) | 5 9 | 11 00 | Liverpool | 19 | 5 80 | Liverpool |
| Nowland Adam (F) | 5 11 | 11 06 | Preston | 6 | 7 81 | Trainee |
| O'Connor Jon (D) | 6 0 | 12 03 | Darlington | 29 10 76 | | Sheffield U |
| Ormerod Brett (F) | 5 11 | 11 04 | Blackburn | 18 10 76 | | Accrington S |
| Parkinson Gary (D) | 5 10 | 11 10 | Middlesbrough | 10 | 1 68 | Preston NE |
| Reid Brian (D) | 6 3 | 13 08 | Paisley | 15 | 6 70 | Dunfermline Ath |
| Simpson Paul (M) | 5 8 | 11 11 | Carlisle | 26 | 7 66 | Wolverhampton W |
| Thompson Phil (D) | 5 11 | 12 00 | Blackpool | 1 | 4 81 | Trainee |
| Wellens Richard (M) | 5 9 | 11 05 | Manchester | 26 | 3 80 | Manchester U |

**League Appearances:** Barnes, P. 34; Bushell, S. 16(8); Caig, T. 6; Clarkson, P. 16(12); Coid, D. 45(1); Collins, L. 23(5); Hawe, S. 2; Hills, J. 18; Hughes, I. 31(3); Jaszczun, T. 32(3); Jones, E. 4(3); Kennedy, J. 6; Maley, M. 2; Milligan, J. 1(5); Milligan, M. 24(2); Morrison, A. 6; Murphy, J. 44(2); Murphy, N. 3(3); Newell, M. 4(1); Nowland, A. (10); O'Connor, J. 10(1); Ormerod, B. 36(5); Parkinson, G. 9; Reid, B. 29; Shittu, D. 15(2); Simpson, P. 44; Thompson, P. 6(2); Walker, R. 6(12); Wellens, R. 34(2).
**Goals – League** (74): Murphy J 18 (1 pen), Ormerod 17, Simpson 12 (2 pens), Wellens 8, Clarkson 5, Walker 3, Hills 2, Reid 2, Shittu 2, Bushell 1, Coid 1, Hughes 1, Milligan M 1, Morrison 1.
**Worthington Cup** (7): Murphy J 5, Nowland 1, Ormerod 1.
**FA Cup** (3): Ormerod 2, Murphy J 1.

**Ground:** Bloomfield Rd Ground, Blackpool FY1 6JJ. Telephone (01253) 404331.
**Record attendance:** 38,098 v Wolverhampton W, Division 1, 17 September 1955.
**Capacity:** 11,295.
**Manager:** Steve McMahon.
**Secretary:** Carol Banks.
**Most League Goals:** 98, Division 2, 1929–30.
**Highest League Scorer in Season:** Jimmy Hampson, 45, Division 2, 1929–30.
**Most League Goals in Total Aggregate:** Jimmy Hampson, 246, 1927–38.
**Most Capped Player:** Jimmy Armfield, 43, England.
**Most League Appearances:** Jimmy Armfield, 568, 1952–71.
**Honours – Football League:** Division 2 Champions – 1929–30. **FA Cup:** Winners 1953. **Anglo-Italian Cup:** Winners 1971.
**Colours:** All tangerine.


# BOLTON WANDERERS                    FA PREMIERSHIP

| | | | | | | |
|---|---|---|---|---|---|---|
| Baldacchino Ryan (F) | 5 9 | 12 03 | Leicester | 13 1 81 | Blackburn R |
| Banks Steve (G) | 6 0 | 13 12 | Hillingdon | 9 2 72 | Blackpool |
| Barness Anthony (D) | 5 11 | 11 10 | Lewisham | 25 3 73 | Charlton Ath |
| Charlton Simon (D) | 5 8 | 11 00 | Huddersfield | 25 10 71 | Birmingham C |
| Evans James (G) | 6 0 | 12 00 | Glasgow | 27 1 82 | Scholar |
| Farrelly Gareth (M) | 6 1 | 13 07 | Dublin | 28 8 75 | Everton |
| Frandsen Per (M) | 5 11 | 12 10 | Copenhagen | 6 2 70 | Blackburn R |
| Gardner Ricardo (M) | 5 9 | 11 01 | St Andrews | 25 9 78 | Harbour View |
| Glennon Matthew (G) | 6 2 | 14 09 | Stockport | 8 10 78 | Trainee |
| Hansen Bo (F) | 6 1 | 12 02 | Jutland | 16 6 72 | Brondby |
| Hendry Colin (D) | 6 1 | 12 07 | Keith | 7 12 65 | Coventry C |
| Holden Dean (D) | 6 0 | 12 03 | Salford | 15 9 79 | |
| Jaaskelainen Jussi (G) | 6 3 | 13 05 | Mikkeli | 19 4 75 | VPS |
| Morini Emmanuelle (F) | | | Rome | 31 1 82 | Roma |
| Nolan Kevin (D) | 6 0 | 14 00 | Liverpool | 24 6 82 | Scholar |
| Norris David (M) | 5 7 | 11 06 | Peterborough | 22 2 81 | Boston U |
| Richardson Leam (D) | 5 8 | 11 04 | Leeds | 19 11 79 | Blackburn R |
| Ricketts Michael (F) | 6 2 | 11 12 | Birmingham | 4 12 78 | Walsall |
| Smith Jeff (M) | 5 10 | 11 01 | Middlesbrough | 28 6 80 | Hartlepool U |
| Snorrason Olaf (F) | 5 10 | 11 00 | Reykjavik | 22 4 82 | |
| Wheatcroft Paul (F) | 5 9 | 9 11 | Manchester | 22 11 80 | Manchester U |
| Whitlow Mike (D) | 6 1 | 13 03 | Northwich | 13 1 68 | Leicester C |

**League Appearances:** Banks, S. 8(1); Barness, A. 17(3); Bergsson, G. 44; Campbell, A. 3(3); Charlton, S. 18(4); Clarke, M. 8; Downey, C. (1); Elliott, R. 31(2); Farrelly, G. 36(5); Fish, M. 13(1); Frandsen, P. 35(4); Fredgaard, C. 1(4); Gardner, R. 27(5); Gope-Fenepej, J. (2); Hansen, B. 38(3); Hendry, C. 22; Holden, D. 1; Holdsworth, D. 22(9); Hunt, N. (1); Jaaskelainen, J. 27; Marshall, I. 13(23); Morini, E. 1(1); Nolan, K. 25(6); O'Kane, S. 25(2); Passi, F. 14(9); Rankin, I. 9(7); Richardson, L. 5(7); Ricketts, M. 24(15); Smith, J. 1; Summerbee, N. 9(3); Warhurst, P. 19(1); Whitlow, M. 7(1); Wright, T. 3(1).
**Goals – League** (76): Ricketts 19, Holdsworth 11, Bergsson 8, Frandsen 7 (1 pen), Marshall 6, Hansen 5, Farrelly 3, Gardner 3, Hendry 3, Elliott 2, Rankin 2, Holden 1, Nolan 1, O'Kane 1, Summerbee 1, Whitlow 1, own goals 2.
**Worthington Cup** (2): Holdsworth 1, Ricketts 1.
**FA Cup** (8): Holdsworth 3, Nolan 2, Ricketts 2, O'Kane 1.
**Ground:** Reebok Stadium, Burnden Way, Lostock, Bolton BL6 6JW. Telephone Bolton (01204) 673673.
**Record attendance:** 69,912 v Manchester C, FA Cup 5th rd, 18 February 1933.

**Capacity:** 27,879.
**Manager:** Sam Allardyce.
**Secretary:** Simon Marland.
**Most League Goals:** 100, Division 1, 1996–97.
**Highest League Scorer in Season:** Joe Smith, 38, Division 1, 1920–21.
**Most League Goals in Total Aggregate:** Nat Lofthouse, 255, 1946–61.
**Most Capped Player:** Mark Fish, 34, South Africa.
**Most League Appearances:** Eddie Hopkinson, 519, 1956–70.
**Honours – Football League:** Division 1 Champions – 1996–97. Division 2
Champions – 1908–09, 1977–78. Division 3 Champions – 1972–73. **FA Cup winners**
1923, 1926, 1929, 1958. **Sherpa Van Trophy:** Winners 1989.
**Colours:** White shirts, navy blue shorts, blue stockings.

---

## AFC BOURNEMOUTH                                    DIV. 2

| | | | | | |
|---|---|---|---|---|---|
| Bernard Narada (M) | | | Bristol | 30 1 81 | Trainee |
| Broadhurst Karl (D) | 6 1 | 11 07 | Portsmouth | 18 3 80 | Trainee |
| Elliott Wade (M) | 5 9 | 11 01 | Southampton | 14 12 78 | |
| Eribenne Chukkie (F) | 5 10 | 11 12 | London | 2 11 80 | Coventry C |
| Fletcher Carl (M) | 5 10 | 11 07 | Camberley | 7 4 80 | Trainee |
| Fletcher Steve (F) | 6 2 | 14 09 | Hartlepool | 26 6 72 | Hartlepool U |
| Ford James (M) | 5 8 | 11 00 | Portsmouth | 23 10 81 | Trainee |
| Grant Peter (M) | 5 8 | 11 00 | Bellshill | 30 8 65 | Reading |
| Hayter James (F) | 5 9 | 10 13 | Newport (IW) | 9 4 79 | Trainee |
| Howe Eddie (D) | 5 9 | 11 02 | Amersham | 29 11 77 | Trainee |
| Huck Willie (M) | 5 10 | 11 09 | Paris | 17 3 79 | Monaco |
| Hughes Richard (M) | 6 2 | 12 00 | Glasgow | 25 6 79 | Atalanta |
| Menetrier Michael (G) | | | Reims | 23 9 78 | Metz |
| O'Connor Gareth (F) | | | Dublin | 10 11 78 | Bohemians |
| Purches Stephen (M) | | | Redbridge | 14 1 80 | West Ham U |
| Smith Danny (D) | 5 11 | 11 04 | Southampton | 17 8 82 | Trainee |
| Stewart Gareth (G) | 6 0 | 12 08 | Preston | 3 2 80 | Blackburn R |
| Stock Brian (M) | 5 11 | 11 02 | Winchester | 24 12 81 | Trainee |
| Tindall Jason (M) | 6 1 | 12 01 | Stepney | 15 11 77 | Charlton Ath |
| Young Neil (D) | 5 9 | 12 00 | Harlow | 31 8 73 | Tottenham H |

**League Appearances:** Angus, S. 7(2); Bernard, N. 6(8); Broadhurst, K. 25(5);
Cummings, W. 10; Day, J. 6(1); Defoe, J. 27(2); Elliott, W. 27(9); Eribenne, C.
6(11); Feeney, W. 3(7); Fenton, N. 4(1); Fletcher, C. 43; Fletcher, S. 45; Ford, J. (3);
Grant, P. 14(1); Hayter, J. 29(11); Howe, E. 30(1); Huck, W. 1(7); Hughes, R. 44;
Jorgensen, C. 43; Keeler, J. (1); Menetrier, M. 11(1); O'Connor, G. 1(21); O'Neill,
J. (3); Purches, S. 25(9); Smith, D. 7(7); Stewart, G. 35; Stock, B. (1); Tindall, J.
44(1); Woozley, D. 6; Young, N. 7.
**Goals – League** (79): Defoe 18, Hayter 11, Elliott 9, Fletcher S 9, Hughes 8
(5 pens), Jorgensen 8, Fletcher C 6, Feeney 4, Howe 2, Cummings 1, Eribenne 1,
O'Connor 1, Tindall 1.
**Worthington Cup** (1): Jorgensen 1.
**FA Cup** (7): Elliott 2, Defoe 1, Fletcher C 1, Hayter 1, Hughes 1, O'Connor 1.
**Ground:** Dean Court Ground, Bournemouth BH7 7AF. Telephone (01202) 395381.
**Record attendance:** 28,799 v Manchester U, FA Cup 6th rd, 2 March 1957.
**Capacity:** 9600 rising to 12,000.
**Manager:** Sean O'Driscoll.
**Secretary:** K. R. J. MacAlister.
**Most League Goals:** 88, Division 3 (S), 1956–57.
**Highest League Scorer in Season:** Ted MacDougall, 42, 1970–71.
**Most League Goals in Total Aggregate:** Ron Eyre, 202, 1924–33.

**Most Capped Player:** Gerry Peyton, 7 (33), Republic of Ireland.
**Most League Appearances:** Sean O'Driscoll, 423, 1984–95.
**Honours – Football League:** Division 3 Champions – 1986–87. **Associate Members' Cup:** Winners 1984.
**Colours:** Red and black striped shirts, black shorts, black stockings.

---

# BRADFORD CITY                                         DIV. 1

| | | | | | | |
|---|---|---|---|---|---|---|
| Atherton Peter (D) | 5 11 | 13 12 | Wigan | 6 4 70 | Sheffield W |
| Blake Robbie (F) | 5 8 | 12 00 | Middlesbrough | 4 3 76 | Darlington |
| Bower Mark (D) | 5 10 | 11 00 | Bradford | 23 1 80 | Trainee |
| Carbone Benito (F) | 5 6 | 10 08 | Begnara | 14 8 71 | Aston Villa |
| Clarke Matthew (G) | 6 3 | 11 07 | Sheffield | 3 11 73 | Sheffield W |
| Davison Aidan (G) | 6 1 | 13 12 | Sedgefield | 11 5 68 | Sheffield U |
| Grant Gareth (F) | 6 1 | 11 00 | Leeds | 6 9 80 | Trainee |
| Halle Gunnar (D) | 5 11 | 11 00 | Oslo | 11 8 65 | Leeds U |
| Jacobs Wayne (D) | 5 9 | 11 00 | Sheffield | 3 2 69 | Rotherham U |
| Jess Eoin (F) | 5 10 | 11 06 | Aberdeen | 13 12 70 | Aberdeen |
| Kerr Scott (M) | 5 9 | 10 07 | Leeds | 11 12 81 | Scholar |
| Lawrence Jamie (M) | 6 0 | 12 00 | Balham | 8 3 70 | Leicester C |
| Locke Gary (D) | 6 1 | 12 06 | Edinburgh | 16 6 75 | Hearts |
| McCall Stuart (M) | 5 8 | 11 12 | Leeds | 10 6 64 | Rangers |
| Molenaar Robert (D) | 6 2 | 14 09 | Zaandam | 27 2 69 | Leeds U |
| Myers Andy (D) | 5 10 | 12 11 | Isleworth | 3 11 73 | Chelsea |
| Sharpe Lee (M) | 6 0 | 12 10 | Halesowen | 27 5 71 | Sampdoria |
| Walsh Gary (G) | 6 3 | 14 13 | Wigan | 21 3 68 | Middlesbrough |
| Ward Ashley (F) | 6 1 | 11 07 | Manchester | 24 11 70 | Blackburn R |
| Wetherall David (D) | 6 3 | 13 02 | Sheffield | 14 3 71 | Leeds U |
| Whalley Gareth (M) | 5 10 | 11 00 | Manchester | 19 12 73 | Crewe Alex |

**League Appearances:** Atherton, P. 25; Beagrie, P. 9(10); Blake, R. 14(7); Carbone, B. 29(2); Clarke, M. 17; Collymore, S. 5(2); Davison, A. 2; Grant, G. (5); Halle, G. 10(3); Hopkin, D. 8(3); Jacobs, W. 19(2); Jess, E. 17; Kerr, S. (1); Lawrence, J. 15(2); Locke, G. 6(1); McCall, S. 36(1); McKinlay, B. 10(1); Molenaar, R. 21; Myers, A. 15(5); Nolan, I. 17(4); O'Brien, A. 17(1); Petrescu, D. 16(1); Rankin, I. (1); Saunders, D. 4(6); Sharpe, L. 6(5); Walsh, G. 19; Ward, A. 24(9); Wetherall, D. 18; Whalley, G. 17(2); Windass, D. 22(2).
**Goals – League** (30): Carbone 5, Blake 4 (2 pens), Ward 4, Jess 3, Windass 3, Collymore 2, Jacobs 2, Beagrie 1, Lawrence 1, McCall 1, Molenaar 1, Myers 1, Petrescu 1, Wetherall 1.
**Worthington Cup** (11): Carbone 2, Ward 2, Whalley 2, Windass 2, Grant 1, Halle 1, Nolan 1.
**FA Cup** (0).
**Ground:** Valley Parade, Bradford BD8 7DY. Telephone (01274) 773355.
**Record attendance:** 39,146 v Burnley, FA Cup 4th rd, 11 March 1911. **Capacity:** 25,000.
**Manager:** Jim Jefferies.
**Secretary:** Jon Pollard.
**Most League Goals:** 128, Division 3 (N), 1928–29.
**Highest League Scorer in Season:** David Layne, 34, Division 4, 1961–62.
**Most League Goals in Total Aggregate:** Bobby Campbell, 121, 1981–84, 1984–86.
**Most Capped Player:** Harry Hampton, 9, Northern Ireland.
**Most League Appearances:** Cec Podd, 502, 1970–84.
**Honours – Football League:** Division 2 Champions – 1907–08. Division 3 Champions – 1984–85. Division 3 (N) Champions – 1928–29. **FA Cup:** Winners 1911.
**Colours:** Claret and amber shirts, black shorts, amber stockings.

# BRENTFORD                                          DIV. 2

| | | | | | |
|---|---|---|---|---|---|
| Anderson Ijah (D) | 5 8 | 10 06 | Hackney | 30 12 75 | Tottenham H |
| Boxall Danny (D) | 5 8 | 11 06 | Croydon | 24 8 77 | Crystal Palace |
| Bryan Derek (F) | 5 10 | 11 05 | London | 11 11 74 | Hampton |
| Charles Julian (F) | 5 9 | 11 00 | Plaistow | 5 2 77 | Hampton & Richmond B |
| Dobson Michael (D) | 5 11 | 12 04 | Isleworth | 9 4 81 | Trainee |
| Evans Paul (M) | 5 8 | 11 06 | Oswestry | 1 9 74 | Shrewsbury T |
| Folan Tony (F) | 5 11 | 11 08 | Lewisham | 18 9 78 | Crystal Palace |
| Gibbs Paul (D) | 5 10 | 11 09 | Gorleston | 26 10 72 | Plymouth Arg |
| Gottskalksson Olafur (G) | 6 3 | 13 12 | Keflavik | 12 3 68 | Hibernian |
| Hutchinson Eddie (M) | 6 1 | 13 00 | Surrey | 23 2 82 | Sutton U |
| Ingimarsson Ivar (M) | 6 0 | 12 07 | Reykjavik | 20 8 77 | Torquay U |
| Lovett Jay (D) | 6 0 | 12 00 | Sussex | 22 1 78 | Crawley T |
| Mahon Gavin (M) | 6 0 | 13 02 | Birmingham | 2 1 77 | Hereford U |
| Marshall Scott (D) | 6 2 | 12 12 | Edinburgh | 1 5 73 | Southampton |
| McCammon Mark (F) | 6 2 | 14 06 | Barnet | 7 8 78 | Charlton Ath |
| O'Connor Kevin (F) | 5 11 | 12 00 | Blackburn | 24 2 82 | Trainee |
| Owusu Lloyd (F) | 6 0 | 14 00 | Slough | 12 12 76 | Slough T |
| Partridge Scott (F) | 5 9 | 11 02 | Leicester | 13 10 74 | Torquay U |
| Pinamonte Lorenzo (F) | 6 3 | 13 04 | Foggia | 9 5 78 | Bristol C |
| Powell Darren (D) | 6 3 | 13 02 | Hammersmith | 10 3 76 | Hampton |
| Rowlands Martin (M) | 5 9 | 10 10 | Hammersmith | 8 2 79 | Farnborough T |
| Smith Jay (M) | 5 11 | 12 00 | London | 29 12 81 | Trainee |
| Smith Paul (G) | 6 3 | 12 04 | Epsom | 17 12 79 | Charlton Ath |
| Theobald David (D) | 6 2 | 11 00 | Cambridge | 15 12 78 | Ipswich T |
| Williams Mark (F) | 5 11 | 12 00 | London | 9 4 82 | Scholar |

**League Appearances:** Anderson, I. 1; Austin, K. 3; Charles, J. 4(6); Crowe, J. 9; Dobson, M. 23(3); Evans, P. 43; Folan, T. 11(10); Gibbs, P. 26(1); Gottskalksson, O. 45; Graham, G. (1); Hutchinson, E. 5(2); Ingimarsson, I. 42; Javary, J. 4(2); Kennedy, R. 1; Lovett, J. 21(4); Mahon, G. 40; Marsh, S. 3(1); Marshall, S. 29; McCammon, M. 14(10); O'Connor, K. 5(6); Owusu, L. 24(9); Partridge, S. 29(7); Pinamonte, L. 3(5); Powell, D. 18; Quinn, R. 22; Rowlands, M. 32; Scott, A. 22; Smith, J. 2(1); Smith, P. 1(1); Somner, M. 2(1); Tabb, J. 1(1); Theobald, D. 15; Williams, M. 6(24).

**Goals – League** (56): Scott 13, Owusu 10, Partridge 8, Evans 7 (3 pens), Ingimarsson 3, McCammon 3, Folan 2, Rowlands 2, Williams 2, Gibbs 1, Mahon 1, O'Connor 1, Pinamonte 1, Powell 1, own goal 1.

**Worthington Cup** (4): Scott 2, McCammon 1, Rowlands 1.

**FA Cup** (1): Pinamonte 1.

**Ground:** Griffin Park, Braemar Rd, Brentford, Middlesex TW8 0NT. Telephone (020) 8847 2511.

**Record attendance:** 39,626 v Preston NE, FA Cup 6th rd, 5 March 1938. **Capacity:** 12,763.

**Manager:** Steve Coppell.

**Secretary:** Polly Kates.

**Most League Goals:** 98, Division 4, 1962–63.

**Highest League Scorer in Season:** Jack Holliday, 38, Division 3 (S), 1932–33.

**Most League Goals in Total Aggregate:** Jim Towers, 153, 1954–61.

**Most Capped Player:** John Buttigieg, (63), Malta.

**Most League Appearances:** Ken Coote, 514, 1949–64.

**Honours – Football League:** Division 2 Champions – 1934–35. Division 3 Champions – 1991–92, 1998–99. Division 3 (S) Champions – 1932–33. Division 4 Champions – 1962–63.
**Colours:** Red and white vertical striped shirts, black shorts, black stockings.

---

# BRIGHTON & HOVE ALBION                                     DIV. 2

---

| | | | | | |
|---|---|---|---|---|---|
| Brooker Paul (F) | 5 8 | 10 01 | Hammersmith | 25 11 76 | Fulham |
| Carpenter Richard (M) | 6 0 | 13 01 | Sheppey | 30 9 72 | Cardiff C |
| Carr Darren (D) | 6 2 | 13 07 | Bristol | 4 9 68 | Gillingham |
| Crosby Andy (D) | 6 2 | 13 07 | Rotherham | 3 3 73 | Chester C |
| Cullip Danny (D) | 6 1 | 12 07 | Bracknell | 17 9 76 | Brentford |
| Hart Gary (F) | 5 9 | 12 08 | Harlow | 6 11 75 | Stansted |
| Jones Nathan (D) | 5 7 | 10 05 | Rhondda | 28 5 73 | Southend U |
| Kuipers Michels (G) | 6 2 | 14 03 | Amsterdam | 26 6 74 | Bristol R |
| Mayo Kerry (D) | 5 8 | 11 07 | Cuckfield | 21 9 77 | Trainee |
| Melton Steve (M) | 5 10 | 10 08 | Lincoln | 31 10 78 | Stoke C |
| Oatway Charlie (M) | 5 7 | 10 10 | Hammersmith | 28 11 73 | Brentford |
| Packham Will (G) | 6 2 | 13 00 | Brighton | 13 1 81 | Trainee |
| Ramsay Scott (F) | 6 0 | 13 00 | Hastings | 16 10 80 | Trainee |
| Steele Lee (F) | 5 8 | 12 05 | Liverpool | 2 12 73 | Shrewsbury T |
| Virgo Adam (D) | 6 1 | 12 00 | Brighton | 25 1 83 | |
| Watson Paul (D) | 5 8 | 10 10 | Hastings | 4 1 75 | Brentford |
| Wicks Matthew (D) | 6 2 | 13 05 | Reading | 8 9 78 | Peterborough U |
| Zamora Bobby (F) | 6 1 | 11 08 | Barking | 16 1 81 | Trainee |

**League Appearances:** Aspinall, W. (1); Brooker, P. 25(16); Carpenter, R. 42; Carr, D. 2; Cartwright, M. 12(1); Crosby, A. 28(6); Cullip, D. 38; Freeman, D. 5(11); Hart, G. 43(2); Jones, N. 27(13); Kuipers, M. 34; Mayo, K. 43(2); Melton, S. 10(18); Oatway, C. 36(2); Packham, W. (1); Ramsay, S. 2(9); Rogers, P. 41(4); Stant, P. (7); Steele, L. 4(19); Thomas, M. 1(7); Thomas, R. (2); Virgo, A. 2(4); Watson, P. 46; Wicks, M. 23(1); Wilkinson, S. (1); Zamora, B. 42(1).
**Goals – League** (73): Zamora 28 (3 pens), Hart 7, Carpenter 6, Rogers 6, Watson 5 (2 pens), Jones 4, Brooker 3, Wicks 3, Crosby 2, Cullip 2, Steele 2, Mayo 1, Melton 1, Stant 1, own goals 2.
**Worthington Cup** (2): Jones 1, Watson 1.
**FA Cup** (7): Watson 2 (2 pens), Zamora 2, Carpenter 1, Oatway 1, Wicks 1.
**Offices:** Hanover House, 118 Queens Road, Brighton BN1 3XG. Telephone: (01273) 778855. **Ground:** Withdean Stadium, Tongdean Lane, Brighton.
**Record attendance:** 36,747 v Fulham, Division 2, 27 December 1958.
**Capacity:** 6960.
**Manager:** Micky Adams.
**Secretary:** Derek Allan.
**Most League Goals:** 112, Division 3 (S), 1955–56.
**Highest League Scorer in Season:** Peter Ward, 32, Division 3, 1976–77.
**Most League Goals in Total Aggregate:** Tommy Cook, 114, 1922–29.
**Most Capped Player:** Steve Penney, 17, Northern Ireland.
**Most League Appearances:** 'Tug' Wilson, 509, 1922–36.
**Honours – Football League:** Division 3 Champions – 2000–01. Division 3 (S) Champions – 1957–58. Division 4 Champions – 1964–65.
**Colours:** Blue and white striped shirts, white shorts, blue stockings.

| Name | | | Place | | | Prev Club |
|---|---|---|---|---|---|---|
| Amankwaah Kevin (D) | 6 1 | 12 00 | London | 19 | 5 82 | Scholar |
| Beadle Peter (F) | 6 2 | 14 07 | Lambeth | 13 | 5 72 | Notts Co |
| Bell Mickey (D) | 5 8 | 11 13 | Newcastle | 15 | 11 71 | Wycombe W |
| Brown Aaron (M) | 5 10 | 11 12 | Bristol | 14 | 3 80 | Trainee |
| Brown Marvin (F) | 5 9 | 11 01 | Bristol | 6 | 7 83 | |
| Burke Andrew (M) | | | Camden | 9 | 1 83 | |
| Burnell Joe (D) | 5 9 | 11 11 | Bristol | 10 | 10 80 | Trainee |
| Burns John (M) | 5 8 | 11 04 | Dublin | 4 | 12 77 | Nottingham F |
| Carey Louis (D) | 5 10 | 12 05 | Bristol | 22 | 1 77 | Trainee |
| Clist Simon (M) | 5 9 | 11 00 | Bournemouth | 13 | 6 81 | Tottenham H |
| Coles Daniel (D) | 6 1 | 11 05 | Bristol | 30 | 10 81 | Scholar |
| Correia Albano (M) | | | Guinea Bissau | 18 | 10 81 | |
| Dew Simon (M) | | | Bristol | 21 | 7 83 | Scholar |
| Doherty Tom (M) | 5 8 | 11 07 | Bristol | 17 | 3 79 | Trainee |
| Edwards Jamie (M) | | | Hereford | 18 | 2 83 | Scholar |
| Fortune Clayton (D) | | | Forest Gate | 10 | 11 82 | Tottenham H |
| Goodridge Greg (M) | 5 6 | 11 02 | Barbados | 10 | 7 71 | QPR |
| Harrhy Nicholas (M) | | | Abergavenny | 14 | 9 82 | |
| Hill Matt (M) | 5 8 | 11 09 | Bristol | 26 | 3 81 | Trainee |
| Holland Paul (M) | 5 9 | 13 05 | Lincoln | 8 | 7 73 | Chesterfield |
| Hulbert Robin (M) | 5 9 | 10 05 | Plymouth | 14 | 3 80 | Swindon T |
| Jones Darren (D) | | | Newport | 26 | 8 83 | Scholar |
| Jones Steve (F) | 6 1 | 12 07 | Cambridge | 17 | 3 70 | Charlton Ath |
| Jordan Thomas (M) | | | Manchester | 25 | 5 81 | Schoolboy |
| Lavin Gerard (D) | 5 10 | 11 10 | Corby | 5 | 2 74 | Millwall |
| Lever Mark (D) | 6 3 | 14 03 | Hull | 29 | 3 70 | Grimsby T |
| Lourenco (F) | | | Luanda | 5 | 6 83 | Sporting Lisbon |
| Matthews Lee (F) | 6 2 | 13 03 | Middlesbrough | 6 | 1 79 | Leeds U |
| Mercer Billy (G) | 6 1 | 11 00 | Liverpool | 22 | 5 69 | Chesterfield |
| Millen Keith (D) | 6 1 | 13 02 | Croydon | 26 | 9 66 | Watford |
| Murray Scott (M) | 5 8 | 11 00 | Aberdeen | 26 | 5 74 | Aston Villa |
| Odejayi Kayode (F) | 6 2 | 12 02 | Ibadon | 21 | 2 82 | Scholar |
| Peacock Lee (F) | 6 1 | 13 12 | Paisley | 9 | 10 76 | Manchester C |
| Phillips Steve (G) | 6 1 | 12 07 | Bath | 6 | 5 78 | Paulton R |
| Pike James (F) | 5 9 | 11 00 | Bristol | 15 | 11 82 | Scholar |
| Shanahan Aaron (M) | | | Coventry | 10 | 9 82 | |
| Sheppard Kyle (D) | | | Cardiff | 4 | 12 82 | Chelsea |
| Spencer Damien (F) | 6 1 | 14 05 | Ascot | 19 | 9 81 | Scholar |
| Testimitanu Ivan (M) | 5 10 | 11 02 | Moldova | 27 | 4 74 | Zimbru Chisinau |
| Thorpe Tony (F) | 5 8 | 12 06 | Leicester | 10 | 4 74 | Fulham |
| Tinnion Brian (M) | 5 11 | 12 13 | Stanley | 23 | 2 68 | Bradford C |
| Woodman Craig (M) | | | Tiverton | 22 | 12 82 | Trainee |

**League Appearances:** Amankwaah, K. 8(6); Beadle, P. 18(15); Bell, M. 41; Brown, A. 27(8); Brown, M. (5); Burnell, J. 19(4); Carey, L. 46; Clist, S. 36(2); Coles, D. 1(1); Dunning, D. 9; Goodridge, G. 1(6); Hill, M. 32(2); Holland, P. 5; Hulbert, R. 14(5); Jordan, A. 1(1); Lavin, G. 3; Lever, M. 2; Lourenco. 1(2); Maddison, N. 4(3); Malessa, A. (1); Matthews, L. 4(2); Millen, K. 28(1); Miller, A. 4; Murray, S. 46; Odejayi, K. (3); Peacock, L. 31(4); Phillips, S. 42; Rodrigues, D. 3(1); Spencer, D. 2(2); Testimitanu, I. 4(7); Thorpe, T. 33(6); Tinnion, B. 40(2); Woodman, C. 1(1).
**Goals – League** (70): Thorpe 19 (2 pens), Peacock 13 (2 pens), Murray 10, Beadle 4, Bell 4, Clist 4, Carey 3, Matthews 3 (1 pen), Brown A 2, Millen 2, Holland 1, Lourenco 1, Maddison 1, Tinnion 1, own goals 2.
**Worthington Cup** (3): Holland 1, Peacock 1 (pen), Thorpe 1 (pen).

**FA Cup** (8): Thorpe 3, Clist 2, Beadle 1, Murray 1, Peacock 1.
**Ground:** Ashton Gate, Bristol BS3 2EJ. Telephone (0117) 9630630.
**Record attendance:** 43,335 v Preston NE, FA Cup 5th rd, 16 February 1935.
**Capacity:** 21,479.
**Manager:** Danny Wilson.
**Secretary:** Michelle McDonald.
**Most League Goals:** 104, Division 3 (S), 1926–27.
**Highest League Scorer in Season:** Don Clark, 36, Division 3 (S), 1946–47.
**Most League Goals in Total Aggregate:** John Atyeo, 314, 1951–66.
**Most Capped Player:** Billy Wedlock, 26, England.
**Most League Appearances:** John Atyeo, 597, 1951–66.
**Honours – Football League:** Division 2 Champions – 1905–06. Division 3 (S) Champions – 1922–23, 1926–27, 1954–55. **Welsh Cup winners** 1934. **Anglo-Scottish Cup:** Winners 1977–78. **Freight Rover Trophy winners** 1985–86.
**Colours:** Red shirts, red shorts, white stockings.

---

# BRISTOL ROVERS                                                    DIV. 3

| | | | | | |
|---|---|---|---|---|---|
| Andreasson Marcus (D) | 6 4 | 13 02 | Liberia | 13 7 78 | Osters |
| Astafjevs Vitalijs (M) | 5 11 | 12 05 | Riga | 3 4 71 | Skonto Riga |
| Bryant Simon (M) | 5 11 | 12 11 | Bristol | 22 11 82 | Scholar |
| Cameron Martin (F) | 6 1 | 12 12 | Dunfermline | 16 6 78 | |
| Challis Trevor (D) | 5 8 | 11 06 | Paddington | 23 10 75 | QPR |
| Ellington Nathan (F) | 5 10 | 12 10 | Bradford | 2 7 81 | Walton & Hersham |
| Ellis Clinton (F) | 5 6 | 12 06 | Ealing | 7 7 77 | |
| Foran Mark (D) | 6 3 | 13 04 | Aldershot | 30 10 73 | Crewe Alex |
| Foster Stephen (D) | 6 1 | 13 00 | Mansfield | 3 12 74 | Trainee |
| Gall Kevin (F) | 5 9 | 11 01 | Merthyr | 4 2 82 | Newcastle U |
| Hillier David (M) | 5 10 | 12 07 | Blackheath | 19 12 69 | Portsmouth |
| Hogg Lewis (M) | 5 8 | 10 07 | Bristol | 13 9 82 | Trainee |
| Jones Scott (D) | 5 10 | 12 01 | Sheffield | 1 5 75 | Barnsley |
| Mauge Ronnie (M) | 5 10 | 10 06 | Islington | 10 3 69 | Plymouth Arg |
| McKeever Mark (M) | 5 9 | 11 08 | Derry | 16 11 78 | Sheffield W |
| Pierre Nigel (F) | 5 11 | 11 11 | Port of Spain | 2 6 79 | Joe Public |
| Plummer Dwayne (F) | 5 9 | 10 12 | Bristol | 12 5 78 | Bristol C |
| Richards Justin (F) | 6 0 | 11 10 | Sandwell | 16 10 80 | WBA |
| Shore Jamie (M) | 5 9 | 12 05 | Bristol | 1 9 77 | Norwich C |
| Smith Mark (D) | 6 0 | 13 07 | Bristol | 13 9 79 | Trainee |
| Thomson Andy (D) | 6 3 | 14 03 | Swindon | 28 3 74 | Portsmouth |
| Trought Michael (D) | 6 2 | 14 03 | Bristol | 19 10 80 | Trainee |
| Walters Mark (M) | 5 9 | 11 05 | Birmingham | 2 6 64 | Swindon T |
| Wilson Che (M) | 5 11 | 11 10 | Ely | 17 1 79 | Norwich C |

**League Appearances:** Allsopp, D. 4(2); Andreasson, M. 4; Astafjevs, V. 34(7); Barrett, G. (1); Bignot, M. 26; Bryant, S. 27(3); Cameron, M. 6(8); Challis, T. 19(3); Culkin, N. 45; Cureton, J. 1; Dagnogo, M. (2); Ellington, N. 36(6); Ellis, C. 2(13); Evans, M. 19(2); Foran, M. 9(3); Foster, S. 44; Gall, K. 3(7); Glennon, M. 1; Hillier, D. 3(1); Hogg, L. 31(3); Johansen, R. (2); Jones, S. 37(2); Lee, C. 8(1); Mauge, R. 14(2); McKeever, M. 7(5); Meaker, M. 2(3); Owusu, A. 11(6); Parkin, B. (2); Partridge, R. 4(2); Pethick, R. 11(2); Plummer, D. 17(3); Richards, J. 3(4); Thomson, A. 31(1); Walters, M. 11(5); Wilson, C. 36(1).
**Goals – League** (53): Ellington 15, Astafjevs 5, Evans 4 (1 pen), Foster 4, Walters 4 (2 pens), Hogg 3, Jones 3, Cameron 2, Gall 2, Lee 2, Andreasson 1, Bignot 1, Bryant 1, Cureton 1 (pen), Ellis 1, Partridge 1, Plummer 1, Thomson 1, own goal 1.
**Worthington Cup** (6): Bignot 2, Ellington 2, Cameron 1, Hogg 1.
**FA Cup** (1): own goal 1.

**Ground:** The Memorial Ground, Filton Avenue, Horfield, Bristol BS7 0BF.
**Record attendance:** 9464 v Liverpool, FA Cup 4th rd, 8 February 1992
(Twerton Park). 38,472 v Preston NE, FA Cup 4th rd, 30 January 1960 (Eastville).
11,433 v Sunderland, League Cup 3rd rd, 31 October 2000 (Memorial Ground).
**Capacity:** 11,976.
**Director of Football/Team Manager:** Gerry Francis.
**Secretary:** Roger Brinsford.
**Most League Goals:** 92, Division 3 (S), 1952–53.
**Highest League Scorer in Season:** Geoff Bradford, 33, Division 3 (S), 1952–53.
**Most League Goals in Total Aggregate:** Geoff Bradford, 242, 1949–64.
**Most Capped Player:** Neil Slatter, 10 (22), Wales.
**Most League Appearances:** Stuart Taylor, 546, 1966–80.
**Honours – Football League:** Division 3 (S) Champions – 1952–53. Division 3
Champions – 1989–90.
**Colours:** Blue and white quartered shirts, blue shorts, blue stockings.

---

# BURNLEY                                                    DIV. 1

| | | | | | |
|---|---|---|---|---|---|
| Ball Kevin (M) | 5 10 | 12 04 | Hastings | 12 11 64 | Fulham |
| Branch Graham (F) | 6 2 | 12 02 | Liverpool | 12  2 72 | Stockport Co |
| Briscoe Lee (D) | 5 11 | 11 12 | Pontefract | 30  9 75 | Sheffield W |
| Cook Paul (M) | 5 11 | 11 00 | Liverpool | 22  6 67 | Stockport Co |
| Cox Ian (D) | 6 0 | 12 00 | Croydon | 25  3 71 | Bournemouth |
| Crichton Paul (G) | 6 1 | 13 08 | Pontefract | 3 10 68 | WBA |
| Davis Steve (D) | 6 2 | 14 07 | Hexham | 30 10 68 | Luton T |
| Johnrose Lenny (M) | 5 11 | 12 06 | Preston | 27 11 69 | Bury |
| Little Glen (M) | 6 3 | 13 00 | Wimbledon | 15 10 75 | Glentoran |
| Maylett Bradley (M) | 5 8 | 10 07 | Manchester | 24 12 80 | Trainee |
| Michopoulos Nick (G) | 6 3 | 14 00 | Greece | 20  2 70 | PAOK Salonika |
| Moore Ian (F) | 5 11 | 12 02 | Birkenhead | 26  8 76 | Stockport Co |
| Mullin John (F) | 6 0 | 11 05 | Bury | 11  8 75 | Sunderland |
| Payton Andy (F) | 5 9 | 11 13 | Burnley | 23 10 67 | Huddersfield T |
| Shandran Anthony (F) | | | North Shields | 17  9 81 | Scholar |
| Thomas Mitchell (D) | 6 2 | 14 00 | Luton | 2 10 64 | Luton T |
| Weller Paul (M) | 5 8 | 11 02 | Brighton | 6  3 75 | Trainee |
| West Dean (D) | 5 10 | 11 07 | Leeds | 5 12 72 | Bury |
| Williamson John (D) | 6 1 | 11 06 | Derby | 3  3 81 | Trainee |

**League Appearances:** Armstrong, G. 14(5); Ball, K. 40; Branch, G. 26(9); Briscoe,
L. 25(4); Cook, P. 38(2); Cooke, A. 10(1); Cox, I. 35(3); Crichton, P. 7(1); Davis, S.
44; Gray, P. 5; Jepson, R. (13); Johnrose, L. 9(10); Little, G. 27(7); Maylett, B.
2(10); Mellon, M. 19(3); Michopoulos, N. 39; Moore, I. 26(1); Mullin, J. 11(25);
Payton, A. 18(22); Robinson, P. (4); Shandran, A. (1); Smith, P. 10(4); Taylor, G.
15; Thomas, M. 41(2); Weller, P. 39(5); West, D. 6(1).
**Goals – League** (50): Payton 9 (2 pens), Branch 5, Davis 5, Moore 5, Taylor 4,
Cook 3 (1 pen), Little 3, Mullin 3, Weller 3, Ball 2, Cooke 2, Cox 1, Gray 1,
Johnrose 1, Smith 1, own goals 2.
**Worthington Cup** (9): Payton 5 (2 pens), Cooke 3, Davis 1.
**FA Cup** (3): Johnrose 1, Moore 1, Payton 1.
**Ground:** Turf Moor, Burnley BB10 4BX. Telephone (01282) 700000.
**Record attendance:** 54,775 v Huddersfield T, FA Cup 3rd rd, 23 February 1924.
**Capacity:** 22,546.
**Manager:** Stan Ternent.
**Secretary:** Cathy Pickup.
**Most League Goals:** 102, Division 1, 1960–61.
**Highest League Scorer in Season:** George Beel, 35, Division 1, 1927–28.

**Most League Goals in Total Aggregate:** George Beel, 178, 1923–32.
**Most Capped Player:** Jimmy McIlroy, 51 (55), Northern Ireland.
**Most League Appearances:** Jerry Dawson, 522, 1907–28.
**Honours – Football League:** Division 1 Champions – 1920–21, 1959–60. Division 2 Champions – 1897–98, 1972–73. Division 3 Champions – 1981–82. Division 4 Champions – 1991–92. **FA Cup winners** 1913–14. **Anglo-Scottish Cup:** Winners 1978–79.
**Colours:** Claret and blue shirts, white shorts, white stockings.

# BURY                                                                    DIV. 2

| Name | ht | wt | Birthplace | Birthdate | From |
|---|---|---|---|---|---|
| Armstrong Christopher (D) | 5 9 | 10 08 | Newcastle | 5 8 82 | Scholar |
| Barrass Matt (D) | 5 11 | 12 00 | Bury | 28 2 81 | Trainee |
| Bhutia Baichung (F) | 5 8 | 10 02 | Sikkim | 15 6 76 | East Bengal |
| Bullock Darren (M) | 5 9 | 12 10 | Worcester | 12 2 69 | Swindon T |
| Collins Sam (D) | 6 2 | 14 04 | Pontefract | 5 6 77 | Huddersfield T |
| Connell Lee (M) | 6 0 | 12 00 | Bury | 24 6 81 | Trainee |
| Forrest Martyn (M) | 5 10 | 12 02 | Bury | 2 1 79 | Trainee |
| Garner Glyn (G) | | | Pontypool | 9 12 76 | Llanelli |
| Halford Stephen (D) | 5 10 | 12 10 | Bury | 21 9 80 | Trainee |
| Hill Nicky (D) | 6 0 | 12 03 | Accrington | 26 2 81 | Trainee |
| Jarrett Jason (M) | 6 0 | 12 04 | Bury | 14 9 79 | Wrexham |
| Kenny Paddy (G) | 6 1 | 14 06 | Halifax | 17 5 78 | Bradford PA |
| Newby Jon (F) | 6 0 | 12 00 | Warrington | 28 11 78 | Liverpool |
| Peyton Warren (M) | 5 9 | 11 03 | Manchester | 13 12 79 | |
| Swailes Danny (D) | 6 3 | 12 06 | Bolton | 1 4 79 | Trainee |

**League Appearances:** Armstrong, C. 22; Barnes, P. 12(4); Barrass, M. 4(1); Barrick, D. 9(1); Bhutia, B. 11(9); Billy, C. 46; Bullock, D. 9(1); Collins, S. 33(1); Connell, L. (1); Cramb, C. 15; Crowe, D. 1(6); Daws, N. 44; Forrest, M. 20(7); Halford, S. 2(1); Hill, N. 8(2); James, L. 7(21); Jarrett, J. 13(12); Kenny, P. 46; Littlejohn, A. 24(13); Nelson, M. 2; Newby, J. 17; Peyton, W. (1); Preece, A. 13(17); Redmond, S. 39; Reid, P. 42(1); Smith, A. 2; Swailes, C. 43; Swailes, D. 10(1); Unsworth, L. 12(3).
**Goals – League** (45): Cramb 5, Newby 5, Barnes 4, Littlejohn 4, Reid 4 (3 pens), Swailes C 4, Daws 3, Bullock 2, Collins 2, Jarrett 2, Preece 2 (1 pen), Redmond 2, Armstrong 1, Bhutia 1, Connell 1, Crowe 1, Nelson 1, own goal 1.
**Worthington Cup** (3): Bullock 2 (1 pen), Littlejohn 1.
**FA Cup** (1): Daws 1.
**Ground:** Gigg Lane, Bury BL9 9HR. Telephone (0161) 764 4881.
**Record attendance:** 35,000 v Bolton W, FA Cup 3rd rd, 9 January 1960. **Capacity:** 11,669.
**Manager:** Andy Preece.
**Secretary:** Jill Neville.
**Most League Goals:** 108, Division 3, 1960–61.
**Highest League Scorer in Season:** Craig Madden, 35, Division 4, 1981–82.
**Most League Goals in Total Aggregate:** Craig Madden, 129, 1978–86.
**Most Capped Player:** Bill Gorman, 11 (13), Republic of Ireland and (4), Northern Ireland.
**Most League Appearances:** Norman Bullock, 506, 1920–35.
**Honours – Football League:** Division 2 Champions – 1894–95, 1996–97. Division 3 Champions – 1960–61. **FA Cup winners** 1900, 1903. **Auto Windscreens Shield winners** 1997.
**Colours:** White shirts, royal blue shorts, royal blue stockings.

| | | | | | | |
|---|---|---|---|---|---|---|
| Ashbee Ian (M) | 6 1 | 14 04 | Birmingham | 6 | 9 76 | Derby Co |
| Butterworth Adam (D) | | | Paignton | 9 | 8 82 | |
| Chillingworth Daniel (F) | 6 0 | 12 06 | Cambridge | 13 | 9 81 | Scholar |
| Cockrill Dale (D) | | | Great Yarmouth | 23 | 11 81 | |
| Cowan Tom (D) | 5 8 | 11 10 | Bothwell | 28 | 8 69 | Burnley |
| Dreyer John (D) | 6 1 | 13 02 | Alnwick | 11 | 6 63 | Bradford C |
| Duncan Andy (D) | 5 11 | 14 03 | Hexham | 20 | 10 77 | Manchester U |
| Fleming Terry (M) | 5 8 | 10 01 | Marston Green | 5 | 1 73 | Plymouth Arg |
| Greene David (D) | 6 3 | 14 03 | Luton | 26 | 10 73 | Cardiff C |
| Guttridge Luke (M) | 5 5 | 8 06 | Barnstaple | 27 | 3 82 | Torquay U |
| Hansen John (M) | 5 11 | 13 01 | Mannheim | 17 | 9 73 | |
| Kitson Dave (F) | | | Hitchin | 21 | 1 80 | Arlesey |
| Marshall Shaun (G) | 6 1 | 13 03 | Fakenham | 3 | 10 78 | Trainee |
| McAnespie Steve (D) | 5 9 | 10 09 | Kilmarnock | 1 | 2 72 | Fulham |
| McNeil Martin (D) | 6 0 | 13 02 | Rutherglen | 28 | 9 80 | Trainee |
| Mustoe Neil (M) | 5 9 | 12 02 | Gloucester | 5 | 11 76 | Manchester U |
| Nacca Francesco (M) | | | Venezuela | 9 | 11 81 | Scholar |
| Perez Lionel (G) | 5 11 | 13 04 | Bagnols Coze | 24 | 4 67 | Newcastle U |
| Preece David (M) | 5 6 | 11 05 | Bridgnorth | 28 | 5 63 | Derby Co |
| Prokas Richard (M) | 5 9 | 11 05 | Penrith | 22 | 1 76 | Carlisle U |
| Revell Alexander (F) | | | Cambridge | 7 | 7 83 | Scholar |
| Richardson Marcus (F) | | | Reading | 31 | 8 77 | Harrow B |
| Tann Adam (D) | 6 0 | 11 05 | Fakenham | 12 | 5 82 | Scholar |
| Taylor John (F) | 6 2 | 15 00 | Norwich | 24 | 10 64 | Luton T |
| Traore Demba (M) | 6 0 | 12 00 | Sweden | 22 | 4 82 | |
| Wanless Paul (M) | 6 1 | 14 08 | Banbury | 14 | 12 73 | Lincoln C |
| Youngs Tom (F) | 5 9 | 11 01 | Bury St Edmunds | 31 | 8 79 | Trainee |

**League Appearances:** Abbey, Z. 14; Ashbee, I. 43(1); Axeldal, J. 12(6); Butterworth, A. (1); Chillingworth, D. (1); Connor, P. 12(1); Cowan, T. 41; Dreyer, J. 40; Duncan, A. 39; Fleming, T. 9(1); Greene, D. 1; Gudmundsson, J. 3; Guttridge, L. 1; Hansen, J. 7(5); Hanson, C. 8; Humphreys, R. 7; Joseph, M. 29(1); Kitson, D. 6(2); Lamey, N. (3); Logan, R. 5; MacKenzie, N. 1(5); Marshall, S. 10(1); McAnespie, S. 20(3); McNeil, M. 5(1); Mustoe, N. 15(12); Oakes, S. 7(11); Perez, L. 36(1); Pilvi, T. 3(2); Preece, D. (2); Prokas, R. 1(2); Revell, A. 2(2); Richardson, M. 3(7); Riza, O. 10(2); Russell, A. 22(7); Slade, S. 4(5); Tann, A. 1; Taylor, J. 12(18); Traore, D. (1); Wanless, P. 42(1); Wilson, S. 3(3); Youngs, T. 32(6).

**Goals – League** (61): Youngs 14, Wanless 10 (3 pens), Abbey 5, Connor 5, Ashbee 4, Humphreys 3, Riza 3, Taylor 3 (1 pen), Axeldal 2, Cowan 2, Richardson 2, Russell 2, Duncan 1, Fleming 1, Guttridge 1, Kitson 1, Logan 1, Mustoe 1 (pen), Slade 1.

**Worthington Cup** (0).

**FA Cup** (3): Axeldal 1, Hansen 1, Youngs 1.

**Ground:** Abbey Stadium, Newmarket Rd, Cambridge CB5 8LN. Telephone (01223) 566500. **Capacity:** 9247.

**Record attendance;** 14,000 v Chelsea, Friendly, 1 May 1970.

**Manager:** John Beck.

**Secretary:** Andrew Pincher.

**Most League Goals:** 87, Division 4, 1976–77.

**Highest League Scorer in Season:** David Crown, 24, Division 4, 1985–86.

**Most League Goals in Total Aggregate:** John Taylor, 86, 1988–92; 1996–01.

**Most Capped Player:** Tom Finney, 7 (15), Northern Ireland.

**Most League Appearances:** Steve Spriggs, 416, 1975–87.

**Honours – Football League:** Division 3 Champions – 1990–91. Division 4 Champions – 1976–77.
**Colours:** Amber shirts with black trim, black shorts, amber stockings.

# CARDIFF CITY                                          DIV. 2

| | | | | | | |
|---|---|---|---|---|---|---|
| Boland Willie (M) | 5 9 | 11 02 | Ennis | 6 | 8 75 | Coventry C |
| Bonner Mark (M) | 5 8 | 11 00 | Ormskirk | 7 | 6 74 | Blackpool |
| Bowen Jason (F) | 5 8 | 11 02 | Merthyr | 24 | 8 72 | Reading |
| Brayson Paul (F) | 5 4 | 10 10 | Newcastle | 16 | 9 77 | Reading |
| Brazier Matt (M) | 5 8 | 11 08 | Whipps Cross | 2 | 7 76 | Fulham |
| Collins James (F) | | | Newport | 23 | 8 83 | Scholar |
| Earnshaw Robert (F) | 5 6 | 9 09 | Zambia | 6 | 4 81 | Trainee |
| Eckhardt Jeff (D) | 6 0 | 12 00 | Sheffield | 7 | 10 65 | Stockport Co |
| Evans Kevin (D) | 6 2 | 12 10 | Carmarthen | 16 | 12 80 | Leeds U |
| Fortune-West Leo (F) | 6 4 | 13 01 | Stratford | 9 | 4 71 | Rotherham U |
| Fowler Jason (M) | 6 3 | 12 04 | Bristol | 20 | 8 74 | Bristol C |
| Gabbidon Daniel (D) | 5 10 | 11 02 | Cwmbran | 8 | 8 79 | WBA |
| Giles Martyn (D) | | | Cardiff | 10 | 4 83 | Scholar |
| Gordon Gavin (F) | 6 2 | 12 00 | Manchester | 24 | 6 79 | Lincoln C |
| Hughes David (D) | 6 4 | 13 06 | Wrexham | 1 | 2 78 | Shrewsbury T |
| Jones Gethin (M) | | | Carmarthen | 8 | 8 81 | Carmarthen T |
| Jordan Andrew (D) | 6 2 | 13 04 | Manchester | 14 | 12 79 | Bristol C |
| Kendall Lee (G) | 5 10 | 10 05 | Newport | 8 | 1 81 | Crystal Palace |
| Legg Andy (D) | 5 8 | 11 01 | Swansea | 28 | 7 66 | Reading |
| Low Josh (F) | 6 0 | 14 00 | Bristol | 15 | 2 79 | Leyton Orient |
| McCulloch Scott (D) | 6 0 | 13 04 | Cumnock | 29 | 11 75 | Dundee U |
| Nogan Kurt (F) | 5 10 | 11 01 | Cardiff | 9 | 9 70 | Preston NE |
| Nugent Kevin (F) | 6 2 | 13 00 | Edmonton | 10 | 4 69 | Bristol C |
| Perrett Russell (D) | 6 2 | 13 00 | Barton-on-Sea | 18 | 6 73 | Portsmouth |
| Sheridan Tony (F) | 6 0 | 11 08 | Dublin | 21 | 10 74 | Portadown |
| Thompson Andy (D) | 5 5 | 10 06 | Cannock | 9 | 11 67 | Tranmere R |
| Walton Mark (G) | 6 4 | 15 08 | Merthyr | 1 | 6 69 | Brighton & HA |
| Weston Rhys (D) | 6 0 | 12 03 | Kingston | 27 | 10 80 | Arsenal |
| Young Scott (D) | 6 2 | 13 04 | Llywnypia | 14 | 1 76 | Trainee |

**League Appearances:** Boland, W. 25; Bonner, M. 17(7); Bowen, J. 35(5); Brayson, P. 25(15); Brazier, M. 23(3); Collins, J. (3); Earnshaw, R. 21(15); Eckhardt, J. 6(2); Evans, K. 24(6); Fortune-West, L. 28(9); Fowler, J. 3(2); Gabbidon, D. 42(1); Giles, M. 1(4); Gordon, G. 4(6); Greene, D. 10; Harper, J. 3; Hill, D. 7(2); Hughes, D. 11(1); Jones, G. (2); Jordan, A. 3(2); Legg, A. 39; Lightbourne, K. 2(1); Low, J. 31(5); McCulloch, S. 9(12); Muggleton, C. 6; Nogan, K. (12); Nugent, K. 14; Perrett, R. 2; Thompson, A. 5(2); Walton, M. 40; Weston, R. 25(3); Young, S. 45.
**Goals – League (95):** Earnshaw 19, Brayson 15 (1 pen), Bowen 12, Fortune-West 12, Young 10, Low 4, Nugent 4, Evans 3, Gabbidon 3, Legg 3, Brazier 2, Boland 1 (pen), Bonner 1, Gordon 1, Hill 1, McCulloch 1, Nogan 1, own goals 2.
**Worthington Cup (1):** Young 1.
**FA Cup (10):** Earnshaw 6 (1 pen), Evans 2, Fortune-West 1, Young 1.
**Ground:** Ninian Park, Cardiff CF11 8SX. Telephone (029) 2022 1001.
**Record attendance:** 61,566, Wales v England, 14 October 1961. **Capacity:** 15,585.
**Manager:** Alan Cork.
**Secretary:** Jim Finney.
**Most League Goals:** 95, Division 3, 2000–01.
**Highest League Scorer in Season:** Stan Richards, 30, Division 3 (S), 1946–47.
**Most League Goals in Total Aggregate:** Len Davies, 128, 1920–31.

**Most Capped Player:** Alf Sherwood, 39 (41), Wales.
**Most League Appearances:** Phil Dwyer, 471, 1972–85.
**Honours – Football League:** Division 3 (S) Champions – 1946–47. **FA Cup winners** 1926–27 (only occasion the Cup has been won by a club outside England). **Welsh Cup winners** 21 times.
**Colours:** Blue shirts, white shorts, blue stockings.

---

## CARLISLE UNITED DIV. 3

| Name | | | | Previous Club | | | Signed From |
|------|---|---|---|---|---|---|---|
| Allan Jonathan (M) | | | | Carlisle | 24 | 5 83 | Trainee |
| Antony Paul (M) | 5 10 | 11 00 | | Barnet | 4 | 3 82 | Trainee |
| Dobie Scott (F) | 6 2 | 12 09 | | Workington | 10 10 78 | | Trainee |
| Galloway Mick (M) | 5 11 | 11 05 | | Nottingham | 13 10 74 | | Chesterfield |
| Halliday Stephen (F) | 5 10 | 12 07 | | Sunderland | 3 | 5 76 | Motherwell |
| Heggs Carl (F) | 6 1 | 12 10 | | Leicester | 11 10 70 | | Chester C |
| Hore John (F) | 5 11 | 11 12 | | Liverpool | 18 | 8 82 | Trainee |
| Maddison Lee (D) | 6 0 | 12 10 | | Bristol | 5 10 72 | | Dundee |
| McAughtrie Craig (D) | 6 2 | 14 07 | | Burton-on-Trent | 3 | 3 81 | Trainee |
| Morley David (D) | 6 2 | 13 05 | | St Helens | 25 | 9 77 | Southend U |
| Soley Steve (M) | 5 11 | 12 08 | | Widnes | 22 | 4 71 | Portsmouth |
| Thurston Mark (M) | 6 2 | 11 08 | | Carlisle | 10 | 2 80 | Trainee |
| Thwaites Adam (M) | 5 10 | 11 00 | | Kendal | 0 | 0 | Trainee |
| Weaver Luke (G) | 6 2 | 13 02 | | Woolwich | 26 | 6 79 | Sunderland |
| Whitehead Stuart (D) | 6 0 | 12 02 | | Bromsgrove | 17 | 7 76 | Bolton W |

**League Appearances:** Birch, M. 44; Carr, D. 10; Carss, T. 6(1); Connelly, G. 21(7); Cullen, J. 10(1); Darby, J. 15(3); Dobie, S. 41(3); Galloway, M. 26; Glennon, M. 29; Halliday, S. 3(21); Heggs, C. 16(14); Hemmings, T. 16(6); Hopper, T. 4(5); Hore, J. 1; Inglis, J. 8; Keen, P. 3; Lee, D. 1(12); Lemarchand, S. 4(1); Maddison, L. 34; McAughtrie, C. (5); Morley, D. 23; Pitts, M. 1(4); Prokas, R. 26(3); Soley, S. 21(4); Squires, J. 2(3); Stevens, I. 41; Thurston, M. 3(2); Tracey, R. 4(2); Weaver, L. 14; Whitehead, S. 45; Winstanley, M. 34(2).
**Goals – League** (42): Stevens 12, Dobie 10, Heggs 5 (1 pen), Soley 4 (1 pen), Connelly 1, Darby 1, Galloway 1, Halliday 1, Keen 1, Lemarchand 1, Morley 1, Tracey 1, Whitehead 1, own goals 2.
**Worthington Cup** (1): Stevens 1.
**FA Cup** (7): Stevens 4, Dobie 2, Connelly 1.
**Ground:** Brunton Park, Carlisle CA1 1LL. Telephone (01228) 526237.
**Record attendance:** 27,500 v Birmingham C, FA Cup 3rd rd, 5 January 1957 and v Middlesbrough, FA Cup 5th rd, 7 February 1970. **Capacity:** 16,651.
**Manager:**
**Secretary:** Sarah McKnight.
**Most League Goals:** 113, Division 4, 1963–64.
**Highest League Scorer in Season:** Jimmy McConnell, 42, Division 3 (N), 1928–29.
**Most League Goals in Total Aggregate:** Jimmy McConnell, 126, 1928–32.
**Most Capped Player:** Eric Welsh, 4, Northern Ireland.
**Most League Appearances:** Allan Ross, 466, 1963–79.
**Honours – Football League:** Division 3 Champions – 1964–65, 1994–95. **Auto Windscreens Shield winners:** 1997
**Colours:** Blue shirts, white shorts, white stockings.

# CHARLTON ATHLETIC                     FA PREMIERSHIP

| Bagheri Karim (M) | 6 1 | 12 04 | Tabriz | 20 2 74 | Arminia Bielefeld |
|---|---|---|---|---|---|
| Bartlett Shaun (F) | 6 2 | 12 04 | Cape Town | 31 10 72 | Zurich |
| Brennan Martin (G) | | | | | |
| Brown Steve (D) | 6 1 | 14 10 | Brighton | 13 5 72 | Trainee |
| Collis Dave (D) | 5 10 | 10 12 | London | 8 11 81 | Trainee |
| De Bolla Mark (F) | | | London | 1 1 83 | Aston Villa |
| Dincer Fatih (M) | | | Stockholm | 13 7 83 | |
| Fish Mark (D) | 6 4 | 13 06 | Cape Town | 14 3 74 | Bolton W |
| Fortune Jonathan (D) | 6 2 | 12 12 | Islington | 23 8 80 | Trainee |
| George Kevin (M) | 5 11 | 12 04 | London | 21 11 82 | Scholar |
| Hunt Andy (F) | 6 1 | 12 08 | Thurrock | 9 6 70 | WBA |
| Ilic Sasa (G) | 6 4 | 14 12 | Melbourne | 18 7 72 | St Leonards Stamcroft |
| Jensen Claus (M) | 6 1 | 13 04 | Nykobing | 29 4 77 | Bolton W |
| Johansson Jonatan (F) | 6 1 | 12 08 | Stockholm | 16 8 75 | Rangers |
| Kiely Dean (G) | 6 0 | 12 13 | Salford | 10 10 70 | Bury |
| Kinsella Mark (M) | 5 8 | 12 01 | Dublin | 12 8 72 | Colchester U |
| Kishishev Radostin (D) | 5 10 | 12 08 | Bourgas | 30 7 74 | Litets Lovech |
| Konchesky Paul (D) | 5 10 | 11 07 | Barking | 15 5 81 | Trainee |
| Lisbie Kevin (F) | 5 10 | 11 01 | Hackney | 17 10 78 | Trainee |
| MacDonald Charlie (F) | 5 8 | 12 10 | Southwark | 13 2 81 | Trainee |
| Martin Alex (M) | 5 8 | 11 04 | Harlow | 2 5 83 | Scholar |
| Mendonca Clive (F) | 5 10 | 12 10 | Islington | 9 9 68 | Grimsby T |
| Newton Shaun (M) | 5 8 | 11 12 | Camberwell | 20 8 75 | Trainee |
| Parker Scott (M) | 5 9 | 10 12 | Lambeth | 13 10 80 | Trainee |
| Powell Chris (D) | 5 10 | 11 13 | Lambeth | 8 9 69 | Derby Co |
| Pringle Martin (F) | 6 2 | 12 03 | Gothenburg | 18 11 70 | Benfica |
| Roberts Ben (G) | 6 2 | 13 00 | Bishop Auckland | 22 6 75 | Middlesbrough |
| Robinson John (F) | 5 10 | 12 01 | Bulawayo | 29 8 71 | Brighton & HA |
| Rufus Richard (D) | 6 1 | 12 12 | Lewisham | 12 1 75 | Trainee |
| Salako John (F) | 5 9 | 11 12 | Nigeria | 11 2 69 | Fulham |
| Shields Greg (D) | 5 10 | 11 06 | Falkirk | 21 8 76 | Dunfermline Ath |
| Shittu Dan (D) | 6 2 | 16 03 | Lagos | 2 9 80 | |
| Stuart Graham (M) | 5 8 | 12 00 | Tooting | 24 10 70 | Sheffield U |
| Svensson Mathias (F) | 6 1 | 12 08 | Boras | 24 9 74 | Crystal Palace |
| Todd Andy (D) | 5 11 | 13 04 | Derby | 21 9 74 | Bolton W |
| Youds Eddie (D) | 6 2 | 14 10 | Liverpool | 3 5 70 | Bradford C |

**League Appearances:** Bagheri, K. (1); Bartlett, S. 16(2); Brown, S. 15(10); Caig, T. (1); Fish, M. 24; Hunt, A. 8; Ilic, S. 13; Jensen, C. 37(1); Johansson, J. 27(4); Kiely, D. 25; Kinsella, M. 27(5); Kishishev, R. 25(2); Konchesky, P. 11(12); Lisbie, K. 5(13); MacDonald, C. 1(2); Newton, S. 1(9); Parker, S. 15(5); Powell, C. 31(2); Pringle, M. 1(7); Robinson, J. 21(8); Rufus, R. 32; Salako, J. 4(13); Shields, G. 2(2); Stuart, G. 33(2); Svensson, M. 18(4); Tiler, C. 7; Todd, A. 19(4).
**Goals – League** (50): Johansson 11, Bartlett 7, Jensen 5 (1 pen), Stuart 5 (2 pens), Svensson 5, Hunt 4, Kinsella 2, Robinson 2, Rufus 2, Fish 1, Parker 1, Pringle 1, Todd 1, own goals 3.
**Worthington Cup** (5): Johansson 3, Lisbie 2.
**FA Cup** (4): Newton 1, Powell 1, Salako 1, Svensson 1.
**Ground:** The Valley, Floyd Road, Charlton, London SE7 8BL. Telephone (020) 8333 4000.
**Record attendance:** 75,031 v Aston Villa, FA Cup 5th rd, 12 February 1938 (at The Valley). **Capacity:** 20,043 rising to 26,500.
**Manager:** Alan Curbishley.

**Secretary:** Chris Parkes.
**Most League Goals:** 107, Division 2, 1957–58.
**Highest League Scorer in Season:** Ralph Allen, 32, Division 3 (S), 1934–35.
**Most League Goals in Total Aggregate:** Stuart Leary, 153, 1953–62.
**Most Capped Player:** John Robinson, 26, Wales.
**Most League Appearances:** Sam Bartram, 583, 1934–56.
**Honours – Football League:** Division 1 Champions – 1999–2000. Division 3 (S) Champions – 1928–29, 1934–35. **FA Cup winners** 1947.
**Colours:** Red shirts, white shorts, red stockings.

# CHELSEA                                    FA PREMIERSHIP

| Name | | | Birthplace | Birthdate | Previous club |
|---|---|---|---|---|---|
| Aleksidze Rati (F) | 6 0 | 12 02 | Georgia | 3 8 78 | Dynamo Tbilisi |
| Ambrosetti Gabriele (M) | 5 11 | 11 05 | Varese | 7 8 73 | Vicenza |
| Babayaro Celestine (D) | 5 9 | 11 09 | Kaduna | 29 8 78 | Anderlecht |
| Bogarde Winston (D) | 6 3 | 14 04 | Rotterdam | 22 10 70 | Barcelona |
| Bosnich Mark (G) | 6 2 | 14 08 | Fairfield | 13 1 72 | Manchester U |
| Cole Carlton (F) | 6 3 | 12 13 | Surrey | 12 11 83 | Scholar |
| Cudicini Carlo (G) | 6 1 | 12 02 | Milan | 6 9 73 | Castel di Sangro |
| Cummings Warren (D) | 5 9 | 11 05 | Aberdeen | 15 10 80 | Trainee |
| Dalla Bona Samuele (F) | 6 0 | 13 03 | San Dona di Piave | 6 2 81 | |
| De Goey Ed (G) | 6 6 | 14 05 | Gouda | 20 12 66 | Feyenoord |
| Desailly Marcel (D) | 6 0 | 13 05 | Accra | 7 9 68 | AC Milan |
| Di Cesare Valerio (M) | | | Rome | 23- 5 83 | |
| Di Matteo Roberto (M) | 5 10 | 12 04 | Schaffhausen | 29 5 70 | Lazio |
| Evans Rhys (G) | 6 1 | 11 12 | Swindon | 27 1 82 | Trainee |
| Ferrer Albert (D) | 5 6 | 12 02 | Barcelona | 6 6 70 | Barcelona |
| Forssell Mikael (F) | 6 0 | 12 08 | Steinfurt | 15 3 81 | HJK Helsinki |
| Gronkjaer Jesper (M) | 6 2 | 13 03 | Nuuk | 12 8 77 | Ajax |
| Gudjohnsen Eidur (F) | 6 1 | 14 05 | Reykjavik | 15 9 78 | Bolton W |
| Harley Jon (D) | 5 9 | 11 05 | Maidstone | 26 9 79 | Trainee |
| Hasselbaink Jimmy Floyd (F) | 5 11 | 13 09 | Paramaribo | 27 3 72 | Atletico Madrid |
| Issa Pierre (D) | 6 4 | 13 07 | Johannesburg | 11 9 75 | Marseille |
| Jokanovic Slavisa (M) | 6 3 | 13 03 | Novi Sad | 16 8 68 | La Coruna |
| Keenan Joseph (M) | 5 7 | 10 00 | Southampton | 14 10 82 | Trainee |
| Kitamirike Joel (D) | | | Uganda | 5 4 84 | Scholar |
| Kneissl Sebastian (F) | 5 11 | 11 05 | Germany | 13 1 83 | |
| Knight Leon (F) | 5 4 | 9 06 | Hackney | 16 9 82 | Trainee |
| Lambourde Bernard (D) | 6 0 | 13 05 | Pointe-A-Pitre | 11 5 71 | Bordeaux |
| Le Saux Graeme (D) | 5 10 | 11 09 | Jersey | 17 10 68 | Blackburn R |
| Leboeuf Franck (D) | 6 1 | 11 11 | Marseille | 22 1 68 | Strasbourg |
| Melchiot Mario (D) | 6 2 | 11 11 | Amsterdam | 4 11 76 | Ajax |
| Morris Jody (M) | 5 5 | 10 03 | Hammersmith | 22 12 78 | Trainee |
| Parkin Sam (F) | 6 2 | 13 03 | Roehampton | 14 3 81 | School |
| Pitt Courtney (M) | 5 7 | 10 08 | London | 17 12 81 | Scholar |
| Poyet Gustavo (M) | 6 1 | 12 13 | Montevideo | 15 11 67 | Zaragoza |
| Reddington Stuart (D) | 6 3 | 13 08 | Lincoln | 21 2 78 | Lincoln U |
| Slatter Danny (D) | 5 7 | 10 01 | Cardiff | 15 11 80 | Trainee |
| Stanic Mario (M) | 6 2 | 13 00 | Sarajevo | 10 4 72 | Parma |
| Terry John (D) | 6 1 | 12 13 | Barking | 7 12 80 | Trainee |
| Thornton Paul (D) | 5 7 | 11 00 | Surrey | 7 1 83 | Trainee |
| Wise Dennis (M) | 5 6 | 10 11 | Kensington | 16 12 66 | Wimbledon |
| Wolleaston Robert (M) | 5 11 | 11 07 | Perivale | 21 12 79 | Trainee |
| Zola Gianfranco (F) | 5 6 | 10 08 | Oliena | 5 7 66 | Parma |

**League Appearances:** Aleksidze, R. (2); Babayaro, C. 19(5); Bogarde, W. 2(7); Cudicini, C. 23(1); Dalla Bona, S. 26(3); De Goey, E. 15; Desailly, M. 34; Di Matteo, R. 7; Emerson, 1; Ferrer, A. 12(2); Flo, T. 5(9); Gronkjaer, J. 6(8); Gudjohnsen, E. 17(13); Harley, J. 6(4); Hasselbaink, J. 35; Jokanovic, S. 7(12); Lambourde, B. (1); Le Saux, G. 18(2); Leboeuf, F. 23(2); Melchiot, M. 27(4); Morris, J. 13(8); Panucci, C. 7(1); Poyet, G. 22(8); Stanic, M. 8(4); Terry, J. 19(3); Wise, D. 35(1); Zola, G. 31(5).
**Goals – League (68):** Hasselbaink 23 (4 pens), Poyet 11, Gudjohnsen 10, Zola 9, Flo 3, Wise 3, Dalla Bona 2, Desailly 2, Stanic 2, Gronkjaer 1, Terry 1, own goal 1.
**Worthington Cup (1):** Zola 1.
**FA Cup (10):** Gudjohnsen 3, Gronkjaer 2, Hasselbaink 2, Zola 2, Poyet 1.
**Ground:** Stamford Bridge, London SW6 1HS. Telephone (020) 7385 5545.
**Record attendance:** 82,905 v Arsenal, Division 1, 12 October 1935.
**Capacity:** 42,420.
**Manager:** Claudio Ranieri.
**Secretary:** Alan Shaw.
**Most League Goals:** 98, Division 1, 1960–61.
**Highest League Scorer in Season:** Jimmy Greaves, 41, 1960–61.
**Most League Goals in Total Aggregate:** Bobby Tambling, 164, 1958–70.
**Most Capped Player:** Dan Petrescu, 43 (95), Romania.
**Most League Appearances:** Ron Harris, 655, 1962–80.
**Honours – Football League:** Division 1 Champions – 1954–55. **FA Cup winners** 1970, 1997, 2000. **Football League Cup winners** 1964–65, 1997–98. **Full Members' Cup winners** 1985–86. **Zenith Data Systems Cup winners** 1989–90. **European Cup-Winners' Cup winners** 1970–71, 1997–98. **Super Cup Winners:** 1999.
**Colours:** Royal blue shirts and shorts with white trim, white stockings with royal blue trim.

## CHELTENHAM TOWN                                            DIV. 3

| | | | | | | | |
|---|---|---|---|---|---|---|---|
| Alsop Julian (F) | 6 5 | 14 08 | Nuneaton | 28 | 5 73 | Swansea C |
| Banks Chris (D) | 5 11 | 12 04 | Stone | 22 | 11 65 | Exeter C |
| Book Steve (G) | 5 11 | 11 02 | Bournemouth | 7 | 7 69 | Lincoln C |
| Brough John (D) | 6 0 | 12 11 | Ilkeston | 8 | 1 73 | Hereford U |
| Devaney Martin (F) | 5 11 | 12 06 | Cheltenham | 1 | 6 80 | Coventry C |
| Duff Michael (D) | 6 1 | 11 08 | Belfast | 11 | 1 78 | Trainee |
| Duff Shane (D) | | | Swindon | 2 | 4 82 | |
| Freeman Mark (D) | 6 2 | 13 08 | Walsall | 27 | 1 70 | Bilston T |
| Grayson Neil (F) | 5 10 | 12 09 | York | 1 | 11 64 | Northampton T |
| Griffin Anthony (M) | 5 11 | 11 03 | Bournemouth | 22 | 3 79 | Bournemouth |
| Higgs Shane (G) | 6 3 | 14 02 | Oxford | 13 | 5 77 | Bristol R |
| Hopkins Gareth (F) | 6 2 | 13 08 | Cheltenham | 14 | 6 80 | Trainee |
| Howarth Neil (D) | 6 2 | 13 06 | Bolton | 15 | 11 71 | Macclesfield T |
| Howells Lee (M) | 5 11 | 11 02 | Fremantle | 14 | 10 68 | Apprentice |
| Jackson Michael D (M) | 5 7 | 10 10 | Cheltenham | 26 | 6 80 | Trainee |
| McAuley Hugh (F) | 5 10 | 11 06 | Plymouth | 13 | 5 77 | Leek T |
| Milton Russell (M) | 5 8 | 12 01 | Folkestone | 12 | 1 69 | Arsenal |
| Mitchinson Stuart (F) | 5 6 | 10 08 | Cheltenham | 15 | 10 80 | Trainee |
| Victory Jamie (D) | 5 11 | 12 02 | London | 14 | 11 75 | Bournemouth |
| Walker Richard (D) | 5 10 | 11 09 | Derby | 9 | 11 71 | Notts Co |
| White Jason (F) | 6 1 | 12 12 | Meriden | 19 | 10 71 | Rotherham U |
| Yates Mark (M) | 5 11 | 13 02 | Birmingham | 24 | 1 70 | Doncaster R |

**League Appearances:** Alsop, J. 29(10); Banks, C. 40; Bloomer, B. 5(7); Book, S. 46; Brough, J. 4(6); Clare, D. 4; Devaney, M. 23(11); Duff, M. 39; Freeman, M. 25(2); Goodridge, G. 10(1); Grayson, N. 23(8); Griffin, A. 14(8); Higgs, S. (1);

Hopkins, G. 1(3); Howarth, N. 19(4); Howells, L. 36; Iwelumo, C. 2(2); Jackson, M. 2(4); Jones, M. 1(1); MacDonald, C. 7(1); McAuley, H. 30(5); McCann, G. 27(3); Milton, R. 18(1); Sertori, M. 10; Victory, J. 3; Walker, R. 35(1); White, J. 8(19); Yates, M. 45.

**Goals – League** (59): Grayson 13, Devaney 10 (1 pen), Yates 6, Alsop 5, Duff 5, Howarth 3, McAuley 3, McCann 3, MacDonald 2, Banks 1, Bloomer 1, Goodridge 1, Griffin 1, Howells 1, Iwelumo 1, Milton 1, Victory 1, own goal 1.

**Worthington Cup** (0).

**FA Cup** (5): Grayson 2, Alsop 1, Howells 1, Milton 1.

**Ground:** Whaddon Road, Cheltenham, Gloucester GL52 5NA. Telephone (01242) 573558.

**Record attendance:** at Whaddon Road: 8326 v Reading, FA Cup 1st rd, 17 November 1956; at Cheltenham Athletic Ground: 10,389 v Blackpool, FA Cup 3rd rd, 13 January 1934.

**Capacity:** 6114.

**Manager:** Steve Cotterill.

**Secretary:** Bob Hands.

**Most League Goals:** 115, Southern League, 1957–58.

**Highest League Scorer in Season:** Dave Lewis, 33 (53 in all competitions), Southern League Division 1, 1974–75.

**Most League Goals in Total Aggregate:** Dave Lewis, 205 (290 in all competitions), 1970–83.

**Most League Appearances:** Roger Thorndale, 523 (702 in all competitions), 1958–76.

**Honours – Football Conference:** Champions – 1998–99. **FA Trophy winners** 1997–98.

**Colours:** Red and white striped shirts, white shorts, red stockings.

---

# CHESTERFIELD                                         DIV. 2

| | | | | | |
|---|---|---|---|---|---|
| Barrett Danny (M) | 6 0 | 11 12 | Bradford | 25 9 80 | Trainee |
| Beckett Luke (F) | 5 11 | 11 06 | Sheffield | 25 11 76 | Chester C |
| Breckin Ian (D) | 5 11 | 11 07 | Rotherham | 24 2 75 | Rotherham U |
| D'Auria David (M) | 5 9 | 11 11 | Swansea | 26 3 70 | Hull C |
| Ebdon Marcus (M) | 5 10 | 11 02 | Pontypool | 17 10 70 | Peterborough U |
| Edwards Rob (M) | 5 9 | 12 04 | Manchester | 23 2 70 | Huddersfield T |
| Hewitt Jamie (M) | 5 10 | 10 08 | Chesterfield | 17 5 68 | Doncaster R |
| Ingledow Jamie (M) | 5 7 | 11 01 | Barnsley | 23 8 80 | Rotherham U |
| Parrish Sean (M) | 5 10 | 11 05 | Wrexham | 14 3 72 | Northampton T |
| Payne Steve (D) | 5 11 | 12 05 | Castleford | 1 8 75 | Macclesfield T |
| Pearce Greg (M) | 6 0 | 11 00 | Bolton | 26 5 80 | Trainee |
| Pollitt Mike (G) | 6 3 | 14 12 | Farnworth | 29 2 72 | Rotherham U |
| Reeves David (F) | 6 0 | 12 06 | Birkenhead | 19 11 67 | Preston NE |
| Richardson Lee J (M) | 5 11 | 10 06 | Halifax | 12 3 69 | Livingston |
| Simpkins Mike (D) | 6 0 | 11 11 | Sheffield | 28 11 78 | Trainee |
| Tutill Steve (D) | 5 10 | 12 06 | Derwent | 1 10 69 | Darlington |
| Williams Danny (D) | 5 9 | 9 13 | Sheffield | 2 3 81 | Trainee |
| Williams Ryan (F) | 5 4 | 11 02 | Chesterfield | 31 8 78 | Tranmere R |

**League Appearances:** Armstrong, J. (1); Barrett, D. (1); Beaumont, C. 4(10); Beckett, L. 38(3); Blatherwick, S. 38; Breckin, I. 45; D'Auria, D. 4(2); Dudfield, L. 4(10); Ebdon, M. 41; Edwards, R. 34; Galloway, M. 4(1); Howard, J. 13(18); Ingledow, J. 14(10); Jones, M. (3); Parrish, S. 33(2); Payne, S. 33(2); Pearce, G. 1; Perkins, C. 8; Pollitt, M. 46; Reeves, D. 34(3); Richardson, L. 30; Rushbury, A. (2); Simpkins, M. 14(2); Tutill, S. 17(2); Williams, D. 1(1); Williams, R. 39(6); Willis, R. 11(21).

43

**Goals – League** (79): Beckett 16, Reeves 13 (2 pens), Parrish 10 (1 pen), Williams R 8 (1 pen), Howard 5, Willis 5, Edwards 4, Breckin 3, Dudfield 3, Ebdon 3, Ingledow 3, Blatherwick 1, Payne 1, Tutill 1, own goals 3.
**Worthington Cup** (5): Beckett 2, Breckin 1, Parrish 1, Reeves 1.
**FA Cup** (0).
**Ground:** Recreation Ground, Chesterfield S40 4SX. Telephone (01246) 209765.
**Record attendance:** 30,968 v Newcastle U, Division 2, 7 April 1939. **Capacity:** 8880.
**Manager:** Nicky Law.
**Secretary:** Stephanie Otter.
**Most League Goals:** 102, Division 3 (N), 1930–31.
**Highest League Scorer in Season:** Jimmy Cookson, 44, Division 3 (N), 1925–26.
**Most League Goals in Total Aggregate:** Ernie Moss, 161, 1969–76, 1979–81 and 1984–86.
**Most Capped Player:** Walter McMillen, 4 (7), Northern Ireland; Mark Williams, 4 (17), Northern Ireland.
**Most League Appearances:** Dave Blakey, 613, 1948–67.
**Honours – Football League:** Division 3 (N) Champions – 1930–31, 1935–36. Division 4 Champions – 1969–70, 1984–85. **Anglo-Scottish Cup winners** 1980–81.
**Colours:** Blue shirts, white shorts, blue stockings.

---

# COLCHESTER UNITED                                          DIV. 2

| | | | | | |
|---|---|---|---|---|---|
| Clark Simon (D) | 6 0 | 12 10 | Boston | 12 3 67 | Leyton Orient |
| Duguid Karl (F) | 5 11 | 11 00 | Letchworth | 21 3 78 | Trainee |
| Fitzgerald Scott (D) | 5 11 | 12 08 | Westminster | 13 8 69 | Millwall |
| Izzet Kemal (M) | 5 6 | 10 03 | Whitechapel | 29 9 80 | Charlton Ath |
| Johnson Ross (D) | 6 0 | 13 00 | Brighton | 2 1 76 | Brighton & HA |
| Keeble Chris (M) | 5 9 | 11 00 | Colchester | 17 9 78 | Ipswich T |
| Keith Joey (D) | 5 7 | 10 06 | London | 1 10 78 | West Ham U |
| McGleish Scott (F) | 5 10 | 11 07 | Camden Town | 10 2 74 | Barnet |
| Pinault Thomas (M) | 5 10 | 11 01 | Grasse | 4 12 81 | Cannes |
| White Alan (D) | 6 1 | 13 07 | Darlington | 22 3 76 | Luton T |
| Woodman Andy (G) | 6 3 | 13 07 | Camberwell | 11 8 71 | Brentford |

**League Appearances:** Arnott, A. 1(2); Brown, S. 18; Clark, S. 33(1); Conlon, B. 23(3); Dozzell, J. 22; Duguid, K. 34(7); Dunne, J. 31(3); Fitzgerald, S. 30; Gregory, D. 27(1); Izzet, K. 5(1); Johnson, G. 33(4); Johnson, R. 17(1); Keeble, C. 10(6); Keith, J. 21(6); Lock, T. 3(11); Lua-Lua, L. 7; McGavin, S. 19(22); McGleish, S. 11(10); Morgan, D. (4); Nicholls, M. 3(1); Opara, C. (2); Pinault, T. 3(2); Scott, K. 8(1); Skelton, A. 43(1); Stockwell, M. 46; Tanner, A. 1(3); White, A. 29(3); Woodman, A. 28.

**Goals – League** (55): Stockwell 11, Conlon 8, Skelton 6 (4 pens), Duguid 5, McGleish 5, Gregory 3, Keith 3, Johnson G 2, Lock 2, Lua-Lua 2, McGavin 2 (1 pen), Dunne 1, Izzet 1, Keeble 1, Pinault 1, Scott 1, own goal 1.
**Worthington Cup** (4): Lua-Lua 3, McGavin 1.
**FA Cup** (1): Duguid 1.
**Ground:** Layer Rd Ground, Colchester CO2 7JJ. Telephone (01206) 508800.
**Record attendance:** 19,072 v Reading, FA Cup 1st rd, 27 Nov, 1948. **Capacity:** 7556.
**Manager:** Steve Whitton.
**Secretary:** Miss Sonya Constantine.
**Most League Goals:** 104, Division 4, 1961–62.
**Highest League Scorer in Season:** Bobby Hunt, 38, Division 4, 1961–62.
**Most League Goals in Total Aggregate:** Martyn King, 130, 1956–64.
**Most Capped Player:** None.
**Most League Appearances:** Micky Cook, 613, 1969–84.

**Honours – GM Vauxhall Conference winners** 1991–92. **FA Trophy winners** 1991–92.
**Colours:** Blue and white striped shirts, navy shorts, white stockings.

## COVENTRY CITY                                                    DIV. 1

| Name | | | Birthplace | | Previous Club |
|---|---|---|---|---|---|
| Aloisi John (F) | 6 1 | 12 06 | Adelaide | 5 2 76 | Portsmouth |
| Bellamy Craig (F) | 5 8 | 11 00 | Cardiff | 13 7 79 | Norwich C |
| Betts Robert (D) | 5 10 | 11 00 | Doncaster | 21 12 81 | School |
| Bothroyd Jay (F) | 6 3 | 13 00 | Islington | 7 5 82 | Trainee |
| Brancati Marco (M) | 5 10 | 11 05 | Rome | 16 4 83 | |
| Breen Gary (D) | 6 1 | 11 12 | London | 12 12 73 | Birmingham C |
| Carsley Lee (M) | 5 10 | 12 06 | Birmingham | 28 2 74 | Blackburn R |
| Chippo Youssef (M) | 5 11 | 12 00 | Rabat | 10 6 73 | Porto |
| Cudworth Thomas (D) | 5 10 | 11 00 | Coventry | 3 8 82 | Trainee |
| Davenport Calum (D) | 6 4 | 14 00 | Bedford | 1 1 83 | Trainee |
| Delorge Laurent (M) | 5 10 | 11 12 | Leuven | 21 7 79 | |
| Edworthy Marc (D) | 5 11 | 10 03 | Barnstaple | 24 12 72 | Crystal Palace |
| Eustace John (M) | 5 11 | 11 12 | Solihull | 3 11 79 | Dundee U |
| Fahlman Per (M) | | | Sweden | 26 4 84 | |
| Ferguson Barry (D) | 6 3 | 13 00 | Dublin | 7 9 79 | Home Farm |
| Ford Brian (D) | 5 11 | 12 00 | Edinburgh | 23 9 82 | Trainee |
| Fowler Lee (M) | 5 7 | 10 00 | Cardiff | 10 6 83 | Scholar |
| Froggatt Steve (F) | 5 11 | 11 00 | Lincoln | 9 3 73 | Wolverhampton W |
| Gallieri Antonio (F) | 5 8 | 11 00 | Rome | 5 7 83 | |
| Guerrero Ivan (D) | 5 7 | 10 00 | Comayagua | 30 11 77 | Motagua |
| Gustafsson Tomas (D) | 5 10 | 11 00 | Stockholm | 7 5 73 | AIK Stockholm |
| Hadji Mustapha (M) | 6 0 | 12 00 | Ifrane | 16 11 71 | La Coruna |
| Hall Marcus (D) | 6 1 | 12 02 | Coventry | 24 3 76 | Trainee |
| Hartson John (F) | 6 0 | 13 07 | Swansea | 5 4 75 | Wimbledon |
| Hedman Magnus (G) | 6 3 | 14 00 | Stockholm | 19 3 73 | AIK Stockholm |
| Hope Shaun (D) | 5 11 | 12 00 | Hartlepool | 15 12 82 | Scholar |
| Hyldgaard Morten (G) | 6 6 | 14 00 | Herning | 26 1 78 | Ikast |
| Kirkland Christopher (G) | 6 3 | 11 07 | Leicester | 2 5 81 | Trainee |
| Konjic Muhamed (D) | 6 3 | 13 00 | Bosnia | 14 5 70 | Monaco |
| Magennis Mark (M) | | | Newtonards | 15 3 83 | Scholar |
| Martinez Jairo (M) | | | Honduras | 14 5 78 | |
| McSheffrey Gary (F) | 5 8 | 10 06 | Coventry | 13 8 82 | Trainee |
| Miller Kirk (M) | | | Coventry | 15 9 83 | Scholar |
| Montgomery Gary (M) | | | Leamington Spa | 8 10 82 | Scholar |
| Normann Runar (M) | 5 11 | 12 00 | Harstad | 1 3 78 | Lillestrom |
| Palmer Carlton (M) | 6 3 | 13 00 | Oldbury | 5 12 65 | Nottingham F |
| Pead Craig (M) | 5 9 | 11 06 | Bromsgrove | 15 9 81 | Trainee |
| Pipe David (M) | | | Caerphilly | 5 11 83 | Scholar |
| Quinn Barry (M) | 6 0 | 12 02 | Dublin | 9 5 79 | Trainee |
| Shaw Richard (D) | 5 9 | 12 08 | Brentford | 11 9 68 | Crystal Palace |
| Spong Richard (M) | | | Falun | 23 9 83 | Scholar |
| Strachan Craig (M) | 5 8 | 10 06 | Aberdeen | 19 5 82 | Trainee |
| Strachan Gavin (M) | 5 10 | 11 07 | Aberdeen | 23 12 78 | Trainee |
| Telfer Paul (M) | 5 9 | 11 06 | Edinburgh | 21 10 71 | Luton T |
| Thompson David (M) | 5 7 | 10 00 | Birkenhead | 12 9 77 | Liverpool |
| Williams Paul (D) | 5 11 | 12 10 | Burton | 26 3 71 | Derby Co |
| Zuniga Ysrael (F) | 5 9 | 11 00 | Lima | 27 8 76 | |

**League Appearances:** Aloisi, J. 8(11); Bellamy, C. 33(1); Betts, R. (1); Bothroyd, J. 3(5); Breen, G. 29(2); Carsley, L. 21; Chippo, Y. 18(14); Davenport, C. (1);

45

Edworthy, M. 18(6); Eustace, J. 22(10); Guerrero, I. 3; Hadji, M. 28(1); Hall, M. 21; Hartson, J. 12; Hedman, M. 15; Hendry, C. 1(1); Kirkland, C. 23; Konjic, M. 8; Miller, A. (1); Palmer, C. 12(3); Quinn, B. 25; Roussel, C. 10(7); Shaw, R. 23(1); Strachan, G. 2; Telfer, P. 27(4); Thompson, D. 22(3); Williams, P. 27(3); Zuniga, Y. 7(8).

**Goals – League** (36): Bellamy 6 (2 pens), Hadji 6, Hartson 6, Aloisi 3, Thompson 3, Carsley 2 (1 pen), Eustace 2, Roussel 2, Breen 1, Edworthy 1, Zuniga 1, own goals 3.

**Worthington Cup** (9): Aloisi 3 (1 pen), Eustace 2, Bellamy 1 (pen), Hall 1, Strachan 1 (pen), Zuniga 1.

**FA Cup** (2): Bellamy 1, Hadji 1.

**Ground:** Highfield Road Stadium, King Richard Street, Coventry CV2 4FW. Telephone (024) 7623 4000.

**Record attendance:** 51,455 v Wolverhampton W, Division 2, 29 April 1967.

**Capacity:** 23,633.

**Manager:** Gordon Strachan.

**Secretary:** Graham Hover.

**Most League Goals:** 108, Division 3 (S), 1931–32.

**Highest League Scorer in Season:** Clarrie Bourton, 49, Division 3 (S), 1931–32.

**Most League Goals in Total Aggregate:** Clarrie Bourton, 171, 1931–37.

**Most Capped Player:** Marcus Hedman, 31 (36), Sweden.

**Most League Appearances:** Steve Ogrizovic, 507, 1984–2000.

**Honours – Football League:** Division 2 Champions – 1966–67. Division 3 Champions – 1963–64. Division 3 (S) Champions 1935–36. **FA Cup winners** 1986–87.

**Colours:** All sky blue with black piping.

---

# CREWE ALEXANDRA                                    DIV. 1

| | | | | | |
|---|---|---|---|---|---|
| Ashton Dean (F) | | | Swindon | 24 11 83 | Schoolboy |
| Bankole Ademola (G) | 6 3 | 14 11 | Lagos | 9 9 69 | QPR |
| Bell Lee (M) | | | Crewe | 26 1 83 | Scholar |
| Betts Thomas (M) | | | Stone | 3 12 82 | Scholar |
| Charles Anthony (D) | 6 0 | 12 00 | Isleworth | 11 3 81 | Brook House |
| Charnock Phil (M) | 5 10 | 11 03 | Southport | 14 2 75 | Liverpool |
| Cramb Colin (F) | 6 0 | 12 09 | Lanark | 23 6 74 | Bristol C |
| Edwards Paul (M) | | | Derby | 10 11 82 | Scholar |
| Foster Stephen (D) | 5 11 | 11 00 | Warrington | 10 9 80 | Trainee |
| Frost Carl (M) | | | Chester | 19 7 83 | Scholar |
| Grant John (F) | 5 11 | 10 08 | Manchester | 9 8 81 | Trainee |
| Higdon Michael (M) | | | Liverpool | 2 9 83 | School |
| Hulse Robert (F) | 6 1 | 12 00 | Crewe | 25 10 79 | Trainee |
| Ince Clayton (G) | 6 3 | 13 00 | Trinidad | 13 7 72 | Defence Force |
| Jack Rodney (F) | 5 7 | 10 07 | Kingston, Jamaica | 28 9 72 | Torquay U |
| Jeffs Ian (M) | | | Chester | 12 10 82 | Scholar |
| Kearton Jason (G) | 6 1 | 12 03 | Ipswich (Aus) | 9 7 69 | Everton |
| Liddle Gareth (D) | 6 0 | 12 00 | Manchester | 10 8 82 | Scholar |
| Little Colin (F) | 5 10 | 11 00 | Wythenshaw | 4 11 72 | Hyde U |
| Lunt Kenny (M) | 5 10 | 10 00 | Runcorn | 20 11 79 | Trainee |
| Macauley Steve (D) | 6 1 | 12 03 | Lytham | 4 3 69 | Fleetwood T |
| McCready Christopher (M) | | | Chester | 5 9 81 | Scholar |
| Morris Alexander (M) | | | Stoke | 5 10 82 | Scholar |
| Rivers Mark (F) | 5 10 | 11 00 | Crewe | 26 11 75 | Trainee |
| Rix Benjamin (M) | | | Wolverhampton | 11 12 82 | Scholar |
| Smith Shaun (D) | 5 10 | 11 00 | Leeds | 9 4 71 | Halifax T |
| Sorvel Neil (M) | 6 0 | 12 09 | Widnes | 2 3 73 | Macclesfield T |

| Street Kevin (M) | 5 10 | 11 00 | Crewe | 25 11 77 | Trainee |
|---|---|---|---|---|---|
| Tait Paul (F) | 6 1 | 11 00 | Newcastle | 24 10 74 | Wigan Ath |
| Trainer Phil (M) | 6 0 | 12 00 | Wolverhampton | 3 7 81 | |
| Vaughan David (M) | | | St Asaph | 18 2 83 | Scholar |
| Walker Richard (D) | 6 2 | 13 00 | Stafford | 17 9 80 | Trainee |
| Walton David (D) | 6 2 | 14 07 | Bellingham | 10 4 73 | Shrewsbury T |
| Wright David (D) | 5 11 | 10 09 | Warrington | 1 5 80 | Trainee |
| Yates Adam (M) | | | Stoke | 28 5 83 | Scholar |

**League Appearances:** Ashton, D. 12(9); Bankole, A. 21; Charnock, P. 4(5); Collins, J. 2(2); Cramb, C. 10(3); Foster, S. 21(9); Gannon, J. 5(2); Grant, J. (2); Howell, D. (1); Hulse, R. 22(11); Ince, C. (1); Jack, R. 23(7); Kearton, J. 25(1); Little, C. 24(3); Lumsdon, C. 14(2); Lunt, K. 46; Macauley, S. 30; Maybury, A. 6; Navarro, A. 5(3); Rivers, M. 32(1); Smith, P. 2(3); Smith, S. 44(1); Sodje, E. 29(3); Sorvel, N. 42(4); Street, K. 16(7); Tait, P. 9(9); Vaughan, D. 1; Walker, R. 2(1); Walton, D. 17(3); Wright, D. 42.
**Goals – League** (47): Hulse 11, Ashton 8, Rivers 7, Cramb 4, Jack 4, Little 4, Smith S 4 (3 pens), Lunt 1, Macauley 1, Navarro 1, Sorvel 1, Street 1.
**Worthington Cup** (4): Rivers 2, Foster 1, Little 1.
**FA Cup** (3): Rivers 1, Smith S 1 (pen), own goal 1.
**Ground:** Football Ground, Gresty Rd, Crewe CW2 6EB. Telephone (01270) 213014.
**Record attendance:** 20,000 v Tottenham H, FA Cup 4th rd, 30 January 1960.
**Capacity:** 10,046.
**Manager:** Dario Gradi MBE.
**Secretary:** Mrs Gill Palin.
**Most League Goals:** 95, Division 3 (N), 1931–32.
**Highest League Scorer in Season:** Terry Harkin, 35, Division 4, 1964–65.
**Most League Goals in Total Aggregate:** Bert Swindells, 126, 1928–37.
**Most Capped Player:** Bill Lewis, 9 (27), Wales.
**Most League Appearances:** Tommy Lowry, 436, 1966–78.
**Honours – Welsh Cup:** Winners 1936, 1937.
**Colours:** Red shirts, white shorts, red stockings.

---

# CRYSTAL PALACE                                    DIV. 1

| Austin Dean (D) | 5 11 | 11 11 | Hemel Hempstead | 26 4 70 | Tottenham H |
|---|---|---|---|---|---|
| Black Tommy (M) | 5 7 | 11 04 | Chigwell | 26 11 79 | Arsenal |
| Boardman Jonathan (M) | | | Reading | 27 1 81 | Trainee |
| Carlisle Wayne (M) | 6 0 | 11 06 | Lisburn | 9 9 79 | Trainee |
| Dimond Kristian (M) | | | Cardiff | 1 2 83 | Trainee |
| Evans Stephen (M) | 5 11 | 11 02 | Caerphilly | 25 9 80 | Trainee |
| Frampton Andrew (D) | 5 11 | 10 10 | Wimbledon | 3 9 79 | Trainee |
| Freedman Dougie (F) | 5 9 | 12 05 | Glasgow | 21 1 74 | Nottingham F |
| Fuller Ricardo (F) | | | Kingston, Jamaica | 31 10 79 | Tivoli Gardens |
| Gray Julian (M) | 6 1 | 11 00 | Lewisham | 21 9 79 | Arsenal |
| Gregg Matt (G) | 5 11 | 12 00 | Cheltenham | 30 11 78 | Torquay U |
| Gwillim Gareth (M) | | | Farnborough | 9 2 83 | |
| Hankin Sean (M) | 5 11 | 12 04 | Camberley | 28 2 81 | Trainee |
| Harris Richard (M) | 5 11 | 10 09 | Croydon | 23 10 80 | Trainee |
| Harrison Craig (D) | 6 0 | 11 08 | Gateshead | 10 11 77 | Middlesbrough |
| Hopkin David (M) | 6 1 | 13 13 | Greenock | 21 8 70 | Bradford C |
| Howell Richard (M) | | | Hitchin | 29 8 82 | |
| Kabba Steven (D) | 5 10 | 11 12 | Lambeth | 7 3 81 | Trainee |
| Kember Robert (M) | | | Wimbledon | 21 8 81 | |
| Kolinko Aleksandrs (G) | 6 3 | 13 08 | Latvia | 18 6 75 | Skonto Riga |
| Martin Andrew (F) | 6 0 | 10 12 | Cardiff | 28 2 80 | Trainee |

| Morrison Clinton (F) | 6 1 | 11 02 | Tooting | 14 5 79 | Trainee |
| Mullins Hayden (M) | 6 0 | 11 12 | Reading | 27 3 79 | Trainee |
| Pollock Jamie (M) | 6 0 | 13 03 | Stockton | 16 2 74 | Manchester C |
| Riihilahti Aki (M) | 6 1 | 12 06 | Helsinki | 9 6 76 | |
| Rubins Andrejs (M) | 5 9 | 10 03 | Latvia | 26 11 78 | Skonto Riga |
| Ruddock Neil (D) | 6 2 | 12 12 | Wandsworth | 9 5 68 | West Ham U |
| Sharpling Christopher (F) | 5 11 | 11 10 | Bromley | 21 4 81 | Trainee |
| Thomson Steve (M) | 5 8 | 10 04 | Glasgow | 23 1 78 | Trainee |
| Warren Steven (M) | | | London | 27 9 83 | |
| Windegaard Stephen (M) | | | Chertsey | 6 8 82 | |
| Woozley David (D) | 6 0 | 12 10 | Berkshire | 6 12 79 | Trainee |
| Zhiyi Fan (M) | 6 0 | 12 01 | Shanghai | 22 1 70 | Shanghai Shenhua |

**League Appearances:** Austin, D. 38(1); Berhalter, G. 4(1); Black, T. 30(10); Carlisle, W. 4(10); Evans, S. (1); Forssell, M. 31(8); Frampton, A. 8(2); Freedman, D. 16(10); Fullarton, J. 1(1); Fuller, R. 2(6); Gray, J. 12(11); Gregg, M. 1; Harris, R. 1(1); Harrison, C. 30(2); Hopkin, D. 8(1); Kabba, S. (1); Karic, A. 3; Kitson, P. 4; Kolinko, A. 35; Linighan, A. (1); McKenzie, L. 2(6); Morrison, A. 5; Morrison, C. 41(4); Mullins, H. 40(1); Pollock, J. 29(2); Riihilahti, A. 9; Rodger, S. 28(5); Rubins, A. 17(5); Ruddock, N. 19(1); Smith, J. 25(4); Staunton, S. 6; Taylor, S. 10; Thomson, S. 12(6); Upson, M. 7; Verhoene, K. (1); Zhiyi, F. 28.
**Goals – League** (57): Morrison C 14, Forssell 13, Freedman 11 (1 pen), Black 4, Pollock 4, Austin 3 (1 pen), Ruddock 2, Gray 1, Hopkin 1, Mullins 1, Riihilahti 1, Staunton 1, Zhiyi 1.
**Worthington Cup** (12): Morrison C 4, Forssell 2, Rubins 2, Black 1, Linighan 1, Ruddock 1, Thomson 1.
**FA Cup** (2): Morrison C 1, Thompson 1.
**Ground:** Selhurst Park, London SE25 6PU. Telephone (0181) 768 6000.
**Record attendance:** 51,482 v Burnley, Division 2, 11 May 1979. **Capacity:** 26,400.
**Manager:** Steve Bruce.
**Club Secretary:** Mike Hurst.
**Most League Goals:** 110, Division 4, 1960–61.
**Highest League Scorer in Season:** Peter Simpson, 46, Division 3 (S), 1930–31.
**Most League Goals in Total Aggregate:** Peter Simpson, 153, 1930–36.
**Most Capped Player:** Eric Young, 19 (21), Wales.
**Most League Appearances:** Jim Cannon, 571, 1973–88.
**Honours – Football League:** Division 1 – Champions 1993–94. Division 2 Champions – 1978–79. Division 3 (S) 1920–21. **Zenith Data Systems Cup winners** 1991.
**Colours:** Red shirts with blue trim, red shorts with blue and white trim, red stockings.

---

# DARLINGTON                                                    DIV. 3

| Atkinson Brian (M) | 5 10 | 12 10 | Darlington | 19 1 71 | Sunderland |
| Brightwell David (D) | 6 2 | 12 09 | Lutterworth | 7 1 71 | Hull C |
| Brumwell Phil (M) | 5 8 | 11 00 | Darlington | 8 8 75 | Hull C |
| Campbell Paul (M) | 6 1 | 11 00 | Middlesbrough | 29 1 80 | Trainee |
| Cau Jean-Michel (F) | | | Corsica | 27 10 80 | Gazelec |
| Collett Andy (G) | 6 0 | 12 10 | Stockton | 28 10 73 | Bristol R |
| Convery Mark (F) | 5 6 | 10 05 | Newcastle | 29 5 81 | Sunderland |
| Ford Mark (M) | 5 7 | 10 08 | Pontefract | 10 10 75 | Torquay U |
| Gray Martin (M) | 5 9 | 11 05 | Stockton | 17 8 71 | Oxford U |
| Harper Steve (M) | 5 10 | 11 12 | Newcastle-under-Lyme | 3 2 69 | Hull C |
| Heckingbottom Paul (D) | 6 0 | 12 03 | Barnsley | 17 7 77 | Sunderland |
| Himsworth Gary (M) | 5 8 | 11 00 | York | 19 12 69 | York C |

| Hodgson Richard (F) | 5 10 | 11 06 | Sunderland | 1 10 79 | Scunthorpe U |
| Jackson Kirk (F) | 5 10 | 11 07 | Barnsley | 16 10 76 | Worksop T |
| Jeannin Alexandre (D) | | | Troyes | 30 12 77 | Troyes |
| Kilty Mark (D) | 6 0 | 12 00 | Sunderland | 24 6 81 | Trainee |
| Liddle Craig (D) | 5 11 | 12 07 | Chester-le-Street | 21 10 71 | Middlesbrough |
| Marcelle Clint (M) | 5 5 | 10 00 | Port of Spain | 9 11 68 | Barnsley |
| Marsh Adam (M) | | | Sheffield | 20 2 82 | Worksop T |
| Naylor Glenn (F) | 5 10 | 11 10 | York | 11 8 72 | York C |
| Raymond Christophe | | | Amiens | 1 9 69 | Amiens FC |
| Reed Adam (D) | 6 1 | 11 00 | Bishop Auckland | 18 2 75 | Blackburn R |
| Van der Geest Frank (G) | | | Beverwijk | 30 4 73 | Heracles |

**League Appearances:** Angel, M. 1(4); Aspin, N. 21; Atkinson, B. 17(6); Beavers, P. 3(4); Bernard, O. 9(1); Brightwell, D. 12(2); Brumwell, P. 19(2); Butler, T. 8; Campbell, P. 11(5); Cau, J. (1); Collett, A. 37; Convery, M. 5(6); Elliott, S. 20(4); Ford, M. 11; Gray, M. 25; Harper, S. 17; Heckingbottom, P. 17(1); Himsworth, G. 14(1); Hjorth, J. 8(15); Hodgson, R. 20(15); Jackson, K. 5(5); Jeannin, A. 11; Kaak, T. 7(1); Keen, P. 7; Kilty, M. 18; Kyle, K. 5; Liddle, C. 45; Marcelle, C. 8(4); Marsh, A. 1(6); McMahon, D. 5(3); Naylor, G. 42(2); Nogan, L. 18; Reed, A. 28(6); Skelton, C. (1); Tait, J. 2(1); Van der Geest, F. 2; Walklate, S. 2(4); Williams, J. 23(1); Williamson, G. 1(5); Zeghdane, L. 1(2).

**Goals – League** (44): Naylor 11 (1 pen), Williams 5, Atkinson 4 (4 pens) Nogan 4, Bernard 2, Ford 2 (1 pen), Hodgson 2, Kaak 2, Liddle 2, Beavers 1, Campbell 1, Heckingbottom 1, Hjorth 1, Jackson 1, Kilty 1, Kyle 1, McMahon 1, own goals 2.
**Worthington Cup** (6): Elliott 3 (1 pen), Angel 1, Campbell 1, Naylor 1.
**FA Cup** (6): Naylor 3, Hodgson 2, Kyle 1.
**Ground:** Feethams Ground, Darlington DL1 5JB. Telephone (01325) 240240.
**Record attendance:** 21,023 v Bolton W, League Cup 3rd rd, 14 November 1960.
**Capacity:** 8500.
**Manager:** Gary Bennett.
**Secretary:** Lisa Charlton.
**Most League Goals:** 108, Division 3 (N), 1929–30.
**Highest League Scorer in Season:** David Brown, 39, Division 3 (N), 1924–25.
**Most League Goals in Total Aggregate:** Alan Walsh, 90, 1978–84.
**Most Capped Player:** Jason Devos, 3, Canada.
**Most League Appearances:** Ron Greener, 442, 1955–68.
**Honours – Football League:** Division 3 (N) Champions – 1924–25. Division 4 Champions – 1990–91.
**Colours:** Black and white.

---

# DERBY COUNTY                          FA PREMIERSHIP

| Bannister Patrick (M) | | | Walsall | 3 12 83 | Scholar |
| Blatsis Con (D) | 6 3 | 14 06 | Australia | 5 7 77 | |
| Boertien Paul (D) | 5 11 | 11 11 | Carlisle | 21 1 79 | Carlisle U |
| Bolder Adam (M) | 5 8 | 11 13 | Hull | 25 10 80 | Hull C |
| Bragstad Bjorn (D) | 6 3 | 14 06 | Trondheim | 5 1 71 | Rosenborg |
| Burley Craig (M) | 6 1 | 13 03 | Ayr | 24 9 71 | Celtic |
| Burton Deon (F) | 5 9 | 12 08 | Reading | 25 10 77 | Portsmouth |
| Carbonari Horace | 6 3 | 14 08 | Rosario | 2 5 71 | Rosario Central |
|    Angel (D) | | | | | |
| Christie Malcolm (F) | 6 0 | 12 06 | Peterborough | 11 4 79 | Nuneaton B |
| Delap Rory (M) | 6 1 | 13 00 | Sutton Coldfield | 6 7 76 | Carlisle U |
| Elliott Steve (D) | 6 2 | 14 08 | Derby | 29 10 78 | Trainee |
| Evatt Ian (D) | 6 3 | 14 04 | Coventry | 23 11 81 | Trainee |

49

| | | | | | |
|---|---|---|---|---|---|
| Flanagan Martin (M) | | | Omagh | 13 1 84 | Scholar |
| Grant Lee (G) | 6 2 | 13 00 | Watford | 27 1 83 | Scholar |
| Gudjonsson Thordur (F) | 5 9 | 12 04 | Akranes | 14 10 73 | Las Palmas |
| Higginbotham Danny (D) | 6 1 | 13 03 | Manchester | 29 12 78 | Manchester U |
| Hunt Lewis (D) | 5 11 | 12 08 | Birmingham | 25 8 82 | Scholar |
| Jackson Richard (D) | 5 7 | 11 02 | Whitby | 18 4 80 | Scarborough |
| Johnson Seth (M) | 5 11 | 12 11 | Birmingham | 12 3 79 | Crewe Alex |
| Kinkladze Georgiou (M) | 5 6 | 11 05 | Tbilisi | 6 7 73 | Ajax |
| Mawene Youl (D) | 6 1 | 13 05 | Caen | 16 7 79 | |
| McArdle Fiachra (M) | | | Newry | 18 8 83 | Scholar |
| Morris Lee (F) | 5 9 | 11 02 | Driffield | 30 4 80 | Sheffield U |
| Moukoko Tonton (M) | | | Congo | 22 12 83 | Scholar |
| Murray Adam (M) | 5 9 | 11 11 | Birmingham | 30 9 81 | Trainee |
| O'Neil Brian (M) | 6 0 | 13 10 | Paisley | 6 9 72 | Wolfsburg |
| Oakes Andy (G) | 6 1 | 12 04 | Crewe | 11 1 77 | Hull C |
| Poom Mart (G) | 6 4 | 14 03 | Tallinn | 3 2 72 | Flora Tallinn |
| Powell Darryl (M) | 6 1 | 13 03 | Lambeth | 15 11 71 | Portsmouth |
| Riggott Chris (D) | 6 2 | 13 09 | Derby | 1 9 80 | Trainee |
| Robinson Marvin (F) | 6 0 | 13 05 | Crewe | 11 4 80 | Trainee |
| Strupar Branko (F) | 6 3 | 14 06 | Zagreb | 9 2 70 | Genk |
| Twigg Gary (M) | | | Glasgow | 19 3 84 | Scholar |
| Valakari Simo (M) | 5 11 | 12 08 | Helsinki | 24 4 73 | Motherwell |
| Weckstrom Kristoffer (M) | | | Helsinki | 26 5 83 | IFK Mariehamn |

**League Appearances:** Blatsis, C. 2; Boertien, P. 7(1); Bohinen, L. 1(1); Bolder, A. (2); Bragstad, B. 10(2); Burley, C. 24; Burton, D. 25(7); Carbonari, H. 27; Christie, M. 29(5); Delap, R. 32(1); Elliott, S. 5(1); Eranio, S. 25(3); Evatt, I. (1); Gudjonsson, T. 2(8); Higginbotham, D. 23(3); Jackson, R. 1(1); Johnson, S. 30; Kinkladze, G. 13(11); Martin, L. 7(2); Mawene, Y. 7(1); Morris, L. 4(16); Murray, A. 4(10); O'Neil, B. 3(1); Oakes, A. 6; Poom, M. 32(1); Powell, D. 27; Riggott, C. 29(2); Schnoor, S. 6(2); Strupar, B. 7(2); Sturridge, D. 3(11); Valakari, S. 9(2); West, T. 18.

**Goals – League** (37): Christie 8, Strupar 6 (1 pen), Burton 5 (1 pen), Delap 3, Riggott 3, Burley 2, Eranio 2, Boertien 1, Carbonari 1, Gudjonsson 1, Johnson 1, Kinkladze 1, Powell 1, Sturridge 1, Valakari 1.

**Worthington Cup** (10): Bragstad 2, Burley 2 (1 pen), Christie 2, Burton 1, Delap 1, Powell 1, Riggott 1.

**FA Cup** (5): Christie 2, Eranio 2, Riggott 1.

**Ground:** Pride Park Stadium, Derby DE24 8XL. Telephone: (01332) 202202.

**Record attendance:** 41,826 v Tottenham H, Division 1, 20 September 1969.

**Capacity:** 33,597.

**Manager:** Jim Smith.

**Secretary:** Keith Pearson ACIS.

**Most League Goals:** 111, Division 3 (N), 1956–57.

**Highest League Scorer in Season:** Jack Bowers, 37, Division 1, 1930–31; Ray Straw, 37 Division 3 (N), 1956–57.

**Most League Goals in Total Aggregate:** Steve Bloomer, 292, 1892–1906 and 1910–14.

**Most Capped Player:** Deon Burton, 35, Jamaica.

**Most League Appearances:** Kevin Hector, 486, 1966–78 and 1980–82.

**Honours – Football League:** Division 1 Champions – 1971–72, 1974–75. Division 2 Champions – 1911–12, 1914–15, 1968–69, 1986–87. Division 3 (N) 1956–57. **FA Cup winners** 1945–46.

**Colours:** White shirts with black trim, black shorts with white stripes, white stockings.

| | | | | | |
|---|---|---|---|---|---|
| Alexandersson Niclas (M) | 5 9 | 11 08 | Halmstad | 29 12 71 | Sheffield W |
| Ball Michael (D) | 5 11 | 11 12 | Liverpool | 2 10 79 | Trainee |
| Cadamarteri Danny (F) | 5 10 | 12 13 | Bradford | 12 10 79 | Trainee |
| Campbell Kevin (F) | 6 0 | 13 13 | Lambeth | 4 2 70 | Trabzonspor |
| Carney David (M) | | | Sydney | 30 11 83 | Scholar |
| Chadwick Nick (F) | 6 0 | 12 04 | Stoke | 26 10 82 | |
| Clarke Peter (D) | 6 0 | 12 00 | Southport | 3 1 82 | Trainee |
| Cleland Alec (D) | 5 10 | 11 07 | Glasgow | 10 12 70 | Rangers |
| Curran Damien (M) | 5 9 | 12 01 | Antrim | 17 10 81 | Trainee |
| Degn Peter (D) | 5 10 | 12 06 | Denmark | 6 4 77 | Aarhus |
| Ferguson Duncan (F) | 6 4 | 13 07 | Stirling | 27 12 71 | Newcastle U |
| Gascoigne Paul (M) | 5 10 | 11 12 | Gateshead | 27 5 67 | Middlesbrough |
| Gemmill Scot (M) | 5 10 | 11 08 | Paisley | 2 1 71 | Nottingham F |
| Gerrard Paul (G) | 6 2 | 13 11 | Heywood | 22 1 73 | Oldham Ath |
| Gravesen Thomas (M) | 5 11 | 13 06 | Vejle | 11 3 76 | Hamburg |
| Hibbert Tony (D) | 5 8 | 11 01 | Liverpool | 20 2 81 | Trainee |
| Jeffers Francis (F) | 5 10 | 10 07 | Liverpool | 25 1 81 | Trainee |
| Jevons Phil (F) | 5 11 | 12 00 | Liverpool | 1 8 79 | Trainee |
| Kearney Tom (M) | 5 9 | 10 12 | Liverpool | 7 10 81 | Trainee |
| Lester John (M) | 5 11 | 12 09 | Dublin | 5 8 82 | Trainee |
| McKay Matt (M) | 6 0 | 11 05 | Warrington | 21 1 81 | Trainee |
| McLeod Kevin (M) | 5 11 | 11 00 | Liverpool | 12 9 80 | Trainee |
| Moogan Alan (M) | | | Liverpool | 22 2 84 | Scholar |
| Moore Joe-Max (F) | 5 8 | 11 06 | USA | 23 2 71 | New England Rev |
| Myhre Thomas (G) | 6 3 | 13 13 | Sarpsborg | 16 10 73 | Viking |
| Naysmith Gary (D) | 5 7 | 11 08 | Edinburgh | 16 11 78 | Hearts |
| Nyarko Alex (M) | 6 0 | 13 00 | Accra | 15 10 73 | Lens |
| O'Hanlon Sean (D) | 6 1 | 12 02 | Liverpool | 2 1 83 | |
| Osman Leon (M) | 5 8 | 9 11 | Billinge | 17 5 81 | Trainee |
| Pembridge Mark (M) | 5 7 | 11 09 | Merthyr | 29 11 70 | Benfica |
| Penman Craig (D) | 5 11 | 11 06 | Falkirk | 9 9 82 | Trainee |
| Pettinger Andrew (G) | | | Scunthorpe | 21 4 84 | Scholar |
| Pilkington George (D) | 5 11 | 11 00 | Rugeley | 7 11 81 | Trainee |
| Pistone Alessandro (D) | 5 11 | 11 08 | Milan | 27 7 75 | Newcastle U |
| Schumacher Steven (M) | | | Liverpool | 30 4 84 | Scholar |
| Simonsen Steve (G) | 6 2 | 14 00 | South Shields | 3 4 79 | Tranmere R |
| Southern Keith (M) | | | Gateshead | 24 4 81 | Trainee |
| Southern Robert (M) | | | Gateshead | 24 9 83 | Scholar |
| Tal Idan (M) | 5 9 | 11 07 | Petah Tikva | 13 9 75 | Merida |
| Unsworth Dave (D) | 6 1 | 15 02 | Chorley | 16 10 73 | Aston Villa |
| Valentine Ryan (D) | 5 10 | 11 07 | Wrexham | 19 8 82 | Trainee |
| Watson Steve (D) | 6 0 | 12 07 | North Shields | 1 4 74 | Aston Villa |
| Weir David (D) | 6 5 | 14 03 | Falkirk | 10 5 70 | Hearts |
| Xavier Abel (D) | 6 2 | 13 06 | Mozambique | 30 11 72 | PSV Eindhoven |

**League Appearances:** Alexandersson, N. 17(3); Ball, M. 29; Cadamarteri, D. 7(9); Campbell, K. 27(2); Clarke, P. (1); Cleland, A. 2(3); Dunne, R. 3; Ferguson, D. 9(3); Gascoigne, P. 10(4); Gemmill, S. 25(3); Gerrard, P. 32; Gough, R. 9; Gravesen, T. 30(2); Hibbert, A. 1(2); Hughes, M. 6(3); Hughes, S. 16(2); Jeffers, F. 10(2); Jevons, P. (4); McLeod, K. (5); Moore, J. 8(13); Myhre, T. 6; Naysmith, G. 17(3); Nyarko, A. 19(3); Pembridge, M. 20(1); Pistone, A. 5(2); Simonsen, S. (1); Tal, I. 12(10); Unsworth, D. 17(12); Watson, S. 34; Weir, D. 37; Xavier, A. 10(1).

Goals – League (45): Campbell 9, Ferguson 6, Jeffers 6, Unsworth 5 (3 pens), Cadamarteri 4, Ball 3 (2 pens), Alexandersson 2, Gemmill 2, Gravesen 2, Naysmith 2, Tal 2, Nyarko 1, Weir 1.
Worthington Cup (2): Campbell 1, Jeffers 1.
FA Cup (2): Hughes 1, Watson 1.
Ground: Goodison Park, Liverpool L4 4EL. Telephone (0151) 330 2200.
Record attendance: 78,299 v Liverpool, Division 1, 18 September 1948. Capacity: 40,200.
Manager: Walter Smith OBE.
Secretary: Michael J. Dunford.
Most League Goals: 121, Division 2, 1930–31.
Highest League Scorer in Season: William Ralph 'Dixie' Dean, 60, Division 1, 1927–28 (All-time League record).
Most League Goals in Total Aggregate: William Ralph 'Dixie' Dean, 349, 1925–37.
Most Capped Player: Neville Southall, 92, Wales.
Most League Appearances: Neville Southall, 578, 1981–98.
Honours – Football League: Division 1 Champions – 1890–91, 1914–15, 1927–28, 1931–32, 1938–39, 1962–63, 1969–70, 1984–85, 1986–87. Division 2 Champions – 1930–31. FA Cup: Winners 1906, 1933, 1966, 1984, 1995. European Competitions: European Cup-Winners' Cup winners: 1984–85.
Colours: Royal blue shirts with white trim, white shorts, royal blue stockings.

---

# EXETER CITY                                    DIV. 3

| | | | | | |
|---|---|---|---|---|---|
| Ampadu Kwame (M) | 5 10 | 11 10 | Bradford | 20 12 70 | Leyton Orient |
| Breslan Geoff (M) | 5 9 | 10 05 | Torbay | 4 6 80 | Trainee |
| Burrows Mark (D) | 6 3 | 12 08 | Kettering | 14 8 80 | Coventry C |
| Campbell Jamie (D) | 6 1 | 12 07 | Birmingham | 21 10 72 | Brighton & HA |
| Cronin Glenn (M) | 5 8 | 10 11 | Dublin | 14 9 81 | Trainee |
| Flack Steve (F) | 6 1 | 14 07 | Cambridge | 29 5 71 | Cardiff C |
| Fraser Stuart (G) | 6 0 | 12 00 | Cheltenham | 1 8 78 | Stoke C |
| McConnell Barry (F) | 5 11 | 10 10 | Exeter | 1 1 77 | Trainee |
| Read Paul (F) | 5 8 | 12 06 | Harlow | 25 9 73 | Wycombe W |
| Roberts Chris (F) | 5 10 | 12 03 | Cardiff | 22 10 79 | Cardiff C |
| Roscoe Andy (M) | 5 9 | 12 00 | Liverpool | 4 6 73 | Mansfield T |
| Tomlinson Graeme (F) | 5 10 | 12 00 | Watford | 10 12 75 | Macclesfield T |
| Van Heusden Arjan (G) | 6 4 | 14 05 | Alphen | 11 12 72 | Cambridge U |
| Whitworth Neil (D) | 6 0 | 12 13 | Ince | 12 4 72 | Hull C |
| Zabek Lee (M) | 6 0 | 13 08 | Bristol | 13 10 78 | Bristol R |

League Appearances: Ampadu, K. 29(7); Ashton, J. 7(6); Birch, G. 6(3); Blake, N. 3(2); Breslan, G. (2); Buckle, P. 39(2); Burrows, M. 21(8); Campbell, J. 42; Cornforth, J. 11(1); Curran, C. 26; Epesse-Titi, S. 5(1); Flack, S. 33(7); Francis, K. 3(4); Fraser, S. 5(1); Holligan, G. 3; Holloway, C. (4); Hutchings, C. 2; Inglethorpe, A. 11(7); McConnell, B. 3(1); Mudge, J. (3); Power, G. 34(1); Rapley, K. 6(1); Rawlinson, M. 18(7); Read, P. 10(1); Roberts, C. 33(9); Roberts, D. 3(5); Roscoe, A. 33(10); Speakman, R. (1); Spencer, D. 2(4); Tierney, F. 4(3); Tomlinson, G. 13(11); Van Heusden, A. 41; Whitworth, N. 34; Wilkinson, J. (1); Zabek, L. 26(5).
Goals – League (40): Flack 13, Roberts C 8, Buckle 3, Birch 2, Campbell 2, Inglethorpe 2, Rawlinson 2 (1 pen), Francis 1, Power 1, Read 1, Roscoe 1, Tierney 1, Tomlinson 1, Whitworth 1, own goal 1.
Worthington Cup (2): Ampadu 1, Rawlinson 1.
FA Cup (0).
Ground: St James Park, Exeter EX4 6PX. Telephone (01392) 254073.
Record attendance: 20,984 v Sunderland, FA Cup 6th rd (replay), 4 March 1931.
Capacity: 9036.

**Manager:** Noel Blake.
**Secretary:** Stuart Brailey.
**Most League Goals:** 88, Division 3 (S), 1932–33.
**Highest League Scorer in Season:** Fred Whitlow, 33, Division 3 (S), 1932–33.
**Most League Goals in Total Aggregate:** Tony Kellow, 129, 1976–78, 1980–83, 1985–88.
**Most Capped Player:** Dermot Curtis, 1 (17), Eire.
**Most League Appearances:** Arnold Mitchell, 495, 1952–66.
**Honours – Football League:** Division 4 Champions – 1989–90. **Division 3 (S) Cup:** Winners 1934.
**Colours:** Red and white striped shirts, black shorts and stockings.

---

# FULHAM                                      FA PREMIERSHIP

| | | | | | |
|---|---|---|---|---|---|
| Betsy Kevin (F) | 6 0 | 12 03 | Seychelles | 20  3 78 | Woking |
| Clark Lee (M) | 5 8 | 11 09 | Wallsend | 27 10 72 | Sunderland |
| Coleman Chris (D) | 6 2 | 14 04 | Swansea | 10  6 70 | Blackburn R |
| Collins John (M) | 5 7 | 10 10 | Galashiels | 30  1 68 | Everton |
| Cornwall Luke (F) | 5 9 | 10 11 | Lambeth | 23  7 80 | Trainee |
| Davis Sean (M) | 5 11 | 12 10 | Clapham | 20  9 79 | Trainee |
| Finnan Steve (D) | 6 0 | 12 03 | Limerick | 20  4 76 | Notts Co |
| Goldbaek Bjarne (M) | 5 9 | 12 08 | Denmark | 6 10 68 | Chelsea |
| Goma Alain (D) | 6 0 | 13 08 | Sault | 5 10 72 | Newcastle U |
| Hahnemann Marcus (G) | 6 3 | 16 02 | Seattle | 15  6 72 | Colorado Rapids |
| Hammond Elvis (F) | 5 11 | 11 09 | Accra | 6 10 80 | Trainee |
| Hayles Barry (F) | 5 9 | 13 00 | London | 17  5 72 | Bristol R |
| Hudson Mark (D) | 6 2 | 12 08 | Guildford | 30  3 82 | Trainee |
| Hutchinson Tom (D) | 6 0 | 12 08 | Kingston | 23  2 82 | |
| Knight Zatyiah (D) | 6 6 | 14 00 | Solihull | 2  5 80 | |
| Lewis Eddie (M) | 5 9 | 11 05 | California | 17  5 74 | San Jose Clash |
| McAnespie Kieran (D) | 5 8 | 11 05 | Gosport | 11  9 79 | St Johnstone |
| Melville Andy (D) | 6 1 | 12 10 | Swansea | 29 11 68 | Sunderland |
| Peschisolido Paul (F) | 5 7 | 11 03 | Canada | 25  5 71 | WBA |
| Saha Louis (F) | 6 0 | 12 04 | Paris | 8  8 78 | Metz |
| Shevel David (M) | | | Croydon | 14  9 83 | Scholar |
| Stolcers Andrejs (M) | 5 8 | 11 00 | Latvia | 8  7 74 | Spartak Moscow |
| Symons Kit (D) | 6 3 | 13 02 | Basingstoke | 8  3 71 | Manchester C |
| Taylor Maik (G) | 6 3 | 14 02 | Hildeshein | 4  9 71 | Southampton |
| Thompson Glyn (G) | 6 3 | 12 08 | Shrewsbury | 24  2 81 | Shrewsbury T |
| Trollope Paul (M) | 6 0 | 11 05 | Swindon | 3  6 72 | Derby Co |
| Willock Calum (F) | 6 1 | 12 08 | London | 29 10 81 | Scholar |

**League Appearances:** Betsy, K. 2(3); Boa Morte, L. 21(18); Brevett, R. 39; Clark, L. 45; Coleman, C. 25; Collins, J. 25(2); Collins, W. 3(2); Davis, S. 37(3); Fernandes, F. 23(6); Finnan, S. 45; Goldbaek, B. 41(3); Goma, A. 3; Hahnemann, M. 2; Hayles, B. 28(7); Hayward, S. 1; Lewis, E. 1(6); Melville, A. 42(1); Moller, P. 2(3); Morgan, S. 1; Neilson, A. (3); Phelan, T. 1(1); Riedle, K. 1(13); Saha, L. 39(4); Sahnoun, N. 2(5); Stolcers, A. 8(7); Symons, K. 22(2); Taylor, M. 44; Trollope, P. 5(5); Willock, C. (1).
**Goals – League** (90): Saha 27 (10 pens), Boa Morte 18 (1 pen) Hayles 18, Clark 7, Davis 6, Collins J 3, Fernandes 2, Finnan 2, Goldbaek 2, Stolcers 2, Melville 1, Moller 1, Riedle 1.
**Worthington Cup** (14): Saha 5, Boa Morte 3, Davis 1, Fernandes 1, Hayles 1, Hayward 1, Lewis 1.
**FA Cup** (1): Fernandes 1.

**Ground:** Craven Cottage, Stevenage Rd, Fulham, London SW6 6HH. Telephone (020) 7893 8383.
**Record attendance:** 49,335 v Millwall, Division 2, 8 October 1938. **Capacity:** 20,787.
**Manager:** Jean Tigana.
**Secretary:** Lee Hoos.
**Most League Goals:** 111, Division 3 (S), 1931–32.
**Highest League Scorer in Season:** Frank Newton, 43, Division 3 (S), 1931–32.
**Most League Goals in Total Aggregate:** Gordon Davies, 159, 1978–84, 1986–91.
**Most Capped Player:** Johnny Haynes, 56, England.
**Most League Appearances:** Johnny Haynes, 594, 1952–70.
**Honours – Football League:** Division 1 Champions – 2000–01. Division 2 Champions – 1948–49, 1998–99. Division 3 (S) Champions – 1931–32.
**Colours:** White shirts, red and black trim, black shorts, white stockings red and black trim.

---

# GILLINGHAM                                            DIV. 1

| | | | | | |
|---|---|---|---|---|---|
| Ashby Barry (D) | 6 2 | 13 08 | London | 2 11 70 | Brentford |
| Bartram Vince (G) | 6 2 | 13 04 | Birmingham | 8 8 68 | Arsenal |
| Brown Jason (G) | | | Southwark | 18 5 82 | Charlton Ath |
| Browning Marcus (M) | 6 0 | 12 10 | Bristol | 22 4 71 | Huddersfield T |
| Butters Guy (D) | 6 3 | 13 12 | Hillingdon | 30 10 69 | Portsmouth |
| Edge Roland (D) | 5 10 | 11 10 | Gillingham | 25 11 78 | Trainee |
| Gooden Ty (M) | 5 8 | 12 06 | Canvey Island | 23 10 72 | Swindon T |
| Hope Chris (D) | 6 1 | 12 08 | Sheffield | 14 11 73 | Scunthorpe U |
| Ipoua Guy (F) | 6 1 | 13 02 | Douala | 14 1 76 | Scunthorpe U |
| James Kevin (F) | 5 9 | 10 07 | Southwark | 3 1 80 | Charlton Ath |
| King Marlon (F) | 6 1 | 12 03 | Dulwich | 26 4 80 | Barnet |
| Mitten Charlie (G) | 6 2 | 12 07 | Woolwich | 9 10 74 | Dover Ath |
| Nosworthy Nayron (M) | 6 1 | 12 07 | London | 11 10 80 | Trainee |
| Onuora Iffy (F) | 6 1 | 13 10 | Glasgow | 28 7 67 | Swindon T |
| Patterson Mark (D) | 5 9 | 12 04 | Leeds | 13 9 68 | Plymouth Arg |
| Pennock Adrian (M) | 6 1 | 13 05 | Ipswich | 27 3 71 | Bournemouth |
| Rose Richard (D) | | | Tonbridge Wells | 8 9 82 | Trainee |
| Saunders Mark (M) | 5 11 | 11 12 | Reading | 23 7 71 | Plymouth Arg |
| Shaw Paul (F) | 5 10 | 12 10 | Burnham | 4 9 73 | Millwall |
| Smith Paul (M) | 5 11 | 12 08 | East Ham | 18 9 71 | Brentford |
| Spiller Daniel (M) | | | Maidstone | 10 10 81 | Trainee |
| White Ben (D) | 6 1 | 13 00 | Hastings | 2 6 82 | Trainee |

**League Appearances:** Asaba, C. 18(7); Ashby, B. 38(2); Bartram, V. 46; Browning, M. 22(9); Butters, G. 12; Crofts, A. (1); Edge, R. 19(1); Gooden, T. 17(1); Hessenthaler, A. 19(4); Hope, C. 46; Ipoua, G. (9); James, K. 1(6); King, M. 26(12); Lewis, J. 10(7); Lovell, M. (1); McGlinchey, B. 1; Nosworthy, N. 8(2); Onuora, I. 17(14); Patterson, M. 26(2); Pennock, A. 34(1); Phillips, M. (1); Rose, R. 1(3); Saunders, M. 24(11); Shaw, P. 27(6); Smith, P. 42; Southall, N. 40(4); Thomson, A. 12(12).
**Goals – League** (61): King 15 (2 pens), Asaba 10, Onuora 9, Saunders 5, Thomson 5, Butters 3, Smith 3, Hessenthaler 2, Hope 2, Lewis 2, Southall 2 (1 pen), Ashby 1, Shaw 1, own goal 1.
**Worthington Cup** (7): Thomson 3, Asaba 2, Smith 1, own goal 1.
**FA Cup** (5): Shaw 2, Hessenthaler 1, Hope 1, Onuora 1.
**Ground:** Priestfield Stadium, Gillingham ME7 4DD. Telephone (01634) 851854, 576828.
**Record attendance:** 23,002 v QPR, FA Cup 3rd rd 10 January 1948. **Capacity:** 10,600.

**Player-Manager:** Andy Hessenthaler.
**Secretary:** Mrs G. E. Poynter.
**Most League Goals:** 90, Division 4, 1973–74.
**Highest League Scorer in Season:** Ernie Morgan, 31, Division 3 (S), 1954–55; Brian Yeo, 31, Division 4, 1973–74.
**Most League Goals in Total Aggregate:** Brian Yeo, 135, 1963–75.
**Most Capped Player:** Tony Cascarino, 3 (88), Republic of Ireland.
**Most League Appearances:** John Simpson, 571, 1957–72.
**Honours – Football League:** Division 4 Champions – 1963–64.
**Colours:** Blue and black.

---

# GRIMSBY TOWN                                                    DIV. 1

| | | | | | | |
|---|---|---|---|---|---|---|
| Allen Bradley (F) | 5 8 | 11 00 | Harold Wood | 13 9 71 | Charlton Ath | |
| Buckley Adam (M) | 5 9 | 11 07 | Nottingham | 2 8 79 | WBA | |
| Butterfield Danny (D) | 5 10 | 11 06 | Boston | 21 11 79 | Trainee | |
| Chapman Ben (D) | 5 6 | 11 05 | Scunthorpe | 2 3 79 | Trainee | |
| Coyne Danny (G) | 6 0 | 13 04 | Prestatyn | 27 8 73 | Tranmere R | |
| Cranley Morgan (M) | | | Dublin | 12 1 84 | | |
| Croudson Steve (G) | 6 0 | 11 12 | Grimsby | 14 9 79 | Trainee | |
| Jeffrey Mike (F) | 6 1 | 11 09 | Liverpool | 11 8 71 | Kilmarnock | |
| Livingstone Steve (F) | 6 1 | 15 03 | Middlesbrough | 8 9 68 | Chelsea | |
| McDermott John (D) | 5 7 | 10 13 | Middlesbrough | 3 2 69 | Trainee | |
| Pouton Alan (M) | 6 0 | 12 10 | Newcastle | 1 2 77 | York C | |
| Raven Paul (D) | 6 1 | 12 11 | Salisbury | 28 7 70 | WBA | |
| Rowan Jonathan (F) | 5 10 | 11 00 | Grimsby | 29 11 81 | | |
| Smith David (M) | 5 7 | 11 11 | Gloucester | 29 5 68 | WBA | |
| Ward Iain (M) | | | Cleethorpes | 13 5 83 | | |
| Willems Menno (M) | 6 0 | 11 13 | Amsterdam | 10 3 77 | Vitesse | |

**League Appearances:** Allen, B. 15(6); Black, K. 4(1); Bloomer, M. 3(3); Burnett, W. 20(3); Butterfield, D. 23(7); Campbell, S. 38; Chapman, B. (2); Clare, D. 6(11); Coldicott, S. 34(3); Cornwall, L. 9(1); Coyne, D. 46; Donovan, K. 36(5); Enhua, Z. 16(1); Fostervold, K. 9(1); Gallimore, T. 26(2); Groves, P. 45; Handyside, P. 17(2); Jeffrey, M. 15(14); Livingstone, S. 27(5); McDermott, J. 36; Murray, N. 1(1); Nielsen, D. 16(1); Pouton, A. 16(5); Raven, P. 11(4); Rowan, J. 2(3); Smith, D. 16(8); Smith, R. 2(4); Willems, M. 17(7).
**Goals – League** (43): Livingstone 5, Donovan 5, Nielsen 5, Cornwall 4, Groves 4, Allen 3, Enhua 3, Campbell 2, Burnett 1, Butterfield 1, Coldicott 1, Handyside 1, Jeffrey 1, Pouton 1 (pen), Smith D 1, Smith R 1, Willems 1, own goal 1.
**Worthington Cup** (6): Allen 3, Coldicott 1, Gallimore 1, Rowan 1.
**FA Cup** (2): Jeffrey 1, Nielsen 1.
**Ground:** Blundell Park, Cleethorpes, North-East Lincolnshire DN35 7PY. Telephone (01472) 605050.
**Record attendance:** 31,651 v Wolverhampton W, FA Cup 5th rd, 20 February 1937.
**Capacity:** 10,033.
**Manager:** Lennie Lawrence.
**Secretary:** Ian Fleming.
**Most League Goals:** 103, Division 2, 1933–34.
**Highest League Scorer in Season:** Pat Glover, 42, Division 2, 1933–34.
**Most League Goals in Total Aggregate:** Pat Glover, 180, 1930–39.
**Most Capped Player:** Pat Glover, 7, Wales.
**Most League Appearances:** Keith Jobling, 448, 1953–69.

**Honours – Football League:** Division 2 Champions – 1900–01, 1933–34. Division 3 (N) Champions – 1925–26, 1955–56. Division 3 Champions – 1979–80. Division 4 Champions – 1971-72. **League Group Cup:** Winners 1981–82. **Auto Windscreens Shield:** Winners 1997–98.

**Colours:** Black and white striped shirts, black shorts, black stockings.

# HALIFAX TOWN                    DIV. 3

| | | | | | | |
|---|---|---|---|---|---|---|
| Butler Lee (G) | 6 1 | 13 08 | Sheffield | 30 | 5 66 | Dunfermline Ath |
| Clarke Chris (D) | 6 3 | 12 02 | Leeds | 18 12 80 | | Wolverhampton W |
| Clarke Matthew (F) | 6 3 | 13 00 | Leeds | 18 12 80 | | Wolverhampton W |
| Fitzpatrick Ian (F) | 5 9 | 10 00 | Manchester | 22 | 9 80 | Manchester U |
| Herbert Robert (M) | 5 10 | 11 00 | Durham | 29 | 8 83 | Scholar |
| Jones Gary (F) | 6 1 | 12 08 | Huddersfield | 6 | 4 69 | Hartlepool U |
| Kerrigan Steve (F) | 6 1 | 12 04 | Bailleston | 9 10 72 | | Shrewsbury T |
| Middleton Craig (M) | 5 11 | 12 00 | Nuneaton | 10 | 9 70 | Cardiff C |
| Mitchell Graham (D) | 6 1 | 13 01 | Shipley | 16 | 2 68 | Cardiff C |
| Oleksewycz Stephen (F) | | | Halifax | 24 | 2 83 | |
| Parks Tony (G) | 5 10 | 11 05 | Hackney | 28 | 1 63 | Scarborough |
| Potter Lee (F) | 5 11 | 12 10 | Salford | 3 | 9 78 | Bolton W |
| Redfearn Neil (M) | 5 8 | 12 00 | Dewsbury | 20 | 6 65 | Wigan Ath |
| Reilly Alan (M) | 5 11 | 12 01 | Dublin | 22 | 8 80 | Manchester C |
| Rezai Carl (D) | 5 9 | 11 00 | Manchester | 16 10 82 | | |
| Stoneman Paul (D) | 6 0 | 13 06 | Whitley Bay | 26 | 2 73 | Blackpool |
| Wilder Chris (D) | 5 11 | 12 07 | Stocksbridge | 23 | 9 67 | Brighton & HA |

**League Appearances:** Bradshaw, M. 15(2); Brass, C. 6; Butler, L. 33; Clarke, C. 26; Clarke, M. 12(7); Fitzpatrick, I. 9(3); Gaughan, S. 6(3); Harrison, G. 7(2); Hawe, S. 6(2); Herbert, R. 3(6); Holt, G. (2); Jones, G. 30(3); Jules, M. 16(4); Kerrigan, S. 40(1); Matthews, R. 8; Mawson, C. 9; Middleton, C. 35(2); Mike, L. 2(5); Mitchell, G. 42; Mitchell, P. 11; Morgan, S. 1; Murphy, P. 18(3); Myers, P. (1); Oleksewycz, S. (3); Painter, R. 8(8); Parks, T. 4(1); Parnaby, S. 6; Potter, L. (3); Proctor, M. 11(1); Redfearn, N. 12; Reilly, A. 15(8); Rezai, C. 8(3); Richards, I. 8(10); Stansfield, J. 2; Stoneman, P. 29(1); Thompson, S. 35(1); Wainwright, N. 13; Wilder, C. 20.

**Goals – League** (54): Kerrigan 19, Jones 5, Middleton 5, Proctor 4, Bradshaw 2, Fitzpatrick 2, Matthews 2, Reilly 2, Stoneman 2 (1 pen), Thompson 2, Clarke C 1, Clarke M 1, Gaughan 1, Harrison 1, Herbert 1, Jules 1, Mitchell G 1, Murphy 1, own goal 1.

**Worthington Cup** (1): Holt 1.

**FA Cup** (0).

**Ground:** The Shay Stadium, Shaw Hill, Halifax HX1 2YS. Telephone Halifax (01422) 345543.

**Record attendance:** 36,885 v Tottenham H, FA Cup 5th rd, 15 February 1953.

**Capacity:** 9,900.

**Manager:** Paul Bracewell.

**Secretary:** Mike Riley.

**Most League Goals:** 83, Division 3 (N), 1957–58.

**Highest League Scorer in Season:** Albert Valentine, 34, Division 3 (N), 1934–35.

**Most League Goals in Total Aggregate:** Ernest Dixon, 129, 1922–30.

**Most Capped Player:** None.

**Most League Appearances:** John Pickering, 367, 1965–74.

**Honours – Football League:** Division 3 (N)—Runners-up 1934–35; Division 4: Runners-up 1968–69. **Vauxhall Conference:** Champions 1997–98.

**Colours:** Blue shirts, white trim, blue shorts, white trim, white stockings.

| | | | | | | |
|---|---|---|---|---|---|---|
| Arnison Paul (D) | 5 10 | 11 08 | Hartlepool | 18 | 9 77 | Newcastle U |
| Barron Micky (D) | 5 11 | 11 11 | Lumley | 22 12 74 | | Middlesbrough |
| Boyd Adam (F) | 5 9 | 10 12 | Hartlepool | 25 | 5 82 | Scholar |
| Easter Jermaine (F) | 5 9 | 10 11 | Cardiff | 15 | 1 82 | Trainee |
| Henderson Kevin (F) | 5 11 | 13 04 | Ashington | 8 | 6 74 | Burnley |
| Lee Graeme (D) | 6 2 | 13 07 | Middlesbrough | 31 | 5 78 | Trainee |
| Lormor Tony (F) | 6 1 | 14 02 | Ashington | 29 10 70 | | Mansfield T |
| Miller Tommy (M) | 6 1 | 12 01 | Easington | 8 | 1 79 | Trainee |
| Robinson Mark (D) | 5 9 | 11 00 | Guisborough | 24 | 7 81 | Trainee |
| Sharp James (D) | 6 2 | 13 07 | Reading | 2 | 1 76 | Andover T |
| Simms Gordon (D) | 6 2 | 12 06 | Larne | 23 | 3 81 | Wolverhampton W |
| Stephenson Paul (M) | 5 10 | 12 06 | Wallsend | 2 | 1 68 | York C |
| Tinkler Mark (M) | 6 2 | 13 00 | Bishop Auckland | 24 10 74 | | Southend U |
| Westwood Chris (D) | 5 11 | 12 03 | Dudley | 13 | 2 77 | Wolverhampton W |
| Williams Anthony (G) | 6 1 | 12 13 | Ogwr | 20 | 9 77 | Blackburn R |

**League Appearances:** Arnison, P. 26(1); Aspin, N. 5(5); Baker, S. 9; Barron, M. 27(1); Boyd, A. 3(2); Clark, I. 15(9); Easter, J. (4); Ferguson, B. 4; Fitzpatrick, L. 12(11); Henderson, K. 40; Hollund, M. 5; Knowles, D. 22(3); Lee, G. 3(3); Lormor, T. 22(9); McAvoy, A. 2(3); Midgley, C. 24(17); Miller, T. 46; Robinson, M. 5(1); Sharp, J. 31(3); Shilton, S. 29(4); Sperrevik, T. 4(11); Stephenson, P. 40; Strodder, G. 17(2); Tennebo, T. (2); Tinkler, M. 28; Westwood, C. 46; Williams, A. 41.
**Goals – League** (71): Henderson 17, Miller 16 (5 pens), Lormor 8, Midgley 8, Fitzpatrick 4, Shilton 4, Tinkler 3, Sharp 2, Stephenson 2, Arnison 1, Knowles 1, Sperrevik 1, Westwood 1, own goals 3.
**Worthington Cup** (4): Miller 2 (1 pen), Fitzpatrick 1, Stephenson 1.
**FA Cup** (1): Midgley 1.
**Ground:** Victoria Park, Clarence Road, Hartlepool TS24 8BZ. Telephone (01429) 272584.
**Record attendance:** 17,426 v Manchester U, FA Cup 3rd rd, 5 January 1957.
**Capacity:** 7229.
**Manager:** Chris Turner.
**Secretary:** Maureen Smith.
**Most League Goals:** 90, Division 3 (N), 1956–57.
**Highest League Scorer in Season:** William Robinson, 28, Division 3 (N), 1927–28; Joe Allon, 28, Division 4, 1990–91.
**Most League Goals in Total Aggregate:** Ken Johnson, 98, 1949–64.
**Most Capped Player:** Ambrose Fogarty, 1 (11), Republic of Ireland.
**Most League Appearances:** Wattie Moore, 447, 1948–64.
**Honours – Nil.**
**Colours:** Royal blue and white stripes.

# HUDDERSFIELD TOWN    DIV. 2

| | | | | | | |
|---|---|---|---|---|---|---|
| Armstrong Craig (D) | 5 11 | 12 10 | South Shields | 23 | 5 75 | Nottingham F |
| Baldry Simon (M) | 5 10 | 11 06 | Huddersfield | 12 | 2 76 | Trainee |
| Beech Chris (M) | 5 10 | 11 12 | Blackpool | 16 | 9 74 | Hartlepool U |
| Booth Andy (F) | 6 0 | 13 00 | Huddersfield | 6 12 73 | | Sheffield W |
| Brown Nathaniel (F) | 6 2 | 12 05 | Sheffield | 15 | 6 81 | Trainee |
| Facey Delroy (F) | 6 0 | 13 00 | Huddersfield | 22 | 4 80 | Trainee |
| Gorre Dean (M) | 5 8 | 11 07 | Surinam | 10 | 9 70 | Ajax |
| Gray Kevin (D) | 6 0 | 14 00 | Sheffield | 7 | 1 72 | Mansfield T |
| Hay Chris (F) | 5 11 | 11 07 | Glasgow | 28 | 8 74 | Swindon T |

| Heary Thomas (D) | 5 10 | 11 03 | Dublin | 14 2 79 | Trainee |
| Holland Chris (M) | 5 9 | 11 05 | Whalley | 11 9 75 | Birmingham C |
| Irons Kenny (M) | 5 10 | 11 02 | Liverpool | 4 11 70 | Tranmere R |
| Jenkins Steve (D) | 5 11 | 12 03 | Merthyr | 16 7 72 | Swansea C |
| Lucketti Chris (D) | 6 1 | 13 04 | Littleborough | 21 9 71 | Bury |
| Macari Paul (F) | 5 8 | 11 11 | Manchester | 23 8 76 | Sheffield U |
| Margetson Martyn (G) | 6 0 | 14 00 | West Neath | 8 9 71 | Southend U |
| Mattis Dwayne (M) | 5 10 | 11 00 | Huddersfield | 31 7 81 | Trainee |
| Moses Adi (D) | 6 0 | 12 07 | Doncaster | 4 5 75 | Barnsley |
| Schofield Danny (F) | 5 10 | 11 06 | Doncaster | 10 4 80 | Brodsworth |
| Scott Paul (M) | 5 11 | 12 00 | Wakefield | 5 11 79 | Trainee |
| Senior Michael (M) | 5 9 | 11 06 | Huddersfield | 3 3 81 | Trainee |
| Senior Philip (M) | | | Huddersfield | 30 10 82 | Trainee |
| Smith Martin (F) | 5 11 | 12 00 | Sunderland | 13 11 74 | Sheffield U |
| Thorrington John (F) | 5 7 | 10 05 | Johannesburg | 17 10 79 | Manchester U |
| Vaesen Nico (G) | 6 1 | 13 08 | Hasselt | 28 9 69 | Aalst |
| Wijnhard Clyde (F) | 5 10 | 13 04 | Paramaribo | 1 11 73 | Leeds U |

**League Appearances:** Armstrong, C. 44; Baldry, S. 26(9); Beech, C. 10; Beresford, D. (2); Booth, A. 8; Brennan, J. (2); Dyson, J. 25(5); Facey, D. 22(12); Gallen, K. 30(8); Gorre, D. 23(11); Gray, K. 13(4); Hay, C. (4); Heary, T. 25(3); Holland, C. 29; Irons, K. 18(15); Jenkins, S. 30; Kozluk, R. 14; Kyle, K. (4); Lucketti, C. 40; Margetson, M. 1(1); Monkou, K. 2; Morris, L. 5; Moses, A. 10(2); Ndlovu, P. 6; Schofield, D. (1); Sellars, S. 6(8); Senior, M. (4); Smith, M. 27(3); Thornley, B. 29(7); Vaesen, N. 45; Vincent, J. 14(2); Wijnhard, C. 4.

**Goals – League** (48): Facey 10, Gallen 10, Smith 8 (1 pen), Ndlovu 4, Armstrong 3, Booth 3, Dyson 3, Baldry 2, Gorre 2 (1 pen), Lucketti 1, Morris 1, own goal 1.

**Worthington Cup** (0).

**FA Cup** (0).

**Ground:** The Alfred McAlpine Stadium, Leeds Road, Huddersfield HD1 6PX. Telephone (01484) 484100.

**Record attendance:** 67,037 v Arsenal, FA Cup 6th rd, 27 February 1932. **Capacity:** 25,000.

**Manager:** Lou Macari.

**Secretary:** Ann Hough.

**Most League Goals:** 101, Division 4, 1979–80.

**Highest League Scorer in Season:** Sam Taylor, 35, Division 2, 1919–20; George Brown, 35, Division 1, 1925–26.

**Most League Goals in Total Aggregate:** George Brown, 142, 1921–29; Jimmy Glazzard, 142, 1946–56.

**Most Capped Player:** Jimmy Nicholson, 31 (41), Northern Ireland.

**Most League Appearances:** Billy Smith, 520, 1914–34.

**Honours – Football League:** Division 1 Champions – 1923–24, 1924–25, 1925–26. Division 2 Champions – 1969–70. Division 4 Champions – 1969–70. **FA Cup winners** 1922.

**Colours:** Blue and white striped shirts, white shorts, white stockings with blue trim.

# HULL CITY                                               DIV. 3

| Brabin Gary (M) | 5 11 | 14 08 | Liverpool | 9 12 70 | Blackpool |
| Bracey Lee (G) | 6 2 | 13 02 | Barking | 11 9 68 | Ipswich T |
| Bradshaw Gary (F) | 5 6 | 10 06 | Beverley | 30 12 82 | Scholar |
| Brown David (F) | 5 10 | 12 07 | Bolton | 2 10 78 | Manchester U |
| Edwards Mike (D) | 6 1 | 12 00 | Hessle | 25 4 80 | Trainee |
| Eyre John (F) | 6 0 | 12 06 | Hull | 9 10 74 | Scunthorpe U |
| Goodison Ian (D) | 6 1 | 12 06 | St James, Jamaica | 5 8 72 | Olympic Gardens |

| | | | | | | |
|---|---|---|---|---|---|---|
| Greaves Mark (D) | 6 1 | 13 00 | Hull | 22 1 75 | Brigg Town |
| Harris Jason (F) | 6 1 | 11 07 | Sutton | 24 11 76 | Preston NE |
| Joyce Warren (M) | 5 9 | 12 00 | Oldham | 20 1 65 | Burnley |
| Mann Neil (M) | 5 10 | 12 01 | Nottingham | 19 11 72 | Grantham T |
| Matthews Rob (F) | 6 0 | 12 05 | Slough | 14 10 70 | Stockport Co |
| Musselwhite Paul (G) | 6 2 | 14 04 | Portsmouth | 22 12 68 | Port Vale |
| Philpott Lee (M) | 5 11 | 11 08 | Barnet | 21 2 70 | Lincoln C |
| Rowe Rodney (F) | 5 8 | 12 08 | Plymouth | 30 7 75 | Gillingham |
| Whitmore Theodore (M) | 6 2 | 12 10 | Jamaica | 21 11 72 | Seba U |
| Whitney Jon (M) | 5 10 | 13 08 | Nantwich | 23 12 70 | Lincoln C |
| Whittle Justin (D) | 6 1 | 12 12 | Derby | 18 3 71 | Stoke C |

**League Appearances:** Atkins, M. 8; Brabin, G. 31(6); Bracey, L. 9(1); Bradshaw, G. (2); Brightwell, D. 24(3); Brown, D. 24(13); Brumwell, P. 1(3); Edwards, M. 40(2); Eyre, J. 19(9); Fletcher, G. 1(4); Francis, K. 22; Goodison, I. 36; Greaves, M. 28(2); Harper, S. 27; Harris, J. 1(8); Holt, A. 10; Mann, N. 11(2); Marcelle, C. 16(7); Matthews, R. 8; Morley, B. (2); Musselwhite, P. 37; Perry, J. 6; Philpott, L. 36(6); Rowe, R. 14(7); Swales, S. 20(6); Whitmore, T. 23(3); Whitney, J. 14(1); Whittle, J. 38; Wood, J. 2(13).

**Goals – League** (47): Rowe 6 (4 pens), Eyre 5 (1 pen), Francis 5, Whitmore 5, Brown 4, Edwards 4, Brabin 2, Brightwell 2, Greaves 2, Holt 2, Marcelle 2, Goodison 1, Philpott 1, Whitney 1, own goals 5.
**Worthington Cup** (1): Eyre 1.
**FA Cup** (0).
**Ground:** Boothferry Park, Hull HU4 6EU. Telephone (01482) 575263.
**Record attendance:** 55,019 v Manchester U, FA Cup 6th rd, 26 February 1949.
**Capacity:** 15,159.
**Manager:** Brian Little.
**Assistant Secretary:** Jackie Bell.
**Most League Goals:** 109, Division 3, 1965–66.
**Highest League Scorer in Season:** Bill McNaughton, 39, Division 3 (N), 1932–33.
**Most League Goals in Total Aggregate:** Chris Chilton, 195, 1960–71.
**Most Capped Player:** Terry Neill, 15 (59), Northern Ireland.
**Most League Appearances:** Andy Davidson, 520, 1952–67.
**Honours – Football League:** Division 3 (N) Champions – 1932–33, 1948–49. Division 3 Champions – 1965–66.
**Colours:** Amber shirts, black and white trim, black shorts, black stockings with amber turnovers.

## IPSWICH TOWN                    FA PREMIERSHIP

| | | | | | | |
|---|---|---|---|---|---|---|
| Abidallah Nabil (M) | 5 7 | 9 00 | Amsterdam | 5 8 82 | |
| Armstrong Alun (F) | 6 0 | 13 08 | Gateshead | 22 2 75 | Middlesbrough |
| Artun Erdem (D) | | | London | 11 11 82 | Trainee |
| Beevers Lee (M) | | | Doncaster | 4 12 83 | Scholar |
| Bramble Titus (D) | 6 2 | 14 10 | Ipswich | 21 7 81 | Trainee |
| Branagan Keith (G) | 6 0 | 14 00 | Fulham | 10 7 66 | Bolton W |
| Brown Wayne (D) | 6 0 | 12 06 | Barking | 20 8 77 | Trainee |
| Clapham Jamie (M) | 5 9 | 11 05 | Lincoln | 7 12 75 | Tottenham H |
| Croft Gary (D) | 5 8 | 11 08 | Stafford | 17 2 74 | Blackburn R |
| Dickinson Robert (M) | | | Leeds | 27 11 83 | Scholar |
| Graaven Guillermo (M) | 6 0 | 11 06 | Amsterdam | 17 1 82 | |
| Holland Matt (M) | 5 9 | 12 07 | Bury | 11 4 74 | Bournemouth |
| Hreidarsson Hermann (D) | 6 3 | 13 01 | Iceland | 11 7 74 | Wimbledon |
| Karic Amir (D) | 5 11 | 12 08 | Oramovica Ponja | 31 12 73 | Maribor |
| Logan Richard (F) | 6 0 | 12 05 | Bury St Edmunds | 4 1 82 | Ipswich T |

| Name | Ht | Wt | Birthplace | Date | Previous club |
|---|---|---|---|---|---|
| Magilton Jim (M) | 6 0 | 13 10 | Belfast | 6 5 69 | Sheffield W |
| Makin Chris (D) | 5 11 | 12 11 | Manchester | 8 5 73 | Sunderland |
| McGreal John (D) | 5 11 | 13 00 | Birkenhead | 2 6 72 | Tranmere R |
| Miller Justin (D) | 6 0 | 11 07 | Johannesburg | 16 12 80 | Academy |
| Naylor Richard (F) | 6 1 | 13 07 | Leeds | 28 2 77 | Trainee |
| Nicholls Ashley (M) | 5 11 | 11 11 | Suffolk | 30 10 81 | Ipswich W |
| Pullen James (G) | 6 2 | 14 00 | Chelmsford | 18 3 82 | Heybridge S |
| Reuser Martijn (M) | 5 7 | 12 10 | Amsterdam | 1 2 75 | Vitesse |
| Salmon Mike (G) | 6 2 | 14 00 | Leyland | 14 7 64 | Charlton Ath |
| Scowcroft James (F) | 6 1 | 14 02 | Bury St Edmunds | 15 11 75 | Trainee |
| Stewart Marcus (F) | 5 10 | 11 08 | Bristol | 7 11 72 | Huddersfield T |
| Venus Mark (D) | 6 0 | 13 02 | Hartlepool | 6 4 67 | Wolverhampton W |
| Wilnis Fabian (D) | 5 8 | 12 06 | Paramaribo | 23 8 70 | De Graafschap |
| Wright Jermaine (M) | 5 10 | 12 07 | Greenwich | 21 10 75 | Crewe Alex |
| Wright Richard (G) | 6 2 | 14 04 | Ipswich | 5 11 77 | Trainee |

**League Appearances:** Abidallah, N. (2); Armstrong, A. 15(6); Bramble, T. 23(3); Branagan, K. 2; Brown, W. (4); Burchill, M. 2(5); Clapham, J. 28(7); Croft, G. 6(2); Holland, M. 38; Hreidarsson, H. 35(1); Johnson, D. 6(8); Magilton, J. 32(1); Makin, C. 10; McGreal, J. 25(3); Naylor, R. 5(8); Reuser, M. 13(13); Scales, J. 2; Scowcroft, J. 22(12); Stewart, M. 33(1); Venus, M. 23(2); Wilnis, F. 27(2); Wright, J. 35(2); Wright, R. 36.

**Goals – League** (57): Stewart 19 (2 pens), Armstrong 7, Reuser 6, Scowcroft 4, Holland 3, Venus 3, Clapham 2, Wilnis 2, Wright J 2, Bramble 1, Burchill 1, Hreidarsson 1, Magilton 1 (pen), McGreal 1, Naylor 1, own goals 3.

**Worthington Cup** (13): Johnson 3, Bramble 2, Holland 2, Scowcroft 2, Clapham 1, Magilton 1, Stewart 1, Venus 1.

**FA Cup** (3): Armstrong 1, Stewart 1, Wright J 1.

**Ground:** Portman Road, Ipswich, Suffolk IP1 2DA. Telephone (01473) 400500.

**Record attendance:** 38,010 v Leeds U, FA Cup 6th rd, 8 March 1975.

**Capacity:** 22,700 rising to 30,300.

**Manager:** George Burley.

**Secretary:** David C. Rose.

**Most League Goals:** 106, Division 3 (S), 1955–56.

**Highest League Scorer in Season:** Ted Phillips, 41, Division 3 (S), 1956–57.

**Most League Goals in Total Aggregate:** Ray Crawford, 203, 1958–63 and 1966–69.

**Most Capped Player:** Allan Hunter, 47 (53), Northern Ireland.

**Most League Appearances:** Mick Mills, 591, 1966–82.

**Honours – Football League:** Division 1 Champions – 1961–62. Division 2 Champions – 1960–61, 1967–68, 1991–92. Division 3 (S) Champions – 1953–54, 1956–57. **FA Cup:** Winners 1977–78. **European Competitions: UEFA Cup winners:** 1980–81.

**Colours:** Blue shirts, white shorts, blue stockings.

## KIDDERMINSTER HARRIERS                    DIV. 3

| Name | Ht | Wt | Birthplace | Date | Previous club |
|---|---|---|---|---|---|
| Barnett Gary (M) | 5 6 | 9 13 | Stratford upon Avon | 11 3 63 | Leyton Orient |
| Bennett Dean (F) | 5 10 | 11 00 | Wolverhampton | 13 12 77 | WBA |
| Bird Tony (F) | 5 11 | 12 10 | Cardiff | 1 9 74 | Swansea C |
| Brock Stuart (G) | 6 1 | 13 03 | Sandwell | 26 9 76 | Northampton T |
| Broughton Drewe (F) | 6 3 | 12 04 | Hitchin | 25 10 78 | Peterborough U |
| Clarkson Ian (D) | 5 10 | 12 00 | Solihull | 4 12 70 | Northampton T |
| Corbett Andy (F) | | | Worcester | 20 2 82 | |
| Davies Ben (M) | | | Birmingham | 27 5 81 | Walsall |
| Doyle Daire (M) | 5 10 | 11 06 | Dublin | 18 10 80 | Coventry C |
| Ducros Andy (F) | 5 6 | 9 08 | Evesham | 16 9 77 | Coventry C |

| Foster Ian (F) | 5 7 | 10 07 | Merseyside | 11 11 76 | Liverpool |
| Hadley Stewart (F) | 5 11 | 13 05 | Stourbridge | 30 12 73 | Mansfield T |
| Hinton Craig (D) | 5 11 | 11 00 | Wolverhampton | 26 11 77 | Birmingham C |
| Medou-Otye Parfait (D) | 5 10 | 12 00 | Ekoundendi | 29 11 76 | Morton |
| Murphy Brendan (G) | 5 11 | 11 12 | Wexford | 19 8 75 | Wimbledon |
| Shail Mark (D) | 6 1 | 12 06 | Sweden | 15 10 66 | Bristol C |
| Smith Adie (D) | | | Birmingham | 11 8 73 | Bromsgrove R |
| Stamps Scott (D) | 5 11 | 11 09 | Edgbaston | 20 3 75 | Colchester U |
| Webb Paul (M) | | | Wolverhampton | 30 11 67 | Bromsgrove R |

**League Appearances:** Barnett, G. 2; Bennett, D. 35(7); Bird, T. 16(9); Bogie, I. 14(7); Brock, S. 21; Broughton, D. 19; Clarke, T. 25; Clarkson, I. 37(1); Corbett, A. 3(3); Davies, B. 2(1); Doyle, D. 13(2); Ducros, A. 29(5); Durnin, J. 28(3); Foster, I. 9(1); Hadley, S. 18(15); Hinton, C. 46; Horne, B. 21(6); Kerr, D. (1); MacKenzie, N. 20(3); Medou-Otye, P. 16(1); Shail, M. 36; Skovbjerg, T. 7(5); Smith, A. 32(2); Stamps, S. 34; Webb, P. 23(9).
**Goals – League** (47): Durnin 9, Broughton 7, Hadley 6, Smith 5, Bennett 4, MacKenzie 3, Ducros 2, Foster 2, Hinton 2, Bird 1, Bogie 1, Horne 1, Shail 1, Skovbjerg 1, Webb 1, own goal 1.
**Worthington Cup** (1): Hadley 1.
**FA Cup** (4): Hadley 2, Bird 1, Bogie 1.
**Ground:** Aggborough Stadium, Hoo Road, Kidderminster DY10 1NB. Telephone (01562) 823 931.
**Record attendance:** 9,155 v Hereford U, 27 November 1948.
**Capacity:** 6,293 (1,100 seated).
**Manager:** Jan Molby.
**Football Secretary:** Roger Barlow.
**Most League Goals:** 98, Division 2, 1927–28.
**Honours – Conference:** Champions 1993–94, 1999–2000; Runners-up 1996–97. **FA Trophy:** 1986–87 (winners); 1990–91 (runners-up), 1994–95 (runners-up). **League Cup:** 1996–97 (winners). **Welsh FA Cup:** 1985–86 (runners-up), 1988–89 (runners-up). **Southern League Cup:** 1979–80 (winners). **Worcester Senior Cup:** (21). **Birmingham Senior Cup:** (7). **Staffordshire Senior Cup:** (4). **West Midland League Champions:** (6), Runners-up (3). **Southern Premier:** Runners-up (1). **West Midland League Cup:** Winners (7). **Keys Cup:** Winners (7). **Border Counties Floodlit League Champions:** (3). **Camkin Floodlit Cup:** Winners (3). **Bass County Vase:** Winners (1). **Conference Fair Play Trophy:** (5)
**Colours:** Red shirts with white flash, red shorts and stockings with white trim.

# LEEDS UNITED                         FA PREMIERSHIP

| Allaway Shaun (G) | 6 2 | 11 06 | Reading | 16 2 83 | Trainee |
| Bakke Eirik (M) | 6 1 | 12 06 | Sogndal | 13 9 77 | Sogndal |
| Batty David (M) | 5 8 | 11 09 | Leeds | 2 12 68 | Newcastle U |
| Bowyer Lee (M) | 5 9 | 10 07 | London | 3 1 77 | Charlton Ath |
| Boyle Wes (F) | 5 10 | 12 00 | Portadown | 30 3 79 | Trainee |
| Breen Gerard (M) | 5 7 | 11 08 | County Louth | 29 3 84 | Scholar |
| Bridges Michael (F) | 6 1 | 12 04 | North Shields | 5 8 78 | Sunderland |
| Burns Jacob (M) | 5 10 | 11 06 | Sydney | 21 4 78 | Paramatta Power |
| Cansdell-Sheriff Shane (M) | 6 0 | 11 12 | Sydney | 10 11 82 | NSW Academy |
| Cramer Martin (M) | 5 4 | 10 07 | Dublin | 15 11 82 | Maryland Boys |
| Dacourt Olivier (M) | 5 10 | 11 06 | Montreuil | 25 9 74 | Lens |
| Duberry Michael (D) | 6 1 | 14 00 | Enfield | 14 10 75 | Chelsea |
| Evans Gareth (D) | 6 0 | 12 00 | Leeds | 15 2 81 | Trainee |
| Farrell Craig (F) | 5 11 | 12 13 | Middlesbrough | 5 12 82 | Trainee |
| Farren Larry (D) | 5 10 | 11 09 | Donegal | 29 7 83 | Scholar |

| Name | Ht | Wt | Birthplace | Birthdate | Source |
|------|----|----|-----------|-----------|--------|
| Ferdinand Rio (D) | 6 3 | 14 01 | Peckham | 7 11 78 | West Ham U |
| Ferguson Steven (M) | 5 6 | 9 12 | Newry | 25 2 83 | St Andrew's |
| Folan Caleb (F) | 6 1 | 12 10 | Leeds | 26 10 82 | Trainee |
| Hackworth Tony (F) | 6 1 | 13 05 | Durham | 19 5 80 | Trainee |
| Harte Ian (D) | 6 0 | 12 03 | Drogheda | 31 8 77 | Trainee |
| Hay Danny (D) | 6 4 | 14 00 | Auckland | 15 5 75 | Perth Glory |
| Johnson Simon (F) | 5 9 | 11 09 | West Bromwich | 9 3 83 | Scholar |
| Kamara Christopher (D) | 5 6 | 11 07 | York | 27 2 84 | Scholar |
| Keane Robbie (F) | 5 9 | 12 00 | Dublin | 8 7 80 | Internazionale |
| Kelly Gary (D) | 5 8 | 11 00 | Drogheda | 9 7 74 | Home Farm |
| Kewell Harry (F) | 6 0 | 13 00 | Sydney | 22 9 78 | NSW Academy |
| Kilgallon Matthew (D) | 6 0 | 12 00 | York | 8 1 84 | Scholar |
| Kinsella Alan (F) | 5 6 | 11 00 | Dublin | 2 2 84 | Scholar |
| Lennon Anthony (F) | 5 9 | 10 08 | Leeds | 16 5 82 | Trainee |
| Martyn Nigel (G) | 6 2 | 14 08 | St Austell | 11 8 66 | Crystal Palace |
| Matteo Dominic (D) | 6 1 | 12 07 | Dumfries | 28 4 74 | Liverpool |
| Maybury Alan (D) | 5 9 | 11 05 | Dublin | 8 8 78 | Trainee |
| McCargo Gerard (F) | 5 4 | 10 03 | Belfast | 3 11 82 | Celtic (Belfast) Boy |
| McMaster Jamie (M) | 5 10 | 11 12 | Sydney | 29 11 82 | NSW Academy |
| McPhail Stephen (M) | 5 10 | 12 00 | London | 9 12 79 | Trainee |
| Mills Danny (D) | 6 0 | 12 05 | Norwich | 18 5 77 | Charlton Ath |
| Milosevic Danny (G) | 6 3 | 14 12 | Carlton | 26 6 78 | Perth Glory |
| Newey Tom (D) | 5 9 | 10 07 | Sheffield | 31 10 82 | Scholar |
| Radebe Lucas (D) | 6 1 | 12 01 | Johannesburg | 12 4 69 | Kaiser Chiefs |
| Richardson Frazer (D) | 5 11 | 11 12 | Rotherham | 29 10 82 | Trainee |
| Robinson Paul (G) | 6 4 | 14 04 | Beverley | 15 10 79 | Trainee |
| Shields Robbie (M) | 5 5 | 10 05 | Dublin | 1 5 84 | Scholar |
| Singh Harpal (F) | 5 7 | 10 09 | Bradford | 15 9 81 | Trainee |
| Smith Alan (F) | 5 9 | 11 05 | Leeds | 28 10 80 | Trainee |
| Viduka Marko (F) | 6 2 | 14 08 | Melbourne | 9 10 75 | Celtic |
| Ward Michael (F) | 5 6 | 10 03 | Omagh | 17 4 84 | Scholar |
| Wilcox Jason (M) | 6 0 | 12 00 | Bolton | 15 7 71 | Blackburn R |
| Woodgate Jonathan (D) | 6 2 | 13 05 | Middlesbrough | 22 1 80 | Trainee |

**League Appearances:** Bakke, E. 24(5); Batty, D. 13(3); Bowyer, L. 38; Bridges, M. 6(1); Burns, J. 3(1); Dacourt, O. 33; Duberry, M. 5; Evans, G. (1); Ferdinand, R. 23; Harte, I. 29; Hay, D. 2(2); Huckerby, D. 2(5); Jones, M. 3(1); Keane, R. 12(6); Kelly, G. 22(2); Kewell, H. 12(5); Martyn, N. 23; Matteo, D. 30; McPhail, S. 3(4); Mills, D. 20(3); Radebe, L. 19(1); Robinson, P. 15(1); Smith, A. 26(7); Viduka, M. 34; Wilcox, J. 7(10); Woodgate, J. 14.

**Goals – League** (64): Viduka 17, Smith 11, Bowyer 9, Keane 9 (1 pen), Harte 7 (2 pens), Dacourt 3, Bakke 2, Ferdinand 2, Kewell 2, Woodgate 1, own goal 1.

**Worthington Cup** (2): Huckerby 2.

**FA Cup** (1): Viduka 1.

**Ground:** Elland Road, Leeds LS11 0ES. Telephone (0113) 2266000.

**Record attendance:** 57,892 v Sunderland, FA Cup 5th rd (replay), 15 March 1967.

**Capacity:** 40,204.

**Manager:** David O'Leary.

**Secretary:** Ian Silvester.

**Most League Goals:** 98, Division 2, 1927–28.

**Highest League Scorer in Season:** John Charles, 42, Division 2, 1953–54.

**Most League Goals in Total Aggregate:** Peter Lorimer, 168, 1965–79 and 1983–86.

**Most Capped Player:** Billy Bremner, 54, Scotland.

**Most League Appearances:** Jack Charlton, 629, 1953–73.

**Honours – Football League:** Division 1 Champions – 1968–69, 1973–74, 1991–92. Division 2 Champions – 1923–24, 1963–64, 1989–90. **FA Cup:** Winners 1972. **Football League Cup:** Winners 1967–68. **European Competitions: European Fairs Cup winners:** 1967–68, 1970–71.
**Colours:** All white, yellow and blue trim.

## LEICESTER CITY          FA PREMIERSHIP

| Name | Ht | Wt | Birthplace | D.O.B. | Previous Club |
|---|---|---|---|---|---|
| Akinbiyi Ade (F) | 6 1 | 13 09 | Hackney | 10 10 74 | Wolverhampton W |
| Ashton Jonathan (M) | | | Nuneaton | 4 10 82 | Scholar |
| Benjamin Trevor (F) | 6 2 | 14 02 | Kettering | 8 2 79 | Cambridge U |
| Campbell Stuart (M) | 5 10 | 10 13 | Corby | 9 12 77 | Trainee |
| Cresswell Richard (F) | 6 0 | 11 08 | Bridlington | 20 9 77 | Sheffield W |
| Darby Brett (M) | | | Leicester | 10 11 83 | Scholar |
| Davidson Callum (D) | 5 10 | 12 07 | Stirling | 25 6 76 | Blackburn R |
| Delaney Damien (D) | | | Cork | 20 7 81 | |
| Dudfield Lawrie (F) | 6 0 | 12 04 | London | 7 5 80 | Kettering T |
| Eadie Darren (F) | 5 7 | 10 09 | Chippenham | 10 6 75 | Norwich C |
| Elliott Matt (D) | 6 3 | 15 00 | Roehampton | 1 11 68 | Oxford U |
| Ellison Kevin (F) | | | Liverpool | 23 2 79 | Altrincham |
| Flowers Tim (G) | 6 2 | 14 00 | Kenilworth | 3 2 67 | Blackburn R |
| Gunnlaugsson Arnar (F) | 5 10 | 11 06 | Akranes | 6 3 73 | Bolton W |
| Guppy Steve (M) | 5 11 | 11 11 | Winchester | 29 3 69 | Port Vale |
| Heath Matthew (M) | | | Leicester | 1 11 81 | Scholar |
| Impey Andrew (M) | 5 8 | 11 06 | Hammersmith | 13 9 71 | West Ham U |
| Izzet Muzzy (M) | 5 10 | 11 02 | Hackney | 31 10 74 | Chelsea |
| Jones Matthew (M) | 5 11 | 11 09 | Llanelli | 1 9 80 | Leeds U |
| Lewis Junior (F) | 6 2 | 11 08 | Wembley | 9 10 73 | Gillingham |
| Lyth Ashley (M) | | | Whitby | 14 6 83 | |
| Marshall Lee (M) | 6 2 | 12 00 | Islington | 21 1 79 | Norwich C |
| Mortimer Alex (M) | 5 10 | 10 06 | Manchester | 28 11 82 | Trainee |
| Oakes Stefan (M) | 5 11 | 12 08 | Leicester | 6 9 78 | Trainee |
| Piper Matt (M) | 6 1 | 13 02 | Leicester | 29 9 81 | Trainee |
| Price Michael (M) | | | Ashington | 3 4 83 | Scholar |
| Reeves Martin (M) | | | Birmingham | 7 9 81 | Scholar |
| Rowett Gary (D) | 6 0 | 12 10 | Bromsgrove | 6 3 74 | Birmingham C |
| Royce Simon (G) | 6 2 | 12 10 | Newham | 9 9 71 | Charlton Ath |
| Savage Robbie (M) | 5 11 | 11 02 | Wrexham | 18 10 74 | Crewe Alex |
| Sherman David (D) | 5 9 | 12 07 | Wegberg | 19 5 83 | Scholar |
| Sinclair Frank (D) | 5 10 | 12 03 | Lambeth | 3 12 71 | Chelsea |
| Smith Matthew (M) | | | Northampton | 28 10 82 | Derby Co |
| Stevenson Jonathan (M) | | | Leicester | 13 10 82 | Scholar |
| Stewart Jordan (M) | 6 0 | 12 04 | Birmingham | 3 3 82 | Trainee |
| Sturridge Dean (F) | 5 8 | 12 02 | Birmingham | 27 7 73 | Derby Co |
| Taggart Gerry (D) | 6 2 | 14 01 | Belfast | 18 10 70 | Bolton W |
| Thomas Danny (M) | 5 7 | 10 10 | Leamington Spa | 1 5 81 | Trainee |
| Webb Mark (M) | | | Wolverhampton | 21 9 82 | Scholar |

**League Appearances:** Akinbiyi, A. 33(4); Benjamin, T. 7(14); Collymore, S. 1(4); Cottee, T. (2); Cresswell, R. 3(5); Davidson, C. 25(3); Delaney, D. 3(2); Dudfield, D. 16(8); Elliott, M. 34; Ellison, K. (1); Flowers, T. 22; Gilchrist, P. 6(6); Gunnlaugsson, A. 3(14); Guppy, S. 17(11); Impey, A. 29(4); Izzet, M. 27; Jones, M. 10(1); Lennon, N. 15; Lewis, J. 15; Mancini, R. 3(1); Marshall, L. 7(2); Oakes, S. 5(8); Rowett, G. 38; Royce, S. 16(3); Savage, R. 33; Sinclair, F. 14(3); Sturridge, D. 12(1); Taggart, G. 24; Walsh, S. (1).

**Goals – League** (39): Akinbiyi 9, Izzet 7 (2 pens), Savage 4 (1 pen), Gunnlaugsson 3, Sturridge 3, Eadie 2, Elliott 2, Rowett 2, Taggart 2, Benjamin 1, Collymore 1, Davidson 1, Guppy 1, own goal 1.
**Worthington Cup** (0).
**FA Cup** (9): Izzet 3 (2 pens), Akinbiyi 1, Cresswell 1, Gunnlaugsson 1, Rowett 1, Sturridge 1, own goal 1.
**Ground:** City Stadium, Filbert St, Leicester LE2 7FL. Telephone (0116) 2915000.
**Record attendance:** 47,298 v Tottenham H, FA Cup 5th rd, 18 February 1928.
**Capacity:** 22,868.
**Manager:** Peter Taylor.
**Secretary:** Andrew Neville.
**Most League Goals:** 109, Division 2, 1956–57.
**Highest League Scorer in Season:** Arthur Rowley, 44, Division 2, 1956–57.
**Most League Goals in Total Aggregate:** Arthur Chandler, 259, 1923–35.
**Most Capped Player:** John O'Neill, 39, Northern Ireland.
**Most League Appearances:** Adam Black, 528, 1920–35.
**Honours – Football League:** Division 2 Champions – 1924–25, 1936–37, 1953–54, 1956–57, 1970–71, 1979–80. **Football League Cup:** Winners 1964, 1997, 2000.
**Colours:** Royal blue shirts, white shorts, blue stockings.

# LEYTON ORIENT                                        DIV. 3

| | | | | | |
|---|---|---|---|---|---|
| Bayes Ashley (G) | 6 1 | 13 05 | Lincoln | 19 4 72 | Exeter C |
| Beall Billy (M) | 5 6 | 12 00 | Enfield | 4 12 77 | Cambridge U |
| Castle Steve (M) | 5 11 | 11 07 | Ilford | 17 5 66 | Peterborough U |
| Christie Iyseden (F) | 5 10 | 12 02 | Coventry | 14 11 76 | Mansfield T |
| Dorrian Chris (D) | | | Harlow | 3 4 82 | Trainee |
| Downer Simon (D) | 5 11 | 12 08 | Romford | 19 10 81 | Trainee |
| Gough Neil (F) | 5 11 | 11 08 | Harlow | 1 9 81 | Trainee |
| Gould Ronnie (M) | 5 11 | 11 05 | London | 27 9 82 | Trainee |
| Griffiths Carl (F) | 5 9 | 11 04 | Welshpool | 15 7 71 | Port Vale |
| Houghton Scott (M) | 5 5 | 12 02 | Hitchin | 22 10 71 | Southend U |
| Joseph Matt (D) | 5 7 | 10 02 | Bethnal Green | 30 9 72 | Cambridge U |
| Ling Martin (M) | 5 7 | 10 08 | West Ham | 15 7 66 | Leyton Orient |
| Lockwood Matt (D) | 5 9 | 10 12 | Rochford | 17 10 76 | Bristol R |
| Martin John (M) | 5 5 | 10 00 | Bethnal Green | 15 7 81 | Trainee |
| McElholm Brendan (M) | 5 11 | 12 02 | Omagh | 7 7 82 | Trainee |
| McGhee Dave (D) | 6 0 | 12 01 | Worthing | 19 6 76 | Brentford |
| Murray Jade (F) | 5 9 | 11 05 | Islington | 23 9 81 | Trainee |
| Parsons David (M) | 6 1 | 12 07 | Greenwich | 25 2 82 | Trainee |
| Smith Dean (D) | 6 0 | 13 00 | West Bromwich | 19 3 71 | Hereford U |
| Tate Chris (F) | 6 0 | 12 03 | York | 27 12 77 | Scarborough |
| Uka Niam (M) | 5 7 | 10 01 | Kosovo | 26 10 81 | Partizani |
| Watts Steve (F) | 6 1 | 13 00 | Peckham | 11 7 76 | Fisher Ath |

**League Appearances:** Barrett, S. 7; Bayes, A. 39; Beall, B. 12(5); Brissett, J. 2(2); Brkovic, A. 34(6); Cadiou, F. (3); Castle, S. 2(7); Christie, I. 1(6); Dorrian, C. 2; Downer, S. 20(11); Forge, N. 1; Garcia, R. 18; Griffiths, C. 35(2); Harris, A. 44; Hatcher, D. (2); Houghton, S. 17(4); Ibehre, J. 1(4); Jones, B. 1; Joseph, M. 44; Lee, C. 2(1); Lockwood, M. 31(1); Mansley, C. (1); Martin, J. 15(4); McElholm, B. 3(9); McGhee, D. 39; McLean, A. 1(1); Opara, C. 3(3); Opinel, S. 9(2); Pinamonte, L. 5(6); Shorey, N. 8; Smith, D. 43; Tate, C. 9(13); Vasseur, E. (2); Walschaerts, W. 44(1); Watts, S. 14(22).
**Goals – League** (59): Griffiths 14 (2 pens), Watts 8, Lockwood 7 (6 pens), Smith 5, Garcia 4, Brkovic 3, McGhee 3, Tate 3, Walschaerts 3, Christie 2, Ibehre 2,

Pinamonte 2, Houghton 1, McLean 1, Opinel 1.
**Worthington Cup** (4): Brkovic 2, Christie 1, Watts 1.
**FA Cup** (8): Griffiths 4, Houghton 1, Tate 1, Watts 1, own goal 1.
**Ground:** Leyton Stadium, Brisbane Road, Leyton, London E10 5NE. Telephone (020) 8926 1111.
**Record attendance:** 34,345 v West Ham U, FA Cup 4th rd, 25 January 1964.
**Capacity:** 13,842.
**Manager:** Tommy Taylor.
**Secretary:** Kirstine Nicholson.
**Most League Goals:** 106, Division 3 (S), 1955–56.
**Highest League Scorer in Season:** Tom Johnston, 35, Division 2, 1957–58.
**Most League Goals in Total Aggregate:** Tom Johnston, 121, 1956–58, 1959–61.
**Most Capped Players:** Tunji Banjo, 7 (7), Nigeria; John Chiedozie, 7 (9), Nigeria; Tony Grealish, 7 (45), Eire.
**Most League Appearances:** Peter Allen, 432, 1965–78.
**Honours – Football League:** Division 3 Champions – 1969–70. Division 3 (S) Champions – 1955–56.
**Colours:** Red and white check shirts, black shorts with red and white check trim.

---

# LINCOLN CITY                                              DIV. 3

| Barnett Jason (D) | 5 9 | 10 10 | Shrewsbury | 21 4 76 | Wolverhampton W |
|---|---|---|---|---|---|
| Battersby Tony (F) | 6 0 | 12 09 | Doncaster | 30 8 75 | Bury |
| Cameron Dave (F) | 6 1 | 12 05 | Bangor | 24 8 75 | Brighton & HA |
| Camm Mark (D) | 5 8 | 10 12 | Mansfield | 1 10 81 | Trainee |
| Finnigan John (M) | 5 8 | 10 11 | Wakefield | 29 3 76 | Nottingham F |
| Gain Peter (M) | 5 9 | 11 00 | Hammersmith | 2 11 76 | Tottenham H |
| Holmes Steve (D) | 6 2 | 13 00 | Middlesbrough | 13 1 71 | Preston NE |
| Marriott Alan (G) | 5 11 | 12 05 | Bedford | 3 9 78 | Tottenham H |
| Mayo Paul (D) | 5 11 | 11 09 | Lincoln | 13 10 81 | Scholar |
| Sedgemore Ben (M) | 6 0 | 12 07 | Wolverhampton | 5 8 75 | Macclesfield T |
| Smith Paul (M) | 5 11 | 11 07 | Hastings | 25 1 76 | Nottingham F |
| Thorpe Lee (F) | 6 0 | 11 06 | Wolverhampton | 14 12 75 | Blackpool |
| Walker Justin (M) | 6 0 | 13 03 | Nottingham | 6 9 75 | Scunthorpe U |

**League Appearances:** Barnett, J. 27(6); Battersby, T. 24(11); Bimson, S. 17(3); Black, K. 5; Brown, G. 20; Bullock, T. 2; Cameron, D. 10(6); Camm, M. 3; Carr, D. 3; Day, C. 14; Dudfield, L. 2(1); Dudgeon, J. 20(2); Eustace, S. (1); Finnigan, J. 40; Gain, P. 19(5); Garratt, M. 2; Ghent, M. (1); Gordon, G. 18; Grant, G. 3; Henry, A. 1; Holmes, S. 37(1); Lewis, G. (2); Logan, R. 4(1); Marriott, A. 30; Mayo, P. 26(1); Miller, P. 10(9); Peacock, R. 22(12); Perkins, C. 11(1); Schofield, J. 13(6); Sedgemore, B. 3(7); Smith, P. 35(5); Stergiopoulos, M. 2(5); Thorpe, L. 29(2); Walker, J. 44(1); Welsh, S. 10(1).
**Goals – League** (58): Holmes 11 (5 pens), Gordon 9, Smith 7, Thorpe 7, Battersby 6, Gain 5, Dudgeon 3, Peacock 3, Brown 2, Cameron 2, Barnett J 1, Sedgemore 1, Walker 1.
**Worthington Cup** (2): Smith 1, Stergiopoulos 1.
**FA Cup** (4): Gain 1, Gordon 1, Peacock 1, own goal 1.
**Ground:** Sincil Bank, Lincoln LN5 8LD. Telephone (01522) 880011.
**Record attendance:** 23,196 v Derby Co, League Cup 4th rd, 15 November 1967.
**Capacity:** 10,147.
**Manager:** Alan Buckley.
**Secretary:** F. J. Martin.
**Most League Goals:** 121, Division 3 (N), 1951–52.
**Highest League Scorer in Season:** Allan Hall, 42, Division 3 (N), 1931–32.

**Most League Goals in Total Aggregate:** Andy Graver, 144, 1950–55 and 1958–61.
**Most Capped Player:** David Pugh, 3 (7), Wales; George Moulson, 3, Republic of Ireland.
**Most League Appearances:** Tony Emery, 402, 1946–59.
**Honours – Football League:** Division 3 (N) Champions – 1931–32, 1947–48, 1951–52. Division 4 Champions – 1975–76.
**Colours:** Red and white striped shirts, red shorts and stockings.

---

# LIVERPOOL                                      FA PREMIERSHIP

| | | | | | | |
|---|---|---|---|---|---|---|
| Arphexad Pegguy (G) | 6 2 | 13 07 | Abymes | 18 | 5 73 | Leicester C |
| Babbel Markus (D) | 6 0 | 13 03 | Munich | 8 | 9 72 | Bayern Munich |
| Barmby Nick (M) | 5 6 | 11 04 | Hull | 11 | 2 74 | Everton |
| Berger Patrik (M) | 6 1 | 13 00 | Prague | 10 | 11 73 | Borussia Dortmund |
| Biscan Igor (M) | 6 3 | 12 08 | Zagreb | 4 | 5 78 | Dinamo Zagreb |
| Carragher Jamie (M) | 6 1 | 12 05 | Liverpool | 28 | 1 78 | Trainee |
| Diomede Bernard (M) | 5 9 | 12 04 | Bourges | 23 | 1 74 | Auxerre |
| Foley-Sheridan Michael (M) | | | Dublin | 9 | 3 83 | |
| Fowler Robbie (F) | 5 11 | 11 12 | Liverpool | 9 | 4 75 | Trainee |
| Gerrard Steven (M) | 6 1 | 12 03 | Whiston | 30 | 5 80 | Trainee |
| Hamann Dietmar (M) | 6 2 | 12 01 | Waldasson | 27 | 8 73 | Newcastle U |
| Heggem Vegard (D) | 5 11 | 12 04 | Trondheim | 13 | 7 75 | Rosenborg |
| Henchoz Stephane (D) | 6 1 | 12 13 | Billens | 7 | 9 74 | Blackburn R |
| Heskey Emile (F) | 6 1 | 14 04 | Leicester | 11 | 1 78 | Leicester C |
| Hyypia Sami (D) | 6 4 | 13 11 | Porvoo | 7 | 10 73 | Willem II |
| Kippe Frode (D) | 6 4 | 14 02 | Oslo | 17 | 1 78 | Lillestrom |
| Litmanen Jari (F) | 6 0 | 12 10 | Lahti | 20 | 2 71 | Barcelona |
| McAllister Gary (M) | 6 1 | 11 11 | Motherwell | 25 | 12 64 | Coventry C |
| Miles John (F) | | | Fazackerley | 28 | 9 81 | Trainee |
| Murphy Danny (M) | 5 9 | 12 08 | Chester | 18 | 3 77 | Crewe Alex |
| Navarro Alan (M) | 5 10 | 11 07 | Liverpool | 31 | 5 81 | Trainee |
| Nielsen Jorgen (G) | 6 0 | 12 11 | Nykobing | 6 | 5 71 | Hvidovre |
| O'Brien Chris (M) | | | Liverpool | 13 | 1 82 | Trainee |
| Otsemobor John (D) | | | Liverpool | 23 | 3 83 | Trainee |
| Owen Michael (F) | 5 8 | 10 13 | Chester | 14 | 12 79 | Trainee |
| Partridge Richie (M) | 5 8 | 10 07 | Dublin | 12 | 9 80 | Trainee |
| Redknapp Jamie (M) | 6 0 | 13 04 | Barton-on-Sea | 25 | 6 73 | Bournemouth |
| Sjolund Danny (F) | 5 11 | 12 00 | Mariehamn | 22 | 4 83 | West Ham U |
| Smicer Vladimir (M) | 5 10 | 12 02 | Degin | 24 | 5 73 | Lens |
| Traore Djimi (D) | 6 1 | 12 06 | Saint-Ouen | 1 | 3 80 | Laval |
| Vignal Gregory (D) | 5 11 | 12 03 | Montpellier | 19 | 7 81 | |
| Warnock Stephen (M) | | | Ormskirk | 12 | 12 81 | Trainee |
| Welsh John (D) | | | Liverpool | 10 | 1 84 | Scholar |
| Westerveld Sander (G) | 6 4 | 13 08 | Enschede | 23 | 10 74 | Vitesse |
| Wright Stephen (M) | 6 0 | 11 11 | Liverpool | 8 | 2 80 | Trainee |
| Ziege Christian (D) | 6 1 | 12 04 | Berlin | 1 | 2 72 | Middlesbrough |

**League Appearances:** Babbel, M. 38; Barmby, N. 21(5); Berger, P. 11(3); Biscan, I. 8(5); Carragher, J. 30(4); Diomede, B. 1(1); Fowler, R. 15(12); Gerrard, S. 29(4); Hamann, D. 26(4); Heggem, V. 1(2); Henchoz, S. 32; Heskey, E. 33(3); Hyypia, S. 35; Litmanen, J. 4(1); McAllister, G. 21(9); Meijer, E. (3); Murphy, D. 13(14); Owen, M. 20(8); Smicer, V. 16(11); Song, R. 3; Staunton, S. 1; Traore, D. 8; Vignal, G. 4(2); Westerveld, S. 38; Wright, S. (2); Ziege, C. 11(5).
**Goals – League** (71): Owen 16, Heskey 14, Fowler 8, Gerrard 7, McAllister 5

66

(1 pen), Murphy 4, Babbel 3, Hyypia 3, Barmby 2, Berger 2 (1 pen), Hamann 2, Smicer 2, Litmanen 1 (pen), Ziege 1, own goal 1.
**Worthington Cup** (20): Fowler 6 (1 pen), Murphy 4, Smicer 4, Babbel 1, Barmby 1, Biscan 1, Hyypia 1, Owen 1, Ziege 1.
**FA Cup** (17): Heskey 5, Owen 3, Fowler 2 (1 pen), Babbel 1, Barmby 1, Gerrard 1, Hamann 1, Litmanen 1 (pen), Murphy 1, Smicer 1 (pen).
**Ground:** Anfield Road, Liverpool L4 0TH. Telephone (0151) 263 2361.
**Record attendance:** 61,905 v Wolverhampton W, FA Cup 4th rd, 2 February 1952.
**Capacity:** 45,362.
**Manager:** Gerard Houllier.
**Secretary:** Bryce Morrison.
**Most League Goals:** 106, Division 2, 1895–96.
**Highest League Scorer in Season:** Roger Hunt, 41, Division 2, 1961–62.
**Most League Goals in Total Aggregate:** Roger Hunt, 245, 1959–69.
**Most Capped Player:** Ian Rush, 67 (73), Wales.
**Most League Appearances:** Ian Callaghan, 640, 1960–78.
**Honours – Football League:** Division 1 – Champions 1900–01, 1905–06, 1921–22, 1922–23, 1946–47, 1963–64, 1965–66, 1972–73, 1975–76, 1976–77, 1978–79, 1979–80, 1981–82, 1982–83, 1983–84, 1985–86, 1987–88, 1989–90 (Liverpool have a record number of 18 League Championship wins). Division 2 Champions – 1893–94, 1895–96, 1904–05, 1961–62. **FA Cup:** Winners 1965, 1974, 1986, 1989, 1992, 2001.
**League Cup:** Winners 1981, 1982, 1983, 1984, 1995, 2001. Super Cup: Winners 1985–86. **European Competitions: European Cup winners:** 1976–77, 1977–78, 1980–81, 1983–84. **UEFA Cup winners:** 1972–73, 1975–76, 2001. **Super Cup winners:** 1977.
**Colours:** All red.

# LUTON TOWN                                                DIV. 3

| | | | | | |
|---|---|---|---|---|---|
| Boyce Emmerson (D) | 5 11 | 11 02 | Aylesbury | 24 9 79 | Trainee |
| Brennan Dean (M) | 5 9 | 11 08 | Dublin | 17 6 80 | Sheffield W |
| Bruce Joseph (M) | | | London | 5 7 83 | |
| Douglas Stuart (F) | 5 8 | 11 05 | London | 9 4 78 | Trainee |
| Dryden Richard (D) | 6 0 | 13 10 | Stroud | 14 6 69 | Southampton |
| Fotiadis Andrew (F) | 5 11 | 11 07 | Hitchin | 6 9 77 | School |
| Fraser Stuart (D) | 5 9 | 10 06 | Edinburgh | 9 1 80 | Trainee |
| George Liam (F) | 5 11 | 11 04 | Luton | 2 2 79 | Trainee |
| Helin Petri (D) | 5 10 | 13 00 | Helsinki | 13 12 69 | Jokerit |
| Holmes Peter (M) | 5 10 | 10 00 | Bishop Auckland | 18 11 80 | Sheffield W |
| Howard Steve (M) | 6 3 | 14 06 | Durham | 10 5 76 | Northampton T |
| Johnson Marvin (D) | 6 1 | 13 00 | Wembley | 29 10 68 | Apprentice |
| Karlsen Kent (D) | 6 2 | 13 00 | Norway | 17 2 73 | Haugesund |
| Locke Adam (M) | 5 11 | 12 07 | Croydon | 20 8 70 | Bristol C |
| Mansell Lee (M) | | | Gloucester | 23 9 82 | Scholar |
| Murphy Daryl (M) | | | Ireland | 15 3 83 | |
| Ovendale Mark (G) | 6 2 | 13 10 | Leicester | 22 11 73 | Bournemouth |
| Spring Matthew (M) | 5 11 | 11 07 | Harlow | 17 11 79 | Trainee |
| Standen Dean (M) | 5 10 | 11 00 | Lewisham | 23 3 82 | Welling U |
| Stirling Jude (D) | 6 2 | 11 12 | Enfield | 29 6 82 | Trainee |
| Taylor Matthew (D) | 5 10 | 11 08 | Oxford | 27 11 81 | Trainee |
| Thomson Peter (F) | 6 3 | 13 04 | Crumpsall | 30 6 77 | NAC Breda |
| Ward Scott (G) | 6 2 | 13 00 | Brent | 5 10 81 | Trainee |

**League Appearances:** Abbey, N. 20; Baptiste, R. (3); Boyce, E. 42; Breitenfelder, F. 2(3); Brennan, D. 2(7); Douglas, S. 15(6); Dryden, R. 20; Fotiadis, A. 12(10); Fraser, S. 10(5); George, L. 37(6); Helin, P. 23; Holmes, P. 12(6); Howard, S. 12; Johnson,

M. 9; Kandol, T. 6(7); Karlsen, K. 4(2); Locke, A. 17(8); Mansell, L. 17(1); McGowan, G. 5(1); McLaren, P. 35; Nogan, L. 7; Ovendale, M. 26; Rowland, K. 12; Scarlett, A. 5(4); Shepherd, P. 7; Spring, M. 41; Stein, M. 19(11); Stirling, J. 5(4); Taylor, M. 45; Thomson, P. 4(7); Ward, S. (1); Watts, J. 26(2); Whitbread, A. 9.
**Goals – League** (52): George 7, Mansell 5, Douglas 4, Spring 4 (2 pens), Watts 4, Boyce 3, Fotiadis 3, Howard 3 (1 pen), Kandol 3, Stein 3, Locke 2, McLaren 2, Rowland 2, Thomson 2, Helin 1, Holmes 1, Nogan 1, Taylor 1, own goal 1.
**Worthington Cup** (3): Kandol 1, Scarlett 1, Stein 1.
**FA Cup** (7): George 2, Douglas 1, Fotiadis 1, McLaren 1, Mansell 1, Nogan 1.
**Ground:** Kenilworth Road Stadium, 1 Maple Rd, Luton, Beds. LU4 8AW. Telephone (01582) 411622.
**Record attendance:** 30,069 v Blackpool, FA Cup 6th rd replay, 4 March 1959.
**Capacity:** 9975.
**Manager:** Joe Kinnear.
**Secretary:** Cherry Newbery.
**Most League Goals:** 103, Division 3 (S), 1936–37.
**Highest League Scorer in Season:** Joe Payne, 55, Division 3 (S), 1936–37.
**Most League Goals in Total Aggregate:** Gordon Turner, 243, 1949–64.
**Most Capped Player:** Mal Donaghy, 58 (91), Northern Ireland.
**Most League Appearances:** Bob Morton, 494, 1948–64.
**Honours – Football League:** Division 2 Champions – 1981–82. Division 4 Champions – 1967–68. Division 3 (S) Champions – 1936–37. **Football League Cup winners** 1987–88.
**Colours:** White shirts with orange and black trim, black shorts with orange and white trim, black stockings with two white hoops.

## MACCLESFIELD TOWN                          DIV. 3

| | | | | | |
|---|---|---|---|---|---|
| Abbey George (D) | 5 8 | 10 08 | Port Harcourt | 20 10 78 | Sharks |
| Adams Daniel (D) | | | Manchester | 3 1 76 | Altrincham |
| Bamber Michael (D) | 5 7 | 10 02 | Preston | 1 10 80 | Blackpool |
| Came Shaun (D) | 6 3 | 13 00 | Crewe | 15 6 83 | Trainee |
| Glover Lee (F) | 5 11 | 11 09 | Kettering | 24 4 70 | Rotherham U |
| Hitchen Steve (D) | 5 8 | 11 07 | Salford | 28 11 76 | Blackburn R |
| Keen Kevin (M) | 5 6 | 10 10 | Amersham | 25 2 67 | Stoke C |
| Martin Lee (G) | 6 0 | 13 07 | Huddersfield | 9 9 68 | Halifax T |
| Munroe Karl (M) | 6 0 | 10 08 | Manchester | 23 9 79 | Swansea C |
| O'Neill Paul (D) | 5 11 | 11 02 | Bolton | 17 6 82 | Trainee |
| Priest Chris (M) | 5 10 | 12 00 | Leigh | 18 10 73 | Chester C |
| Tinson Darren (D) | 6 0 | 13 07 | Birmingham | 15 11 69 | Northwich V |
| Tracey Richard (F) | 5 11 | 12 04 | Muirfield | 9 7 79 | Carlisle U |
| Whitehead Damien (F) | 5 10 | 12 00 | Whiston | 24 4 79 | Warrington T |
| Whittaker Dan (M) | 5 10 | 11 00 | Manchester | 14 11 80 | |
| Woolley Matt (M) | | | Manchester | 22 2 82 | |

**League Appearances:** Abbey, G. 13(5); Adams, D. 36(1); Askey, J. 29(8); Bamber, M. 2(3); Barker, R. 23; Bettney, C. (2); Bullock, T. 24; Came, S. 3(4); Collins, S. 15(2); Connell, D. (1); Durkan, K. 26(5); Glover, L. 29(8); Hitchen, S. 37; Ingram, R. 32(1); Keen, K. 30(2); Lambert, R. 4(5); Martin, L. 21; Munroe, K. 19(4); O'Neill, P. 5(7); Priest, C. 14(1); Rioch, G. 16(1); Sedgemore, B. 23(4); Shuker, C. 6(3); Tereskinas, A. (1); Tinson, D. 45; Tracey, R. 11(2); Twynham, G. 5(4); Whitehead, D. 9(24); Wilson, S. 1; Wood, S. 27(3); Woolley, M. 1(1).
**Goals – League** (51): Glover 8 (2 pens), Whitehead 8, Barker 7, Durkan 4 (1 pen), Priest 4, Askey 3, Sedgemore 3, Tinson 3, Tracey 3, Keen 2, Ingram 1, Munroe 1, Rioch 1, Shuker 1, Wood 1, own goal 1.

**Worthington Cup** (5): Barker 2, Sedgemore 2 (1 pen), Munroe 1.
**FA Cup** (0).
**Ground:** The Moss Rose Ground, London Road, Macclesfield, Cheshire SK11 7SP.
Telephone: (01625) 264686.
**Record attendance:** 9008 v Winsford U, Cheshire Senior Cup 2nd rd, 4 February
1948. **Capacity:** 6028 (seated 1053, standing 4975).
**Manager:** Gil Prescott.
**Secretary:** Colin Garlick.
**Most League Goals:** 66, Division 3, 1999–2000.
**Highest League Scorer in Season:** Richard Barker, 16, Division 3, 1999–2000.
**Most League Goals in Total Aggregate:** John Askey, 25, 1997–2000.
**Most League Appearances:** Darren Tinson, 127, 1997–2000.
**Honours** – Nil.
**Colours:** Royal blue shirts, white shorts, blue stockings.

---

# MANCHESTER CITY                                              DIV. 1

---

| Player | | | Birthplace | | | Previous club |
|---|---|---|---|---|---|---|
| Almond James (F) | | | Northallerton | 5 10 | 83 | Scholar |
| Browne Gary (F) | | | Ireland | 17 1 | 83 | Scholar |
| Charvet Laurent (D) | 5 11 | 12 03 | Beziers | 8 5 | 73 | Newcastle U |
| Cooke Terry (M) | 5 7 | 10 08 | Marston Green | 5 8 | 76 | Manchester U |
| Day Rhys (D) | 6 2 | 13 00 | Bridgend | 31 8 | 82 | Scholar |
| Dickov Paul (F) | 5 6 | 10 10 | Glasgow | 1 11 | 72 | Arsenal |
| Dunfield Terry (M) | 5 10 | 11 03 | Canada | 20 2 | 82 | Trainee |
| Dunne Richard (D) | 6 2 | 14 06 | Dublin | 21 9 | 79 | Everton |
| Edghill Richard (D) | 5 9 | 12 03 | Oldham | 23 9 | 74 | Trainee |
| Elliott Stephen (F) | | | Dublin | 6 1 | 84 | School |
| Etuhu Dixon (M) | 6 2 | 13 00 | Kano | 8 6 | 82 | Scholar |
| Goater Shaun (F) | 6 0 | 13 00 | Bermuda | 25 2 | 70 | Bristol C |
| Grant Tony (M) | 5 10 | 10 10 | Liverpool | 14 11 | 74 | Everton |
| Granville Danny (D) | 6 2 | 12 13 | Islington | 19 1 | 75 | Leeds U |
| Haaland Alf-Inge (D) | 6 1 | 12 06 | Bryne | 23 11 | 72 | Leeds U |
| Hogan Barry (M) | | | Whiston | 15 2 | 83 | Scholar |
| Holmes Shaun (D) | 5 9 | 11 03 | Derry | 27 12 | 80 | Trainee |
| Horlock Kevin (M) | 5 11 | 12 06 | Erith | 1 11 | 72 | Swindon T |
| Howey Steve (D) | 6 1 | 13 10 | Sunderland | 26 10 | 71 | Newcastle U |
| Huckerby Darren (F) | 5 11 | 11 04 | Nottingham | 23 4 | 76 | Leeds U |
| Jordan Stephen (D) | 6 0 | 11 05 | Warrington | 6 3 | 82 | Scholar |
| Joyce Damien (M) | | | Dublin | 8 3 | 83 | Scholar |
| Kennedy Mark (M) | 6 1 | 12 09 | Dublin | 15 5 | 76 | Wimbledon |
| Killen Chris (F) | 6 0 | 11 03 | Wellington | 8 10 | 81 | Miramar R |
| McCarthy Patrick (D) | | | Dublin | 31 5 | 83 | Scholar |
| McDowall Ryan (M) | | | Knowsley | 30 3 | 84 | School |
| Mears Tyrone (D) | | | Stockport | 18 2 | 83 | |
| Mike Leon (F) | 5 10 | 13 02 | Manchester | 4 9 | 81 | Scholar |
| Morrison Andy (D) | 5 11 | 12 12 | Inverness | 30 7 | 70 | Huddersfield T |
| Murphy Brian (M) | | | Waterford | 7 5 | 83 | |
| Nash Carlo (G) | 6 5 | 14 01 | Bolton | 13 9 | 73 | Stockport Co |
| Paisley Stephen (D) | | | Dublin | 28 7 | 83 | Scholar |
| Prior Spencer (D) | 6 3 | 13 09 | Rochford | 22 4 | 71 | Derby Co |
| Ritchie Paul (D) | 5 11 | 12 06 | Kirkcaldy | 21 8 | 75 | Bolton W |
| Shuker Chris (F) | 5 4 | 9 08 | Liverpool | 9 5 | 82 | Scholar |
| Tiatto Danny (D) | 5 7 | 11 03 | Melbourne | 22 5 | 73 | Stoke C |
| Tunnicliffe Andrew (M) | | | Stockport | 25 5 | 83 | Scholar |
| Wanchope Paulo (F) | 6 3 | 13 08 | Heredia | 31 7 | 76 | West Ham U |
| Weaver Nick (G) | 6 4 | 14 10 | Sheffield | 2 3 | 79 | Mansfield T |

| Whelan Glenn (M) | | | Dublin | 13 1 84 | Scholar |
|---|---|---|---|---|---|
| Whitley Jeff (M) | 5 8 | 10 05 | Zambia | 28 1 79 | Trainee |
| Wiekens Gerard (D) | 6 0 | 13 04 | Tolhuiswyk | 25 2 73 | |
| Wright-Phillips Shaun (F) | 5 4 | 9 08 | London | 25 10 81 | |

**League Appearances:** Allsopp, D. (1); Bishop, I. 3(7); Charvet, L. 16(4); Crooks, L. (2); Dickov, P. 15(6); Dunfield, T. (1); Dunne, R. 24(1); Edghill, R. 6; Goater, S. 20(6); Grant, T. 5(5); Granville, D. 16(3); Haaland, A. 35; Horlock, K. 14; Howey, S. 36; Huckerby, D. 8(5); Kanchelskis, A. 7(3); Kennedy, M. 15(10); Morrison, A. 3; Nash, C. 6; Ostenstad, E. 1(3); Prior, S. 18(3); Ritchie, P. 11(1); Tiatto, D. 31(2); Wanchope, P. 25(2); Weah, G. 5(2); Weaver, N. 31; Whitley, J. 28(3); Wiekens, G. 29(5); Wright, T. 1; Wright-Phillips, S. 9(6).

**Goals – League** (41): Wanchope 9, Goater 6, Howey 6, Dickov 4, Haaland 3, Horlock 2 (1 pen), Tiatto 2, Wiekens 2, Huckerby 1 (pen), Prior 1, Weah 1, Whitley 1, own goals 3.

**Worthington Cup** (9): Weah 3, Dickov 1, Goater 1, Horlock 1 (pen), Kennedy 1, Wanchope 1.

**FA Cup** (6): Goater 3 (1 pen), Huckerby 1, Kanchelskis 1, Morrison 1.

**Ground:** Maine Road, Moss Side, Manchester M14 7WN. Telephone (0161) 232 3000.

**Record attendance:** 84,569 v Stoke C, FA Cup 6th rd, 3 March 1934 (British record for any game outside London or Glasgow). **Capacity:** 31,458.

**Manager:** Kevin Keegan.

**General Secretary:** J. B. Halford.

**Most League Goals:** 108, Division 2, 1926–27.

**Highest League Scorer in Season:** Tommy Johnson, 38, Division 1, 1928–29.

**Most League Goals in Total Aggregate:** Tommy Johnson, 158, 1919–30.

**Most Capped Player:** Colin Bell, 48, England.

**Most League Appearances:** Alan Oakes, 565, 1959–76.

**Honours – Football League:** Division 1 Champions – 1936–37, 1967–68. Division 2 Champions – 1898–99, 1902–03, 1909–10, 1927–28, 1946–47, 1965–66. **FA Cup winners** 1904, 1934, 1956, 1969. **Football League Cup winners** 1970, 1976. **European Competitions:** European Cup-Winners' Cup winners: 1969–70.

**Colours:** Lazer blue shirts, white shorts, navy stockings.

## MANCHESTER UNITED                    FA PREMIERSHIP

| Barthez Fabien (G) | 5 11 | 12 08 | Lavelanet | 28 6 71 | Monaco |
|---|---|---|---|---|---|
| Baxter Nick (G) | 6 3 | 13 10 | Bridlington | 25 3 83 | Scholar |
| Beckham David (M) | 6 0 | 11 13 | Leytonstone | 2 5 75 | Trainee |
| Brown Wes (D) | 6 1 | 13 11 | Manchester | 13 10 79 | Trainee |
| Butt Nicky (M) | 5 10 | 11 11 | Manchester | 21 1 75 | Trainee |
| Chadwick Luke (F) | 5 11 | 11 08 | Cambridge | 18 11 80 | Trainee |
| Clegg Michael (D) | 5 8 | 11 10 | Ashton-under-Lyne | 3 7 77 | Trainee |
| Clegg Steven (D) | 5 9 | 12 08 | Ashton-under-Lyne | 16 4 82 | Scholar |
| Coates Craig (F) | 5 7 | 10 11 | Dryburn | 26 10 82 | Trainee |
| Cole Andy (F) | 5 11 | 12 02 | Nottingham | 15 10 71 | Newcastle U |
| Culkin Nick (G) | 6 2 | 13 09 | York | 6 7 78 | York C |
| Davis Jimmy (F) | 5 8 | 11 05 | Bromsgrove | 6 2 82 | Trainee |
| Djordjic Bojan (F) | 5 10 | 11 01 | Belgrade | 6 2 82 | |
| Fletcher Darren (M) | 6 0 | 13 01 | Edinburgh | 1 2 84 | Scholar |
| Fortune Quinton (F) | 5 9 | 11 09 | Cape Town | 21 5 77 | Atletico Madrid |
| Fox David (M) | 5 9 | 12 02 | Stoke | 13 12 83 | Scholar |
| Giggs Ryan (F) | 5 11 | 11 00 | Cardiff | 29 11 73 | School |
| Greening Jonathan (F) | 6 0 | 11 13 | Scarborough | 2 1 79 | York C |
| Heath Colin (F) | 6 0 | 13 01 | Chesterfield | 31 12 83 | Scholar |

| Name | Ht | | Birthplace | DOB | Previous club |
|---|---|---|---|---|---|
| Hilton Kirk (D) | 5 7 | 10 01 | Flixton | 2 4 81 | Trainee |
| Johnsen Ronny (D) | 6 3 | 13 06 | Sandefjord | 10 6 69 | Besiktas |
| Jowsey James (G) | 6 0 | 12 04 | Scarborough | 24 11 83 | Scholar |
| Keane Roy (M) | 5 11 | 11 10 | Cork | 10 8 71 | Nottingham F |
| Lynch Mark (D) | 5 11 | 11 03 | Manchester | 2 9 81 | Trainee |
| May David (D) | 6 0 | 13 05 | Oldham | 24 6 70 | Blackburn R |
| McDermott Alan (D) | 6 1 | 11 07 | Dublin | 22 1 82 | Trainee |
| Mooniaruck Kalam (F) | 5 8 | 11 09 | Yeovil | 22 11 83 | Scholar |
| Moran David (G) | 6 0 | 14 05 | Ballinasloe | 16 4 82 | Scholar |
| Muirhead Ben (F) | 5 9 | 10 05 | Doncaster | 5 1 83 | Trainee |
| Nardiello Daniel (F) | 5 11 | 11 04 | Coventry | 22 10 82 | Trainee |
| Neville Gary (D) | 5 11 | 12 04 | Bury | 18 2 75 | Trainee |
| Neville Phil (D) | 5 11 | 12 00 | Bury | 21 1 77 | Trainee |
| O'Shea John (D) | 6 3 | 12 10 | Waterford | 30 4 81 | Waterford |
| Pugh Danny (M) | 6 0 | 12 10 | Manchester | 19 10 82 | Scholar |
| Rachubka Paul (G) | 6 1 | 13 01 | San Luis Opispo | 21 5 81 | Trainee |
| Rankin John (M) | 5 8 | 12 08 | Bellshill | 27 6 83 | Scholar |
| Roche Lee (D) | 5 10 | 10 10 | Bolton | 28 10 80 | Trainee |
| Sampson Gary (M) | 5 9 | 11 02 | Manchester | 13 9 82 | Scholar |
| Scholes Paul (M) | 5 7 | 11 00 | Salford | 16 11 74 | Trainee |
| Silvestre Mikael (D) | 6 0 | 13 01 | Chambray les Tours | 9 8 77 | Internazionale |
| Solskjaer Ole Gunnar (F) | 5 10 | 11 11 | Kristiansund | 26 2 73 | Molde |
| Stam Jaap (D) | 6 3 | 15 00 | Kampen | 17 7 72 | PSV Eindhoven |
| Stewart Michael (M) | 5 11 | 11 11 | Edinburgh | 26 2 81 | Trainee |
| Tate Alan (D) | 6 1 | 13 05 | Easington | 2 9 82 | Scholar |
| Taylor Andrew (M) | 5 9 | 12 10 | Exeter | 17 9 82 | Scholar |
| Taylor Kris (M) | 5 9 | 13 05 | Stafford | 12 1 84 | Scholar |
| Tierney Paul (M) | 5 10 | 12 10 | Salford | 15 9 82 | Scholar |
| Wallwork Ronnie (D) | 5 10 | 13 01 | Manchester | 10 9 77 | Trainee |
| Webber Danny (F) | 5 9 | 10 08 | Manchester | 28 12 81 | Trainee |
| Whiteman Marc (F) | 5 10 | 13 12 | St Hellier | 1 10 82 | Scholar |
| Williams Matthew (F) | 5 8 | 9 11 | St Asaph | 5 11 82 | |
| Wilson Mark (M) | 6 0 | 12 07 | Scunthorpe | 9 2 79 | Trainee |
| Wood Neil (F) | 5 10 | 13 02 | Manchester | 4 1 83 | Trainee |
| Yorke Dwight (F) | 5 10 | 12 03 | Canaan | 3 11 71 | Aston Villa |

**League Appearances:** Barthez, F. 30; Beckham, D. 29(2); Berg, H. (1); Brown, W. 25(3); Butt, N. 24(4); Chadwick, L. 6(10); Cole, A. 15(4); Djordjic, B. (1); Fortune, Q. 6(1); Giggs, R. 24(7); Goram, A. 2; Greening, J. 3(4); Healy, D. (1); Irwin, D. 20(1); Johnsen, R. 11; Keane, R. 28; May, D. 1(1); Neville, G. 32; Neville, P. 24(5); Rachubka, P. 1; Scholes, P. 28(4); Sheringham, T. 23(6); Silvestre, M. 25(5); Solskjaer, O. 19(12); Stam, J. 15; Stewart, M. 3; Van der Gouw, R. 5(5); Wallwork, R. 4(8); Yorke, D. 15(7).

**Goals – League** (79): Sheringham 15 (1 pen), Solskjaer 10, Beckham 9 (1 pen), Cole 9, Yorke 9, Scholes 6, Giggs 5, Butt 3, Chadwick 2, Fortune 2, Keane 2, Johnsen 1, Neville G 1, Neville P 1, Silvestre 1, own goals 3.

**Worthington Cup** (4): Solskjaer 2, Yorke 2.

**FA Cup** (2): Sheringham 1, Solskjaer 1.

**Ground:** Old Trafford, Sir Matt Busby Way, Manchester M16 0RA. Telephone (0161) 868 8000.

**Record attendance:** 76,962 Wolverhampton W v Grimsby T, FA Cup semi-final. 25 March 1939. **Capacity:** 68,174.

**Manager:** Sir Alex Ferguson CBE.

**Secretary:** Kenneth Merrett.

**Most League Goals:** 103, Division 1, 1956–57 and 1958–59.

**Highest League Scorer in Season:** Dennis Viollet, 32, 1959–60.

**Most League Goals in Total Aggregate:** Bobby Charlton, 199, 1956–73.

**Most Capped Player:** Bobby Charlton, 106, England.
**Most League Appearances:** Bobby Charlton, 606, 1956–73.
**Honours – FA Premier League:** Champions – 1992–93, 1993–94, 1995–96, 1996–97, 1998–99, 1999–2000, 2000–01. **Football League:** Division 1 Champions – 1907–8, 1910–11, 1951–52, 1955–56, 1956–57, 1964–65, 1966–67. Division 2 Champions – 1935–36, 1974–75. **FA Cup winners** 1909, 1948, 1963, 1977, 1983, 1985, 1990, 1994, 1996, 1999. **Football League Cup winners** 1991–92. **European Competitions: European Cup winners:** 1967–68, 1998–99. **European Cup-Winners' Cup winners:** 1990–91. **Super Cup winners:** 1991. **Inter-Continental Cup winners:** 1999.
**Colours:** Red shirts, white shorts, black stockings.

---

# MANSFIELD TOWN                                        DIV. 3

---

| | | | | | | |
|---|---|---|---|---|---|---|
| Andrews John (D) | 6 1 | 12 08 | Cork | 27 9 78 | Coventry C |
| Asher Alistair (D) | 5 11 | 11 07 | Leicester | 14 10 80 | Trainee |
| Bacon Danny (F) | 5 10 | 10 12 | Mansfield | 20 9 80 | Trainee |
| Barrett Adam (M) | 5 10 | 12 00 | Dagenham | 29 11 79 | Plymouth Arg |
| Bradley Shayne (F) | 5 11 | 13 13 | Gloucester | 8 12 79 | Southampton |
| Clarke Darrell (M) | 5 10 | 11 06 | Mansfield | 16 12 77 | Trainee |
| Corden Wayne (M) | 5 10 | 11 05 | Leek | 1 11 75 | Port Vale |
| Disley Craig (M) | 5 10 | 10 12 | Worksop | 24 8 81 | Trainee |
| Greenacre Chris (F) | 5 11 | 10 06 | Halifax | 23 12 77 | Manchester C |
| Hassell Bobby (D) | 5 9 | 12 04 | Derby | 4 6 80 | Trainee |
| Hicks Stuart (D) | 6 1 | 13 03 | Peterborough | 30 5 67 | Chester C |
| Jervis David (D) | 5 8 | 10 08 | Worksop | 18 1 82 | Trainee |
| Lawrence Liam (M) | 5 10 | 11 03 | Retford | 14 12 81 | Trainee |
| Pilkington Kevin (G) | 6 1 | 13 00 | Hitchin | 8 3 74 | Wigan Ath |
| Robinson Les (D) | 5 9 | 12 02 | Shirebrook | 1 3 67 | Oxford U |
| Sisson Michael (M) | 5 10 | 11 05 | Sutton-in-Ashfield | 24 11 78 | Trainee |
| White Andy (F) | | | Derby | 6 11 81 | Hucknall T |
| Williams Lee (D) | 5 7 | 11 08 | Edgbaston | 3 2 73 | Tranmere R |
| Williamson Lee (M) | 5 10 | 10 04 | Derby | 7 6 82 | Trainee |

**League Appearances:** Andrews, J. 5(3); Asher, A. 23(5); Bacon, D. 7(15); Barrett, A. 8; Blake, M. 38(3); Boulding, M. 12(21); Bowling, I. 4; Bradley, S. 21(5); Clarke, D. 30(2); Corden, W. 31(3); Disley, C. 16(8); Fortune, J. 14; Greenacre, C. 46; Hassell, B. 39(1); Hicks, S. 25; Jervis, D. 17(5); Lawrence, L. 7(11); Lomas, J. 4(2); Mimms, B. 40; Pemberton, M. 16(2); Pilkington, K. 2; Reddington, S. 9; Robinson, L. 44; Sisson, M. 2(2); White, A. (4); Williams, L. 36(5); Williamson, L. 10(5).
**Goals – League** (64): Greenacre 19 (2 pens), Blake 8, Bradley 7, Boulding 6, Clarke 6, Lawrence 4, Williams 4, Corden 3, Bacon 1, Barrett 1, Hassell 1, Pemberton 1, own goals 3.
**Worthington Cup** (4): Corden 2, Clarke 1, Greenacre 1.
**FA Cup** (1): Greenacre 1 (pen).
**Ground:** Field Mill Ground, Quarry Lane, Mansfield NG18 5DA. Telephone (01623) 482482.
**Record attendance:** 24,467 v Nottingham F, FA Cup 3rd rd, 10 January 1953.
**Capacity:** 9990.
**Manager:** Bill Dearden.
**Secretary:** Christine Reynolds.
**Most League Goals:** 108, Division 4, 1962–63.
**Highest League Scorer in Season:** Ted Harston, 55, Division 3 (N), 1936–37.
**Most League Goals in Total Aggregate:** Harry Johnson, 104, 1931–36.
**Most Capped Player:** John McClelland, 6 (53), Northern Ireland.
**Most League Appearances:** Rod Arnold, 440, 1970–83.
**Honours – Football League:** Division 3 Champions – 1976–77. Division 4

Champions – 1974–75. **Freight Rover Trophy winners** 1986–87.
**Colours:** Amber & royal blue shirts, royal blue shorts with amber trim, amber stockings with blue trim.

---

# MIDDLESBROUGH                    FA PREMIERSHIP

| Player | Ht | Wt | Birthplace | DOB | Previous |
|---|---|---|---|---|---|
| Baker Steve (D) | 6 0 | 12 04 | Pontefract | 8 9 78 | Trainee |
| Bennion Chris (G) | 6 2 | 12 00 | Edinburgh | 30 8 80 | Trainee |
| Beresford Marlon (G) | 6 1 | 13 00 | Lincoln | 2 9 69 | Burnley |
| Bernhardt Arturo (F) | 6 1 | 12 02 | Santa Catarina | 27 8 82 | Nova Hamburgo |
| Boksic Alen (F) | 6 1 | 14 01 | Niakarska | 21 1 70 | Lazio |
| Brackstone Stephen (M) | 5 11 | 10 08 | Hartlepool | 19 9 82 | Scholar |
| Campbell Andy (F) | 6 0 | 12 00 | Middlesbrough | 18 4 79 | Trainee |
| Close Brian (M) | 5 10 | 11 08 | Belfast | 27 1 82 | |
| Cooper Colin (D) | 5 11 | 11 09 | Sedgefield | 28 2 67 | Nottingham F |
| Crossley Mark (G) | 6 4 | 15 09 | Barnsley | 16 6 69 | Nottingham F |
| Deane Brian (F) | 6 3 | 14 05 | Leeds | 7 2 68 | Sheffield U |
| Dove Craig (M) | 5 10 | 10 08 | Hartlepool | 16 8 83 | Scholar |
| Ehiogu Ugo (D) | 6 2 | 14 10 | Hackney | 3 11 72 | Aston Villa |
| Festa Gianluca (D) | 5 11 | 13 03 | Cagliari | 15 3 69 | Internazionale |
| Fleming Curtis (D) | 5 10 | 12 11 | Manchester | 8 10 68 | St Patrick's Ath |
| Gavin Jason (D) | 6 0 | 12 04 | Dublin | 14 3 80 | Trainee |
| Gilroy Keith (M) | 5 10 | 10 13 | Sligo | 8 7 83 | |
| Gordon Dean (D) | 6 0 | 14 03 | Thornton Heath | 10 2 73 | Crystal Palace |
| Gulliver Philip (D) | 6 2 | 13 05 | Bishop Auckland | 12 9 82 | Scholar |
| Hanson Christian (D) | 6 1 | 12 11 | Middlesbrough | 3 8 81 | Trainee |
| Hudson Mark (M) | 5 10 | 11 02 | Bishop Auckland | 24 10 80 | Trainee |
| Ince Paul (M) | 5 10 | 12 13 | Ilford | 21 10 67 | Liverpool |
| Job Joseph-Desire (F) | 5 11 | 11 08 | Venissieux | 1 12 77 | Lens |
| Jones Brad (G) | 6 3 | 11 07 | Armadale | 19 3 82 | Trainee |
| Karembeu Christian (M) | 6 0 | 12 06 | Lifou | 3 12 70 | Real Madrid |
| Kilgannon Sean (M) | 5 11 | 12 04 | Stirling | 8 3 81 | Trainee |
| Marinelli Carlos (M) | 5 8 | 11 09 | Buenos Aires | 14 3 82 | Boca Juniors |
| Mustoe Robbie (M) | 6 0 | 11 13 | Oxford | 28 8 68 | Oxford U |
| Nelson Craig (F) | 5 9 | 9 12 | South Shields | 14 10 81 | Scholar |
| O'Neill Keith (M) | 6 1 | 13 03 | Dublin | 16 2 76 | Norwich C |
| Okon Paul (M) | 5 10 | 13 03 | Sydney | 5 4 72 | Fiorentina |
| Ormerod Anthony (M) | 5 10 | 11 13 | Middlesbrough | 31 3 79 | Trainee |
| Parnaby Stuart (D) | 5 11 | 11 02 | Durham City | 19 7 82 | Trainee |
| Ricard Hamilton (F) | 6 1 | 14 05 | Choco | 12 1 74 | Deportivo Cali |
| Robinson Gerard (F) | 6 0 | 14 04 | Dublin | 9 6 82 | Trainee |
| Russell Sam (G) | 6 0 | 10 13 | Middlesbrough | 4 10 82 | Scholar |
| Schwarzer Mark (G) | 6 4 | 15 01 | Sydney | 6 10 72 | Bradford C |
| Stamp Phil (M) | 5 11 | 14 09 | Middlesbrough | 12 12 75 | Trainee |
| Stephenson Paul (D) | 6 2 | 11 12 | Hartlepool | 3 1 82 | Scholar |
| Stockdale Robbie (D) | 6 0 | 12 03 | Redcar | 30 11 79 | Trainee |
| Summerbell Mark (M) | 5 9 | 10 07 | Durham | 30 10 76 | Trainee |
| Vickers Steve (D) | 6 2 | 13 01 | Bishop Auckland | 13 10 67 | Tranmere R |
| Whelan Noel (F) | 6 0 | 13 05 | Leeds | 30 12 74 | Coventry C |
| Wilford Aaron (D) | 6 3 | 14 07 | Scarborough | 14 1 82 | Harrogate College |
| Wilkshire Luke (M) | 5 9 | 11 05 | Wollongong | 2 10 81 | |
| Windass Dean (F) | 5 10 | 12 06 | Hull | 1 4 69 | Bradford C |

**League Appearances:** Beresford, M. (1); Boksic, A. 26(2); Campbell, A. 5(2); Cooper, C. 26(1); Crossley, M. 4(1); Deane, B. 13(12); Ehiogu, U. 21; Festa, G. 21(4); Fleming, C. 29(1); Gavin, J. 10(4); Gordon, D. 12(8); Hudson, M. (3); Ince,

73

P. 30; Job, J. 8(4); Karembeu, C. 31(2); Marinelli, C. 2(11); Mustoe, R. 13(12); O'Neill, K. 14(1); Okon, P. 23(1); Pallister, G. 8; Ricard, H. 22(5); Schwarzer, M. 31; Stamp, P. 11(8); Summerbell, M. 5(2); Vickers, S. 29(1); Walsh, G. 3; Whelan, N. 13(14); Windass, D. 8.
**Goals – League** (44): Boksic 12 (2 pens), Karembeu 4, Ricard 4 (1 pen), Ehiogu 3, Job 3, Cooper 2, Deane 2, Festa 2, Ince 2, Windass 2, Gordon 1, Stamp 1, Summerbell 1, Whelan 1, own goals 4.
**Worthington Cup** (5): Ricard 3, Summerbell 1, Whelan 1.
**FA Cup** (2): Ricard 2.
**Ground:** Cellnet Riverside Stadium, Middlesbrough, Cleveland TS3 6RS. Telephone (01642) 877700
**Record attendance:** 53,596 v Newcastle U, Division 1, 27 December 1949 (at Ayresome Park) and 34,800 v Leeds U, Premier League, 26 February 2000.
**Capacity:** 35,049.
**Manager:** Steve McClaren.
**Secretary:** Karen Nelson.
**Most League Goals:** 122, Division 2, 1926–27.
**Highest League Scorer in Season:** George Camsell, 59, Division 2, 1926–27 (Second Division record).
**Most League Goals in Total Aggregate:** George Camsell, 325, 1925–39.
**Most Capped Player:** Wilf Mannion, 26, England.
**Most League Appearances:** Tim Williamson, 563, 1902–23.
**Honours – Football League:** Division 1 Champions 1994–95. Division 2 Champions 1926–27, 1928–29, 1973–74. **Amateur Cup winners** 1895, 1898, **Anglo-Scottish Cup:** Winners 1975–76.
**Colours:** All red with white facing.

---

# MILLWALL                                                        DIV. 1

| Bircham Marc (D) | 5 11 | 12 02 | Brent | 11 5 78 | Trainee |
|---|---|---|---|---|---|
| Booth Stuart (M) | | | Roehampton | 7 12 83 | School |
| Braniff Kevin (F) | 5 11 | 12 00 | Belfast | 4 3 83 | Scholar |
| Bull Ronnie (D) | 5 7 | 10 11 | Hackney | 27 12 80 | Trainee |
| Cahill Tim (M) | 5 10 | 10 10 | Sydney | 6 12 79 | Sydney U |
| Constantine Leon (F) | 6 2 | 11 10 | Hackney | 24 2 78 | Edgware T |
| Dolan Joe (D) | 6 3 | 13 05 | Harrow | 27 5 80 | Chelsea |
| Dunne Alan (D) | 5 10 | 11 12 | Dublin | 23 8 82 | |
| Dyche Sean (D) | 6 0 | 13 07 | Kettering | 28 6 71 | Bristol C |
| Gueret Willy (G) | | | Saint Claude | 3 8 73 | |
| Harris Neil (F) | 5 11 | 12 04 | Orsett | 12 7 77 | Cambridge C |
| Hearn Charley (M) | | | Ashford | 5 11 83 | School |
| Hicks Mark (F) | 5 8 | 10 04 | Belfast | 24 7 81 | |
| Ifill Paul (M) | 6 0 | 12 09 | Brighton | 20 10 79 | Trainee |
| Kinet Christophe (M) | 5 8 | 10 12 | Huy | 31 12 74 | Strasbourg |
| Lawrence Matthew (D) | 6 1 | 12 12 | Northampton | 19 6 74 | Wycombe W |
| Livermore David (M) | 5 11 | 12 04 | Edmonton | 20 5 80 | Trainee |
| May Ben (M) | | | Gravesend | 10 3 84 | |
| Moody Paul (F) | 6 3 | 14 08 | Portsmouth | 13 6 67 | Fulham |
| Neill Lucas (M) | 6 0 | 12 03 | Sydney | 9 3 78 | NSW Academy |
| Odunsi Leke (M) | 5 9 | 11 07 | Walworth | 5 12 80 | Trainee |
| Phillips Mark (D) | 6 2 | 13 00 | Lambeth | 27 1 82 | Scholar |
| Rees Matthew (D) | 6 3 | 13 06 | Swansea | 2 9 82 | Trainee |
| Reid Steven (F) | 6 0 | 12 03 | Kingston | 10 3 81 | Trainee |
| Robinson Paul (D) | 6 1 | 11 09 | Barnet | 7 1 82 | Scholar |
| Ryan Robbie (D) | 5 10 | 12 03 | Dublin | 6 5 77 | Huddersfield T |
| Sadlier Richard (F) | 6 2 | 13 01 | Dublin | 14 1 79 | Belvedere |

| Tuttle David (D) | 6 2 | 14 02 | Reading | 6 2 72 | Barnsley |
| Warner Tony (G) | 6 4 | 15 01 | Liverpool | 11 5 74 | Liverpool |

**League Appearances:** Bircham, M. 13(7); Bowry, B. (1); Braniff, K. 2(3); Bubb, B. 2(1); Bull, R. 2; Cahill, T. 40(1); Claridge, S. 6; Constantine, L. (1); Cottee, T. (2); Dolan, J. 20; Dyche, S. 33; Fitzgerald, S. (1); Gilkes, M. 2(1); Gueret, W. 11; Harris, N. 39(3); Ifill, P. 28(7); Kinet, C. 18(9); Lawrence, M. 45; Livermore, D. 39; Moody, P. 21(6); Neill, L. 19(5); Nethercott, S. 33(2); Odunsi, L. 2(6); Parkin, S. 5(2); Reid, S. 27(10); Ryan, R. 42; Sadlier, R. 16(13); Stuart, J. (1); Tuttle, D. 6(3); Tyne, T. (3); Warner, T. 35.

**Goals – League** (89): Harris 27 (5 pens), Moody 13, Cahill 9, Reid 7, Ifill 6, Sadlier 6, Parkin 4, Claridge 3, Livermore 3, Bircham 2, Kinet 2, Neill 2, Nethercott 2, Dolan 1, own goals 2.

**Worthington Cup** (5): Braniff 1, Cahill 1, Ifill 1, Kinet 1, Livermore 1.

**FA Cup** (4): Bircham 1, Dolan 1, Harris 1 (pen), Moody 1.

**Ground:** The Den, Zampa Road, Bermondsey SE16 3LN. Telephone (020) 7232 1222.

**Record attendance:** 20,093 v Arsenal, FA Cup 3rd rd, 10 January 1994. **Capacity:** 20,146.

**Manager:** Mark McGhee.

**Secretary:** Yvonne Haines.

**Most League Goals:** 127, Division 3 (S), 1927–28.

**Highest League Scorer in Season:** Richard Parker, 37, Division 3 (S), 1926–27.

**Most League Goals in Total Aggregate:** Teddy Sheringham, 93, 1984–91.

**Most Capped Player:** Eamonn Dunphy, 22 (23), Republic of Ireland.

**Most League Appearances:** Barry Kitchener, 523, 1967–82.

**Honours – Football League:** Division 2 Champions – 1987–88, 2000–01. Division 3 (S) Champions – 1927–28, 1937–38. Division 4 Champions – 1961–62. **Football League Trophy winners** 1982–83.

**Colours:** White with black trim.

---

# NEWCASTLE UNITED        FA PREMIERSHIP

| Acuna Clarence (M) | 5 10 | 12 00 | Rancagua | 8 2 75 | Univ de Chile |
| Ameobi Foluwashola (F) | 6 3 | 12 03 | Zaria | 12 10 81 | Trainee |
| Barton Warren (D) | 6 3 | 12 00 | Islington | 19 3 69 | Wimbledon |
| Bassedas Christian (M) | 5 8 | 11 9 | Buenos Aires | 16 2 73 | Velez Sarsfield |
| Beharall David (D) | 6 2 | 11 12 | Newcastle | 8 3 79 | Trainee |
| Bernard Olivier (D) | 5 7 | 10 11 | Lyon | 14 10 79 | |
| Bonvin Pablo (F) | 5 10 | 11 11 | Concepcion | 15 4 81 | |
| Boyd Mark (M) | 5 10 | 12 04 | Carlisle | 22 10 81 | Trainee |
| Brennan Stephen (D) | 5 8 | 11 10 | Dublin | 26 3 83 | |
| Caldwell Gary (D) | 5 11 | 11 10 | Stirling | 12 4 82 | Trainee |
| Caldwell Steven (D) | 6 0 | 11 05 | Stirling | 12 9 80 | Trainee |
| Chopra Michael (F) | 5 8 | 9 06 | Newcastle | 23 12 83 | Scholar |
| Coppinger James (F) | 5 7 | 10 03 | Middlesbrough | 18 1 81 | Darlington |
| Cort Carl (F) | 6 4 | 12 07 | Southwark | 1 11 77 | Wimbledon |
| Cowan David (D) | 5 11 | 11 02 | Whitehaven | 5 3 82 | Trainee |
| Dabizas Nikos (D) | 6 1 | 12 07 | Amindeo | 3 8 73 | Olympiakos |
| Dimas Pedro (M) | 6 0 | 11 00 | Dexira | 22 4 82 | Porto |
| Dixon Kevin (M) | 5 9 | 10 11 | Preston | 17 3 83 | Scholar |
| Dyer Kieron (M) | 5 7 | 9 07 | Ipswich | 29 12 78 | Ipswich T |
| Gavilan Diego (M) | 5 8 | 10 07 | Asuncion | 1 3 80 | Cerro Porteno |
| Given Shay (G) | 6 1 | 13 04 | Lifford | 20 4 76 | Blackburn R |
| Green Stuart (M) | 5 10 | 11 00 | Carlisle | 15 6 81 | Trainee |
| Griffin Andy (D) | 5 9 | 10 10 | Billinge | 7 3 79 | Stoke C |

| Harper Steve (G) | 6 2 | 13 00 | Easington | 14 3 75 | Seaham Red Star |
| Hughes Aaron (D) | 6 1 | 11 02 | Cookstown | 8 11 79 | Trainee |
| Karelse John (G) | 6 3 | 13 07 | Kapelle | 17 5 70 | NAC Breda |
| Kendrick Joseph (D) | 6 0 | 11 05 | Dublin | 26 6 83 | Scholar |
| Kerr Brian (M) | 5 10 | 10 11 | Motherwell | 12 10 81 | Trainee |
| Lee Robert (M) | 5 10 | 11 13 | Plaistow | 1 2 66 | Charlton Ath |
| Lua-Lua Lomano (F) | 5 8 | 12 00 | Kinshasa | 28 12 80 | Colchester U |
| Mann Jonathan (F) | 5 9 | 10 00 | Blyth | 21 11 82 | Scholar |
| Marcelino Elena (D) | 6 2 | 13 00 | Gijon | 26 9 71 | Mallorca |
| McClen Jamie (M) | 5 8 | 10 07 | Newcastle | 13 5 79 | Trainee |
| McGuffie Ryan (D) | 6 0 | 11 01 | Dumfries | 22 7 80 | |
| McMenamin Colin (F) | 5 9 | 10 12 | Glasgow | 12 2 81 | |
| O'Brien Andy (D) | 6 3 | 11 05 | Harrogate | 29 6 79 | Bradford C |
| Pringle Philip (G) | 6 1 | 14 09 | Newcastle | 1 1 83 | Scholar |
| Quinn Wayne (D) | 5 10 | 11 12 | Truro | 19 11 76 | Sheffield U |
| Robson Damon (M) | 5 7 | 13 06 | Co Durham | 19 9 83 | Scholar |
| Shearer Alan (F) | 6 0 | 12 06 | Newcastle | 13 8 70 | Blackburn R |
| Solano Nolberto (M) | 5 9 | 11 02 | Callao | 12 12 74 | Boca Juniors |
| Speed Gary (M) | 5 10 | 10 12 | Deeside | 8 9 69 | Everton |

**League Appearances:** Acuna, C. 23(3); Ameobi, F. 12(8); Barton, W. 27(2); Bassedas, C. 17(5); Caldwell, S. 5(4); Charvet, L. 6(1); Coppinger, J. (1); Cordone, D. 12(9); Cort, C. 13; Dabizas, N. 9; Domi, D. 11(3); Dyer, K. 25(1); Gallacher, K. 12(7); Gavilan, D. (1); Given, S. 34; Glass, S. 5(9); Goma, A. 18(1); Griffin, A. 14(5); Harper, S. 4(1); Hughes, A. 34(1); Kerr, B. (1); Lee, R. 21(1); Lua-Lua, L. 3(18); Marcelino, E. 5(1); O'Brien, A. 9; Quinn, W. 14(1); Shearer, A. 19; Solano, N. 31(2); Speed, G. 35.

**Goals – League** (44): Cort 6, Solano 6 (2 pens), Dyer 5 (1 pen), Shearer 5 (2 pens), Speed 5, Acuna 3, Glass 3, Ameobi 2, Cordone 2, Gallacher 2, Bassedas 1, Goma 1, O'Brien 1, own goals 2.

**Worthington Cup** (8): Shearer 2, Caldwell 1, Cordone 1, Cort 1, Dyer 1, Gallacher 1, Speed 1.

**FA Cup** (1): Solano 1.

**Ground:** St James' Park, Newcastle-upon-Tyne NE1 4ST. Telephone (0191) 201 8400.

**Record attendance:** 68,386 v Chelsea, Division 1, 3 Sept 1930. **Capacity:** 52,167.

**Manager:** Bobby Robson CBE.

**Secretary:** Russell Cushing.

**Most League Goals:** 98, Division 1, 1951–52.

**Highest League Scorer in Season:** Hughie Gallacher, 36, Division 1, 1926–27.

**Most League Goals in Total Aggregate:** Jackie Milburn, 177, 1946–57.

**Most Capped Player:** Alf McMichael, 40, Northern Ireland.

**Most League Appearances:** Jim Lawrence, 432, 1904–22.

**Honours – Football League:** Division 1 – Champions 1904–05, 1906–07, 1908–09, 1926–27, 1992–93. Division 2 Champions – 1964–65. **FA Cup winners** 1910, 1924, 1932, 1951, 1952, 1955. **Texaco Cup winners** 1973–74, 1974–75. **European Competitions: European Fairs Cup winners:** 1968–69. **Anglo-Italian Cup winners:** 1973.

**Colours:** Black and white striped shirts, white and blue shorts and stockings.

---

# NORTHAMPTON TOWN                                    DIV. 2

---

| Forrester Jamie (F) | 5 6 | 10 12 | Bradford | 1 11 74 | Walsall |
| Frain John (D) | 5 10 | 12 04 | Birmingham | 8 10 68 | Birmingham C |
| Gabbiadini Marco (F) | 5 10 | 13 04 | Nottingham | 21 1 68 | Darlington |

| | | | | | |
|---|---|---|---|---|---|
| Hargreaves Chris (M) | 5 11 | 12 02 | Cleethorpes | 12 5 72 | Plymouth Arg |
| Hodge John (F) | 5 7 | 11 06 | Skelmersdale | 1 4 69 | Gillingham |
| Hope Richard (D) | 6 3 | 13 05 | Stockton | 22 6 78 | Darlington |
| Hunt James (M) | 5 11 | 12 07 | Derby | 17 12 76 | Notts Co |
| Hunter Roy (M) | 5 10 | 12 08 | Saltburn | 29 10 73 | WBA |
| Sampson Ian (D) | 6 2 | 13 05 | Wakefield | 14 11 68 | Sunderland |
| Sollitt Adam (G) | | | Sheffield | 22 6 77 | Barnsley |
| Spedding Duncan (M) | 6 2 | 12 01 | Frimley | 7 9 77 | Southampton |
| Welch Keith (G) | 6 2 | 13 07 | Bolton | 3 10 68 | Bristol C |

**League Appearances:** Canoville, L. 2; Carruthers, C. 1(2); Chilvers, L. 7; Clare, D. 3(1); Crooks, L. 3; Dempsey, P. 5(1); Dryden, R. 9(1); Ferguson, B. 1(2); Forrester, J. 42(1); Frain, J. 27; Gabbiadini, M. 34(10); Gould, J. (1); Green, R. 34(4); Hargreaves, C. 29(2); Hendon, I. 9; Hodge, J. 24(9); Hope, R. 30(3); Howard, S. 23(10); Howey, L. 2(1); Hughes, G. 12(4); Hunt, J. 41; Hunter, R. 1(3); Lopes, R. 3(3); Lowe, D. (4); Maley, M. 2; Morrow, A. 2(2); Nicholson, K. 6(1); Sampson, I. 41; Savage, D. 37(6); Sollitt, A. 6; Spedding, D. 17(4); Thompson, R. (2); Welch, K. 40; Whitley, J. 13; Wilson, K. (6).
**Goals – League (46):** Forrester 17, Howard 8, Savage 8 (6 pens), Gabbiadini 6, Sampson 2, Frain 1, Hendon 1 (pen), Hodge 1, Hughes 1, Hunt 1.
**Worthington Cup (2):** Gabbiadini 1, Sampson 1.
**FA Cup (4):** Forrester 2, Frain 1, Hunt 1.
**Ground:** Sixfields Stadium, Upton Way, Northampton NN5 5QA. Telephone (01604) 757773.
**Record attendance:** 24,523 v Fulham, Division 1, 23 April 1966. **Capacity:** 7653.
**Manager:** Kevin WIlson.
**Secretary:** Norman Howells.
**Most League Goals:** 109, Division 3, 1962–63 and Division 3 (S), 1952–53.
**Highest League Scorer in Season:** Cliff Holton, 36, Division 3, 1961–62.
**Most League Goals in Total Aggregate:** Jack English, 135, 1947–60.
**Most Capped Player:** E. Lloyd Davies, 12 (16), Wales.
**Most League Appearances:** Tommy Fowler, 521, 1946–61.
**Honours – Football League:** Division 3 Champions – 1962–63. Division 4 Champions – 1986–87.
**Colours:** Claret shirts with white trim, white shorts, claret stockings.

---

# NORWICH CITY                                                    DIV. 1

| | | | | | |
|---|---|---|---|---|---|
| Abbey Zema (F) | 6 1 | 12 11 | Luton | 17 4 77 | Cambridge U |
| Anselin Cedric (M) | 5 7 | 11 02 | Lens | 24 7 77 | Bordeaux |
| Bloomfield Daniel (M) | | | Ipswich | 28 7 82 | Felixstowe & Walton |
| Coote Adrian (F) | 6 1 | 11 11 | Gt Yarmouth | 30 9 78 | Trainee |
| Dalglish Paul (F) | 5 10 | 11 00 | Glasgow | 18 2 77 | Newcastle U |
| Derveld Fernando (D) | 6 2 | 13 00 | Vlissingen | 22 10 76 | Haarlem |
| Drury Adam (D) | 5 10 | 11 04 | Cottenham | 29 8 78 | Peterborough U |
| Fleming Craig (D) | 5 11 | 12 10 | Halifax | 6 10 71 | Oldham Ath |
| Forbes Adrian (F) | 5 7 | 11 04 | Greenford | 23 1 79 | Trainee |
| Giallanza Gaetano (F) | 5 11 | 11 09 | Basle | 6 6 74 | Lugano |
| Green Robert (G) | 6 3 | 13 00 | Chertsey | 18 1 80 | Trainee |
| Holt Gary (M) | 6 1 | 11 11 | Irvine | 9 3 73 | Kilmarnock |
| Jackson Matt (D) | 6 0 | 12 09 | Leeds | 19 10 71 | Everton |
| Kenton Darren (D) | 5 11 | 11 10 | Wandsworth | 13 9 78 | Trainee |
| Llewellyn Chris (F) | 6 0 | 11 11 | Merthyr | 29 8 79 | Trainee |
| Mackay Malky (D) | 6 3 | 13 03 | Bellshill | 19 2 72 | Celtic |
| McGovern Brian (D) | 6 3 | 12 07 | Dublin | 28 4 80 | Arsenal |

| | | | | | |
|---|---|---|---|---|---|
| McVeigh Paul (F) | 5 6 | 10 06 | Belfast | 6 12 77 | Tottenham H |
| Mulryne Phil (M) | 5 9 | 11 05 | Belfast | 1 1 78 | Manchester U |
| Nedergaard Steen (M) | 6 1 | 11 11 | Denmark | 25 2 70 | Odense |
| Notman Alex (F) | 5 7 | 10 11 | Edinburgh | 10 12 79 | Manchester U |
| Roberts Iwan (F) | 6 3 | 13 01 | Bangor | 26 6 68 | Wolverhampton W |
| Russell Darel (M) | 6 0 | 12 02 | Mile End | 22 10 80 | Trainee |
| Sutch Daryl (D) | 5 11 | 12 06 | Lowestoft | 11 9 71 | Trainee |

**League Appearances:** Abbey, Z. 11(9); Bellamy, C. 1; Brady, G. 2; Coote, A. 3(11); Cottee, T. 5(2); Dalglish, P. (7); De Blasiis, Y. 2(5); De Waard, R. (6); Derveld, F. 15(2); Drury, A. 6; Fleming, C. 39; Forbes, A. 13(16); Giallanza, G. 5(6); Granville, D. 6; Green, R. 5; Holt, G. 3(1); Jackson, M. 26; Kenton, D. 24(5); Llewellyn, C. 41(1); MacKay, M. 34(4); Marshall, A. 41; Marshall, L. 34(2); McGovern, B. 3(9); McVeigh, P. 6(5); Mulryne, P. 27(1); Nedergaard, S. 10(5); Notman, A. 10(5); Parker, S. 6; Peschisolido, P. 3(2); Roberts, I. 44; Russell, D. 34(7); Sutch, D. 39(1); Walsh, S. 1(3); Whitley, J. 7(1).
**Goals – League** (46): Roberts 15 (2 pens), Llewellyn 8, Forbes 3, Marshall L 3, Giallanza 2, Kenton 2, Russell 2, Abbey 1, Cottee 1, Derveld 1, MacKay 1, McGovern 1, McVeigh 1, Mulryne 1, Nedergaard 1, Notman 1, Parker 1, Whitley.
**Worthington Cup** (10): Giallanza 3, Roberts 3 (1 pen), Russell 2, Cottee 1, Marshall L 1.
**FA Cup** (1): Roberts 1.
**Ground:** Carrow Road, Norwich NR1 1JE. Telephone (01603) 760760.
**Record attendance:** 43,984 v Leicester C, FA Cup 6th rd, 30 March 1963. **Capacity:** 21,468.
**Manager:** Nigel Worthington.
**Secretary:** Kevin Platt.
**Most League Goals:** 99, Division 3 (S), 1952–53.
**Highest League Scorer in Season:** Ralph Hunt, 31, Division 3 (S), 1955–56.
**Most League Goals in Total Aggregate:** Johnny Gavin, 122, 1945–54, 1955–58.
**Most Capped Player:** Mark Bowen, 35 (41), Wales.
**Most League Appearances:** Ron Ashman, 592, 1947–64.
**Honours – Football League:** Division 2 Champions – 1971–72, 1985–86. Division 3 (S) Champions – 1933–34. **Football League Cup:** Winners 1962, 1985.
**Colours:** All yellow.

---

# NOTTINGHAM FOREST     DIV. 1

| | | | | | |
|---|---|---|---|---|---|
| Allou Bernard (M) | 5 8 | 11 00 | Cocody | 19 6 75 | Paris St Germain |
| Bart-Williams Chris (M) | 5 11 | 12 07 | Freetown | 16 6 74 | Sheffield W |
| Bopp Eugene (M) | 5 10 | 12 00 | Kiev | 5 9 83 | Bayern Munich |
| Brennan Jim (D) | 5 9 | 11 06 | Toronto | 8 5 77 | Bristol C |
| Byrne Michael (M) | | | Dublin | 14 2 84 | Scholar |
| Calderwood Colin (D) | 6 0 | 13 00 | Stranraer | 20 1 65 | Aston Villa |
| Cash Brian (M) | 5 9 | 12 00 | Dublin | 24 11 82 | Trainee |
| Dawson Kevin | | | | | |
| Dawson Michael (D) | | | Northallerton | 18 11 83 | School |
| Doig Chris (D) | 6 2 | 12 06 | Dumfries | 13 2 81 | Trainee |
| Edds Gareth (M) | 5 11 | 10 12 | Sydney | 3 2 81 | Trainee |
| Fenton Paul (F) | 5 7 | 10 10 | Cork | 8 3 83 | Scholar |
| Formann Pascal (M) | | | Werne | 16 11 82 | |
| Foy Keith (M) | 5 11 | 12 03 | Crumlin | 30 12 81 | Trainee |
| Freeman David (F) | 5 10 | 11 07 | Dublin | 25 11 79 | Cherry Orchard |
| Gray Andy (M) | 6 0 | 13 00 | Harrogate | 15 11 77 | Leeds U |
| Haigh Philip (M) | | | Boston | 27 9 82 | |

| Harewood Marlon (F) | 6 1 | 13 03 | Hampstead | 25  8 79 | Trainee |
|---|---|---|---|---|---|
| Hjelde Jon Olav (D) | 6 2 | 13 05 | Levanger | 30  7 72 | Rosenborg |
| Hudson Niall (M) | 5 10 | 10 02 | Ilkeston | 7  1 82 | Trainee |
| Jeffrey Richard (F) | 5 9 | 11 00 | Derby | 4 11 83 | Scholar |
| Jenas Jermaine (M) | 5 10 | 12 00 | Nottingham | 18  2 83 | Scholar |
| John Stern (F) | 6 1 | 13 07 | Trinidad | 30 10 76 | Columbus Crew |
| Johnson Andy (M) | 6 1 | 13 03 | Bristol | 2  5 74 | Norwich C |
| Johnson David (F) | 5 6 | 12 00 | Kingston, Jam | 15  8 76 | Ipswich T |
| Jones Gary (F) | 6 3 | 13 05 | Chester | 10  5 75 | Tranmere R |
| Kearney Liam (M) | 5 7 | 10 12 | Dublin | 10  1 83 | Scholar |
| Lester Jack (F) | 5 10 | 11 10 | Sheffield | 8 10 75 | Grimsby T |
| Louis-Jean Mathieu (D) | 5 9 | 10 08 | Mont-St-Aignan | 22  2 76 | Le Havre |
| Love Gordon (F) | 5 7 | 10 00 | Bellshill | 17  3 83 | Scholar |
| Petrachi Gianluca (M) | 5 9 | 11 05 | Lecce | 14  1 69 | Perugia |
| Peyton Emmet (M) | | | Castlebar | 26 10 83 | |
| Prutton David (D) | 6 1 | 11 06 | Hull | 12  9 81 | Trainee |
| Reid Andrew (F) | 5 7 | 11 00 | Dublin | 29  7 82 | Trainee |
| Robertson Gregor (M) | | | Edinburgh | 19  1 84 | |
| Roche Barry (G) | 6 4 | 12 06 | Dublin | 6  4 82 | Trainee |
| Rogers Alan (D) | 5 10 | 12 08 | Liverpool | 3  1 77 | Tranmere R |
| Scimeca Riccardo (D) | 6 0 | 13 11 | Leamington Spa | 13  6 75 | Aston Villa |
| Thompson John (D) | | | Dublin | 12 10 81 | |
| Vaughan Tony (D) | 6 1 | 12 10 | Manchester | 11 10 75 | Manchester C |
| Williams Gareth (M) | 5 11 | 11 08 | Glasgow | 16 12 81 | Trainee |

**League Appearances:** Bart-Williams, C. 46; Beasant, D. 45; Benali, F. 15; Blake, R. 9(2); Brennan, J. 9(3); Calderwood, C. 1(1); Cooper, R. (2); Dawson, K. 1; Doig, C. 14(1); Edds, G. 9(4); Edwards, C. 35(1); Foy, K. 17(3); Freedman, D. 2(3); Freeman, D. 2(3); Gray, A. 11(7); Harewood, M. 13(20); Hjelde, J. 10(1); Jenas, J. 1; John, S. 16(13); Johnson, A. 29(2); Johnson, D. 19; Jones, G. 22(9); Lester, J. 18(1); Louis-Jean, M. 10(3); Olsen, B. 14(4); Platt, D. 2; Prutton, D. 41(1); Reid, A. 9(5); Roche, B. 1(1); Rogers, A. 16(1); Scimeca, R. 34(2); Upson, M. 1; Vaughan, T. 23(2); Williams, G. 11(6).

**Goals – League (55):** Bart-Williams 14 (7 pens), Lester 7, Scimeca 4, Edwards 3, Harewood 3, Johnson A 3, Rogers 3, Hjelde 2, John 2, Johnson D 2, Olsen 2, Reid 2, Blake 1, Edds 1, Foy 1, Jones 1, Platt 1, Prutton 1, Vaughan 1, own goal 1.

**Worthington Cup (3):** Bart-Williams 1 (pen), John 1, Rogers 1.

**FA Cup (0).**

**Ground:** City Ground, Nottingham NG2 5FJ. Telephone (0115) 9824444.

**Record attendance:** 49,945 v Manchester U, Division 1, 28 October 1967. **Capacity:** 30,602.

**Manager:** Paul Hart.

**Secretary:** Paul White.

**Most League Goals:** 110, Division 3 (S), 1950–51.

**Highest League Scorer in Season:** Wally Ardron, 36, Division 3 (S), 1950–51.

**Most League Goals in Total Aggregate:** Grenville Morris, 199, 1898–1913.

**Most Capped Player:** Stuart Pearce, 76 (78), England.

**Most League Appearances:** Bob McKinlay, 614, 1951–70.

**Honours – Football League: Division 1** – Champions 1977–78, 1997–98. **Division 2** Champions – 1906–07, 1921–22. **Division 3 (S)** Champions – 1950–51. **FA Cup:** Winners 1898, 1959. **Football League Cup:** Winners 1977–78, 1978–79, 1988–89, 1989–90. **Anglo-Scottish Cup:** Winners 1976–77. **Simod Cup:** Winners 1989. **Zenith Data Systems Cup:** Winners 1991–92. **European Competitions: European Cup winners:** 1978–79, 1979–80. **Super Cup winners:** 1979–80.

**Colours:** Red shirts, white shorts, red stockings.

| | | | | | |
|---|---|---|---|---|---|
| Allsopp Danny (F) | 6 0 | 14 02 | Melbourne | 10 8 78 | Manchester C |
| Bolland Paul (M) | 6 0 | 12 01 | Bradford | 23 12 79 | Bradford C |
| Brough Michael (M) | 6 0 | 11 07 | Nottingham | 1 8 81 | Trainee |
| Deeney Saul (G) | | | Londonderry | 12 3 83 | Scholar |
| Fenton Nick (D) | 6 2 | 11 10 | Preston | 23 11 79 | Manchester C |
| Ford Ryan (M) | 5 10 | 10 05 | Worksop | 3 9 78 | Manchester U |
| Hamilton Ian (M) | 5 10 | 12 07 | Stevenage | 14 12 67 | Sheffield U |
| Heffernan Paul (F) | 5 10 | 11 00 | Dublin | 29 12 81 | Newton |
| Holmes Richard (D) | 5 11 | 10 12 | Grantham | 7 11 80 | Trainee |
| Hughes Andy (M) | 6 0 | 12 07 | Manchester | 2 1 78 | Oldham Ath |
| Jorgensen Henrik (D) | | | Bogense | 12 1 79 | B1909 |
| Liburd Richard (D) | 5 9 | 11 06 | Nottingham | 26 9 73 | Carlisle U |
| McCaig John (D) | 6 1 | 12 06 | Ayr | 19 11 82 | |
| McDermott Andy (D) | 5 9 | 11 03 | Sydney | 24 3 77 | WBA |
| Nicholson Kevin (D) | 5 9 | 11 07 | Derby | 2 10 80 | Northampton T |
| Owers Gary (M) | 6 0 | 12 09 | Newcastle | 3 10 68 | Bristol C |
| Rapley Kevin (F) | 5 10 | 11 07 | Reading | 21 9 77 | Brentford |
| Richardson Ian (D) | 5 10 | 12 00 | Barking | 22 1 70 | Dagenham & Redbridge |
| Stallard Mark (F) | 6 0 | 12 13 | Derby | 24 10 74 | Wycombe W |
| Warren Mark (D) | 6 0 | 12 08 | Clapton | 12 11 74 | Leyton Orient |

**League Appearances:** Allsopp, D. 26(3); Bolland, P. 7; Brough, M. 11(5); Calderwood, C. 5; Cramb, C. 2(1); Dyer, A. 8(1); Farrell, S. 9(10); Fenton, N. 30; Gibson, P. 9; Hamilton, I. 23(2); Heffernan, P. (1); Holmes, R. 3(2); Hughes, A. 20(10); Ireland, C. 16; Jacobsen, A. 27(2); Jorgensen, H. 3(2); Joseph, D. 13(14); Liburd, R. 28(3); Lindley, J. 2; McCann, G. 2; McDermott, A. 20(5); Moreau, F. 2(3); Murray, S. 7(4); Newton, A. 13(7); Nicholson, K. 9(2); Owers, G. 40; Pearce, D. 26(1); Ramage, C. 14(1); Rapley, K. (7); Redmile, M. 7(1); Richardson, I. 24(1); Stallard, M. 42; Thomas, G. 8; Ward, D. 35; Warren, M. 15(1).

**Goals – League (62):** Stallard 17 (2 pens), Allsopp 13 (4 pens), Hughes 5, Joseph 4 (1 pen), Owers 4, Farrell 3, Liburd 3, Ramage 3, Fenton 2, Jacobsen 2, Nicholson 2, Brough 1, Newton 1, Richardson 1, Thomas 1.

**Worthington Cup (5):** Stallard 3 (2 pens), Hughes 1, McDermott 1.

**FA Cup (7):** Stallard 3, Hughes 2, Liburd 2.

**Ground:** County Ground, Meadow Lane, Nottingham NG2 3HJ. Telephone (0115) 952 9000.

**Record attendance:** 47,310 v York C, FA Cup 6th rd, 12 March 1955. **Capacity:** 20,300.

**Manager:** Jocky Scott.

**Secretary:** Tony Cuthbert.

**Most League Goals:** 107, Division 4, 1959–60.

**Highest League Scorer in Season:** Tom Keetley, 39, Division 3 (S), 1930–31.

**Most League Goals in Total Aggregate:** Les Bradd, 124, 1967–78.

**Most Capped Player:** Kevin Wilson, 15 (42), Northern Ireland.

**Most League Appearances:** Albert Iremonger, 564, 1904–26.

**Honours – Football League:** Division 2 Champions – 1896–97, 1913–14, 1922–23. Division 3 Champions – 1997–98. Division 3 (S) Champions – 1930–31, 1949–50. Division 4 Champions – 1970–71. **FA Cup:** Winners 1893–94. **Anglo-Italian Cup:** Winners 1995.

**Colours:** Black and white striped shirts, black shorts, black stockings.

# OLDHAM ATHLETIC                                     DIV. 2

| | | | | | |
|---|---|---|---|---|---|
| Allott Mark (F) | 5 11 | 10 12 | Middleton | 16  3 78 | Trainee |
| Boshell Daniel (M) | 5 11 | 11 10 | Bradford | 30  5 81 | Trainee |
| Carss Tony (M) | 5 10 | 11 08 | Alnwick | 31  3 76 | Carlisle U |
| Corazzin Carlo (F) | 5 10 | 12 07 | Canada | 25 12 71 | Northampton T |
| Dudley Craig (F) | 5 11 | 11 06 | Ollerton | 12  9 79 | Notts Co |
| Duxbury Lee (M) | 5 10 | 10 07 | Keighley | 7 10 69 | Bradford C |
| Eyres David (F) | 5 11 | 11 06 | Liverpool | 26  2 64 | Preston NE |
| Futcher Ben (D) | 6 6 | 12 02 | Bradford | 4  6 81 | Trainee |
| Garnett Shaun (D) | 6 2 | 13 01 | Wallasey | 22 11 69 | Swansea C |
| Holt Andy (D) | 6 1 | 11 02 | Manchester | 21  5 78 | Trainee |
| Hotte Mark (M) | 5 11 | 11 00 | Bradford | 27  9 78 | Trainee |
| Innes Mark (D) | 5 10 | 12 04 | Bellshill | 27  9 78 | Trainee |
| Jones Paul (D) | 6 1 | 11 09 | Liverpool | 3  6 78 | Tranmere R |
| Kelly Gary (G) | 5 11 | 12 08 | Fulwood | 3  8 66 | Bury |
| McNiven Scott (D) | 5 10 | 10 08 | Leeds | 27  5 78 | Trainee |
| Miskelly David (G) | 6 0 | 12 02 | Ards | 3  9 79 | Trainee |
| Rickers Paul (M) | 5 10 | 11 04 | Dewsbury | 9  5 75 | Trainee |
| Roach Neville (F) | 5 11 | 11 09 | Reading | 29  9 78 | Southend U |
| Salt Philip (M) | 5 10 | 11 02 | Huddersfield | 2  3 79 | Trainee |
| Sheridan John (M) | 5 10 | 11 12 | Stretford | 1 10 64 | Bolton W |
| Sugden Ryan (F) | 6 0 | 12 07 | Bradford | 26 12 80 | Trainee |
| Tipton Matthew (F) | 5 10 | 11 02 | Bridgend | 29  6 80 | Trainee |

**League Appearances:** Adams, N. 18; Allott, M. 26(13); Boshell, D. 11(7); Carss, T. 35; Corazzin, C. 37(1); Dudley, C. 10(16); Duxbury, L. 40; Eyres, D. 30; Futcher, B. 1(4); Garnett, S. 39; Holt, A. 12(8); Hotte, M. 25(3); Innes, M. 27(3); Jones, P. 10(2); Kelly, G. 45; Lightfoot, C. 3; McNiven, S. 43(2); Miskelly, D. 1(1); Parkin, S. 3(4); Prenderville, B. 6(3); Rickers, P. 38; Roach, N. (1); Salt, P. 4(2); Sheridan, J. 22(3); Smith, P. 3(1); Sugden, R. 1(1); Tipton, M. 15(15); Watson, M. 1(1); Whitehall, S. 2.
**Goals – League** (53): Duxbury 8, Allott 7, Corazzin 7, Tipton 5, Dudley 4, Sheridan 4 (2 pens), Eyres 3, Parkin 3, Adams 2, Carss 2, Jones 2, Rickers 2, Boshell 1, Garnett 1, Holt 1, own goal 1.
**Worthington Cup** (5): Rickers 2, Boshell 1, Corazzin 1, Duxbury 1.
**FA Cup** (5): Dudley 2, Corazzin 1, Duxbury 1, Tipton 1.
**Ground:** Boundary Park, Oldham OL1 2PA. Telephone (0161) 624 4972.
**Record attendance:** 47,671 v Sheffield W, FA Cup 4th rd. 25 January 1930.
**Capacity:** 13,559.
**Manager:** Andy Ritchie.
**Secretary:** Alan Hardy.
**Most League Goals:** 95, Division 4, 1962–63.
**Highest League Scorer in Season:** Tom Davis, 33, Division 3 (N), 1936–37.
**Most League Goals in Total Aggregate:** Roger Palmer, 141, 1980–94.
**Most Capped Player:** Gunnar Halle, 24 (62), Norway.
**Most League Appearances:** Ian Wood, 525, 1966–80.
**Honours – Football League:** Division 2 Champions – 1990–91, Division 3 (N) Champions – 1952–53. Division 3 Champions – 1973–74.
**Colours:** White shirts with blue panel, blue shorts and stockings.

# OXFORD UNITED                                       DIV. 3

| | | | | | |
|---|---|---|---|---|---|
| Beauchamp Joey (M) | 5 10 | 12 07 | Oxford | 13  3 71 | Swindon T |
| Brooks Jamie (M) | | | Oxford | 12  8 83 | Scholar |
| Folland Robbie (F) | 5 9 | 10 07 | Swansea | 16  9 79 | Trainee |

| Gray Phil (F) | 5 9 | 12 07 | Belfast | 2 10 68 | Burnley |
| Hackett Christopher (M) | 6 0 | 11 06 | Oxford | 1 3 83 | Scholar |
| Hatswell Wayne (D) | | | Swindon | 8 2 79 | Forest Green R |
| King Simon (D) | | | Oxford | 11 4 83 | Scholar |
| Knight Richard (G) | 6 1 | 14 00 | Burton | 3 8 79 | Derby Co |
| McGuckin Ian (D) | 6 2 | 14 01 | Middlesbrough | 24 4 73 | Fulham |
| Omoyinmi Emmanuel (M) | 5 7 | 10 01 | Nigeria | 28 12 77 | West Ham U |
| Patterson Darren (D) | 6 1 | 12 10 | Belfast | 15 10 69 | York C |
| Powell Paul (M) | 5 8 | 11 01 | Wallingford | 30 6 78 | Trainee |
| Quinn Robert (D) | 5 11 | 11 02 | Sidcup | 8 11 76 | Brentford |
| Richardson Jon (D) | 6 1 | 12 02 | Nottingham | 29 8 75 | Exeter C |
| Ricketts Sam (D) | 6 1 | 13 00 | Aylesbury | 11 10 81 | Trainee |
| Scott Andy (F) | 6 1 | 11 05 | Epsom | 2 8 72 | Brentford |
| Shepheard Jon (D) | 6 2 | 12 04 | Oxford | 31 3 81 | Trainee |
| Tait Paul (M) | 5 11 | 11 10 | Sutton Coldfield | 31 7 71 | Birmingham C |
| Whitehead Dean (M) | 5 11 | 12 01 | Oxford | 12 1 82 | Trainee |

**League Appearances:** Andrews, K. 4; Anthrobus, S. 13(7); Beauchamp, J. 32(11); Brooks, J. 3(1); Brown, K. 3; Busby, H. (1); Cook, J. 4(5); Cutler, N. 11; Fear, P. 14(5); Folland, R. 1(4); Ford, M. 1; Glass, J. 1; Gray, P. 21(2); Hackett, C. 10(6); Hatswell, W. 26(1); Holder, J. (2); Jarman, L. 15(6); King, S. 2; Knight, R. 33; Lilley, D. 15(4); Linighan, A. 12(1); McGowan, N. 11; McGuckin, I. 6(1); Mike, L. 1(2); Monk, G. 5; Murphy, M. 37(3); Omoyinmi, E. 16(8); Patterson, D. 18; Powell, P. 15(5); Quinn, R. 12(1); Richardson, J. 41; Ricketts, S. 13(1); Robertson, J. 37(3); Scott, A. 21; Shepheard, J. 5; Tait, P. 22(4); Weatherstone, R. 1; Weatherstone, S. 6(1); Whitehead, D. 16(4); Whittingham, G. 1; Wilson, P. 1(1).
**Goals – League** (53): Beauchamp 7, Gray 7 (3 pens), Murphy 6, Scott 5, Omoyinmi 3, Tait 3, Fear 2, Hackett 2, Lilley 2, Quinn 2, Richardson 2, Andrews 1, Anthrobus 1, Brooks 1, Cook 1, Folland 1, Jarman 1, Patterson 1, Powell 1, Whittingham 1, own goals 3.
**Worthington Cup** (2): Murphy 1, Shepheard 1.
**FA Cup** (3): Gray 2, Murphy 1.
**Ground:** The Kassam Stadium, Grenoble Road, Oxford OX4 4XP. Telephone (01865) 337500.
**Record attendance:** 22,750 (at Manor Ground) v Preston NE, FA Cup 6th rd, 29 February 1964. **Capacity:** 9650.
**Manager:** Mark Wright.
**Secretary:** Mick Brown.
**Most League Goals:** 91, Division 3, 1983–84.
**Highest League Scorer in Season:** John Aldridge, 30, Division 2, 1984–85.
**Most League Goals in Total Aggregate:** Graham Atkinson, 77, 1962–73.
**Most Capped Player:** Jim Magilton, 18 (47), Northern Ireland.
**Most League Appearances:** John Shuker, 478, 1962–77.
**Honours – Football League:** Division 2 Champions – 1984–85. Division 3 Champions – 1967–68, 1983–84. **Football League Cup:** Winners 1985–86.
**Colours:** Yellow shirts with navy trim, navy shorts and stockings.

---

# PETERBOROUGH UNITED                                           DIV. 2

| Chapple Phil (D) | 6 2 | 13 01 | Norwich | 21 11 66 | Charlton Ath |
| Clarke Andy (F) | 5 10 | 11 07 | Islington | 22 7 67 | Wimbledon |
| Connor Dan (G) | 6 2 | 13 04 | Dublin | 31 1 81 | Trainee |
| Cullen Jon (M) | 6 0 | 13 00 | Durham | 10 1 73 | Sheffield U |
| Danielsson Helgi (M) | 6 0 | 12 00 | Reykjavik | 13 7 81 | Fylkir |
| Edwards Andy (D) | 6 2 | 12 13 | Epping | 17 9 71 | Birmingham C |

| Farrell Dave (M) | 5 11 | 11 08 | Birmingham | 11 11 71 | Wycombe W |
| Forinton Howard (F) | 5 11 | 12 04 | Boston | 18 9 75 | Birmingham C |
| Forsyth Richard (M) | 5 11 | 13 00 | Dudley | 3 10 70 | Blackpool |
| French Daniel (M) | 5 11 | 11 00 | Peterborough | 25 11 79 | Trainee |
| Gill Matthew (M) | 5 11 | 11 07 | Cambridge | 8 11 80 | Trainee |
| Green Francis (F) | 5 9 | 11 04 | Derby | 23 4 80 | Ilkeston T |
| Hanlon Ritchie (M) | 6 1 | 12 13 | Kenton | 25 5 78 | Southend U |
| Hooper Dean (D) | 5 11 | 12 06 | Harefield | 13 4 71 | Swindon T |
| Jelleyman Gareth (D) | 5 10 | 10 03 | Holywell | 14 11 80 | Trainee |
| Lee Jason (F) | 6 3 | 13 03 | Newham | 9 5 71 | Chesterfield |
| MacDonald Gary (M) | 6 1 | 12 00 | Germany | 25 10 79 | Portsmouth |
| McKenzie Leon (F) | 5 10 | 10 03 | Croydon | 17 5 78 | Crystal Palace |
| Murray Dan (D) | 6 2 | 12 12 | Cambridge | 16 5 82 | Scholar |
| Oldfield David (M) | 6 1 | 13 04 | Perth (Aus) | 30 5 68 | Stoke C |
| Pearce Dennis (D) | 5 9 | 11 07 | Wolverhampton | 10 9 74 | Notts Co |
| Rea Simon (D) | 6 1 | 13 00 | Coventry | 20 9 76 | Birmingham C |
| Shields Tony (M) | 5 8 | 10 01 | Derry | 4 6 80 | Trainee |
| Tyler Mark (G) | 5 11 | 12 00 | Norwich | 2 4 77 | Trainee |

**League Appearances:** Clarke, A. 36(6); Cullen, J. 12(6); Danielsson, H. 3(3); Drury, A. 29; Edwards, A. 43; Farrell, D. 39(5); Forinton, H. 2(6); Forsyth, R. 25(5); French, D. 1(1); Gill, M. 11(6); Green, F. 18(14); Hanlon, R. 21(5); Hooper, D. 28(5); Jelleyman, G. 6(2); Lee, J. 14(16); MacDonald, G. 1; McKenzie, L. 30; Morrow, S. 11; Murray, D. 1(2); Oldfield, D. 32(7); Rea, S. 35(1); Rogers, D. 1(2); Scott, R. 18(2); Shields, T. 28(5); Taylor, S. 6; Tyler, M. 40; Whittingham, G. 1(4); Williams, M. 13(2); Williams, T. 1(1).
**Goals – League** (61): McKenzie 13 (2 pens), Clarke 9, Lee 8, Farrell 7, Green 6, Oldfield 3, Forsyth 2 (1 pen), Rea 2, Cullen 1 (pen), Edwards 1, Forinton 1, Gill 1, Hanlon 1, Williams M 1, Shields 1, Whittingham 1, own goals 3.
**Worthington Cup** (2): Clarke 1, Farrell 1.
**FA Cup** (7): Clarke 1, Edwards 1, Farrell 1, Forsyth 1, Lee 1, Oldfield 1, Shields 1.
**Ground:** London Road Ground, Peterborough PE2 8AL. Telephone (01733) 563947.
**Record attendance:** 30,096 v Swansea T, FA Cup 5th rd, 20 February 1965.
**Capacity:** 15,314.
**Manager:** Barry Fry.
**Secretary:** Julie Etherington.
**Most League Goals:** 134, Division 4, 1960–61.
**Highest League Scorer in Season:** Terry Bly, 52, Division 4, 1960–61.
**Most League Goals in Total Aggregate:** Jim Hall, 122, 1967–75.
**Most Capped Player:** Tony Millington, 8 (21), Wales.
**Most League Appearances:** Tommy Robson, 482, 1968–81.
**Honours – Football League:** Division 4 Champions – 1960–61, 1973–74.
**Colours:** Royal blue shirts, white shorts, blue stockings with white tops.


# PLYMOUTH ARGYLE                                    DIV. 3

| Adams Steve (D) | 6 0 | 12 00 | Plymouth | 25 9 80 | Trainee |
| Bastow Darren (M) | 5 11 | 12 00 | Torquay | 22 12 81 | Trainee |
| Beswetherick John (D) | 5 11 | 11 04 | Liverpool | 15 1 78 | Trainee |
| Broad Joseph (M) | | | Bristol | 24 8 82 | Trainee |
| Evans Micky (F) | 6 0 | 12 03 | Plymouth | 1 1 73 | Bristol R |
| Evers Sean (M) | 5 9 | 9 07 | Hitchin | 10 10 77 | Reading |
| Friio David (M) | | | Thionville | 17 2 73 | ASOA Valence |
| Gritton Martin (F) | 6 1 | 12 02 | Glasgow | 1 6 78 | Porthleven |
| Guinan Stephen (F) | 6 1 | 13 06 | Birmingham | 24 12 75 | Cambridge U |

| | | | | | |
|---|---|---|---|---|---|
| Javary Jean-Philippe (M) | | | Montpellier | 10 1 78 | Brentford |
| McGlinchey Brian (D) | 5 8 | 10 05 | Derry | 26 10 77 | Gillingham |
| Phillips Martin (M) | 5 8 | 10 03 | Exeter | 13 3 76 | Portsmouth |
| Sheffield Jon (G) | 5 11 | 11 06 | Bedworth | 1 2 69 | Peterborough U |
| Stonebridge Ian (F) | 6 0 | 11 04 | Lewisham | 30 8 81 | Tottenham H |
| Taylor Craig (D) | 6 1 | 12 03 | Plymouth | 24 1 74 | Swindon T |
| Wills Kevin (F) | 5 7 | 10 04 | Torbay | 15 10 80 | Trainee |
| Worrell David (D) | 5 11 | 12 04 | Dublin | 12 1 78 | Dundee U |
| Wotton Paul (M) | 5 11 | 11 08 | Plymouth | 17 8 77 | Trainee |

**League Appearances:** Adams, S. 12(5); Bance, D. 1; Barlow, M. 17(3); Barrett, A. 9; Beswetherick, J. 44(1); Betts, R. 3(1); Connolly, P. (1); Elliott, S. 11(1); Evans, M. 10; Evers, S. 2(5); Fleming, T. 15(2); Friio, D. 26; Gritton, M. 1(9); Guinan, S. 7(15); Heathcote, M. 4(1); Hodges, J. 2; Javary, J. 4; Larrieu, R. 14(1); Leadbitter, C. 9; Mardon, P. 3; McCarthy, S. 31(6); McCormick, L. 1; McGlinchey, B. 17(3); McGregor, P. 31(2); Meaker, M. 5(6); Nancekivell, K. (6); O'Sullivan, W. 38(2); Peake, J. 7(3); Phillips, L. 4(2); Phillips, M. 36(6); Sheffield, J. 29; Stonebridge, I. 17(14); Taylor, C. 38(1); Trudgian, R. (1); Wilkie, L. 2; Wills, K. 4(6); Worrell, D. 14; Wotton, P. 38(4).
**Goals – League** (54): Stonebridge 11, McCarthy 10, McGregor 6, Friio 5, Evans 4, Wotton 4 (3 pens), Taylor 3, Peake 2, Gritton 1, Guinan 1, Mardon 1, Meaker 1, Nancekivell 1, O'Sullivan 1, Phillips M 1, Wills 1, own goal 1.
**Worthington Cup** (2): McCarthy 1, McGregor 1.
**FA Cup** (2): McGregor 2, Peake 1.
**Ground:** Home Park, Plymouth, Devon PL2 3DQ. Telephone (01752) 562561.
**Record attendance:** 43,596 v Aston Villa, Division 2, 10 October 1936.
**Capacity:** 19,630.
**Manager:** Paul Sturrock.
**Secretary:** Roger Matthews.
**Most League Goals:** 107, Division 3 (S), 1925–26 and 1951–52.
**Highest League Scorer in Season:** Jack Cock, 32, Division 3 (S), 1925–26.
**Most League Goals in Total Aggregate:** Sammy Black, 180, 1924–38.
**Most Capped Player:** Moses Russell, 20 (23), Wales.
**Most League Appearances:** Kevin Hodges, 530, 1978–92.
**Honours – Football League:** Division 3 (S) Champions – 1929–30, 1951–52. Division 3 Champions – 1958–59.
**Colours:** Green and white shirts, white shorts, green, black and white stockings.

---

# PORTSMOUTH                                        DIV. 1

| | | | | | |
|---|---|---|---|---|---|
| Allen Rory (F) | 5 11 | 11 10 | Beckenham | 17 10 77 | Tottenham H |
| Bradbury Lee (F) | 6 2 | 13 10 | Isle of Wight | 3 7 75 | Crystal Palace |
| Buxton Lewis (M) | | | Newport (IW) | 10 12 83 | School |
| Claridge Steve (F) | 5 9 | 12 09 | Portsmouth | 10 4 66 | Portsmouth |
| Cooper Shaun (M) | | | Isle of Wight | 5 10 83 | School |
| Crowe Jason (D) | 5 9 | 11 02 | Sidcup | 30 9 78 | Arsenal |
| Curtis Tom (M) | 5 8 | 10 08 | Exeter | 1 3 73 | Chesterfield |
| Derry Shaun (M) | 5 10 | 13 02 | Nottingham | 6 12 77 | Sheffield U |
| Edinburgh Justin (D) | 5 10 | 12 01 | Basildon | 18 12 69 | Tottenham H |
| Flahavan Aaron (G) | 6 1 | 11 12 | Southampton | 15 12 75 | Trainee |
| Griffiths Ben (D) | | | Bournemouth | 27 11 81 | Trainee |
| Harper Kevin (F) | 5 7 | 12 00 | Oldham | 15 1 76 | Derby Co |
| Hughes Ceri (M) | 5 10 | 12 07 | Pontypridd | 26 2 71 | Wimbledon |
| Lovell Stephen (F) | 5 11 | 11 08 | Amersham | 6 12 80 | Bournemouth |
| Miglioranzi Stefani (M) | 6 1 | 12 12 | Pacos de Caldas | 20 9 77 | St Johns Univ |
| Mills Lee (F) | 6 2 | 12 09 | Mexborough | 10 7 70 | Bradford C |

84

| Moore Darren (D) | 6 3 | 15 08 | Birmingham | 22 4 74 | Bradford C |
|---|---|---|---|---|---|
| Nightingale Luke (F) | 5 11 | 11 07 | Portsmouth | 22 12 80 | Trainee |
| O'Neil Gary (M) | 5 10 | 11 00 | Beckenham | 18 5 83 | Trainee |
| Panopoulos Mike (M) | 6 1 | 12 10 | Melbourne | 9 10 76 | Heidelberg U |
| Pettefer Carl (M) | 5 7 | 10 02 | Taplow | 22 3 81 | Trainee |
| Petterson Andy (G) | 6 2 | 15 02 | Fremantle | 29 9 69 | Charlton Ath |
| Primus Linvoy (D) | 6 0 | 12 04 | Forest Gate | 14 9 73 | Reading |
| Quashie Nigel (M) | 5 9 | 12 08 | Nunhead | 20 7 78 | Nottingham F |
| Rudonja Mladen (F) | 5 9 | 11 07 | Slovenia | 26 7 71 | St Truiden |
| Tardif Chris (G) | 5 11 | 12 07 | Guernsey | 19 9 79 | Trainee |
| Thogersen Thomas (M) | 6 2 | 13 01 | Copenhagen | 2 4 68 | Brondby |
| Tiler Carl (D) | 6 2 | 14 03 | Sheffield | 11 2 70 | Charlton Ath |
| Vincent Jamie (D) | 5 10 | 11 09 | London | 18 6 75 | Huddersfield T |
| Vine Rowan (F) | | | Basingstoke | 21 9 82 | Scholar |
| White Tom (D) | | | Chichester | 30 10 81 | Trainee |

**League Appearances:** Awford, A. 2; Bradbury, L. 35(4); Brady, G. 8; Claridge, S. 24(7); Crowe, J. 21(2); Curtis, T. 4; Derry, S. 27(1); Edinburgh, J. 16(1); Flahavan, A. 20; Harper, K. 15(9); Hiley, S. 34; Hoult, R. 22; Hughes, C. 16(3); Keller, M. 3; Lambourde, B. 6; Lovell, S. 5(4); Miglioranzi, S. 8(4); Mills, L. 22(2); Moore, D. 31(1); Nightingale, L. 7(12); O'Neil, G. 7(3); Panopoulos, M. 26(4); Pettefer, C. (1); Petterson, A. 2; Primus, L. 23; Quashie, N. 29(2); Rudonja, M. 2(9); Sharpe, L. 17; Tardif, C. 2(2); Thogersen, T. 32(2); Tiler, C. 9; Vincent, J. 14; Vine, R. (2); Waterman, D. 12(10); Whittingham, G. (1); Wolleaston, R. 5(1).
**Goals – League** (47): Claridge 11 (2 pens), Bradbury 10 (1 pen), Panopoulos 6 (1 pen), Quashie 5, Mills 4, Thogersen 3, Harper 2, Lovell 1, Moore 1, Nightingale 1, O'Neil 1, Tiler 1, own goal 1.
**Worthington Cup** (2): Mills 1, Nightingale 1.
**FA Cup** (1): Bradbury 1.
**Ground:** Fratton Park, Frogmore Rd, Portsmouth PO4 8RA. Telephone (01705) 731204.
**Record attendance:** 51,385 v Derby Co, FA Cup 6th rd, 26 February 1949.
**Capacity:** 19,179.
**Manager:** Graham Rix.
**Secretary:** Paul Weld.
**Most League Goals:** 91, Division 4, 1979–80.
**Highest League Scorer in Season:** Guy Whittingham, 42, Division 1, 1992–93.
**Most League Goals in Total Aggregate:** Peter Harris, 194, 1946–60.
**Most Capped Player:** Jimmy Dickinson, 48, England.
**Most League Appearances:** Jimmy Dickinson, 764, 1946–65.
**Honours – Football League:** Division 1 Champions – 1948–49, 1949–50. Division 3 (S) Champions – 1923–24. Division 3 Champions – 1961–62, 1982–83. **FA Cup:** Winners 1939.
**Colours:** Blue shirts, white shorts, red stockings.

---

# PORT VALE                                                    DIV. 2

| Brammer Dave (M) | 5 11 | 12 00 | Bromborough | 28 2 75 | Wrexham |
|---|---|---|---|---|---|
| Bridge-Wilkinson Marc (M) | 5 6 | 10 08 | Nuneaton | 16 3 79 | Derby Co |
| Brisco Neil (M) | 5 11 | 13 01 | Billinge | 26 1 78 | Manchester C |
| Brooker Stephen (F) | 5 10 | 12 04 | Newport Pagnell | 21 5 81 | Watford |
| Burgess Richard (F) | 5 8 | 11 00 | Bromsgrove | 18 8 78 | Stoke C |
| Burns Liam (D) | 6 0 | 13 03 | Belfast | 30 10 78 | Trainee |
| Burton Sagi (D) | 6 2 | 13 06 | Birmingham | 25 11 77 | Sheffield U |
| Carragher Matthew (D) | 5 9 | 11 06 | Liverpool | 14 1 76 | Wigan Ath |

| Cummins Michael (M) | 6 0 | 12 08 | Dublin | 1 | 6 78 | Middlesbrough |
| Delany Dean (G) | | | Dublin | 15 | 9 80 | Everton |
| Donnelly Paul (D) | 5 7 | 11 00 | Newcastle under Lyme | 16 | 2 81 | Trainee |
| Goodlad Mark (G) | 6 0 | 13 02 | Barnsley | 9 | 9 80 | Nottingham F |
| O'Callaghan George (M) | 6 1 | 10 05 | Cork | 5 | 9 79 | Trainee |
| Taylor Paul (M) | 5 11 | 12 06 | Stoke | 16 | 9 80 | Trainee |
| Walsh Michael (D) | 6 0 | 12 08 | Rotherham | 5 | 8 77 | Scunthorpe U |

**League Appearances:** Beresford, D. 4; Brammer, D. 33(2); Bridge-Wilkinson, M. 40(2); Brisco, N. 16(1); Brooker, S. 20(3); Burgess, R. (1); Burns, L. 5(8); Burton, S. 24(5); Byrne, P. 1; Carragher, M. 45; Cummins, M. 43(2); Delany, D. 7(1); Dodd, A. 3; Donnelly, P. (1); Eyre, R. 1(5); Freeman, D. 2(1); Goodlad, M. 39(1); Gray, W. 2(1); Lowe, O. 4(1); Minton, J. 11(2); Naylor, T. 41(1); O'Callaghan, G. 2(6); Olaoye, D, (1); Paynter, B. (1); Smith, A. 36(1); Tankard, A. 28(5); Twiss, M. 15(3); Viljanen, V. 15(4); Walsh, M. 38(1); Widdrington, T. 31(4).
**Goals – League** (55): Naylor 14, Bridge-Wilkinson 9 (3 pens), Brooker 8, Tankard 4, Brammer 3, Twiss 3, Cummins 2, Smith 2, Viljanen 2, Widdrington 2, Brisco 1, Lowe 1, Minton 1, O'Callaghan 1, Walsh 1, own goal 1.
**Worthington Cup** (3): Bridge-Wilkinson 1, Burton 1, Minton 1.
**FA Cup** (5): Minton 2, Brammer 1, Bridge-Wilkinson 1, Naylor 1.
**Ground:** Vale Park, Burslem, Stoke-on-Trent ST6 1AW. Telephone (01782) 814134.
**Record attendance:** 50,000 v Aston Villa, FA Cup 5th rd, 20 February 1960.
**Capacity:** 22,356
**Manager:** Brian Horton.
**Secretary:** F. W. Lodey.
**Most League Goals:** 110, Division 4, 1958–59.
**Highest League Scorer in Season:** Wilf Kirkham 38, Division 2, 1926–27.
**Most League Goals in Total Aggregate:** Wilf Kirkham, 154, 1923–29, 1931–33.
**Most Capped Player:** Tony Rougier, Trinidad and Tobago.
**Most League Appearances:** Roy Sproson, 761, 1950–72.
**Honours – Football League:** Division 3 (N) Champions – 1929–30, 1953–54. Division 4 Champions – 1958–59. **LDV Vans Trophy winners:** 2001
**Colours:** White shirts, black shorts, black and white stockings.

# PRESTON NORTH END DIV. 1

| Abbott Pawel (F) | | | York | 5 | 5 82 | LKS Lodz |
| Alexander Graham (D) | 5 10 | 12 00 | Coventry | 10 10 71 | | Luton T |
| Anderson Iain (F) | 5 8 | 9 07 | Glasgow | 23 | 7 77 | Toulouse |
| Barry-Murphy Brian (M) | 6 0 | 12 04 | Cork | 27 | 7 78 | Cork City |
| Basham Steve (F) | 5 11 | 12 05 | Southampton | 2 12 77 | | Southampton |
| Cartwright Lee (F) | 5 8 | 10 07 | Rossendale | 19 | 9 72 | Trainee |
| Eaton Adam (D) | 5 10 | 11 08 | Wigan | 2 | 5 80 | Everton |
| Edwards Robert (D) | 6 0 | 12 07 | Kendal | 1 | 7 73 | Bristol C |
| Gregan Sean (M) | 6 2 | 12 03 | Stockton | 29 | 3 74 | Darlington |
| Gunnlaugsson Bjarki (F) | 5 9 | 11 05 | Iceland | 6 | 3 73 | KR |
| Healy David (F) | 5 8 | 11 01 | Downpatrick | 5 | 8 79 | Manchester U |
| Jackson Michael (D) | 5 11 | 11 10 | Chester | 4 12 73 | | Bury |
| Keane Michael (M) | | | Dublin | 29 12 82 | | Scholar |
| Kidd Ryan (D) | 5 11 | 10 10 | Radcliffe | 16 10 71 | | Port Vale |
| Lonergan Andrew (G) | | | Preston | 19 10 83 | | Scholar |
| Lucas David (G) | 6 1 | 11 06 | Preston | 23 11 77 | | Trainee |
| Macken Jonathan (F) | 5 10 | 12 00 | Manchester | 7 | 9 77 | Trainee |
| McKenna Paul (M) | 5 8 | 11 11 | Chorley | 20 10 77 | | Trainee |

86

| | | | | | |
|---|---|---|---|---|---|
| Moilanen Teuvo (G) | 6 5 | 12 09 | Oulu | 12 12 73 | Jaro |
| Morgan Paul (D) | 6 0 | 11 05 | Belfast | 23 10 78 | Trainee |
| Murdock Colin (D) | 6 1 | 12 00 | Ballymena | 2 7 75 | Manchester U |
| Quinn Patrick (M) | | | | 3 12 81 | |
| Rankine Mark (M) | 5 9 | 11 05 | Doncaster | 30 9 69 | Wolverhampton W |
| Robinson Steve (F) | 5 9 | 11 02 | Crumlin | 10 12 74 | Bournemouth |
| Wright Mark (F) | 5 10 | 11 05 | Chorley | 4 9 81 | Schoolboy |

**League Appearances:** Alexander, G. 34; Anderson, I. 19(12); Appleton, M. 25(1); Barry-Murphy, B. 2(12); Basham, S. 11; Cartwright, L. 29(9); Cresswell, R. 5(6); Eaton, A. 1; Edwards, R. 41(1); Eyres, D. (5); Gregan, S. 39(2); Gunnlaugsson, B. 5(14); Healy, D. 19(3); Jackson, M. 27(3); Keane, M. (2); Kidd, R. 13(2); Lonergan, A. 1; Lucas, D. 28(1); Ludden, D. (2); Macken, J. 37(1); McBride, B. 8(1); McKenna, P. 43(1); Meijer, E. 9; Moilanen, T. 17; Murdock, C. 33(4); O'Hanlon, K. (1); Parkinson, G. 11; Rankine, M. 43(1); Robinson, S. 6(16).
**Goals – League** (64): Macken 19, Healy 9 (1 pen), Anderson 6, Alexander 5 (3 pens), Appleton 5, McKenna 5, Rankine 4, Basham 2, Cresswell 2, Gregan 2, Gunnlaugsson 1, Jackson 1, McBride 1, Robinson 1, own goal 1.
**Worthington Cup** (6): Macken 3, Alexander 2 (1 pen), Rankine 1.
**FA Cup** (0).
**Ground:** Deepdale, Preston PR1 6RU. Telephone (01772) 902020.
**Record attendance:** 42,684 v Arsenal, Division 1, 23 April 1938. **Capacity:** 21,412.
**Manager:** David Moyes.
**Secretary:** G. E. Harrison.
**Most League Goals:** 100, Division 2, 1927–28 and Division 1, 1957–58.
**Highest League Scorer in Season:** Ted Harper, 37, Division 2, 1932–33.
**Most League Goals in Total Aggregate:** Tom Finney, 187, 1946–60.
**Most Capped Player:** Tom Finney, 76, England.
**Most League Appearances:** Alan Kelly, 447, 1961–75.
**Honours – Football League:** Division 1 Champions – 1888–89 (first champions), 1889–90. Division 2 Champions – 1903–04, 1912–13, 1950–51, 1999–2000. Division 3 Champions – 1970–71, 1995–96. **FA Cup winners** 1889, 1938.
**Colours:** White shirts, navy shorts, white stockings.

# QUEENS PARK RANGERS
## DIV. 2

| | | | | | |
|---|---|---|---|---|---|
| Bignot Marcus (D) | 5 9 | 11 00 | Birmingham | 28 8 74 | Bristol R |
| Brady Richard (F) | 5 8 | 10 04 | Dartford | 17 9 82 | Trainee |
| Brown Carlos (D) | 6 0 | 11 07 | Edmonton | 22 4 81 | Trainee |
| Browne Rickey (D) | 6 1 | 12 05 | Edmonton | 19 10 81 | Scholar |
| Bull Nikki (G) | 6 1 | 11 13 | Hastings | 2 10 81 | Scholar |
| Carlisle Clarke (D) | 6 1 | 12 07 | Preston | 14 10 79 | Blackpool |
| Cochrane Justin (M) | 5 11 | 11 07 | Hackney | 26 1 82 | Scholar |
| Connolly Karl (F) | 5 10 | 11 01 | Prescot | 9 2 70 | Wrexham |
| Crouch Peter (F) | 6 2 | 11 12 | Macclesfield | 30 1 81 | Tottenham H |
| Currie Michael (F) | 5 10 | 11 00 | Westminster | 19 10 79 | Trainee |
| D'Austin Ryan (M) | 5 9 | 10 13 | Edgware | 29 11 82 | Trainee |
| Darlington Jermaine (D) | 5 9 | 13 00 | Hackney | 11 4 74 | Aylesbury U |
| Dick Alexander (M) | | | Paddington | 2 9 82 | Scholar |
| Duncan Lyndon (D) | 5 8 | 11 02 | Ealing | 12 1 83 | Trainee |
| Fitzgerald Brian (M) | | | Perivale | 23 10 83 | School |
| Gradley Patrick (M) | | | London | 1 6 83 | Scholar |
| Graham Richard (M) | 5 8 | 10 06 | Newry | 5 8 79 | Trainee |
| Koejoe Sammy (F) | 6 2 | 14 07 | Surinam | 17 8 74 | Salzburg |
| Langley Richard (M) | 5 10 | 11 04 | London | 27 12 79 | Trainee |
| Lusardi Mario (F) | 5 9 | 12 00 | Islington | 27 9 79 | Trainee |

| | | | | | | |
|---|---|---|---|---|---|---|
| Mills Danny (G) | 6 0 | 12 07 | Sidcup | 8 | 9 82 | Trainee |
| Murphy Danny (D) | 5 6 | 10 04 | London | 4 | 12 82 | Trainee |
| Nugent Marcel (M) | | | London | 10 | 9 82 | Scholar |
| Pacquette Richard (F) | 6 0 | 12 07 | Paddington | 28 | 1 83 | Trainee |
| Peacock Gavin (M) | 5 9 | 11 08 | Eltham | 18 | 11 67 | Chelsea |
| Perry Mark (M) | 5 11 | 13 06 | Perivale | 19 | 10 78 | Trainee |
| Plummer Chris (D) | 6 2 | 12 12 | Isleworth | 12 | 10 76 | Trainee |
| Robertson Kristoffer (M) | | | Paisley | 24 | 9 82 | Scholar |
| Rustem Adam (F) | 6 0 | 11 07 | Whipps Cross | 18 | 9 81 | Scholar |
| Sodje Iroroakpeyere (M) | | | Greenwich | 31 | 1 81 | |
| Thomson Andy (F) | 5 10 | 11 05 | Motherwell | 1 | 4 71 | Gillingham |
| Walshe Benjamin (M) | | | London | 24 | 5 83 | Scholar |
| Wardley Stuart (M) | 5 11 | 12 03 | Cambridge | 10 | 9 75 | Saffron Walden T |
| Warren Christer (F) | 5 10 | 11 12 | Poole | 10 | 10 74 | Bournemouth |
| Wattley David (M) | | | Enfield | 5 | 9 83 | School |
| Wright Danny (M) | 5 7 | 10 13 | London | 24 | 9 81 | Trainee |

**League Appearances:** Baraclough, I. 26(3); Bignot, M. 8(1); Breacker, T. 8(2); Broomes, M. 5; Brown, W. 2; Bruce, P. 5(2); Bubb, A. (1); Burgess, O. (1); Carlisle, C. 27; Cochrane, J. (1); Connolly, K. 17(6); Crouch, P. 38(4); Darlington, J. 32(1); Dowie, I. (1); Furlong, P. 3; Harper, L. 29; Heinola, A. (1); Higgins, A. (1); Kiwomya, C. 20(6); Knight, L. 10(1); Koejoe, S. 8(13); Kulcsar, G. 9(5); Langley, R. 26; Lisbie, K. 1(1); Maddix, D. 1(1); McFlynn, T. 1(1); Miklosko, L. 17; Morrow, S. 18(6); Murray, P. 4(2); Ngonge, M. 7(6); Pacquette, R. 1(1); Peacock, G. 31(1); Perry, M. 23(6); Peschisolido, P. 5; Plummer, C. 24(1); Ready, K. 19(4); Rose, M. 27; Rowland, K. 4; Scully, T. 1(1); Thomson, A. 7(1); Walshe, B. (1); Wardley, S. 26(8); Warren, C. 16(6).
**Goals – League** (45): Crouch 10, Kiwomya 6, Connolly 4, Thomson 4, Carlisle 3, Ngonge 3 (1 pen), Peacock 3 (2 pens), Wardley 3, Koejoe 2, Plummer 2, Bignot 1, Bruce 1, Furlong 1, Langley 1, Peschisolido 1.
**Worthington Cup** (2): Kiwomya 2.
**FA Cup** (5): Crouch 2, Kiwomya 2, Peacock 1 (pen).
**Ground:** South Africa Road, W12 7PA. Telephone (020) 8743 0262.
**Record attendance:** 35,353 v Leeds U, Division 1, 27 April 1974. **Capacity:** 19,148.
**Manager:** Ian Holloway.
**Secretary:** Sheila Marson.
**Most League Goals:** 111, Division 3, 1961–62.
**Highest League Scorer in Season:** George Goddard, 37, Division 3 (S), 1929–30.
**Most League Goals in Total Aggregate:** George Goddard, 172, 1926–34.
**Most Capped Player:** Alan McDonald, 52, Northern Ireland.
**Most League Appearances:** Tony Ingham, 519, 1950–63.
**Honours – Football League:** Division 2 Champions – 1982–83. Division 3 (S) Champions – 1947–48. Division 3 Champions – 1966–67. **Football League Cup winners** 1966–67.
**Colours:** Blue and white hooped shirts, white shorts, white stockings.

---

# READING                                               DIV. 2

| | | | | | | |
|---|---|---|---|---|---|---|
| Allaway Ricky (D) | 6 2 | 11 08 | Reading | 16 | 2 83 | Trainee |
| Ashdown Jamie (G) | 6 3 | 14 07 | Wokingham | 30 | 11 80 | |
| Butler Martin (F) | 6 0 | 11 07 | Wordsley | 15 | 9 74 | Cambridge U |
| Casper Chris (D) | 6 0 | 11 02 | Burnley | 28 | 4 75 | Manchester U |
| Cureton Jamie (F) | 5 7 | 11 00 | Bristol | 28 | 8 75 | Bristol R |
| Forster Nicky (F) | 5 9 | 10 11 | Caterham | 8 | 9 73 | Birmingham C |
| Gamble Joe (M) | | | Cork | 14 | 1 82 | Cork C |

| Harper James (M) | 5 9 | 11 06 | Chelmsford | 9 11 80 | Arsenal |
|---|---|---|---|---|---|
| Henderson Darius (F) | 6 1 | 13 09 | Doncaster | 7 9 81 | Trainee |
| Hunter Barry (D) | 6 4 | 12 00 | Coleraine | 18 11 68 | Wrexham |
| Igoe Sammy (M) | 5 6 | 10 08 | Spelthorne | 30 9 75 | Portsmouth |
| Jones Keith (M) | 5 9 | 11 07 | Dulwich | 14 10 65 | Charlton Ath |
| Lockwood Adam (D) | 6 0 | 12 00 | Wakefield | 26 10 81 | Trainee |
| Mackie John (D) | 6 0 | 12 06 | London | 5 7 76 | Sutton U |
| Murty Graeme (M) | 5 10 | 11 10 | Saltburn | 13 11 74 | York C |
| Robinson Matt (D) | 5 10 | 11 02 | Exeter | 23 12 74 | Portsmouth |
| Rougier Tony (F) | 5 10 | 14 07 | Trinidad | 17 7 71 | Port Vale |
| Shorey Nicky (D) | 5 9 | 10 08 | Romford | 19 2 81 | Leyton Orient |
| Smith Neil (M) | 5 9 | 12 00 | Lambeth | 30 9 71 | Fulham |
| Tyson Nathan (F) | 6 0 | 10 01 | Reading | 4 5 82 | Trainee |
| Viveash Adrian (D) | 6 2 | 12 13 | Swindon | 30 9 69 | Walsall |
| Whitehead Phil (G) | 6 3 | 13 07 | Halifax | 17 12 69 | WBA |
| Williams Adrian (D) | 6 2 | 12 06 | Reading | 16 8 71 | Wolverhampton W |

**League Appearances:** Ashdown, J. (1); Butler, M. 42(3); Caskey, D. 35(8); Cureton, J. 37(6); Forster, N. (9); Gamble, J. (1); Gray, S. 2(1); Gurney, A. 15(6); Haddow, A. (1); Harper, J. 9(3); Henderson, D. (4); Hodges, L. 23(6); Hunter, B. 21(2); Igoe, S. 15(16); Jones, K. 18(5); Mackie, J. 7(3); McIntyre, J. 25(8); Murty, G. 18(5); Newman, R. 37(2); Parkinson, P. 44; Robinson, M. 29(3); Rougier, T. 14(17); Scott, K. 1; Smith, N. 4(11); Viveash, A. 40; Whitbread, A. 19; Whitehead, P. 46; Williams, A. 5.

**Goals** (86): Cureton 26, Butler 24, Caskey 9 (4 pens), Igoe 6, McIntyre 4, Parkinson 4, Hodges 2, Rougier 2, Viveash 2, Forster 1, Gurney 1, Harper 1, Hunter 1, Murty 1, Smith 1, own goal 1.

**Worthington Cup** (1): Cureton 1.

**FA Cup** (7): Butler 2, Caskey 1, Cureton 1, Hodges 1, Jones 1, Newman 1.

**Ground:** Madejski Stadium, Junction 11, M4, Reading, Berks RG2 0FL. Telephone (0118) 968 1100.

**Record attendance:** 33,042 v Brentford, FA Cup 5th rd, 19 February 1927.

**Capacity:** 15,000.

**Manager:** Alan Pardew.

**Secretary:** Sue Hewett.

**Most League Goals:** 112, Division 3 (S), 1951–52.

**Highest League Scorer in Season:** Ronnie Blackman, 39, Division 3 (S), 1951–52.

**Most League Goals in Total Aggregate:** Ronnie Blackman, 158, 1947–54.

**Most Capped Player:** Jimmy Quinn, 17 (46), Northern Ireland.

**Most League Appearances:** Martin Hicks, 500, 1978–91.

**Honours – Football League:** Division 2 Champions – 1993–94. Division 3 Champions – 1985–86. Division 3 (S) Champions – 1925–26. Division 4 Champions – 1978–79. **Simod Cup winners** 1987–88.

**Colours:** Royal blue and white hooped shirts, blue shorts, white and blue stockings.

---

## ROCHDALE                                    DIV. 3

| Coleman Simon (D) | 6 1 | 12 10 | Mansfield | 13 6 68 | Southend U |
|---|---|---|---|---|---|
| Connor Paul (F) | 6 2 | 11 08 | Bishop Auckland | 12 1 79 | Stoke C |
| Edwards Neil (G) | 5 9 | 11 11 | Aberdare | 5 12 70 | Stockport Co |
| Evans Wayne (D) | 5 10 | 12 03 | Welshpool | 25 8 71 | Walsall |
| Ford Tony (M) | 5 9 | 13 00 | Grimsby | 14 5 59 | Mansfield T |
| Hadland Phil (M) | 5 11 | 11 11 | Warrington | 20 10 80 | Trainee |
| Hicks Graham (D) | 5 10 | 13 05 | Oldham | 17 2 81 | Trainee |
| Jones Gary (M) | 5 11 | 11 07 | Birkenhead | 3 6 77 | Caernarfon Town |

| | | | | | |
|---|---|---|---|---|---|
| McAuley Sean (D) | 5 9 | 11 13 | Sheffield | 23 6 72 | Scunthorpe U |
| Oliver Michael (M) | 5 10 | 11 04 | Middlesbrough | 2 8 75 | Darlington |
| Parkin Steve (D) | 5 6 | 11 01 | Mansfield | 7 11 65 | Mansfield T |
| Platt Clive (F) | 6 3 | 12 13 | Wolverhampton | 27 10 77 | Walsall |
| Todd Lee (D) | 5 7 | 11 01 | Hartlepool | 7 3 72 | Bradford C |
| Townson Kevin (F) | | | Liverpool | 19 4 83 | |
| Ware Paul (M) | 5 9 | 11 05 | Congleton | 7 11 70 | Macclesfield T |

**League Appearances:** Bayliss, D. 41; Buggie, L. (2); Coleman, S. 5; Connor, P. 14; Davies, S. 7(5); Edwards, N. 44; Ellis, T. 25(3); Evans, W. 45; Flitcroft, D. 40(1); Ford, T. 36(2); Gilks, M. 2(1); Hadland, P. 12(20); Hamilton, G. (3); Hill, K. 22(3); Howell, D. 2(1); Jones, G. 44; Kyle, K. 3(3); Lancashire, G. 6(10); Lee, C. 2(3); McAuley, S. 1; Monington, M. 31(3); Oliver, M. 25(13); Platt, C. 39(4); Todd, L. 40; Townson, K. 1(2); Turner, A. 2(2); Ware, P. 17(13).
**Goals – League** (59): Connor 10, Jones 8 (3 pens), Platt 8, Monington 7, Ellis 6, Bayliss 3, Lancashire 3, Todd 3, Evans 2, Ford 2, Hadland 2, Ware 2, Davies 1 (pen), Lee 1, own goal 1.
**Worthington Cup** (2): Ellis 1, Platt 1.
**FA Cup** (1): Platt 1.
**Ground:** Spotland, Sandy Lane, Rochdale OL11 5DS. Telephone (01706) 644648.
**Record attendance:** 24,231 v Notts Co, FA Cup 2nd rd, 10 December 1949.
**Capacity:** 10,249.
**Manager:** Steve Parkin.
**Secretary:** Hilary Molyneux Dearden.
**Most League Goals:** 105, Division 3 (N), 1926–27.
**Highest League Scorer in Season:** Albert Whitehurst, 44, Division 3 (N), 1926–27.
**Most League Goals in Total Aggregate:** Reg Jenkins, 119, 1964–73.
**Most Capped Player:** None.
**Most League Appearances:** Graham Smith, 317, 1966–74.
**Honours – Nil.**
**Colours:** Blue shirts with white trim, blue shorts, blue stockings with white hoop.

---

# ROTHERHAM UNITED　　　　　　　　　　　　　　DIV. 1

| | | | | | |
|---|---|---|---|---|---|
| Artell David (D) | 6 2 | 13 00 | Rotherham | 22 11 80 | Trainee |
| Barker Richard (F) | 6 1 | 13 12 | Sheffield | 30 5 75 | Macclesfield T |
| Berry Trevor (M) | 5 6 | 11 00 | Haslemere | 1 8 74 | Aston Villa |
| Branston Guy (D) | 6 1 | 13 11 | Leicester | 9 1 79 | Leicester C |
| Bryan Marvin (D) | 6 0 | 12 02 | Paddington | 2 8 75 | Bury |
| Garner Darren (M) | 5 9 | 12 07 | Plymouth | 10 12 71 | Plymouth Arg |
| Gray Ian (G) | 6 2 | 13 00 | Manchester | 25 2 75 | Stockport Co |
| Hudson Danny (M) | 5 8 | 10 03 | Mexborough | 25 6 79 | Trainee |
| Hurst Paul (D) | 5 4 | 9 00 | Sheffield | 25 9 74 | Trainee |
| Lee Alan (F) | 6 2 | 13 09 | Galway | 21 8 78 | Burnley |
| Monkhouse Andy (F) | 6 0 | 13 09 | Leeds | 23 10 80 | Trainee |
| Robins Mark (F) | 5 8 | 11 08 | Ashton-under-Lyne | 22 12 69 | Walsall |
| Scott Rob (F) | 6 1 | 12 04 | Epsom | 15 8 73 | Fulham |
| Sedgwick Chris (F) | 5 11 | 10 10 | Sheffield | 28 4 80 | Trainee |
| Talbot Stuart (M) | 5 11 | 13 07 | Birmingham | 14 6 73 | Port Vale |
| Warne Paul (F) | 5 8 | 11 01 | Norwich | 8 5 73 | Wigan Ath |
| Watson Kevin (M) | 5 10 | 12 08 | Hackney | 3 1 74 | Swindon T |

**League Appearances:** Artell, D. 35(1); Barker, R. 7(12); Beech, C. 8(7); Berry, T. 5(6); Bolima, C. (1); Branston, G. 41; Bryan, M. 23(5); Carr, D. 1; Fortune-West, L. 5; Garner, D. 30(1); Gray, I. 33; Hudson, D. 1(4); Hurst, P. 42(2); Lee, A. 29(2); Minton, J. 5(4); Monkhouse, A. 1(11); Pettinger, P. 13; Robins, M. 42; Scott, R. 39;

Sedgwick, C. 2(19); Talbot, S. 37(1); Turner, A. 3(1); Varty, W. 5(1); Warne, P. 44; Watson, K. 46; Wilsterman, B. 9(1).
**Goals – League** (79): Robins 24 (4 pens), Lee 13 (1 pen), Warne 7, Branston 6, Talbot 5, Watson 5, Artell 4, Hurst 3, Minton 2, Scott 2, Sedgwick 2, Barker 1, Fortune-West 1, Garner 1, Wilsterman 1, own goals 2.
**Worthington Cup** (2): Robins 1, Watson 1.
**FA Cup** (2): Lee 1, own goal 1.
**Ground:** Millmoor Ground, Rotherham S60 1HR. Telephone (01709) 512434.
**Record attendance:** 25,000 v Sheffield U, Division 2, 13 December 1952 and v Sheffield W, Division 2, 26 January 1952. **Capacity:** 11,514
**Manager:** Ronnie Moore.
**Most League Goals:** 114, Division 3 (N), 1946–47.
**Highest League Scorer in Season:** Wally Ardron, 38, Division 3 (N), 1946–47.
**Most League Goals in Total Aggregate:** Gladstone Guest, 130, 1946–56.
**Most Capped Player:** Shaun Goater, 19, Bermuda.
**Most League Appearances:** Danny Williams, 459, 1946–62.
**Honours – Football League:** Division 3 Champions – 1980–81. Division 3 (N) Champions – 1950–51. Division 4 Champions – 1988–89. **Auto Windscreens Shield:** Winners 1996
**Colours:** Red shirts, white shorts, red stockings.

## RUSHDEN & DIAMONDS                                   DIV. 3

**Conference Appearances:** Bradshaw, 0(1); Brady, 39(2); Burgess, 37(3); Butterworth, 40(1); Carey, 32(1); Collins, 0(1); Darby 38; Essandoh, 0(2); Gray, 4(2); Iga, 0(1); Jackson, 40; Mills, 12(9); Mustafa, 41; Naylor, 0(1); Peters 20(2); Rogers, 1; Rodwell, 28(2); Sale, 0(2); Setchell, 19(10); Sigere, 5(15); Solkhon, 1; Town, 1(2); Turley, 41; Underwood, 23(2); Warburton, 37; Wormull, 3(5).
**Goals – League** (78): Darby 24 (3 pens), Jackson 18 (1 pen), Brady 11, Burgess 7, Sigere 6; Underwood 3 (2 pens), Peters 2, Butterworth 1, Carey 1, Setchell 1, Town 1, Warburton 1, Wormull 1, own goal 1.
**Ground:** Nene Park, Diamond Way, Earthlingborough, Northants NN9 5QF. Telephone (01933) 652 000.
**Record Attendance:** 6,431 v Leeds U, F.A. Cup 3rd rd, 2 January 1999.
**Ground Capacity:** 6,553
**Manager:** Brian Talbot.
**Secretary:** David Joyce.
**Most League Goals:** 109, Southern League Midland Division, 1993–94.
**Honours – Conference:** Champions 2000–01. **Southern League Midland Division:** Champions 1993–94. **Premier Division:** Champions 1995–96. **FA Trophy:** Semi-finalists 1994. **Northants FA Hillier Senior Cup:** Winners 1993–94, 1998–99. **Maunsell Premier Cup:** Winners 1994–95, 1998–99.
**Colours:** White shirts with blue sleeves, blue shorts with white trim, white stockings.

## SCUNTHORPE UNITED                                     DIV. 3

| | | | | | |
|---|---|---|---|---|---|
| Brough Scott (M) | | | Doncaster | 10 2 83 | |
| Calvo-Garcia Alexander (M) | 5 11 | 11 10 | Ordizia | 1 1 72 | Eibar |
| Carruthers Martin (F) | 5 10 | 12 02 | Nottingham | 7 8 72 | Southend U |
| Dawson Andrew (D) | 5 9 | 11 05 | Northallerton | 20 10 78 | Nottingham F |
| Graves Wayne (M) | 5 8 | 10 09 | Scunthorpe | 18 9 80 | Trainee |
| Hodges Lee (M) | 5 5 | 11 00 | Newham | 2 3 78 | West Ham U |

91

| Jackson Mark (D) | 5 11 | 12 04 | Barnsley | 30 | 9 77 | Leeds U |
| Pepper Nigel (M) | 5 10 | 11 13 | Rotherham | 25 | 4 68 | Southend U |
| Quailey Brian (F) | 6 0 | 13 04 | Leicester | 21 | 3 78 | WBA |
| Sheldon Gareth (F) | 5 11 | 12 06 | Birmingham | 31 | 1 80 | Trainee |
| Stanton Nathan (D) | 5 9 | 12 06 | Nottingham | 6 | 5 81 | Trainee |
| Thom Stuart (D) | 6 3 | 13 01 | Dewsbury | 27 12 76 | | Oldham Ath |
| Torpey Steve (F) | 6 3 | 13 06 | Islington | 8 12 70 | | Bristol C |

**League Appearances:** Banger, N. (1); Berry, T. 6; Brough, S. (4); Calvo-Garcia, A. 30(4); Carruthers, M. 8; Cotterill, J. 4; Dawson, A. 41; Evans, T. 46; Fickling, A. 3(6); Graves, W. 25(9); Harsley, P. 22(11); Hodges, L. 32(6); Ipoua, G. 22(3); Jackson, M. 28(4); Larusson, B. 33; Mamoum, B. (1); Morrison, P. 8(10); Pepper, N. 2; Quailey, B. 11(16); Rapley, K. 1(4); Ridley, L. 1(1); Rogers, D. 1; Sheldon, G. 33(6); Shepherd, P. (1); Sparrow, M. 9(2); Stamp, D. 4(8); Stanton, N. 34(4); Thom, S. 17(4); Torpey, S. 40; Wilcox, R. 33(3); Woodward, A. 12.
**Goals – League** (62): Ipoua 14 (1 pen), Torpey 10, Hodges 8 (2 pens), Calvo-Garcia 4, Dawson 4, Larusson 4, Sparrow 4, Quailey 3, Graves 2, Berry 1, Carruthers 1, Harsley 1, Jackson 1, Sheldon 1, Stamp 1, Wilcox 1, own goals 2.
**Worthington Cup** (1): Torpey 1.
**FA Cup** (9): Ipoua 4, Calvo-Garcia 1, Dawson 1, Hodges 1, Sheldon 1, Torpey 1.
**Ground:** Glanford Park, Scunthorpe, South Humberside DN15 8TD. Telephone (01724) 848077.
**Record attendance:** Old Showground: 23,935 v Portsmouth, FA Cup 4th rd, 30 January 1954. Glanford Park: 8775 v Rotherham U, Division 4, 1 May 1989.
**Capacity:** 9183.
**Manager:** Brian Laws.
**Secretary:** A. D. Rowing.
**Most League Goals:** 88, Division 3 (N), 1957–58.
**Highest League Scorer in Season:** Barrie Thomas, 31, Division 2, 1961–62.
**Most League Goals in Total Aggregate:** Steve Cammack, 110, 1979–81, 1981–86.
**Most Capped Player:** None.
**Most League Appearances:** Jack Brownsword, 595, 1950–65.
**Honours –** Division 3 (N) Champions – 1957–58.
**Colours:** White shirt with claret and blue trim, white shorts and stockings with claret and blue trim.

---

# SHEFFIELD UNITED                                    DIV. 1

| Asaba Carl (F) | 6 2 | 13 00 | London | 28 | 1 73 | Gillingham |
| Brown Michael R (M) | 5 9 | 10 07 | Hartlepool | 25 | 1 77 | Manchester C |
| Burley Adam (M) | 5 10 | 12 06 | Sheffield | 27 11 80 | | Trainee |
| Cryan Colin (M) | 5 10 | 13 00 | Dublin | 23 | 3 81 | Scholar |
| Curle Keith (D) | 6 0 | 12 07 | Bristol | 14 11 63 | | Wolverhampton W |
| D'Jaffo Laurent (F) | 6 0 | 13 05 | Aquitane | 5 11 70 | | Stockport Co |
| Devlin Paul (F) | 5 8 | 11 08 | Birmingham | 14 | 4 72 | Birmingham C |
| Doane Ben (D) | 5 10 | 10 05 | Sheffield | 22 12 79 | | Trainee |
| Ford Bobby (M) | 5 8 | 10 07 | Bristol | 22 | 9 74 | Oxford U |
| Gijsbrechts Davy (D) | 6 1 | 13 08 | Heusden | 20 | 9 72 | Lokeren |
| Jagielka Philip (M) | | | Manchester | 17 | 8 82 | Scholar |
| Kozluk Robert (D) | 5 8 | 10 07 | Sutton-in-Ashfield | 5 | 8 77 | Derby Co |
| Montgomery Nick (M) | 5 9 | 11 08 | Leeds | 28 10 81 | | Scholar |
| Murphy Shaun (D) | 6 1 | 13 10 | Sydney | 5 11 70 | | WBA |
| Ndlovu Peter (F) | 5 8 | 10 02 | Zimbabwe | 25 | 2 73 | Birmingham C |
| Quinn Gerry (M) | | | Dublin | 16 | 9 83 | |
| Ribeiro Bruno (M) | 5 8 | 12 07 | Setubal | 22 10 75 | | Leeds U |
| Sandford Lee (D) | 6 0 | 13 06 | Basingstoke | 22 | 4 68 | Stoke C |

92

| | | | | | | |
|---|---|---|---|---|---|---|
| Santos Georges (D) | 6 3 | 14 08 | Marseille | 15 8 70 | WBA | |
| Smith Andy (F) | 5 11 | 11 10 | Lisburn | 25 9 80 | | |
| Suffo Patrick (F) | 5 8 | 12 13 | Ebolowa | 17 1 78 | Nantes | |
| Thompson Lee (G) | | | Sheffield | 25 3 82 | | |
| Thompson Tyrone (F) | 5 9 | 11 02 | Sheffield | 8 5 82 | Scholar | |
| Tonge Michael (M) | | | Manchester | 7 4 83 | Scholar | |
| Tracey Simon (G) | 6 0 | 14 00 | Woolwich | 9 12 67 | Wimbledon | |
| Travers Mervyn (G) | | | Dublin | 22 11 82 | Trainee | |
| Uhlenbeek Gus (D) | 5 9 | 12 05 | Paramaribo | 20 8 70 | Fulham | |
| Ward Mark (F) | | | Sheffield | 27 1 82 | Sheffield Colleges | |
| Woodward Andy (D) | 6 0 | 13 04 | Stockport | 13 9 73 | Bury | |
| Yohanna Buba (M) | | | Yaounde | 16 6 82 | | |

**League Appearances:** Asaba, C. 10; Bent, M. 16; Brown, M. 36; Bullock, D. 6; Burley, A. (1); Cryan, C. (1); Curle, K. 23(2); D'Jaffo, L. 16(6); Devlin, P. 41; Doane, B. 3; Ford, B. 33(2); Jagielka, P. 3(12); Kelly, D. 21(14); Kozluk, R. 23(4); Montgomery, N. 14(13); Morrison, A. 3(1); Murphy, S. 46; Ndlovu, P. 15; Newby, J. 3(10); Peschisolido, P. 4(1); Quinn, W. 21(3); Ribeiro, B. 3(2); Sandford, L. 20(2); Santos, G. 23(8); Smith, A. (6); Suffo, P. 6(10); Talia, F. 6; Thetis, M. (1); Thomas, J. 3(7); Tonge, M. 1(1); Tracey, S. 40; Uhlenbeek, G. 28(3); Ullathorne, R. 13(1); Ward, M. (1); Weber, N. 3(1); Woodhouse, C. 23(2).
**Goals – League** (52): Kelly 6, Asaba 5, Bent 5, D'Jaffo 5, Devlin 5 (2 pens), Murphy 5, Ndlovu 4, Santos 4, Ford 3 (3 pens), Peschisolido 2, Quinn 2 (1 pen), Brown 1, Sandford 1, Suffo 1, Thomas 1, own goals 2.
**Worthington Cup** (11): Bent 3, Devlin 3 (1 pen), Kelly 2, Brown 1, own goals 2.
**FA Cup** (0).
**Ground:** Bramall Lane Ground, Sheffield S2 4SU. Telephone (0114) 2215757
**Record attendance:** 68,287 v Leeds U, FA Cup 5th rd, 15 February 1936.
**Capacity:** 30,936.
**Manager:** Neil Warnock.
**Secretary:** D. Capper AFA.
**Most League Goals:** 102, Division 1, 1925–26.
**Highest League Scorer in Season:** Jimmy Dunne, 41, Division 1, 1930–31.
**Most League Goals in Total Aggregate:** Harry Johnson, 205, 1919–30.
**Most Capped Player:** Billy Gillespie, 25, Northern Ireland.
**Most League Appearances:** Joe Shaw, 629, 1948–66.
**Honours – Football League:** Division 1 Champions – 1897–98. Division 2 Champions – 1952–53. Division 4 Champions – 1981–82. **FA Cup:** Winners 1899, 1902, 1915, 1925.
**Colours:** Red and white striped shirts with black trim, black shorts and black stockings with red trim.

---

# SHEFFIELD WEDNESDAY                                        DIV. 1

| | | | | | | |
|---|---|---|---|---|---|---|
| Bettney Scott (D) | 5 9 | 13 00 | Hull | 12 3 80 | Trainee | |
| Bromby Leigh (D) | 5 11 | 11 06 | Dewsbury | 2 6 80 | | |
| Cawley Alan (M) | 6 2 | 10 00 | Sligo | 3 1 82 | Leeds U | |
| Colley Karl (M) | | | Sheffield | 13 10 83 | | |
| Connolly Calem (M) | | | Leeds | 12 2 82 | | |
| Crane Anthony (M) | 6 1 | 12 06 | Liverpool | 8 9 82 | Trainee | |
| De Bilde Gilles (F) | 5 11 | 11 04 | Brussels | 9 6 71 | PSV Eindhoven | |
| Di Piedi Michaelli (F) | 6 6 | 13 05 | Palermo | 4 12 08 | | |
| Donnelly Simon (M) | 5 9 | 10 06 | Glasgow | 1 12 74 | Celtic | |
| Geary Derek (D) | 5 6 | 10 08 | Dublin | 19 6 80 | | |
| Gibson Neil (M) | 5 11 | 11 08 | St Asaph | 10 10 79 | Tranmere R | |
| Hamshaw Matthew (M) | 5 9 | 11 09 | Rotherham | 1 1 82 | Trainee | |

93

| | | | | | | |
|---|---|---|---|---|---|---|
| Harkness Steve (D) | 5 9 | 11 09 | Carlisle | 27 8 71 | Blackburn R |
| Haslam Steven (D) | 5 11 | 10 10 | Sheffield | 6 9 79 | Trainee |
| Hendon Ian (D) | 6 1 | 13 08 | Ilford | 5 12 71 | Northampton T |
| Hinchcliffe Andy (D) | 5 10 | 13 07 | Manchester | 5 2 69 | Everton |
| Houlahan Martin (M) | 6 0 | 12 13 | Bishop Auckland | 17 9 81 | Trainee |
| Lescott Aaron (M) | 5 8 | 10 10 | Birmingham | 2 12 78 | Aston Villa |
| Morrison Owen (F) | 5 8 | 11 12 | Derry | 8 12 81 | Trainee |
| Muller Adam (F) | 5 11 | 12 02 | Thackley | 17 4 82 | |
| O'Donnell Phil (M) | 5 10 | 11 07 | Bellshill | 25 3 72 | Celtic |
| Quinn Alan (F) | 5 9 | 10 02 | Dublin | 13 6 79 | Cherry Orchard |
| Rand Craig (M) | 6 1 | 11 00 | Bishop Auckland | 24 6 82 | Trainee |
| Scott Philip (M) | 5 9 | 11 01 | Perth | 14 11 74 | St Johnstone |
| Sibon Gerald (F) | 6 3 | 13 04 | Emmen | 19 4 74 | Ajax |
| Soltvedt Trond Egil (M) | 6 1 | 12 09 | Voss | 15 2 67 | Southampton |
| Staniforth Thomas (D) | 5 10 | 13 00 | Carlisle | 15 12 80 | Trainee |
| Stringer Chris (G) | 6 6 | 12 00 | Grimsby | 2 6 83 | Scholar |
| Westwood Ashley (D) | 5 11 | 11 02 | Bridgnorth | 31 8 76 | Bradford C |

**League Appearances:** Beresford, M. 4; Blatsis, C. 6; Booth, A. 17(1); Bromby, L. 17(1); Cooke, T. 16(1); Crane, A. 7(8); Cresswell, R. 4; De Bilde, G. 13(8); Di Piedi, M. 6(19); Donnelly, S. (3); Ekoku, E. 31(1); Geary, D. 1(4); Grayson, S. 5; Hamshaw, M. 9(9); Harkness, S. 28(2); Haslam, S. 24(3); Hendon, I. 31; Hinchcliffe, A. 9; Humphreys, R. 7; Jonk, W. 2; Lescott, A. 17(13); Morrison, O. 20(10); Muller, A. 1(4); Nicholson, K. (1); O'Donnell, P. 7(4); Palmer, C. 12; Pressman, K. 38(1); Quinn, A. 37; Ripley, S. 5(1); Rudi, P. (1); Sibon, G. 32(9); Soltvedt, T. 15; Stockdale, R. 6; Stringer, C. 4(1); Walker, D. 43; Westwood, A. 32(1).
**Goals – League** (52): Sibon 13 (2 pens), Ekoku 7, Morrison 6, Di Piedi 4, Booth 3, De Bilde 3, Crane 2, Hendon 2, Hinchcliffe 2 (2 pens), Quinn 2, Westwood 2, Cooke 1, Donnelly 1, Harkness 1, Haslam 1, Ripley 1, Soltvedt 1.
**Worthington Cup** (12): Ekoku 2, Morrison 2, Westwood 2, Crane 1, De Bilde 1, Di Piedi 1, Hamshaw 1, Quinn 1, Sibon 1.
**FA Cup** (3): Booth 1, Hamshaw 1, Sibon 1.
**Ground:** Hillsborough, Sheffield, S6 1SW. Telephone (0114) 2212121
**Record attendance:** 72,841 v Manchester C, FA Cup 5th rd, 17 February 1934.
**Capacity:** 39,859
**Manager:** Peter Shreeves.
**Secretary:** Alan D. Sykes.
**Most League Goals:** 106, Division 2, 1958–59.
**Highest League Scorer in Season:** Derek Dooley, 46, Division 2, 1951–52.
**Most League Goals in Total Aggregate:** Andy Wilson, 199, 1900–20.
**Most Capped Player:** Nigel Worthington, 50 (66), Northern Ireland.
**Most League Appearances:** Andy Wilson, 502, 1900–20.
**Honours – Football League:** Division 1 Champions – 1902–03, 1903–04, 1928–29, 1929–30. Division 2 Champions – 1899–1900, 1925–26, 1951–52, 1955–56, 1958–59.
**FA Cup winners** 1896, 1907, 1935. **Football League Cup winners** 1990–91.
**Colours:** Blue and white striped shirts, black shorts, blue stockings.

# SHREWSBURY TOWN                                    DIV. 3

| | | | | | | |
|---|---|---|---|---|---|---|
| Aiston Sam (M) | 6 0 | 13 09 | Newcastle | 21 11 76 | Sunderland |
| Drysdale Leon (D) | 5 9 | 10 12 | Walsall | 3 2 81 | Trainee |
| Dunbavin Ian (G) | 6 1 | 10 10 | Knowsley | 27 5 80 | Liverpool |
| Freestone Chris (F) | 5 11 | 12 05 | Nottingham | 4 9 71 | Hartlepool U |
| Jagielka Steve (F) | 5 8 | 11 03 | Manchester | 10 3 78 | Trainee |
| Jenkins Iain (D) | 5 9 | 11 10 | Whiston | 24 12 72 | Chester C |

| Lowe Ryan (F) | | | Liverpool | 18  9 78 | Burscough |
| Murray Karl (M) | 5 10 | 12 00 | Islington | 24  6 82 | Trainee |
| Redmile Matt (D) | 6 3 | 15 03 | Nottingham | 12 11 76 | Notts Co |
| Rioch Greg (D) | 5 10 | 12 08 | Sutton Coldfield | 24  6 75 | Macclesfield T |
| Rodgers Luke (F) | 5 6 | 10 05 | Birmingham | 1  1 82 | Trainee |
| Seabury Kevin (D) | 5 10 | 11 06 | Shrewsbury | 24 11 73 | Trainee |
| Tolley Jamie (M) | 6 1 | 10 08 | Shrewsbury | 12  5 83 | Scholar |
| Tretton Andrew (D) | 6 0 | 12 08 | Derby | 9 10 76 | Chesterfield |

**League Appearances:** Aiston, S. 40(2); Brown, M. 20(14); Collins, S. 12; Davidson, R. 31(2); Drysdale, L. 16(2); Dunbavin, I. 20(2); Edwards, P. 26; Freestone, C. 16(4); Gayle, J. (1); Hanmer, G. 18(4); Harris, J. 1(3); Hughes, D. 24; Jagielka, S. 21(10); Jemson, N. 41; Jenkins, I. 16; Jones, M. 5(1); Keister, J. 8; Lowe, R. 13(17); Murphy, C. (1); Murray, K. 29(6); Peer, D. 34(3); Redmile, M. 24; Rioch, G. 8; Rodgers, L. 13(13); Seabury, K. 9(2); Sertori, M. (1); Thomas, W. 4; Tolley, J. 22(2); Tretton, A. 21(1); Wilding, P. 14(7).
**Goals – League** (49): Jemson 15 (5 pens), Rodgers 7 (1 pen), Jagielka 6 (1 pen), Brown 4, Lowe 4, Redmile 3, Aiston 2, Hughes 2, Tolley 2, Tretton 2, Wilding 1, own goal 1.
**Worthington Cup** (2): Davidson 1, Freestone 1.
**FA Cup** (1): Freestone 1.
**Ground:** Gay Meadow, Shrewsbury SY2 6AB. Telephone (01743) 360111.
**Record attendance:** 18,917 v Walsall, Division 3, 26 April 1961. **Capacity:** 8000.
**Manager:** Kevin Ratcliffe.
**Secretary:** M. J. Starkey.
**Most League Goals:** 101, Division 4, 1958–59.
**Highest League Scorer in Season:** Arthur Rowley, 38, Division 4, 1958–59.
**Most League Goals in Total Aggregate:** Arthur Rowley, 152, 1958–65 (completing his League record of 434 goals).
**Most Capped Player:** Jimmy McLaughlin, 5 (12), Northern Ireland; Bernard McNally, 5, Northern Ireland.
**Most League Appearances:** Colin Griffin, 406, 1975–89.
**Honours – Football League:** Division 3 Champions – 1978–79, 1993–94. **Welsh Cup winners** 1891, 1938, 1977, 1979, 1984, 1985.
**Colours:** Amber and blue shirts, blue shorts, blue stockings with amber trim.

# SOUTHAMPTON                                        FA PREMIERSHIP

| Ashford Ryan (D) | | | Honiton | 13 10 81 | Scholar |
| Baird Christopher (D) | 6 1 | 12 00 | Ballymena | 25  2 82 | Scholar |
| Beattie James (F) | 6 1 | 13 08 | Lancaster | 27  2 78 | Blackburn R |
| Benali Francis (M) | 5 9 | 11 00 | Southampton | 30 12 68 | Apprentice |
| Bevan Scott (G) | 6 6 | 15 06 | Southampton | 16  9 79 | Trainee |
| Bleidelis Imants (F) | 5 10 | 12 01 | Latvia | 16  8 75 | Skonto Riga |
| Boa Morte Luis (F) | 5 9 | 11 11 | Lisbon | 4  8 77 | Arsenal |
| Bridge Wayne (F) | 5 10 | 12 04 | Southampton | 5  8 80 | Trainee |
| Caceres Adrian (F) | 5 10 | 12 05 | Buenos Aires | 10  1 82 | Perth SC |
| Davies Kevin (F) | 6 0 | 14 09 | Sheffield | 26  3 77 | Blackburn R |
| Dodd Jason (D) | 5 10 | 12 05 | Bath | 2 11 70 | Bath C |
| Draper Mark (M) | 5 10 | 12 04 | Long Eaton | 11 11 70 | Aston Villa |
| El Khalej Tahar (D) | 6 2 | 13 06 | Morocco | 16  6 68 | Benfica |
| Gibbens Kevin (M) | 5 10 | 13 06 | Southampton | 4 11 79 | Trainee |
| Gray Steven (M) | | | Dublin | 17 10 81 | |
| Howard Brian (M) | | | Winchester | 23  1 83 | Trainee |
| Jones Paul (G) | 6 3 | 14 08 | Chirk | 18  4 67 | Stockport Co |
| Kachloul Hassan (M) | 6 1 | 12 13 | Agadir | 19  2 73 | St Etienne |

95

| | | | | | |
|---|---|---|---|---|---|
| Le Tissier Matthew (F) | 6 1 | 14 01 | Guernsey | 14 10 68 | Trainee |
| Lundekvam Claus (D) | 6 3 | 12 11 | Austevoll | 22 2 73 | Brann |
| Marsden Chris (M) | 5 11 | 12 03 | Sheffield | 3 1 69 | Birmingham C |
| McDonald Scott (F) | 5 8 | 12 04 | Melbourne | 21 8 83 | |
| Mills Jonathan (M) | | | Swindon | 8 9 83 | Oxford U |
| Monk Garry (D) | 6 0 | 13 10 | Bedford | 6 3 79 | Trainee |
| Moss Neil (G) | 6 2 | 13 12 | New Milton | 10 5 75 | Bournemouth |
| Oakley Matthew (M) | 5 10 | 12 01 | Peterborough | 17 8 77 | Trainee |
| Pahars Marian (F) | 5 8 | 10 09 | Latvia | 5 8 76 | Skonto Riga |
| Peters Mark (F) | 5 8 | 10 08 | Frimley | 4 10 83 | Scholar |
| Petrescu Dan (M) | 5 10 | 11 02 | Bucharest | 22 12 67 | Bradford C |
| Richards Dean (D) | 6 2 | 13 12 | Bradford | 9 6 74 | Wolverhampton W |
| Ripley Stuart (F) | 6 0 | 13 06 | Middlesbrough | 20 11 67 | Blackburn R |
| Rodrigues Danny (F) | 5 11 | 11 02 | Madeira | 3 3 80 | Farense |
| Rosier Matthew (M) | | | Australia | 7 1 83 | |
| Rosler Uwe (F) | 6 0 | 12 09 | Altenburg | 15 11 68 | Tennis Berlin |
| Tessem Jo (M) | 6 2 | 13 02 | Norway | 28 2 72 | Molde |
| Warner Phil (D) | 5 10 | 11 12 | Southampton | 2 2 79 | Trainee |

**League Appearances:** Beattie, J. 29(8); Benali, F. (4); Bleidelis, I. (1); Bridge, W. 38; Davies, K. 21(6); Dodd, J. 29(2); Draper, M. 16(6); El Khalej, T. 25(7); Gibbens, K. 1(2); Jones, P. 35; Kachloul, H. 26(6); Le Tissier, M. 2(6); Lundekvam, C. 38; Marsden, C. 19(4); Monk, G. 2; Moss, N. 3; Oakley, M. 35; Pakhar (Pahars), M. 26(5); Petrescu, D. 8(1); Richards, D. 28; Ripley, S. 1(2); Rosler, U. 6(14); Soltvedt, T. 3(3); Tessem, J. 27(6).

**Goals – League (40):** Beattie 11, Pakhar (Pahars) 9, Kachloul 4, Tessem 4, Petrescu 2, Davies 1, Dodd 1, Draper 1, El Khalej 1, Le Tissier 1, Oakley 1, Richards 1, Soltvedt 1, own goals 2.

**Worthington Cup (5):** Soltvedt 2, Le Tissier 1, Rosler 1, Tessem 1.

**FA Cup (7):** Dodd 2 (2 pens), Beattie 1, Davies 1, Kachloul 1, Richards 1, Tessem 1.

**Ground:** The Friends Provident St Mary's Stadium, Britannia Road, Southampton SO14 5FP. Telephone (0870) 220 0000.

**Record attendance:** 31,044 (at The Dell) v Manchester U, Division 1, 8 October 1969. **Capacity:** 32,000.

**Manager:** Stuart Gray.

**Secretary:** Brian Truscott.

**Most League Goals:** 112, Division 3 (S), 1957–58.

**Highest League Scorer in Season:** Derek Reeves, 39, Division 3, 1959–60.

**Most League Goals in Total Aggregate:** Mike Channon, 185, 1966–77, 1979–82.

**Most Capped Player:** Peter Shilton, 49 (125), England.

**Most League Appearances:** Terry Paine, 713, 1956–74.

**Honours – Football League:** Division 3 (S) Champions – 1921–22. Division 3 Champions – 1959–60. **FA Cup:** Winners 1975–76.

**Colours:** Red and white striped shirts, black shorts, white stockings with black and red trim.

# SOUTHEND UNITED                                   DIV. 3

| | | | | | |
|---|---|---|---|---|---|
| Booty Martyn (D) | 5 8 | 12 03 | Kirby Muxloe | 30 5 71 | Reading |
| Bramble Tesfaye (F) | | | Ipswich | 20 7 80 | Cambridge C |
| Capleton Mel (G) | 6 0 | 13 00 | London | 24 10 73 | Leyton Orient |
| Flahavan Darryl (G) | 5 10 | 12 01 | Southampton | 28 11 78 | Woking |
| Johnson Leon (M) | 6 0 | 12 00 | London | 10 5 81 | Scholar |
| Kerrigan Danny (M) | 5 7 | 10 04 | Basildon | 4 7 82 | Trainee |
| Lee David (M) | 5 11 | 11 08 | Basildon | 28 3 80 | Tottenham H |

| McSweeney Dave (D) | | | Basildon | 28 12 81 | Scholar |
| Rawle Mark (F) | | | Leicester | 27 4 79 | Boston U |
| Searle Damon (M) | 5 10 | 11 00 | Cardiff | 26 10 71 | Carlisle U |
| Thurgood Stuart (M) | | | Enfield | 4 11 81 | Shimizu S-Pulse |
| Wardley Shane (M) | | | Ipswich | 26 2 80 | Cambridge C |
| Webb Daniel (F) | 6 0 | 11 08 | Poole | 2 7 83 | |
| Whelan Phil (D) | 6 4 | 14 04 | Stockport | 7 3 72 | Oxford U |

**League Appearances:** Abbey, B. 15(9); Black, M. 10(5); Booty, M. 32; Bramble, T. 12(4); Broad, S. 10; Capleton, M. (1); Carruthers, M. 31(1); Connelly, G. 8(1); Cross, G. 4(4); Edwards, C. (1); Fitzpatrick, T. 8(3); Flahavan, D. 29; Forbes, S. 27(7); Houghton, S. 7(2); Hutchings, C. 14; Johnson, L. 19(1); Lee, D. 37(5); Maher, K. 40(1); McDonald, T. (1); McSweeney, D. 10(1); Morley, D. 8(9); Newman, R. 3(3); Rawle, M. 11(3); Roget, L. 26; Searle, D. 46; Thurgood, S. 8(5); Tinkler, M. 14(1); Tolson, N. 5; Wardley, S. (2); Webb, D. 6(9); Whelan, P. 40(2); Williamson, R. 9(3); Woodman, A. 17.
**Goals – League** (55): Abbey 8, Lee 8 (1 pen), Carruthers 7 (1 pen), Bramble 6, Roget 4, Fitzpatrick 3, Forbes 3, Houghton 2, Maher 2 (1 pen), Newman 2, Black 1, Johnson 1, Rawle 1, Searle 1, Thurgood 1, Tinkler 1, Tolson 1, Webb 1, Whelan 1, own goal 1.
**Worthington Cup** (0).
**FA Cup** (5): Williamson 2, Abbey 1, Forbes 1, Roget 1.
**Ground:** Roots Hall Football Ground, Victoria Avenue, Southend-on-Sea SS2 6NQ. Telephone (01702) 304050
**Record attendance:** 31,090 v Liverpool FA Cup 3rd rd, 10 January 1979. **Capacity:** 12,306
**Manager:** David Webb.
**Secretary:** Miss H. Giles.
**Most League Goals:** 92, Division 3 (S), 1950–51.
**Highest League Scorer in Season:** Jim Shankly, 31, 1928–29; Sammy McCrory, 1957–58, both in Division 3 (S).
**Most League Goals in Total Aggregate:** Roy Hollis, 122, 1953–60.
**Most Capped Player:** George Mackenzie, 9, Eire.
**Most League Appearances:** Sandy Anderson, 452, 1950–63.
**Honours – Football League:** Division 4 Champions – 1980–81.
**Colours:** Royal blue and white.

---

# STOCKPORT COUNTY                                    DIV. 1

| Briggs Keith (D) | 6 0 | 11 00 | Glossop | 11 12 81 | Trainee |
| Bryngelsson Fredrik (D) | 6 2 | 11 13 | Sweden | 10 4 75 | Hacken |
| Carratt Philip (F) | | | Stockport | 22 10 81 | Scholar |
| Carrigan Brian (F) | 5 8 | 10 07 | Glasgow | 26 9 79 | Clyde |
| Clare Robert (M) | | | Belper | 28 2 83 | Trainee |
| Clark Peter (D) | 6 1 | 12 04 | Romford | 10 12 79 | Carlisle U |
| Daly Jon (F) | 6 3 | 12 00 | Dublin | 8 1 83 | Trainee |
| Flynn Mike (D) | 6 0 | 11 02 | Oldham | 23 2 69 | Preston NE |
| Fradin Karim (M) | 5 11 | 12 00 | Ste Martin d'Hyeres | 2 2 72 | Nice |
| Gibb Ali (F) | 5 9 | 11 07 | Salisbury | 17 2 76 | Northampton T |
| Hancock Glynn (D) | 6 0 | 12 02 | Biddulph | 24 5 82 | Trainee |
| Hurst Glynn (F) | 5 10 | 11 06 | Barnsley | 17 1 76 | Ayr U |
| Jones Lee (G) | 6 3 | 14 10 | Pontypridd | 9 8 70 | Bristol R |
| Kuqi Shefki (F) | 6 2 | 13 13 | Albania | 10 11 76 | HJK Helsinki |
| Larsson Jonas (M) | | | Vanersborg | 1 4 82 | Trainee |
| Lawson Ian (F) | 5 11 | 11 00 | Huddersfield | 4 11 77 | Bury |
| Roget Leo (D) | 6 1 | 12 02 | Ilford | 1 8 77 | Southend U |

| Turner Sam (G) | 6 1 | 12 05 | Pontypool | 9 | 9 80 | Charlton Ath |
| Wilbraham Aaron (F) | 6 3 | 12 04 | Knutsford | 21 10 79 | Trainee |
| Wiss Jarkko (M) | 6 0 | 12 08 | Finland | 17 4 72 | Moss |

**League Appearances:** Bailey, A. 1(3); Bergersen, K. 8(1); Brebner, G. 3(3); Bryngelsson, F. 4(1); Byrne, C. (1); Carratt, P. (2); Carrigan, B. 3(10); Clare, R. 19(3); Clark, P. 33(4); Connelly, S. 11(2); Cooper, K. 34; Dibble, A. 9(1); Dinning, T. 6; Flynn, M. 44; Fradin, K. 27(4); Gibb, A. 38(1); Gray, K. 1; Grayson, S. 13; Hancock, G. 1(1); Hurst, G. 10(1); Jones, L. 27; Kelly, A. 2; Kuqi, S. 17; Lawson, I. 1(9); Matthews, R. 7(4); Maxwell, L. 8(12); Moore, I. 17; Nash, C. 8; Nicholson, S. 31(4); Roget, L. 8(1); Smith, D. 31(3); Tod, A. 11; Wilbraham, A. 32(4); Wiss, J. 27(3); Woodthorpe, C. 14(10).
**Goals – League** (58): Wilbraham 12, Moore 7, Fradin 6, Kuqi 6 (1 pen), Wiss 6, Cooper 5, Tod 3, Clark 2, Maxwell 2, Nicholson 2 (2 pens), Bergersen 1, Carrigan 1, Matthews 1, Smith 1, Woodthorpe 1, own goals 2.
**Worthington Cup** (2): Dinning 1, Moore 1.
**FA Cup** (2): Fradin 1, Wiss 1.
**Ground:** Edgeley Park, Hardcastle Road, Stockport, Cheshire SK3 9DD. Telephone (0161) 286 8888.
**Record attendance:** 27,833 v Liverpool, FA Cup 5th rd, 11 February 1950.
**Capacity:** 11,541.
**Manager:** Andy Kilner.
**Secretary:** Gary Glendenning BA (HONS) FCCA.
**Most League Goals:** 115, Division 3 (N), 1933–34.
**Highest League Scorer in Season:** Alf Lythgoe, 46, Division 3 (N), 1933–34.
**Most League Goals in Total Aggregate:** Jack Connor, 132, 1951–56.
**Most Capped Player:** Martin Nash, 4, Canada.
**Most League Appearances:** Andy Thorpe, 489, 1978–86, 1988–92.
**Honours – Football League:** Division 3 (N) Champions – 1921–22, 1936–37. Division 4 Champions – 1966–67.
**Colours:** Blue shirts with white chest band, blue shorts, white stockings.

---

## STOKE CITY                                                   DIV. 2

| Bullock Matthew (M) | 5 8 | 11 00 | Stoke | 1 11 80 | Trainee |
| Clarke Clive (D) | 6 1 | 12 03 | Dublin | 14 1 80 | Trainee |
| Commons Kristian (M) | | | Nottingham | 30 8 83 | Scholar |
| Cooke Andy (F) | 5 11 | 12 08 | Stoke | 20 1 74 | Burnley |
| Crowe Dean (F) | 5 5 | 11 02 | Stockport | 6 6 79 | Trainee |
| Dadason Rikhardur (F) | 6 2 | 13 04 | Iceland | 26 4 72 | Viking |
| Foster Ben (G) | | | Leamington | 3 4 83 | Racing Club Warwick |
| Goodfellow Marc (M) | 5 8 | 10 00 | Burton | 20 9 81 | |
| Gudjonsson Bjarni (F) | 5 8 | 11 02 | Reykjavik | 26 2 79 | Genk |
| Gunnarsson Brynjar (M) | 6 1 | 11 00 | Reykjavik | 16 10 75 | Moss |
| Hansson Mikael (D) | 5 8 | 11 08 | Norrkoping | 15 3 68 | Norrkoping |
| Heath Robert (M) | 5 9 | 10 00 | Newcastle-Under-Lyme | 31 8 78 | |
| Henry Karl (M) | 6 0 | 12 00 | Wolverhampton | 26 11 82 | Trainee |
| Iwelumo Chris (F) | 6 4 | 13 00 | Coatbridge | 1 8 78 | Aarhus Fremad |
| Kavanagh Graham (M) | 5 10 | 12 06 | Dublin | 2 12 73 | Middlesbrough |
| Mohan Nicky (D) | 6 1 | 14 00 | Middlesbrough | 6 10 70 | Wycombe W |
| Neal Lewis (M) | 6 0 | 11 00 | Leicester | 14 7 81 | |
| O'Connor James (M) | 5 8 | 11 00 | Dublin | 1 9 79 | Trainee |
| Petty Ben (D) | 6 0 | 12 05 | Solihull | 22 3 77 | Aston Villa |
| Thomas Wayne (D) | 5 11 | 11 02 | Gloucester | 17 5 79 | Torquay U |

Thordarson Stefan (F) 6 1 12 01 Akranes 27 3 75
Thorne Peter (F) 6 0 13 07 Manchester 21 6 73 Swindon T
Ward Gavin (G) 6 2 12 02 Sutton Coldfield 30 6 70 Bolton W

**League Appearances:** Clarke, C. 12(9); Connor, P. 1(6); Cooke, A. 21(1); Dadason, R. 13(15); Dorigo, T. 34(2); Fenton, G. 2(3); Goodfellow, M. (7); Gudjonsson, B. 41(1); Gunnarsson, B. 46; Hansson, M. 36(2); Iwelumo, C. (2); Kavanagh, G. 42(1); Kippe, F. 15(4); Kristinsson, B. 18; Lightbourne, K. 11(11); Mohan, N. 37; Muggleton, C. 11(1); Neal, L. (1); O'Connor, J. 44; Petty, B. 10(12); Risom, H. 9(16); Robinson, M. 3; Thomas, W. 33(1); Thordarson, S. 15(15); Thorne, P. 35(3); Ward, G. 17.
**Goals – League** (74): Thorne 16, Kavanagh 8 (3 pens), O'Connor 8, Cooke 6, Dadason 6, Gudjonsson 6, Gunnarsson 5, Lightbourne 5, Thordarson 4 (1 pen), Hansson 2, Fenton 1, Iwelumo 1, Mohan 1, Robinson 1, own goals 4.
**Worthington Cup** (13): Connor 2, Gudjonsson 2, O'Connor 2, Thordarson 2 (1 pen), Dadason 1, Goodfellow 1, Gunnarsson 1, Heath 1, Iwelumo 1.
**FA Cup** (0).
**Ground:** Britannia Stadium, Stoke-on-Trent ST4 4EG. Telephone: (01782) 592222.
**Record attendance:** 51,380 v Arsenal, Division 1, 29 March 1937. **Capacity:** 28,384.
**Manager:** Gudjon Thordarson.
**Most League Goals:** 92, Division 3 (N), 1926–27.
**Highest League Scorer in Season:** Freddie Steele, 33, Division 1, 1936–37.
**Most League Goals in Total Aggregate:** Freddie Steele, 142, 1934–49.
**Most Capped Player:** Gordon Banks, 36 (73), England.
**Most League Appearances:** Eric Skeels, 506, 1958–76.
**Honours – Football League:** Division 2 Champions – 1932–33, 1962–63, 1992–93. Division 3 (N) Champions – 1926–27. **Football League Cup:** Winners 1971–72.
**Autoglass Trophy winners** 1992. **Auto Windscreens Shield winners** 2000.
**Colours:** Red and white striped shirts, white shorts, red and white stockings.

# SUNDERLAND                                          FA PREMIERSHIP

| Arca Julio (D) | 6 2 | 11 00 | Quilmes | 31 1 81 | Argentinos Jnrs |
|---|---|---|---|---|---|
| Black Christopher (M) | | | Ashington | 7 9 82 | Scholar |
| Butler Thomas (M) | 5 7 | 10 06 | Ballymun | 25 4 81 | Trainee |
| Byrne Clifford (M) | | | Dublin | 27 4 82 | |
| Clark Ben (D) | 6 2 | 12 06 | Shotley Bridge | 24 1 83 | Manchester U |
| Craddock Jody (D) | 6 2 | 12 00 | Bromsgrove | 25 7 75 | Cambridge U |
| Dichio Danny (F) | 6 4 | 13 09 | Hammersmith | 19 10 74 | Lecce |
| Dickman Jonjo (D) | 5 8 | 10 05 | Hexham | 22 9 81 | |
| Dowell Adam (G) | | | Gateshead | 6 12 82 | Scholar |
| Emerson (D) | 6 2 | 13 04 | Porto Alegre | 30 3 72 | Chelsea |
| Fredgaard Carsten (M) | 6 1 | 12 01 | Hillerod | 20 5 76 | |
| Gray Michael (D) | 5 9 | 10 07 | Sunderland | 3 8 74 | Trainee |
| Graydon Keith (M) | | | Dublin | 10 2 83 | |
| Harrison Steve (D) | | | Hexham | 3 2 82 | Scholar |
| Hutchison Don (M) | 6 1 | 12 04 | Gateshead | 9 5 71 | Everton |
| Ingham Michael (G) | 6 4 | 13 10 | Preston | 7 9 80 | Malachians |
| James Craig (D) | | | Middlesbrough | 15 11 82 | Scholar |
| Kennedy Jon (G) | | | Rotherham | 30 11 80 | Worksop T |
| Kilbane Kevin (M) | 6 0 | 12 07 | Preston | 1 2 77 | WBA |
| Kyle Kevin (F) | 6 3 | 13 00 | Stranraer | 7 6 81 | |
| Lacey Glenn (M) | | | Dublin | 5 6 83 | Scholar |
| Lumsden Chris (M) | 5 10 | 10 09 | Newcastle | 15 12 79 | Trainee |
| Macho Jurgen (G) | 6 4 | 13 12 | Vienna | 24 8 77 | First Vienna |
| Maley Mark (D) | 6 0 | 13 00 | Newcastle | 26 1 81 | Trainee |

| Name | Ht | Wt | Birthplace | DOB | From |
|---|---|---|---|---|---|
| Marchant Ross (M) | | | Bournemouth | 6 4 82 | Scholar |
| McCann Gavin (M) | 6 1 | 12 08 | Blackpool | 10 1 78 | Everton |
| McCartney George (D) | 5 11 | 10 10 | Belfast | 29 4 81 | Trainee |
| McGill Brendan (M) | 5 8 | 9 02 | Dublin | 22 3 81 | |
| Mordey Gareth (D) | | | Sunderland | 28 1 83 | Scholar |
| Oster John (M) | 5 9 | 10 09 | Boston | 8 12 78 | Everton |
| Peeters Tom (M) | 5 10 | 11 00 | Bornem | 25 9 78 | Ekeren |
| Phillips Kevin (F) | 5 8 | 11 05 | Hitchin | 25 7 73 | Watford |
| Proctor Michael (F) | 6 0 | 11 08 | Sunderland | 3 10 80 | Trainee |
| Quinn Niall (F) | 6 5 | 14 08 | Dublin | 6 10 66 | Manchester C |
| Rae Alex (M) | 5 10 | 11 09 | Glasgow | 30 6 69 | Millwall |
| Ramsden Simon (D) | | | Bishop Auckland | 17 12 81 | Scholar |
| Reddy Michael (F) | 6 1 | 11 07 | Graignamanagh | 24 3 80 | Kilkenny C |
| Rossiter Mark (M) | | | Sligo | 27 5 83 | Scholar |
| Schwarz Stefan (M) | 6 0 | 12 00 | Malmo | 18 4 69 | Valencia |
| Shields Dene (F) | 5 9 | 12 00 | Edinburgh | 16 9 82 | Raith R |
| Sorensen Thomas (G) | 6 4 | 13 08 | Odense | 12 6 76 | Odense |
| Thirlwell Paul (M) | 5 11 | 11 04 | Springwell Village | 13 2 79 | Trainee |
| Turns Craig (G) | | | Easington | 4 11 82 | Scholar |
| Varga Stanislav (D) | 6 5 | 14 09 | Lipany | 8 10 72 | Slovan Bratislava |
| Wainwright Neil (M) | 6 1 | 11 07 | Warrington | 4 11 77 | Wrexham |
| Williams Darren (D) | 5 11 | 12 00 | Middlebrough | 28 4 77 | York C |

**League Appearances:** Arca, J. 26(1); Bould, S. (1); Butler, P. 3; Butler, T. (4); Carteron, P. 8; Craddock, J. 33(1); Dichio, D. 2(13); Emerson, 30(1); Gray, M. 36; Holloway, D. 5; Hutchison, D. 30(2); Kilbane, K. 26(4); Kyle, K. (3); Macho, J. 4(1); Makin, C. 21(2); McCann, G. 22; McCartney, G. 1(1); Oster, J. 2(6); Phillips, K. 34; Quinn, N. 32(2); Rae, A. 18; Reddy, M. (2); Roy, E. 1(2); Schwarz, S. 17(3); Sorensen, T. 34; Thirlwell, P. 3(2); Varga, S. 9(3); Williams, D. 21(7).

**Goals – League** (46): Phillips 14 (2 pens), Hutchison 8, Quinn 7, Kilbane 4, McCann 3, Arca 2, Rae 2, Carteron 1, Dichio 1, Emerson 1, Gray 1, Schwarz 1, Varga 1.

**Worthington Cup** (10): Hutchison 2, Phillips 2 (1 pen), Arca 1, Butler P 1, Oster 1, Rae 1, Reddy 1, Thirlwell 1.

**FA Cup** (5): Phillips 2, Dichio 1, Kilbane 1, Quinn 1.

**Ground:** Sunderland Stadium of Light, Sunderland, Tyne and Wear SR5 1SU. Telephone: (0191) 551 5000.

**Record attendance:** 75,118 v Derby Co, FA Cup 6th rd replay, 8 March 1933 (Roker Park). 48,285 v Leeds U, FA Premier League, 31 March 2001 (Stadium of Light). **Capacity:** 48,500.

**Manager:** Peter Reid.

**Secretary:** Mark Blackbourne.

**Most League Goals:** 109, Division 1, 1935–36.

**Highest League Scorer in Season:** Dave Halliday, 43, Division 1, 1928–29.

**Most League Goals in Total Aggregate:** Charlie Buchan, 209, 1911–25.

**Most Capped Player:** Charlie Hurley, 38 (40), Republic of Ireland.

**Most League Appearances:** Jim Montgomery, 537, 1962–77.

**Honours – Football League:** Division 1 Champions – 1891–92, 1892–93, 1894–95, 1901–02, 1912–13, 1935–36, 1995–96, 1998–99. Division 2 Champions – 1975–76. Division 3 Champions – 1987–88. **FA Cup:** Winners 1937, 1973.

**Colours:** Red and white striped shirts with black trim, black shorts, black stockings, red turnover.

| | | | | | |
|---|---|---|---|---|---|
| Appleby Ritchie (M) | 5 9 | 11 04 | Stockton | 18 9 75 | Ipswich T |
| Bound Matthew (D) | 6 2 | 14 00 | Bradford-on-Avon | 9 11 72 | Stockport Co |
| Casey Ryan (M) | 6 2 | 12 05 | Coventry | 3 1 79 | Trainee |
| Coates Jonathan (M) | 5 8 | 11 04 | Swansea | 27 6 75 | Trainee |
| Cusack Nick (M) | 6 0 | 12 05 | Rotherham | 24 12 65 | Fulham |
| De-Vulgt Leigh (M) | 5 10 | 10 07 | Swansea | 17 3 81 | Trainee |
| Freestone Roger (G) | 6 2 | 14 04 | Newport | 19 8 68 | Chelsea |
| Howard Mike (D) | 5 7 | 10 07 | Birkenhead | 2 12 78 | Tranmere R |
| Jenkins Lee (M) | 5 8 | 11 02 | Pontypool | 28 6 79 | Trainee |
| Jones Jason (G) | 6 2 | 12 10 | Wrexham | 10 5 79 | Liverpool |
| Keegan Michael (M) | 5 10 | 11 00 | Liskeard | 12 5 81 | Trainee |
| Lacey Damien (D) | 5 8 | 11 10 | Bridgend | 3 8 77 | Trainee |
| O'Leary Kristian (D) | 6 0 | 13 07 | Port Talbot | 30 8 77 | Trainee |
| Phillips Gareth (M) | 5 7 | 11 02 | Pontypridd | 19 8 79 | Trainee |
| Roberts Stuart (M) | 5 6 | 9 08 | Carmarthen | 22 7 80 | Trainee |
| Romo David (M) | | | Nimes | 7 8 78 | Guingamp |
| Smith Jason (D) | 6 3 | 14 00 | Bromsgrove | 6 9 74 | Coventry C |
| Todd Chris (D) | 6 0 | 13 00 | Swansea | 22 8 81 | Trainee |
| Watkin Steve (F) | 5 10 | 11 12 | Wrexham | 16 6 71 | Wrexham |

**League Appearances:** Appleby, R. (5); Bound, M. 39(1); Boyd, W. 14(3); Casey, R. 3(6); Coates, J. 16(3); Cusack, N. 30(10); Davies, A. (1); De-Vulgt, L. 6(1); Fabiano, N. 12(4); Freestone, R. 43; Howard, M. 39(2); Jenkins, L. 29(10); Jones, J. 3; Jones, S. 13; Keegan, M. 4; Lacey, D. 17(1); Morgan, B. (5); Mumford, A. 2(4); Mutton, T. 3(2); O'Leary, K. 22(2); Phillips, G. 9(6); Price, J. 41; Roberts, S. 21(15); Romo, D. 28(5); Savarese, G. 28(3); Smith, J. 22; Thomas, M. 12(9); Todd, C. 11; Verschave, M. 12; Watkin, S. 27(8).
**Goals – League** (47): Savarese 12, Watkin 7 (1 pen), Roberts 5, Price 4, Bound 3 (2 pens), Boyd 3, Verschave 3, Cusack 2, O'Leary 2, Casey 1, Coates 1, Fabiano 1, Jones S 1, Thomas 1, Todd 1.
**Worthington Cup** (1): Bound 1 (pen).
**FA Cup** (0).
**Ground:** Vetch Field, Swansea SA1 3SU. Telephone (01792) 474114.
**Record attendance:** 32,796 v Arsenal, FA Cup 4th rd, 17 February 1968. **Capacity:** 10,402.
**Team Manager:** John Hollins MBE.
**Secretary:** Jackie Rockey.
**Most League Goals:** 90, Division 2, 1956–57.
**Highest League Scorer in Season:** Cyril Pearce, 35, Division 2, 1931–32.
**Most League Goals in Total Aggregate:** Ivor Allchurch, 166, 1949–58, 1965–68.
**Most Capped Player:** Ivor Allchurch, 42 (68), Wales.
**Most League Appearances:** Wilfred Milne, 585, 1919–37.
**Honours – Football League:** Division 3 Champions – 1999–2000. Division 3 (S) Champions – 1924–25, 1948–49. **Autoglass Trophy:** Winners 1994. **Welsh Cup:** Winners 9 times.
**Colours:** White shirts with maroon and black trim, white shorts, white stockings.

# SWINDON TOWN

DIV. 2

| | | | | | |
|---|---|---|---|---|---|
| Alexander Gary (F) | 6 0 | 12 00 | South London | 15 8 79 | West Ham U |
| Cobian Juan (D) | 5 6 | 10 10 | Buenos Aires | 11 9 75 | Aberdeen |
| Davies Gareth (D) | 6 1 | 11 12 | Hereford | 11 12 73 | Reading |
| Davis Sol (D) | 5 8 | 11 00 | Cheltenham | 4 9 79 | Trainee |

| | | | | | | |
|---|---|---|---|---|---|---|
| Duke David (M) | 5 10 | 11 01 | Inverness | 7 11 78 | Sunderland |
| Grazioli Guiliano (F) | 5 11 | 12 11 | London | 23 3 75 | Peterborough U |
| Griemink Bart (G) | 6 3 | 15 02 | Holland | 29 3 72 | Peterborough U |
| Hewlett Matt (M) | 6 2 | 12 12 | Bristol | 25 2 76 | Bristol C |
| Heywood Matthew (M) | 6 3 | 14 00 | Chatham | 26 8 79 | Burnley |
| Howe Bobby (M) | 5 7 | 10 04 | Annisford | 6 11 73 | Nottingham F |
| Invincible Danny (M) | 6 0 | 12 02 | Australia | 31 3 79 | Marconi Stallions |
| McAreavey Paul (M) | 5 10 | 11 00 | Belfast | 3 12 80 | Trainee |
| Mildenhall Steve (G) | 6 5 | 13 05 | Swindon | 13 5 78 | Trainee |
| O'Halloran Keith (D) | 5 9 | 11 06 | Ireland | 10 11 75 | St Johnstone |
| Robinson Mark (D) | 5 9 | 12 04 | Rochdale | 21 11 68 | Newcastle U |
| Robinson Steve (M) | 5 9 | 11 00 | Nottingham | 17 10 75 | Birmingham C |
| Williams James (M) | 5 7 | 10 08 | Liverpool | 15 7 82 | Trainee |
| Willis Adam (D) | 6 1 | 12 02 | Nuneaton | 21 9 76 | Coventry C |
| Young Alan (D) | | | Swindon | 12 8 83 | Scholar |

**League Appearances:** Alexander, G. 30(7); Bakalli, A. 1; Cobian, J. 3; Cowe, S. 5(4); Davis, S. 35(1); Dryden, R. 7; Duke, D. 24(8); Grazioli, G. 10(18); Griemink, B. 24(1); Griffin, C. 1(1); Hall, G. 3(4); Heiselberg, K. 1; Hewlett, M. 25(1); Heywood, M. 21; Howe, B. 17(2); Invincible, D. 32(10); Lightbourne, K. 2; McAreavey, P. 2(1); McHugh, F. 3(1); Mildenhall, S. 22(1); Mills, J. (2); O'Halloran, K. 40; Reddy, M. 17(1); Reeves, A. 42(2); Robertson, M. 4(6); Robinson, M. 29(5); Robinson, S. 18; Tuomela, 1(1); Van der Linden, A. 17(16); Whitley, J. 2; Williams, A. 3(5); Williams, J. 6(1); Williams, M. 17(2); Willis, A. 21; Woan, I. 21(1); Young, A. (4).
**Goals – League (47):** Invincible 9, Alexander 7, O'Halloran 5 (4 pens), Reddy 4, Reeves 3, Woan 3, Grazioli 2, Heywood 2, Robinson S 2, Williams M 2, Cowe 1, Duke 1, Howe 1, McAreavey 1, Robertson 1 (pen), Robinson M 1, Van der Linden 1, own goal 1.
**Worthington Cup (4):** Howe 1, Invincible 1, Reeves 1, own goal 1.
**FA Cup (9):** Cowe 2, Howe 2, O'Halloran 2, Williams M 1, Willis 1, Young 1.
**Ground:** County Ground, Swindon, Wiltshire SN1 2ED. Telephone (01793) 333 700.
**Record attendance:** 32,000 v Arsenal, FA Cup 3rd rd, 15 January 1972. **Capacity:** 15,728.
**Manager:** Andy King.
**Secretary:** Steve Jones.
**Most League Goals:** 100, Division 3 (S), 1926–27.
**Highest League Scorer in Season:** Harry Morris, 47, Division 3 (S), 1926–27.
**Most League Goals in Total Aggregate:** Harry Morris, 216, 1926–33.
**Most Capped Player:** Rod Thomas, 30 (50), Wales.
**Most League Appearances:** John Trollope, 770, 1960–80.
**Honours – Football League:** Division 2 Champions – 1995–96. Division 4 Champions – 1985–86. **Football League Cup:** Winners 1968–69. **Anglo-Italian Cup:** Winners 1970.
**Colours:** Red shirts, white shorts, red stockings.

---

# TORQUAY UNITED                                    DIV. 3

| | | | | | | |
|---|---|---|---|---|---|---|
| Aggrey Jimmy (D) | 6 3 | 13 06 | London | 26 10 78 | Chelsea |
| Bedeau Anthony (F) | 5 10 | 11 00 | Hammersmith | 24 3 79 | Trainee |
| Brandon Chris (M) | 5 7 | 10 00 | Bradford | 7 4 76 | Bradford PA |
| Chalqi Khalid (M) | | | Oujda | 28 4 71 | Cretail |
| Douglin Troy (D) | 6 2 | 13 00 | Coventry | 7 5 82 | Trainee |
| Healy Brian (M) | 6 1 | 13 02 | Glasgow | 27 12 68 | Morecambe |
| Hill Kevin (M) | 5 8 | 10 03 | Exeter | 6 3 76 | Torrington |

| | | | | | |
|---|---|---|---|---|---|
| Hockley Matthew (D) | 5 11 | 12 00 | Paignton | 5 6 82 | Trainee |
| Holmes Paul (D) | 5 10 | 11 00 | Stocksbridge | 18 2 68 | WBA |
| Jones Stuart (G) | 6 0 | 13 07 | Bristol | 24 10 77 | Sheffield W |
| Kell Richard (M) | 6 1 | 11 00 | Bishop Auckland | 15 9 79 | Middlesbrough |
| Law Gareth (F) | | | Torquay | 20 8 82 | Scholar |
| Mendy Jules (M) | | | Pikine | 4 9 73 | |
| Northmore Ryan (G) | 6 1 | 13 00 | Plymouth | 5 9 80 | Trainee |
| O'Brien Mick (M) | 5 5 | 10 06 | Liverpool | 25 9 79 | Everton |
| Parker Kevin (F) | 5 10 | 11 06 | Plymouth | 20 9 79 | Trainee |
| Russell Lee (D) | 5 10 | 11 09 | Southampton | 3 9 69 | Portsmouth |
| Tully Stephen (M) | 5 7 | 10 04 | Paignton | 10 2 80 | Trainee |
| Watson Alex (D) | 6 1 | 12 00 | Liverpool | 5 4 68 | Bournemouth |
| Williams Eifion (F) | 5 11 | 11 00 | Bangor | 15 11 75 | Barry T |

**League Appearances:** Aggrey, J. 41; Ashington, R. 9(5); Bedeau, A. 33(1); Benefield, J. (1); Brandon, C. 1(1); Chalqi, K. 20(1); Douglin, T. 3; Ford, M. 28; Gayle, J. 5(8); Graham, D. 5; Green, R. 10; Herrera, R. 29; Hill, K. 43(1); Hockley, M. 4(2); Holmes, P. 28(4); Jones, S. 16; Kell, R. 15; Law, G. 2(8); Lyons, S. (9); Mendy, J. 7(14); Neil, G. 9(4); Northmore, R. 24(1); O'Brien, M. 7(14); Parker, K. 8(7); Petterson, A. 6; Platts, M. 2(2); Rees, J. 25; Rowbotham, J. 4(1); Russell, L. 27; Sissoko, H. 7(7); Stocco, T. (2); Tully. S. 28(1); Watson, A. 29(1); Williams, E. 31(6).
**Goals – League** (52): Hill 9, Williams 9, Bedeau 5, Ford 3 (3 pens), Kell 3 (2 pens), Aggrey 2, Graham 2, Holmes 2, Mendy 2, Parker 2, Rees 2, Sissoko 2, Chalqi 1, Gayle 1, Herrera 1, Hockley 1, Law 1, Lyons 1, Neil 1 (pen), O'Brien 1, Tully 1.
**Worthington Cup** (3): Bedeau 2, Hill 1.
**FA Cup** (2): Chalqi 1, Ford 1 (pen).
**Ground:** Plainmoor Ground, Torquay, Devon TQ1 3PS. Telephone (01803) 328666.
**Record attendance:** 21,908 v Huddersfield T, FA Cup 4th rd, 29 January 1955.
**Capacity:** 6283.
**Manager:**
**Secretary:** Mrs H. Kindeleit-Badcock.
**Most League Goals:** 89, Division 3 (S), 1956–57.
**Highest League Scorer in Season:** Sammy Collins, 40, Division 3 (S), 1955–56.
**Most League Goals in Total Aggregate:** Sammy Collins, 204, 1948–58.
**Most Capped Player:** Rodney Jack, St Vincent.
**Most League Appearances:** Dennis Lewis, 443, 1947–59.
**Honours – Nil**
**Colours:** Yellow shirts with navy and white trim, navy shorts with yellow stripe, yellow stockings.

# TOTTENHAM HOTSPUR      FA PREMIERSHIP

| | | | | | |
|---|---|---|---|---|---|
| Anderton Darren (M) | 6 1 | 12 08 | Southampton | 3 3 72 | Portsmouth |
| Armstrong Chris (F) | 6 0 | 13 00 | Newcastle | 19 6 71 | Crystal Palace |
| Bowditch Ben (D) | | | Harlow | 19 2 84 | Scholar |
| Campbell Sol (D) | 6 2 | 14 02 | Newham | 18 9 74 | Trainee |
| Carr Stephen (D) | 5 9 | 13 00 | Dublin | 29 8 76 | Trainee |
| Clemence Stephen (M) | 5 11 | 12 05 | Liverpool | 31 3 78 | Trainee |
| Consorti Maurizio (M) | | | Rome | 6 3 82 | Trainee |
| Davies Simon (M) | 5 10 | 11 02 | Haverfordwest | 23 10 79 | Peterborough U |
| Doherty Gary (D) | 6 0 | 12 13 | Carndonagh | 31 1 80 | Luton T |
| Etherington Matthew (F) | 5 9 | 10 11 | Truro | 14 8 81 | Peterborough U |
| Ferdinand Les (F) | 6 0 | 13 08 | Paddington | 8 12 66 | Newcastle U |
| Ferguson Steven (F) | 5 11 | 11 00 | Dunfermline | 1 4 82 | Musselburgh Windsor |

| Name | Ht | | Birthdate | Birthplace | Signed | | | Previous club |
|---|---|---|---|---|---|---|---|---|
| Freund Steffen (M) | 5 | 11 | 12 04 | Brandenburg | 9 | 1 | 70 | Borussia Dortmund |
| Gardner Anthony (D) | 6 | 5 | 12 13 | Stafford | 19 | 9 | 80 | Port Vale |
| Hillier Ian (M) | 6 | 0 | 11 07 | Neath | 26 | 12 | 79 | Trainee |
| Iversen Steffen (F) | 6 | 1 | 12 05 | Oslo | 10 | 11 | 76 | |
| Jackson Johnnie (M) | | | | Camden | 15 | 8 | 82 | Trainee |
| Jonsson Jon (M) | | | | Kristianstad | 8 | 7 | 83 | |
| Kamanan Yannick (F) | | | | St Pol-sur-Mer | 5 | 10 | 82 | Le Mans |
| Kelly Gavin (G) | 6 | 0 | 13 05 | Hammersmith | 3 | 6 | 81 | Trainee |
| Kelly Stephen (D) | | | | Dublin | 6 | 9 | 83 | |
| King Ledley (D) | 6 | 2 | 14 02 | Bow | 12 | 10 | 80 | Trainee |
| Korsten Willem (M) | 6 | 4 | 12 13 | Boxtel | 21 | 1 | 75 | Leeds U |
| Leonhardsen Oyvind (M) | 5 | 10 | 11 02 | Kristiansund | 17 | 8 | 70 | Liverpool |
| Perry Chris (D) | 5 | 8 | 10 11 | Carshalton | 26 | 4 | 73 | Wimbledon |
| Piercy John (F) | 5 | 11 | 12 04 | Forest Gate | 18 | 9 | 79 | Trainee |
| Rebrov Sergei (F) | 5 | 7 | 10 11 | Gorlovka | 3 | 6 | 74 | Dynamo Kiev |
| Sherwood Tim (M) | 6 | 1 | 11 04 | St Albans | 2 | 2 | 69 | Blackburn R |
| Snee George (F) | | | | Dublin | 26 | 1 | 83 | Scholar |
| Sullivan Neil (G) | 6 | 2 | 14 10 | Sutton | 24 | 2 | 70 | Wimbledon |
| Taricco Mauricio (D) | 5 | 8 | 10 01 | Buenos Aires | 10 | 3 | 73 | Ipswich T |
| Thatcher Ben (D) | 5 | 11 | 12 02 | Swindon | 30 | 11 | 75 | Wimbledon |
| Thelwell Alton (D) | 6 | 0 | 12 05 | Holloway | 5 | 9 | 80 | Trainee |
| Toner Ciaran (M) | 6 | 1 | 12 02 | Craigavon | 30 | 6 | 81 | Trainee |
| Vedeux Ghyslain (F) | | | | Yaounde | 23 | 10 | 83 | |
| Walker Ian (G) | 6 | 2 | 13 08 | Watford | 31 | 10 | 71 | Trainee |
| Young Luke (D) | 6 | 0 | 12 04 | Harlow | 19 | 7 | 79 | Trainee |

**League Appearances:** Anderton, D. 22(1); Armstrong, C. 3(6); Booth, A. 3(1); Campbell, S. 21; Carr, S. 27(1); Clemence, S. 27(2); Davies, S. 9(4); Doherty, G. 18(4); Dominguez, J. (2); Etherington, M. 1(5); Ferdinand, L. 25(3); Freund, S. 19(2); Gardner, A. 5(3); Iversen, S. 10(4); King, L. 18; Korsten, W. 8(6); Leonhardsen, O. 23(2); McEwen, D. (3); Perry, C. 30(2); Piercy, J. (5); Rebrov, S. 28(1); Sherwood, T. 31(2); Sullivan, N. 35; Taricco, M. 2(3); Thatcher, B. 10(2); Thelwell, A. 13(3); Vega, R. 8(2); Walker, I. 3(1); Young, L. 19(4).

**Goals – League** (47): Ferdinand 10, Rebrov 9 (1 pen), Carr 3, Doherty 3, Korsten 3, Leonhardsen 3, Anderton 2 (2 pens), Armstrong 2, Campbell 2, Davies 2, Iversen 2, Sherwood 2, Clemence 1, King 1, Perry 1, own goal 1.

**Worthington Cup** (3): Ferdinand 1 (pen), Iversen 1, Leonhardsen 1.

**FA Cup** (13): Doherty 3, Rebrov 3, Davies 2, Anderton 1, King 1, Leonhardsen 1, own goals 2.

**Ground:** 748 High Rd, Tottenham, London N17 0AP. Telephone (020) 8365 5000.

**Record attendance:** 75,038 v Sunderland, FA Cup 6th rd, 5 March 1938.

**Capacity:** 36,236.

**Manager:** Glenn Hoddle.

**Secretary:** John Alexander.

**Most League Goals:** 115, Division 1, 1960–61.

**Highest League Scorer in Season:** Jimmy Greaves, 37, Division 1, 1962–63.

**Most League Goals in Total Aggregate:** Jimmy Greaves, 220, 1961–70.

**Most Capped Player:** Pat Jennings, 74 (119), Northern Ireland.

**Most League Appearances:** Steve Perryman, 655, 1969–86.

**Honours – Football League:** Division 1 Champions – 1950–51, 1960–61. Division 2 Champions – 1919–20, 1949–50. **FA Cup:** Winners 1901 (as non-League club), 1921, 1961, 1962, 1967, 1981, 1982, 1991. **Football League Cup:** Winners 1970–71, 1972–73, 1998–99. **European Competitions:** European Cup-Winners' Cup winners: 1962–63. **UEFA Cup winners:** 1971–72, 1983–84.

**Colours:** White shirts, navy blue shorts, navy blue stockings.

# TRANMERE ROVERS

| Player | | | Previous Club | | | Birthplace |
|---|---|---|---|---|---|---|
| Achterberg John (G) | 6 1 | 13 00 | Utrecht | 8 | 7 71 | Eindhoven |
| Aldridge Paul (F) | 5 11 | 11 07 | Liverpool | 2 12 81 | | Scholar |
| Allison Wayne (F) | 6 0 | 14 07 | Huddersfield | 16 10 68 | | Huddersfield T |
| Barlow Stuart (F) | 5 10 | 11 03 | Liverpool | 16 | 7 68 | Wigan Ath |
| Challinor Dave (D) | 6 1 | 12 00 | Chester | 2 10 75 | | Brombrough Pool |
| Flynn Sean (M) | 5 8 | 11 09 | Birmingham | 13 | 3 68 | WBA |
| Gill Wayne (M) | 5 9 | 11 00 | Chorley | 28 11 75 | | Blackpool |
| Hay Alexander (F) | 5 10 | 11 05 | Wirral | 14 10 81 | | Scholar |
| Hazell Reuben (D) | 5 11 | 11 11 | Birmingham | 24 | 4 79 | Aston Villa |
| Hill Clint (D) | 6 0 | 11 06 | Liverpool | 19 10 78 | | Trainee |
| Hinds Richard (D) | 6 2 | 12 00 | Sheffield | 22 | 8 80 | Schoolboy |
| Hume Iain (F) | 5 7 | 11 02 | Edinburgh | 31 10 83 | | |
| Jobson Richard (D) | 6 2 | 12 10 | Holderness | 9 | 5 63 | Manchester C |
| Koumas Jason (M) | 5 10 | 11 06 | Wrexham | 25 | 9 79 | Trainee |
| Mellon Micky (D) | 5 10 | 12 11 | Paisley | 18 | 3 72 | Burnley |
| Morgan Alan (D) | 5 9 | 11 00 | Aberystwyth | 2 11 73 | | Trainee |
| Murphy Joe (G) | 6 2 | 13 06 | Dublin | 21 | 8 81 | Trainee |
| N'Diaye Seyni (F) | 6 2 | 13 06 | Dakar | 6 | 1 73 | Caen |
| Olsen James (M) | | | Bootle | 23 10 81 | | Liverpool |
| Parkinson Andy (F) | 5 8 | 10 12 | Liverpool | 27 | 5 79 | Liverpool |
| Rideout Paul (F) | 5 11 | 12 00 | Bournemouth | 14 | 8 64 | Everton |
| Roberts Gareth (D) | 5 8 | 11 00 | Wrexham | 6 | 2 78 | Liverpool |
| Sharps Ian (M) | 6 3 | 13 05 | Warrington | 23 10 80 | | Trainee |
| Yates Steve (D) | 5 10 | 12 02 | Bristol | 29 | 1 70 | QPR |

**League Appearances:** Achterberg, J. 24(1); Aldridge, P. (2); Allen, G. 21(1); Allison, W. 32(4); Barlow, S. 12(15); Challinor, D. 18(4); Flynn, S. 35; Gill, W. 7(9); Hamilton, D. 5(1); Hazell, R. 11(2); Henry, N. 17(3); Hill, C. 34; Hinds, R. 24(5); Hume, I. (10); Jobson, R. 16; Kenna, J. 11; Koumas, J. 34(5); Mellon, M. 11(2); Morgan, A. 3(4); Murphy, J. 19(1); Myhre, T. 3; N'Diaye, S. 5(3); Olsen, J. (1); Osborn, S. 9; Parkinson, A. 29(10); Rideout, P. 28(3); Roberts, G. 33(1); Taylor, S. 24(13); Yates, S. 41(2).

**Goals – League (46):** Koumas 10, Allison 6, Parkinson 6, Hill 5, Taylor 5, Barlow 2 (1 pen), Gill 2 (1 pen), N'Diaye 2, Rideout 2, Yates 2, Flynn 1, Mellon 1, Osborn 1, own goal 1.

**Worthington Cup (10):** Parkinson 2, Rideout 2, Allison 1, Barlow 1, Gill 1, Hill 1, Taylor 1, Yates 1.

**FA Cup (11):** Yates 4, Rideout 3, Allison 1, Barlow 1, Koumas 1, Parkinson 1.

**Ground:** Prenton Park, Prenton Road West, Prenton, Wirral L42 9PN. Telephone (0151) 608 4194.

**Record attendance:** 24,424 v Stoke C, FA Cup 4th rd, 5 February 1972.

**Capacity:** 16,487.

**Manager:** Dave Watson.

**Secretary:** Mick Horton.

**Most League Goals:** 111, Division 3 (N), 1930–31.

**Highest League Scorer in Season:** Bunny Bell, 35, Division 3 (N), 1933–34.

**Most League Goals in Total Aggregate:** Ian Muir, 142, 1985–95.

**Most Capped Player:** John Aldridge, 30 (69), Republic of Ireland.

**Most League Appearances:** Harold Bell, 595, 1946–64 (incl. League record 401 consecutive appearances).

**Honours – Football League** Division 3 (N) Champions – 1937–38. **Welsh Cup:** Winners 1935. **Leyland Daf Cup:** Winners 1990.

**Colours:** White shirts, white shorts with blue trim.

# WALSALL                                            DIV. 1

| | | | | | | |
|---|---|---|---|---|---|---|
| Angell Brett (F) | 6 2 | 13 10 | Marlborough | 20 8 68 | Stockport Co |
| Aranalde Zigor (D) | 6 0 | 12 00 | Ibarra | 28 2 73 | Logrones |
| Bennett Tom (M) | 5 11 | 11 08 | Falkirk | 12 12 69 | Stockport Co |
| Birch Gary (F) | 6 0 | 12 03 | Birmingham | 8 10 81 | Trainee |
| Gadsby Matthew (D) | 6 1 | 11 12 | Sutton Coldfield | 6 9 79 | Trainee |
| Hall Paul (F) | 5 8 | 10 02 | Manchester | 3 7 72 | Coventry C |
| Hawley Karl (F) | 5 7 | 10 06 | Walsall | 6 12 81 | Scholar |
| Keates Dean (M) | 5 5 | 10 06 | Walsall | 30 6 78 | Trainee |
| Leitao Jorge (F) | 5 11 | 13 05 | Oporto | 14 1 74 | Feirense |
| Roper Ian (D) | 6 3 | 14 00 | Nuneaton | 20 6 77 | Trainee |
| Scott Dion (D) | 5 11 | 11 00 | Bearwood | 24 12 80 | Trainee |
| Tillson Andy (D) | 6 2 | 13 05 | Huntingdon | 30 6 66 | Bristol R |
| Walker James (G) | 5 11 | 12 13 | Sutton-in-Ashfield | 9 7 73 | Notts Co |
| Wrack Darren (F) | 5 9 | 12 02 | Cleethorpes | 5 5 76 | Grimsby T |
| Wright Mark (M) | 5 11 | 12 06 | Wolverhampton | 24 2 82 | Scholar |

**League Appearances:** Angell, B. 23(18); Aranalde, Z. 45; Barras, T. 33(3); Bennett, T. 34(4); Brightwell, I. 43(1); Bukran, G. 30(6); Byfield, D. 21(19); Carter, A. (1); Ekelund, R. 2(7); Emberson, C. 3; Gadsby, M. 2(3); Goodman, D. 8; Hall, P. 36(6); Horne, B. 1(2); Keates, D. 21(12); Leitao, J. 40(4); Marsh, C. 4(3); Matias, P. 36(4); Roper, I. 20(5); Scott, D. (1); Simpson, F. 8(2); Tillson, A. 42; Walker, J. 43(1); Wrack, D. 11(17); Wright, M. (4).
**Goals – League** (79): Leitao 18, Angell 13, Byfield 9, Matias 9, Hall 6, Bennett 5, Keates 4 (1 pen), Wrack 4, Bukran 2, Goodman 2, Barras 1, Ekelund 1 (pen), Simpson 1, Tillson 1, own goals 3.
**Worthington Cup** (3): Leitao 2, Byfield 1.
**FA Cup** (8): Tillson 2, Angell 1, Barras 1, Hall 1, Leitao 1, Matias 1, Wrack 1.
**Ground:** Bescot Stadium, Bescot Cresent, Walsall WS1 4SA. Telephone (01922) 622791.
**Record attendance:** 10,628 B International, England v Switzerland, 20 May 1991.
**Capacity:** 9000.
**Manager:** Ray Graydon.
**Secretary/Commercial Manager:** Roy Whalley.
**Most League Goals:** 102, Division 4, 1959–60.
**Highest League Scorer in Season:** Gilbert Alsop, 40, Division 3 (N), 1933–34 and 1934–35.
**Most League Goals in Total Aggregate:** Tony Richards, 184, 1954–63; Colin Taylor, 184, 1958–63, 1964–68, 1969–73.
**Most Capped Player:** Mick Kearns, 15 (18), Republic of Ireland.
**Most League Appearances:** Colin Harrison, 467, 1964–82.
**Honours – Football League:** Division 4 Champions – 1959–60.
**Colours:** Red shirts with black trim, black shorts with white trim, red stockings with white band.

---

# WATFORD                                            DIV. 1

| | | | | | | |
|---|---|---|---|---|---|---|
| Baardsen Espen (G) | 6 5 | 13 03 | San Rafael | 7 12 77 | Tottenham H |
| Chamberlain Alec (G) | 6 2 | 13 10 | March | 20 6 64 | Sunderland |
| Cook Lee (F) | 5 9 | 11 04 | Hammersmith | 3 8 82 | Aylesbury U |
| Cox Neil (D) | 6 0 | 12 01 | Scunthorpe | 8 10 71 | Bolton W |
| Doyley Lloyd (M) | | | London | 1 12 82 | Scholar |
| Easton Clint (M) | 5 11 | 10 04 | Barking | 1 11 77 | Trainee |
| Fisken Gary (M) | | | Watford | 27 10 81 | Scholar |

| Player | | | Birthplace | Birthdate | Status |
|---|---|---|---|---|---|
| Forde Fabian (F) | | | London | 26 10 81 | Scholar |
| Gibbs Nigel (D) | 5 7 | 11 06 | St Albans | 20 11 65 | Apprentice |
| Godfrey Elliott (M) | | | Toronto | 22 2 83 | Scholar |
| Helguson Heidar (F) | 5 10 | 11 00 | Akureyri | 22 8 77 | Lillestrom |
| Hyde Micah (M) | 5 10 | 11 07 | Newham | 10 11 74 | Cambridge U |
| Ifil Jerel (D) | 6 1 | 12 11 | London | 27 6 82 | Academy |
| Johnson Richard (M) | 5 10 | 11 13 | Kurri Kurri | 27 4 74 | Trainee |
| Kennedy Peter (M) | 5 10 | 11 11 | Lisburn | 10 9 73 | Portadown |
| Langston Matthew (D) | 6 2 | 12 04 | Brighton | 2 4 81 | Trainee |
| Lee Richard (M) | | | Oxford | 5 10 82 | Scholar |
| Matthews Barrie (M) | | | Forest of Dean | 1 2 83 | Scholar |
| Neill Thomas (M) | | | Harrow | 13 11 81 | Scholar |
| Nielsen Allan (M) | 5 8 | 11 02 | Esbjerg | 13 3 71 | Tottenham H |
| Noel-Williams Gifton (F) | 6 1 | 12 04 | Islington | 21 1 80 | Trainee |
| Page Robert (D) | 6 0 | 12 05 | Llwynipia | 9 9 74 | Trainee |
| Palmer Steve (M) | 6 1 | 12 03 | Brighton | 31 3 68 | Ipswich T |
| Panayi James (D) | 6 1 | 12 06 | Hammersmith | 24 1 80 | Trainee |
| Patterson Simon (M) | | | Northwick | 4 9 82 | |
| Perpetuini David (D) | 5 9 | 10 00 | Hitchin | 26 9 79 | Trainee |
| Robinson Paul (D) | 5 9 | 11 11 | Watford | 14 12 78 | Trainee |
| Smart Allan (F) | 6 2 | 12 04 | Perth | 8 7 74 | Carlisle U |
| Smith Tommy (F) | 5 9 | 10 00 | Hemel Hempstead | 22 5 80 | Trainee |
| Swonnell Sam (M) | | | Havering | 13 9 82 | Scholar |
| Vernazza Paulo (M) | 5 10 | 10 13 | Islington | 1 11 79 | Arsenal |
| Ward Darren (D) | 6 3 | 12 11 | Kenton | 13 9 78 | Trainee |
| Williams Nicholas (M) | | | Cheltenham | 16 2 83 | |
| Wooter Nordin (F) | 5 6 | 10 08 | Breda | 24 8 76 | Zaragoza |
| Wright Nick (F) | 5 10 | 11 08 | Derby | 15 10 75 | Carlisle U |

**League Appearances:** Armstrong, S. (3); Baardsen, E. 27; Chamberlain, A. 19(2); Cook, L. 2(2); Cox, N. 43(1); Easton, C. 5(6); Foley, D. (5); Forde, F. (1); Gibbs, N. 3(3); Helguson, H. 23(10); Hyde, M. 17(9); Jobson, R. 2; Johnson, R. 1(2); Kennedy, P. 11(6); Mooney, T. 38(1); Ngonge, M. (2); Nielsen, A. 45; Noel-Williams, G. 28(4); Page, R. 36; Palmer, C. 5; Palmer, S. 37(2); Panayi, J. 8(1); Perpetuini, D. 4(1); Robinson, P. 39; Smart, A. 1(7); Smith, T. 38(5); Vernazza, P. 20(3); Ward, D. 40; Wooter, N. 14(12).

**Goals – League** (76): Mooney 19 (1 pen), Smith 11, Nielsen 10, Helguson 8, Noel-Williams 8, Hyde 6, Cox 5, Vernazza 2, Foley 1, Page 1, Palmer S 1, Ward 1, Wooter 1, own goals 2.

**Worthington Cup** (6): Mooney 2, Helguson 1, Palmer 1, Smith 1, Ward 1.

**FA Cup** (1): Mooney 1.

**Ground:** Vicarage Road Stadium, Watford WD18 0ER. Telephone (01923) 496000.

**Record attendance:** 34,099 v Manchester U, FA Cup 4th rd (replay), 3 February 1969. **Capacity:** 20,800.

**Manager:** Gianluca Vialli.

**Secretary:** Catherine Alexander.

**Most League Goals:** 92, Division 4, 1959–60.

**Highest League Scorer in Season:** Cliff Holton, 42, Division 4, 1959–60.

**Most League Goals in Total Aggregate:** Luther Blissett, 148, 1976–83, 1984–88, 1991–92.

**Most Capped Player:** John Barnes, 31 (79), England and Kenny Jackett, 31, Wales.

**Most League Appearances:** Luther Blissett, 415, 1976–83, 1984–88, 1991–92.

**Honours – Football League:** Division 3 Champions – 1968–69. Division 2 Champions – 1997–98. Division 4 Champions – 1977–78.

**Colours:** Yellow shirts, red shorts, red stockings with black and yellow trim.

# WEST BROMWICH ALBION                                           DIV. 1

| Adamson Chris (G) | 6 3 | 12 00 | Ashington | 4 11 78 | Trainee |
| Appleton Michael (M) | 5 8 | 11 00 | Salford | 4 12 75 | Preston NE |
| Balis Igor (M) | 5 11 | 11 00 | Czech Republic | 5 1 70 | Spartak Trnava |
| Butler Tony (D) | 6 2 | 12 00 | Stockport | 28 9 72 | Port Vale |
| Chambers Adam (D) | 5 10 | 11 08 | Sandwell | 20 11 80 | Trainee |
| Chambers James (D) | 5 10 | 11 08 | Sandwell | 20 11 80 | Trainee |
| Clement Neil (D) | 6 0 | 14 07 | Reading | 3 10 78 | Chelsea |
| Collins Matthew (M) | 5 10 | 10 12 | Hitchen | 10 2 82 | Scholar |
| Fox Ruel (F) | 5 6 | 10 05 | Ipswich | 14 1 68 | Tottenham H |
| Gilchrist Phil (D) | 6 0 | 13 03 | Stockton | 25 8 73 | Leicester C |
| Hoult Russell (G) | 6 4 | 14 07 | Ashby | 22 11 72 | Portsmouth |
| Hughes Lee (F) | 5 10 | 11 06 | Birmingham | 22 5 76 | Kidderminster H |
| Iezzi Massamiliano (M) | | | Rome | 1 2 81 | |
| Jensen Brian (G) | 6 1 | 12 04 | Copenhagen | 8 6 75 | AZ |
| Jordao (M) | | | Malanje | 30 8 71 | Braga |
| Lyttle Des (D) | 5 9 | 12 00 | Wolverhampton | 24 9 71 | Watford |
| McInnes Derek (M) | 5 7 | 11 04 | Paisley | 5 7 71 | Toulouse |
| Morris Elliott (G) | 5 11 | 11 07 | Belfast | 4 5 81 | Trainee |
| Oliver Adam (M) | 5 9 | 11 02 | Sandwell | 25 10 80 | Trainee |
| Quinn James (F) | 6 1 | 12 10 | Coventry | 15 12 74 | Blackpool |
| Roberts Jason (F) | 6 1 | 13 06 | Park Royal | 25 1 78 | Bristol R |
| Scott Mark (F) | 6 1 | 12 02 | Birmingham | 16 7 82 | Scholar |
| Sigurdsson Larus (D) | 6 0 | 13 11 | Akureyri | 4 6 73 | Stoke C |
| Taylor Bob (F) | 5 11 | 13 05 | Easington | 3 2 67 | Bolton W |
| Turner Matthew (F) | 5 9 | 10 00 | Nottingham | 29 12 81 | Nottingham F |

**League Appearances:** Appleton, M. 15; Balis, I. 1(6); Burgess, D. 1(2); Butler, T. 44; Carbon, M. 19(5); Chambers, A. 4(7); Chambers, J. 27(4); Clement, N. 45; Cummings, W. 1(2); Derveld, F. 1(1); Fox, R. 36(2); Gilchrist, P. 8; Grant, T. 3(2); Hoult, R. 13; Hughes, L. 41; Jensen, B. 33; Jordao, 28(7); Lyttle, D. 38(2); McInnes, D. 14; Oliver, A. 1(6); Quinn, J. 3(11); Roberts, J. 32(11); Sigurdsson, L. 7(5); Sneekes, R. 39(6); Taylor, B. 17(23); Van Blerk, J. 35(1).
**Goals – League** (60): Hughes 21 (3 pens), Roberts 14, Clement 5, Taylor 5, Sneekes 3, Van Blerk 2, Butler 1, Chambers A 1, Fox 1, Jordao 1, Lyttle 1, McInnes 1, Quinn 1, own goals 3.
**Worthington Cup** (6): Clement 2, Roberts 2, Jordao 1, Sneekes 1.
**FA Cup** (2): Hughes 1, Taylor 1.
**Ground:** The Hawthorns, West Bromwich B71 4LF. Telephone (0121) 525 8888.
**Record attendance:** 64,815 v Arsenal, FA Cup 6th rd, 6 March 1937. **Capacity:** 25,396.
**Manager:** Gary Megson.
**Secretary:** Dr. John J. Evans BA, PHD. (Wales).
**Most League Goals:** 105, Division 2, 1929–30.
**Highest League Scorer in Season:** William 'Ginger' Richardson, 39, Division 1, 1935–36.
**Most League Goals in Total Aggregate:** Tony Brown, 218, 1963–79.
**Most Capped Player:** Stuart Williams, 33 (43), Wales.
**Most League Appearances:** Tony Brown, 574, 1963–80.
**Honours – Football League:** Division 1 Champions – 1919–20. Division 2 Champions – 1901–02, 1910–11. **FA Cup:** Winners 1888, 1892, 1931, 1954, 1968. **Football League Cup:** Winners 1965–66.
**Colours:** Navy blue and white striped shirts, white shorts, blue and white stockings.

# WEST HAM UNITED                    FA PREMIERSHIP

| Name | | | Birthplace | D.O.B. | Previous Club |
|---|---|---|---|---|---|
| Britton Leon (M) | | | London | 16 9 82 | Trainee |
| Byrne Shaun (D) | 5 9 | 11 08 | Taplow | 21 1 81 | Trainee |
| Bywater Steve (G) | 6 2 | 12 00 | Manchester | 7 6 81 | Trainee |
| Camara Titi (F) | 6 0 | 13 00 | Donka | 17 11 72 | Liverpool |
| Carrick Michael (M) | 6 0 | 11 10 | Wallsend | 28 7 81 | Trainee |
| Cascione Emmanuel (M) | | | Catanzaro | 22 9 83 | Lucchese |
| Charles Gary (D) | 5 9 | 11 08 | East London | 13 4 70 | Benfica |
| Cole Joe (M) | 5 7 | 9 08 | Islington | 8 11 81 | Trainee |
| Dailly Christian (D) | 6 0 | 12 10 | Dundee | 23 10 73 | Blackburn R |
| Defoe Jermaine (F) | 5 7 | 10 04 | Beckton | 7 10 82 | Charlton Ath |
| Di Canio Paolo (F) | 5 9 | 11 09 | Rome | 9 7 68 | Sheffield W |
| Ferrante Michael (M) | | | Melbourne | 28 4 81 | Australia IOS |
| Forrest Craig (G) | 6 4 | 14 04 | Vancouver | 20 9 67 | Ipswich T |
| Foxe Hayden (D) | 6 3 | 13 05 | Sydney | 23 6 77 | Ajax |
| Garcia Richard (F) | | | Perth | 4 9 81 | Trainee |
| Hislop Shaka (G) | 6 4 | 14 04 | Hackney | 22 2 69 | Newcastle U |
| Iriekpen Ezomo (D) | 6 1 | 12 02 | East London | 14 5 82 | Trainee |
| Kanoute Frederic (F) | 6 3 | 13 08 | Ste. Foy-Les-Lyon | 2 9 77 | Lyon |
| Kitson Paul (F) | 5 11 | 10 12 | Murton | 9 1 71 | Newcastle U |
| Lampard Frank (M) | 6 0 | 11 12 | Romford | 20 6 78 | Trainee |
| Laurie Steve (D) | | | Melbourne | 30 10 82 | |
| Lomas Steve (M) | 6 0 | 12 08 | Hanover | 14 3 72 | Manchester C |
| McCann Grant (M) | | | Belfast | 14 4 80 | Trainee |
| McMahon Daryl (M) | | | Dublin | 10 10 83 | |
| Minto Scott (D) | 5 10 | 10 00 | Wirral | 6 8 71 | Benfica |
| Moncur John (M) | 5 8 | 9 10 | Mile End | 22 9 66 | Swindon T |
| Newton Adam (D) | 5 10 | 11 00 | Ascot | 4 12 80 | Trainee |
| Pearce Ian (D) | 6 3 | 14 04 | Bury St Edmunds | 7 5 74 | Blackburn R |
| Potts Steve (D) | 5 7 | 10 11 | Hartford (USA) | 7 5 67 | Apprentice |
| Riza Omer (F) | | | Edmonton | 8 11 79 | Arsenal |
| Sinclair Trevor (M) | 5 10 | 12 05 | Dulwich | 2 3 73 | QPR |
| Soma Ragnvald (D) | 6 2 | 12 02 | Norway | 10 11 79 | Bryne |
| Song Rigobert (D) | 6 2 | 13 00 | Nkenlicock | 1 7 76 | Liverpool |
| Stimac Igor (D) | 6 2 | 13 00 | Metkovic | 6 9 67 | Derby Co |
| Todorov Svetoslav (F) | 6 0 | 11 11 | Bulgaria | 30 8 78 | Litets Lovech |
| Williams Tommy (M) | | | Carshalton | 8 7 80 | Walton & Hersham |
| Winterburn Nigel (D) | 5 8 | 11 04 | Coventry | 11 12 63 | Arsenal |

**League Appearances:** Bassila, C. (3); Bywater, S. 1; Camara, T. 5(1); Carrick, M. 32(1); Charles, G. (1); Cole, J. 24(6); Dailly, C. 11(1); Defoe, J. (1); Di Canio, P. 31; Diawara, K. 6(5); Ferdinand, R. 12; Forrest, C. 3(1); Foxe, H. 3(2); Hislop, S. 34; Kanoute, F. 32; Kitson, P. (2); Lampard, F. 30; Lomas, S. 20; Margas, J. 3; McCann, G. (1); Minto, S. 1; Moncur, J. 6(10); Pearce, I. 13(2); Pearce, S. 34; Potts, S. 2(6); Schemmel, 10(2); Sinclair, T. 19; Soma, R. 2(2); Song, R. 18(1); Stimac, I. 19; Suker, D. 7(4); Tihinen, H. 5(3); Todorov, S. 2(6); Winterburn, N. 33.
**Goals – League** (45): Kanoute 11, Di Canio 9 (3 pens), Lampard 7 (1 pen), Cole 5, Sinclair 3, Pearce S 2, Suker 2, Carrick 1, Lomas 1, Pearce I 1, Todorov 1, Winterburn 1, own goal 1.
**Worthington Cup** (5): Defoe 1, Di Canio 1, Lampard 1, Lomas 1, Suker 1.
**FA Cup** (7): Kanoute 3, Di Canio 1, Lampard 1, Pearce S 1, Todorov 1.
**Ground:** Boleyn Ground, Green Street, Upton Park, London E13 9AZ. Telephone (020) 8548 2748.
**Record attendance:** 42,322 v Tottenham H, Division 1, 17 October 1970. **Capacity:** 26,012.

**Manager:** Glenn Roeder.
**Secretary:** Peter Barnes.
**Most League Goals:** 101, Division 2, 1957–58.
**Highest League Scorer in Season:** Vic Watson, 42, Division 1, 1929–30.
**Most League Goals in Total Aggregate:** Vic Watson, 298, 1920–35.
**Most Capped Player:** Bobby Moore, 108, England.
**Most League Appearances:** Billy Bonds, 663, 1967–88.
**Honours – Football League:** Division 2 Champions – 1957–58, 1980–81. **FA Cup:** Winners 1964, 1975, 1980. **European Competitions: European Cup-Winners' Cup winners:** 1964–65. **Intertoto Cup winners** 1999.
**Colours:** Claret shirt with sky blue sleeves, white shorts, white stockings.

## WIGAN ATHLETIC                                      DIV. 2

| | | | | | | |
|---|---|---|---|---|---|---|
| Ashcroft Lee (F) | 5 9 | 12 07 | Preston | 7 | 9 72 | Grimsby T |
| Bidstrup Stefan (D) | 6 2 | 13 08 | Helsinger | 24 | 2 75 | Lyngby |
| Brannan Ged (D) | 6 0 | 12 05 | Liverpool | 15 | 1 72 | Motherwell |
| Carroll Roy (G) | 6 2 | 13 12 | Enniskillen | 30 | 9 77 | Hull C |
| De Zeeuw Arjan (D) | 6 3 | 13 07 | Castricum | 16 | 4 70 | Barnsley |
| Dickson Hugh (D) | | | Down Patrick | 28 | 8 81 | |
| Green Scott (D) | 5 10 | 12 09 | Walsall | 15 | 1 70 | Bolton W |
| Haworth Simon (F) | 6 1 | 14 02 | Cardiff | 30 | 3 77 | Coventry C |
| Kilford Ian (M) | 5 10 | 11 04 | Bristol | 6 | 10 73 | Nottingham F |
| Liddell Andy (F) | 5 8 | 11 05 | Leeds | 28 | 6 73 | Barnsley |
| McCulloch Lee (M) | 5 11 | 12 05 | Bellshill | 14 | 5 78 | Motherwell |
| McGibbon Pat (D) | 6 2 | 13 09 | Lurgan | 6 | 9 73 | Manchester U |
| McLaughlin Brian (M) | 5 5 | 9 02 | Bellshill | 14 | 5 74 | Dundee U |
| McLoughlin Alan (M) | 5 8 | 10 10 | Manchester | 20 | 4 67 | Portsmouth |
| McMillan Stephen (M) | 5 10 | 11 00 | Edinburgh | 19 | 1 76 | Motherwell |
| Mitchell Paul (D) | 6 0 | 12 00 | Manchester | 26 | 8 81 | Scholar |
| Nicholls Kevin (M) | 5 11 | 12 04 | Newham | 2 | 1 79 | Charlton Ath |
| Roberts Neil (F) | 5 10 | 11 02 | Wrexham | 7 | 4 78 | Wrexham |
| Sharp Kevin (D) | 5 9 | 11 04 | Ontario | 19 | 9 74 | Leeds U |
| Stillie Derek (G) | 6 0 | 12 05 | Cumnock | 3 | 12 73 | Aberdeen |

**League Appearances:** Ashcroft, L. 23(7); Balmer, S. 22(2); Beagrie, P. 7(3); Bidstrup, S. 10(5); Bradshaw, C. 22(5); Brannan, G. 12(1); Carroll, R. 29; Dalglish, P. 5(1); De Zeeuw, A. 45; Dickson, H. (1); Gillespie, K. 4(1); Green, S. 27(8); Griffiths, G. 14(3); Haworth, S. 25(5); Kilford, I. 23(1); Liddell, A. 37; Martinez, R. 25(9); McCulloch, L. 10; McGibbon, P. 38(2); McLaughlin, B. 13(5); McLoughlin, A. (4); McMillan, S. 6; Mitchell, P. (1); Nicholls, K. 13(7); Padula, G. 2(2); Redfearn, N. 6(4); Roberts, N. 17(17); Sharp, K. 29(2); Sheridan, D. 25(2); Stillie, D. 17(1).
**Goals – League** (53): Haworth 11, Liddell 9, Roberts 6, Ashcroft 5 (1 pen), Bradshaw 3 (2 pens), McCulloch 3, Bidstrup 2, Green 2, Kilford 2, McGibbon 2, Balmer 1, Beagrie 1, De Zeeuw 1, Griffiths 1, Redfearn 1 (pen), own goals 3.
**Worthington Cup** (6): Haworth 2, Kilford 1, Liddell 1, Roberts 1, Sharp 1.
**FA Cup** (5): Ashcroft 1, Bidstrup 1, Kilford 1, Roberts 1, own goal 1.
**Ground:** J. J. B. Stadium, Robin Park, Newtown, Wigan WN6 7BA. Telephone (01942) 774 000.
**Record attendance:** 27,500 v Hereford U, FA Cup 2nd rd, 12 December 1953.
**Capacity:** 25,000
**Manager:** Paul Jewell.
**Secretary:** Mrs Brenda Spencer.
**Most League Goals:** 84, Division 3, 1996–97.
**Highest League Scorer in Season:** Graeme Jones, 31, Division 3, 1996–97.
**Most League Goals in Total Aggregate:** David Lowe, 66, 1982–87 and 1995–99.
**Most Capped Player:** Roy Carroll, 9, Northern Ireland.

**Most League Appearances:** Kevin Langley, 317, 1981–86, 1990–94.
**Honours – Football League:** Division 3 Champions – 1996–97. **Freight Rover Trophy:** Winners 1984–85. **Auto Windscreens Shield:** Winners 1998–99.
**Colours:** All blue.

---

# WIMBLEDON                                                    DIV. 1

---

| | | | | | | |
|---|---|---|---|---|---|---|
| Agyemang Patrick (F) | 6 1 | 12 00 | Walthamstow | 29 9 80 | Trainee |
| Ainsworth Gareth (M) | 5 9 | 11 00 | Blackburn | 10 5 73 | Port Vale |
| Andersen Trond (M) | 6 0 | 11 06 | Kristiansund | 6 1 75 | Molde |
| Berni Tommaso (G) | | | Firenze | 6 3 83 | Internazionale |
| Blackwell Dean (D) | 6 1 | 12 10 | Camden | 5 12 69 | Trainee |
| Bolger Gavin (M) | | | Dublin | 7 8 82 | |
| Byrne Des (D) | 6 1 | 12 07 | Dublin | 10 4 81 | Sr Patrick's Ath |
| Cooper Kevin (F) | 5 8 | 10 07 | Derby | 8 2 75 | Stockport Co |
| Cunningham Kenny (D) | 5 11 | 11 04 | Dublin | 28 6 71 | Millwall |
| Davis Kelvin (G) | 6 1 | 11 02 | Bedford | 29 9 76 | Luton T |
| Euell Jason (F) | 5 11 | 11 02 | Lambeth | 6 2 77 | Trainee |
| Feuer Ian (G) | 6 6 | 15 06 | Las Vegas | 20 5 71 | West Ham U |
| Francis Damien (M) | 6 0 | 10 10 | Wandsworth | 27 2 79 | Trainee |
| Gier Robert (M) | 5 9 | 11 07 | Ascot | 6 1 80 | Trainee |
| Gray Wayne (F) | 5 10 | 11 10 | South London | 7 11 80 | Trainee |
| Haara Heikki (M) | | | Lahti | 20 11 82 | |
| Hawkins Peter (D) | 6 0 | 11 04 | Maidstone | 19 9 78 | Trainee |
| Heald Paul (G) | 6 2 | 12 05 | Wath-on-Dearne | 20 9 68 | Leyton Orient |
| Holloway Darren (D) | 6 0 | 12 09 | Crook | 3 10 77 | Sunderland |
| Hughes Michael (M) | 5 6 | 10 08 | Larne | 2 8 71 | West Ham U |
| Jenkins Neil (M) | | | Carshalton | 6 1 82 | Scholar |
| Jupp Duncan (D) | 6 0 | 12 11 | Guildford | 25 1 75 | Fulham |
| Karlsson Par (M) | 5 7 | 10 11 | Sweden | 29 5 78 | IFK Gothenburg |
| Kimble Alan (D) | 5 10 | 12 04 | Poole | 6 8 66 | Cambridge U |
| Lund Andreas (F) | 6 1 | 11 04 | Kristiansand | 7 5 75 | Molde |
| McAnuff Joel (M) | | | Edmonton | 9 11 81 | Scholar |
| Mensing Simon (M) | 5 10 | 11 06 | Woifenbuttel | 27 6 82 | |
| Morgan Lionel (F) | | | Enfield | 17 2 83 | Scholar |
| Nielsen David (F) | 6 0 | 11 11 | Denmark | 1 12 76 | Grimsby T |
| Owusu Ansah (M) | 5 11 | 11 02 | Hackney | 22 11 79 | Trainee |
| Roberts Andy (M) | 5 10 | 13 00 | Dartford | 20 3 74 | Crystal Palace |
| Robinson Paul (F) | 5 11 | 12 11 | Sunderland | 20 11 78 | Newcastle U |
| Selley Ian (M) | 5 10 | 10 09 | Chertsey | 14 6 74 | Fulham |
| Tapp Alex (M) | 5 8 | 11 10 | Redhill | 7 6 82 | Trainee |
| Thomas Michael (M) | 5 9 | 12 06 | Lambeth | 24 8 67 | Liverpool |
| Waehler Kjetil (M) | 5 10 | 11 00 | Oslo | 16 3 76 | Lyn |
| Williams Mark (D) | 6 0 | 12 04 | Stalybridge | 28 9 70 | Watford |
| Willmott Chris (D) | 5 11 | 10 12 | Bedford | 30 9 77 | Luton T |

**League Appearances:** Agyemang, P. 16(13); Ainsworth, G. 8(4); Andersen, T. 40(2); Ardley, N. 36(1); Blackwell, D. 5(1); Cooper, K. 11; Cunningham, K. 15; Davis, K. 45; Euell, J. 33(3); Francis, D. 29; Gayle, M. 24(8); Gier, R. 13(1); Gray, W. 1(10); Harley, J. 6; Hartson, J. 19; Hawkins, P. 29(1); Heald, P. 1(2); Holloway, D. 30(1); Hreidarsson, H. 1; Hughes, M. 5(5); Hunt, J. 8(4); Jupp, D. 4; Karlsson, P. 7(9); Kimble, A. 21(4); Leaburn, C. 2(1); Morgan, L. 1(4); Nielsen, D. 9(2); Owusu, A. 1(3); Roberts, A. 25(2); Robinson, P. (3); Selley, I. 1(3); Thomas, M. 5(3); Williams, M. 42; Willmott, C. 13(1).

**Goals – League** (71): Euell 19 (2 pens), Francis 8, Hartson 8, Williams 6, Andersen 5, Agyemang 4, Ardley 3 (1 pen), Cooper 3, Gayle 3, Ainsworth 2, Harley 2, Nielsen 2, Roberts 2, Hughes 1, Willmott 1, own goals 2.

**Worthington Cup** (4): Hartson 2 (1 pen), Gayle 1, Roberts 1.
**FA Cup** (9): Ardley 2 (1 pen), Ageymang 1, Ainsworth 1, Andersen 1, Euell 1, Hunt 1, Karlsson 1, Williams 1.
**Ground:** Selhurst Park, South Norwood, London SE25 6PY. Telephone (020) 8771 2233.
**Record attendance:** 30,115 v Manchester U, FA Premier League, 9 May 1993.
**Capacity:** 26,297.
**Manager:** Terry Burton.
**Secretary:** Steve Rooke.
**Most League Goals:** 97, Division 3, 1983–84.
**Highest League Scorer in Season:** Alan Cork, 29, 1983–84.
**Most League Goals in Total Aggregate:** Alan Cork, 145, 1977–92.
**Most Capped Player:** Kenny Cunningham, 33, Republic of Ireland.
**Most League Appearances:** Alan Cork, 430, 1977–92.
**Honours – Football League:** Division 4 Champions – 1982–83. **FA Cup:** Winners 1987–88.
**Colours:** All navy blue with yellow trim.

# WOLVERHAMPTON WANDERERS                    DIV. 1

| | | | | | |
|---|---|---|---|---|---|
| Andrews Keith (M) | 5 10 | 12 04 | Dublin | 13 9 80 | Trainee |
| Barrett Shane (F) | 5 10 | 11 00 | Luton | 23 11 81 | Trainee |
| Bazeley Darren (D) | 5 11 | 10 09 | Northampton | 5 10 72 | Watford |
| Branch Michael (F) | 5 10 | 11 09 | Liverpool | 18 10 78 | Everton |
| Butler Paul (D) | 6 3 | 14 09 | Manchester | 2 11 72 | Sunderland |
| Camara Mohammed (D) | 5 11 | 11 09 | Conakry | 25 6 75 | Le Havre |
| Coleman Kenneth (M) | | | Cork | 20 9 82 | Scholar |
| Dickson Andrew (M) | | | Belfast | 3 8 82 | Scholar |
| Dinning Tony (M) | 6 0 | 12 04 | Wallsend | 24 7 75 | Stockport Co |
| Emblen Neil (M) | 6 1 | 13 03 | Bromley | 19 6 71 | Crystal Palace |
| Green Ryan (D) | 5 8 | 10 10 | Cardiff | 20 10 80 | Danes Court |
| Ketsbaia Temuri (F) | 5 8 | 10 12 | Gale | 18 3 68 | Newcastle U |
| Larkin Colin (F) | 5 9 | 11 07 | Dundalk | 27 4 82 | Trainee |
| Lescott Jolean (D) | 6 2 | 13 00 | Birmingham | 16 8 82 | Trainee |
| McQuade Scott (M) | 5 7 | 10 06 | Dumfries | 7 1 82 | Trainee |
| Melligan John (M) | | | Dublin | 11 2 82 | Trainee |
| Murray Matt (G) | 6 3 | 13 07 | Solihull | 2 5 81 | Trainee |
| Muscat Kevin (D) | 5 11 | 11 07 | Crawley | 7 8 73 | Crystal Palace |
| Naylor Lee (D) | 5 8 | 12 00 | Bloxwich | 19 3 80 | Trainee |
| Ndah George (F) | 6 1 | 11 04 | Dulwich | 23 12 74 | Swindon T |
| Niestroj Robert (M) | 5 10 | 11 03 | Oppeln | 2 12 74 | Fortuna Dusseldorf |
| Oakes Michael (G) | 6 2 | 14 07 | Northwich | 30 10 73 | Aston Villa |
| Pollet Ludovic (D) | 6 0 | 12 06 | Vieux-conde | 18 6 70 | Le Havre |
| Proudlock Adam (M) | 6 0 | 13 00 | Wellington | 9 5 81 | Trainee |
| Robinson Carl (M) | 5 10 | 12 10 | Llandrindod Wells | 13 10 76 | Trainee |
| Roussel Cedric (F) | 6 3 | 13 00 | Mons | 6 1 78 | Coventry C |
| Taylor Robert (F) | 6 1 | 13 08 | Norwich | 30 4 71 | Manchester C |
| Tudor Shane (M) | 5 8 | 11 00 | Wolverhampton | 10 2 82 | Trainee |
| Ward Graham (M) | | | Dublin | 25 2 83 | Scholar |

**League Appearances:** Al-Jaber, S. (4); Andrews, K. 20(2); Bazeley, D. 23(1); Branch, M. 31(7); Butler, P. 12; Camara, M. 4(14); Connelly, S. 6; Dinning, T. 31; Emblen, N. 21(7); Green, R. 5(2); Ketsbaia, T. 14(8); Larkin, C. (2); Lescott, J. 31(6); Muscat, K. 37; Naylor, L. 44(2); Ndah, G. 23(6); Oakes, M. 46; Osborn, S. 16(4); Peacock, D. 2(2); Pollet, L. 29; Proudlock, A. 28(7); Robinson, C. 36(4); Roussel, C. 3(6); Sedgley, S. 5; Sinton, A. 28(2); Stowell, M. (1); Taylor, R. 5(4); Taylor, S. 3(1); Thetis, M. 3; Tudor, S. (1).

**Goals – League** (45): Proudlock 8, Dinning 6 (1 pen), Ndah 6 (1 pen), Branch 4, Ketsbaia 3, Muscat 3 (1 pen), Robinson 3, Lescott 2, Pollet 2, Sinton 2, Bazeley 1, Naylor 1, Sedgley 1, own goals 3.
**Worthington Cup** (9): Taylor 3, Proudlock 2, Ketsbaia 1, Muscat 1 (pen), Osborn 1, Robinson 1.
**FA Cup** (2): Proudlock 1, Robinson 1.
**Ground:** Molineux Grounds, Wolverhampton WV1 4QR. Telephone (01902) 655000.
**Record attendance:** 61,315 v Liverpool, FA Cup 5th rd, 11 February 1939.
**Capacity:** 28,525.
**Manager:** Dave Jones.
**Secretary:** Richard Skirrow.
**Most League Goals:** 115, Division 2, 1931–32.
**Highest League Scorer in Season:** Dennis Westcott, 38, Division 1, 1946–47.
**Most League Goals in Total Aggregate:** Steve Bull, 250, 1986–99.
**Most Capped Player:** Billy Wright, 105, England (70 consecutive).
**Most League Appearances:** Derek Parkin, 501, 1967–82.
**Honours – Football League:** Division 1 Champions – 1953–54, 1957–58, 1958–59. Division 2 Champions – 1931–32, 1976–77. Division 3 (N) Champions – 1923–24. Division 3 Champions – 1988–89. Division 4 Champions – 1987–88. **FA Cup:** Winners 1893, 1908, 1949, 1960. **Football League Cup:** Winners 1973–74, 1979–80. **Sherpa Van Trophy winners** 1988.
**Colours:** Old gold shirts, black shorts, old gold stockings.

## WREXHAM                                                           DIV. 2

| | | | | | |
|---|---|---|---|---|---|
| Barrett Paul (M) | 5 9 | 11 04 | Newcastle | 13 4 78 | Newcastle U |
| Blackwood Michael (F) | 5 11 | 11 10 | Birmingham | 30 9 79 | Aston Villa |
| Edwards Carlos (F) | 5 10 | 12 00 | Trinidad | 24 10 78 | |
| Faulconbridge Craig (F) | 6 1 | 13 00 | Nuneaton | 20 4 78 | Dunfermline Ath |
| Ferguson Darren (M) | 5 10 | 11 10 | Glasgow | 9 2 72 | Wolverhampton W |
| Gibson Robin (F) | 5 7 | 10 07 | Crewe | 15 11 79 | Trainee |
| Lawrence Dennis (F) | 6 7 | 14 00 | Trinidad | 1 8 74 | Defence Force |
| Morrell Andy (F) | 5 11 | 11 06 | Doncaster | 28 9 74 | Newcastle Blue Star |
| Phillips Wayne (M) | 5 11 | 11 00 | Bangor | 15 12 70 | Stockport Co |
| Roberts Steve (D) | 6 2 | 11 06 | Wrexham | 24 2 80 | Trainee |
| Rogers Kristian (G) | 6 2 | 11 07 | Chester | 2 10 80 | |
| Sam Hector (F) | 5 9 | 11 04 | Trinidad | 25 2 78 | San Juan Jabloteh |
| Thomas Steve (M) | 5 10 | 11 07 | Hartlepool | 23 6 79 | Trainee |
| Trundle Lee (F) | | | Liverpool | 10 10 76 | Rhyl |
| Walsh Dave (G) | 6 1 | 12 05 | Wrexham | 29 4 79 | Trainee |
| Warren David (M) | 5 10 | 11 05 | Cork | 28 2 81 | Mayfield U |

**League Appearances:** Barrett, P. 22(2); Blackwood, M. 3(12); Bouanane, E. 13(4); Carey, B. 33; Chalk, M. 22(2); Dearden, K. 36; Edwards, C. 31(5); Faulconbridge, C. 33(6); Ferguson, D. 43; Gibson, R. 17(11); Hardy, P. 13; Killen, C. 11(1); Lawrence, D. 1(2); Mardon, P. 6(1); McGregor, M. 43; Moody, A. 2(1); Morrell, A. 10(10); Owen, G. 18(4); Pejic, S. 1; Phillips, W. 4(3); Ridler, D. 22(2); Roberts, S. 6(1); Roche, L. 41; Rogers, K. 5; Russell, K. 24(2); Sam, H. 11(9); Thomas, S. 4(2); Trundle, L. 12(2); Walsh, D. 5; Williams, D. 14(1).
**Goals – League** (65): Faulconbridge 10, Ferguson 9 (4 pens), Trundle 8, Sam 6, McGregor 5, Chalk 4, Edwards 4, Russell 4, Carey 3, Killen 3, Morrell 3, Owen 2, Williams 2, Gibson 1, Phillips 1.
**Worthington Cup** (1): Ferguson 1.
**FA Cup** (0).
**Ground:** Racecourse Ground, Mold Road, Wrexham LL11 2AH. Telephone (01978) 262129.

**Record attendance:** 34,445 v Manchester U, FA Cup 4th rd, 26 January 1957.
**Capacity:** 15,500.
**Manager:** Brian Flynn.
**Secretary:** D. L. Rhodes.
**Most League Goals:** 106, Division 3 (N), 1932–33.
**Highest League Scorer in Season:** Tom Bamford, 44, Division 3 (N), 1933–34.
**Most Goals in Total Aggregate:** Tom Bamford, 175, 1928–34.
**Most Capped Player:** Joey Jones, 29 (72), Wales.
**Most League Appearances:** Arfon Griffiths, 592, 1959–61, 1962–79.
**Honours – Football League:** Division 3 Champions – 1977–78. **Welsh Cup:** Winners 22 times.
**Colours:** Red shirts, white shorts, red stockings.

---

# WYCOMBE WANDERERS                                             DIV. 2

| Name | | | Birthplace | | | Previous Club |
|---|---|---|---|---|---|---|
| Baird Andy (F) | 5 10 | 11 13 | East Kilbride | 18 1 79 | | Trainee |
| Bates Jamie (D) | 6 2 | 14 06 | Croydon | 24 2 68 | | Brentford |
| Brown Steve (M) | 5 10 | 11 12 | Northampton | 6 7 66 | | Northampton T |
| Bulman Dannie (M) | 5 9 | 11 12 | Ashford | 24 1 79 | | Ashford T |
| Castleline Stewart (M) | 6 1 | 12 00 | Wandsworth | 22 1 73 | | Wimbledon |
| Cousins Jason (D) | 5 10 | 12 07 | Hayes | 4 10 70 | | Brentford |
| Devine Sean (F) | 5 11 | 13 00 | Lewisham | 6 9 72 | | Barnet |
| Lee Martyn (M) | 5 6 | 9 00 | Guilford | 10 8 80 | | Trainee |
| Marsh Chris (D) | 5 11 | 13 02 | Dudley | 14 1 70 | | Walsall |
| McCarthy Paul (D) | 5 10 | 13 10 | Cork | 4 8 71 | | Brighton & HA |
| McSporran Jermaine (F) | 5 10 | 10 12 | Manchester | 1 1 77 | | Oxford C |
| Osborn Mark (G) | 6 0 | 14 01 | Bletchley | 19 6 81 | | Trainee |
| Rammell Andy (F) | 6 1 | 13 12 | Nuneaton | 10 2 67 | | Walsall |
| Rogers Mark (D) | 5 11 | 12 12 | Geulph | 3 11 75 | | |
| Ryan Keith (M) | 5 10 | 12 06 | Northampton | 25 6 70 | | Berkhamsted T |
| Senda Danny (F) | 5 10 | 10 02 | Harrow | 17 4 81 | | Southampton |
| Simpson Michael (M) | 5 8 | 11 07 | Nottingham | 28 2 74 | | Notts Co |
| Taylor Martin (G) | 6 0 | 13 11 | Tamworth | 9 12 66 | | Derby Co |
| Townsend Ben (D) | 5 10 | 11 03 | Reading | 8 10 81 | | Scholar |
| Vinnicombe Chris (D) | 5 9 | 10 12 | Exeter | 20 10 70 | | Burnley |

**League Appearances:** Baird, A. 9(4); Bates, J. 37(2); Beeton, A. 3; Brady, M. 2(3); Brown, S. 30(2); Bulman, D. 36; Carroll, D. 8(4); Castleline, S. 6(11); Clegg, G. 2(8); Cousins, J. 26(6); Essandoh, R. 8(5); Harkin, M. 10(5); Johnson, R. (1); Jones, S. 5; Lavin, G. 2; Lee, M. 13(8); Marsh, C. 11; McCarthy, P. 38; McSporran, J. 20; Nutter, J. 1; Parkin, S. 5(3); Phelan, L. (2); Rammell, A. 25(1); Rogers, M. 19(3); Ryan, K. 21(9); Senda, D. 12(19); Simpson, M. 45; Taylor, M. 46; Thompson, N. 6(2); Townsend, B. 9(1); Vinnicombe, C. 42; Whittingham, G. 9(3).
**Goals – League (46):** Rammell 10, Brown 4 (2 pens), Bulman 4, Ryan 4, Baird 3, Bates 3, Lee 3, Simpson 3, Carroll 2, McCarthy 2, McSporran 2, Senda 2, Parkin 1, Rogers 1, Vinnicombe 1, Whittingham 1.
**Worthington Cup (7):** Baird 1, Bates 1, Castleline 1, McCarthy 1, McSporran 1, Rammell 1, Rogers 1.
**FA Cup (17):** McCarthy 4, Simpson 3 (1 pen), Bates 2, Rammell 2, Brown 1, Carroll 1, Essendoh 1, Parkin 1, Rogers 1, Ryan 1.
**Ground:** Adams Park, Hillbottom Road, Sands, High Wycombe HP12 4HJ. Telephone (01494) 472100.
**Record attendance:** 9002 v West Ham U, FA Cup 3rd rd, 7 January 1995. **Capacity:** 10,000 (7350 seats).
**Manager:** Lawrie Sanchez.
**Secretary:** Keith J. Allen.

**Most League Goals:** 67, Division 3, 1993–94.
**Highest League Goalscorer in Season:** Sean Devine, 23, 1999–2000.
**Most League Goals in Total Aggregate:** Dave Carroll, 40, 1993–2001.
**Most Capped Player:** None.
**Most League Appearances:** Dave Carroll, 290, 1993–2001.
**Honours – GM Vauxhall Conference winners:** 1993. **FA Trophy winners:** 1991, 1993.
**Colours:** Light & dark blue quartered shirts, navy shorts, light blue stockings.

---

# YORK CITY                                        DIV. 3

| | | | | | | |
|---|---|---|---|---|---|---|
| Alcide Colin (F) | 6 2 | 13 11 | Huddersfield | 14 | 4 72 | Hull C |
| Brass Chris (D) | 5 9 | 12 06 | Easington | 24 | 7 75 | Burnley |
| Bullock Lee (M) | 6 1 | 12 07 | Stockton | 22 | 5 81 | Trainee |
| Conlon Barry (F) | 6 2 | 13 07 | Drogheda | 1 | 10 78 | Southend U |
| Cooper Richard (D) | 5 9 | 10 07 | Nottingham | 4 | 9 79 | Nottingham F |
| Duffield Peter (F) | 5 6 | 10 04 | Middlesbrough | 4 | 2 69 | Darlington |
| Edmondson Darren (D) | 6 0 | 12 10 | Ulverston | 4 | 11 71 | Huddersfield T |
| Fettis Alan (G) | 6 2 | 13 00 | Newtownards | 1 | 2 71 | Blackburn R |
| Fox Christian (M) | 5 11 | 11 00 | Auchenbrae | 11 | 4 81 | Trainee |
| Hobson Gary (D) | 6 2 | 13 02 | North Ferriby | 12 | 11 72 | Chester C |
| Hocking Matt (D) | 5 11 | 12 00 | Boston | 30 | 1 78 | Hull C |
| Howarth Russell (G) | 6 1 | 12 00 | York | 27 | 3 82 | Scholar |
| Mathie Alex (F) | 5 10 | 11 13 | Bathgate | 20 | 12 68 | Preston NE |
| Potter Graham (D) | 6 1 | 11 12 | Solihull | 20 | 5 75 | WBA |
| Skinner Craig (M) | 5 8 | 11 00 | Bury | 21 | 10 70 | Wrexham |
| Stamp Neville (D) | 5 11 | 12 07 | Reading | 7 | 7 81 | Reading |
| Thompson Marc (D) | 5 10 | 12 03 | York | 15 | 1 82 | |

**League Appearances:** Agnew, S. 37(2); Alcide, C. 24(14); Basham, M. 6(1); Bower, M. 21; Brass, C. 8(2); Bullock, L. 29(4); Conlon, B. 2(6); Cooper, R. 14; Darlow, K. (1); Duffield, P. 6; Durkan, K. 7; Edmondson, D. 22(1); Emmerson, S. 3(5); Fettis, A. 46; Fox, C. 3(5); Hall, W. 16(3); Hobson, G. 8(3); Hocking, M. 24(2); Hulme, K. 11(4); Iwelumo, C. 11(1); Jones, B. 28(1); Jordan, S. 6(6); Mathie, A. 13(6); McNiven, D. 25(16); Nogan, L. 16; Patterson, D. 4(2); Potter, G. 34(4); Reed, M. 1(1); Richardson, N. 16(1); Sertori, M. 26; Stamp, N. 12(1); Swan, P. 2; Tarrant, N. 6(1); Thompson, M. 9(3); Turley, J. 5(5); Williams, J. 1(5); Wood, L. 4(1).
**Goals – League** (42): McNiven 8, Nogan 6, Alcide 5, Bullock 3, Duffield 3 (2 pens), Hulme 3, Agnew 2, Iwelumo 2, Potter 2, Basham 1, Bower 1, Brass 1 (pen), Emmerson 1, Mathie 1, Richardson 1, Sertori 1, Tarrant 1.
**Worthington Cup** (1): Jones 1.
**FA Cup** (9): McNiven 2, Agnew 1, Alcide 1, Bullock 1, Iwelumo 1, Jordan 1, Mathie 1, Potter 1.
**Ground:** Bootham Crescent, York YO3 7AQ. Telephone (01904) 624447.
**Record attendance:** 28,123 v Huddersfield T, FA Cup 6th rd, 5 March 1938.
**Capacity:** 9534.
**Manager:** Terry Dolan.
**Secretary:** Keith Usher.
**Most League Goals:** 96, Division 4, 1983–84.
**Highest League Scorer in Season:** Bill Fenton, 31, Division 3 (N), 1951–52; Arthur Bottom, 31, Division 3 (N), 1954–55 and 1955–56.
**Most League Goals in Total Aggregate:** Norman Wilkinson, 125, 1954–66.
**Most Capped Player:** Peter Scott, 7 (10), Northern Ireland.
**Most League Appearances:** Barry Jackson, 481, 1958–70.
**Honours – Football League:** Division 4 Champions – 1983–84.
**Colours:** Red shirts, navy shorts, navy stockings.

## LEAGUE POSITIONS: FA PREMIER from 1992–93 and DIVISION 1 1975–76 to 1991–92

| | 1999–2000 | 1998–99 | 1997–98 | 1996–97 | 1995–96 | 1994–95 | 1993–94 | 1992–93 | 1991–92 | 1990–91 | 1989–90 | 1988–89 | 1987–88 |
|---|---|---|---|---|---|---|---|---|---|---|---|---|---|
| Arsenal | 2 | 2 | 1 | 3 | 5 | 12 | 4 | 10 | 4 | 1 | 4 | 1 | 6 |
| Aston Villa | 6 | 6 | 7 | 5 | 4 | 18 | 10 | 2 | 7 | 17 | 2 | 17 | – |
| Barnsley | – | – | 19 | – | – | – | – | – | – | – | – | – | – |
| Birmingham C | – | – | – | – | – | – | – | – | – | – | – | – | – |
| Blackburn R | – | 19 | 6 | 13 | 7 | 1 | 2 | 4 | – | – | – | – | – |
| Bolton W | – | – | 18 | – | 20 | – | – | – | – | – | – | – | – |
| Bradford C | 17 | – | – | – | – | – | – | – | – | – | – | – | – |
| Brighton & HA | – | – | – | – | – | – | – | – | – | – | – | – | – |
| Bristol C | – | – | – | – | – | – | – | – | – | – | – | – | – |
| Burnley | – | – | – | – | – | – | – | – | – | – | – | – | – |
| Charlton Ath | – | 18 | – | – | – | – | – | – | – | – | 19 | 14 | 17 |
| Chelsea | 5 | 3 | 4 | 6 | 11 | 11 | 14 | 11 | 14 | 11 | 5 | – | 18 |
| Coventry C | 14 | 15 | 11 | 17 | 16 | 16 | 11 | 15 | 19 | 16 | 12 | 7 | 10 |
| Crystal Palace | – | – | 20 | – | – | 19 | – | 20 | 10 | 3 | 15 | – | – |
| Derby Co | 16 | 8 | 9 | 12 | – | – | – | – | – | – | 20 | 5 | 15 |
| Everton | 13 | 14 | 17 | 15 | 6 | 15 | 17 | 13 | 12 | 9 | 6 | 8 | 4 |
| Ipswich T | – | – | – | – | 22 | 19 | 16 | – | – | – | – | – | – |
| Leeds U | 3 | 4 | 5 | 11 | 13 | 5 | 5 | 17 | 1 | 4 | – | – | – |
| Leicester C | 8 | 10 | 10 | 9 | – | 21 | – | – | – | – | – | – | – |
| Liverpool | 4 | 7 | 3 | 4 | 3 | 4 | 8 | 6 | 6 | 2 | 1 | 2 | 1 |
| Luton T | – | – | – | – | – | – | – | – | 20 | 18 | 17 | 16 | 9 |
| Manchester C | – | – | – | – | 18 | 17 | 16 | 9 | 5 | 5 | 14 | – | – |
| Manchester U | 1 | 1 | 2 | 1 | 1 | 2 | 1 | 1 | 2 | 6 | 13 | 11 | 2 |
| Middlesbrough | 12 | 9 | – | 19 | 12 | – | – | 21 | – | – | – | 18 | – |
| Millwall | – | – | – | – | – | – | – | – | – | – | 20 | 10 | – |
| Newcastle U | 11 | 13 | 13 | 2 | 2 | 6 | 3 | – | – | – | – | 20 | 8 |
| Norwich C | – | – | – | – | – | 20 | 12 | 3 | 18 | 15 | 10 | 4 | 14 |
| Nottingham F | – | 20 | – | 20 | 9 | 3 | – | 22 | 8 | 8 | 9 | 3 | 3 |
| Notts Co | – | – | – | – | – | – | – | 21 | – | – | – | – | – |
| Oldham Ath | – | – | – | – | – | 21 | 19 | 17 | – | – | – | – | – |
| Oxford U | – | – | – | – | – | – | – | – | – | – | – | – | 21 |
| Portsmouth | – | – | – | – | – | – | – | – | – | – | – | – | 19 |
| QPR | – | – | – | – | 19 | 8 | 9 | 5 | 11 | 12 | 11 | 9 | 5 |
| Sheffield U | – | – | – | – | – | 20 | 14 | 9 | 13 | – | – | – | – |
| Sheffield W | 19 | 12 | 16 | 7 | 15 | 13 | 7 | 7 | 3 | – | 18 | 15 | 11 |
| Southampton | 15 | 17 | 12 | 16 | 17 | 10 | 18 | 18 | 16 | 14 | 7 | 13 | 12 |
| Stoke C | – | – | – | – | – | – | – | – | – | – | – | – | – |
| Sunderland | 7 | – | – | 18 | – | – | – | – | – | 19 | – | – | – |
| Swansea C | – | – | – | – | – | – | – | – | – | – | – | – | – |
| Swindon T | – | – | – | – | – | 22 | – | – | – | – | – | – | – |
| Tottenham H | 10 | 11 | 14 | 10 | 8 | 7 | 15 | 8 | 15 | 10 | 3 | 6 | 13 |
| Watford | 20 | – | – | – | – | – | – | – | – | – | – | – | 20 |
| WBA | – | – | – | – | – | – | – | – | – | – | – | – | – |
| West Ham U | 9 | 5 | 8 | 14 | 10 | 14 | 13 | – | 22 | – | – | 19 | 16 |
| Wimbledon | 18 | 16 | 15 | 8 | 14 | 9 | 6 | 12 | 13 | 7 | 8 | 12 | 7 |
| Wolv'hampton W | – | – | – | – | – | – | – | – | – | – | – | – | – |

| 1986-87 | 1985-86 | 1984-85 | 1983-84 | 1982-83 | 1981-82 | 1980-81 | 1979-80 | 1978-79 | 1977-78 | 1976-77 | 1975-76 | |
|---|---|---|---|---|---|---|---|---|---|---|---|---|
| 4 | 7 | 7 | 6 | 10 | 5 | 3 | 4 | 7 | 5 | 8 | 17 | Arsenal |
| 22 | 16 | 10 | 10 | 6 | 11 | 1 | 7 | 8 | 8 | 4 | 16 | Aston Villa |
| – | – | – | – | – | – | – | – | – | – | – | – | Barnsley |
| – | 21 | – | 20 | 17 | 16 | 13 | – | 21 | 11 | 13 | 19 | Birmingham C |
| – | – | – | – | – | – | – | – | – | – | – | – | Blackburn R |
| – | – | – | – | – | – | – | 22 | 17 | – | – | – | Bolton W |
| – | – | – | – | – | – | – | – | – | – | – | – | Bradford C |
| – | – | – | – | 22 | 13 | 19 | 16 | – | – | – | – | Brighton & HA |
| – | – | – | – | – | – | – | 20 | 13 | 17 | 18 | – | Bristol C |
| – | – | – | – | – | – | – | – | – | – | – | 21 | Burnley |
| 19 | – | – | – | – | – | – | – | – | – | – | – | Charlton Ath |
| 14 | 6 | 6 | – | – | – | – | – | 22 | 16 | – | – | Chelsea |
| 10 | 17 | 18 | 19 | 19 | 14 | 16 | 15 | 10 | 7 | 19 | 14 | Coventry C |
| – | – | – | – | – | – | 22 | 13 | – | – | – | – | Crystal Palace |
| – | – | – | – | – | – | – | 21 | 19 | 12 | 15 | 4 | Derby Co |
| 1 | 2 | 1 | 7 | 7 | 8 | 15 | 19 | 4 | 3 | 9 | 11 | Everton |
| – | 20 | 17 | 12 | 9 | 2 | 2 | 3 | 6 | 18 | 3 | 6 | Ipswich T |
| – | – | – | – | – | 20 | 9 | 11 | 5 | 9 | 10 | 5 | Leeds U |
| 20 | 19 | 15 | 15 | – | – | 21 | – | – | 22 | 11 | 7 | Leicester C |
| 2 | 1 | 2 | 1 | 1 | 1 | 5 | 1 | 1 | 2 | 1 | 1 | Liverpool |
| 7 | 9 | 13 | 16 | 18 | – | – | – | – | – | – | – | Luton T |
| 21 | 15 | – | – | 20 | 10 | 12 | 17 | 15 | 4 | 2 | 8 | Manchester C |
| 11 | 4 | 4 | 4 | 3 | 3 | 8 | 2 | 9 | 10 | 6 | 3 | Manchester U |
| – | – | – | – | – | 22 | 14 | 9 | 12 | 14 | 12 | 13 | Middlesbrough |
| – | – | – | – | – | – | – | – | – | – | – | – | Millwall |
| 17 | 11 | 14 | – | – | – | – | – | – | 21 | 5 | 15 | Newcastle U |
| 5 | – | 20 | 14 | 14 | – | 20 | 12 | 16 | 13 | 16 | 10 | Norwich C |
| 8 | 8 | 9 | 3 | 5 | 12 | 7 | 5 | 2 | 1 | – | – | Nottingham F |
| – | – | – | 21 | 15 | 15 | – | – | – | – | – | – | Notts Co |
| – | – | – | – | – | – | – | – | – | – | – | – | Oldham Ath |
| 18 | 18 | – | – | – | – | – | – | – | – | – | – | Oxford U |
| – | – | – | – | – | – | – | – | – | – | – | – | Portsmouth |
| 16 | 13 | 19 | 5 | – | – | – | – | 20 | 19 | 14 | 2 | QPR |
| – | – | – | – | – | – | – | – | – | – | – | 22 | Sheffield U |
| 13 | 5 | 8 | – | – | – | – | – | – | – | – | – | Sheffield W |
| 12 | 14 | 5 | 2 | 12 | 7 | 6 | 8 | 14 | – | – | – | Southampton |
| – | – | 22 | 18 | 13 | 18 | 11 | 18 | – | – | 21 | 12 | Stoke C |
| – | – | 21 | 13 | 16 | 19 | 17 | – | – | – | 20 | – | Sunderland |
| – | – | – | – | 21 | 6 | – | – | – | – | – | – | Swansea C |
| – | – | – | – | – | – | – | – | – | – | – | – | Swindon T |
| 3 | 10 | 3 | 8 | 4 | 4 | 10 | 14 | 11 | – | 22 | 9 | Tottenham H |
| 9 | 12 | 11 | 11 | 2 | – | – | – | – | – | – | – | Watford |
| – | 22 | 12 | 17 | 11 | 17 | 4 | 10 | 3 | 6 | 7 | – | WBA |
| 15 | 3 | 16 | 9 | 8 | 9 | – | – | – | 20 | 17 | 18 | West Ham U |
| 6 | – | – | – | – | – | – | – | – | – | – | – | Wimbledon |
| – | – | – | 22 | – | 21 | 18 | 6 | 18 | 15 | – | 20 | Wolv'hampton W |

# LEAGUE POSITIONS: DIVISION 1 from 1992–93 and DIVISION 2 1975–76 to 1991–92

| | 1999-2000 | 1998-99 | 1997-98 | 1996-97 | 1995-96 | 1994-95 | 1993-94 | 1992-93 | 1991-92 | 1990-91 | 1989-90 | 1988-89 | 1987-88 |
|---|---|---|---|---|---|---|---|---|---|---|---|---|---|
| Aston Villa | – | – | – | – | – | – | – | – | – | – | – | – | 2 |
| Barnsley | 4 | 13 | – | 2 | 10 | 6 | 18 | 13 | 16 | 8 | 19 | 7 | 14 |
| Birmingham C | 5 | 4 | 7 | 10 | 15 | – | 22 | 19 | – | – | – | 23 | 19 |
| Blackburn R | 11 | – | – | – | – | – | – | – | 6 | 19 | 5 | 5 | 5 |
| Blackpool | – | – | – | – | – | – | – | – | – | – | – | – | – |
| Bolton W | 6 | 6 | – | 1 | – | 3 | 14 | – | – | – | – | – | – |
| Bournemouth | – | – | – | – | – | – | – | – | – | – | 22 | 12 | 17 |
| Bradford C | – | 2 | 13 | 21 | – | – | – | – | – | – | 23 | 14 | 4 |
| Brentford | – | – | – | – | – | – | – | 22 | – | – | – | – | – |
| Brighton & HA | – | – | – | – | – | – | – | – | 23 | 6 | 18 | 19 | – |
| Bristol C | – | 24 | – | – | – | 23 | 13 | 15 | 17 | 9 | – | – | – |
| Bristol R | – | – | – | – | – | – | – | 24 | 13 | 13 | – | – | – |
| Burnley | – | – | – | – | – | 22 | – | – | – | – | – | – | – |
| Bury | – | 22 | 17 | – | – | – | – | – | – | – | – | – | – |
| Cambridge U | – | – | – | – | – | – | – | 23 | 5 | – | – | – | – |
| Cardiff C | – | – | – | – | – | – | – | – | – | – | – | – | – |
| Carlisle U | – | – | – | – | – | – | – | – | – | – | – | – | – |
| Charlton Ath | 1 | – | 4 | 15 | 6 | 15 | 11 | 12 | 7 | 16 | – | – | – |
| Chelsea | – | – | – | – | – | – | – | – | – | – | – | 1 | – |
| Crewe Alex | 19 | 18 | 11 | – | – | – | – | – | – | – | – | – | – |
| Crystal Palace | 15 | 14 | – | 6 | 3 | – | 1 | – | – | – | – | 3 | 6 |
| Derby Co | – | – | – | – | 2 | 9 | 6 | 8 | 3 | – | – | – | – |
| Fulham | 9 | – | – | – | – | – | – | – | – | – | – | – | – |
| Grimsby T | 20 | 11 | – | 22 | 17 | 10 | 16 | 9 | 19 | – | – | – | – |
| Hereford U | – | – | – | – | – | – | – | – | – | – | – | – | – |
| Huddersfield T | 8 | 10 | 16 | 20 | 8 | – | – | – | – | – | – | – | 23 |
| Hull C | – | – | – | – | – | – | – | – | – | 24 | 14 | 21 | 15 |
| Ipswich T | 3 | 3 | 5 | 4 | 7 | – | – | – | 1 | 14 | 9 | 8 | 8 |
| Leeds U | – | – | – | – | – | – | – | – | – | – | 1 | 10 | 7 |
| Leicester C | – | – | – | – | 5 | – | 4 | 6 | 4 | 22 | 13 | 15 | 13 |
| Leyton Orient | – | – | – | – | – | – | – | – | – | – | – | – | – |
| Luton T | – | – | – | – | 24 | 16 | 20 | 20 | – | – | – | – | – |
| Manchester C | 2 | – | 22 | 14 | – | – | – | – | – | – | – | 2 | 9 |
| Mansfield T | – | – | – | – | – | – | – | – | – | – | – | – | – |
| Middlesbrough | – | – | 2 | – | – | 1 | 9 | – | 2 | 7 | 21 | – | 3 |
| Millwall | – | – | – | – | 22 | 12 | 3 | 7 | 15 | 5 | – | – | 1 |
| Newcastle U | – | – | – | – | – | – | – | 1 | 20 | 11 | 3 | – | – |
| Norwich C | 12 | 9 | 15 | 13 | 16 | – | – | – | – | – | – | – | – |
| Nottingham F | 14 | – | 1 | – | – | – | 2 | – | – | – | – | – | – |
| Notts Co | – | – | – | – | – | 24 | 7 | 17 | – | 4 | – | – | – |
| Oldham Ath | – | – | – | 23 | 18 | 14 | – | – | – | 1 | 8 | 16 | 10 |
| Oxford U | – | 23 | 12 | 17 | – | – | 23 | 14 | 21 | 10 | 17 | 17 | – |
| Peterborough U | – | – | – | – | – | – | 24 | 10 | – | – | – | – | – |
| Plymouth Arg | – | – | – | – | – | – | – | – | 22 | 18 | 16 | 18 | 16 |
| Port Vale | 23 | 21 | 19 | 8 | 12 | 17 | – | – | 24 | 15 | 11 | – | – |
| Portsmouth | 18 | 19 | 20 | 7 | 21 | 18 | 17 | 3 | 9 | 17 | 12 | 20 | – |
| Preston NE | – | – | – | – | – | – | – | – | – | – | – | – | – |
| QPR | 10 | 20 | 21 | 9 | – | – | – | – | – | – | – | – | – |

| | 1986–87 | 1985–86 | 1984–85 | 1983–84 | 1982–83 | 1981–82 | 1980–81 | 1979–80 | 1978–79 | 1977–78 | 1976–77 | 1975–76 |
|---|---|---|---|---|---|---|---|---|---|---|---|---|
| Aston Villa | – | – | – | – | – | – | – | – | – | – | – | – |
| Barnsley | 11 | 12 | 11 | 14 | 10 | 6 | – | – | – | – | – | – |
| Birmingham C | 19 | – | 2 | – | – | – | – | 3 | – | – | – | – |
| Blackburn R | 12 | 19 | 5 | 6 | 11 | 10 | 4 | – | 22 | 5 | 12 | 15 |
| Blackpool | – | – | – | – | – | – | – | – | – | 20 | 5 | 10 |
| Bolton W | – | – | – | – | 22 | 19 | 18 | – | 1 | 4 | 4 | |
| Bournemouth | – | – | – | – | – | – | – | – | – | – | – | – |
| Bradford C | 10 | 13 | – | – | – | – | – | – | – | – | – | – |
| Brentford | – | – | – | – | – | – | – | – | – | – | – | – |
| Brighton & HA | 22 | 11 | 6 | 9 | – | – | – | – | 2 | 4 | – | 2 |
| Bristol C | – | – | – | – | – | – | 21 | – | – | – | – | 2 |
| Bristol R | – | – | – | – | – | 22 | 19 | 16 | 18 | 15 | 18 | |
| Burnley | – | – | – | 21 | – | – | 21 | 13 | 11 | 16 | – | |
| Bury | – | – | – | – | – | – | – | – | – | – | – | – |
| Cambridge U | – | – | 22 | 12 | 14 | 13 | 8 | 12 | – | – | | |
| Cardiff C | – | – | 21 | 15 | – | 20 | 19 | 15 | 9 | 19 | 18 | – |
| Carlisle U | – | 20 | 16 | 7 | 14 | – | – | – | – | 20 | 19 | |
| Charlton Ath | – | 2 | 17 | 13 | 17 | 13 | – | 22 | 19 | 17 | 7 | 9 |
| Chelsea | – | – | – | 1 | 18 | 12 | 12 | 4 | – | – | 2 | 11 |
| Crewe Alex | – | – | – | – | – | – | – | – | – | – | – | – |
| Crystal Palace | 6 | 5 | 15 | 18 | 15 | 15 | – | – | 1 | 9 | – | – |
| Derby Co | 1 | – | – | 20 | 13 | 16 | 6 | – | – | – | – | – |
| Fulham | – | 22 | 9 | 11 | 4 | – | 20 | 10 | 10 | 17 | 12 | |
| Grimsby T | 21 | 15 | 10 | 5 | 19 | 17 | 7 | – | – | – | – | |
| Hereford U | – | – | – | – | – | – | – | – | – | – | 22 | – |
| Huddersfield T | 17 | 16 | 13 | 12 | – | – | – | – | – | – | – | |
| Hull C | 14 | 6 | – | – | – | – | – | – | 22 | 14 | 14 | |
| Ipswich T | 5 | – | – | – | – | – | – | – | – | – | – | |
| Leeds U | 4 | 14 | 7 | 10 | 8 | – | – | – | – | – | – | |
| Leicester C | – | – | – | – | 3 | 8 | – | 1 | 17 | – | – | |
| Leyton Orient | – | – | – | – | 22 | 17 | 14 | 11 | 14 | 19 | 13 | |
| Luton T | – | – | – | – | 1 | 5 | 6 | 18 | 13 | 6 | 7 | |
| Manchester C | – | – | 3 | 4 | – | – | – | – | – | – | – | |
| Mansfield T | – | – | – | – | – | – | – | – | 21 | – | – | |
| Middlesbrough | – | 21 | 19 | 17 | 16 | – | – | – | – | – | – | |
| Millwall | 16 | 9 | – | – | – | – | – | – | – | – | – | |
| Newcastle U | – | – | – | 3 | 5 | 9 | 11 | 9 | 8 | – | – | |
| Norwich C | – | 1 | – | – | – | 3 | – | – | – | – | – | |
| Nottingham F | – | – | – | – | – | – | – | – | – | – | 3 | 8 |
| Notts Co | – | – | 20 | – | – | 2 | 17 | 6 | 15 | 8 | 5 | |
| Oldham Ath | 3 | 8 | 14 | 19 | 7 | 11 | 15 | 11 | 14 | 8 | 13 | 17 |
| Oxford U | – | – | 1 | – | – | – | – | – | – | – | – | 20 |
| Peterborough U | – | – | – | – | – | – | – | – | – | – | – | – |
| Plymouth Arg | 7 | – | – | – | – | – | – | – | – | – | 21 | 16 |
| Port Vale | – | – | – | – | – | – | – | – | – | – | – | – |
| Portsmouth | 2 | 4 | 4 | 16 | – | – | – | – | – | – | – | 22 |
| Preston NE | – | – | – | – | – | – | 20 | 10 | 7 | – | – | – |
| QPR | – | – | – | – | 1 | 5 | 8 | 5 | – | – | – | – |

# LEAGUE POSITIONS: DIVISION 1 from 1992–93 and DIVISION 2 1975–76 to 1991–92 (cont.)

| | 1999–2000 | 1998–99 | 1997–98 | 1996–97 | 1995–96 | 1994–95 | 1993–94 | 1992–93 | 1991–92 | 1990–91 | 1989–90 | 1988–89 | 1987–88 |
|---|---|---|---|---|---|---|---|---|---|---|---|---|---|
| Reading | – | – | 24 | 18 | 19 | 2 | – | – | – | – | – | – | 22 |
| Rotherham U | – | – | – | – | – | – | – | – | – | – | – | – | – |
| Sheffield U | 16 | 8 | 6 | 5 | 9 | 8 | – | – | – | – | 2 | – | 21 |
| Sheffield W | – | – | – | – | – | – | – | – | – | 3 | – | – | – |
| Shrewsbury T | – | – | – | – | – | – | – | – | – | – | – | 22 | 18 |
| Southampton | – | – | – | – | – | – | – | – | – | – | – | – | – |
| Southend U | – | – | – | 24 | 14 | 13 | 15 | 18 | 12 | – | – | – | – |
| Stockport Co | 17 | 16 | 8 | – | – | – | – | – | – | – | – | – | – |
| Stoke C | – | – | 23 | 12 | 4 | 11 | 10 | – | – | – | 24 | 13 | 11 |
| Sunderland | – | 1 | 3 | – | 1 | 20 | 12 | 21 | 18 | – | 6 | 11 | – |
| Swansea C | – | – | – | – | – | – | – | – | – | – | – | – | – |
| Swindon T | 24 | 17 | 18 | 19 | – | 21 | – | 5 | 8 | 21 | 4 | 6 | 12 |
| Tottenham H | – | – | – | – | – | – | – | – | – | – | – | – | – |
| Tranmere R | 13 | 15 | 14 | 11 | 13 | 5 | 5 | 4 | 14 | – | – | – | – |
| Walsall | 22 | – | – | – | – | – | – | – | – | – | – | 24 | – |
| Watford | – | 5 | – | – | 23 | 7 | 19 | 16 | 10 | 20 | 15 | 4 | – |
| WBA | 21 | 12 | 10 | 16 | 11 | 19 | 21 | – | – | 23 | 20 | 9 | 20 |
| West Ham U | – | – | – | – | – | – | – | 2 | – | 2 | 7 | – | – |
| Wimbledon | – | – | – | – | – | – | – | – | – | – | – | – | – |
| Wolv'hampton W | 7 | 7 | 9 | 3 | 20 | 4 | 8 | 11 | 11 | 12 | 10 | – | – |
| Wrexham | – | – | – | – | – | – | – | – | – | – | – | – | – |
| York C | – | – | – | – | – | – | – | – | – | – | – | – | – |

# LEAGUE POSITIONS: DIVISION 2 from 1992–93 and DIVISION 3 1975–76 to 1991–92

| | 1999–2000 | 1998–99 | 1997–98 | 1996–97 | 1995–96 | 1994–95 | 1993–94 | 1992–93 | 1991–92 | 1990–91 | 1989–90 | 1988–89 | 1987–88 |
|---|---|---|---|---|---|---|---|---|---|---|---|---|---|
| Aldershot | – | – | – | – | – | – | – | – | – | – | – | 24 | 20 |
| Barnet | – | – | – | – | – | – | 24 | – | – | – | – | – | – |
| Barnsley | – | – | – | – | – | – | – | – | – | – | – | – | – |
| Birmingham C | – | – | – | – | – | 1 | – | – | 2 | 12 | 7 | – | – |
| Blackburn R | – | – | – | – | – | – | – | – | – | – | – | – | – |
| Blackpool | 22 | 14 | 12 | 7 | 3 | 12 | 20 | 18 | – | – | 23 | 19 | 10 |
| Bolton W | – | – | – | – | – | – | – | 2 | 13 | 4 | 6 | 10 | – |
| Bournemouth | 16 | 7 | 9 | 16 | 14 | 19 | 17 | 17 | 8 | 9 | – | – | – |
| Bradford C | – | – | – | – | 6 | 14 | 7 | 10 | 16 | 8 | – | – | – |
| Brentford | 17 | – | 21 | 4 | 15 | 2 | 16 | – | 1 | 6 | 13 | 7 | 12 |
| Brighton & HA | – | – | – | – | 23 | 16 | 14 | 9 | – | – | – | – | 2 |
| Bristol C | 9 | – | 2 | 5 | 13 | – | – | – | – | – | 2 | 11 | 5 |
| Bristol R | 7 | 13 | 5 | 17 | 10 | 4 | 8 | – | – | – | 1 | 5 | 8 |

| | 1986-87 | 1985-86 | 1984-85 | 1983-84 | 1982-83 | 1981-82 | 1980-81 | 1979-80 | 1978-79 | 1977-78 | 1976-77 | 1975-76 |
|---|---|---|---|---|---|---|---|---|---|---|---|---|
| Reading | 13 | – | – | – | 20 | 7 | – | – | – | – | – | – |
| Rotherham U | – | – | – | – | 20 | 7 | – | – | – | – | – | – |
| Sheffield U | 9 | 7 | 18 | – | – | – | – | 20 | 12 | 11 | – | – |
| Sheffield W | – | – | – | 2 | 6 | 4 | 10 | – | – | – | – | – |
| Shrewsbury T | 18 | 17 | 8 | 8 | 9 | 18 | 14 | 13 | – | – | – | – |
| Southampton | – | – | – | – | – | – | – | – | – | 2 | 9 | 6 |
| Southend U | – | – | – | – | – | – | – | – | – | – | – | – |
| Stockport Co | – | – | – | – | – | – | – | – | – | – | – | – |
| Stoke C | 8 | 10 | – | – | – | – | – | – | 3 | 7 | – | – |
| Sunderland | 20 | 18 | – | – | – | – | 2 | 4 | 6 | – | – | 1 |
| Swansea C | – | – | – | 21 | – | – | 3 | 12 | – | – | – | – |
| Swindon T | – | – | – | – | – | – | – | – | – | – | – | – |
| Tottenham H | – | – | – | – | – | – | – | – | 3 | – | – | – |
| Tranmere R | – | – | – | – | – | – | – | – | – | – | – | – |
| Walsall | – | – | – | – | – | – | – | – | – | – | – | – |
| Watford | – | – | – | – | – | 2 | 9 | 18 | – | – | – | – |
| WBA | 15 | – | – | – | – | – | – | – | – | – | – | 3 |
| West Ham U | – | – | – | – | – | – | 1 | 7 | 5 | – | – | – |
| Wimbledon | – | 3 | 12 | – | – | – | – | – | – | – | – | – |
| Wolv'hampton W | – | – | 22 | – | – | 2 | – | – | – | – | 1 | – |
| Wrexham | – | – | – | – | – | 21 | 16 | 16 | 15 | – | – | – |
| York C | – | – | – | – | – | – | – | – | – | – | – | 21 |

| | 1986-87 | 1985-86 | 1984-85 | 1983-84 | 1982-83 | 1981-82 | 1980-81 | 1979-80 | 1978-79 | 1977-78 | 1976-77 | 1975-76 |
|---|---|---|---|---|---|---|---|---|---|---|---|---|
| Aldershot | – | – | – | – | – | – | – | – | – | – | – | 21 |
| Barnet | – | – | – | – | – | – | – | – | – | – | – | – |
| Barnsley | – | – | – | – | – | – | 2 | 11 | – | – | – | – |
| Birmingham C | – | – | – | – | – | – | – | 2 | – | – | – | – |
| Blackburn R | – | – | – | – | – | – | – | – | – | – | – | – |
| Blackpool | 9 | 12 | – | – | – | – | 23 | 18 | 12 | – | – | – |
| Bolton W | 21 | 18 | 17 | 10 | – | – | – | – | – | – | – | – |
| Bournemouth | 1 | 15 | 10 | 17 | 14 | – | – | – | – | – | – | – |
| Bradford C | – | – | 1 | 7 | 12 | – | – | – | – | 22 | – | – |
| Brentford | 11 | 10 | 13 | 20 | 9 | 8 | 9 | 19 | 10 | – | – | – |
| Brighton & HA | – | – | – | – | – | – | – | – | – | – | 2 | 4 |
| Bristol C | 6 | 9 | 5 | – | – | 23 | – | – | – | – | – | – |
| Bristol R | 19 | 16 | 6 | 5 | 7 | 15 | – | – | – | – | – | – |

# LEAGUE POSITIONS: DIVISION 2 from 1992–93 and DIVISION 3 1975–76 to 1991–92 (cont.)

| | 1999–2000 | 1998–99 | 1997–98 | 1996–97 | 1995–96 | 1994–95 | 1993–94 | 1992–93 | 1991–92 | 1990–91 | 1989–90 | 1988–89 | 1987–88 |
|---|---|---|---|---|---|---|---|---|---|---|---|---|---|
| Burnley | 2 | 15 | 20 | 9 | 17 | – | 6 | 13 | – | – | – | – | – |
| Bury | 15 | – | – | 1 | – | – | – | – | 21 | 7 | 5 | 13 | 14 |
| Cambridge U | 19 | – | – | – | 20 | 10 | – | – | – | 1 | – | – | – |
| Cardiff C | 21 | – | – | – | – | 22 | 19 | – | – | – | 21 | 16 | – |
| Carlisle U | – | – | 23 | – | 21 | – | – | – | – | – | – | – | – |
| Charlton Ath | – | – | – | – | – | – | – | – | – | – | – | – | – |
| Chester C | – | – | – | – | – | 23 | – | 24 | 18 | 19 | 16 | 8 | 15 |
| Chesterfield | 24 | 9 | 10 | 10 | 7 | – | – | – | – | – | – | 22 | 18 |
| Colchester U | 18 | 18 | – | – | – | – | – | – | – | – | – | – | – |
| Crewe Alex | – | – | – | 6 | 5 | 3 | – | – | – | 22 | 12 | – | – |
| Crystal Palace | – | – | – | – | – | – | – | – | – | – | – | – | – |
| Darlington | – | – | – | – | – | – | – | – | 24 | – | – | – | – |
| Derby Co | – | – | – | – | – | – | – | – | – | – | – | – | – |
| Doncaster R | – | – | – | – | – | – | – | – | – | – | – | – | 24 |
| Exeter C | – | – | – | – | – | – | 22 | 19 | 20 | 16 | – | – | – |
| Fulham | – | 1 | 6 | – | – | – | 21 | 12 | 9 | 21 | 20 | 4 | 9 |
| Gillingham | 3 | 4 | 8 | 11 | – | – | – | – | – | – | – | 23 | 13 |
| Grimsby T | – | – | 3 | – | – | – | – | – | 3 | – | – | 22 | – |
| Halifax T | – | – | – | – | – | – | – | – | – | – | – | – | – |
| Hartlepool U | – | – | – | – | – | 23 | 16 | 11 | – | – | – | – | – |
| Hereford U | – | – | – | – | – | – | – | – | – | – | – | – | – |
| Huddersfield T | – | – | – | – | – | 5 | 11 | 15 | 3 | 11 | 8 | 14 | – |
| Hull C | – | – | – | – | 24 | 8 | 9 | 20 | 14 | – | – | – | – |
| Leyton Orient | – | – | – | – | – | 24 | 18 | 7 | 10 | 13 | 14 | – | – |
| Lincoln C | – | 23 | – | – | – | – | – | – | – | – | – | – | – |
| Luton T | 13 | 12 | 17 | 3 | – | – | – | – | – | – | – | – | – |
| Macclesfield T | – | 24 | – | – | – | – | – | – | – | – | – | – | – |
| Manchester C | – | 3 | – | – | – | – | – | – | – | – | – | – | – |
| Mansfield T | – | – | – | – | – | – | – | 22 | – | 24 | 15 | 15 | 19 |
| Middlesbrough | – | – | – | – | – | – | – | – | – | – | – | – | – |
| Millwall | 5 | 10 | 18 | 14 | – | – | – | – | – | – | – | – | – |
| Newport Co | – | – | – | – | – | – | – | – | – | – | – | – | – |
| Northampton T | – | 22 | 4 | – | – | – | – | – | – | – | 22 | 20 | 6 |
| Notts Co | 8 | 16 | – | 24 | 4 | – | – | – | – | – | 3 | 9 | 4 |
| Oldham Ath | 14 | 20 | 13 | – | – | – | – | – | – | – | – | – | – |
| Oxford U | 20 | – | – | – | 2 | 7 | – | – | – | – | – | – | – |
| Peterborough U | – | – | – | 21 | 19 | 15 | – | – | 6 | – | – | – | – |
| Plymouth Arg | – | – | 22 | 19 | – | 21 | 3 | 14 | – | – | – | – | – |
| Portsmouth | – | – | – | – | – | – | – | – | – | – | – | – | – |
| Port Vale | – | – | – | – | – | – | 2 | 3 | – | – | – | 3 | 11 |
| Preston NE | 1 | 5 | 15 | 15 | – | – | – | 21 | 17 | 17 | 19 | 6 | 16 |
| Reading | 10 | 11 | – | – | – | – | 1 | 8 | 12 | 15 | 10 | 18 | – |
| Rochdale | – | – | – | – | – | – | – | – | – | – | – | – | – |
| Rotherham U | – | – | – | 23 | 16 | 17 | 15 | 11 | – | 23 | 9 | – | 21 |
| Scunthorpe U | 23 | – | – | – | – | – | – | – | – | – | – | – | – |
| Sheffield U | – | – | – | – | – | – | – | – | – | – | – | 2 | – |
| Sheffield W | – | – | – | – | – | – | – | – | – | – | – | – | – |
| Shrewsbury T | – | – | – | 22 | 18 | 18 | – | – | 22 | 18 | 11 | – | – |
| Southend U | – | – | 24 | – | – | – | – | – | – | 2 | – | 21 | 17 |

| 1986-87 | 1985-86 | 1984-85 | 1983-84 | 1982-83 | 1981-82 | 1980-81 | 1979-80 | 1978-79 | 1977-78 | 1976-77 | 1975-76 | |
|---|---|---|---|---|---|---|---|---|---|---|---|---|
| - | - | 21 | 12 | - | 1 | 8 | - | - | - | - | - | Burnley |
| 16 | 20 | - | - | - | - | - | 21 | 19 | 15 | 7 | 13 | Bury |
| - | - | 24 | - | - | - | - | - | - | 2 | - | - | Cambridge U |
| - | 22 | - | - | 2 | - | - | - | - | - | - | 2 | Cardiff C |
| 22 | - | - | - | 2 | 19 | 6 | 6 | 13 | - | - | - | Carlisle U |
| - | - | - | - | - | 3 | - | - | - | - | - | - | Charlton Ath |
| 15 | - | - | - | - | 24 | 18 | 9 | 16 | 5 | 13 | 17 | Chester C |
| 17 | 17 | - | - | 24 | 11 | 5 | 4 | 20 | 9 | 18 | 15 | Chesterfield |
| - | - | - | - | - | - | 22 | 5 | 7 | 8 | - | 22 | Colchester U |
| - | - | - | - | - | - | - | - | - | - | - | - | Crewe Alex |
| - | - | - | - | - | - | - | - | - | - | 3 | 5 | Crystal Palace |
| 22 | 13 | - | - | - | - | - | - | - | - | - | - | Darlington |
| - | 3 | 7 | - | - | - | - | - | - | - | - | - | Derby C |
| 13 | 11 | 14 | - | 23 | 19 | - | - | - | - | - | - | Doncaster R |
| - | - | - | 24 | 19 | 18 | 11 | 8 | 9 | 17 | - | - | Exeter C |
| 18 | - | - | - | - | 3 | 13 | - | - | - | - | - | Fulham |
| 5 | 5 | 4 | 8 | 13 | 6 | 15 | 16 | 4 | 7 | 12 | 14 | Gillingham |
| - | - | - | - | - | - | - | 1 | - | - | 23 | 18 | Grimsby T |
| - | - | - | - | - | - | - | - | - | - | - | 24 | Halifax T |
| - | - | - | - | - | - | - | - | - | 23 | - | 1 | Hartlepool U |
| - | - | - | 3 | 17 | 4 | - | - | - | - | - | - | Hereford U |
| - | - | 3 | 4 | - | 24 | 20 | 8 | - | - | - | - | Huddersfield T |
| - | - | 22 | 11 | 20 | - | - | - | - | - | - | - | Hull C |
| 21 | 19 | 14 | 6 | 4 | - | - | 24 | 16 | 9 | - | - | Leyton Orient |
| - | - | - | - | - | - | - | - | - | - | - | - | Lincoln C |
| - | - | - | - | - | - | - | - | - | - | - | - | Luton T |
| - | - | - | - | - | - | - | - | - | - | - | - | Macclesfield T |
| - | - | - | - | - | - | - | - | - | - | - | - | Manchester C |
| 10 | - | - | - | - | - | 23 | 18 | - | 1 | 11 | - | Mansfield T |
| 2 | - | - | - | - | - | - | - | - | - | - | 3 | Middlesbrough |
| - | - | 2 | 9 | 17 | 9 | 16 | 14 | - | - | - | 3 | Millwall |
| 23 | 19 | 18 | 13 | 4 | 16 | 12 | - | - | - | - | - | Newport Co |
| - | - | - | - | - | - | - | - | - | - | 22 | - | Northampton T |
| 7 | 8 | - | - | - | - | - | - | - | - | - | - | Notts Co |
| - | - | - | - | - | - | - | - | - | - | - | - | Oldham Ath |
| - | - | - | 1 | 5 | 5 | 14 | 17 | 11 | 18 | 17 | - | Oxford U |
| - | - | - | - | - | - | - | 21 | 4 | 16 | 10 | - | Peterborough U |
| - | 2 | 15 | 19 | 8 | 10 | 7 | 15 | 15 | 19 | - | - | Plymouth Arg |
| - | - | - | - | 1 | 13 | 6 | - | - | 24 | 20 | - | Portsmouth |
| 12 | - | - | 23 | - | - | - | - | - | 21 | 19 | 12 | Port Vale |
| - | - | 23 | 16 | 16 | 14 | - | - | - | 3 | 6 | 8 | Preston NE |
| - | 1 | 9 | - | 21 | 12 | 10 | 7 | - | - | 21 | - | Reading |
| - | - | - | - | - | - | - | - | - | - | - | - | Rochdale |
| 14 | 14 | 12 | 18 | - | - | 1 | 13 | 17 | 20 | 4 | 16 | Rotherham U |
| - | - | - | 21 | - | - | - | - | - | - | - | - | Scunthorpe U |
| - | - | - | 3 | 11 | - | 21 | 12 | - | - | - | - | Sheffield U |
| - | - | - | - | - | - | 3 | 14 | 14 | 8 | 20 | - | Sheffield W |
| - | - | - | - | - | - | - | - | 1 | 11 | 10 | 9 | Shrewsbury T |
| - | - | - | 22 | 15 | 7 | - | 22 | 13 | - | - | 23 | Southend U |

# LEAGUE POSITIONS: DIVISION 2 from 1992–93 and DIVISION 3 1975–76 to 1991–92 (cont.)

| | 1999–2000 | 1998–99 | 1997–98 | 1996–97 | 1995–96 | 1994–95 | 1993–94 | 1992–93 | 1991–92 | 1990–91 | 1989–90 | 1988–89 | 1987–88 |
|---|---|---|---|---|---|---|---|---|---|---|---|---|---|
| Stockport Co | – | – | – | 2 | 9 | 11 | 4 | 6 | 5 | – | – | – | – |
| Stoke C | 6 | 8 | – | – | – | – | – | 1 | 4 | 14 | – | – | – |
| Sunderland | – | – | – | – | – | – | – | – | – | – | – | – | 1 |
| Swansea C | – | – | – | – | 22 | 10 | 13 | 5 | 19 | 20 | 17 | 12 | – |
| Swindon T | – | – | – | – | 1 | – | – | – | – | – | – | – | – |
| Torquay U | – | – | – | – | – | – | – | – | 23 | – | – | – | – |
| Tranmere R | – | – | – | – | – | – | – | – | – | 5 | 4 | – | – |
| Walsall | – | 2 | 19 | 12 | 11 | – | – | 5 | – | – | 24 | – | 3 |
| Watford | – | – | 1 | 13 | – | – | – | – | – | – | – | – | – |
| WBA | – | – | – | – | – | – | – | 4 | 7 | – | – | – | – |
| Wigan Ath | 4 | 6 | 11 | – | – | – | – | 23 | 15 | 10 | 18 | 17 | 7 |
| Wimbledon | – | – | – | – | – | – | – | – | – | – | – | – | – |
| Wolv'hampton W | – | – | – | – | – | – | – | – | – | – | – | 1 | – |
| Wrexham | 11 | 17 | 7 | 8 | 8 | 13 | 12 | – | – | – | – | – | – |
| Wycombe W | 12 | 19 | 14 | 18 | 12 | 6 | – | – | – | – | – | – | – |
| York C | – | 21 | 16 | 20 | 20 | 9 | 5 | – | – | – | – | – | 23 |

# LEAGUE POSITIONS: DIVISION 3 from 1992–93 and DIVISION 4 1975–76 to 1991–92

| | 1999–2000 | 1998–99 | 1997–98 | 1996–97 | 1995–96 | 1994–95 | 1993–94 | 1992–93 | 1991–92 | 1990–91 | 1989–90 | 1988–89 | 1987–88 |
|---|---|---|---|---|---|---|---|---|---|---|---|---|---|
| Aldershot | – | – | – | – | – | – | – | – | * | 23 | 22 | – | – |
| Barnet | 6 | 16 | 7 | 15 | 9 | 11 | – | 3 | 7 | – | – | – | – |
| Barnsley | – | – | – | – | – | – | – | – | – | – | – | – | – |
| Blackpool | – | – | – | – | – | – | – | – | 4 | 5 | – | – | – |
| Bolton W | – | – | – | – | – | – | – | – | – | – | – | – | 3 |
| Bournemouth | – | – | – | – | – | – | – | – | – | – | – | – | – |
| Bradford C | – | – | – | – | – | – | – | – | – | – | – | – | – |
| Brentford | – | – | – | – | – | – | – | – | – | – | – | – | – |
| Brighton & HA | 11 | 17 | 23 | 23 | – | – | – | – | – | – | – | – | – |
| Bristol C | – | – | – | – | – | – | – | – | – | – | – | – | – |
| Burnley | – | 15 | – | – | – | – | – | – | 1 | 6 | 16 | 16 | 10 |
| Bury | – | – | – | – | 3 | 4 | 13 | 7 | – | – | – | – | – |
| Cambridge U | – | 2 | 16 | 10 | 16 | – | – | – | – | – | 6 | 8 | 15 |
| Cardiff C | – | 3 | 21 | 7 | 22 | – | – | 1 | 9 | 13 | – | – | 2 |
| Carlisle U | 23 | 23 | – | 3 | – | 1 | 7 | 18 | 22 | 20 | 8 | 12 | 23 |
| Cheltenham T | 8 | – | – | – | – | – | – | – | – | – | – | – | – |
| Chester C | 24 | 14 | 14 | 6 | 8 | – | 2 | – | – | – | – | – | – |
| Chesterfield | – | – | – | – | – | 3 | 8 | 12 | 13 | 18 | 7 | – | – |

*Record expunged

| | 1986–87 | 1985–86 | 1984–85 | 1983–84 | 1982–83 | 1981–82 | 1980–81 | 1979–80 | 1978–79 | 1977–78 | 1976–77 | 1975–76 |
|---|---|---|---|---|---|---|---|---|---|---|---|---|
| Stockport Co | – | – | – | – | – | – | – | – | – | – | – | – |
| Stoke C | – | – | – | – | – | – | – | – | – | – | – | – |
| Sunderland | – | – | – | – | – | – | – | – | – | – | – | – |
| Swansea C | – | 24 | 20 | – | – | – | – | – | 3 | – | – | – |
| Swindon T | 3 | – | – | – | – | 22 | 17 | 10 | 5 | 10 | 11 | 19 |
| Torquay U | – | – | – | – | – | – | – | – | – | – | – | – |
| Tranmere R | – | – | – | – | – | – | – | – | 23 | 12 | 14 | – |
| Walsall | 8 | 6 | 11 | 6 | 10 | 20 | 20 | – | 22 | 6 | 15 | 7 |
| Watford | – | – | – | – | – | – | – | – | 2 | – | – | – |
| WBA | – | – | – | – | – | – | – | – | – | – | – | – |
| Wigan Ath | 4 | 4 | 16 | 15 | 18 | – | – | – | – | – | – | – |
| Wimbledon | – | – | – | 2 | – | 21 | – | 24 | – | – | – | – |
| Wolv'hampton W | – | 23 | – | – | – | – | – | – | – | – | – | – |
| Wrexham | – | – | – | – | 22 | – | – | – | – | 1 | 5 | 6 |
| Wycombe W | – | – | – | – | – | – | – | – | – | – | – | – |
| York C | 20 | 7 | 8 | – | – | – | – | – | – | – | 24 | – |

| | 1985–86 | 1984–85 | 1983–84 | 1982–83 | 1981–82 | 1980–81 | 1979–80 | 1978–79 | 1977–78 | 1976–77 | 1975–76 | 1974–75 |
|---|---|---|---|---|---|---|---|---|---|---|---|---|
| Aldershot | 6 | 16 | 13 | 5 | 18 | 16 | 6 | 10 | 5 | 5 | 17 | – |
| Barnet | – | – | – | – | – | – | – | – | – | – | – | – |
| Barnsley | – | – | – | – | – | – | – | 4 | 7 | 6 | 12 | – |
| Blackpool | – | – | 2 | 6 | 21 | 12 | – | – | – | – | – | – |
| Bolton W | – | – | – | – | – | – | – | – | – | – | – | – |
| Bournemouth | – | – | – | – | 4 | 13 | 11 | 18 | 17 | 13 | 6 | – |
| Bradford C | – | – | – | – | 2 | 14 | 5 | 15 | – | 4 | 17 | – |
| Brentford | – | – | – | – | – | – | – | – | 4 | 15 | 18 | – |
| Brighton & HA | – | – | – | – | – | – | – | – | – | – | – | – |
| Bristol C | – | – | – | 4 | 14 | – | – | – | – | – | – | – |
| Burnley | 22 | 14 | – | – | – | – | – | – | – | – | – | – |
| Bury | – | – | 4 | 15 | 5 | 9 | 12 | – | – | – | – | – |
| Cambridge U | 11 | 22 | – | – | – | – | – | – | – | 1 | 13 | – |
| Cardiff C | 13 | – | – | – | – | – | – | – | – | – | – | – |
| Carlisle U | – | – | – | – | – | – | – | – | – | – | – | – |
| Cheltenham T | – | – | – | – | – | – | – | – | – | – | – | – |
| Chester C | – | 2 | 16 | 24 | 13 | 9 | – | – | – | – | – | – |
| Chesterfield | – | – | 1 | 13 | – | – | – | – | – | – | – | – |

# LEAGUE POSITIONS: DIVISION 3 from 1992–93 and DIVISION 4 1975–76 to 1991–92 (cont.)

| | 1999–2000 | 1998–99 | 1997–98 | 1996–97 | 1995–96 | 1994–95 | 1993–94 | 1992–93 | 1991–92 | 1990–91 | 1989–90 | 1988–89 | 1987–88 |
|---|---|---|---|---|---|---|---|---|---|---|---|---|---|
| Colchester U | – | – | 4 | 8 | 7 | 10 | 17 | 10 | – | – | 24 | 22 | 9 |
| Crewe Alex | – | – | – | – | – | 3 | 6 | 6 | – | – | – | 3 | 17 |
| Darlington | 4 | 11 | 19 | 18 | 5 | 20 | 21 | 15 | – | 1 | – | 24 | 13 |
| Doncaster R | – | – | 24 | 19 | 13 | 9 | 15 | 16 | 21 | 11 | 20 | 23 | – |
| Exeter C | 21 | 12 | 15 | 22 | 14 | 22 | – | – | – | – | 1 | 13 | 22 |
| Fulham | – | – | – | 2 | 17 | 8 | – | – | – | – | – | – | – |
| Gillingham | – | – | – | – | 2 | 19 | 16 | 21 | 11 | 15 | 14 | – | – |
| Grimsby T | – | – | – | – | – | – | – | – | – | – | – | 2 | 9 |
| Halifax T | 18 | 10 | – | – | – | – | – | 22 | 20 | 22 | 23 | 21 | 18 |
| Hartlepool U | 7 | 22 | 17 | 20 | 20 | 18 | – | – | – | 3 | 19 | 19 | 16 |
| Hereford U | – | – | – | 24 | 6 | 16 | 20 | 17 | 17 | 17 | 17 | 15 | 19 |
| Huddersfield T | – | – | – | – | – | – | – | – | – | – | – | 1 | – |
| Hull C | 14 | 21 | 22 | 17 | – | – | – | – | – | – | – | – | – |
| Leyton Orient | 19 | 6 | 11 | 16 | 21 | – | – | – | – | – | – | 6 | 8 |
| Lincoln C | 15 | – | 3 | 9 | 18 | 12 | 18 | 8 | 10 | 14 | 10 | 10 | – |
| Macclesfield T | 13 | – | 2 | – | – | – | – | – | – | – | – | – | – |
| Maidstone U | – | – | – | – | – | – | – | 18 | 19 | 5 | – | – | – |
| Mansfield T | 17 | 8 | 12 | 11 | 19 | 6 | 12 | – | 3 | – | – | – | – |
| Newport Co | – | – | – | – | – | – | – | – | – | – | – | – | 24 |
| Northampton T | 3 | – | 1 | 4 | 11 | 17 | 22 | 20 | 16 | 10 | – | – | – |
| Notts Co | – | – | 1 | – | – | – | – | – | – | – | – | – | – |
| Peterborough U | 5 | 9 | 10 | – | – | – | – | – | – | 4 | 9 | 17 | 7 |
| Plymouth Arg | 12 | 13 | – | – | 4 | – | – | – | – | – | – | – | – |
| Portsmouth | – | – | – | – | – | – | – | – | – | – | – | – | – |
| Port Vale | – | – | – | – | – | – | – | – | – | – | – | – | – |
| Preston NE | – | – | – | – | 1 | 5 | 5 | – | – | – | – | – | – |
| Reading | – | – | – | – | – | – | – | – | – | – | – | – | – |
| Rochdale | 10 | 19 | 18 | 14 | 15 | 15 | 9 | 11 | 8 | 12 | 12 | 18 | 21 |
| Rotherham U | 2 | 5 | 9 | – | – | – | – | – | – | 2 | – | 1 | – |
| Scarborough | – | 24 | 6 | 12 | 23 | 21 | 14 | 13 | 12 | 9 | 18 | 5 | 12 |
| Scunthorpe U | – | 4 | 8 | 13 | 12 | 7 | 11 | 14 | 5 | 8 | 11 | 4 | 4 |
| Sheffield U | – | – | – | – | – | – | – | – | – | – | – | – | – |
| Shrewsbury T | 22 | 15 | 13 | – | – | – | 1 | 9 | – | – | – | – | – |
| Southend U | 16 | 18 | – | – | – | – | – | – | – | – | 3 | – | – |
| Southport | – | – | – | – | – | – | – | – | – | – | – | – | – |
| Stockport Co | – | – | – | – | – | – | – | – | – | 2 | 4 | 20 | 20 |
| Swansea C | 1 | 7 | 20 | 5 | – | – | – | – | – | – | – | – | 6 |
| Swindon T | – | – | – | – | – | – | – | – | – | – | – | – | – |
| Torquay U | 9 | 20 | 5 | 21 | 24 | 13 | 6 | 19 | – | 7 | 15 | 14 | 5 |
| Tranmere R | – | – | – | – | – | – | – | – | – | – | – | 2 | 14 |
| Walsall | – | – | – | – | – | 2 | 10 | 5 | 15 | 16 | – | – | – |
| Watford | – | – | – | – | – | – | – | – | – | – | – | – | – |
| Wigan Ath | – | – | – | 1 | 10 | 14 | 19 | – | – | – | – | – | – |
| Wimbledon | – | – | – | – | – | – | – | – | – | – | – | – | – |
| Wolv'hampton W | – | – | – | – | – | – | – | – | – | – | – | – | 1 |
| Workington | – | – | – | – | – | – | – | – | – | – | – | – | – |
| Wrexham | – | – | – | – | – | – | – | 2 | 14 | 24 | 21 | 7 | 11 |
| Wycombe W | – | – | – | – | – | – | 4 | – | – | – | – | – | – |
| York C | 20 | – | – | – | – | – | – | 4 | 19 | 21 | 13 | 11 | – |

| 1986-87 | 1985-86 | 1984-85 | 1983-84 | 1982-83 | 1981-82 | 1980-81 | 1979-80 | 1978-79 | 1977-78 | 1976-77 | 1975-76 | |
|---|---|---|---|---|---|---|---|---|---|---|---|---|
| 5 | 6 | 7 | 8 | 6 | 6 | – | – | – | – | 3 | – | Colchester U |
| 17 | 12 | 10 | 16 | 23 | 24 | 18 | 23 | 24 | 15 | 12 | 16 | Crewe Alex |
| – | – | 3 | 14 | 17 | 3 | 8 | 22 | 21 | 19 | 11 | 20 | Darlington |
| – | – | – | 2 | – | – | 3 | 12 | 22 | 12 | 8 | 10 | Doncaster R |
| 14 | 21 | 18 | – | – | – | – | – | – | – | 2 | 7 | Exeter C |
|  |  |  |  |  |  |  |  |  |  |  |  | Fulham |
|  |  |  |  |  |  |  |  |  |  |  |  | Gillingham |
| – | – | – | – | – | – | – | – | 2 | 6 | – | – | Grimsby T |
| 15 | 20 | 21 | 21 | 11 | 19 | 23 | 18 | 23 | 20 | 21 | – | Halifax T |
| 18 | 7 | 19 | 23 | 22 | 14 | 9 | 19 | 13 | 21 | 22 | 14 | Hartlepool U |
| 16 | 10 | 5 | 11 | 24 | 10 | 22 | 21 | 14 | – | – | – | Hereford U |
| – | – | – | – | – | – | – | 1 | 9 | 11 | 9 | 5 | Huddersfield T |
|  |  |  |  |  |  |  |  |  |  |  |  | Hull C |
| 7 | 5 | – | – | 2 | 8 | – | – | – | – | – | – | Leyton Orient |
| 24 | – | – | – | – | 2 | 7 | – | – | – | – | 1 | Lincoln C |
|  |  |  |  |  |  |  |  |  |  |  |  | Macclesfield T |
|  |  |  |  |  |  |  |  |  |  |  |  | Maidstone U |
| – | 3 | 14 | 19 | 10 | 20 | 7 | – | – | – | – | – | Mansfield T |
| – | – | – | – | – | – | 3 | 8 | 16 | 19 | 22 | | Newport C |
| 1 | 8 | 23 | 18 | 15 | 22 | 10 | 13 | 19 | 10 | – | 2 | Northampton T |
|  |  |  |  |  |  |  |  |  |  |  |  | Notts Co |
| 10 | 17 | 11 | 7 | 9 | 5 | 5 | 8 | – | – | – | – | Peterborough U |
|  |  |  |  |  |  |  |  |  |  |  |  | Plymouth Arg |
| – | – | – | – | – | – | – | 4 | 7 | – | – | – | Portsmouth |
| – | 4 | 12 | – | 3 | 7 | 19 | 20 | 16 | – | – | – | Port Vale |
| 2 | 23 | – | – | – | – | – | – | – | – | – | – | Preston NE |
| – | – | – | 3 | – | – | – | – | 1 | 8 | – | 3 | Reading |
| 21 | 18 | 17 | 22 | 20 | 21 | 15 | 24 | 20 | 24 | 18 | 15 | Rochdale |
|  |  |  |  |  |  |  |  |  |  |  |  | Rotherham U |
|  |  |  |  |  |  |  |  |  |  |  |  | Scarborough |
| 8 | 15 | 9 | – | 4 | 23 | 16 | 14 | 12 | 14 | 20 | 19 | Scunthorpe U |
| – | – | – | – | 1 | – | – | – | – | – | – | – | Sheffield U |
|  |  |  |  |  |  |  |  |  |  |  |  | Shrewsbury T |
| 3 | 9 | 20 | – | – | – | 1 | – | – | 2 | 10 | – | Southend U |
| – | – | – | – | – | – | – | – | – | 23 | 23 | 23 | Southport |
| 19 | 11 | 22 | 12 | 16 | 18 | 20 | 16 | 17 | 18 | 14 | 21 | Stockport Co |
| 12 | – | – | – | – | – | – | – | – | 3 | 5 | 11 | Swansea C |
| – | 1 | 8 | 17 | 8 | – | – | – | – | – | – | – | Swindon T |
| 23 | 24 | 24 | 9 | 12 | 15 | 17 | 9 | 11 | 9 | 16 | 9 | Torquay U |
| 20 | 19 | 6 | 10 | 19 | 11 | 21 | 15 | – | – | – | 4 | Tranmere R |
| – | – | – | – | – | – | 2 | – | – | – | – | – | Walsall |
| – | – | – | – | – | – | – | – | – | 1 | 7 | 8 | Watford |
| – | – | – | – | 3 | 11 | 6 | 6 | – | – | – | – | Wigan Ath |
| – | – | – | 1 | – | 4 | – | 3 | 13 | – | – | – | Wimbledon |
| 4 | – | – | – | – | – | – | – | – | – | – | – | Wolv'hampton W |
| – | – | – | – | – | – | – | – | – | – | 24 | 24 | Workington |
| 9 | 13 | 15 | 20 | – | – | – | – | – | – | – | – | Wrexham |
|  |  |  |  |  |  |  |  |  |  |  |  | Wycombe W |
| – | – | – | 1 | 7 | 17 | 24 | 17 | 10 | 22 | – | – | York C |

# LEAGUE CHAMPIONSHIP HONOURS

## FA PREMIER LEAGUE

*Maximum points:* 126

|  | *First* | *Pts* | *Second* | *Pts* | *Third* | *Pts* |
|---|---|---|---|---|---|---|
| 1992–93 | Manchester U | 84 | Aston Villa | 74 | Norwich C | 72 |
| 1993–94 | Manchester U | 92 | Blackburn R | 84 | Newcastle U | 77 |
| 1994–95 | Blackburn R | 89 | Manchester U | 88 | Nottingham F | 77 |

*Maximum points:* 114

|  | | | | | | |
|---|---|---|---|---|---|---|
| 1995–96 | Manchester U | 82 | Newcastle U | 78 | Liverpool | 71 |
| 1996–97 | Manchester U | 75 | Newcastle U* | 68 | Arsenal* | 68 |
| 1997–98 | Arsenal | 78 | Manchester U | 77 | Liverpool | 65 |
| 1998–99 | Manchester U | 79 | Arsenal | 78 | Chelsea | 75 |
| 1999–00 | Manchester U | 91 | Arsenal | 73 | Leeds U | 69 |
| 2000–01 | Manchester U | 80 | Arsenal | 70 | Liverpool | 69 |

## DIVISION 1

*Maximum points:* 138

|  | | | | | | |
|---|---|---|---|---|---|---|
| 1992–93 | Newcastle U | 96 | West Ham U* | 88 | Portsmouth†† | 88 |
| 1993–94 | Crystal Palace | 90 | Nottingham F | 83 | Millwall†† | 74 |
| 1994–95 | Middlesbrough | 82 | Reading†† | 79 | Bolton W | 77 |
| 1995–96 | Sunderland | 83 | Derby Co | 79 | Crystal Palace†† | 75 |
| 1996–97 | Bolton W | 98 | Barnsley | 80 | Wolverhampton W†† | 76 |
| 1997–98 | Nottingham F | 94 | Middlesbrough | 91 | Sunderland†† | 90 |
| 1998–99 | Sunderland | 105 | Bradford C | 87 | Ipswich T†† | 86 |
| 1999–00 | Charlton Ath | 91 | Manchester C | 89 | Ipswich T | 87 |
| 2000–01 | Fulham | 101 | Blackburn R | 91 | Bolton W | 87 |

## DIVISION 2

*Maximum points:* 138

|  | | | | | | |
|---|---|---|---|---|---|---|
| 1992–93 | Stoke C | 93 | Bolton W | 90 | Port Vale†† | 89 |
| 1993–94 | Reading | 89 | Port Vale | 88 | Plymouth Arg†† | 85 |
| 1994–95 | Birmingham C | 89 | Brentford†† | 85 | Crewe Alex†† | 83 |
| 1995–96 | Swindon T | 92 | Oxford U | 83 | Blackpool†† | 82 |
| 1996–97 | Bury | 84 | Stockport Co | 82 | Luton T†† | 78 |
| 1997–98 | Watford | 88 | Bristol C | 85 | Grimsby T | 72 |
| 1998–99 | Fulham | 101 | Walsall | 87 | Manchester C | 82 |
| 1999–00 | Preston NE | 95 | Burnley | 88 | Gillingham | 85 |
| 2000–01 | Millwall | 93 | Rotherham U | 91 | Reading†† | 86 |

## DIVISION 3

*Maximum points:* 126

|  | | | | | | |
|---|---|---|---|---|---|---|
| 1992–93 | Cardiff C | 83 | Wrexham | 80 | Barnet | 79 |
| 1993–94 | Shrewsbury T | 79 | Chester C | 74 | Crewe Alex | 73 |
| 1994–95 | Carlisle U | 91 | Walsall | 83 | Chesterfield | 81 |

*Maximum points:* 138

|  | | | | | | |
|---|---|---|---|---|---|---|
| 1995–96 | Preston NE | 86 | Gillingham | 83 | Bury | 79 |
| 1996–97 | Wigan Ath* | 87 | Fulham | 87 | Carlisle U | 84 |
| 1997–98 | Notts Co | 99 | Macclesfield T | 82 | Lincoln C | 75 |
| 1998–99 | Brentford | 85 | Cambridge U | 81 | Cardiff C | 80 |
| 1999–00 | Swansea C | 85 | Rotherham U | 84 | Northampton T | 82 |
| 2000–01 | Brighton & HA | 92 | Cardiff C | 82 | Chesterfield¶ | 80 |

†† *Not promoted after play-offs.* ¶ *9 pts deducted for irregularities.*

## FOOTBALL LEAGUE

*Maximum points: a* 44; *b* 60

|  | | | | | | |
|---|---|---|---|---|---|---|
| 1888–89*a* | Preston NE | 40 | Aston Villa | 29 | Wolverhampton W | 28 |
| 1889–90*a* | Preston NE | 33 | Everton | 31 | Blackburn R | 27 |
| 1890–91*a* | Everton | 29 | Preston NE | 27 | Notts Co | 26 |
| 1891–92*b* | Sunderland | 42 | Preston NE | 37 | Bolton W | 36 |

*Maximum points: a 44; b 52; c 60; d 68; e 76; f 84; g 126; h 120; k 114.*

| | First | Pts | Second | Pts | Third | Pts |
|---|---|---|---|---|---|---|
| 1892–93c | Sunderland | 48 | Preston NE | 37 | Everton | 36 |
| 1893–94c | Aston Villa | 44 | Sunderland | 38 | Derby Co | 36 |
| 1894–95c | Sunderland | 47 | Everton | 42 | Aston Villa | 39 |
| 1895–96c | Aston Villa | 45 | Derby Co | 41 | Everton | 39 |
| 1896–97c | Aston Villa | 47 | Sheffield U* | 36 | Derby Co | 36 |
| 1897–98c | Sheffield U | 42 | Sunderland | 37 | Wolverhampton W* | 35 |
| 1898–99d | Aston Villa | 45 | Liverpool | 43 | Burnley | 39 |
| 1899–1900d | Aston Villa | 50 | Sheffield U | 48 | Sunderland | 41 |
| 1900–01d | Liverpool | 45 | Sunderland | 43 | Notts Co | 40 |
| 1901–02d | Sunderland | 44 | Everton | 41 | Newcastle U | 37 |
| 1902–03d | The Wednesday | 42 | Aston Villa* | 41 | Sunderland | 41 |
| 1903–04d | The Wednesday | 47 | Manchester C | 44 | Everton | 43 |
| 1904–05d | Newcastle U | 48 | Everton | 47 | Manchester C | 46 |
| 1905–06e | Liverpool | 51 | Preston NE | 47 | The Wednesday | 44 |
| 1906–07e | Newcastle U | 51 | Bristol C | 48 | Everton* | 45 |
| 1907–08e | Manchester U | 52 | Aston Villa* | 43 | Manchester C | 43 |
| 1908–09e | Newcastle U | 53 | Everton | 46 | Sunderland | 44 |
| 1909–10e | Aston Villa | 53 | Liverpool | 48 | Blackburn R* | 45 |
| 1910–11e | Manchester U | 52 | Aston Villa | 51 | Sunderland* | 45 |
| 1911–12e | Blackburn R | 49 | Everton | 46 | Newcastle U | 44 |
| 1912–13e | Sunderland | 54 | Aston Villa | 50 | Sheffield W | 49 |
| 1913–14e | Blackburn R | 51 | Aston Villa | 44 | Middlesbrough* | 43 |
| 1914–15e | Everton | 46 | Oldham Ath | 45 | Blackburn R* | 43 |
| 1919–20f | WBA | 60 | Burnley | 51 | Chelsea | 49 |
| 1920–21f | Burnley | 59 | Manchester C | 54 | Bolton W | 52 |
| 1921–22f | Liverpool | 57 | Tottenham H | 51 | Burnley | 49 |
| 1922–23f | Liverpool | 60 | Sunderland | 54 | Huddersfield T | 53 |
| 1923–24f | Huddersfield T* | 57 | Cardiff C | 57 | Sunderland | 53 |
| 1924–25f | Huddersfield T | 58 | WBA | 56 | Bolton W | 55 |
| 1925–26f | Huddersfield T | 57 | Arsenal | 52 | Sunderland | 48 |
| 1926–27f | Newcastle U | 56 | Huddersfield T | 51 | Sunderland | 49 |
| 1927–28f | Everton | 53 | Huddersfield T | 51 | Leicester C | 48 |
| 1928–29f | Sheffield W | 52 | Leicester C | 51 | Aston Villa | 50 |
| 1929–30f | Sheffield W | 60 | Derby Co | 50 | Manchester C* | 47 |
| 1930–31f | Arsenal | 66 | Aston Villa | 59 | Sheffield W | 52 |
| 1931–32f | Everton | 56 | Arsenal | 54 | Sheffield W | 50 |
| 1932–33f | Arsenal | 58 | Aston Villa | 54 | Sheffield W | 51 |
| 1933–34f | Arsenal | 59 | Huddersfield T | 56 | Tottenham H | 49 |
| 1934–35f | Arsenal | 58 | Sunderland | 54 | Sheffield W | 49 |
| 1935–36f | Sunderland | 56 | Derby Co* | 48 | Huddersfield T | 48 |
| 1936–37f | Manchester C | 57 | Charlton Ath | 54 | Arsenal | 52 |
| 1937–38f | Arsenal | 52 | Wolverhampton W | 51 | Preston NE | 49 |
| 1938–39f | Everton | 59 | Wolverhampton W | 55 | Charlton Ath | 50 |
| 1946–47f | Liverpool | 57 | Manchester U* | 56 | Wolverhampton W | 56 |
| 1947–48f | Arsenal | 59 | Manchester U* | 52 | Burnley | 52 |
| 1948–49f | Portsmouth | 58 | Manchester U* | 53 | Derby Co | 53 |
| 1949–50f | Portsmouth* | 53 | Wolverhampton W | 53 | Sunderland | 52 |
| 1950–51f | Tottenham H | 60 | Manchester U | 56 | Blackpool | 50 |
| 1951–52f | Manchester U | 57 | Tottenham H* | 53 | Arsenal | 53 |
| 1952–53f | Arsenal* | 54 | Preston NE | 54 | Wolverhampton W | 51 |
| 1953–54f | Wolverhampton W | 57 | WBA | 53 | Huddersfield T | 51 |
| 1954–55f | Chelsea | 52 | Wolverhampton W* | 48 | Portsmouth* | 48 |
| 1955–56f | Manchester U | 60 | Blackpool* | 49 | Wolverhampton W | 49 |
| 1956–57f | Manchester U | 64 | Tottenham H* | 56 | Preston NE | 56 |
| 1957–58f | Wolverhampton W | 64 | Preston NE | 59 | Tottenham H | 51 |
| 1958–59f | Wolverhampton W | 61 | Manchester U | 55 | Arsenal* | 50 |

|  | First | Pts | Second | Pts | Third | Pts |
|---|---|---|---|---|---|---|
| 1959–60f | Burnley | 55 | Wolverhampton W | 54 | Tottenham H | 53 |
| 1960–61f | Tottenham H | 66 | Sheffield W | 58 | Wolverhampton W | 57 |
| 1961–62f | Ipswich T | 56 | Burnley | 53 | Tottenham H | 52 |
| 1962–63f | Everton | 61 | Tottenham H | 55 | Burnley | 54 |
| 1963–64f | Liverpool | 57 | Manchester U | 53 | Everton | 52 |
| 1964–65f | Manchester U* | 61 | Leeds U | 61 | Chelsea | 56 |
| 1965–66f | Liverpool | 61 | Leeds U* | 55 | Burnley | 55 |
| 1966–67f | Manchester U | 60 | Nottingham F* | 56 | Tottenham H | 56 |
| 1967–68f | Manchester C | 58 | Manchester U | 56 | Liverpool | 55 |
| 1968–69f | Leeds U | 67 | Liverpool | 61 | Everton | 57 |
| 1969–70f | Everton | 66 | Leeds U | 57 | Chelsea | 55 |
| 1970–71f | Arsenal | 65 | Leeds U | 64 | Tottenham H* | 52 |
| 1971–72f | Derby Co | 58 | Leeds U* | 57 | Liverpool* | 57 |
| 1972–73f | Liverpool | 60 | Arsenal | 57 | Leeds U | 53 |
| 1973–74f | Leeds U | 62 | Liverpool | 57 | Derby Co | 48 |
| 1974–75f | Derby Co | 53 | Liverpool* | 51 | Ipswich T | 51 |
| 1975–76f | Liverpool | 60 | QPR | 59 | Manchester U | 56 |
| 1976–77f | Liverpool | 57 | Manchester C | 56 | Ipswich T | 52 |
| 1977–78f | Nottingham F | 64 | Liverpool | 57 | Everton | 55 |
| 1978–79f | Liverpool | 68 | Nottingham F | 60 | WBA | 59 |
| 1979–80f | Liverpool | 60 | Manchester U | 58 | Ipswich T | 53 |
| 1980–81f | Aston Villa | 60 | Ipswich T | 56 | Arsenal | 53 |
| 1981–82g | Liverpool | 87 | Ipswich T | 83 | Manchester U | 78 |
| 1982–83g | Liverpool | 82 | Watford | 71 | Manchester U | 70 |
| 1983–84g | Liverpool | 80 | Southampton | 77 | Nottingham F* | 74 |
| 1984–85g | Everton | 90 | Liverpool* | 77 | Tottenham H | 77 |
| 1985–86g | Liverpool | 88 | Everton | 86 | West Ham U | 84 |
| 1986–87g | Everton | 86 | Liverpool | 77 | Tottenham H | 71 |
| 1987–88h | Liverpool | 90 | Manchester U | 81 | Nottingham F | 73 |
| 1988–89k | Arsenal* | 76 | Liverpool | 76 | Nottingham F | 64 |
| 1989–90k | Liverpool | 79 | Aston Villa | 70 | Tottenham H | 63 |
| 1990–91k | Arsenal† | 83 | Liverpool | 76 | Crystal Palace | 69 |
| 1991–92g | Leeds U | 82 | Manchester U | 78 | Sheffield W | 75 |

*No official competition during 1915–19 and 1939–46; Regional Leagues operating.*
*\* Won or placed on goal average (ratio)/goal difference.*
*† 2 pts deducted*

## DIVISION 2 to 1991–92

*Maximum points: a 44; b 56; c 60; d 68; e 76; f 84; g 126; h 132; k 138.*

|  | First | Pts | Second | Pts | Third | Pts |
|---|---|---|---|---|---|---|
| 1892–93a | Small Heath | 36 | Sheffield U | 35 | Darwen | 30 |
| 1893–94b | Liverpool | 50 | Small Heath | 42 | Notts Co | 39 |
| 1894–95c | Bury | 48 | Notts Co | 39 | Newton Heath* | 38 |
| 1895–96c | Liverpool* | 46 | Manchester C | 46 | Grimsby T* | 42 |
| 1896–97c | Notts Co | 42 | Newton Heath | 39 | Grimsby T | 38 |
| 1897–98c | Burnley | 48 | Newcastle U | 45 | Manchester C | 39 |
| 1898–99d | Manchester C | 52 | Glossop NE | 46 | Leicester Fosse | 45 |
| 1899–1900d | The Wednesday | 54 | Bolton W | 52 | Small Heath | 46 |
| 1900–01d | Grimsby T | 49 | Small Heath | 48 | Burnley | 44 |
| 1901–02d | WBA | 55 | Middlesbrough | 51 | Preston NE* | 42 |
| 1902–03d | Manchester C | 54 | Small Heath | 51 | Woolwich A | 48 |
| 1903–04d | Preston NE | 50 | Woolwich A | 49 | Manchester U | 48 |
| 1904–05d | Liverpool | 58 | Bolton W | 56 | Manchester U | 53 |
| 1905–06e | Bristol C | 66 | Manchester U | 62 | Chelsea | 53 |
| 1906–07e | Nottingham F | 60 | Chelsea | 57 | Leicester Fosse | 48 |
| 1907–08e | Bradford C | 54 | Leicester Fosse | 52 | Oldham Ath | 50 |
| 1908–09e | Bolton W | 52 | Tottenham H* | 51 | WBA | 51 |
| 1909–10e | Manchester C | 54 | Oldham Ath* | 53 | Hull C* | 53 |
| 1910–11e | WBA | 53 | Bolton W | 51 | Chelsea | 49 |

130

| | First | Pts | Second | Pts | Third | Pts |
|---|---|---|---|---|---|---|
| 1911–12e | Derby Co* | 54 | Chelsea | 54 | Burnley | 52 |
| 1912–13e | Preston NE | 53 | Burnley | 50 | Birmingham | 46 |
| 1913–14e | Notts Co | 53 | Bradford PA* | 49 | Woolwich A | 49 |
| 1914–15e | Derby Co | 53 | Preston NE | 50 | Barnsley | 47 |
| 1919–20f | Tottenham H | 70 | Huddersfield T | 64 | Birmingham | 56 |
| 1920–21f | Birmingham* | 58 | Cardiff C | 58 | Bristol C | 51 |
| 1921–22f | Nottingham F | 56 | Stoke C* | 52 | Barnsley | 52 |
| 1922–23f | Notts Co | 53 | West Ham U* | 51 | Leicester C | 51 |
| 1923–24f | Leeds U | 54 | Bury* | 51 | Derby Co | 51 |
| 1924–25f | Leicester C | 59 | Manchester U | 57 | Derby Co | 55 |
| 1925–26f | Sheffield W | 60 | Derby Co | 57 | Chelsea | 52 |
| 1926–27f | Middlesbrough | 62 | Portsmouth* | 54 | Manchester C | 54 |
| 1927–28f | Manchester C | 59 | Leeds U | 57 | Chelsea | 54 |
| 1928–29f | Middlesbrough | 55 | Grimsby T | 53 | Bradford PA* | 48 |
| 1929–30f | Blackpool | 58 | Chelsea | 55 | Oldham Ath | 53 |
| 1930–31f | Everton | 61 | WBA | 54 | Tottenham H | 51 |
| 1931–32f | Wolverhampton W | 56 | Leeds U | 54 | Stoke C | 52 |
| 1932–33f | Stoke C | 56 | Tottenham H | 55 | Fulham | 50 |
| 1933–34f | Grimsby T | 59 | Preston NE | 52 | Bolton W* | 51 |
| 1934–35f | Brentford | 61 | Bolton W* | 56 | West Ham U | 56 |
| 1935–36f | Manchester U | 56 | Charlton Ath | 55 | Sheffield U* | 52 |
| 1936–37f | Leicester C | 56 | Blackpool | 55 | Bury | 52 |
| 1937–38f | Aston Villa | 57 | Manchester U* | 53 | Sheffield U | 53 |
| 1938–39f | Blackburn R | 55 | Sheffield U | 54 | Sheffield W | 53 |
| 1946–47f | Manchester C | 62 | Burnley | 58 | Birmingham C | 55 |
| 1947–48f | Birmingham C | 59 | Newcastle U | 56 | Southampton | 52 |
| 1948–49f | Fulham | 57 | WBA | 56 | Southampton | 55 |
| 1949–50f | Tottenham H | 61 | Sheffield W* | 52 | Sheffield U* | 52 |
| 1950–51f | Preston NE | 57 | Manchester C | 52 | Cardiff C | 50 |
| 1951–52f | Sheffield W | 53 | Cardiff C* | 51 | Birmingham C | 51 |
| 1952–53f | Sheffield U | 60 | Huddersfield T | 58 | Luton T | 52 |
| 1953–54f | Leicester C* | 56 | Everton | 56 | Blackburn R | 55 |
| 1954–55f | Birmingham C* | 54 | Luton T* | 54 | Rotherham U | 54 |
| 1955–56f | Sheffield W | 55 | Leeds U | 52 | Liverpool* | 48 |
| 1956–57f | Leicester C | 61 | Nottingham F | 54 | Liverpool | 53 |
| 1957–58f | West Ham U | 57 | Blackburn R | 56 | Charlton Ath | 55 |
| 1958–59f | Sheffield W | 62 | Fulham | 60 | Sheffield U* | 53 |
| 1959–60f | Aston Villa | 59 | Cardiff C | 58 | Liverpool* | 50 |
| 1960–61f | Ipswich T | 59 | Sheffield U | 58 | Liverpool | 52 |
| 1961–62f | Liverpool | 62 | Leyton Orient | 54 | Sunderland | 53 |
| 1962–63f | Stoke C | 53 | Chelsea* | 52 | Sunderland | 52 |
| 1963–64f | Leeds U | 63 | Sunderland | 61 | Preston NE | 56 |
| 1964–65f | Newcastle U | 57 | Northampton T | 56 | Bolton W | 50 |
| 1965–66f | Manchester C | 59 | Southampton | 54 | Coventry C | 53 |
| 1966–67f | Coventry C | 59 | Wolverhampton W | 58 | Carlisle U | 52 |
| 1967–68f | Ipswich T | 59 | QPR* | 58 | Blackpool | 58 |
| 1968–69f | Derby Co | 63 | Crystal Palace | 56 | Charlton Ath | 50 |
| 1969–70f | Huddersfield T | 60 | Blackpool | 53 | Leicester C | 51 |
| 1970–71f | Leicester C | 59 | Sheffield U | 56 | Cardiff C* | 53 |
| 1971–72f | Norwich C | 57 | Birmingham C | 56 | Millwall | 55 |
| 1972–73f | Burnley | 62 | QPR | 61 | Aston Villa | 50 |
| 1973–74f | Middlesbrough | 65 | Luton T | 50 | Carlisle U | 49 |
| 1974–75f | Manchester U | 61 | Aston Villa | 58 | Norwich C | 53 |
| 1975–76f | Sunderland | 56 | Bristol C* | 53 | WBA | 53 |
| 1976–77f | Wolverhampton W | 57 | Chelsea | 55 | Nottingham F | 53 |
| 1977–78f | Bolton W | 58 | Southampton | 57 | Tottenham H* | 56 |
| 1978–79f | Crystal Palace | 57 | Brighton & HA* | 56 | Stoke C | 56 |
| 1979–80f | Leicester C | 55 | Sunderland | 54 | Birmingham C* | 53 |
| 1980–81f | West Ham U | 66 | Notts Co | 53 | Swansea C* | 50 |

| | First | Pts | Second | Pts | Third | Pts |
|---|---|---|---|---|---|---|
| 1981–82g | Luton T | 88 | Watford | 80 | Norwich C | 71 |
| 1982–83g | QPR | 85 | Wolverhampton W | 75 | Leicester C | 70 |
| 1983–84g | Chelsea* | 88 | Sheffield W | 88 | Newcastle U | 80 |
| 1984–85g | Oxford U | 84 | Birmingham C | 82 | Manchester C | 74 |
| 1985–86g | Norwich C | 84 | Charlton Ath | 77 | Wimbledon | 76 |
| 1986–87g | Derby Co | 84 | Portsmouth | 78 | Oldham Ath†† | 75 |
| 1987–88h | Millwall | 82 | Aston Villa* | 78 | Middlesbrough | 78 |
| 1988–89k | Chelsea | 99 | Manchester C | 82 | Crystal Palace | 81 |
| 1989–90k | Leeds U* | 85 | Sheffield U | 85 | Newcastle U†† | 80 |
| 1990–91k | Oldham Ath | 88 | West Ham U | 87 | Sheffield W | 82 |
| 1991–92k | Ipswich T | 84 | Middlesbrough | 80 | Derby Co | 78 |

*No official competition during 1915–19 and 1939–46; Regional Leagues operating.*
*\* Won or placed on goal average (ratio)/goal difference.*
*†† Not promoted after play-offs.*

## DIVISION 3 to 1991–92

*Maximum points: 92; 138 from 1981–82.*

| | | | | | | |
|---|---|---|---|---|---|---|
| 1958–59 | Plymouth Arg | 62 | Hull C | 61 | Brentford* | 57 |
| 1959–60 | Southampton | 61 | Norwich C | 59 | Shrewsbury T* | 52 |
| 1960–61 | Bury | 68 | Walsall | 62 | QPR | 60 |
| 1961–62 | Portsmouth | 65 | Grimsby T | 62 | Bournemouth* | 59 |
| 1962–63 | Northampton T | 62 | Swindon T | 58 | Port Vale | 54 |
| 1963–64 | Coventry C* | 60 | Crystal Palace | 60 | Watford | 58 |
| 1964–65 | Carlisle U | 60 | Bristol C* | 59 | Mansfield T | 59 |
| 1965–66 | Hull C | 69 | Millwall | 65 | QPR | 57 |
| 1966–67 | QPR | 67 | Middlesbrough | 55 | Watford | 54 |
| 1967–68 | Oxford U | 57 | Bury | 56 | Shrewsbury T | 55 |
| 1968–69 | Watford* | 64 | Swindon T | 64 | Luton T | 61 |
| 1969–70 | Orient | 62 | Luton T | 60 | Bristol R | 56 |
| 1970–71 | Preston NE | 61 | Fulham | 60 | Halifax T | 56 |
| 1971–72 | Aston Villa | 70 | Brighton & HA | 65 | Bournemouth* | 62 |
| 1972–73 | Bolton W | 61 | Notts Co | 57 | Blackburn R | 55 |
| 1973–74 | Oldham Ath | 62 | Bristol R* | 61 | York C | 61 |
| 1974–75 | Blackburn R | 60 | Plymouth Arg | 59 | Charlton Ath | 55 |
| 1975–76 | Hereford U | 63 | Cardiff C | 57 | Millwall | 56 |
| 1976–77 | Mansfield T | 64 | Brighton & HA | 61 | Crystal Palace* | 59 |
| 1977–78 | Wrexham | 61 | Cambridge U | 58 | Preston NE* | 56 |
| 1978–79 | Shrewsbury T | 61 | Watford* | 60 | Swansea C | 60 |
| 1979–80 | Grimsby T | 62 | Blackburn R | 59 | Sheffield W | 58 |
| 1980–81 | Rotherham U | 61 | Barnsley* | 59 | Charlton Ath | 59 |
| 1981–82 | Burnley* | 80 | Carlisle U | 80 | Fulham | 78 |
| 1982–83 | Portsmouth | 91 | Cardiff C | 86 | Huddersfield T | 82 |
| 1983–84 | Oxford U | 95 | Wimbledon | 87 | Sheffield U* | 83 |
| 1984–85 | Bradford C | 94 | Millwall | 90 | Hull C | 87 |
| 1985–86 | Reading | 94 | Plymouth Arg | 87 | Derby Co | 84 |
| 1986–87 | Bournemouth | 97 | Middlesbrough | 94 | Swindon T | 87 |
| 1987–88 | Sunderland | 93 | Brighton & HA | 84 | Walsall | 82 |
| 1988–89 | Wolverhampton W | 92 | Sheffield U* | 84 | Port Vale | 84 |
| 1989–90 | Bristol R | 93 | Bristol C | 91 | Notts Co | 87 |
| 1990–91 | Cambridge U | 86 | Southend U | 85 | Grimsby T* | 83 |
| 1991–92 | Brentford | 82 | Birmingham C | 81 | Huddersfield T | 78 |

*\* Won or placed on goal average (ratio)/goal difference.*

## DIVISION 4 (1958–1992)
*Maximum points: 92; 138 from 1981–82.*

| | First | Pts | Second | Pts | Third | Pts |
|---|---|---|---|---|---|---|
| 1958–59 | Port Vale | 64 | Coventry C* | 60 | York C | 60 |
| 1959–60 | Walsall | 65 | Notts Co* | 60 | Torquay U | 60 |
| 1960–61 | Peterborough U | 66 | Crystal Palace | 64 | Northampton T* | 60 |
| 1961–62† | Millwall | 56 | Colchester U | 55 | Wrexham | 53 |
| 1962–63 | Brentford | 62 | Oldham Ath* | 59 | Crewe Alex | 59 |
| 1963–64 | Gillingham* | 60 | Carlisle U | 60 | Workington | 59 |
| 1964–65 | Brighton & HA | 63 | Millwall* | 62 | York C | 62 |
| 1965–66 | Doncaster R* | 59 | Darlington | 59 | Torquay U | 58 |
| 1966–67 | Stockport Co | 64 | Southport* | 59 | Barrow | 59 |
| 1967–68 | Luton T | 66 | Barnsley | 61 | Hartlepools U | 60 |
| 1968–69 | Doncaster R | 59 | Halifax T | 57 | Rochdale* | 56 |
| 1969–70 | Chesterfield | 64 | Wrexham | 61 | Swansea C | 60 |
| 1970–71 | Notts Co | 69 | Bournemouth | 60 | Oldham Ath | 59 |
| 1971–72 | Grimsby T | 63 | Southend U | 60 | Brentford | 59 |
| 1972–73 | Southport | 62 | Hereford U | 58 | Cambridge U | 57 |
| 1973–74 | Peterborough U | 65 | Gillingham | 62 | Colchester U | 60 |
| 1974–75 | Mansfield T | 68 | Shrewsbury T | 62 | Rotherham U | 59 |
| 1975–76 | Lincoln C | 74 | Northampton T | 68 | Reading | 60 |
| 1976–77 | Cambridge U | 65 | Exeter C | 62 | Colchester U* | 59 |
| 1977–78 | Watford | 71 | Southend U | 60 | Swansea C* | 56 |
| 1978–79 | Reading | 65 | Grimsby T* | 61 | Wimbledon* | 61 |
| 1979–80 | Huddersfield T | 66 | Walsall | 64 | Newport Co | 61 |
| 1980–81 | Southend U | 67 | Lincoln C | 65 | Doncaster R | 56 |
| 1981–82 | Sheffield U | 96 | Bradford C* | 91 | Wigan Ath | 91 |
| 1982–83 | Wimbledon | 98 | Hull C | 90 | Port Vale | 88 |
| 1983–84 | York C | 101 | Doncaster R | 85 | Reading* | 82 |
| 1984–85 | Chesterfield | 91 | Blackpool | 86 | Darlington | 85 |
| 1985–86 | Swindon T | 102 | Chester C | 84 | Mansfield T | 81 |
| 1986–87 | Northampton T | 99 | Preston NE | 90 | Southend U | 80 |
| 1987–88 | Wolverhampton W | 90 | Cardiff C | 85 | Bolton W | 78 |
| 1988–89 | Rotherham U | 82 | Tranmere R | 80 | Crewe Alex | 78 |
| 1989–90 | Exeter C | 89 | Grimsby T | 79 | Southend U | 75 |
| 1990–91 | Darlington | 83 | Stockport Co* | 82 | Hartlepool U | 82 |
| 1991–92†* | Burnley | 83 | Rotherham U* | 77 | Mansfield T | 77 |

†*Maximum points:* 88 owing to Accrington Stanley's resignation. ††*Not promoted after play-offs.*
†*\*Maximum points:* 126 owing to Aldershot being expelled.

## DIVISION 3—SOUTH (1920–1958)
*1920–21 Season as Division 3.*
*Maximum points: a 84; b 92.*

| | First | | Second | | Third | |
|---|---|---|---|---|---|---|
| 1920–21a | Crystal Palace | 59 | Southampton | 54 | QPR | 53 |
| 1921–22a | Southampton* | 61 | Plymouth Arg | 61 | Portsmouth | 53 |
| 1922–23a | Bristol C | 59 | Plymouth Arg* | 53 | Swansea T | 53 |
| 1923–24a | Portsmouth | 59 | Plymouth Arg | 55 | Millwall | 54 |
| 1924–25a | Swansea T | 57 | Plymouth Arg | 56 | Bristol C | 53 |
| 1925–26a | Reading | 57 | Plymouth Arg | 56 | Millwall | 53 |
| 1926–27a | Bristol C | 62 | Plymouth Arg | 60 | Millwall | 56 |
| 1927–28a | Millwall | 65 | Northampton T | 55 | Plymouth Arg | 53 |
| 1928–29a | Charlton Ath* | 54 | Crystal Palace | 54 | Northampton T* | 52 |
| 1929–30a | Plymouth Arg | 68 | Brentford | 61 | QPR | 51 |
| 1930–31a | Notts Co | 59 | Crystal Palace | 51 | Brentford | 50 |
| 1931–32a | Fulham | 57 | Reading | 55 | Southend U | 53 |
| 1932–33a | Brentford | 62 | Exeter C | 58 | Norwich C | 57 |
| 1933–34a | Norwich C | 61 | Coventry C* | 54 | Reading* | 54 |

133

| | First | Pts | Second | Pts | Third | Pts |
|---|---|---|---|---|---|---|
| 1934–35a | Charlton Ath | 61 | Reading | 53 | Coventry C | 51 |
| 1935–36a | Coventry C | 57 | Luton T | 56 | Reading | 54 |
| 1936–37a | Luton T | 58 | Notts Co | 56 | Brighton & HA | 53 |
| 1937–38a | Millwall | 56 | Bristol C | 55 | QPR* | 53 |
| 1938–39a | Newport Co | 55 | Crystal Palace | 52 | Brighton & HA | 49 |
| 1939–46 | Competition cancelled owing to war. | | | | | |
| 1946–47a | Cardiff C | 66 | QPR | 57 | Bristol C | 51 |
| 1947–48a | QPR | 61 | Bournemouth | 57 | Walsall | 51 |
| 1948–49a | Swansea T | 62 | Reading | 55 | Bournemouth | 52 |
| 1949–50a | Notts Co | 58 | Northampton T* | 51 | Southend U | 51 |
| 1950–51b | Nottingham F | 70 | Norwich C | 64 | Reading* | 57 |
| 1951–52b | Plymouth Arg | 66 | Reading* | 61 | Norwich C | 61 |
| 1952–53b | Bristol R | 64 | Millwall* | 62 | Northampton T | 62 |
| 1953–54b | Ipswich T | 64 | Brighton & HA | 61 | Bristol C | 56 |
| 1954–55b | Bristol C | 70 | Leyton Orient | 61 | Southampton | 59 |
| 1955–56b | Leyton Orient | 66 | Brighton & HA | 65 | Ipswich T | 64 |
| 1956–57b | Ipswich T* | 59 | Torquay U | 59 | Colchester U | 58 |
| 1957–58b | Brighton & HA | 60 | Brentford* | 58 | Plymouth Arg | 58 |

* Won or placed on goal average (ratio).

## DIVISION 3—NORTH (1921–1958)
*Maximum points: a 76; b 84; c 80; d 92.*

| | First | Pts | Second | Pts | Third | Pts |
|---|---|---|---|---|---|---|
| 1921–22a | Stockport Co | 56 | Darlington* | 50 | Grimsby T | 50 |
| 1922–23a | Nelson | 51 | Bradford PA | 47 | Walsall | 46 |
| 1923–24b | Wolverhampton W | 63 | Rochdale | 62 | Chesterfield | 54 |
| 1924–25b | Darlington | 58 | Nelson* | 53 | New Brighton | 53 |
| 1925–26b | Grimsby T | 61 | Bradford PA | 60 | Rochdale | 59 |
| 1926–27b | Stoke C | 63 | Rochdale | 58 | Bradford PA | 55 |
| 1927–28b | Bradford PA | 63 | Lincoln C | 55 | Stockport Co | 54 |
| 1928–29g | Bradford C | 63 | Stockport Co | 62 | Wrexham | 52 |
| 1929–30b | Port Vale | 67 | Stockport Co | 63 | Darlington* | 50 |
| 1930–31b | Chesterfield | 58 | Lincoln C | 57 | Wrexham* | 54 |
| 1931–32c | Lincoln C* | 57 | Gateshead | 57 | Chester | 50 |
| 1932–33b | Hull C | 59 | Wrexham | 57 | Stockport Co | 54 |
| 1933–34b | Barnsley | 62 | Chesterfield | 61 | Stockport Co | 59 |
| 1934–35b | Doncaster R | 57 | Halifax T | 55 | Chester | 54 |
| 1935–36b | Chesterfield | 60 | Chester* | 55 | Tranmere R | 55 |
| 1936–37b | Stockport Co | 60 | Lincoln C | 57 | Chester | 53 |
| 1937–38b | Tranmere R | 56 | Doncaster R | 54 | Hull C | 53 |
| 1938–39b | Barnsley | 67 | Doncaster R | 56 | Bradford C | 52 |
| 1939–46 | Competition cancelled owing to war. | | | | | |
| 1946–47b | Doncaster R | 72 | Rotherham U | 60 | Chester | 56 |
| 1947–48b | Lincoln C | 60 | Rotherham U | 59 | Wrexham | 50 |
| 1948–49b | Hull C | 65 | Rotherham U | 62 | Doncaster R | 50 |
| 1949–50b | Doncaster R | 55 | Gateshead | 53 | Rochdale* | 51 |
| 1950–51d | Rotherham U | 71 | Mansfield T | 64 | Carlisle U | 62 |
| 1951–52d | Lincoln C | 69 | Grimsby T | 66 | Stockport Co | 59 |
| 1952–53d | Oldham Ath | 59 | Port Vale | 58 | Wrexham | 56 |
| 1953–54d | Port Vale | 69 | Barnsley | 58 | Scunthorpe U | 57 |
| 1954–55d | Barnsley | 65 | Accrington S | 61 | Scunthorpe U* | 58 |
| 1955–56d | Grimsby T | 68 | Derby Co | 63 | Accrington S | 59 |
| 1956–57d | Derby Co | 63 | Hartlepools U | 59 | Accrington S* | 58 |
| 1957–58d | Scunthorpe U | 66 | Accrington S | 59 | Bradford C | 57 |

* Won or placed on goal average (ratio).

134

PROMOTED AFTER PLAY-OFFS
(Not accounted for in previous section)
1986–87   Aldershot to Division 3.
1987–88   Swansea C to Divison 3.
1988–89   Leyton Orient to Division 3.
1989–90   Cambridge U to Division 3; Notts Co to Division 2; Sunderland to Division 1.
1990–91   Notts Co to Division 1; Tranmere R to Division 2; Torquay U to Division 3.
1991–92   Blackburn R to Premier League; Peterborough U to Division 1.
1992–93   Swindon T to Premier League; WBA to Division 1; York C to Division 2.
1993–94   Leicester C to Premier League; Burnley to Division 1; Wycombe W to
          Division 2.
1994–95   Huddersfield T to Division 1.
1995–96   Leicester C to Premier League; Bradford C to Division 1; Plymouth Arg to
          Division 2.
1996–97   Crystal Palace to Premier League; Crewe Alex to Division 1; Northampton T
          to Division 2.
1997–98   Charlton Ath to Premier League; Colchester U to Division 2.
1998–99   Watford to Premier League; Scunthorpe to Division 2.
1999–00   Peterborough U to Division 2.
2000–01   Walsall to Division 1; Blackpool to Division 2.

# RELEGATED CLUBS

## FA PREMIER LEAGUE TO DIVISION 1

1992–93   Crystal Palace, Middlesbrough, Nottingham F
1993–94   Sheffield U, Oldham Ath, Swindon T
1994–95   Crystal Palace, Norwich C, Leicester C, Ipswich T
1995–96   Manchester C, QPR, Bolton W
1996–97   Sunderland, Middlesbrough, Nottingham F
1997–98   Bolton W, Barnsley, Crystal Palace
1998–99   Charlton Ath, Blackburn R, Nottingham F
1999–00   Wimbledon, Sheffield W, Watford
2000–01   Manchester C, Coventry C, Bradford C.

## DIVISION 1 TO DIVISION 2

| | |
|---|---|
| 1898–99 Bolton W and Sheffield W | 1926–27 Leeds U and WBA |
| 1899–1900 Burnley and Glossop | 1927–28 Tottenham H and |
| 1900–01 Preston NE and WBA | Middlesbrough |
| 1901–02 Small Heath and Manchester C | 1928–29 Bury and Cardiff C |
| 1902–03 Grimsby T and Bolton W | 1929–30 Burnley and Everton |
| 1903–04 Liverpool and WBA | 1930–31 Leeds U and Manchester U |
| 1904–05 League extended. Bury and | 1931–32 Grimsby T and West Ham U |
| Notts Co, two bottom clubs in | 1932–33 Bolton W and Blackpool |
| First Division, re-elected. | 1933–34 Newcastle U and Sheffield U |
| 1905–06 Nottingham F and | 1934–35 Leicester C and Tottenham H |
| Wolverhampton W | 1935–36 Aston Villa and Blackburn R |
| 1906–07 Derby Co and Stoke C | 1936–37 Manchester U and Sheffield W |
| 1907–08 Bolton W and Birmingham C | 1937–38 Manchester C and WBA |
| 1908–09 Manchester C and Leicester | 1938–39 Birmingham C and Leicester C |
| Fosse | 1946–47 Brentford and Leeds U |
| 1909–10 Bolton W and Chelsea | 1947–48 Blackburn R and Grimsby T |
| 1910–11 Bristol C and Nottingham F | 1948–49 Preston NE and Sheffield U |
| 1911–12 Preston NE and Bury | 1949–50 Manchester C and |
| 1912–13 Notts Co and Woolwich Arsenal | Birmingham C |
| 1913–14 Preston NE and Derby Co | 1950–51 Sheffield W and Everton |
| 1914–15 Tottenham H and Chelsea* | 1951–52 Huddersfield T and Fulham |
| 1919–20 Notts Co and Sheffield W | 1952–53 Stoke C and Derby Co |
| 1920–21 Derby Co and Bradford PA | 1953–54 Middlesbrough and Liverpool |
| 1921–22 Bradford C and Manchester U | 1954–55 Leicester C and Sheffield W |
| 1922–23 Stoke C and Oldham Ath | 1955–56 Huddersfield T and Sheffield U |
| 1923–24 Chelsea and Middlesbrough | 1956–57 Charlton Ath and Cardiff C |
| 1924–25 Preston NE and Nottingham F | 1957–58 Sheffield W and Sunderland |
| 1925–26 Manchester C and Notts Co | 1958–59 Portsmouth and Aston Villa |

135

| | |
|---|---|
| 1959–60 Luton T and Leeds U | 1982–83 Manchester C, Swansea C, Brighton & HA |
| 1960–61 Preston NE and Newcastle U | 1983–84 Birmingham C, Notts Co, Wolverhampton W |
| 1961–62 Chelsea and Cardiff C | 1984–85 Norwich C, Sunderland, Stoke C |
| 1962–63 Manchester C and Leyton Orient | 1985–86 Ipswich T, Birmingham C, WBA |
| 1963–64 Bolton W and Ipswich T | 1986–87 Leicester C, Manchester C, Aston Villa |
| 1964–65 Wolverhampton W and Birmingham C | 1987–88 Chelsea**, Portsmouth, Watford, Oxford U |
| 1965–66 Northampton T and Blackburn R | 1988–89 Middlesbrough, West Ham U, Newcastle U |
| 1966–67 Aston Villa and Blackpool | 1989–90 Sheffield W, Charlton Ath, Millwall |
| 1967–68 Fulham and Sheffield U | 1990–91 Sunderland and Derby Co |
| 1968–69 Leicester C and QPR | 1991–92 Luton T, Notts Co, West Ham U |
| 1969–70 Sunderland and Sheffield W | 1992–93 Brentford, Cambridge U, Bristol R |
| 1970–71 Burnley and Blackpool | 1993–94 Birmingham C, Oxford U, Peterborough U |
| 1971–72 Huddersfield T and Nottingham F | 1994–95 Swindon T, Burnley, Bristol C, Notts Co |
| 1972–73 Crystal Palace and WBA | 1995–96 Millwall, Watford, Luton T |
| 1973–74 Southampton, Manchester U, Norwich C | 1996–97 Grimsby T, Oldham Ath, Southend U |
| 1974–75 Luton T, Chelsea, Carlisle U | 1997–98 Manchester C, Stoke C, Reading |
| 1975–76 Wolverhampton W, Burnley, Sheffield U | 1998–99 Bury, Oxford U, Bristol C |
| 1976–77 Sunderland, Stoke C, Tottenham H | 1999–00 Walsall, Port Vale, Swindon T |
| 1977–78 West Ham U, Newcastle U, Leicester C | 2000–01 Huddersfield T, QPR, Tranmere R |
| 1978–79 QPR, Birmingham C, Chelsea | |
| 1979–80 Bristol C, Derby Co, Bolton W | |
| 1980–81 Norwich C, Leicester C, Crystal Palace | |
| 1981–82 Leeds U, Wolverhampton W, Middlesbrough | |

**Relegated after play-offs.*

*Subsequently re-elected to Division 1 when League was extended after the War.*

# DIVISION 2 TO DIVISION 3

| | |
|---|---|
| 1920–21 Stockport Co | 1952–53 Southampton and Barnsley |
| 1921–22 Bradford PA and Bristol C | 1953–54 Brentford and Oldham Ath |
| 1922–23 Rotherham Co and Wolverhampton W | 1954–55 Ipswich T and Derby Co |
| 1923–24 Nelson and Bristol C | 1955–56 Plymouth Arg and Hull C |
| 1924–25 Crystal Palace and Coventry C | 1956–57 Port Vale and Bury |
| 1925–26 Stoke C and Stockport Co | 1957–58 Doncaster R and Notts Co |
| 1926–27 Darlington and Bradford C | 1958–59 Barnsley and Grimsby T |
| 1927–28 Fulham and South Shields | 1959–60 Bristol C and Hull C |
| 1928–29 Port Vale and Clapton Orient | 1960–61 Lincoln C and Portsmouth |
| 1929–30 Hull C and Notts Co | 1961–62 Brighton & HA and Bristol R |
| 1930–31 Reading and Cardiff C | 1962–63 Walsall and Luton T |
| 1931–32 Barnsley and Bristol C | 1963–64 Grimsby T and Scunthorpe U |
| 1932–33 Chesterfield and Charlton Ath | 1964–65 Swindon T and Swansea T |
| 1933–34 Millwall and Lincoln C | 1965–66 Middlesbrough and Leyton Orient |
| 1934–35 Oldham Ath and Notts Co | 1966–67 Northampton T and Bury |
| 1935–36 Port Vale and Hull C | 1967–68 Plymouth Arg and Rotherham U |
| 1936–37 Doncaster R and Bradford C | 1968–69 Fulham and Bury |
| 1937–38 Barnsley and Stockport Co | 1969–70 Preston NE and Aston Villa |
| 1938–39 Norwich C and Tranmere R | 1970–71 Blackburn R and Bolton W |
| 1946–47 Swansea T and Newport Co | 1971–72 Charlton Ath and Watford |
| 1947–48 Doncaster R and Millwall | 1972–73 Huddersfield T and Brighton & HA |
| 1948–49 Nottingham F and Lincoln C | 1973–74 Crystal Palace, Preston NE, Swindon T |
| 1949–50 Plymouth Arg and Bradford PA | 1974–75 Millwall, Cardiff C, Sheffield W |
| 1950–51 Grimsby T and Chesterfield | |
| 1951–52 Coventry C and QPR | |

| | |
|---|---|
| 1975–76 | Oxford U, York C, Portsmouth |
| 1976–77 | Carlisle U, Plymouth Arg, Hereford U |
| 1977–78 | Blackpool, Mansfield T, Hull C |
| 1978–79 | Sheffield U, Millwall, Blackburn R |
| 1979–80 | Fulham, Burnley, Charlton Ath |
| 1980–81 | Preston NE, Bristol C, Bristol R |
| 1981–82 | Cardiff C, Wrexham, Orient |
| 1982–83 | Rotherham U, Burnley, Bolton W |
| 1983–84 | Derby Co, Swansea C, Cambridge U |
| 1984–85 | Notts Co, Cardiff C, Wolverhampton W |
| 1985–86 | Carlisle U, Middlesbrough, Fulham |
| 1986–87 | Sunderland**, Grimsby T, Brighton & HA |
| 1987–88 | Huddersfield T, Reading, Sheffield U** |
| 1988–89 | Shrewsbury T, Birmingham C, Walsall |
| 1989–90 | Bournemouth, Bradford C, |
| 1990–91 | WBA and Hull C |
| 1991–92 | Plymouth Arg, Brighton & HA, Port Vale |
| 1992–93 | Preston NE, Mansfield T, Wigan Ath, Chester C |
| 1993–94 | Fulham, Exeter C, Hartlepool U, Barnet |
| 1994–95 | Cambridge U, Plymouth Arg, Cardiff C, Chester C, Leyton Orient |
| 1995–96 | Carlisle U, Swansea C, Brighton & HA, Hull C |
| 1996–97 | Peterborough U, Shrewsbury T, Rotherham U, Notts Co |
| 1997–98 | Brentford, Plymouth Arg, Carlisle U, Southend U |
| 1998–99 | York C, Northampton T, Lincoln C, Macclesfield T |
| 1999–00 | Cardiff C, Blackpool, Scunthorpe U, Chesterfield |
| 2000–01 | Bristol R, Luton T, Swansea C, Oxford U |

## DIVISION 3 TO DIVISION 4

| | |
|---|---|
| 1958–59 | Rochdale, Notts Co, Doncaster R, Stockport Co |
| 1959–60 | Accrington S, Wrexham, Mansfield T, York C |
| 1960–61 | Chesterfield, Colchester U, Bradford C, Tranmere R |
| 1961–62 | Newport Co, Brentford, Lincoln C, Torquay U |
| 1962–63 | Bradford PA, Brighton & HA, Carlisle U, Halifax T |
| 1963–64 | Millwall, Crewe Alex, Wrexham, Notts Co |
| 1964–65 | Luton T, Port Vale, Colchester U, Barnsley |
| 1965–66 | Southend U, Exeter C, Brentford, York C |
| 1966–67 | Doncaster R, Workington, Darlington, Swansea T |
| 1967–68 | Scunthorpe U, Colchester U, Grimsby T, Peterborough U (demoted) |
| 1968–69 | Oldham Ath, Crewe Alex, Hartlepool, Northampton T |
| 1969–70 | Bournemouth, Southport, Barrow, Stockport Co |
| 1970–71 | Reading, Bury, Doncaster R, Gillingham |
| 1971–72 | Mansfield T, Barnsley, Torquay U, Bradford C |
| 1972–73 | Rotherham U, Brentford, Swansea C, Scunthorpe U |
| 1973–74 | Cambridge U, Shrewsbury T, Southport, Rochdale |
| 1974–75 | Bournemouth, Tranmere R, Watford, Huddersfield T |
| 1975–76 | Aldershot, Colchester U, Southend U, Halifax T |
| 1976–77 | Reading, Northampton T, Grimsby T, York C |
| 1977–78 | Port Vale, Bradford C, Hereford U, Portsmouth |
| 1978–79 | Peterborough U, Walsall, Tranmere R, Lincoln C |
| 1979–80 | Bury, Southend U, Mansfield T, Wimbledon |
| 1980–81 | Sheffield U, Colchester U, Blackpool, Hull C |
| 1981–82 | Wimbledon, Swindon T, Bristol C, Chester |
| 1982–83 | Reading, Wrexham, Doncaster R, Chesterfield |
| 1983–84 | Scunthorpe U, Southend U, Port Vale, Exeter C |
| 1984–85 | Burnley, Orient, Preston NE, Cambridge U |
| 1985–86 | Lincoln C, Cardiff C, Wolverhampton W, Swansea C |
| 1986–87 | Bolton W**, Carlisle U, Darlington, Newport Co |
| 1987–88 | Doncaster R, York C, Grimsby T, Rotherham U** |
| 1988–89 | Southend U, Chesterfield, Gillingham, Aldershot |
| 1989–90 | Cardiff C, Northampton T, Blackpool, Walsall |
| 1990–91 | Crewe Alex, Rotherham U, Mansfield T |
| 1991–92 | Bury, Shrewsbury T, Torquay U, Darlington |

*\*\*Relegated after play-offs.*

# LEAGUE TITLE WINS

FA PREMIER LEAGUE – Manchester U 7, Arsenal 1, Blackburn R 1.

LEAGUE DIVISION 1 – Liverpool 18, Arsenal 10, Everton 9, Sunderland 8, Manchester U 7, Aston Villa 7, Newcastle U 5, Sheffield W 4, Huddersfield T 3, Leeds U 3, Wolverhampton W 3, Blackburn R 2, Nottingham F 2, Portsmouth 2, Preston NE 2, Burnley 2, Manchester C 2, Tottenham H 2, Derby Co 2, Bolton W 1, Chelsea 1, Sheffield U 1, WBA 1, Ipswich T 1, Crystal Palace 1, Middlesbrough 1, Charlton Ath 1, Fulham 1.

LEAGUE DIVISION 2 – Leicester C 6, Manchester C 6, Sheffield W 5, Birmingham C (one as Small Heath) 5, Derby Co 4, Liverpool 4, Preston NE 4, Ipswich T 3, Leeds U 3, Notts Co 3, Middlesbrough 3, Stoke C 3, Bury 2, Grimsby T 2, Norwich C 2, Nottingham F 2, Tottenham H 2, WBA 2, Aston Villa 2, Burnley 2, Chelsea 2, Manchester U 2, Millwall 2, West Ham U 2, Wolverhampton W 2, Bolton W 2, Fulham 2, Swindon T, Huddersfield T, Bristol C, Brentford, Bradford C, Everton, Sheffield U, Newcastle U, Coventry C, Blackpool, Blackburn R, Sunderland, Crystal Palace, Luton T, QPR, Oxford U, Oldham Ath, Reading, Watford 1 each.

LEAGUE DIVISION 3 – Portsmouth 2, Oxford U 2, Carlisle U 2, Preston NE 2, Shrewsbury T 2, Brentford 2, Plymouth Arg, Southampton, Bury, Northampton T, Coventry C, Hull C, QPR, Watford, Leyton Orient, Aston Villa, Bolton W, Oldham Ath, Blackburn R, Hereford U, Mansfield T, Wrexham, Grimsby T, Rotherham U, Burnley, Bradford C, Bournemouth, Reading, Sunderland, Wolverhampton W, Bristol R, Cambridge U, Cardiff C, Wigan Ath, Notts Co, Swansea C, Brighton & HA 1 each.

LEAGUE DIVISION 4 – Chesterfield 2, Doncaster R 2, Peterborough U 2, Port Vale, Walsall, Millwall, Brentford, Gillingham, Brighton, Stockport Co, Luton T, Notts Co, Grimsby T, Southport, Mansfield T, Lincoln C, Cambridge U, Watford, Reading, Huddersfield T, Southend U, Sheffield U, Wimbledon, York C, Swindon T, Northampton T, Wolverhampton W, Rotherham U, Exeter C, Darlington, Burnley 1 each.

## To 1957–58

DIVISION 3 (South) – Bristol C 3; Charlton Ath, Ipswich T, Millwall, Notts Co, Plymouth Arg, Swansea T 2 each; Brentford, Bristol R, Cardiff C, Crystal Palace, Coventry C, Fulham, Leyton Orient, Luton T, Newport Co, Nottingham F, Norwich C, Portsmouth, QPR, Reading, Southampton, Brighton & HA 1 each.

DIVISION 3 (North) – Barnsley, Doncaster R, Lincoln C 3 each; Chesterfield, Grimsby T, Hull C, Port Vale, Stockport Co 2 each; Bradford PA, Bradford C, Darlington, Derby Co, Nelson, Oldham Ath, Rotherham U, Stoke C, Tranmere R, Wolverhampton W, Scunthorpe U 1 each.

# LEAGUE ATTENDANCES 2000–2001

## FA CARLING PREMIERSHIP ATTENDANCES

| | Average Gate | | | Season 2000/2001 | |
|---|---|---|---|---|---|
| | 1999/2000 | 2000/01 | +/–% | Highest | Lowest |
| Arsenal | 38,033 | 37,975 | –0.15 | 38,146 | 37,318 |
| Aston Villa | 31,697 | 31,597 | –0.32 | 41,366 | 27,056 |
| Bradford City | 18,030 | 18,511 | +2.67 | 22,057 | 15,523 |
| Charlton Athletic | 19,557 | 20,020 | +2.37 | 20,043 | 19,633 |
| Chelsea | 34,531 | 34,698 | +0.48 | 35,196 | 33,159 |
| Coventry City | 20,786 | 20,535 | –1.21 | 23,063 | 17,275 |
| Derby County | 29,351 | 28,551 | –2.73 | 33,239 | 22,310 |
| Everton | 34,880 | 34,130 | –2.15 | 40,260 | 27,670 |
| Ipswich Town | 18,370 | 22,524 | +22.61 | 24,888 | 21,767 |
| Leeds United | 39,155 | 39,016 | –0.35 | 40,055 | 35,552 |
| Leicester City | 19,825 | 20,453 | +3.17 | 22,132 | 18,084 |
| Liverpool | 44,074 | 43,699 | –0.85 | 44,806 | 38,474 |
| Manchester City | 32,088 | 34,058 | +6.14 | 34,629 | 32,053 |
| Manchester United | 58,017 | 67,544 | +16.42 | 67,637 | 67,447 |
| Middlesbrough | 33,263 | 30,730 | –7.61 | 34,696 | 27,556 |
| Newcastle United | 36,311 | 51,290 | +41.25 | 52,134 | 50,159 |
| Southampton | 15,132 | 15,115 | –0.11 | 15,252 | 14,801 |
| Sunderland | 40,495 | 45,069 | +11.29 | 47,250 | 43,185 |
| Tottenham Hotspur | 34,902 | 35,216 | +0.90 | 36,096 | 28,300 |
| West Ham United | 25,093 | 25,697 | +2.41 | 26,048 | 22,586 |

## NATIONWIDE FOOTBALL LEAGUE: DIVISION ONE ATTENDANCES

| | Average Gate | | | Season 2000/2001 | |
|---|---|---|---|---|---|
| | 1999/2000 | 2000/01 | +/–% | Highest | Lowest |
| Barnsley | 15,412 | 14,465 | –6.1 | 19,989 | 12,412 |
| Birmingham City | 21,895 | 21,283 | –2.8 | 29,150 | 15,579 |
| Blackburn Rovers | 19,253 | 20,740 | +7.7 | 29,426 | 16,397 |
| Bolton Wanderers | 14,244 | 16,062 | +12.8 | 24,249 | 10,180 |
| Burnley | 12,973 | 16,234 | +25.1 | 21,369 | 13,189 |
| Crewe Alexandra | 6,222 | 6,698 | +7.7 | 9,415 | 5,215 |
| Crystal Palace | 15,662 | 17,061 | +8.9 | 21,133 | 13,987 |
| Fulham | 13,092 | 14,985 | +14.5 | 19,373 | 10,437 |
| Gillingham | 7,088 | 9,293 | +31.1 | 10,518 | 7,810 |
| Grimsby Town | 6,157 | 5,646 | –8.3 | 8,706 | 3,732 |
| Huddersfield Town | 14,029 | 12,808 | –8.7 | 19,290 | 7,592 |
| Norwich City | 15,539 | 16,525 | +6.3 | 21,241 | 13,688 |
| Nottingham Forest | 17,196 | 20,615 | +19.9 | 28,372 | 17,089 |
| Portsmouth | 13,906 | 13,533 | –2.7 | 19,013 | 9,235 |
| Preston North End | 12,589 | 14,617 | +16.1 | 17,355 | 12,632 |
| Queens Park Rangers | 13,718 | 12,013 | –12.4 | 17,608 | 9,388 |
| Sheffield United | 13,718 | 17,211 | +25.5 | 25,673 | 10,816 |
| Sheffield Wednesday | 24,855 | 19,268 | –22.5 | 38,433 | 14,695 |
| Stockport County | 7,411 | 7,031 | –5.1 | 9,782 | 5,383 |
| Tranmere Rovers | 7,273 | 9,045 | +24.4 | 12,362 | 7,119 |
| Watford | 18,544 | 13,941 | –24.8 | 18,333 | 11,166 |
| West Bromwich Albion | 14,584 | 17,657 | +21.1 | 22,301 | 13,980 |
| Wimbledon | 17,156 | 7,901 | –53.9 | 14,071 | 4,489 |
| Wolverhampton Wanderers | 21,470 | 19,258 | –10.3 | 26,627 | 14,853 |

## NATIONWIDE FOOTBALL LEAGUE: DIVISION TWO ATTENDANCES

| | Average Gate | | | Season 2000/2001 | |
|---|---|---|---|---|---|
| | 1999/2000 | 2000/01 | +/–% | Highest | Lowest |
| AFC Bournemouth | 4,917 | 4,403 | -10.5 | 6,843 | 3,004 |
| Brentford | 5,742 | 4,645 | -19.1 | 7,550 | 3,062 |
| Bristol City | 9,803 | 10,369 | +5.8 | 16,696 | 7,411 |
| Bristol Rovers | 8,402 | 7,275 | -13.4 | 9,361 | 5,502 |
| Bury | 4,025 | 3,444 | -14.4 | 4,976 | 2,274 |
| Cambridge United | 4,403 | 4,403 | +0.0 | 7,505 | 3,027 |
| Colchester United | 3,782 | 3,555 | -6.0 | 5,010 | 2,579 |
| Luton Town | 5,658 | 5,754 | +1.7 | 7,405 | 4,362 |
| Millwall | 9,260 | 11,442 | +23.6 | 18,510 | 7,064 |
| Northampton Town | 5,459 | 5,654 | +3.6 | 7,079 | 4,361 |
| Notts County | 5,667 | 5,201 | -8.2 | 9,125 | 2,860 |
| Oldham Athletic | 5,391 | 4,972 | -7.8 | 9,359 | 3,011 |
| Oxford United | 5,790 | 5,148 | -11.1 | 7,480 | 3,676 |
| Peterborough United | 6,568 | 6,252 | -4.8 | 11,274 | 4,004 |
| Port Vale | 5,997 | 4,458 | -25.7 | 8,948 | 3,192 |
| Reading | 8,985 | 12,647 | +40.8 | 20,589 | 7,768 |
| Rotherham United | 4,426 | 5,652 | +27.7 | 9,760 | 3,545 |
| Stoke City | 11,426 | 13,767 | +20.5 | 22,133 | 9,350 |
| Swansea City | 5,895 | 4,913 | -16.7 | 8,391 | 2,002 |
| Swindon Town | 6,977 | 6,187 | -11.3 | 10,031 | 3,452 |
| Walsall | 6,779 | 5,632 | -16.9 | 7,772 | 4,437 |
| Wigan Athletic | 7,007 | 6,774 | -3.3 | 10,048 | 4,798 |
| Wrexham | 3,952 | 3,600 | -8.9 | 6,447 | 1,584 |
| Wycombe Wanderers | 5,101 | 5,513 | +8.1 | 7,516 | 4,488 |

## NATIONWIDE FOOTBALL LEAGUE: DIVISION THREE ATTENDANCES

| | Average Gate | | | Season 2000/2001 | |
|---|---|---|---|---|---|
| | 1999/2000 | 2000/01 | +/–% | Highest | Lowest |
| Barnet | 2,743 | 2,406 | -12.3 | 5,523 | 1,322 |
| Blackpool | 4,841 | 4,457 | -7.9 | 5,862 | 2,907 |
| Brighton & Hove Albion | 5,733 | 6,603 | +15.2 | 6,995 | 5,804 |
| Cardiff City | 6,895 | 7,962 | +15.5 | 13,602 | 4,625 |
| Carlisle United | 3,192 | 3,670 | +15.0 | 8,194 | 1,309 |
| Cheltenham Town | 4,125 | 3,695 | -10.4 | 5,139 | 2,368 |
| Chesterfield | 2,935 | 4,846 | +65.1 | 7,014 | 3,796 |
| Darlington | 5,523 | 3,844 | -30.4 | 6,717 | 2,689 |
| Exeter City | 3,014 | 3,692 | +22.5 | 5,150 | 2,470 |
| Halifax Town | 2,536 | 2,214 | -12.7 | 3,979 | 1,382 |
| Hartlepool United | 2,982 | 3,423 | +14.8 | 5,324 | 2,130 |
| Hull City | 5,736 | 6,684 | +16.5 | 11,820 | 4,450 |
| Kidderminster Harriers | 2,857 | 3,422 | +19.8 | 5,122 | 2,438 |
| Leyton Orient | 4,357 | 4,528 | +3.9 | 7,958 | 2,200 |
| Lincoln City | 3,405 | 3,273 | -3.9 | 5,487 | 1,853 |
| Macclesfield Town | 2,304 | 2,064 | -10.4 | 3,045 | 1,349 |
| Mansfield Town | 2,594 | 2,706 | +4.3 | 7,899 | 1,623 |
| Plymouth Argyle | 5,372 | 4,945 | -7.9 | 8,671 | 3,378 |
| Rochdale | 2,774 | 3,249 | +17.1 | 5,008 | 2,444 |
| Scunthorpe United | 4,064 | 3,446 | -15.2 | 6,101 | 2,523 |
| Shrewsbury Town | 2,832 | 2,898 | +2.3 | 5,360 | 2,058 |
| Southend United | 4,138 | 4,322 | +4.4 | 9,950 | 2,403 |
| Torquay United | 2,555 | 2,556 | +0.0 | 4,505 | 1,538 |
| York City | 3,048 | 3,026 | -0.7 | 5,493 | 1,981 |

# TRANSFERS 2000–2001

| **May 2000** | *From* | *To* |
|---|---|---|
| 17 Alford, Carl P. | Stevenage Borough | Doncaster Rovers |
| 4 Carlisle, Clarke J. | Blackpool | Queens Park Rangers |
| 24 Kelly, James | Hednesford Town | Doncaster Rovers |
| 22 Marsh, Michael A. | Kidderminster Harriers | Southport |
| 25 Matthews, Colin E. | Bognor Regis Town | Newport (IW) |
| 9 Morrison, Peter A. | Bolton Wanderers | Scunthorpe United |
| 25 Robinson, Stephen | AFC Bournemouth | Preston North End |

| **Temporary transfers** | | |
|---|---|---|
| 8 Coppinger, James | Newcastle United | Hartlepool United |
| 5 Gunnlaugsson, Arnar B. | Leicester City | Stoke City |
| 8 Hendry, Iain | Woking | Kingstonian |
| 9 Myhre, Thomas | Everton | Birmingham City |
| 6 Saunders, Edward | Woking | Kingstonian |
| 7 Simba, Amara S. | Leyton Orient | Kingstonian |
| 6 Stewart, Jordan B. | Leicester City | Bristol Rovers |
| 1 Trundle, Lee C. | Southport | Bamber Bridge |
| 7 Webb, Simon J. | Leyton Orient | Purfleet |

| **June 2000** | | |
|---|---|---|
| 28 Bjornebye, Stig I. | Liverpool | Blackburn Rovers |
| 9 Bramble, Tesfaye | Chelmsford City | Cambridge City |
| 2 Brooker, Paul | Fulham | Brighton & Hove Albion |
| 16 Crossley, Matthew | Kingstonian | Aldershot Town |
| 1 Curtis, John C.K. | Manchester United | Blackburn Rovers |
| 21 Darby, Duane | Notts County | Rushden & Diamonds |
| 14 Delaney, Dean | Everton | Port Vale |
| 12 Flitter, Matthew A.H. | Chesham United | Hampton & Richmond Borough |
| 28 Gabbiadini, Marco | Darlington | Northampton Town |
| 16 Haaland, Alf I.R. | Leeds United | Manchester City |
| 16 Jackson, Justin J. | Morecambe | Rushden & Diamonds |
| 28 King, Marlon F. | Barnet | Gillingham |
| 14 Regan, Carl A. | Everton | Barnsley |
| 27 Shuttlewood, Justin | Forest Green Rovers | Salisbury City |
| 5 Thomas, Wayne | Torquay United | Stoke City |
| 8 Walters, Steven P. | Northwich Victoria | Morecambe |
| 15 Warren, Christer | AFC Bournemouth | Queens Park Rangers |

| **July 2000** | | |
|---|---|---|
| 21 Aiston, Sam J. | Sunderland | Shrewsbury Town |
| 28 Akinbiyi, Adeola P. | Wolverhampton Wanderers | Leicester City |
| 20 Alexandersson, Niclas | Sheffield Wednesday | Everton |
| 24 Ball, Kevin A. | Fulham | Burnley |
| 19 Barmby, Nicholas J. | Everton | Liverpool |
| 14 Benjamin, Trevor J. | Cambridge United | Leicester City |
| 21 Black, Thomas R. | Arsenal | Crystal Palace |
| 13 Bothroyd, Jay | Arsenal | Coventry City |
| 11 Cameron, Martin G.W. | Alloa Athletic | Bristol Rovers |
| 7 Clark, Peter J. | Carlisle United | Stockport County |
| 7 Clement, Neil | Chelsea | West Bromwich Albion |
| 21 Collins, John | Everton | Fulham |
| 6 Cort, Carl E.R. | Wimbledon | Newcastle United |
| 19 Cousins, Ian | Burnham Ramblers | Chelmsford City |
| 24 Crouch, Peter J. | Tottenham Hotspur | Queens Park Rangers |
| 10 Curle, Keith | Wolverhampton Wanderers | Sheffield United |
| 19 Dack, James | Sutton United | Farnborough Town |

| | | |
|---|---|---|
| 12 Davidson, Callum I. | Blackburn Rovers | Leicester City |
| 22 Ducros, Andrew J. | Nuneaton Borough | Kidderminster Harriers |
| 11 Duffield, Peter | Darlington | York City |
| 31 Farrell, Andrew J. | Morecambe | Leigh RMI |
| 14 Forsyth, Richard M. | Blackpool | Peterborough United |
| 24 Frandsen, Per | Blackburn Rovers | Bolton Wanderers |
| 11 Gabbiadini, Marco | Darlington | Northampton Town |
| 21 Gray, Julian R. | Arsenal | Crystal Palace |
| 12 Gudjohnsen, Eidur S. | Bolton Wanderers | Chelsea |
| 25 Hale, Matthew | Yeovil Town | Weymouth |
| 27 Hicks, Stuart J. | Chester City | Mansfield Town |
| 12 Higginbotham, Daniel J. | Manchester United | Derby County |
| 11 Hignett, Craig J. | Barnsley | Blackburn Rovers |
| 21 Hope, Christopher J. | Scunthorpe United | Gillingham |
| 12 Hopkin, David | Leeds United | Bradford City |
| 15 Horsfield, Geoffrey M. | Fulham | Birmingham City |
| 21 Hutchinson, Ed | Sutton United | Brentford |
| 19 Hutchison, Donald | Everton | Sunderland |
| 21 Jensen, Claus W. | Bolton Wanderers | Charlton Athletic |
| 27 Jones, Gary | Hartlepool United | Halifax Town |
| 19 Jones, Lee | Bristol Rovers | Stockport County |
| 3 King, Marlon F. | Barnet | Gillingham |
| 27 Lovett, Jay | Crawley Town | Brentford |
| 18 McCammon, Mark J. | Charlton Athletic | Brentford |
| 12 McGregor, Marc R. | Forest Green Rovers | Nuneaton Borough |
| 27 Mike, Adrian R. | Southport | Northwich Victoria |
| 11 Neil, Alexander | Airdrieonians | Barnsley |
| 28 Piper, Leonard H. | St Albans City | Farnborough Town |
| 12 Pistone, Alessandro | Newcastle United | Everton |
| 3 Reed, Ian P. | Nuneaton Borough | Worcester City |
| 5 Reid, Paul M. | Carlisle United | Rangers |
| 13 Richardson, Leam N. | Blackburn Rovers | Bolton Wanderers |
| 25 Ricketts, Michael B. | Walsall | Bolton Wanderers |
| 24 Roberts, Christian J. | Cardiff City | Exeter City |
| 27 Roberts, Jason A.D. | Bristol Rovers | West Bromwich Albion |
| 7 Rowett, Gary | Birmingham City | Leicester City |
| 28 Ruddock, Neil | West Ham United | Crystal Palace |
| 5 Saunders, Edward | Woking | Kingstonian |
| 21 Shaw, Paul | Millwall | Gillingham |
| 25 Sollitt, Adam J. | Kettering Town | Northampton Town |
| 14 Strong, G. | Bolton Wanderers | Motherwell |
| 12 Thatcher, Ben D. | Wimbledon | Tottenham Hotspur |
| 14 Ward, Mitcham D. | Everton | Barnsley |
| 12 Watson, Stephen C. | Aston Villa | Everton |
| 26 Williams, Mark S. | Watford | Wimbledon |
| 29 Winston, Samuel A. | Sutton United | Kingstonian |
| 5 Winterburn, Nigel | Arsenal | West Ham United |

**Temporary transfers**

| | | |
|---|---|---|
| 28 Boa Morte, Luis P. | Southampton | Fulham |
| 4 Culkin, Nicholas J. | Manchester United | Bristol Rovers |
| 28 Ferguson, Barry | Coventry City | Hartlepool United |
| 28 Forsell, Mikael K. | Chelsea | Crystal Palace |
| 21 Jones, Stephen G. | Bristol City | Wycombe Wanderers |
| 17 Maxwell, Layton J. | Liverpool | Stockport County |
| 27 McGovern, Brian | Arsenal | Norwich City |
| 24 Roche, Lee P. | Manchester United | Wrexham |

**August 2000**

| | | |
|---|---|---|
| 31 Adams, Daniel B. | Altrincham | Macclesfield Town |
| 11 Alexander, Gary G. | West Ham United | Swindon Town |
| 9 Ashcroft, Lee | Grimsby Town | Wigan Athletic |

| | | |
|---|---|---|
| 3 Baardsen, Espen | Tottenham Hotspur | Watford |
| 14 Beard, Robert | Bedworth United | Rugby United |
| 17 Bellamy, Craig D. | Norwich City | Coventry City |
| 10 Bennett, Thomas M. | Stockport County | Walsall |
| 10 Birch, Mark | Northwich Victoria | Carlisle United |
| 11 Black, Thomas R. | Arsenal | Crystal Palace |
| 24 Bradley, Shayne | Southampton | Mansfield Town |
| 31 Constantine, Leon | Edgware Town | Millwall |
| 21 Cureton, Jamie | Bristol Rovers | Reading |
| 4 Curtis, Thomas D. | Chesterfield | Portsmouth |
| 0 Duke, David | Sunderland | Swindon Town |
| 19 Ferguson, Duncan | Newcastle United | Everton |
| 11 Foran, Mark J. | Crewe Alexandra | Bristol Rovers |
| 15 Forbes, Donald | Forest Green Rovers | Basingstoke Town |
| 30 Fox, Ruel A. | Tottenham Hotspur | West Bromwich Albion |
| 1 Ginola, David D.M. | Tottenham Hotspur | Aston Villa |
| 11 Gray, Julian R. | Arsenal | Crystal Palace |
| 1 Holmes, Peter J. | Sheffield Wednesday | Luton Town |
| 14 Howey, Stephen N. | Newcastle United | Manchester City |
| 19 Hreidarsson, Hermann | Wimbledon | Ipswich Town |
| 18 Javary, Jean-Phillipe | Raith Rovers | Brentford |
| 11 Jones, Mark A. | Wolverhampton Wanderers | Chesterfield |
| 10 Ketsbaia, Temuri | Newcastle United | Wolverhampton Wanderers |
| 9 Lormor, Anthony | Mansfield Town | Hartlepool United |
| 24 Matteo, Dominic | Liverpool | Leeds United |
| 11 McAnespie, Kieran | St Johnstone | Fulham |
| 22 McGovern, Brian | Arsenal | Norwich City |
| 11 Mills, Rowan L. | Bradford City | Portsmouth |
| 10 Morley, Dominic A. | Southport | Droylsden |
| 30 Nancekivell, Kevin W. | Tiverton Town | Plymouth Argyle |
| 3 Nielsen, Allan | Tottenham Hotspur | Watford |
| 25 Okita, Jean-Marie | Enfield | Tilbury |
| 10 Ovendale, Mark J. | AFC Bournemouth | Luton Town |
| 10 Peacock, Lee A. | Manchester City | Bristol City |
| 4 Pemberton, Martin C. | Bradford Park Avenue | Mansfield Town |
| 2 Petrescu, Dan V. | Chelsea | Bradford City |
| 11 Phillips, Martin J. | Portsmouth | Plymouth Argyle |
| 11 Pollock, Jamie | Manchester City | Crystal Palace |
| 7 Quashie, Nigel F. | Nottingham Forest | Portsmouth |
| 8 Richardson, Jonathan D. | Exeter City | Oxford United |
| 22 Ritchie, Paul M. | Rangers | Manchester City |
| 9 Robinson, Paul D. | Newcastle United | Wimbledon |
| 1 Rougier, Anthony L. | Port Vale | Reading |
| 3 Ruddock, Neil | West Ham United | Crystal Palace |
| 18 Ruffer, Carl J. | Runcorn | Chester City |
| 19 Skelly, Richard B. | Sutton United | Cambridge City |
| 9 Tate, Steven K. | Weymouth | Newport (IW) |
| 15 Taylor, Robert A. | Manchester City | Wolverhampton Wanderers |
| 8 Thompson, David A. | Liverpool | Coventry City |
| 9 Tillson, Andrew | Bristol Rovers | Walsall |
| 9 Todd, Lee | Bradford City | Rochdale |
| 1 Tutill, Stephen A. | Darlington | Chesterfield |
| 10 Twynham, Gary S. | Hednesford Town | Macclesfield Town |
| 25 Utterson, John | Margate | Ramsgate |
| 16 Wanchope, Watson P. | West Ham United | Manchester City |
| 18 Ward, Ashley S. | Blackburn Rovers | Bradford City |
| 17 Wardley, Shane | Chelmsford City | Cambridge City |
| 4 Whelan, Noel D. | Coventry City | Middlesbrough |
| 2 Williams, Mark S. | Watford | Wimbledon |
| 4 Williams, Stephen J. | Chatham Town | Dartford |
| 3 Windsor, Simon L. | Racing Club Warwick | Stratford Town |

| | | |
|---|---|---|
| 19 Wyatt, Nicky | Havant & Waterlooville | Bognor Regis Town |
| 10 Zabek, Lee K. | Bristol Rovers | Exeter City |
| 10 Zamora, Robert L. | Bristol Rovers | Brighton & Hove Albion |
| 29 Ziege, Christian | Middlesbrough | Liverpool |

**Temporary transfers**

| | | |
|---|---|---|
| 19 Abbey, Benjamin | Oxford United | Aldershot Town |
| 11 Angus, Stevland D. | West Ham United | AFC Bournemouth |
| 22 Blake, Robert J. | Bradford City | Nottingham Forest |
| 22 Bradley, Shayne | Southampton | Mansfield Town |
| 18 Bridge, Mark | Stevenage Borough | Baldock Town |
| 10 Cartwright, Mark N. | Wrexham | Brighton & Hove Albion |
| 11 Collins, Lee D. | Stoke City | Cambridge United |
| 18 Crompton, Paul A. | Lancaster City | Kendal Town |
| 11 Crowe, Dean A. | Stoke City | Bury |
| 12 Dunning, Darren | Blackburn Rovers | Bristol City |
| 26 Evans, David A. | Barnsley | Chester City |
| 18 Evans, Michael J. | West Bromwich Albion | Bristol Rovers |
| 11 Fenton, Nicholas L. | Manchester City | AFC Bournemouth |
| 27 Ferguson, Barry | Coventry City | Hartlepool United |
| 31 Fortune, Jonathan J. | Charlton Athletic | Mansfield Town |
| 26 Fox, Ruel A. | Tottenham Hotspur | West Bromwich Albion |
| 18 Furlong, Paul A. | Birmingham City | Queens Park Rangers |
| 10 Gabbidon, Daniel L. | West Bromwich Albion | Cardiff City |
| 1 Garcia, Richard | West Ham United | Leyton Orient |
| 11 Gray, Kevin J. | Huddersfield Town | Stockport County |
| 11 Grayson, Simon N. | Blackburn Rovers | Sheffield Wednesday |
| 26 Greene, Dennis B. | Windsor & Eton | Harlow Town |
| 5 Haley, Grant R. | Peterborough United | Bedford Town |
| 17 Hamilton, Gary I. | Blackburn Rovers | Rochdale |
| 11 Harrison, Craig | Middlesbrough | Crystal Palace |
| 18 Hasell, James | Stevenage Borough | Ashford Town |
| 11 Hawe, Steven J. | Blackburn Rovers | Blackpool |
| 19 Hayes, Adrian M. | Boston United | Tamworth |
| 24 Hooper, Nicholas | Farnborough Town | Staines Town |
| 26 Inman, Niall E. | Peterborough United | Ketteringn Town |
| 10 Jones, Scott | Barnsley | Bristol Rovers |
| 25 Keeler, Justin J. | AFC Bournemouth | Dorchester Town |
| 2 Kendall, Lee M. | Crystal Palace | Barry Town |
| 26 King, Stuart S.D. | Preston North End | Ross County |
| 11 Lindley, James E. | Notts County | Lincoln City |
| 11 McCann, Grant S. | West Ham United | Notts County |
| 18 McCann, Peter | Barnet | Folkestone Invicta |
| 19 Meechan, Alexander T. | Bristol City | Forest Green Rovers |
| 12 Miller, Alan J. | Blackburn Rovers | Bristol City |
| 25 Nancekivell, Kevin W. | Tiverton Town | Plymouth Argyle |
| 25 Neal, Jon | Folkestone Invicta | St Leonards |
| 4 Newby, Jon P.R. | Liverpool | Sheffield United |
| 21 Okita, Jean-Marie | Enfield | Tilbury |
| 18 Osborn, Mark | Wycombe Wanderers | Marlow |
| 18 Pinnock, James E. | Gillingham | Dover Athletic |
| 1 Proudlock, Adam D. | Wolverhampton Wanderers | Clyde |
| 11 Rankin, Isaiah | Bradford City | Bolton Wanderers |
| 19 Rouco, Daniel | Hampton & Richmond Borough | Chertsey Town |
| 21 Searle, Stuart A. | Aldershot Town | Molesey |
| 9 Taylor, Stuart J. | Arsenal | Crystal Palace |
| 25 Thetis, Jean M. | Ipswich Town | Wolverhampton Wanderers |
| 10 Thom, Stuart P. | Oldham Athletic | Scunthorpe United |
| 31 Thomas, Anthony | Burton Albion | Kings Lynn |
| 10 Westwood, Ashley M. | Bradford City | Sheffield Wednesday |

| 24 Whitley, James | Manchester City | Norwich City |
|---|---|---|
| 25 Whittingham, Guy | Portsmouth | Peterborough United |
| 27 Willmott, Richard | Hitchin Town | Hendon |
| 8 Woodman, Andrew J. | Brentford | Southend United |

**September 2000**

| 14 Cartwright, Mark N. | Wrexham | Brighton & Hove Albion |
|---|---|---|
| 11 Cottee, Anthony R. | Leicester City | Norwich City |
| 5 Cresswell, Richard P.W. | Sheffield Wednesday | Leicester City |
| 22 Dinning, Tony | Stockport County | Wolverhampton Wanderers |
| 8 Edwards, Robert | Huddersfield Town | Chesterfield |
| 11 Emerson, Thome A. | Chelsea | Sunderland |
| 11 Evans, Michael J. | West Bromwich Albion | Bristol Rovers |
| 11 Fortune-West, Leopold O. | Rotherham United | Cardiff City |
| 1 Foster, Adrian M. | Yeovil Town | Forest Green Rovers |
| 21 Gabbidon, Daniel L. | West Bromwich Albion | Cardiff City |
| 29 Harkness, Steven | Blackburn Rovers | Sheffield Wednesday |
| 1 Harrison, Craig | Middlesbrough | Crystal Palace |
| 11 Jones, Scott | Barnsley | Bristol Rovers |
| 22 Lua-Lua, Lomano T. | Colchester United | Newcastle United |
| 1 McCulloch, Scott A. | Dundee United | Cardiff City |
| 7 Rammell, Andrew V. | Walsall | Wycombe Wanderers |
| 18 Thomas, Anthony | Burton Albion | Kings Lynn |
| 11 Thom, Stuart P. | Oldham Athletic | Scunthorpe United |
| 18 Walsh, Steven | Leicester City | Norwich City |
| 12 Westwood, Ashley M. | Bradford City | Sheffield Wednesday |

**Temporary transfers**

| 29 Ayres, James M. | Luton Town | Stevenage Borough |
|---|---|---|
| 28 Baker, Steven R. | Middlesbrough | Hartlepool United |
| 8 Ball, Alex I. | Bristol City | Salisbury City |
| 15 Beresford, David | Huddersfield Town | Port Vale |
| 8 Berg, Henning | Manchester United | Blackburn Rovers |
| 4 Brady, Gary | Newcastle United | Norwich City |
| 22 Brass, Christopher P. | Burnley | Halifax Town |
| 21 Broughton, Drewe O. | Peterborough United | Dagenham & Redbridge |
| 15 Buggie, Lee D. | Bury | Rochdale |
| 22 Burchill, Mark J. | Celtic | Birmingham City |
| 23 Campbell, James R. | Peterborough United | St Albans City |
| 15 Campbell, Stuart P. | Leicester City | Grimsby Town |
| 9 Caton, Sean T. | Heybridge Swifts | Barking |
| 15 Charles, Gary A. | West Ham United | Birmingham City |
| 1 Clarke, Matthew P. | Halifax Town | Gainsborough Trinity |
| 21 Cooke, Terence J. | Manchester City | Sheffield Wednesday |
| 11 Cramb, Colin | Crewe Alexandra | Notts County |
| 1 Cramman, Kenneth W. | Boston United | Slough Town |
| 12 Crowe, Jason W.R. | Portsmouth | Brentford |
| 22 Devenney, Michael P. | Burnley | Leigh RMI |
| 8 Dryden, Richard A. | Southampton | Northampton Town |
| 1 Dudfield, Lawrie G. | Leicester City | Lincoln City |
| 18 Fenton, Nicholas L. | Manchester City | Notts County |
| 29 Fortune, Jonathan J. | Charlton Athletic | Mansfield Town |
| 23 Foster, Martin | Doncaster Rovers | Ilkeston Town |
| 8 Freeman, David B. | Nottingham Forest | Port Vale |
| 12 Garcia, Richard | West Ham United | Leyton Orient |
| 15 Glennon, Matthew W. | Bolton Wanderers | Bristol Rovers |
| 22 Goodyear, Craig | Barnsley | Frickley Athletic |
| 23 Haley, Grant R. | Peterborough United | Bedford Town |
| 22 Hann, Matthew | Peterborough United | Stamford |
| 5 Harvey, Lee | St Albans City | Enfield |
| 21 Hodson, Benjamin M. | Hayes | Sutton United |

| 22 Hollis, Simon | Solihull Borough | Paget Rangers |
|---|---|---|
| 21 Holmes, David J. | Burton Albion | Ilkeston Town |
| 22 Hooper, Nicholas | Farnborough Town | Staines Town |
| 29 Johnson, Ben | Stockport County | Carlisle United |
| 5 Jones, Daniel | Enfield | St Albans City |
| 22 Jones, Dean | Ilkeston Town | Frickley Athletic |
| 26 Keeler, Justin J. | AFC Bournemouth | Dorchester Town |
| 22 Keller, Marc | West Ham United | Portsmouth |
| 8 Killen, Christopher J. | Manchester City | Wrexham |
| 14 Kitson, Paul | West Ham United | Crystal Palace |
| 7 Kozluk, Robert | Sheffield United | Huddersfield Town |
| 8 Kyle, Kevin A. | Sunderland | Huddersfield Town |
| 8 Lambourde, Bernard | Chelsea | Portsmouth |
| 21 Lee, Alan D. | Burnley | Rotherham United |
| 15 Lightfoot, Christopher I. | Crewe Alexandra | Oldham Athletic |
| 1 Lumsdon, Christopher | Sunderland | Crewe Alexandra |
| 21 Mardon, Paul J. | West Bromwich Albion | Plymouth Argyle |
| 1 Marsh, Simon T. | Birmingham City | Brentford |
| 15 Matassa, Vincent | Basingstoke Town | Dorchester Town |
| 27 Mawson, Craig J. | Burnley | Lincoln City |
| 21 McConnell, Barry | Exeter City | Weston-Super-Mare |
| 18 Meechan, Alexander T. | Bristol City | Forest Green Rovers |
| 21 Mike, Leon J. | Manchester City | Oxford United |
| 5 Miller, Alan J. | Bristol City | Blackburn Rovers |
| 29 Miller, Barry S. | Gillingham | Doncaster Rovers |
| 1 Morrison, Andrew C. | Manchester City | Blackpool |
| 22 Morrison-Hill, Jamie S. | Plymouth Argyle | Tiverton Town |
| 20 Murray, Matthew W. | Wolverhampton Wanderers | Slough Town |
| 21 Newell, Paul C. | Billericay Town | Sutton United |
| 20 Osborn, Mark | Wycombe Wanderers | Hampton & Richmond Borough |
| 26 Packham, William J. | Brighton & Hove Albion | Bognor Regis Town |
| 12 Parkin, Sam | Chelsea | Millwall |
| 16 Parsons, David | Leyton Orient | Purfleet |
| 22 Patton, Aaron | Slough Town | Oxford City |
| 4 Peacock, Darren | Blackburn Rovers | West Ham United |
| 18 Pinnock, James | Gillingham | Dover Athletic |
| 20 Randall, Martin J. | St Albans City | Woking |
| 3 Read, David | Stafford Rangers | Sutton Coldfield Town |
| 4 Robertson, Mark W. | Burnley | Swindon Town |
| 13 Robinson, Marvin L.S. | Derby County | Stoke City |
| 22 Scott, Christopher J. | Burnley | Leigh RMI |
| 4 Searle, Stephen | Barnet | Stevenage Borough |
| 21 Searle, Stuart A. | Aldershot Town | Molesey |
| 30 Sills, Timothy | Basingstoke Town | Staines Town |
| 22 Smith, Darren K. | Gravesend & Northfleet | Ashford Town |
| 22 Smith, Ian P. | Burnley | Oldham Athletic |
| 20 Smith, Peter E. | Exeter City | Cambridge City |
| 1 Smith, Philip A. | Millwall | Croydon |
| 21 Speakman, Robert | Exeter City | Bashley |
| 13 Stockdale, Robert K. | Middlesbrough | Sheffield Wednesday |
| 9 Sullivan, Martyn G. | Forest Green Rovers | Weymouth |
| 7 Taylor, Leigh D. | Boston United | Wisbech Town |
| 12 Taylor, Stuart J. | Arsenal | Crystal Palace |
| 15 Walsh, Gary | Bradford City | Middlesbrough |
| 16 Whitehall, Steven C. | Oldham Athletic | Chester City |
| 26 Whitley, James | Manchester City | Norwich City |
| 1 Wicks, Matthew J. | Peterborough United | Brighton & Hove Albion |
| 24 Wilmot, Richard | Hitchin Town | Hendon |
| 8 Wilson, Paul R. | Barnet | Boston United |
| 12 Woodman, Andrew J. | Brentford | Southend United |

| 22 | Woodward, Andrew S. | Sheffield United | Scunthorpe United |
| 15 | Woozley, David J. | Crystal Palace | AFC Bournemouth |
| 8 | Wright, Benjamin | Bristol City | Woking |
| 22 | Yeoman, Daniel | Farnborough Town | Northwood |

**October 2000**

| 26 | Charvet, Laurent J. | Newcastle United | Manchester City |
| 27 | Collymore, Stanley V. | Leicester City | Bradford City |
| 20 | Dunne, Richard P. | Everton | Manchester City |
| 20 | Ehiogu, Ugochuku | Aston Villa | Middlesbrough |
| 13 | Eyres, David | Preston North End | Oldham Athletic |
| 18 | Fitzgerald, Scott B. | Millwall | Colchester United |
| 5 | Hayes, Adrian M. | Boston United | Kings Lynn |
| 12 | Hendon, Ian M. | Northampton Town | Sheffield Wednesday |
| 2 | Holloway, Darren | Sunderland | Wimbledon |
| 27 | Hooper, Nicholas | Farnborough Town | Staines Town |
| 27 | Horner, Richard | Farnborough Town | Sutton United |
| 24 | Hughes, Leslie M. | Everton | Blackburn Rovers |
| 26 | Jordan, Andrew J. | Bristol City | Cardiff City |
| 3 | Lescott, Aaron A. | Aston Villa | Sheffield Wednesday |
| 19 | Matassa, Vincent | Basingstoke Town | Woking |
| 13 | McKenzie, Leon M. | Crystal Palace | Peterborough United |
| 19 | Miller, Barry S. | Gillingham | Doncaster Rovers |
| 20 | Naysmith, Gary | Heart of Midlothian | Everton |
| 20 | O'Connor, Joseph N. | Kingstonian | Stafford Rangers |
| 20 | Ormerod, Mark I. | Woking | Dorchester Town |
| 18 | Sullivan, Martyn G. | Forest Green Rovers | Dorchester Town |
| 12 | Tait, Jordan A. | Oldham Athletic | Darlington |
| 23 | Wicks, Matthew J. | Peterborough United | Brighton & Hove Albion |

**Temporary transfers**

| 12 | Allsopp, Daniel | Manchester City | Bristol Rovers |
| 6 | Ashdown, Jamie L. | Reading | Bishop's Stortford |
| 27 | Austin, Kevin L. | Barnsley | Brentford |
| 30 | Baker, Steven R. | Middlesbrough | Hartlepool United |
| 21 | Ball, Alex I. | Bristol City | Clevedon Town |
| 6 | Bartholomew, Matthew P. | Hendon | Yeading |
| 13 | Black, Kingsley T. | Grimsby Town | Lincoln City |
| 25 | Blake, Robert J. | Bradford City | Nottingham Forest |
| 25 | Broomes, Marlon C. | Blackburn Rovers | Queens Park Rangers |
| 18 | Broughton, Drewe O. | Peterborough United | Dagenham & Redbridge |
| 20 | Buggie, Lee D. | Bury | Whitby Town |
| 13 | Butler, Thomas A. | Sunderland | Darlington |
| 19 | Campbell, Stuart P. | Leicester City | Grimsby Town |
| 11 | Caton, Sean T. | Heybridge Swifts | Barking |
| 27 | Clarke, Matthew P. | Halifax Town | Frickley Athletic |
| 20 | Connell, Lee A. | Bury | Whitby Town |
| 23 | Cooke, Terence J. | Manchester City | Sheffield Wednesday |
| 21 | Cowley, Alan D. | Runcorn | Trafford |
| 18 | Cramman, Kenneth W. | Boston United | Farnborough Town |
| 18 | Crowe, Jason W.R. | Portsmouth | Brentford |
| 20 | Cummings, Warren | Chelsea | AFC Bournemouth |
| 6 | D'Arcy, Ross | Barnet | Dover Athletic |
| 13 | Deakin, John | Worcester City | Evesham United |
| 12 | De Bilde, Gilles R.G. | Sheffield Wednesday | Aston Villa |
| 26 | Defoe, Jermaine C. | West Ham United | AFC Bournemouth |
| 6 | Denny, Philip M. | Bradford Park Avenue | Bamber Bridge |
| 18 | De Souza, Juan M. | Boston United | Farnborough Town |
| 20 | Druce, Mark A. | Woking | Oxford City |
| 10 | Dryden, Richard A. | Southampton | Northampton Town |
| 6 | Duerden, Ian C. | Doncaster Rovers | Kingstonian |

|  | | |
|---|---|---|
| 4 Durkan, Kieron J. | Macclesfield Town | York City |
| 13 Evers, Sean A. | Reading | St Johnstone |
| 18 Fenton, Nicholas L. | Manchester City | Notts County |
| 16 Fitzgerald, Scott B. | Millwall | Colchester United |
| 30 Fortune, Jonathan J. | Charlton Athletic | Mansfield Town |
| 30 French, Daniel J. | Peterborough United | Boston United |
| 16 Garcia, Richard | West Ham United | Leyton Orient |
| 27 Granville, Daniel P. | Manchester City | Norwich City |
| 6 Gray, Wayne W. | Wimbledon | Port Vale |
| 13 Griffin, Charles J. | Swindon Town | Woking |
| 25 Hamilton, Derrik V. | Newcastle United | Tranmere Rovers |
| 20 Harley, Jonathan | Chelsea | Wimbledon |
| 4 Harvey, Lee | St Albans City | Enfield |
| 3 Hasell, James | Stevenage Borough | Harlow Town |
| 19 Haworth, Robert J. | Dagenham & Redbridge | Sutton United |
| 2 Hay, Alexander N. | Tranmere Rovers | Altrincham |
| 27 Hicks, Graham | Rochdale | Chorley |
| 17 Holligan, Gavin V. | West Ham United | Exeter City |
| 26 Holt, Grant | Halifax Town | Workington |
| 23 Ince, Clayton | Crewe Alexandra | Dundee |
| 6 Jones, Daniel | Enfield | St Albans City |
| 30 Keeler, Justin J. | AFC Bournemouth | Dorchester Town |
| 17 Kennedy, Jon | Sunderland | Blackpool |
| 13 Kippe, Frode | Liverpool | Stoke City |
| 7 Kozluk, Robert | Sheffield United | Huddersfield Town |
| 23 Lee, Alan D. | Burnley | Rotherham United |
| 20 Lee, Christian | Gillingham | Rochdale |
| 10 Lumsdon, Christopher | Sunderland | Crewe Alexandra |
| 13 Maddison, Lee R. | Dundee United | Carlisle United |
| 6 Maley, Mark | Sunderland | Blackpool |
| 16 Mardon, Paul J. | West Bromwich Albion | Wrexham |
| 20 Martin, Jae A. | Woking | Sutton United |
| 27 Mawson, Craig | Burnley | Lincoln City |
| 8 Maybury, Alan P. | Leeds United | Crewe Alexandra |
| 17 McCann, Grant S. | West Ham United | Cheltenham Town |
| 23 McConnell, Barry | Exeter City | Weston-Super-Mare |
| 27 McKinlay, William | Blackburn Rovers | Leicester City |
| 17 Meijer, Erik | Liverpool | Preston North End |
| 20 Miller, Alan J. | Blackburn Rovers | Coventry City |
| 19 Morris, Elliott J. | West Bromwich Albion | Doncaster Rovers |
| 12 Morrison, Andrew C. | Manchester City | Crystal Palace |
| 20 Mounty, Carl T. | Swansea City | Waterford |
| 24 Murphy, Peter | Blackburn Rovers | Halifax Town |
| 20 Murray, Matthew W. | Wolverhampton Wanderers | Kingstonian |
| 21 Naylor, Dominic J. | Dagenham & Redbridge | Basingstoke Town |
| 5 Nicholls, Mark | Chelsea | Colchester United |
| 31 Parker, Scott M. | Charlton Athletic | Norwich City |
| 11 Parkin, Sam | Chelsea | Millwall |
| 23 Parnaby, Stuart | Middlesbrough | Halifax Town |
| 14 Peacock, Darren | Blackburn Rovers | Wolverhampton Wanderers |
| 27 Prindiville, Steven A. | Nuneaton Borough | Solihull Borough |
| 2 Rachel, Adam | Blackpool | Northwich Victoria |
| 28 Read, David | Stafford Rangers | Bilston Town |
| 6 Reid, Brian R. | Dunfermline Athletic | Blackpool |
| 20 Riza, Omer K. | West Ham United | Barnet |
| 10 Robinson, Paul D. | Wimbledon | Burnley |
| 3 Rodrigues, Daniel F. | Southampton | Bristol City |
| 6 Rogers, David R. | Ayr United | Peterborough United |
| 3 Savic, Sinisa | Barnsley | Scarborough |
| 12 Scott, Keith | Reading | Colchester United |
| 5 Slater, Carl D. | Burton Albion | Rocester |

| | | |
|---|---|---|
| 20 Smith, Philip A. | Millwall | Walton & Hersham |
| 6 Souter, Ryan | Bury | AFC Newport |
| 20 Staunton, Stephen | Liverpool | Crystal Palace |
| 2 Taaffe, Steven L. | Stoke City | Northwich Victoria |
| 19 Tarrant, Neil K. | Aston Villa | York City |
| 6 Tod, Andrew | Dunfermline Athletic | Stockport County |
| 20 Tunnicliffe, Andrew J. | Manchester City | Macclesfield Town |
| 5 Turner, Michael C. | Barnsley | Doncaster Rovers |
| 12 Vanninen, Jukka | Exeter City | Bashley |
| 17 Wainwright, Neil | Sunderland | Halifax Town |
| 6 Whittingham, Guy | Portsmouth | Oxford United |
| 23 Wilmot, Richard | Hitchin Town | Hendon |
| 26 Woodward, Andrew | Sheffield United | Scunthorpe United |
| 20 Yeoman, Daniel | Farnborough Town | Northwood |

### November 2000

| | | |
|---|---|---|
| 24 Bent, Marcus N. | Sheffield United | Blackburn Rovers |
| 30 Brumwell, Phillip | Hull City | Darlington |
| 23 Collins, Darren | Rushden & Diamonds | Kettering Town |
| 10 Edwards, Robert | Huddersfield Town | Chesterfield |
| 10 Fenton, Nicholas L. | Manchester City | Notts County |
| 10 Ferdinand, Rio G. | West Ham United | Leeds United |
| 10 Fish, Mark A. | Bolton Wanderers | Charlton Athletic |
| 7 Friedel, Bradley H. | Liverpool | Blackburn Rovers |
| 10 Hawthorne, Mark D. | Slough Town | Crawley Town |
| 10 Lee, Alan D. | Burnley | Rotherham United |
| 24 McKinlay, William | Blackburn Rovers | Bradford City |
| 20 Moore, Ian R. | Stockport County | Burnley |
| 16 Morgan, John R. | Enfield | Stevenage Borough |
| 28 Notman, Alexander M. | Manchester United | Norwich City |
| 24 Nower, Benjamin E. | Kings Lynn | AFC Sudbury |
| 10 Read, David | Stafford Rangers | Bilston Town |
| 24 Richardson, Stephen J. | Basingstoke Town | Salisbury City |
| 17 Samuels, Anthony | St Albans City | Boreham Wood |
| 10 Smith, Jason J. | Stafford Rangers | Bilston Town |
| 29 Song, Bahanag R. | Liverpool | West Ham United |
| 17 Thompson, Paul S. | Devizes Town | Mangotsfield United |
| 21 Weston, Rhys D. | Arsenal | Cardiff City |
| 17 Wraight, Gary P. | Stevenage Borough | St Albans City |

### Temporary transfers

| | | |
|---|---|---|
| 4 Adebowale, Andrew | St Albans City | Berkhamsted Town |
| 22 Allsopp, Daniel | Manchester City | Notts County |
| 10 Andrews, Keith J. | Wolverhampton Wanderers | Oxford United |
| 17 Aspinall, Brendan J. | Hyde United | Ossett Town |
| 28 All, Alex | Bristol City | Clevedon Town |
| 3 Banger, Nicholas L. | Dundee | Scunthorpe United |
| 7 Bartholomew, Matthew | Hendon | Yeading |
| 30 Bossu, Bertrand | Barnet | Hayes |
| 30 Bower, Mark | Bradford City | York City |
| 10 Boyce, Robert A. | Wealdstone | Boreham Wood |
| 27 Bradshaw, Mark | Halifax Town | Southport |
| 13 Brennan, Karl A. | Nuneaton Borough | Redditch United |
| 24 Breslan, Geoffrey F. | Exeter City | Tamworth |
| 20 Broughton, Drewe O. | Peterborough United | Dagenham & Redbridge |
| 10 Brown, John K. | Barnsley | Oxford United |
| 17 Butler, Paul J. | Sunderland | Wolverhampton Wanderers |
| 13 Butler, Thomas | Sunderland | Darlington |
| 18 Butterfield, John P. | Chesham United | Dulwich Hamlet |
| 30 Caig, Antony | Blackpool | Charlton Athletic |
| 17 Campbell, James R. | Peterborough United | Spalding United |
| 30 Carr, Darren J. | Brighton & Hove Albion | Rotherham United |

|  | | |
|---|---|---|
| 10 Caton, Sean T. | Heybridge Swifts | Chelmsford City |
| 24 Clare, Daryl A. | Grimsby Town | Northampton Town |
| 9 Conlon, Barry J. | York City | Colchester United |
| 9 Connor, Paul | Stoke City | Cambridge United |
| 24 Cooper, Michael E.C. | Exeter City | Weston-Super-Mare |
| 15 Cowley, Alan D. | Runcorn | Trafford |
| 20 Cummings, Warren | Chelsea | AFC Bournemouth |
| 8 Darcy, Ross | Barnet | Dover Athletic |
| 11 Deakin, John | Worcester City | Evesham United |
| 26 Defoe, Jermaine C. | West Ham United | AFC Bournemouth |
| 7 Denny, Philip M. | Bradford Park Avenue | Bamber Bridge |
| 23 De Souza, Juan M. | Boston United | Farnborough Town |
| 24 Drewett, Gary P. | Kingstonian | Woking |
| 18 Druce, Mark A. | Woking | Oxford City |
| 24 Dryden, Richard A. | Southampton | Swindon Town |
| 22 Dudgeon, James F. | Barnsley | Lincoln City |
| 14 Edghill, Richard A. | Manchester City | Birmingham City |
| 17 Fredgaard, Carsten | Sunderland | Bolton Wanderers |
| 1 French, Daniel J. | Peterborough United | Boston United |
| 9 Galloway, Michael A. | Chesterfield | Carlisle United |
| 8 Garcia, Richard | West Ham United | Leyton Orient |
| 10 Glennon, Matthew | Bolton Wanderers | Carlisle United |
| 10 Gray, Simon R. | Wivenhoe Town | Witham Town |
| 9 Gudmundsson, Johann B. | Watford | Cambridge United |
| 16 Hann, Matthew | Peterborough United | Bishop's Stortford |
| 24 Hannigan, Al J. | St Albans City | Hayes |
| 10 Harney, Michael | Welling United | Bromley |
| 4 Harvey, Lee | St Albans City | Enfield |
| 3 Hasell, James | Stevenage Borough | Harlow Town |
| 10 Hawe, Steven J. | Blackburn Rovers | Halifax Town |
| 1 Hay, Alexander N. | Tranmere Rovers | Altrincham |
| 3 Henry, Anthony F. | Lincoln City | Northwich Victoria |
| 23 Hicks, Graham | Rochdale | Chorley |
| 10 Holbrook, Adam P. | Portsmouth | Salisbury City |
| 23 Holt, Grant | Halifax Town | Workington |
| 24 Huckerby, Scott | Telford United | Tamworth |
| 30 Hutchings, Carl E. | Bristol City | Exeter City |
| 15 Inman, Niall E. | Peterborough United | Kettering Town |
| 10 Iwellumo, Chris | Stoke City | York City |
| 7 Jobson, Richard I. | Manchester City | Watford |
| 4 Jones, Daniel | Enfield | St Albans City |
| 24 Kadi, Junior | Kingstonian | Woking |
| 14 Kippe, Frode | Liverpool | Stoke City |
| 9 Kozluk, Robert | Sheffield United | Huddersfield Town |
| 1 Kyle, Kevin | Sunderland | Darlington |
| 10 Lumsdon, Christopher | Sunderland | Crewe Alexandra |
| 4 Maddison, Neil S. | Middlesbrough | Barnsley |
| 24 Maley, Mark | Sunderland | Northampton Town |
| 18 Mason, Andrew | Leigh RMI | Leek Town |
| 24 McAreavey, Paul | Swindon Town | Kilkenny City |
| 26 McCann, Grant S. | West Ham United | Cheltenham Town |
| 17 McCann, Peter | Barnet | Folkestone |
| 27 Meechan, Alexander T. | Bristol City | Yeovil Town |
| 20 Meijer, Erik | Liverpool | Preston North End |
| 23 Miller, Alan J. | Blackburn Rovers | Coventry City |
| 20 Morris, Elliott | West Bromwich Albion | Doncaster Rovers |
| 2 Mumford, Andrew O. | Swansea City | Haverfordwest |
| 28 Myhre, Thomas | Everton | Tranmere Rovers |
| 22 Newton, Adam L. | West Ham United | Notts County |
| 10 O'Reilly, Alexander | West Ham United | Wigan Athletic |

| 24 | Packham, William J. | Brighton & Hove Albion | Bognor Regis Town |
| 30 | Parker, Scott M. | Charlton Athletic | Norwich City |
| 24 | Parkin, Sam | Chelsea | Wycombe Wanderers |
| 23 | Parnaby, Stuart | Middlesbrough | Halifax Town |
| 17 | Patton, Aaron | Slough Town | Hemel Hempstead Town |
| 3 | Peschisolido, Paulo P. | Fulham | Queens Park Rangers |
| 18 | Pope, Steven A. | Kidderminster Harriers | Moor Green |
| 24 | Priestley, Philip A. | Rochdale | Scarborough |
| 24 | Prindiville, Steven A. | Nuneaton Borough | Solihull Borough |
| 1 | Rapley, Kevin J. | Notts County | Exeter City |
| 3 | Redmile, Matthew I. | Notts County | Shrewsbury Town |
| 7 | Ripley, Stuart E. | Southampton | Barnsley |
| 27 | Riza, Omer K. | West Ham United | Barnet |
| 10 | Roberts, Aaron | Basingstoke Town | Leatherhead |
| 10 | Roberts, Darren A. | Exeter City | Barrow |
| 4 | Robinson, Paul D. | Wimbledon | Burnley |
| 17 | Simpson, Phillip M. | Slough Town | Boreham Wood |
| 30 | Smith, Andrew W. | Sheffield United | Bury |
| 9 | Smith, Peter E. | Exeter City | Cambridge City |
| 20 | Smith, Philip A. | Millwall | Walton & Hersham |
| 13 | Speakman, Robert | Exeter City | Tiverton Town |
| 19 | Tarrant, Neil K. | Aston Villa | York City |
| 3 | Tate, Christopher D. | Scarborough | Leyton Orient |
| 17 | Taylor, Mark J. | Barnet | Chelmsford City |
| 24 | Thomas, James A. | Blackburn Rovers | Sheffield United |
| 3 | Trees, Robert V. | Bristol Rovers | Leigh RMI |
| 8 | Turner, Andrew P. | Rotherham United | Boston United |
| 5 | Turner, Michael | Barnsley | Doncaster Rovers |
| 10 | Underwood, Steven | Halifax Town | Harrogate Town |
| 13 | Wainwright, Neil | Sunderland | Halifax Town |
| 10 | Westcott, John P.J. | Sutton United | Langney Sports |
| 23 | Whitbread, Adrian R. | Portsmouth | Luton Town |
| 30 | Wolf, Danny | Bishop's Stortford | Leyton Pennant |
| 10 | Woodman, Andrew J. | Brentford | Colchester United |
| 24 | Worrell, David | Dundee United | Plymouth Argyle |

**December 2000**

| 15 | Abbey, Zema | Cambridge United | Norwich City |
| 21 | Allsopp, Daniel | Manchester City | Notts County |
| 8 | Armstrong, Alun | Middlesbrough | Ipswich Town |
| 1 | Barrett, Adam N. | Plymouth Argyle | Mansfield Town |
| 15 | Berg, Henning | Manchester United | Blackburn Rovers |
| 23 | Betts, Simon R. | Scarborough | Yeovil Town |
| 21 | Camara, Aboubacar S. | Liverpool | West Ham United |
| 1 | Carsley, Lee K. | Blackburn Rovers | Coventry City |
| 1 | Cooke, Andrew R. | Burnley | Stoke City |
| 18 | Gordon, Kenyatta G. | Lincoln City | Cardiff City |
| 1 | Hatswell, Wayne | Forest Green Rovers | Oxford United |
| 1 | Hockton, Danny J. | Stevenage Borough | Dover Athletic |
| 29 | Huckerby, Darren C. | Leeds United | Manchester City |
| 13 | Jones, Matthew G. | Leeds United | Leicester City |
| 22 | Kendall, Lee M. | Crystal Palace | Cardiff City |
| 15 | Lilley, Derek | Oxford United | Dundee United |
| 1 | McGlinchey, Brian K. | Gillingham | Plymouth Argyle |
| 15 | Mills, Jonathan P. | Oxford United | Southampton |
| 1 | Molenaar, Robert | Leeds United | Bradford City |
| 20 | Moses, Adrian P. | Barnsley | Huddersfield Town |
| 13 | Ngonge, Felix M. | Watford | Queens Park Rangers |
| 20 | Reina, Enrique I. | Ramsgate | Folkestone Invicta |
| 1 | Sjolund, Henrik D. | West Ham United | Liverpool |
| 7 | Staunton, Stephen | Liverpool | Aston Villa |

| 14 Vernazza, Paolo | Arsenal | Watford |
| 16 Wardley, Shane | Cambridge City | Southend United |

**Temporary transfers**

| 11 Andrews, Keith J. | Wolverhampton Wanderers | Oxford United |
| 15 Barrett, Graham | Arsenal | Bristol Rovers |
| 8 Birmingham, David P. | Portsmouth | Bognor Regis Town |
| 15 Blackford, Gary | Margate | Dulwich Hamlet |
| 29 Black, Michael J. | Tranmere Rovers | Southend United |
| 29 Blatsis, Con | Derby County | Sheffield Wednesday |
| 15 Brennan, Karl A. | Nuneaton Borough | Redditch United |
| 24 Breslan, Geoff F. | Exeter City | Tamworth |
| 15 Broughton, Drewe O. | Peterborough United | Stevenage Borough |
| 29 Burley, Adam G. | Sheffield United | Burton Albion |
| 3 Caig, Antony | Blackpool | Charlton Athletic |
| 17 Campbell, James R. | Peterborough United | Spalding United |
| 12 Caton, Sean T. | Heybridge Swifts | Chelmsford City |
| 8 Charles, Anthony D. | Crewe Alexandra | Hyde United |
| 22 Chilvers, Liam C. | Arsenal | Northampton Town |
| 30 Clare, Daryl A. | Grimsby Town | Cheltenham Town |
| 10 Conlon, Barry J. | York City | Colchester United |
| 6 Connor, Paul | Stoke City | Cambridge United |
| 15 Cooke, Terence J. | Manchester City | Sheffield Wednesday |
| 15 Cort, Leon T.A. | Millwall | Forest Green Rovers |
| 29 Craker, Lewis | Walton & Hersham | Maidenhead United |
| 26 Crooks, Lee R. | Manchester City | Northampton Town |
| 20 Cummings, Warren | Chelsea | AFC Bournemouth |
| 15 Cutler, Neil A. | Aston Villa | Oxford United |
| 15 Davies, Allan A. | Burton Albion | Worcester City |
| 14 Day, Christopher N. | Watford | Lincoln City |
| 27 Defoe, Jermaine C. | West Ham United | AFC Bournemouth |
| 22 Doherty, Gerard | Derby County | Ilkeston Town |
| 25 Dryden, Richard A. | Southampton | Swindon Town |
| 9 Duckett, Mark | Stevenage Borough | Aylesbury United |
| 14 Dudfield, Lawrie G. | Leicester City | Chesterfield |
| 21 Dudgeon, James F. | Barnsley | Lincoln City |
| 15 Evans, Lee | Stockport County | Radcliffe Borough |
| 29 Ferguson, Barry | Coventry City | Northampton Town |
| 8 Finney, Stephen K. | Chester City | Altrincham |
| 1 Forrester, Scott | Sutton United | Dulwich Hamlet |
| 1 Fredgaard, Carsten | Sunderland | Bolton Wanderers |
| 4 Galloway, Michael A. | Chesterfield | Carlisle United |
| 1 Gillespie, Keith R. | Blackburn Rovers | Wigan Athletic |
| 1 Grant, Anthony J. | Manchester City | West Bromwich Albion |
| 9 Gray, Simon R. | Wivenhoe Town | Witham Town |
| 7 Greatorex, Mark | Margate | Dartford |
| 22 Haley, Grant R. | Peterborough United | Bedford Town |
| 15 Hamsher, John J. | Rushden & Diamonds | Dagenham & Redbridge |
| 15 Harney, Michael | Welling United | Bromley |
| 15 Harper, James A.J. | Arsenal | Cardiff City |
| 29 Healy, David J. | Manchester United | Preston North End |
| 15 Hendry, Edward C.J. | Coventry City | Bolton Wanderers |
| 16 Hibbins, John J. | Worksop Town | Lincoln United |
| 24 Hicks, Graham | Rochdale | Chorley |
| 23 Holt, Grant | Halifax Town | Workington |
| 1 Inglethorpe, Alex M. | Exeter City | Canvey Island |
| 15 Inman, Niall E. | Peterborough United | Kettering Town |
| 10 Iwellumo, Chris | Stoke City | York City |
| 15 Jenkins, Stephen R. | Huddersfield Town | Birmingham City |
| 28 Jobson, Richard I. | Manchester City | Tranmere Rovers |
| 27 Jones, Matthew N. | Shrewsbury Town | Southport |

| | | |
|---|---|---|
| 23 Kadi, Junior | Kingstonian | Woking |
| 31 Kelly, Gavin R. | Tottenham Hotspur | Kingstonian |
| 12 Kippe, Frode | Liverpool | Stoke City |
| 16 Landon, Richard J. | Altrincham | Droylsden |
| 15 Lindley, James E. | Notts County | Mansfield Town |
| 8 Ling, Martin | Leyton Orient | Purfleet |
| 1 Lisbie, Kevin A. | Charlton Athletic | Queens Park Rangers |
| 12 McDonald, Thomas | Southend United | Slough Town |
| 15 McMahon, David | Newcastle United | Darlington |
| 9 Nash, Carlo J. | Stockport County | Wolverhampton Wanderers |
| 8 Ndlovu, Peter | Birmingham City | Huddersfield Town |
| 15 Newell, Paul C. | Billericay Town | Hendon |
| 28 Newton, Adam L. | West Ham United | Notts County |
| 22 Norris, David M. | Bolton Wanderers | Boston United |
| 15 Osborn, Mark | Wycombe Wanderers | Carshalton Athletic |
| 24 Packham, William J. | Brighton & Hove Albion | Bognor Regis Town |
| 15 Palmer, Carlton L. | Coventry City | Watford |
| 21 Peake, Jason W. | Plymouth Argyle | Nuneaton Borough |
| 20 Pearce, Alexander G. | Chesterfield | Worksop Town |
| 22 Phillips, Lee P. | Plymouth Argyle | Weymouth |
| 18 Pope, Steven A. | Kidderminster Harriers | Moor Green |
| 22 Priestley, Philip A. | Rochdale | Scarborough |
| 3 Rapley, Kevin J. | Notts County | Exeter City |
| 21 Redmile, Matthew I. | Notts County | Shrewsbury Town |
| 16 Ricketts, Gary | Hinckley United | Hucknall Town |
| 13 Ripley, Stuart E. | Southampton | Barnsley |
| 12 Roberts, Aaron | Basingstoke Town | Leatherhead |
| 11 Roberts, Darren A. | Exeter City | Barrow |
| 12 Rogers, Kristian R. | Wrexham | Rushden & Diamonds |
| 8 Trainer, Philip A. | Crewe Alexandra | Hyde United |
| 6 Trees, Robert V. | Bristol Rovers | Leigh RMI |
| 12 Trought, Michael | Bristol Rovers | Clevedon Town |
| 5 Turner, Michael | Barnsley | Doncaster Rovers |
| 10 Underwood, Steven | Halifax Town | Harrogate Town |
| 8 Upson, Matthew J. | Arsenal | Nottingham Forest |
| 11 Westcott, John P.J. | Sutton United | Langney Sports |
| 24 Whitbread, Adrian R. | Portsmouth | Luton Town |
| 15 White, Ben | Gillingham | Dover Athletic |
| 15 Whitley, James | Manchester City | Swindon Town |
| 7 Wilkinson, Stephen J. | Kettering Town | Spalding United |
| 24 Winter, Steven D. | Basingstoke Town | Tiverton Town |
| 22 Wooding, Timothy D. | Boston United | Cambridge City |
| 10 Woodman, Andrew J. | Brentford | Colchester United |
| 22 Woodward, Andrew S. | Sheffield United | Scunthorpe United |

**January 2001**

| | | |
|---|---|---|
| 19 Appleton, Michael A. | Preston North End | West Bromwich Albion |
| 3 Barker, Richard I. | Macclesfield Town | Rotherham United |
| 15 Blundell, Gregg | Vauxhall Motors | Northwich Victoria |
| 31 Bradshaw, Darren S. | Rushden & Diamonds | Stevenage Borough |
| 22 Bramble, Tesfaye | Cambridge City | Southend United |
| 29 Brooker, Stephen M. | Watford | Port Vale |
| 31 Butler, Paul J. | Sunderland | Wolverhampton Wanderers |
| 9 Caig, Antony | Blackpool | Charlton Athletic |
| 18 Dailly, Christian E. | Blackburn Rovers | West Ham United |
| 25 De Bolla, Mark | Aston Villa | Charlton Athletic |
| 17 De Souza, Juan M. | Boston United | Farnborough Town |
| 19 Duerden, Ian C. | Doncaster Rovers | Kingstonian |
| 10 Flynn, Lee D. | Hayes | Barnet |
| 9 Forrester, Scott | Sutton United | Dulwich Hamlet |
| 19 Gower, Mark | Tottenham Hotspur | Barnet |

153

| 15 | Hamsher, John J. | Rushden & Diamonds | Stevenage Borough |
|---|---|---|---|
| 3 | Hasell, James | Stevenage Borough | Harlow Town |
| 19 | Hayward, Steve L. | Fulham | Barnsley |
| 3 | Healy, David J. | Manchester United | Preston North End |
| 22 | Heywood, Matthew S. | Burnley | Swindon Town |
| 5 | Hoult, Russell | Portsmouth | West Bromwich Albion |
| 12 | Johnson, David A. | Ipswich Town | Nottingham Forest |
| 25 | Kadi, Junior | Kingstonian | Woking |
| 12 | Keller, Marc | West Ham United | Blackburn Rovers |
| 5 | Lane, Christopher | Hereford United | Southport |
| 25 | Maddison, Lee R. | Dundee United | Carlisle United |
| 12 | McGleish, Scott | Barnet | Colchester United |
| 4 | Mitchell, Richard D. | Nuneaton Borough | Norwich Victoria |
| 12 | Nash, Carlo J. | Stockport County | Manchester City |
| 26 | Nwadike, Chukweumeka | Kings Lynn | Ilkeston Town |
| 5 | Perkins, Christopher P. | Chesterfield | Lincoln City |
| 30 | Piper, Christopher C. | St Albans City | Farnborough Town |
| 12 | Quinn, Robert J. | Brentford | Oxford United |
| 19 | Rankin, Isaiah | Bradford City | Barnsley |
| 12 | Redmile, Matthew I. | Notts County | Shrewsbury Town |
| 12 | Reid, Brian R. | Dunfermline Athletic | Blackpool |
| 19 | Richards, Justin | West Bromwich Albion | Bristol Rovers |
| 2 | Rowe, Rodney C. | Gillingham | Hull City |
| 12 | Scott, Andrew | Brentford | Oxford United |
| 4 | Shields, Dene | Raith Rovers | Sunderland |
| 19 | Sturridge, Dean | Derby County | Leicester City |
| 4 | Summerbee, Nicholas J. | Sunderland | Bolton Wanderers |
| 25 | Worrell, David | Dundee United | Plymouth Argyle |

**Temporary transfers**

| 19 | Alford, Carl P. | Doncaster Rovers | Kettering Town |
|---|---|---|---|
| 12 | Benali, Francis V. | Southampton | Nottingham Forest |
| 12 | Beresford, Marlon | Middlesbrough | Sheffield Wednesday |
| 26 | Blatsis, Con | Derby County | Sheffield Wednesday |
| 30 | Booth, Andrew D. | Sheffield Wednesday | Tottenham Hotspur |
| 19 | Bramble, Tesfaye | Cambridge City | Southend United |
| 12 | Brennan, Karl A. | Nuneaton Borough | Hinckley United |
| 5 | Brooker, Stephen M.L. | Watford | Port Vale |
| 22 | Broughton, Drewe O. | Peterborough United | Kidderminster Harriers |
| 2 | Caig, Antony | Blackpool | Charlton Athletic |
| 26 | Canoville, Lee | Arsenal | Northampton Town |
| 9 | Carr, Darren J. | Brighton & Hove Albion | Lincoln City |
| 25 | Cartwright, James P. | Telford United | Stafford Rangers |
| 5 | Chambers, Leroy D. | Altrincham | Frickley Athletic |
| 6 | Charles, Anthony D. | Crewe Alexandra | Hyde United |
| 26 | Chudy, Lee | Basingstoke Town | Burnham |
| 26 | Coleman, Danny | Farnborough Town | Chalfont St Peter |
| 7 | Connor, Paul | Stoke City | Cambridge United |
| 27 | Cooper, Kevin | Chertsey Town | Molesey |
| 16 | Cort, Leon | Millwall | Forest Green Rovers |
| 3 | Crooks, Lee R. | Manchester City | Northampton Town |
| 21 | Cutler, Neil | Aston Villa | Oxford United |
| 12 | Davies, Allan | Burton Albion | Worcester City |
| 16 | Day, Christopher N. | Watford | Lincoln City |
| 20 | Denny, Philip M. | Bradford Park Avenue | Guiseley |
| 5 | De Souza, Juan M. | Boston United | Farnborough Town |
| 24 | Doherty, Gerard | Derby County | Ilkeston Town |
| 6 | Duckett, Mark | Stevenage Borough | Aylesbury United |
| 4 | Dudfield, Lawrie G. | Leicester City | Chesterfield |
| 9 | Ebanks, Michael | Dulwich Hamlet | Croydon Athletic |
| 26 | Foster, Martin | Doncaster Rovers | Forest Green Rovers |

| | | |
|---|---|---|
| 12 Grayson, Simon N. | Blackburn Rovers | Stockport County |
| 11 Greatorex, Mark | Margate | Dartford |
| 10 Hamilton, Derrik V. | Newcastle United | Tranmere Rovers |
| 12 Harney, Michael | Welling United | Bromley |
| 5 Henry, Anthony F. | Lincoln City | Northwich Victoria |
| 20 Hibbins, John J. | Worksop Town | Lincoln United |
| 5 Hodson, Matthew J. | Hayes | Hampton & Richmond Borough |
| 23 Holsgrove, Lee | Aldershot Town | Boreham Wood |
| 10 Iwelumo, Chris | Stoke City | York City |
| 30 Jobson, Richard I. | Manchester City | Tranmere Rovers |
| 26 Kennerdale, Nick | Eastwood Town | Nuneaton Borough |
| 26 Kirby, Ryan | Stevenage Borough | Aldershot Town |
| 2 Kotylo, Krystof J. | Nuneaton Borough | Eastwood Town |
| 26 Kyle, Kevin A. | Sunderland | Rochdale |
| 17 Landon, Richard J. | Altrincham | Droylsden |
| 19 Lavin, Gerard | Bristol City | Wycombe Wanderers |
| 27 Lenagh, Steven M. | Kettering Town | Kings Lynn |
| 30 Lewis, Karl J. | Gillingham | Leicester City |
| 13 Lightbourne, Kyle L. | Stoke City | Swindon Town |
| 9 Ling, Martin | Leyton Orient | Purfleet |
| 25 Logan, Richard J. | Ipswich Town | Cambridge United |
| 30 Marriott, Andrew | Sunderland | Wigan Athletic |
| 5 Mason, Andrew | Leigh RMI | Chorley |
| 22 McAnespie, Kieran | Fulham | Heart of Midlothian |
| 26 McKenzie, Christy G. | Tamworth | Sutton Coldfield Town |
| 12 Monk, Garry A. | Southampton | Oxford United |
| 26 Morley, David T. | Southend United | Carlisle United |
| 5 Mounty, Carl T. | Swansea City | Bangor |
| 5 Murphy, Brendan F. | Kidderminster Harriers | Redditch United |
| 18 Murray, Jade A. | Leyton Orient | Chelmsford City |
| 5 Mutton, Thomas J. | Swansea City | Merthyr Tydfil |
| 4 Nancekivell, Kevin W.J. | Plymouth Argyle | Tiverton Town |
| 20 Newell, Paul C. | Billericay Town | Grays Athletic |
| 20 Newton, Howard | Hampton & Richmond Borough | Epsom & Ewell |
| 21 Norris, David M. | Bolton Wanderers | Boston United |
| 17 O'Brien, Michael G. | Torquay United | Southport |
| 16 Osborn, Mark | Wycombe Wanderers | Carshalton Athletic |
| 20 Parkin, Sam | Chelsea | Wycombe Wanderers |
| 17 Peake, Jason W. | Plymouth Argyle | Nuneaton Borough |
| 19 Peschisolido, Paolo P. | Fulham | Sheffield United |
| 5 Phillips, Gareth R. | Swansea City | Merthyr Tydfil |
| 22 Phillips, Lee P. | Plymouth Argyle | Weymouth |
| 5 Piearce, Steven | Hereford United | Halesowen Town |
| 19 Pinnock, James E. | Gillingham | Chesham United |
| 20 Pluck, Lee K. | Barnet | Grays Athletic |
| 5 Pope, Steven A. | Kidderminster Harriers | Aberystwyth Town |
| 10 Quinn, Wayne R. | Sheffield United | Newcastle United |
| 27 Reddy, Michael | Sunderland | Swindon Town |
| 5 Robinson, Ian B. | Hednesford Town | Northwich Victoria |
| 11 Ross, Neil J. | Stockport County | Radcliffe Borough |
| 27 Rowland, Keith | Queens Park Rangers | Luton Town |
| 19 Sharpling, Christopher B. | Crystal Palace | Woking |
| 18 Simpson, Phillip M. | Slough Town | Boreham Wood |
| 1 Smith, Andrew W. | Sheffield United | Bury |
| 26 Smith, Darren K. | Gravesend & Northfleet | Aveley |
| 30 Strevens, Benjamin J. | Barnet | St Albans City |
| 4 Summerbee, Nicholas J. | Sunderland | Bolton Wanderers |
| 23 Thompson, Glyn W. | Fulham | Shrewsbury Town |

155

| | | |
|---|---|---|
| 25 Town, David | Rushden & Diamonds | Hayes |
| 6 Trainer, Philip A. | Crewe Alexandra | Hyde United |
| 10 Trought, Michael | Bristol Rovers | Clevedon Town |
| 16 Wakefield, David | Havant & Waterlooville | Salisbury City |
| 5 Walshe, Liam R. | Burton Albion | Shepshed Dynamo |
| 12 Welsby, Kevin J. | Crewe Alexandra | Leek Town |
| 12 Westcott, John P.J. | Sutton United | Langney Sports |
| 12 Wilkie, Lee | Dundee | Plymouth Argyle |
| 23 Williams, Daniel I.L. | Wrexham | Doncaster Rovers |
| 23 Winter, Steven D. | Basingstoke Town | Tiverton Town |
| 4 Wolf, Danny | Bishop's Stortford | Aveley |
| 23 Wooding, Timothy D. | Boston United | Cambridge City |
| 2 Woodward, Andrew | Sheffield United | Scunthorpe United |
| 18 Wright, Thomas J. | Manchester City | Bolton Wanderers |

**February 2001**

| | | |
|---|---|---|
| 16 Beagrie, Peter S. | Bradford City | Wigan Athletic |
| 9 Berkovic, Eyal | Celtic | Blackburn Rovers |
| 16 Brannan, Gerald D. | Motherwell | Wigan Athletic |
| 15 Brightwell, David J. | Hull City | Darlington |
| 2 Brooker, Stephen M.L. | Watford | Port Vale |
| 21 Broughton, Drewe O. | Peterborough United | Kidderminster Harriers |
| 9 Clifford, Mark | Ilkeston Town | Boston United |
| 13 Ellison, Kevin | Altrincham | Leicester City |
| 19 Ford, Mark S. | Torquay United | Darlington |
| 23 Harper, James | Arsenal | Reading |
| 15 Harper, Steven J. | Hull City | Darlington |
| 8 Hartson, John | Wimbledon | Coventry City |
| 14 Haydon, Nicky | Heybridge Swifts | Chelmsford City |
| 12 Hendry, Edward C.J. | Coventry City | Bolton Wanderers |
| 9 Hughes, Robert D. | Shrewsbury Town | Cardiff City |
| 16 Hurst, Glynn | Ayr United | Stockport County |
| 9 Jones, Mark A. | Chesterfield | Raith Rovers |
| 22 Kennerdale, Nick | Eastwood Town | Nuneaton Borough |
| 16 Macdonald, Gary | Havant & Waterlooville | Peterborough United |
| 23 Marcelle, Clinton S. | Hull City | Darlington |
| 16 Mawson, Craig J. | Burnley | Halifax Town |
| 12 McIndoe, Michael | Hereford United | Yeovil Town |
| 2 Ndlovu, Peter | Birmingham City | Sheffield United |
| 21 Quinn, Wayne R. | Sheffield United | Newcastle United |
| 23 Rawle, Mark A. | Boston United | Southend United |
| 9 Ricketts, Gary | Hinckley United | Hucknall Town |
| 12 Robinson, Steven E. | Birmingham City | Swindon Town |
| 15 Roussel, Cedric | Coventry City | Wolverhampton Wanderers |
| 16 Sedgemore, Benjamin R. | Macclesfield Town | Lincoln City |
| 9 Shorey, Nicholas | Leyton Orient | Reading |
| 9 Talbot, Robert T. | Burscough | Morecambe |
| 23 Vincent, Jamie R. | Huddersfield Town | Portsmouth |
| 2 Woodhouse, Curtis | Sheffield United | Birmingham City |

**Temporary transfers**

| | | |
|---|---|---|
| 17 Abbott, Paul | Stevenage Borough | Arlessey Town |
| 17 Alford, Carl P. | Doncaster Rovers | Kettering Town |
| 15 Atherton, Peter | Bradford City | Birmingham City |
| 10 Barrett, Daniel T. | Chesterfield | Stafford Rangers |
| 8 Beall, Matthew J. | Leyton Orient | Dover Athletic |
| 12 Benali, Francis V. | Southampton | Nottingham Forest |
| 9 Bennett, Frank | Forest Green Rovers | Cinderford Town |
| 9 Berry, Trevor J. | Rotherham United | Scunthorpe United |
| 16 Betts, Robert | Coventry City | Plymouth Argyle |
| 16 Brennan, Karl A. | Nuneaton Borough | Hinckley United |
| 9 Carr, Darren J. | Brighton & Hove Albion | Carlisle United |

| | | |
|---|---|---|
| 3 Charles, Anthony D. | Crewe Alexandra | Hyde United |
| 8 Clarke, David L. | Dover Athletic | Chesham United |
| 9 Clark, Richard | Tamworth | Evesham United |
| 16 Collins, Simon J. | Macclesfield Town | Shrewsbury Town |
| 28 Cooper, Kevin | Chertsey Town | Molesey |
| 18 Cort, Leon | Millwall | Forest Green Rovers |
| 16 Cramb, Colin | Crewe Alexandra | Bury |
| 14 Davies, Allan | Burton Albion | Worcester City |
| 4 Day, Christopher N. | Watford | Lincoln City |
| 21 Denny, Philip M. | Bradford Park Avenue | Guiseley |
| 6 Derveld, Fernando | Norwich City | West Bromwich Albion |
| 23 Doherty, Gerard | Derby County | Ilkeston Town |
| 17 Duckett, Mark | Stevenage Borough | Arlessey Town |
| 8 Dudfield, Lawrie G. | Leicester City | Chesterfield |
| 23 Eaton, Jamie | Ilkeston Town | Eastwood Town |
| 9 Ebanks, Michael | Dulwich Hamlet | Croydon Athletic |
| 9 Fewings, Paul J. | Boston United | Kingstonian |
| 4 Forbes, Steven D. | Dagenham & Redbridge | Cambridge City |
| 28 Gittens, Jon | Nuneaton Borough | Dorchester Town |
| 24 Goodridge, Gregory St. C.R. | Bristol City | Cheltenham Town |
| 9 Grant, Gareth M. | Bradford City | Lincoln City |
| 15 Greatorex, Mark | Margate | Dartford |
| 28 Gritton, Martin | Plymouth Argyle | Yeovil Town |
| 2 Hann, Matthew | Peterborough United | Cambridge City |
| 23 Harney, Michael | Welling United | Ashford Town |
| 6 Hodson, Matthew J. | Hayes | Hampton & Richmond Borough |
| 26 Holt, Grant | Halifax Town | Barrow |
| 2 Ireland, Craig | Dundee | Notts County |
| 13 Iwelumo, Chris | Stoke City | Cheltenham Town |
| 21 James, Robert K. | Swansea City | Port Talbot |
| 9 Jefferson, Christopher | Worcester City | Bromsgrove Rovers |
| 8 Kell, Richard | Middlesbrough | Torquay United |
| 1 Kelly, Gavin R. | Tottenham Hotspur | Kingstonian |
| 16 King, Stuart S.E. | Preston North End | Queen of the South |
| 2 Kotylo, Krystof J. | Nuneaton Borough | Eastwood Town |
| 27 Lenagh, Steven M. | Kettering Town | Kings Lynn |
| 20 Lightbourne, Kyle L. | Stoke City | Cardiff City |
| 26 Lindley, James E. | Notts County | Gresley Rovers |
| 9 Matthews, Robert D. | Stockport County | Halifax Town |
| 8 McKeever, Mark A. | Sheffield Wednesday | Bristol Rovers |
| 1 Mensing, Simon R. | Wimbledon | Stenhousemuir |
| 9 Mike, Leon J. | Manchester City | Halifax Town |
| 11 Monk, Garry | Southampton | Oxford United |
| 23 Morris, Elliott J. | West Bromwich Albion | Bromsgrove Rovers |
| 21 Mumford, Andrew O. | Swansea City | Port Talbot |
| 5 Nancekivell, Kevin W.J. | Plymouth Argyle | Tiverton Town |
| 2 Newby, Jon P.R. | Liverpool | Bury |
| 20 Newell, Paul C. | Billericay Town | Grays Athletic |
| 20 Newton, Howard | Hampton & Richmond Borough | Epsom & Euell |
| 17 O'Brien, Michael G. | Torquay United | Southport |
| 17 Osborn, Mark | Wycombe Wanderers | Carshalton Athletic |
| 9 Ostendstad, Egil | Blackburn Rovers | Manchester City |
| 9 Owusu, Ansah O. | Wimbledon | Bristol Rovers |
| 16 Packham, William J. | Brighton & Hove Albion | Langney Sports |
| 13 Palmer, Carlton L. | Coventry City | Sheffield Wednesday |
| 14 Peake, Jason W. | Plymouth Argyle | Nuneaton Borough |
| 13 Pearce, Alexander G. | Chesterfield | Worksop Town |
| 18 Phillips, Lee P. | Plymouth Argyle | Weymouth |

157

| | | |
|---|---|---|
| 2 Piearce, Steven | Hereford United | Halesowen Town |
| 3 Pinamonte, Lorenzo | Brentford | Leyton Orient |
| 19 Pinnock, James | Gillingham | Chesham United |
| 2 Poland, Lee | Northwich Victoria | Leek Town |
| 27 Priestley, Philip A. | Rochdale | Chester City |
| 27 Reddy, Michael | Sunderland | Swindon Town |
| 9 Robinson, Gerard | Middlesbrough | Scarborough |
| 21 Robinson, Paul D. | Wimbledon | Dundee United |
| 2 Sharpe, Lee S. | Bradford City | Portsmouth |
| 16 Shittu, Daniel O. | Charlton Athletic | Blackpool |
| 23 Smith, Darren K. | Gravesend & Northfleet | Aveley |
| 16 Smith, Peter L. | Crewe Alexandra | Doncaster Rovers |
| 3 Soltvedt, Trond E. | Southampton | Sheffield Wednesday |
| 9 Steele, Paul | Yeovil Town | Woking |
| 16 Stoner, Craig J. | Portsmouth | Bognor Regis Town |
| 20 Taylor, Gareth K. | Manchester City | Burnley |
| 15 Taylor, Stuart J. | Arsenal | Peterborough United |
| 19 Thomas, Nathan | Barking | Grays Athletic |
| 9 Tiler, Carl | Charlton Athletic | Birmingham City |
| 3 Trainer, Philip A. | Crewe Alexandra | Hyde United |
| 16 Trundle, Lee C. | Rhyl | Wrexham |
| 9 Tyne, Thomas R. | Millwall | Fisher Athletic |
| 9 Walker, Richard M. | Aston Villa | Blackpool |
| 23 Walsh, David | Wrexham | Rhyl |
| 2 Walshe, Liam R. | Burton Albion | Shepshed Dynamo |
| 8 Wharton, Paul | Farsley Celtic | Bradford Park Avenue |
| 8 Whitbread, Adrian R. | Portsmouth | Reading |
| 27 Whitley, James | Manchester City | Northampton Town |
| 19 Wilkinson, Stephen J. | Kettering Town | Shepshed Dynamo |
| 24 Willmot, Richard | Hitchin Town | Metropolitan Police |
| 23 Winter, Steven D. | Basingstoke Town | Tiverton Town |

**March 2001**

| | | |
|---|---|---|
| 8 Asaba, Carl E. | Gillingham | Sheffield United |
| 16 Baldacchino, Ryan L. | Blackburn Rovers | Bolton Wanderers |
| 14 Basham, Michael | Barnet | York City |
| 16 Bignot, Marcus | Bristol Rovers | Queens Park Rangers |
| 22 Booth, Andrew D. | Sheffield Wednesday | Huddersfield Town |
| 15 Brass, Christopher P. | Burnley | York City |
| 16 Brennan, Karl A. | Nuneaton Borough | Hinckley United |
| 22 Carruthers, Martin G. | Southend United | Scunthorpe United |
| 9 Connor, Paul | Stoke City | Rochdale |
| 16 Cooper, Kevin L. | Stockport County | Wimbledon |
| 16 Cooper, Mark N. | Hednesford Town | Forest Green Rovers |
| 2 Crooks, Lee R. | Manchester City | Barnsley |
| 23 Dixon, Gary J. | Hitchin Town | Boreham Wood |
| 4 Drury, Adam J. | Peterborough United | Norwich City |
| 17 Easter, Jermaine M. | Wolverhampton Wanderers | Hartlepool United |
| 7 Elliott, Stuart T. | Darlington | Plymouth Argyle |
| 22 Epesse-Titi, Steeve | Wolverhampton Wanderers | Exeter City |
| 22 Evans, Michael J. | Bristol Rovers | Plymouth Argyle |
| 8 Evers, Sean A. | Reading | Plymouth Argyle |
| 22 Gall, Kevin A. | Newcastle United | Bristol Rovers |
| 8 Gayle, Marcus A. | Wimbledon | Glasgow Rangers |
| 23 Gilchrist, Philip A. | Leicester City | West Bromwich Albion |
| 16 Goma, Alain | Newcastle United | Fulham |
| 22 Greene, David M. | Cardiff City | Cambridge United |
| 20 Holt, Gary J. | Kilmarnock | Norwich City |
| 16 Hopkin, David | Bradford City | Crystal Palace |
| 22 Howard, Steven J. | Northampton Town | Luton Town |
| 31 Hoyle, Colin | Boston United | Burton Albion |

| | | |
|---|---|---|
| 19 Ipoua, Guy | Scunthorpe United | Gillingham |
| 1 Jackson, Kirk S.S. | Worksop Town | Darlington |
| 2 Jobson, Richard I. | Manchester City | Tranmere Rovers |
| 16 Kitson, David | Arlesey Town | Cambridge United |
| 22 Lee, Christian | Gillingham | Bristol Rovers |
| 16 Lewis, Karl J. | Gillingham | Leicester City |
| 7 Makin, Christopher | Sunderland | Ipswich Town |
| 13 Marriott, Andrew | Sunderland | Barnsley |
| 22 Marsh, Christopher J. | Walsall | Wycombe Wanderers |
| 21 Marshall, Lee | Norwich City | Leicester City |
| 22 Matthews, Lee J. | Leeds United | Bristol City |
| 21 Matthews, Robert D. | Stockport County | Hull City |
| 2 McCulloch, Lee | Motherwell | Wigan Athletic |
| 15 McKeever, Mark A. | Sheffield Wednesday | Bristol Rovers |
| 2 McMillan, Stephen | Motherwell | Wigan Athletic |
| 8 Mellon, Michael J. | Burnley | Tranmere Rovers |
| 22 Milligan, Jamie | Everton | Blackpool |
| 22 Newby, Jon P.R. | Liverpool | Bury |
| 31 Newell, Paul C. | Billericay Town | Grays Athletic |
| 28 O'Brien, Andrew J. | Bradford City | Newcastle United |
| 22 O'Reilly, Alexander | West Ham United | Bristol Rovers |
| 22 Osborn, Simon E. | Wolverhampton Wanderers | Tranmere Rovers |
| 22 Parkinson, Gary A. | Preston North End | Blackpool |
| 22 Prokas, Richard | Carlisle United | Cambridge United |
| 12 Simms, Gordon H. | Wolverhampton Wanderers | Hartlepool United |
| 1 Smith, Craig | Belper Town | Hinckley United |
| 22 Soltvedt, Trond E. | Southampton | Sheffield Wednesday |
| 1 Thomas, Geoffrey R. | Barnsley | Notts County |
| 22 Thomas, Martin R. | Swansea City | Brighton & Hove Albion |
| 9 Thomas, Nathan | Barking | Grays Athletic |
| 22 Thomson, Andrew | Gillingham | Queens Park Rangers |
| 14 Tiler, Carl | Charlton Athletic | Portsmouth |
| 28 Town, David | Rushden & Diamonds | Boston United |
| 15 Windass, Dean | Bradford City | Middlesbrough |
| 20 Wright, Thomas J. | Manchester City | Bolton Wanderers |

**Temporary transfers**

| | | |
|---|---|---|
| 9 Ashdown, Jamie L. | Reading | Gravesend & Northfleet |
| 22 Baptiste, Jairzinho R. | Luton Town | Hayes |
| 29 Barlow, Martin D. | Plymouth Argyle | Yeovil Town |
| 30 Barnes, Paul L. | Bury | Nuneaton Borough |
| 11 Barrett, Daniel | Chesterfield | Stafford Rangers |
| 18 Benali, Francis V. | Southampton | Nottingham Forest |
| 2 Bennetts, Scott | Farnborough Town | Boreham Wood |
| 13 Bernard, Olivier | Newcastle United | Darlington |
| 22 Birch, Gary S. | Walsall | Exeter City |
| 22 Boardman, Jonathan G. | Crystal Palace | Woking |
| 5 Bossu, Bertrand | Barnet | Rushden & Diamonds |
| 21 Brennan, James G. | Nottingham Forest | Huddersfield Town |
| 29 Bridgwater, David | Telford United | Bromsgrove Rovers |
| 21 Broad, Stephen | Chelsea | Southend United |
| 22 Brown, Wayne L. | Ipswich Town | Queens Park Rangers |
| 22 Bullock, Darren J. | Bury | Sheffield United |
| 22 Bunce, Nathan | Stevenage Borough | Hayes |
| 13 Calderwood, Colin | Nottingham Forest | Notts County |
| 9 Campbell, Andrew P. | Middlesbrough | Bolton Wanderers |
| 9 Carr, Darren J. | Brighton & Hove Albion | Carlisle United |
| 13 Carr, David | Solihull Borough | Paget Rangers |
| 30 Charles, Anthony D. | Crewe Alexandra | Stalybridge Celtic |
| 30 Chillingworth, Daniel T. | Cambridge United | Cambridge City |
| 21 Claridge, Stephen E. | Portsmouth | Millwall |

159

| |  | | |
|---|---|---|---|
| 20 | Clarke, Matthew J. | Bradford City | Bolton Wanderers |
| 2 | Clegg, George G. | Manchester United | Wycombe Wanderers |
| 28 | Cockrill, Dale | Cambridge United | Wisbech Town |
| 22 | Collins, Derek | Hibernian | Preston North End |
| 2 | Collins, James I. | Crewe Alexandra | Halesowen Town |
| 16 | Collins, Simon | Macclesfield Town | Shrewsbury Town |
| 11 | Collis, David J. | Charlton Athletic | Barnet |
| 21 | Connelly, Sean P. | Stockport County | Wolverhampton Wanderers |
| 2 | Cooper, Richard A. | Nottingham Forest | York City |
| 5 | Corbett, Andrew J. | Kidderminster Harriers | Redditch United |
| 13 | Cornwall, Lucas C.C. | Fulham | Grimsby Town |
| 29 | Cort, Leon T.A. | Millwall | Stevenage Borough |
| 22 | Cramb, Colin | Crewe Alexandra | Bury |
| 13 | Cresswell, Richard P.W. | Leicester City | Preston North End |
| 22 | Crowe, Seamus M.M. | Wolverhampton Wanderers | Hereford United |
| 16 | Cullen, David J. | Peterborough United | Carlisle United |
| 21 | Cummings, Warren | Chelsea | West Bromwich Albion |
| 22 | Dalglish, Paul | Norwich City | Wigan Athletic |
| 9 | Dawson, Kevin E. | Nottingham Forest | Barnet |
| 22 | Denny, Philip M. | Bradford Park Avenue | Guiseley |
| 22 | Dodd, Ashley M. | Manchester United | Port Vale |
| 22 | Feeney, Warren J. | Leeds United | AFC Bournemouth |
| 30 | Fewings, Paul J. | Boston United | Farnborough Town |
| 2 | Field, Lewis | Stevenage Borough | Hemel Hempstead Town |
| 16 | Fletcher, Gary | Northwich Victoria | Hull City |
| 5 | Fontenelle, Anthony | Arlesey Town | Harrow Borough |
| 29 | Ford, James A. | AFC Bournemouth | Dorchester Town |
| 23 | Forinton, Howard L. | Peterborough United | Yeovil Town |
| 1 | Foster, Martin | Doncaster Rovers | Forest Green Rovers |
| 2 | French, Daniel J. | Peterborough United | Bedford Town |
| 16 | Gamble, Joseph F. | Reading | Crawley Town |
| 22 | Gilchrist, Philip A. | Leicester City | West Bromwich Albion |
| 8 | Giles, Christopher | Yeovil Town | Weston Super Mare |
| 25 | Goodridge, Gregory R. | Bristol City | Cheltenham Town |
| 19 | Grant, John A.C. | Crewe Alexandra | Hyde United |
| 2 | Green, Ryan M. | Wolverhampton Wanderers | Torquay United |
| 1 | Gritton, Martin | Plymouth Argyle | Yeovil Town |
| 22 | Hanson, Christian | Middlesbrough | Cambridge United |
| 16 | Harris, Jason A. | Hull City | Shrewsbury Town |
| 29 | Holligan, Gavin V. | West Ham United | Kingstonian |
| 2 | Holmes, David J. | Burton Albion | Ilkeston Town |
| 15 | Holt, Andrew | Oldham Athletic | Hull City |
| 26 | Holt, Grant | Halifax Town | Barrow |
| 24 | Hopkins, Gareth | Cheltenham Town | Cinderford Town |
| 1 | Howell, Dean G. | Crewe Alexandra | Rochdale |
| 22 | Hyldgaard, Morten L. | Coventry City | Grimsby Town |
| 22 | Izzet, Kemal | Charlton Athletic | Colchester United |
| 2 | Karic, Amir | Ipswich Town | Crystal Palace |
| 13 | Keen, Peter A. | Carlisle United | Darlington |
| 20 | Kenna, Jeffrey J. | Blackburn Rovers | Tranmere Rovers |
| 9 | Knight, Leon L. | Chelsea | Queens Park Rangers |
| 2 | Kotylo, Krystof J. | Nuneaton Borough | Eastwood Town |
| 6 | Lee, Christian | Gillingham | Leyton Orient |
| 28 | Lindley, James E. | Notts County | Gresley Rovers |
| 3 | Lockwood, Adam B. | Reading | Forest Green Rovers |
| 16 | Macdonald, Charles L. | Charlton Athletic | Cheltenham Town |
| 22 | Maddison, Neil S. | Middlesbrough | Bristol City |
| 16 | Matthews, Lee J. | Leeds United | Bristol City |
| 14 | Matthews, Robert | Stockport County | Halifax Town |
| 9 | McKeever, Mark | Sheffield Wednesday | Bristol Rovers |
| 5 | Mellon, Michael J. | Burnley | Tranmere Rovers |

| | | |
|---|---|---|
| 22 Mitchell, Paul A. | Wigan Athletic | Halifax Town |
| 2 Moran, Andrew J. | Hereford United | Bamber Bridge |
| 26 Morris, Elliott | West Bromwich Albion | Bromsgrove Rovers |
| 8 Morris, Lee | Derby County | Huddersfield Town |
| 22 Morrison, Andrew C. | Manchester City | Sheffield United |
| 22 Morrow, Stephen J. | Queens Park Rangers | Peterborough United |
| 26 Moseley, Michael | Runcorn | Vauxhall Motors |
| 1 Mounty, Carl T. | Swansea City | Bangor City |
| 15 Muggleton, Carl D. | Stoke City | Cardiff City |
| 1 Muller, Adam P. | Sheffield Wednesday | Worksop Town |
| 29 Murphy, Brendan F. | Kidderminster Harriers | Solihull Borough |
| 22 Murray, Shaun | Notts County | Kettering Town |
| 22 Navarro, Alan E. | Liverpool | Crewe Alexandra |
| 9 Newby, Jon P.R. | Liverpool | Bury |
| 9 Newby, Keith | Harrow Borough | Yeading |
| 16 Ostenstad, Egil | Blackburn Rovers | Manchester City |
| 12 Owusu, Ansah O. | Wimbledon | Bristol Rovers |
| 22 Parkin, Sam | Chelsea | Oldham Athletic |
| 22 Partridge, Richard J. | Liverpool | Bristol Rovers |
| 28 Pearce, Alexander G. | Chesterfield | Worksop Town |
| 22 Peschisolido, Paulo P. | Fulham | Norwich City |
| 15 Petterson, Andrew K. | Portsmouth | Torquay United |
| 17 Piscopides, Paul | Dagenham & Redbridge | Billericay Town |
| 4 Poland, Lee | Northwich Victoria | Leek Town |
| 16 Pollock, Jamie | Crystal Palace | Birmingham City |
| 28 Priestley, Philip A. | Rochdale | Chester City |
| 14 Proctor, Michael A. | Sunderland | Halifax Town |
| 17 Rapley, Kevin J. | Notts County | Scunthorpe United |
| 16 Reddington, Stuart | Chelsea | Mansfield Town |
| 28 Reddy, Michael | Sunderland | Swindon Town |
| 22 Ripley, Stuart E. | Southampton | Sheffield Wednesday |
| 2 Riza, Omer K. | West Ham United | Cambridge United |
| 1 Roget, Leo T.E. | Southend United | Stockport County |
| 1 Searle, Stuart A. | Aldershot Town | Carshalton Athletic |
| 5 Sharpe, Lee S. | Bradford City | Portsmouth |
| 18 Shittu, Daniel O. | Charlton Athletic | Blackpool |
| 27 Shuker, Christopher A. | Manchester City | Macclesfield Town |
| 1 Simpson, Fitzroy | Heart of Midlothian | Walsall |
| 22 Simpson, Wesley | Northwich Victoria | Winsford United |
| 9 Smith, Mark J.W. | Bristol Rovers | Mangotsfield Town |
| 16 Smith, Peter L. | Crewe Alexandra | Doncaster Rovers |
| 27 Sodje, Akpo | Queens Park Rangers | Stevenage Borough |
| 1 Sodje, Samuel | Stevenage Borough | Grays Athletic |
| 22 Spencer, Damien M. | Bristol City | Exeter City |
| 29 Stamp, Darryn M. | Scunthorpe United | Scarborough |
| 14 Steele, Paul | Yeovil Town | Woking |
| 31 Stoner, Craig J. | Portsmouth | Bognor Regis Town |
| 31 Sugden, Ryan S. | Oldham Athletic | Burton Albion |
| 27 Sykes, Alexander | Nuneaton Borough | Forest Green Rovers |
| 21 Takalogabhashi, Mohammad | Margate | Scunthorpe United |
| 30 Tann, Adam J. | Cambridge United | Cambridge City |
| 22 Taylor, Gareth K. | Manchester City | Burnley |
| 29 Telemaque, Errol | Hayes | Yeading |
| 22 Turner, Andrew P. | Rotherham United | Rochdale |
| 12 Tyne, Thomas R. | Millwall | Fisher Athletic |
| 12 Tyson, Nathan | Reading | Maidenhead United |
| 2 Upson, Matthew J. | Arsenal | Crystal Palace |
| 2 Walker, Richard S. | Crewe Alexandra | Halesowen Town |
| 11 Walker, Richard M. | Aston Villa | Blackpool |
| 27 Wharton, Paul | Farsley Celtic | Bradford Park Avenue |

| 30 Whitley, James | Manchester City | Nottingham Forest |
| 22 Williams, Thomas A. | West Ham United | Peterborough United |
| 22 Wilson, Stephen L. | Hull City | Macclesfield Town |
| 8 Wolleaston, Robert A. | Chelsea | Portsmouth |

**April 2001**

| 26 Cooper, Richard A. | Nottingham Forest | York City |
| 25 Foster, Benjamin | Racing Club Warwick | Stoke City |
| 11 Izzet, Kemal | Charlton Athletic | Colchester United |
| 28 Ward, Christopher | Lancaster City | Birmingham City |

**Temporary transfers**

| 13 Bernard, Olivier | Newcastle United | Darlington |
| 23 Birch, Gary S. | Walsall | Exeter City |
| 9 Carr, Darren J. | Brighton & Hove Albion | Carlisle United |
| 3 Clegg, George G. | Manchester United | Wycombe Wanderers |
| 2 Cooper, Richard A. | Nottingham Forest | York City |
| 17 Cornwall, Lucas C.C. | Fulham | Grimsby Town |
| 13 Cullen, David J. | Peterborough United | Carlisle United |
| 23 Dalglish, Paul | Norwich City | Wigan Athletic |
| 4 Field, Lewis | Stevenage Borough | Hemel Hempstead Town |
| 17 Gamble, Joseph | Reading | Crawley Town |
| 9 Giles, Christopher | Yeovil Town | Weston-Super-Mare |
| 13 Grant, John | Crewe Alexandra | Hyde United |
| 2 Green, Ryan M. | Wolverhampton Wanderers | Torquay United |
| 22 Hanson, Christian | Middlesbrough | Cambridge United |
| 26 Holt, Grant | Halifax Town | Barrow |
| 25 Hopkins, Gareth | Cheltenham Town | Cinderford Town |
| 3 Kelly, Alan T. | Blackburn Rovers | Stockport County |
| 17 Macdonald, Charles L. | Charlton Athletic | Cheltenham Town |
| 17 Maddison, Neil S. | Middlesbrough | Bristol City |
| 22 Mitchell, Paul A. | Wigan Athletic | Halifax Town |
| 8 Newby, Keith | Harrow Borough | Yeading |
| 2 Poland, Lee | Northwich Victoria | Leek Town |
| 17 Pollock, Jamie | Crystal Palace | Birmingham City |
| 18 Rapley, Kevin J. | Notts County | Scunthorpe United |
| 17 Reddington, Stuart | Chelsea | Mansfield Town |
| 1 Riza, Omer K. | West Ham United | Cambridge United |
| 3 Roget, Leo T.E. | Southend United | Stockport County |
| 22 Simpson, Wesley | Northwich Victoria | Winsford United |
| 9 Smith, Mark J.W. | Bristol Rovers | Mangotsfield United |
| 1 Sodje, Samuel | Stevenage Borough | Grays Athletic |
| 22 Spencer, Damien M. | Bristol City | Exeter City |
| 25 Stoner, Craig J. | Portsmouth | Bognor Regis Town |
| 26 Taylor, Gareth K. | Manchester City | Burnley |
| 8 Tyne, Thomas R. | Millwall | Fisher Athletic |
| 9 Tyson, Nathan | Reading | Maidenhead United |

**May 2001**

| 30 Campbell, Stuart P. | Leicester City | Grimsby Town |
| 30 Griffiths, Leroy | Hampton & Richmond Borough | Queens Park Rangers |
| 12 Harford, Paul | Sutton United | Aldershot Town |
| 23 Penny, Andrew J. | Solihull Borough | Hinckley United |
| 3 Roget, Leo T.E. | Southend United | Stockport County |
| 26 Steele, Paul | Yeovil Town | Woking |

**Temporary transfers**

| 8 Broad, Stephen | Chelsea | Southend United |
| 6 Field, Lewis | Stevenage Borough | Hemel Hempstead Town |
| 8 Holt, Andrew | Oldham Athletic | Hull City |
| 7 Lockwood, Adam B. | Reading | Forest Green Rovers |
| 6 Reddington, Stuart | Chelsea | Mansfield Town |

# FA CUP REVIEW 2000–2001

The halfway stage of Liverpool's cup treble was arguably the most difficult to negotiate. In their second visit to Cardiff for a major final of the season, they were on the rack against a wasteful Arsenal for much of the match before a stunning late comeback having gone a goal down to win 2-1.

Three times Sami Hyypia cleared off the Liverpool goal-line and Thierry Henry, though clearly the most gifted player on the park, was the squanderer-in-chief in front of goal for the Gunners. Yet when Fredrik Ljungberg took advantage of a poor kicked clearance by Sander Westerveld and put Arsenal into a 72nd minute lead, the match seemed over. Alas it all fell apart for the Londoners after that.

Curiously whoever is in charge of Arsenal the 'one-nil to the Arsenal' cry often has a negative effect on their attitude and with shrewd substitutions by Liverpool manager Gerard Houllier, the game was turned on its head with two goals in five minutes by Michael Owen.

Sensibly reverting to a third round in the first week of the new year rather than before Christmas, the FA Cup regained much of its lost prestige of the previous season. Manchester United were also back in the competition, but one wondered for how long in the short term. The first round opened on 17 November, a Friday night encounter involving aspiring Conference outfit Rushden & Diamonds. They failed to sparkle at Luton Town and went out 1-0.

But the following day the cluster of other would-be giant-killers proved the day of the minnow was far from over. Brentford were stunned by Kingstonian who won 3-1 at Griffin Park and those perennial cup fighters Yeovil Town crushed Colchester United 5-1. In addition Northwich Victoria held Bury and there were other replays earned for Chester City against Plymouth Argyle, Kettering Town against Hull City, Burton Albion at Kidderminster Harriers and Nuneaton Borough at Stoke City. The following day Canvey Island shared eight goals with Port Vale.

Often such results are overturned in a second meeting. But this time Nuneaton edged out Stoke 1-0 and on 28 November, a night of many replay shocks, Kettering won at Hull, Chester at Plymouth and Canvey at Port Vale. Northwich were successful homers at Bury's expense.

Though some fell by the wayside, it was not the end of the torture for League clubs. Chester had a 3-2 win over Oxford, Dagenham & Redbridge won 1-0 at Lincoln, Morecambe defeated Cambridge United 2-1 and Yeovil won 1-0 at Blackpool. Northwich shared six goals with Leyton Orient. In a non-league domestic affair, Kingstonian won 2-1 at Southport.

Round three saw their numbers further reduced. Chester at Blackburn, Yeovil at Bolton Wanderers, Morecambe at home to Ipswich Town all succumbed, but Dagenham held Charlton Athletic at The Valley 1-1 and Kingstonian won 1-0 at Southend United.

Eventual finalists Arsenal and Liverpool came through respectively 1-0 at Carlisle United and 3-0 at home to Rotherham United. There were no fatal Premiership mishaps. The weather disrupted several fixtures and replays ran into the fourth round, the shock of this stage being Manchester United's 1-0 defeat at home to West Ham United. Liverpool won 2-0 at Leeds United, Arsenal 6-0 at Queens Park Rangers.

Alas Dagenham lost 1-0 to Charlton in their third round replay and Kingstonian, after conceding an injury-time equaliser at Bristol City, lost theirs to another late goal. Best replay result: Blackburn Rovers' winning 5-2 at Derby County though Wimbledon did well to inflict a 3-1 defeat on Middlesbrough.

Both Arsenal and Liverpool put on their Sunday best in fifth round wins against Chelsea 3-1 and Manchester City 4-2 respectively, but arguably the shock of the entire 2000-01 competition came in Southampton's replay at Tranmere Rovers. Cruising 3-0 at half-time the Saints became sinners and lost 4-3!

Wycombe, meanwhile, were making progress and entered the sixth round via an 8-7 penalty shoot-out against Wimbledon. Arsenal took three goals off Blackburn without reply and in the Merseyside derby, Liverpool won 4-2 at Tranmere. Tottenham Hotspur won 3-2 at West Ham, but Wycombe caused more eyebrow-raising with a 2-1 injury-time winner at Leicester City.

Arsenal should have walked the semi-final with Spurs but had to be content with a 2-1 win, and plucky Wycombe restricted Liverpool to just one corner and a dangerous free-kick and thus conceded two goals in a 2-1 defeat.

# AXA FA CUP 2000–2001

## FIRST ROUND

| | | | |
|---|---|---|---|
| Luton T | (0) 1 | Rushden & D | (0) 0 |
| Aldershot T | (1) 2 | Brighton & HA | (2) 6 |
| Barnet | (0) 2 | Hampton & Richmond B | (1) 1 |
| Barrow | (0) 0 | Leyton Orient | (0) 2 |
| Blackpool | (2) 3 | Telford U | (0) 1 |
| Bournemouth | (0) 2 | Swansea C | (0) 0 |
| Brentford | (0) 1 | Kingstonian | (0) 3 |
| Bury | (0) 1 | Northwich Vic | (0) 1 |
| Cambridge U | (1) 2 | Rochdale | (1) 1 |
| Carlisle U | (3) 5 | Woking | (1) 1 |
| Cheltenham T | (1) 4 | Shrewsbury T | (1) 1 |
| Chester C | (0) 1 | Plymouth Arg | (0) 1 |
| Chesterfield | (0) 0 | Bristol C | (0) 1 |
| Dagenham & Redbridge | (1) 3 | Hayes | (1) 1 |
| Darlington | (1) 6 | AFC Sudbury | (1) 1 |
| Forest Green R | (0) 0 | Morecambe | (1) 3 |
| Halifax T | (0) 0 | Gateshead | (1) 2 |
| Havant & Waterlooville | (1) 1 | Southport | (1) 2 |
| Hednesford T | (1) 2 | Oldham Ath | (2) 4 |
| Kettering T | (0) 0 | Hull C | (0) 0 |
| Kidderminster H | (0) 0 | Burton Albion | (0) 0 |
| Lincoln C | (3) 4 | Bracknell T | (0) 0 |
| Macclesfield T | (0) 0 | Oxford U | (0) 1 |
| Mansfield T | (0) 1 | Peterborough U | (1) 1 |
| Northampton T | (1) 4 | Frickley Ath | (0) 0 |
| Reading | (1) 4 | Grays Ath | (0) 0 |
| Scunthorpe U | (1) 3 | Hartlepool U | (1) 1 |
| Stoke C | (0) 0 | Nuneaton B | (0) 0 |
| Swindon T | (1) 4 | Ilkeston T | (0) 1 |
| Torquay U | (0) 1 | Southend U | (1) 1 |
| Walsall | (2) 4 | Exeter C | (0) 0 |
| Wigan Ath | (2) 3 | Dorchester T | (0) 1 |
| Wrexham | (0) 0 | Rotherham U | (1) 1 |
| Wycombe W | (2) 3 | Harrow B | (0) 0 |
| Yeovil T | (0) 5 | Colchester U | (0) 1 |
| Canvey Island | (0) 4 | Port Vale | (2) 4 |
| Cardiff C | (1) 5 | Bristol R | (1) 1 |
| Leigh RMI | (0) 0 | Millwall | (1) 3 |
| *(at Millwall.)* | | | |
| Radcliffe B | (0) 1 | York C | (4) 4 |
| *(at Bury.)* | | | |
| Gravesend & N | (0) 1 | Notts Co | (1) 2 |

## FIRST ROUND REPLAYS

| | | | |
|---|---|---|---|
| Nuneaton B | (0) 1 | Stoke C | (0) 0 |
| Burton Albion | (0) 2 | Kidderminster H | (3) 4 |
| Hull C | (0) 0 | Kettering T | (0) 1 |
| Northwich Vic | (0) 1 | Bury | (0) 0 |
| Peterborough U | (1) 4 | Mansfield T | (0) 0 |
| Plymouth Arg | (0) 1 | Chester C | (1) 2 |
| *(aet.)* | | | |
| Port Vale | (0) 1 | Canvey Island | (0) 2 |
| *(aet.)* | | | |
| Southend U | (0) 2 | Torquay U | (0) 1 |
| *(aet.)* | | | |

## SECOND ROUND

| | | | |
|---|---|---|---|
| Walsall | (2) 2 | Barnet | (0) 1 |
| Bournemouth | (1) 3 | Nuneaton B | (0) 0 |
| Bristol C | (0) 3 | Kettering T | (1) 1 |
| Cardiff C | (2) 3 | Cheltenham T | (1) 1 |
| Chester C | (1) 3 | Oxford U | (2) 2 |
| Darlington | (0) 0 | Luton T | (0) 0 |
| Kidderminster H | (0) 0 | Carlisle U | (1) 2 |
| Lincoln C | (0) 0 | Dagenham & Redbridge | (0) 1 |
| Morecambe | (1) 2 | Cambridge U | (1) 1 |
| Northwich Vic | (0) 3 | Leyton Orient | (1) 3 |
| Rotherham U | (1) 1 | Northampton T | (0) 0 |
| Scunthorpe U | (1) 2 | Brighton & HA | (1) 1 |
| Southport | (1) 1 | Kingstonian | (2) 2 |
| Swindon T | (1) 5 | Gateshead | (0) 0 |
| York C | (0) 2 | Reading | (0) 2 |
| Blackpool | (0) 0 | Yeovil T | (1) 1 |
| Canvey Island | (0) 1 | Southend U | (1) 2 |
| *(at Southend.)* | | | |
| Millwall | (0) 0 | Wycombe W | (0) 0 |
| Peterborough U | (0) 1 | Oldham Ath | (0) 1 |
| Wigan Ath | (0) 1 | Notts Co | (0) 1 |

## SECOND ROUND REPLAYS

| | | | |
|---|---|---|---|
| Luton T | (0) 2 | Darlington | (0) 0 |
| Notts Co | (1) 2 | Wigan Ath | (1) 1 |
| *(aet.)* | | | |
| Oldham Ath | (0) 0 | Peterborough U | (1) 1 |
| Reading | (1) 1 | York C | (1) 3 |
| Wycombe W | (2) 2 | Millwall | (1) 1 |
| Leyton Orient | (0) 3 | Northwich Vic | (2) 2 |
| *(aet.)* | | | |

## THIRD ROUND

| | | | |
|---|---|---|---|
| Blackburn R | (0) 2 | Chester C | (0) 0 |
| Bolton W | (1) 2 | Yeovil T | (1) 1 |
| Bournemouth | (1) 2 | Gillingham | (2) 3 |
| Burnley | (1) 2 | Scunthorpe U | (1) 2 |
| Cardiff C | (0) 1 | Crewe Alex | (1) 1 |
| Carlisle U | (0) 0 | Arsenal | (1) 1 |
| Charlton Ath | (0) 1 | Dagenham & Redbridge | (1) 1 |
| Chelsea | (2) 5 | Peterborough U | (0) 0 |
| Derby Co | (1) 3 | WBA | (0) 2 |
| Huddersfield T | (0) 0 | Bristol C | (0) 2 |
| Leeds U | (1) 1 | Barnsley | (0) 0 |
| Leicester C | (0) 3 | York C | (0) 0 |
| Leyton Orient | (0) 0 | Tottenham H | (0) 1 |
| Liverpool | (0) 3 | Rotherham U | (0) 0 |
| Luton T | (2) 3 | QPR | (0) 3 |
| Manchester C | (3) 3 | Birmingham C | (0) 2 |
| Morecambe | (0) 0 | Ipswich T | (1) 3 |
| Portsmouth | (1) 1 | Tranmere R | (1) 2 |
| Preston NE | (0) 0 | Stockport Co | (0) 1 |
| Sheffield W | (1) 2 | Norwich C | (0) 1 |
| Southampton | (0) 1 | Sheffield U | (0) 0 |
| Southend U | (0) 0 | Kingstonian | (1) 1 |
| Sunderland | (0) 0 | Crystal Palace | (0) 0 |

165

| Swindon T | (0) 0 | Coventry C | (1) 2 |
| Walsall | (1) 2 | West Ham U | (1) 3 |
| Watford | (1) 1 | Everton | (0) 2 |
| Wimbledon | (2) 2 | Notts Co | (1) 2 |
| Wycombe W | (0) 1 | Grimsby T | (1) 1 |
| Fulham | (1) 1 | Manchester U | (1) 2 |
| Newcastle U | (0) 1 | Aston Villa | (0) 1 |
| Nottingham F | (0) 0 | Wolverhampton W | (0) 1 |
| Bradford C | (0) 0 | Middlesbrough | (0) 1 |

## THIRD ROUND REPLAYS

| Crewe Alex | (1) 2 | Cardiff C | (1) 1 |
| Grimsby T | (1) 1 | Wycombe W | (2) 3 |
| Aston Villa | (0) 1 | Newcastle U | (0) 0 |
| Crystal Palace | (1) 2 | Sunderland | (0) 4 |
| *(aet.)* | | | |
| QPR | (0) 2 | Luton T | (1) 1 |
| *(aet.)* | | | |
| Scunthorpe U | (0) 1 | Burnley | (0) 1 |
| *(aet; Scunthorpe U won 5-4 on penalties.)* | | | |
| Dagenham & Redbridge | (0) 0 | Charlton Ath | (0) 1 |
| Notts Co | (0) 0 | Wimbledon | (0) 1 |
| *(aet.)* | | | |

## FOURTH ROUND

| Aston Villa | (0) 1 | Leicester C | (1) 2 |
| Blackburn R | (0) 0 | Derby Co | (0) 0 |
| Bristol C | (0) 1 | Kingstonian | (0) 1 |
| Crewe Alex | (0) 0 | Stockport Co | (0) 1 |
| Everton | (0) 0 | Tranmere R | (2) 3 |
| Leeds U | (0) 0 | Liverpool | (0) 2 |
| Manchester C | (0) 1 | Coventry C | (0) 0 |
| QPR | (0) 0 | Arsenal | (2) 6 |
| Southampton | (1) 3 | Sheffield W | (0) 1 |
| Sunderland | (1) 1 | Ipswich T | (0) 0 |
| Wycombe W | (1) 2 | Wolverhampton W | (0) 1 |
| Bolton W | (2) 5 | Scunthorpe U | (1) 1 |
| Gillingham | (0) 2 | Chelsea | (3) 4 |
| Manchester U | (0) 0 | West Ham U | (0) 1 |
| Middlesbrough | (0) 0 | Wimbledon | (0) 0 |
| Charlton Ath | (1) 2 | Tottenham H | (0) 4 |

## FOURTH ROUND REPLAYS

| Derby Co | (1) 2 | Blackburn R | (0) 5 |
| Kingstonian | (0) 0 | Bristol C | (0) 1 |
| Wimbledon | (0) 3 | Middlesbrough | (1) 1 |
| *(aet.)* | | | |

## FIFTH ROUND

| Bolton W | (0) 1 | Blackburn R | (1) 1 |
| Leicester C | (2) 3 | Bristol C | (0) 0 |
| Southampton | (0) 0 | Tranmere R | (0) 0 |
| Sunderland | (0) 0 | West Ham U | (0) 1 |
| Tottenham H | (3) 4 | Stockport Co | (0) 0 |

| Wycombe W | (0) 2 | Wimbledon | (2) 2 |
| Arsenal | (0) 3 | Chelsea | (0) 1 |
| Liverpool | (2) 4 | Manchester C | (1) 2 |

## FIFTH ROUND REPLAYS

| Tranmere R | (0) 4 | Southampton | (3) 3 |
| Wimbledon | (1) 1 | Wycombe W | (1) 1 |

*(aet; Wycombe W won 8-7 on penalties.)*

| Blackburn R | (0) 3 | Bolton W | (0) 0 |

## SIXTH ROUND

| Arsenal | (3) 3 | Blackburn R | (0) 0 |
| Leicester C | (0) 1 | Wycombe W | (0) 2 |
| Tranmere R | (0) 2 | Liverpool | (2) 4 |
| West Ham U | (1) 2 | Tottenham H | (1) 3 |

## SEMI-FINALS

| Arsenal | (1) 2 | Tottenham H | (1) 1 |

*(at Old Trafford.)*

| Wycombe W | (0) 1 | Liverpool | (0) 2 |

*(at Villa Park.)*

### FINAL (at Millennium Stadium)

### 12 MAY

**Arsenal (0) 1** *(Ljungberg 72)*
**Liverpool (0) 2** *(Owen 83, 88)*                                           74,200

*Arsenal:* Seaman; Dixon (Bergkamp), Cole, Vieira, Keown, Adams, Pires, Grimandi, Wiltord (Parlour), Henry, Ljungberg (Kanu).
*Liverpool:* Westerveld; Babbel, Carragher, Hamann (McAllister), Henchoz, Hyypia, Murphy (Berger), Gerrard, Heskey, Owen, Smicer (Fowler).
*Referee:* S. Dunn (Bristol).

# PAST FA CUP FINALS

*Details of one goalscorer is not available in 1878.*

| | | | | |
|---|---|---|---|---|
| 1872 | The Wanderers .....................1 *Betts* | Royal Engineers ...............................0 | | |
| 1873 | The Wanderers .....................2 *Kinnaird, Wollaston* | Oxford University ............................0 | | |
| 1874 | Oxford University................2 *Mackarness, Patton* | Royal Engineers ..............................0 | | |
| 1875 | Royal Engineers ...................1 *Renny-Tailyour* | Old Etonians ..................................1* *Bonsor* | | |
| Replay | Royal Engineers ...................2 *Renny-Tailyour, Stafford* | Old Etonians ....................................0 | | |
| 1876 | The Wanderers .....................1 *Edwards* | Old Etonians ..................................1* *Bonsor* | | |
| Replay | The Wanderers .....................3 *Wollaston, Hughes 2* | Old Etonians ....................................0 | | |
| 1877 | The Wanderers .....................2 *Lindsay, Kenrick* | Oxford University ...........................1* *Kinnaird (og)* | | |
| 1878 | The Wanderers .....................3 *Kenrick 2, Kinnaird* | Royal Engineers ..............................1 *Unknown* | | |
| 1879 | Old Etonians ........................1 *Clerke* | Clapham Rovers ..............................0 | | |
| 1880 | Clapham Rovers ...................1 *Lloyd-Jones* | Oxford University ............................0 | | |
| 1881 | Old Carthusians ...................3 *Wyngard, Parry, Todd* | Old Etonians ....................................0 | | |
| 1882 | Old Etonians ........................1 *Anderson* | Blackburn Rovers.............................0 | | |
| 1883 | Blackburn Olympic .............2 *Costley, Matthews* | Old Etonians ..................................1* *Goodhart* | | |
| 1884 | Blackburn Rovers.................2 *Sowerbutts, Forrest* | Queen's Park, Glasgow ....................1 *Christie* | | |
| 1885 | Blackburn Rovers.................2 *Forrest, Brown* | Queen's Park, Glasgow ....................0 | | |
| 1886 | Blackburn Rovers.................0 | West Bromwich Albion .....................0 | | |
| Replay | Blackburn Rovers.................2 *Brown, Sowerbutts* | West Bromwich Albion .....................0 | | |
| 1887 | Aston Villa ...........................2 *Hunter, Hodgetts* | West Bromwich Albion .....................0 | | |
| 1888 | West Bromwich Albion ........2 *Woodhall, Bayliss* | Preston NE........................................1 *Dewhurst* | | |
| 1889 | Preston NE ...........................3 *Dewhurst, J. Ross, Thompson* | Wolverhampton W.............................0 | | |
| 1890 | Blackburn Rovers.................6 *Walton, John Southworth, Lofthouse, Townley 3* | Sheffield W.......................................1 *Bennett* | | |
| 1891 | Blackburn Rovers.................3 *Dewar, John Southworth, Townley* | Notts Co............................................1 *Oswald* | | |

| Year | Winner/Team 1 | Score | Team 2 | Score |
|------|---------------|-------|--------|-------|
| 1892 | West Bromwich Albion | 3 | Aston Villa | 0 |
| | *Geddes, Nicholls, Reynolds* | | | |
| 1893 | Wolverhampton W | 1 | Everton | 0 |
| | *Allen* | | | |
| 1894 | Notts Co | 4 | Bolton W | 1 |
| | *Watson, Logan 3* | | *Cassidy* | |
| 1895 | Aston Villa | 1 | West Bromwich Albion | 0 |
| | *J. Devey* | | | |
| 1896 | Sheffield W | 2 | Wolverhampton W | 1 |
| | *Spiksley 2* | | *Black* | |
| 1897 | Aston Villa | 3 | Everton | 2 |
| | *Campbell, Wheldon, Crabtree* | | *Boyle, Bell* | |
| 1898 | Nottingham F | 3 | Derby Co | 1 |
| | *Cape 2, McPherson* | | *Bloomer* | |
| 1899 | Sheffield U | 4 | Derby Co | 1 |
| | *Bennett, Beers, Almond, Priest* | | *Boag* | |
| 1900 | Bury | 4 | Southampton | 0 |
| | *McLuckie 2, Wood, Plant* | | | |
| 1901 | Tottenham H | 2 | Sheffield U | 2 |
| | *Brown 2* | | *Bennett, Priest* | |
| Replay | Tottenham H | 3 | Sheffield U | 1 |
| | *Cameron, Smith, Brown* | | *Priest* | |
| 1902 | Sheffield U | 1 | Southampton | 1 |
| | *Common* | | *Wood* | |
| Replay | Sheffield U | 2 | Southampton | 1 |
| | *Hedley, Barnes* | | *Brown* | |
| 1903 | Bury | 6 | Derby Co | 0 |
| | *Ross, Sagar, Leeming 2, Wood, Plant* | | | |
| 1904 | Manchester C | 1 | Bolton W | 0 |
| | *Meredith* | | | |
| 1905 | Aston Villa | 2 | Newcastle U | 0 |
| | *Hampton 2* | | | |
| 1906 | Everton | 1 | Newcastle U | 0 |
| | *Young* | | | |
| 1907 | Sheffield W | 2 | Everton | 1 |
| | *Stewart, Simpson* | | *Sharp* | |
| 1908 | Wolverhampton W | 3 | Newcastle U | 1 |
| | *Hunt, Hedley, Harrison* | | *Howey* | |
| 1909 | Manchester U | 1 | Bristol C | 0 |
| | *A. Turnbull* | | | |
| 1910 | Newcastle U | 1 | Barnsley | 1 |
| | *Rutherford* | | *Tufnell* | |
| Replay | Newcastle U | 2 | Barnsley | 0 |
| | *Shepherd 2 (1 pen)* | | | |
| 1911 | Bradford C | 0 | Newcastle U | 0 |
| Replay | Bradford C | 1 | Newcastle U | 0 |
| | *Speirs* | | | |
| 1912 | Barnsley | 0 | West Bromwich Albion | 0 |
| Replay | Barnsley | 1 | West Bromwich Albion | 0* |
| | *Tufnell* | | | |

| 1913 | Aston Villa .............................1 | Sunderland .......................................0 |
|---|---|---|
| | *Barber* | |
| 1914 | Burnley ...................................1 | Liverpool .........................................0 |
| | *Freeman* | |
| 1915 | Sheffield U .............................3 | Chelsea ............................................0 |
| | *Simmons, Masterman, Kitchen* | |
| 1920 | Aston Villa .............................1 | Huddersfield T .................................0* |
| | *Kirton* | |
| 1921 | Tottenham H ...........................1 | Wolverhampton W ............................0 |
| | *Dimmock* | |
| 1922 | Huddersfield T ........................1 | Preston NE .......................................0 |
| | *Smith (pen)* | |
| 1923 | Bolton W ................................2 | West Ham U ......................................0 |
| | *Jack, J.R. Smith* | |
| 1924 | Newcastle U ............................2 | Aston Villa .......................................0 |
| | *Harris, Seymour* | |
| 1925 | Sheffield U .............................1 | Cardiff C ..........................................0 |
| | *Tunstall* | |
| 1926 | Bolton W ................................1 | Manchester C ....................................0 |
| | *Jack* | |
| 1927 | Cardiff C ................................1 | Arsenal .............................................0 |
| | *Ferguson* | |
| 1928 | Blackburn Rovers..................3 | Huddersfield T .................................1 |
| | *Roscamp 2, McLean* | *A. Jackson* |
| 1929 | Bolton W ................................2 | Portsmouth ......................................0 |
| | *Butler, Blackmore* | |
| 1930 | Arsenal...................................2 | Huddersfield T .................................0 |
| | *James, Lambert* | |
| 1931 | West Bromwich Albion ........2 | Birmingham .....................................1 |
| | *W.G. Richardson 2* | *Bradford* |
| 1932 | Newcastle U ...........................2 | Arsenal .............................................1 |
| | *Allen 2* | *John* |
| 1933 | Everton ...................................3 | Manchester C ....................................0 |
| | *Stein, Dean, Dunn* | |
| 1934 | Manchester C .........................2 | Portsmouth.......................................1 |
| | *Tilson 2* | *Rutherford* |
| 1935 | Sheffield W ............................4 | West Bromwich Albion ....................2 |
| | *Rimmer 2, Palethorpe, Hooper* | *Boyes, Sandford* |
| 1936 | Arsenal...................................1 | Sheffield U .......................................0 |
| | *Drake* | |
| 1937 | Sunderland ............................3 | Preston NE .......................................1 |
| | *Gurney, Carter, Burbanks* | *F. O'Donnell* |
| 1938 | Preston NE .............................1 | Huddersfield T .................................0* |
| | *Mutch (pen)* | |
| 1939 | Portsmouth.............................4 | Wolverhampton W ............................1 |
| | *Parker 2, Barlow, Anderson* | *Dorsett* |
| 1946 | Derby Co ................................4 | Charlton Ath.....................................1* |
| | *H. Turner (og), Doherty, Stamps 2* | *H. Turner* |

| Year | Winner | Score | Loser | Score |
|---|---|---|---|---|
| 1947 | Charlton Ath | 1 | Burnley | 0* |
| | *Duffy* | | | |
| 1948 | Manchester U | 4 | Blackpool | 2 |
| | *Rowley 2, Pearson, Anderson* | | *Shimwell (pen), Mortensen* | |
| 1949 | Wolverhampton W | 3 | Leicester C | 1 |
| | *Pye 2, Smyth,* | | *Griffiths* | |
| 1950 | Arsenal | 2 | Liverpool | 0 |
| | *Lewis 2* | | | |
| 1951 | Newcastle U | 2 | Blackpool | 0 |
| | *Milburn 2* | | | |
| 1952 | Newcastle U | 1 | Arsenal | 0 |
| | *G. Robledo* | | | |
| 1953 | Blackpool | 4 | Bolton W | 3 |
| | *Mortensen 3, Perry* | | *Lofthouse, Moir, Bell* | |
| 1954 | West Bromwich Albion | 3 | Preston NE | 2 |
| | *Allen 2 (1 pen), Griffin* | | *Morrison, Wayman* | |
| 1955 | Newcastle U | 3 | Manchester C | 1 |
| | *Milburn, Mitchell, Hannah* | | *Johnstone* | |
| 1956 | Manchester C | 3 | Birmingham C | 1 |
| | *Hayes, Dyson, Johnstone* | | *Kinsey* | |
| 1957 | Aston Villa | 2 | Manchester U | 1 |
| | *McParland 2* | | *T. Taylor* | |
| 1958 | Bolton W | 2 | Manchester U | 0 |
| | *Lofthouse 2* | | | |
| 1959 | Nottingham F | 2 | Luton T | 1 |
| | *Dwight, Wilson* | | *Pacey* | |
| 1960 | Wolverhampton W | 3 | Blackburn Rovers | 0 |
| | *McGrath (og), Deeley 2* | | | |
| 1961 | Tottenham H | 2 | Leicester C | 0 |
| | *Smith, Dyson* | | | |
| 1962 | Tottenham H | 3 | Burnley | 1 |
| | *Greaves, Smith, Blanchflower (pen)* | | *Robson* | |
| 1963 | Manchester U | 3 | Leicester C | 1 |
| | *Herd 2, Law* | | *Keyworth* | |
| 1964 | West Ham U | 3 | Preston NE | 2 |
| | *Sissons, Hurst, Boyce* | | *Holden, Dawson* | |
| 1965 | Liverpool | 2 | Leeds U | 1* |
| | *Hunt, St John* | | *Bremner* | |
| 1966 | Everton | 3 | Sheffield W | 2 |
| | *Trebilcock 2, Temple* | | *McCalliog, Ford* | |
| 1967 | Tottenham H | 2 | Chelsea | 1 |
| | *Robertson, Saul* | | *Tambling* | |
| 1968 | West Browmwich Albion | 1 | Everton | 0* |
| | *Astle* | | | |
| 1969 | Manchester C | 1 | Leicester C | 0 |
| | *Young* | | | |
| 1970 | Chelsea | 2 | Leeds U | 2* |
| | *Houseman, Hutchinson* | | *Charlton, Jones* | |

| | | | | |
|---|---|---|---|---|
| Replay | Chelsea | 2 | Leeds U | 1* |
| | Osgood, Webb | | Jones | |
| 1971 | Arsenal | 2 | Liverpool | 1* |
| | Kelly, George | | Heighway | |
| 1972 | Leeds U | 1 | Arsenal | 0 |
| | Clarke | | | |
| 1973 | Sunderland | 1 | Leeds U | 0 |
| | Porterfield | | | |
| 1974 | Liverpool | 3 | Newcastle | 0 |
| | Keegan 2, Heighway | | | |
| 1975 | West Ham U | 2 | Fulham | 0 |
| | A. Taylor 2 | | | |
| 1976 | Southampton | 1 | Manchester U | 0 |
| | Stokes | | | |
| 1977 | Manchester U | 2 | Liverpool | 1 |
| | Pearson, J. Greenhoff | | Case | |
| 1978 | Ipswich T | 1 | Arsenal | 0 |
| | Osborne | | | |
| 1979 | Arsenal | 3 | Manchester U | 2 |
| | Talbot, Stapleton, Sunderland | | McQueen, McIlroy | |
| 1980 | West Ham U | 1 | Arsenal | 0 |
| | Brooking | | | |
| 1981 | Tottenham H | 1 | Manchester C | 1* |
| | Hutchison (og) | | Hutchison | |
| Replay | Tottehham H | 3 | Manchester C | 2 |
| | Villa 2, Crooks | | MacKenzie, Reeves (pen) | |
| 1982 | Tottenham H | 1 | QPR | 1* |
| | Hoddle | | Fenwick | |
| Replay | Tottenham H | 1 | QPR | 0 |
| | Hoddle (pen) | | | |
| 1983 | Manchester U | 2 | Brighton & HA | 2* |
| | Stapleton, Wilkins | | Smith, Stevens | |
| Replay | Manchester U | 4 | Brighton & HA | 0 |
| | Robson 2, Whiteside, Muhren (pen) | | | |
| 1984 | Everton | 2 | Watford | 0 |
| | Sharp, Gray | | | |
| 1985 | Manchester U | 1 | Everton | 0* |
| | Whiteside | | | |
| 1986 | Liverpool | 3 | Everton | 1 |
| | Rush 2, Johnston | | Lineker | |
| 1987 | Coventry C | 3 | Tottenham H | 2* |
| | Bennett, Houchen, Mabbutt (og) | | C. Allen, Kilcline (og) | |
| 1988 | Wimbledon | 1 | Liverpool | 0 |
| | Sanchez | | | |
| 1989 | Liverpool | 3 | Everton | 2* |
| | Aldridge, Rush 2 | | McCall 2 | |
| 1990 | Manchester U | 3 | Crystal Palace | 3* |
| | Robson, Hughes 2 | | O'Reilly, Wright 2 | |
| Replay | Manchester U | 1 | Crystal Palace | 0 |
| | Martin | | | |

| 1991 | Tottenham H | 2 | Nottingham F | 1* |
| | *Stewart, Walker (og)* | | *Pearce* | |
| 1992 | Liverpool | 2 | Sunderland | 0 |
| | *Thomas, Rush* | | | |
| 1993 | Arsenal | 1 | Sheffield W | 1* |
| | *Wright* | | *Hirst* | |
| Replay | Arsenal | 2 | Sheffield W | 1* |
| | *Wright, Linighan* | | *Waddle* | |
| 1994 | Manchester U | 4 | Chelsea | 0 |
| | *Cantona 2 (2 pens),* | | | |
| | *Hughes, McClair* | | | |
| 1995 | Everton | 1 | Manchester U | 0 |
| | *Rideout* | | | |
| 1996 | Manchester U | 1 | Liverpool | 0 |
| | *Cantona* | | | |
| 1997 | Chelsea | 2 | Middlesbrough | 0 |
| | *Di Matteo, Newton* | | | |
| 1998 | Arsenal | 2 | Newcastle U | 0 |
| | *Overmars, Anelka* | | | |
| 1999 | Manchester U | 2 | Newcastle U | 0 |
| | *Sheringham, Scholes* | | | |
| 2000 | Chelsea | 1 | Aston Villa | 0 |
| | *Di Matteo* | | | |

*After extra time

# SUMMARY OF FA CUP WINNERS SINCE 1871

| | |
|---|---|
| Manchester United | 10 |
| Tottenham Hotspur | 8 |
| Arsenal | 7 |
| Aston Villa | 7 |
| Blackburn Rovers | 6 |
| Liverpool | 6 |
| Newcastle United | 6 |
| Everton | 5 |
| The Wanderers | 5 |
| West Bromwich Albion | 5 |
| Bolton Wanderers | 4 |
| Manchester City | 4 |
| Sheffield United | 4 |
| Wolverhampton Wanderers | 4 |
| Chelsea | 3 |
| Sheffield Wednesday | 3 |
| West Ham United | 3 |
| Bury | 2 |
| Nottingham Forest | 2 |
| Old Etonians | 2 |
| Preston North End | 2 |
| Sunderland | 2 |
| Barnsley | 1 |
| Blackburn Olympic | 1 |
| Blackpool | 1 |
| Bradford City | 1 |
| Burnley | 1 |
| Cardiff City | 1 |
| Charlton Athletic | 1 |
| Clapham Rovers | 1 |
| Coventry City | 1 |
| Derby County | 1 |
| Huddersfield Town | 1 |
| Ipswich Town | 1 |
| Leeds United | 1 |
| Notts County | 1 |
| Old Carthusians | 1 |
| Oxford University | 1 |
| Portsmouth | 1 |
| Royal Engineers | 1 |
| Southampton | 1 |
| Wimbledon | 1 |

# APPEARANCES IN FA CUP FINAL

| | |
|---|---|
| Manchester United | 15 |
| Arsenal | 14 |
| Newcastle United | 13 |
| Everton | 12 |
| Liverpool | 12 |
| Aston Villa | 10 |
| West Bromwich Albion | 10 |
| Tottenham Hotspur | 9 |
| Blackburn Rovers | 8 |
| Manchester City | 8 |
| Wolverhampton Wanderers | 8 |
| Bolton Wanderers | 7 |
| Preston North End | 7 |
| Chelsea | 6 |
| Old Etonians | 6 |
| Sheffield United | 6 |
| Sheffield Wednesday | 6 |
| Huddersfield Town | 5 |
| The Wanderers | 5 |
| Derby County | 4 |
| Leeds United | 4 |
| Leicester City | 4 |
| Oxford University | 4 |
| Royal Engineers | 4 |
| Sunderland | 4 |
| West Ham United | 4 |
| Blackpool | 3 |
| Burnley | 3 |
| Nottingham Forest | 3 |
| Portsmouth | 3 |
| Southampton | 3 |
| Barnsley | 2 |
| Birmingham City | 2 |
| Bury | 2 |
| Cardiff City | 2 |
| Charlton Athletic | 2 |
| Clapham Rovers | 2 |
| Notts County | 2 |
| Queen's Park (Glasgow) | 2 |
| Blackburn Olympic | 1 |
| Bradford City | 1 |
| Brighton & Hove Albion | 1 |
| Bristol City | 1 |
| Coventry City | 1 |
| Crystal Palace | 1 |
| Fulham | 1 |
| Ipswich Town | 1 |
| Luton Town | 1 |
| Middlesbrough | 1 |
| Old Carthusians | 1 |
| Queen's Park Rangers | 1 |
| Watford | 1 |
| Wimbledon | 1 |

# WORTHINGTON CUP REVIEW 2000–2001

The Liverpool cup trilogy began in tentative fashion late in February far away in the Millennium Stadium in Cardiff with a none-too-convincing penalty shoot-out win over a determined Birmingham City team keen to fully represent the Football League in an event which was founded more than 40 years previously by Alan Hardaker.

With the advantage of scoring in half an hour through Robbie Fowler from a searing left-foot volley over 20 yards, Liverpool appeared safely to have one hand on the trophy when an injury time penalty gave Birmingham the opportunity of a reprieve. It was a dramatic moment for Darren Purse to level the score after Stephane Henchoz had brought down Martin O'Connor in the box. The City central defender coolly converted to send the final into extra time, the first such occasion in the competition's history.

Though the momentum of the match swung Birmingham's way in the extra period, as one might have expected given the late equaliser, they were unable to topple the Anfield rearguard and it was left to penalties to decide the outcome. It was 5-4 to Liverpool when teenaged Andy Johnson needed to score for City but found Sander Westerveld correctly positioned to save his spot kick.

But of course the Worthington Cup had started back in August when Birmingham made the brightest of starts by taking five goals off Southend United in the first leg of the first round at Roots Hall. Their effort had been topped by Sheffield United, 6-1 winners over Lincoln City. Neither did as well in the return legs, City allowing Southend a goalless draw while United were actually losing at Lincoln 1-0. There was another six when Blackburn took a 6-1 win over Rochdale with David Dunn creating another piece of League Cup history with three successful penalties.

Birmingham were again in scoring mood on their travels in the second round when they took a 4-3 lead over Wycombe Wanderers and also edged the home tie 1-0. But there were serious casualties among the Premier League clubs. Stoke City accounted for Charlton Athletic on away goals and Bristol Rovers disposed of Everton in a penalty shoot-out.

A long pause in proceedings until late October brought the privileged bye-boys hitherto engaged in Europe into the third round fray. Arsenal went down swiftly to Ipswich Town 2-1 at home and Leeds United were nudged out 3-2 at Tranmere Rovers. Liverpool were taken to extra time by Chelsea before emerging 2-1 and Manchester United, never totally committed to the League Cup, won comfortably enough 3-0 at Watford. Yet the sensation was the 3-0 defeat on their own ground of Leicester City against Crystal Palace.

Birmingham impressively led the parade of other upsets with a 3-1 win at Tottenham Hotspur and Wimbledon accounted for Middlesbrough 1-0 at Selhurst Park. Premier pairings cost Aston Villa 1-0 against Manchester City and Southampton similarly against Coventry City. Newcastle United won by the odd goal in seven against Bradford City, leaving the Premier content down to just nine of the last 16.

The draw for round four unkindly pitted four Premiership teams against each other. Ipswich beat Coventry 2-1 and Sunderland had an identical victory over Manchester United. Birmingham kept up their excellent work with a 2-1 victory against Newcastle, Fulham defeated Derby County 3-2 at Craven Cottage and Sheffield Wednesday further cut into the Premier ranks with a 2-1 win at West Ham United. Yet the outstanding result was Liverpool's 8-0 win at Stoke City including a Fowler hat-trick, a record away win for the League Cup. Palace won on penalties against Tranmere and Manchester City beat Wimbledon 2-1. This left four of the last eight clubs representing the elite.

In the quarter-finals, Liverpool needed extra time before taking three goals off Fulham without reply, but Palace again did well beating Sunderland 2-1. Ipswich won 2-1 at Manchester City after a waterlogged abandonment and Birmingham's march continued with a 2-0 win over Wednesday.

Surprise surprise, the semi-final draw kept the Premier teams apart! Despite losing the first leg 1-0 at Ipswich Town, Birmingham won the return 4-1 in extra time and brave Palace's 2-1 lead over Liverpool vanished in a 5-0 drubbing at Anfield to set up the final in Wales.

# PAST LEAGUE CUP FINALS

*Played as two legs up to 1966*

|  | | | | |
|---|---|---|---|---|
| 1961 | Rotherham U | 2 | Aston Villa | 0 |
| | *Webster, Kirkman* | | | |
| | Aston Villa | 3 | Rotherham U | 0* |
| | *O'Neill, Burrows, McParland* | | | |
| 1962 | Rochdale | 0 | Norwich C | 3 |
| | | | *Lythgoe 2, Punton* | |
| | Norwich C | 1 | Rochdale | 0 |
| | *Hill* | | | |
| 1963 | Birmingham C | 3 | Aston Villa | 1 |
| | *Leek 2, Bloomfield* | | *Thomson* | |
| | Aston Villa | 0 | Birmingham C | 0 |
| 1964 | Stoke C | 1 | Leicester C | 1 |
| | *Bebbington* | | *Gibson* | |
| | Leicester C | 3 | Stoke C | 2 |
| | *Stringfellow, Gibson, Riley* | | *Viollet, Kinnell* | |
| 1965 | Chelsea | 3 | Leicester C | 2 |
| | *Tambling, Venables (pen), McCreadie* | | *Appleton, Goodfellow* | |
| | Leicester C | 0 | Chelsea | 0 |
| 1966 | West Ham U | 2 | WBA | 1 |
| | *Moore, Byrne* | | *Astle* | |
| | WBA | 4 | West Ham U | 1 |
| | *Kaye, Brown, Clark, Williams* | | *Peters* | |
| 1967 | QPR | 3 | WBA | 2 |
| | *Morgan R, Marsh, Lazarus* | | *Clark C 2* | |
| 1968 | Leeds U | 1 | Arsenal | 0 |
| | *Cooper* | | | |
| 1969 | Swindon T | 3 | Arsenal | 1* |
| | *Smart, Rogers 2* | | *Gould* | |
| 1970 | Manchester C | 2 | WBA | 1* |
| | *Doyle, Pardoe* | | *Astle* | |
| 1971 | Tottenham H | 2 | Aston Villa | 0 |
| | *Chivers 2* | | | |
| 1972 | Chelsea | 1 | Stoke C | 2 |
| | *Osgood* | | *Conroy, Eastham* | |
| 1973 | Tottenham H | 1 | Norwich C | 0 |
| | *Coates* | | | |
| 1974 | Wolverhampton W | 2 | Manchester C | 1 |
| | *Hibbitt, Richards* | | *Bell* | |
| 1975 | Aston Villa | 1 | Norwich C | 0 |
| | *Graydon* | | | |
| 1976 | Manchester C | 2 | Newcastle U | 1 |
| | *Barnes, Tueart* | | *Gowling* | |
| 1977 | Aston Villa | 0 | Everton | 0 |
| Replay | Aston Villa | 1 | Everton | 1* |
| | *Kenyon (og)* | | *Latchford* | |
| Replay | Aston Villa | 3 | Everton | 2* |
| | *Little 2, Nicholl* | | *Latchford, Lyons* | |

176

| 1978 | Nottingham F | 0 | Liverpool | 0* |
| Replay | Nottingham F | 1 | Liverpool | 0 |
| | *Robertson (pen)* | | | |
| 1979 | Nottingham F | 3 | Southampton | 2 |
| | *Birtles 2, Woodcock* | | *Peach, Holmes* | |
| 1980 | Wolverhampton W | 1 | Nottingham F | 0 |
| | *Gray* | | | |
| 1981 | Liverpool | 1 | West Ham U | 1* |
| | *Kennedy A* | | *Stewart (pen)* | |
| Replay | Liverpool | 2 | West Ham U | 1 |
| | *Dalglish, Hansen* | | *Goddard* | |
| 1982 | Liverpool | 3 | Tottenham H | 1* |
| | *Whelan 2, Rush* | | *Archibald* | |
| 1983 | Liverpool | 2 | Manchester U | 1* |
| | *Kennedy A, Whelan* | | *Whiteside* | |
| 1984 | Liverpool | 0 | Everton | 0* |
| Replay | Liverpool | 1 | Everton | 0 |
| | *Souness* | | | |
| 1985 | Norwich C | 1 | Sunderland | 0 |
| | *Chisholm (og)* | | | |
| 1986 | Oxford U | 3 | QPR | 0 |
| | *Hebberd, Houghton, Charles* | | | |
| 1987 | Arsenal | 2 | Liverpool | 1 |
| | *Nicholas 2* | | *Rush* | |
| 1988 | Luton T | 3 | Arsenal | 2 |
| | *Stein B 2, Wilson* | | *Hayes, Smith* | |
| 1989 | Nottingham F | 3 | Luton T | 1 |
| | *Clough 2, Webb* | | *Harford* | |
| 1990 | Nottingham F | 1 | Oldham Ath | 0 |
| | *Jemson* | | | |
| 1991 | Sheffield W | 1 | Manchester U | 0 |
| | *Sheridan* | | | |
| 1992 | Manchester U | 1 | Nottingham F | 0 |
| | *McClair* | | | |
| 1993 | Arsenal | 2 | Sheffield W | 1 |
| | *Merson, Morrow* | | *Harkes* | |
| 1994 | Aston Villa | 3 | Manchester U | 1 |
| | *Atkinson, Saunders 2 (1 pen)* | | *Hughes* | |
| 1995 | Liverpool | 2 | Bolton W | 1 |
| | *McManaman 2* | | *Thompson* | |
| 1996 | Aston Villa | 3 | Leeds U | 0 |
| | *Milosevic, Taylor, Yorke* | | | |
| 1997 | Leicester C | 1 | Middlesbrough | 1* |
| | *Heskey* | | *Ravanelli* | |
| Replay | Leicester C | 1 | Middlesbrough | 0* |
| | *Claridge* | | | |
| 1998 | Chelsea | 2 | Middlesbrough | 0* |
| | *Sinclair, Di Matteo* | | | |
| 1999 | Tottenham H | 1 | Leicester C | 0 |
| | *Nielsen* | | | |
| 2000 | Leicester C | 2 | Tranmere R | 1 |
| | *Elliott 2* | | *Kelly* | |

*After extra time*

# WORTHINGTON CUP 2000–2001

## FIRST ROUND, FIRST LEG

| | | | |
|---|---|---|---|
| Barnet | (0) 2 | Wycombe W | (0) 1 |
| Bolton W | (0) 1 | Macclesfield T | (0) 0 |
| Brighton & HA | (1) 1 | Millwall | (1) 2 |
| Bristol C | (2) 2 | Brentford | (1) 2 |
| Burnley | (0) 4 | Hartlepool U | (1) 1 |
| Cambridge U | (0) 0 | Portsmouth | (0) 0 |
| Crewe Alex | (0) 2 | Bury | (0) 2 |
| Darlington | (1) 2 | Nottingham F | (1) 2 |
| Gillingham | (1) 2 | Torquay U | (0) 0 |
| Grimsby T | (2) 2 | Carlisle U | (0) 0 |
| Hull C | (1) 1 | Notts Co | (0) 0 |
| Leyton Orient | (0) 1 | Reading | (1) 1 |
| Luton T | (0) 0 | Peterborough U | (0) 0 |
| Mansfield T | (0) 0 | Wrexham | (1) 1 |
| Northampton T | (1) 1 | Fulham | (0) 0 |
| Norwich C | (0) 0 | Bournemouth | (0) 0 |
| Oldham Ath | (1) 1 | Huddersfield T | (0) 0 |
| Port Vale | (1) 1 | Chesterfield | (2) 2 |
| Rochdale | (0) 1 | Blackburn R | (0) 1 |
| Rotherham U | (0) 0 | Barnsley | (1) 1 |
| Sheffield U | (2) 6 | Lincoln C | (1) 1 |
| Shrewsbury T | (0) 1 | Preston NE | (1) 1 |
| Southend U | (0) 0 | Birmingham C | (3) 5 |
| Stockport Co | (0) 0 | Blackpool | (1) 1 |
| Swansea C | (0) 0 | WBA | (0) 0 |
| Swindon T | (1) 1 | Exeter C | (0) 1 |
| Tranmere R | (2) 3 | Halifax T | (0) 0 |
| Walsall | (1) 1 | Kidderminster H | (0) 1 |
| Watford | (0) 0 | Cheltenham T | (0) 0 |
| Wigan Ath | (0) 1 | Scunthorpe U | (0) 0 |
| Wolverhampton W | (0) 0 | Oxford U | (0) 1 |
| York C | (0) 1 | Stoke C | (1) 5 |
| Colchester U | (0) 0 | QPR | (1) 1 |
| Crystal Palace | (2) 2 | Cardiff C | (0) 1 |
| Plymouth Arg | (0) 1 | Bristol R | (2) 2 |

## FIRST ROUND, SECOND LEG

| | | | |
|---|---|---|---|
| Barnsley | (0) 3 | Rotherham U | (1) 2 |
| *(Barnsley won 4-2 on aggregate.)* | | | |
| Birmingham C | (0) 0 | Southend U | (0) 0 |
| *(Birmingham C won 5-0 on aggregate.)* | | | |
| Blackpool | (1) 3 | Stockport Co | (1) 2 |
| *(Blackpool won 4-2 on aggregate.)* | | | |
| Bournemouth | (1) 1 | Norwich C | (0) 2 |
| *(Norwich C won 2-1 on aggregate.)* | | | |
| Brentford | (0) 2 | Bristol C | (1) 1 |
| *(Brentford won 4-3 on aggregate.)* | | | |
| Bristol R | (0) 1 | Plymouth Arg | (0) 1 |
| *(Bristol R won 3-2 on aggregate.)* | | | |
| Bury | (1) 1 | Crewe Alex | (1) 2 |
| *(Crewe Alex won 4-3 on aggregate.)* | | | |
| Cardiff C | (0) 0 | Crystal Palace | (0) 0 |
| *(Crystal Palace won 2-1 on aggregate.)* | | | |
| Carlisle U | (1) 1 | Grimsby T | (1) 1 |
| *(Grimsby T won 3-1 on aggregate.)* | | | |
| Cheltenham T | (0) 0 | Watford | (2) 3 |
| *(Watford won 3-0 on aggregate.)* | | | |
| Chesterfield | (0) 2 | Port Vale | (0) 2 |
| *(aet; Chesterfield won 4-3 on aggregate.)* | | | |

| Exeter C | (0) 1 | Swindon T | (2) 2 |
|---|---|---|---|

*(Swindon T won 3-2 on aggregate.)*

| Fulham | (1) 4 | Northampton T | (1) 1 |
|---|---|---|---|

*(Fulham won 4-2 on aggregate.)*

| Hartlepool U | (2) 3 | Burnley | (1) 2 |
|---|---|---|---|

*(Burnley won 6-4 on aggregate.)*

| Huddersfield T | (0) 0 | Oldham Ath | (1) 2 |
|---|---|---|---|

*(Oldham Ath won 3-0 on aggregate.)*

| Kidderminster H | (0) 0 | Walsall | (0) 1 |
|---|---|---|---|

*(Walsall won 2-1 on aggregate.)*

| Lincoln C | (0) 1 | Sheffield U | (0) 0 |
|---|---|---|---|

*(Sheffield U won 6-2 on aggregate.)*

| Macclesfield T | (2) 3 | Bolton W | (0) 1 |
|---|---|---|---|

*(Macclesfield T won 3-2 on aggregate.)*

| Millwall | (1) 1 | Brighton & HA | (0) 1 |
|---|---|---|---|

*(Millwall won 3-2 on aggregate.)*

| Notts Co | (0) 2 | Hull C | (0) 0 |
|---|---|---|---|

*(aet; Notts Co won 2-1 on aggregate.)*

| Oxford U | (1) 1 | Wolverhampton W | (0) 3 |
|---|---|---|---|

*(Wolverhampton W won 3-2 on aggregate.)*

| Peterborough U | (1) 2 | Luton T | (1) 2 |
|---|---|---|---|

*(aet; Luton T won on away goals rule.)*

| Portsmouth | (0) 1 | Cambridge U | (0) 0 |
|---|---|---|---|

*(Portsmouth won 1-0 on aggregate.)*

| Preston NE | (3) 4 | Shrewsbury T | (0) 1 |
|---|---|---|---|

*(Preston NE won 4-2 on aggregate.)*

| Reading | (0) 0 | Leyton Orient | (0) 2 |
|---|---|---|---|

*(Leyton Orient won 3-1 on aggregate.)*

| Scunthorpe U | (0) 1 | Wigan Ath | (1) 4 |
|---|---|---|---|

*(Wigan Ath won 5-1 on aggregate.)*

| Torquay U | (2) 3 | Gillingham | (1) 2 |
|---|---|---|---|

*(Gillingham won 4-3 on aggregate.)*

| Wrexham | (0) 0 | Mansfield T | (2) 3 |
|---|---|---|---|

*(Mansfield T won 3-1 on aggregate.)*

| Wycombe W | (1) 3 | Barnet | (1) 1 |
|---|---|---|---|

*(aet; Wycombe W won 4-3 on aggregate.)*

| Blackburn R | (2) 6 | Rochdale | (1) 1 |
|---|---|---|---|

*(Blackburn R won 7-2 on aggregate.)*

| Halifax T | (1) 1 | Tranmere R | (1) 2 |
|---|---|---|---|

*(Tranmere R won 5-1 on aggregate; at Valley Parade.)*

| Nottingham F | (1) 1 | Darlington | (0) 2 |
|---|---|---|---|

*(Darlington won 4-3 on aggregate.)*

| QPR | (1) 1 | Colchester U | (2) 4 |
|---|---|---|---|

*(Colchester U won 4-2 on aggregate.)*

| Stoke C | (0) 0 | York C | (0) 0 |
|---|---|---|---|

*(Stoke C won 5-1 on aggregate.)*

| WBA | (0) 2 | Swansea C | (0) 1 |
|---|---|---|---|

*(WBA won 2-1 on aggregate.)*

## SECOND ROUND, FIRST LEG

| Barnsley | (1) 4 | Crewe Alex | (0) 0 |
|---|---|---|---|
| Blackburn R | (2) 4 | Portsmouth | (0) 0 |
| Brentford | (0) 0 | Tottenham H | (0) 0 |
| Burnley | (0) 2 | Crystal Palace | (1) 2 |
| Chesterfield | (0) 1 | Fulham | (0) 0 |
| Darlington | (0) 0 | Bradford C | (1) 1 |
| Derby Co | (1) 1 | WBA | (0) 2 |
| Middlesbrough | (0) 2 | Macclesfield T | (0) 1 |
| Millwall | (1) 2 | Ipswich T | (0) 0 |
| Norwich C | (3) 3 | Blackpool | (2) 3 |
| Notts Co | (0) 1 | Watford | (0) 3 |
| Oldham Ath | (1) 1 | Sheffield W | (1) 3 |
| Preston NE | (0) 1 | Coventry C | (2) 3 |
| Sheffield U | (1) 3 | Colchester U | (0) 0 |
| Sunderland | (0) 3 | Luton T | (0) 0 |

| | | | |
|---|---|---|---|
| Tranmere R | (0) 1 | Swindon T | (0) 1 |
| Walsall | (0) 0 | West Ham U | (0) 1 |
| Wimbledon | (0) 0 | Wigan Ath | (0) 0 |
| Wycombe W | (1) 3 | Birmingham C | (3) 4 |
| Everton | (0) 1 | Bristol R | (0) 1 |
| Manchester C | (0) 1 | Gillingham | (0) 1 |
| Newcastle U | (1) 2 | Leyton Orient | (0) 0 |
| Southampton | (1) 2 | Mansfield T | (0) 0 |
| Stoke C | (1) 2 | Charlton Ath | (1) 1 |
| Grimsby T | (1) 3 | Wolverhampton W | (2) 2 |

## SECOND ROUND, SECOND LEG

| | | | |
|---|---|---|---|
| Birmingham C | (0) 1 | Wycombe W | (0) 0 |
| *(Birmingham C won 5-3 on aggregate.)* | | | |
| Bradford C | (4) 7 | Darlington | (0) 2 |
| *(Bradford C won 8-2 on aggregate.)* | | | |
| Charlton Ath | (1) 4 | Stoke C | (1) 3 |
| *(aet; Stoke C won on away goals rule.)* | | | |
| Crewe Alex | (0) 0 | Barnsley | (1) 3 |
| *(Barnsley won 7-0 on aggregate.)* | | | |
| Crystal Palace | (0) 1 | Burnley | (1) 1 |
| *(aet; Crystal Palace won on away goals rule.)* | | | |
| Gillingham | (1) 2 | Manchester C | (0) 4 |
| *(aet; Manchester C won 5-3 on aggregate.)* | | | |
| Ipswich T | (0) 5 | Millwall | (0) 0 |
| *(aet; Ipswich T won 5-2 on aggregate.)* | | | |
| Leyton Orient | (1) 1 | Newcastle U | (1) 1 |
| *(Newcastle U won 3-1 on aggregate.)* | | | |
| Luton T | (0) 1 | Sunderland | (2) 2 |
| *(Sunderland won 5-1 on aggregate.)* | | | |
| Macclesfield T | (1) 1 | Middlesbrough | (1) 3 |
| *(Middlesbrough won 5-2 on aggregate.)* | | | |
| Mansfield T | (0) 1 | Southampton | (2) 3 |
| *(Southampton won 5-1 on aggregate.)* | | | |
| Portsmouth | (0) 1 | Blackburn R | (0) 1 |
| *(Blackburn R won 5-1 on aggregate.)* | | | |
| Swindon T | (0) 0 | Tranmere R | (1) 1 |
| *(Tranmere R won 2-1 on aggregate.)* | | | |
| Tottenham H | (0) 2 | Brentford | (0) 0 |
| *(Tottenham H won 2-0 on aggregate.)* | | | |
| Watford | (0) 0 | Notts Co | (0) 2 |
| *(aet; Watford won on away goals rule.)* | | | |
| WBA | (2) 2 | Derby Co | (2) 4 |
| *(Derby Co won 5-4 on aggregate.)* | | | |
| Wigan Ath | (0) 1 | Wimbledon | (1) 2 |
| *(Wimbledon won 2-1 on aggregate.)* | | | |
| Bristol R | (0) 1 | Everton | (1) 1 |
| *(aet; Bristol R won 4-2 on penalties.)* | | | |
| Colchester U | (0) 0 | Sheffield U | (0) 1 |
| *(Sheffield U won 4-0 on aggregate.)* | | | |
| Coventry C | (3) 4 | Preston NE | (0) 1 |
| *(Coventry C won 7-2 on aggregate.)* | | | |
| Fulham | (1) 4 | Chesterfield | (0) 0 |
| *(Fulham won 4-1 on aggregate.)* | | | |
| Sheffield W | (1) 5 | Oldham Ath | (1) 1 |
| *(Sheffield W won 8-2 on aggregate.)* | | | |
| West Ham U | (1) 1 | Walsall | (1) 1 |
| *(West Ham U won 2-1 on aggregate.)* | | | |
| Blackpool | (0) 0 | Norwich C | (2) 5 |
| *(Norwich C won 8-3 on aggregate.)* | | | |
| Wolverhampton W | (1) 2 | Grimsby T | (0) 0 |
| *(Wolverhampton W won 4-3 on aggregate.)* | | | |

## THIRD ROUND

| | | | |
|---|---|---|---|
| Bristol R | (0) 1 | Sunderland | (0) 2 |
| Tottenham H | (0) 1 | Birmingham C | (3) 3 |
| Tranmere R | (0) 3 | Leeds U | (2) 2 |
| *(aet.)* | | | |
| Watford | (0) 0 | Manchester U | (1) 3 |
| West Ham U | (0) 2 | Blackburn R | (0) 0 |
| Wimbledon | (0) 1 | Middlesbrough | (0) 0 |
| Arsenal | (1) 1 | Ipswich T | (1) 2 |
| Aston Villa | (0) 0 | Manchester C | (0) 1 |
| Derby Co | (3) 3 | Norwich C | (0) 0 |
| Fulham | (0) 3 | Wolverhampton W | (0) 2 |
| Leicester C | (0) 0 | Crystal Palace | (2) 3 |
| Liverpool | (1) 2 | Chelsea | (1) 1 |
| *(aet.)* | | | |
| Newcastle U | (3) 4 | Bradford C | (1) 3 |
| Sheffield W | (1) 2 | Sheffield U | (1) 1 |
| *(aet.)* | | | |
| Southampton | (0) 0 | Coventry C | (0) 1 |
| *(aet.)* | | | |
| Stoke C | (1) 3 | Barnsley | (1) 2 |

## FOURTH ROUND

| | | | |
|---|---|---|---|
| Crystal Palace | (0) 0 | Tranmere R | (0) 0 |
| *(aet; Crystal Palace won 6-5 on penalties.)* | | | |
| Ipswich T | (1) 2 | Coventry C | (0) 1 |
| Sunderland | (0) 2 | Manchester U | (1) 1 |
| *(aet.)* | | | |
| Birmingham C | (1) 2 | Newcastle U | (1) 1 |
| Fulham | (2) 3 | Derby Co | (2) 2 |
| Manchester C | (1) 2 | Wimbledon | (1) 1 |
| Stoke C | (0) 0 | Liverpool | (4) 8 |
| West Ham U | (0) 1 | Sheffield W | (1) 2 |

## FIFTH ROUND

| | | | |
|---|---|---|---|
| Birmingham C | (1) 2 | Sheffield W | (0) 0 |
| Manchester C | 1 | Ipswich T | 1 |
| *(Abandoned 23 minutes; waterlogged pitch.)* | | | |
| Liverpool | (0) 3 | Fulham | (0) 0 |
| *(aet.)* | | | |
| Crystal Palace | (0) 2 | Sunderland | (0) 1 |
| Manchester C | (1) 1 | Ipswich T | (0) 2 |
| *(aet.)* | | | |

## SEMI-FINAL, FIRST LEG

| | | | |
|---|---|---|---|
| Ipswich T | (1) 1 | Birmingham C | (0) 0 |
| Crystal Palace | (0) 2 | Liverpool | (0) 1 |

## SEMI-FINAL, SECOND LEG

| | | | |
|---|---|---|---|
| Liverpool | (3) 5 | Crystal Palace | (0) 0 |
| Birmingham C | (1) 4 | Ipswich T | (0) 1 |
| *(aet.)* | | | |

### FINAL (at Millennium Stadium)

### 25 FEB

**Birmingham C (0) 1** *(Purse 90 (pen))*
**Liverpool (1) 1** *(Fowler 30)*                                              73,500

*Birmingham C:* Bennett; Eaden, Grainger, Sonner (Hughes), Purse, Johnson M,
McCarthy, O'Connor, Horsfield (Marcelo), Adebola (Johnson A), Lazaridis.
*Liverpool:* Westerveld; Babbel, Carragher, Hamann, Henchoz, Hyypia, Gerrard
(McAllister), Smicer (Barmby), Heskey, Fowler, Biscan (Ziege).
*aet; Liverpool won 5-4 on penalties.*
*Referee:* D. Elleray (Harrow).

# LDV VANS TROPHY 2000–2001

## FIRST ROUND

| | | | |
|---|---|---|---|
| Barnet | (2) 2 | Rushden & D | (0) 0 |
| Lincoln C | (1) 3 | Morecambe | (1) 2 |
| Bournemouth | (0) 1 | Dover Ath | (1) 1 |

*(aet; Bournemouth won 4-2 on penalties.)*

| | | | |
|---|---|---|---|
| Brentford | (3) 4 | Oxford U | (0) 1 |
| Brighton & HA | (2) 2 | Cardiff C | (0) 0 |
| Cambridge U | (2) 2 | Colchester U | (0) 0 |
| Chester C | (0) 1 | Hull C | (0) 0 |
| Doncaster R | (1) 3 | Rochdale | (1) 2 |

*(aet; Doncaster R won on sudden death.)*

| | | | |
|---|---|---|---|
| Millwall | (2) 4 | Northampton T | (0) 1 |
| Peterborough U | (0) 1 | Luton T | (0) 0 |
| Plymouth Arg | (1) 3 | Bristol C | (0) 0 |
| Rotherham U | (0) 3 | Chesterfield | (3) 4 |

*(aet; Chesterfield won on sudden death.)*

| | | | |
|---|---|---|---|
| Southend U | (2) 2 | Cheltenham T | (0) 0 |
| Wycombe W | (0) 1 | Exeter C | (0) 0 |
| Stoke C | (2) 3 | Scarborough | (0) 1 |
| Bury | (1) 2 | Mansfield T | (1) 1 |
| Torquay U | (0) 0 | Bristol R | (0) 2 |
| Wrexham | (0) 0 | Halifax T | (0) 1 |
| Hartlepool U | (2) 3 | Scunthorpe U | (1) 2 |
| Kidderminster H | (1) 2 | Carlisle U | (0) 1 |

*(aet; Kidderminster H won on sudden death.)*

| | | | |
|---|---|---|---|
| Hereford U | (2) 4 | Yeovil T | (0) 0 |
| Oldham Ath | (1) 2 | Wigan Ath | (1) 3 |

*(aet; Wigan Ath won on sudden death.)*

| | | | |
|---|---|---|---|
| Port Vale | (2) 3 | Notts Co | (0) 0 |
| York C | (0) 0 | Darlington | (2) 4 |

## SECOND ROUND

| | | | |
|---|---|---|---|
| Bournemouth | (0) 0 | Swansea C | (0) 1 |
| Brighton & HA | (2) 2 | Brentford | (1) 2 |

*(aet; Brentford won 4-2 on penalties.)*

| | | | |
|---|---|---|---|
| Bristol R | (1) 3 | Plymouth Arg | (0) 0 |
| Chesterfield | (2) 4 | Macclesfield T | (1) 2 |
| Halifax T | (2) 2 | Stoke C | (2) 3 |
| Hartlepool U | (1) 3 | Doncaster R | (0) 1 |
| Hereford U | (0) 1 | Reading | (2) 2 |
| Leyton Orient | (0) 0 | Wycombe W | (1) 2 |
| Lincoln C | (1) 3 | Blackpool | (0) 1 |
| Millwall | (0) 0 | Swindon T | (0) 0 |

*(aet; Swindon T won 3-2 on penalties.)*

| | | | |
|---|---|---|---|
| Peterborough U | (0) 1 | Barnet | (1) 3 |
| Southend U | (2) 3 | Cambridge U | (1) 1 |
| Bury | (2) 2 | Kidderminster H | (0) 0 |
| Darlington | (1) 2 | Shrewsbury T | (0) 0 |
| Port Vale | (1) 2 | Chester C | (0) 0 |
| Walsall | (1) 2 | Wigan Ath | (1) 1 |

## QUARTER-FINALS

| | | | |
|---|---|---|---|
| Barnet | (0) 1 | Brentford | (1) 2 |
| Bury | (0) 0 | Chesterfield | (3) 3 |
| Lincoln C | (1) 1 | Hartlepool U | (0) 0 |
| Southend U | (1) 1 | Bristol R | (0) 0 |

| | | | |
|---|---|---|---|
| Swansea C | (0) 1 | Reading | (0) 0 |
| Swindon T | (2) 2 | Wycombe W | (1) 1 |
| Port Vale | (1) 4 | Darlington | (0) 0 |
| Stoke C | (1) 4 | Walsall | (0) 0 |

## NORTHERN SEMI-FINALS

| | | | |
|---|---|---|---|
| Lincoln C | (1) 4 | Chesterfield | (0) 1 |
| Port Vale | (0) 2 | Stoke C | (0) 1 |

*(aet; Port Vale won on sudden death.)*

## SOUTHERN SEMI-FINALS

| | | | |
|---|---|---|---|
| Southend U | (0) 2 | Swindon T | (0) 1 |

*(aet; Southend U won on sudden death.)*

| | | | |
|---|---|---|---|
| Swansea C | (0) 2 | Brentford | (1) 3 |

## NORTHERN FINAL, FIRST LEG

| | | | |
|---|---|---|---|
| Lincoln C | (0) 0 | Port Vale | (0) 2 |

## NORTHERN FINAL, SECOND LEG

| | | | |
|---|---|---|---|
| Port Vale | (0) 0 | Lincoln C | (0) 0 |

*(Port Vale won 2-0 on aggregate.)*

## SOUTHERN FINAL, FIRST LEG

| | | | |
|---|---|---|---|
| Southend U | (0) 1 | Brentford | (0) 2 |

## SOUTHERN FINAL, SECOND LEG

| | | | |
|---|---|---|---|
| Brentford | (1) 2 | Southend U | (1) 1 |

*(Brentford won 4-2 on aggregate.)*

### FINAL (at Millennium Stadium)

### 22 APR

**Brentford (1) 1** *(Dobson 3)*
**Port Vale (0) 2** *(Bridge-Wilkinson 77 (pen), Brooker 84)* 25,654

*Brentford:* Gottskalksson; Gibbs (Williams), Dobson, Mahon, Powell, Theobald, Ingimarsson, Evans, Owusu, Rowlands (McCammon), Partridge.
*Port Vale:* Goodlad; Burton, Carragher, Brammer, Walsh, Brisco, Bridge-Wilkinson, Cummins, Naylor, Brooker, Smith.
*Referee:* W.C. Burns (Scarborough).

# FA CHARITY SHIELD WINNERS 1908–2000

| 1908 | Manchester U v QPR | |
| | 4-0 after 1-1 draw | |
| 1909 | Newcastle U v Northampton T 2-0 | |
| 1910 | Brighton v Aston Villa | 1-0 |
| 1911 | Manchester U v Swindon T | 8-4 |
| 1912 | Blackburn R v QPR | 2-1 |
| 1913 | Professionals v Amateurs | 7-2 |
| 1920 | Tottenham H v Burnley | 2-0 |
| 1921 | Huddersfield T v Liverpool | 1-0 |
| 1922 | Not played | |
| 1923 | Professionals v Amateurs | 2-0 |
| 1924 | Professionals v Amateurs | 3-1 |
| 1925 | Amateurs v Professionals | 6-1 |
| 1926 | Amateurs v Professionals | 6-3 |
| 1927 | Cardiff C v Corinthians | 2-1 |
| 1928 | Everton v Blackburn R | 2-1 |
| 1929 | Professionals v Amateurs | 3-0 |
| 1930 | Arsenal v Sheffield W | 2-1 |
| 1931 | Arsenal v WBA | 1-0 |
| 1932 | Everton v Newcastle U | 5-3 |
| 1933 | Arsenal v Everton | 3-0 |
| 1934 | Arsenal v Manchester C | 4-0 |
| 1935 | Sheffield W v Arsenal | 1-0 |
| 1936 | Sunderland v Arsenal | 2-1 |
| 1937 | Manchester C v Sunderland | 2-0 |
| 1938 | Arsenal v Preston NE | 2-1 |
| 1948 | Arsenal v Manchester U | 4-3 |
| 1949 | Portsmouth v Wolverhampton W | 1-1* |
| 1950 | World Cup Team v | 4-2 |
| | Canadian Touring Team | |
| 1951 | Tottenham H v Newcastle U | 2-1 |
| 1952 | Manchester U v Newcastle U | 4-2 |
| 1953 | Arsenal v Blackpool | 3-1 |
| 1954 | Wolverhampton W v WBA | 4-4* |
| 1955 | Chelsea v Newcastle U | 3-0 |
| 1956 | Manchester U v Manchester C | 1-0 |
| 1957 | Manchester U v Aston Villa | 4-0 |
| 1958 | Bolton W v Wolverhampton W | 4-1 |
| 1959 | Wolverhampton W v | 3-1 |
| | Nottingham F | |

| 1960 | Burnley v Wolverhampton W | 2-2* |
| 1961 | Tottenham H v FA XI | 3-2 |
| 1962 | Tottenham H v Ipswich T | 5-1 |
| 1963 | Everton v Manchester U | 4-0 |
| 1964 | Liverpool v West Ham U | 2-2* |
| 1965 | Manchester U v Liverpool | 2-2* |
| 1966 | Liverpool v Everton | 1-0 |
| 1967 | Manchester U v Tottenham H | 3-3* |
| 1968 | Manchester C v WBA | 6-1 |
| 1969 | Leeds U v Manchester C | 2-1 |
| 1970 | Everton v Chelsea | 2-1 |
| 1971 | Leicester C v Liverpool | 1-0 |
| 1972 | Manchester C v Aston Villa | 1-0 |
| 1973 | Burnley v Manchester C | 1-0 |
| 1974 | Liverpool† v Leeds U | 1-1 |
| 1975 | Derby Co v West Ham U | 2-0 |
| 1976 | Liverpool v Southampton | 1-0 |
| 1977 | Liverpool v Manchester U | 0-0* |
| 1978 | Nottingham F v Ipswich T | 5-0 |
| 1979 | Liverpool v Arsenal | 3-1 |
| 1980 | Liverpool v West Ham U | 1-0 |
| 1981 | Aston Villa v Tottenham H | 2-2* |
| 1982 | Liverpool v Tottenham H | 1-0 |
| 1983 | Manchester U v Liverpool | 2-0 |
| 1984 | Everton v Liverpool | 1-0 |
| 1985 | Everton v Manchester U | 2-0 |
| 1986 | Everton v Liverpool | 1-1* |
| 1987 | Everton v Coventry C | 1-0 |
| 1988 | Liverpool v Wimbledon | 2-1 |
| 1989 | Liverpool v Arsenal | 1-0 |
| 1990 | Liverpool v Manchester U | 1-1* |
| 1991 | Arsenal v Tottenham H | 0-0* |
| 1992 | Leeds U v Liverpool | 4-3 |
| 1993 | Manchester U† v Arsenal | 1-1 |
| 1994 | Manchester U v Blackburn R | 2-0 |
| 1995 | Everton v Blackburn R | 1-0 |
| 1996 | Manchester U v Newcastle U | 4-0 |
| 1997 | Manchester U† v Chelsea | 1-1 |
| 1998 | Arsenal v Manchester U | 3-0 |
| 1999 | Arsenal v Manchester U | 2-1 |

*Each club retained shield for six months. †Won on penalties.

## ONE2ONE CHARITY SHIELD 2000

### Chelsea (1) 2, Manchester U (0) 0

At Wembley, 13 August 2000, attendance 65,148

*Chelsea:* De Goey; Melchiot, Babayaro, Stanic, Leboeuf, Desailly, Poyet (Le Saux), Di Matteo (Morris), Hasselbaink, Zola (Gudjohnsen), Wise.

*Scorers:* Hasselbaink 22, Melchiot 72.

*Manchester U:* Barthez; Irwin, Silvestre (Stam), Johnsen, Keane, Neville G, Beckham, Scholes, Solskjaer (Cole), Sheringham (Yorke), Giggs (Fortune).

*Referee:* M. Riley (Leeds).

# SCOTTISH LEAGUE REVIEW 2000-2001

Celtic's masterstroke of appointing Martin O'Neill as manager paid off in the most handsome of ways with a clean sweep of domestic trophies: the CIS Insurance Cup, the Tennent's Scottish Cup and the Scottish Premier League.

A Henrik Larsson hat-trick disposed of Kilmarnock in the cup final after a 3-1 semi-final win over Rangers and at the time Celtic were seven points clear of their rivals at the top of the League. And even before the table was split, Celtic had seized the championship. Before the Scottish Cup final wrapped up the season, Celtic could look back having stretched their lead to 15 points.

Celtic's third trophy came from another 3-0 victory, this time against Hibernian and served to underline the total domination the club enjoyed throughout the campaign. Finishing runners-up in Scotland is almost the equivalent of coming second in a two-horse race and Rangers will have been disappointed at the outcome. This was even more of a shock for the Ibrox club since the previous season they had won the title by a staggering 21 point margin.

For Celtic it was their first treble for 32 years and the season was also a milestone one for top scorer Larsson who took his tally to a staggering 53 goals for the club, 35 of them in the League.

However, the early stages had seen Hibernian top of the pile and unbeaten in the first six games until losing predictably perhaps 3-0 at Celtic. The Easter Road club did have a good season overall and merited third place. But foreign packed Dundee found their home form so wretched that they only scraped into the top six on the last day - after winning away.

Tayside neighbours Dundee United looked doomed and after 20 matches had managed only seven points. But they overhauled St Mirren late in February and improved considerably afterwards.

The 2000-01 season was also the first of the new structure whereby 12 teams competed for the championship. The intention was for each one to play three fixtures against the others at which point a split would be introduced dividing top and bottom. The six at the top would play-off for the championship, the rest being concerned with avoiding relegation.

Unfortunately at the time, Celtic had taken the League and there were just European places to be fought for the top half dozen and at the other end, merely a question of whether St Mirren could avoid the drop at the expense of Dundee United.

Again the imbalance of playing just five matches in this second stage served no satisfaction except that it enabled all clubs to play 38 games. The alternative of 44 games overall with every club playing each other four times was deemed unacceptable, especially when you consider a winter break has cut down the number of weeks in which football can be played in the Premier League.

The remaining excitement on the last day was that Kilmarnock secured the last European berth in front of Hearts while St Mirren, already doomed by this time, went back to the Scottish League to be replaced by Livingston. Formerly Meadowbank Thistle, they have only been in existence for 27 years and also reached the Scottish Cup semi-final.

The line-up for Europe in 2001-02 will be: Celtic and Rangers in the Champions League yet again, Hibs and Killie in the UEFA Cup while Dundee accepted an invitation to enter the Intertoto Cup. Whatever criticism there is of the Scottish structure, five places in Europe from only 12 clubs is a remarkable ratio.

Down from the First Division went Morton, one of a number of clubs in financial difficulty, and Alloa. Their replacements are Partick Thistle and Arbroath. Into Division Three went Queen's Park and Stirling Albion, with Hamilton Academical and Cowdenbeath taking their places.

It was a mixed season for newcomers Peterhead and Elgin City. The former finished fifth in Division Three but Elgin found it tougher and had to settle for the wooden spoon.

In terms of European success, neither Celtic nor Rangers covered themselves with any glory last term. Rangers failed to make the cut in the Champions League and Celtic went out of the UEFA Cup by losing 2-1 in the home leg of the second round tie with Bordeaux after extra time.

Expectations will be high at Celtic next season though the pressures on the top two will stay as intense as ever.

# SCOTTISH LEAGUE TABLES 2000–2001

**Premier Division**

| | P | Home | | | Goals | | Away | | | Goals | | GD | Pts |
|---|---|---|---|---|---|---|---|---|---|---|---|---|---|
| | | W | D | L | F | A | W | D | L | F | A | | |
| Celtic | 38 | 17 | 1 | 1 | 49 | 14 | 14 | 3 | 2 | 41 | 18 | 61 | 97 |
| Rangers | 38 | 15 | 0 | 4 | 45 | 16 | 11 | 4 | 4 | 31 | 20 | 40 | 82 |
| Hibernian | 38 | 11 | 6 | 2 | 37 | 15 | 7 | 6 | 6 | 20 | 20 | 22 | 66 |
| Kilmarnock | 38 | 7 | 4 | 8 | 20 | 25 | 8 | 5 | 6 | 24 | 28 | –9 | 54 |
| Hearts | 38 | 11 | 2 | 6 | 36 | 21 | 3 | 8 | 8 | 20 | 29 | 6 | 52 |
| Dundee | 38 | 4 | 7 | 8 | 25 | 24 | 9 | 1 | 9 | 26 | 25 | 2 | 47 |
| Aberdeen | 38 | 6 | 6 | 7 | 24 | 24 | 5 | 6 | 8 | 21 | 28 | –7 | 45 |
| Motherwell | 38 | 5 | 4 | 10 | 22 | 27 | 7 | 3 | 9 | 20 | 29 | –14 | 43 |
| Dunfermline Ath | 38 | 8 | 6 | 5 | 20 | 17 | 3 | 3 | 13 | 14 | 37 | –20 | 42 |
| St Johnstone | 38 | 4 | 6 | 9 | 22 | 31 | 5 | 7 | 7 | 18 | 25 | –16 | 40 |
| Dundee U | 38 | 5 | 6 | 8 | 21 | 28 | 4 | 2 | 13 | 17 | 35 | –25 | 35 |
| St Mirren | 38 | 7 | 3 | 9 | 20 | 25 | 1 | 3 | 15 | 12 | 47 | –40 | 30 |

**First Division**

| | P | Home | | | Goals | | Away | | | Goals | | GD | Pts |
|---|---|---|---|---|---|---|---|---|---|---|---|---|---|
| | | W | D | L | F | A | W | D | L | F | A | | |
| Livingston | 36 | 13 | 2 | 3 | 39 | 14 | 10 | 5 | 3 | 33 | 17 | 41 | 76 |
| Ayr U | 36 | 11 | 6 | 1 | 44 | 19 | 8 | 6 | 4 | 29 | 22 | 32 | 69 |
| Falkirk | 36 | 8 | 6 | 4 | 29 | 24 | 8 | 2 | 8 | 28 | 35 | –2 | 56 |
| Inverness CT | 36 | 9 | 4 | 5 | 42 | 25 | 5 | 8 | 5 | 29 | 29 | 17 | 54 |
| Clyde | 36 | 4 | 10 | 4 | 23 | 24 | 7 | 4 | 7 | 21 | 22 | –2 | 47 |
| Ross Co | 36 | 5 | 3 | 10 | 21 | 25 | 6 | 7 | 5 | 27 | 27 | –4 | 43 |
| Raith R | 36 | 5 | 4 | 9 | 24 | 26 | 5 | 4 | 9 | 17 | 29 | –14 | 38 |
| Airdrieonians | 36 | 4 | 8 | 6 | 25 | 24 | 4 | 6 | 8 | 24 | 43 | –18 | 38 |
| Morton | 36 | 3 | 4 | 11 | 13 | 37 | 6 | 4 | 8 | 21 | 24 | –27 | 35 |
| Alloa Ath | 36 | 5 | 5 | 8 | 21 | 28 | 2 | 6 | 10 | 17 | 33 | –23 | 32 |

**Second Division**

| | P | Home | | | Goals | | Away | | | Goals | | GD | Pts |
|---|---|---|---|---|---|---|---|---|---|---|---|---|---|
| | | W | D | L | F | A | W | D | L | F | A | | |
| Partick T | 36 | 11 | 5 | 2 | 34 | 13 | 11 | 4 | 3 | 32 | 19 | 34 | 75 |
| Arbroath | 36 | 10 | 6 | 2 | 39 | 20 | 5 | 7 | 6 | 15 | 18 | 16 | 58 |
| Berwick R | 36 | 8 | 5 | 5 | 26 | 22 | 6 | 7 | 5 | 25 | 22 | 7 | 54 |
| Stranraer | 36 | 7 | 4 | 7 | 25 | 27 | 8 | 5 | 5 | 26 | 23 | 1 | 54 |
| Clydebank | 36 | 8 | 4 | 6 | 25 | 22 | 4 | 7 | 7 | 17 | 21 | –1 | 47 |
| Queen of the S | 36 | 5 | 5 | 8 | 24 | 30 | 8 | 2 | 8 | 28 | 29 | –7 | 46 |
| Stenhousemuir | 36 | 8 | 4 | 6 | 27 | 19 | 4 | 2 | 12 | 18 | 44 | –18 | 42 |
| Forfar Ath | 36 | 5 | 4 | 9 | 28 | 25 | 5 | 6 | 7 | 20 | 27 | –4 | 40 |
| Queen's Park | 36 | 5 | 6 | 7 | 14 | 16 | 5 | 4 | 9 | 14 | 24 | –12 | 40 |
| Stirling Albion | 36 | 3 | 9 | 6 | 15 | 20 | 2 | 8 | 8 | 19 | 30 | –16 | 32 |

**Third Division**

| | P | Home | | | Goals | | Away | | | Goals | | GD | Pts |
|---|---|---|---|---|---|---|---|---|---|---|---|---|---|
| | | W | D | L | F | A | W | D | L | F | A | | |
| Hamilton A | 36 | 11 | 5 | 2 | 40 | 13 | 11 | 5 | 2 | 35 | 17 | 45 | 76 |
| Cowdenbeath | 36 | 14 | 3 | 1 | 38 | 13 | 9 | 4 | 5 | 20 | 18 | 27 | 76 |
| Brechin C | 36 | 13 | 3 | 2 | 42 | 17 | 9 | 3 | 6 | 29 | 19 | 35 | 72 |
| East Fife | 36 | 8 | 4 | 6 | 24 | 23 | 7 | 4 | 7 | 25 | 23 | 3 | 53 |
| Peterhead | 36 | 7 | 5 | 6 | 24 | 19 | 6 | 5 | 7 | 22 | 27 | 0 | 49 |
| Dumbarton | 36 | 7 | 1 | 10 | 28 | 28 | 6 | 5 | 7 | 18 | 21 | –3 | 45 |
| Albion R | 36 | 4 | 6 | 8 | 16 | 22 | 8 | 3 | 7 | 22 | 21 | –5 | 45 |
| East Stirlingshire | 36 | 4 | 4 | 10 | 11 | 26 | 6 | 3 | 9 | 26 | 43 | –32 | 37 |
| Montrose | 36 | 1 | 6 | 11 | 13 | 29 | 5 | 2 | 11 | 18 | 36 | –34 | 26 |
| Elgin C | 36 | 3 | 2 | 13 | 17 | 37 | 2 | 5 | 11 | 12 | 28 | –36 | 22 |

# BELL'S SCOTTISH LEAGUE—PREMIER DIVISION RESULTS 2000–2001

| | Aberdeen | Celtic | Dundee | Dundee U | Dunfermline Ath | Hearts | Hibernian | Kilmarnock | Motherwell | Rangers | St Johnstone | St Mirren |
|---|---|---|---|---|---|---|---|---|---|---|---|---|
| Aberdeen | — | 1-1 | 0-2 | 4-1 *1-2* | 0-0 *1-0* | 1-1 | 0-2 | 1-2 | 3-3 | 1-2 | 1-1 | 2-1 |
| Celtic | 6-0 | — | 1-0 *0-2* | 2-1 | 3-1 | 1-1 | 1-0 | 6-0 | 1-0 | 6-2 *1-0* | 1-2 | 3-0 |
| Dundee | 2-2 | 0-2 | — | 2-3 | 3-0 | 1-1 | 0-0 | 3-1 | 0-2 | 0-3 | 2-3 | 2-1 |
| Dundee U | 3-1 | 2-1 | 3-0 *2-3* | — | 3-0 *0-1* | 0-4 | 1-1 | 0-1 | 0-0 | 1-0 | 1-0 *2-3* | 1-0 |
| Dunfermline Ath | 3-2 | 0-3 | 3-2 *1-0* | 2-0 *7-1* | — | 1-0 | 2-1 | 1-0 | 4-1 *2-0* | 0-1 *1-2* | 0-2 | 5-0 |
| Hearts | 3-0 | 2-4 | 1-1 | 0-4 *1-1* | 2-0 *3-0* | — | 1-1 *2-1* | 6-2 *0-0* | 0-3 *1-1* | 0-1 *1-4* | 0-3 *2-0 2-2* | 1-0 |
| Hibernian | 0-2 | 0-3 | 1-1 | 2-1 | 0-0 | 1-1 | — | 0-2 | 3-0 | 1-0 *0-0* | 0-3 | 2-0 |
| Kilmarnock | 1-0 | 0-1 *2-5* | 0-2 | 0-0 *2-1* | 2-2 | 2-0 | 0-1 | — | 3-2 *1-2* | 2-4 *1-2* | 0-2 | 4-2 |
| Motherwell | 3-1 | 3-3 | 0-2 | 0-3 | 0-2 | 1-0 | 1-1 | 1-2 | — | 0-1 *1-2* | 0-2 | 2-1 |
| Rangers | 1-0 | 5-1 *0-3* | 3-0 | 0-2 *1-0 2-3* | 4-1 *2-0* | 1-0 *4-0* | 1-0 | 0-3 *5-1* | 2-0 | — | 4-0 *0-1 1-0* | 2-0 *3-3* |
| St Johnstone | 0-0 *0-3* | 1-2 | 2-3 | 0-2 | 0-2 | 2-2 *2-2* | 1-2 | 1-1 *1-2* | 2-3 | 2-1 | — | 2-0 *2-2* |
| St Mirren | 2-0 *2-1* | 0-2 | 2-1 | 1-1 *2-1* | 2-1 *1-1* | 1-2 | 1-1 | 0-1 *1-3* | 0-1 *0-1* | 1-3 *1-3* | 0-1 *1-0* | — |

# BELL'S SCOTTISH LEAGUE—DIVISION ONE RESULTS 2000–2001

| | Airdrieonians | Alloa Ath | Ayr U | Clyde | Falkirk | Inverness CT | Livingston | Morton | Raith R | Ross Co |
|---|---|---|---|---|---|---|---|---|---|---|
| Airdrieonians | — | 2-2 | 0-0 | 1-3 | 1-2 | 1-2 | 1-2 | 1-1 | 1-1 | 5-1 |
| Alloa Ath | 2-0 | — | 1-1 | 1-0 | 1-2 | 1-1 | 1-1 | 0-2 | 3-0 | 2-2 |
| Ayr U | 6-0 | 3-1 | — | 3-1 | 3-2 | 1-4 | 0-6 | 2-1 | 0-1 | 0-0 |
| Clyde | 3-1 | 4-1 | 0-2 | — | 0-1 | 3-3 | 0-2 | 0-3 | 1-2 | 1-1 |
| Falkirk | 2-2 | 0-0 | 2-0 | 2-0 | — | 1-1 | 1-1 | 3-0 | 2-0 | 1-0 |
| Inverness CT | 4-1 | 1-1 | 0-1 | 3-2 | 2-3 | — | 3-2 | 1-0 | 2-1 | 2-0 |
| Livingston | 0-2 | 1-1 | 3-0 | 1-2 | 1-1 | 2-1 | — | 1-3 | 2-0 | 2-3 |
| Morton | 4-0 | 2-2 | 1-0 | 2-2 | 4-1 | 2-1 | 2-3 | — | 1-2 | 1-1 |
| Raith R | 2-2 | 4-0 | 1-0 | 2-0 | 3-0 | 4-1 | 2-3 | 4-2 | — | 0-1 |
| Ross Co. | 5-0 | 1-0 | 0-1 | 2-0 | 4-1 | 0-3 | 0-1 | 0-2 | 4-0 | — |

# BELL'S SCOTTISH LEAGUE—DIVISION TWO RESULTS 2000–2001

| | Arbroath | Berwick R | Clydebank | Forfar Ath | Partick Th | Queen of the S | Queen's Park | Stenhousemuir | Stirling Alb | Stranraer |
|---|---|---|---|---|---|---|---|---|---|---|
| Arbroath | — | 0-2 | 1-0 | 3-4 | 1-1 | 2-0 | 2-2 | 3-0 | 3-2 | 1-1 |
| Berwick R | 2-1 | — | 4-2 | 1-1 | 1-1 | 5-2 | 2-0 | 5-0 | 1-1 | 2-1 |
| Clydebank | 1-0 | 3-1 | — | 1-0 | 1-2 | 0-4 | 1-0 | 4-1 | 2-2 | 1-1 |
| Forfar Ath | 1-2 | 2-2 | 0-2 | — | 0-1 | 2-1 | 0-1 | 1-0 | 4-1 | 0-2 |
| Partick Th | 3-1 | 0-1 | 1-3 | 2-2 | — | 3-1 | 3-0 | 7-0 | 3-0 | 2-3 |
| Queen of the S | 0-1 | 1-1 | 2-0 | 4-0 | 0-1 | — | 2-1 | 3-0 | 1-0 | 0-0 |
| Queen's Park | 1-1 | 1-1 | 1-1 | 0-1 | 3-0 | 1-0 | — | 4-0 | 0-1 | 0-0 |
| Stenhousemuir | 1-1 | 3-3 | 1-0 | 2-3 | 1-3 | 1-0 | 0-1 | — | 3-1 | 2-3 |
| Stirling Alb | 1-0 | 1-0 | 1-1 | 0-0 | 0-3 | 4-3 | 2-0 | 1-3 | — | 0-3 |
| Stranraer | 0-1 | 1-1 | 0-0 | 0-1 | 3-4 | 2-0 | 0-1 | 2-1 | 1-1 | — |

# BELL'S SCOTTISH LEAGUE—DIVISION THREE RESULTS 2000–2001

| | Albion R | Brechin C | Cowdenbeath | Dumbarton | East Fife | East Stirling | Elgin C | Hamilton A | Montrose | Peterhead |
|---|---|---|---|---|---|---|---|---|---|---|
| Albion R | — | 1-1 | 1-0 | 0-1 | 0-1 | 2-1 | 1-1 | 1-1 | 3-2 | 0-0 |
| Brechin C | 2-1 | — | 0-0 | 1-3 | 1-2 | 2-2 | 0-1 | 0-1 | 2-1 | 0-1 |
| Cowdenbeath | 5-0 | 2-1 | — | 3-1 | 3-1 | 4-1 | 2-1 | 0-0 | 6-1 | 3-2 |
| Dumbarton | 1-0 | 0-2 | 2-4 | — | 1-0 | 5-1 | 2-1 | 3-4 | 3-0 | 1-1 |
| East Fife | 0-1 | 1-0 | 3-0 | 1-0 | — | 3-0 | 3-1 | 1-1 | 2-0 | 2-0 |
| East Stirling | 1-4 | 1-0 | 0-2 | 0-1 | 3-2 | — | 1-0 | 2-0 | 2-1 | 4-0 |
| Elgin C | 0-0 | 0-1 | 0-2 | 1-1 | 2-3 | 1-3 | — | 2-3 | 1-0 | 1-3 |
| Hamilton A | 1-1 | 1-4 | 2-3 | 2-0 | 2-0 | 3-2 | 3-0 | — | 1-2 | 2-2 |
| Montrose | 1-2 | 0-1 | 0-2 | 0-3 | 1-3 | 3-0 | 2-0 | 1-2 | — | 1-1 |
| Peterhead | 1-1 | 0-2 | 3-0 | 2-0 | 1-3 | 3-1 | 1-1 | 1-2 | 3-1 | — |

## ABERDEEN                                  PREMIER LEAGUE

**Ground:** Pittodrie Stadium, Aberdeen AB24 5QH (01224) 650400
**Ground capacity:** 22,199. **Colours:** All red with white trim.
**Manager:** Ebbe Skovdahl.
**League Appearances:** Belabed R 5(14); Bernard P 3; Bett C (2); Clark C 14(10); Di Rocco A 7(3); Dow A 4(11); Esson R 36; Guntweit C 28(2); Jess E 12(2); Lilley D 2(6); Mackie D 12(10); Mayer A (7); McAllister J 21(4); McGuire P 26(3); McNaughton K 30(3); Michie S (1); O'Donoghue R (2); Perry M 7(2); Preece D 2; Rowson D 35; Rutkiewicz K (3); Solberg T 20(2); Stavrum A 28(3); Tiernan F (2); Whyte D 29; Winters R 37; Young Darr 31; Young Dere 27(4); Zerouali H 2(3).
**Goals – League (45):** Stavrum 17 (1 pen), Winters 9 (1 pen), Derek Young 6, Di Rocco 3, Mackie 2, Rowson 2, Dow 1, Guntweit 1, Jess 1, Mayer 1, Perry 1, Darren Young 1
**Scottish Cup (3):** Mackie 1, Rowson 1, Winters 1
**CIS Cup (2):** Winters 1, Derek Young 1
**Honours – Division 1:** Champions – 1954-55, **Premier Division:** Champions – 1979-80, 1983-84, 1984-85. **Scottish Cup winners** 1947, 1970, 1982, 1983, 1984, 1986, 1990. **League Cup winners** 1956, 1977, 1986, 1990, 1996. **European Cup-Winners' Cup winners** 1983.

## AIRDRIEONIANS                                    DIV. 1

**Ground:** Shyberry Excelsior Stadium, Airdrie ML6 8QZ (01236) 622000
**Ground capacity:** 10,000 (all seated). **Colours:** White shirts with red diamond, white shorts.
**Manager:** Ian McCall.
**League Appearances:** Aguilar M 1; Alfonso M 11; Armstrong P 26; Bannerman S 9; Boyce S 13(9); Brady D 20(1); Broto J 23; Calderon A 24; Cameron I 9; Capin S 7(7); Clark P 1(2); Coulter R 6; Coyle O 9; Davidson S 2(3); Dunn R 5(6); Elliott B 2(1); Elliott J 7(8); Evans G (4); Ferguson A 3; Fernandez D 19(1); Forrest E 25; Gardner L 9(1); Gonzales R 7(1); Ingram S 2(3); Ireland C 12; May E 4(2); McAlpine J 7(7); McCann A 20; McGuire D 2(11); McKeown S (3); McManus T 1; McPherson C 7; McWilliams D 6; Moreau F 21(3); Nicolas F 1; Phillips T 1(1); Pilvi T 4(5); Prest M 13(5); Sanjuan J 21(1); Struthers W (3); Sweeney S 10; Taylor S 14(5); Wilson S 2(2); Wishart F 9; Zahana-Oni L 1.
**Goals – League (49):** Fernandez 7, Coyle 6 (2 pens), Moreau 6, Sanjuan 5 (2 pens), Prest 4, Taylor 4, Calderon 2, Dunn 2, Elliott J 2, Forrest 2, Ireland 2, Pilvi 2, Bannerman 1, Capin 1, Elliot B 1, McCann 1 (pen), McGuire 1
**Scottish Cup (3):** Moreau 1, Pilvi 1, Sanjuan 1
**CIS Cup (4):** Alfonso 1, Elliott J 1, Fernandez 1, McCann 1
**Bell's League Cup (10):** Prest 3, Calderon 1, Clark 1, Fernandez 1, McGuire 1, McKeown 1, Pacifico 1, Taylor 1
**Honours – Division II:** Champions – 1902-03, 1954-55, 1973-74. **Scottish Cup winners** 1924. **B&Q Cup winners** 1995. **Bell's Challenge Cup winners** 2000-01.

## ALBION ROVERS                                     DIV. 3

**Ground:** Cliffhill Stadium, Main Street, Coatbridge ML5 3RB (01236) 606334
**Ground capacity:** 2496. **Colours:** Yellow shirts with black trim, black shorts.
**Manager:** John McVeigh.

**League Appearances:** Begue Y 11(1); Booth M 33; Carr D (1); Clark S 21(1); Clyde R 17; Coyne T 1; Deegan C (1); Diack I 3(10); Easton S 13(3); Fahey C 34; Grosset W 3(3); Harty M 10(9); Ingram S 4(1); Lumsden T 33; Martin A 1(1); McBride K 2(2); McCormick S 15(1); McKenna G 12(2); McKenzie J 16(6); McLees J 9(8); McMillan A 13; McMullan R 22(7); Rankin I 3(11); Rodden P 2(5); Shearer S 2(1); Shields P 11; Silvestro C 18(3); Smith J 11(4); Stirling J 15; Tait T 26; Waldie C 35(1).
**Goals – League** (38): Booth 6 (1 pen) McCormick 5, Shields 5 (1 pen), Harty 4, Begue 2, Lumsden 2, McLees 2, Smith 2, Clyde 1, Diack 1, Easton 1, Grosset 1, McBride 1, McKenna 1, McKenzie 1, McMullan 1, Stirling 1, Waldie 1
**Scottish Cup** (1): Shields
**CIS Cup** (0):
**Bell's League Cup** (0):
**Honours – Division II:** Champions – 1933-34. **Second Division:** Champions 1988-89.

---

## ALLOA ATHLETIC                                                    DIV. 2

**Ground:** Recreation Park, Alloa FK10 1RY (01259) 722695
**Ground capacity:** 3100. **Colours:** Gold shirts with black trim, black shorts.
**Manager:** Terry Christie.
**League Appearances:** Armstrong G (1); Beaton D (1); Brigain C (2); Cairns M 22; Christie M 25(2); Clark D 28(2); Conway F 19(3); Davidson S 3; Evans G 16(6); French H 21(4); Gardner L 3(4); Hamilton R 32(1); Huxford R 12(5); Irvine W 24(11); Johnston G 16(8); Little I 28(6); McManus A 5; McQueen J 1(1); McQuillan J 11; Murray I 2; Nish C 10; Thomson S 31(3); Valentine C 28(1); Van De Kamp G 13; Watson G 27(1); Wilson M (5); Wood C 9(11).
**Goals – League** (38): Hamilton 9, Irvine 7 (2 pens), Evans 3, Nish 3, Thomson 3, Wood 3, Conway 2, French 2, Little 2, Clark 1, Johnston 1, Watson 1, own goal 1
**Scottish Cup** (0):
**CIS Cup** (2): Wood 2
**Bell's League Cup** (2): Hamilton 2
**Honours – Division II:** Champions – 1921-22. **Third Division:** Champions – 1997-98. **League Challenge Cup winners** 2000.

---

## ARBROATH                                                          DIV. 1

**Ground:** Gayfield Park, Arbroath DD11 1QB (01241) 872157
**Ground capacity:** 4020. **Colours:** Maroon shirts with sky blue trim, white shorts.
**Manager:** John Brownlie.
**League Appearances:** Arbuckle D 2; Brownlie P 16(4); Bryce T 4; Crawford J 25; Cunningham D 2(4); Cusick J 21(8); Florence S 23(1); Fotheringham K 19(1); Good I 5(5); Graham E 1; Heenan K 12(12); Henslee G 1(2); Hinchcliffe C 29; King T 8; Kirk S (1); Mallan S 27(2); Maughan R 4(2); McAulay J 15(14); McDonald C 4(1); McGlashan C 20(7); McGlashan J 23(2); McInally D 7; McKinnon C 11; Mercer J 34(1); Peters S 3(1); Rowe G 33; Steele K 2(17); Swankie G (1); Thomson J 29; Tindal K (3); Webster A 9(4); Wight C 7(1).
**Goals – League** (54): Mallan 10 (1 pen), Brownlie 7, Rowe 6, McGlashan C 5 (2 pens), McGlashan J 5, Fotheringham 4, McDonald 3, McKinnon 3, Mercer 3, Cusick 1, Heenan 1, McAulay 1, Swankie 1, Webster 1, own goals 3
**Scottish Cup** (1): Cusick 1

**CIS Cup** (3): Brownlie 1, McGlashan C 1, Mercer 1
**Bell's League Cup** (7): McGlashan C 2, Brownlie 1, Mallan 1, Mercer 1, Rowe 1, Webster 1
**Honours – Nil.**

---

# AYR UNITED                                                    DIV. 1

---

**Ground:** Somerset Park, Ayr KA8 9NB (01292) 263435
**Ground capacity:** 10,243 (1549 seated). **Colours:** White shirts with black sleeves, black shorts.
**Manager:** Gordon Dalziel.
**League Appearances:** Annand E 26(5); Benlaredj M (1); Boyack S 10; Bradford J 10(12); Burns G 1(2); Campbell M 16(4); Connolly P 6; Craig D 30; Crilly M 5(5); Duffy C 29; Grady J 13(5); Hughes J 18; Hurst G 19; Kean S 2; Lovering P 21(8); McEwan C 24(1); McGinlay P 34; Nelson C 26; Renwick M 13(2); Reynolds M 4(14); Robertson H 8; Rovde M 10; Scally N 13(10); Sharp L 15(2); Teale G 27(2); Wilson M 18(6).
**Goals – League** (73): Annand 18 (5 pens), Hurst 17, McGinlay 13, Teale 5, Boyack 3, Bradford 3 (1 pen), Grady 3, Sharp 3, Connolly 2, Robertson 2, Campbell 1, Craig 1, Hughes 1, Lovering 1
**Scottish Cup** (3): Annand 1, Campbell 1, Wilson 1
**CIS Cup** (0):
**Bell's League Cup** (1): McGinlay 1
**Honours – Division II:** Champions – 1911-12, 1912-13, 1927-28, 1936-37, 1958-59, 1965-66. **Second Division:** Champions – 1987-88, 1996-97.

---

# BERWICK RANGERS                                              DIV. 2

---

**Ground:** Shielfield Park, Berwick-on-Tweed TD15 2EF (01289) 307424
**Ground capacity:** 4131. **Colours:** Black with two inch gold stripe, black shorts.
**Manager:** Paul Smith.
**League Appearances:** Anthony M 27(2); Duthie M 12(5); Elliot B 5(4); Findlay C 6(20); Forrest G 24(8); Graham A 6(1); Gray D 17(2); Haddow L 9(1); Harvey J (1); Laidlaw S 1(5); Magee K 5(5); McCulloch W 15; McDonald C 4; McLean M 11; McMartin G 20(2); McNicoll G 19(2); Neil M 29; Neill A 31(1); O'Connor G 10; O'Neil K 6(2); Oliver N (1); Ritchie I 36; Ronald P 20(9); Smith D 20(11); Walton K 4(6); Watt D 4(5); Whelan J 26(4); Wood G 29(2).
**Goals – League** (51): Wood 14, Anthony 6 (1 pen), Neil M 5, Ronald 5, Findlay 3, Forrest 3, Duthie 2, Elliot 2 (1 pen), Haddow 2 (2 pens), Neill A 2, Ritchie 2, Smith 2, McNicoll 1, O'Neil 1, Walton 1
**Scottish Cup** (9): Anthony 2, Elliot 2, Neill A 2, Ronald 1, Watt 1, Wood 1
**CIS Cup** (0):
**Bell's League Cup** (2): McMartin 1, Oliver 1
**Honours – Second Division:** Champions – 1978-79.

---

# BRECHIN CITY                                                 DIV. 3

---

**Ground:** Glebe Park, Brechin DD9 6BJ (01356) 622856
**Ground capacity:** 3980. **Colours:** Red with white trim.

**Manager:** Dick Campbell.
**League Appearances:** Bailey L 7(10); Bain K 31(1); Black R 19(4); Cairney H 32; Campbell P 5(13); Christie B 1(2); Coulston D 32(1); Dewar G 7(5); Donachie B 9(6); Fotheringham K 12; Gardner L 7; Grant R 32; Honeyman B 12(4); Hutcheon A (1); Kinnaird P 12(1); Leask M 14(11); Mackay D 16; McKeith J 1(2); Miller G 6(6); Nairn J 13(6); O'Sullivan L 1; Parkyn M 5; Raynes S 26(1); Riley P 18(6); Smith D 14(9); Smith G 13(6); Soutar D 31; Sturrock B 20(7); Williamson K (1).
**League (71):** Grant 22, Bain 11 (3 pens), Sturrock 6, Coulston 5, Leask 5, Smith D 4, Bailey 3, Fotheringham 3, Honeyman 3, Black 2, Campbell 1, Christie 1, Dewar 1, Donachie 1, Mackay 1, Nairn 1, Raynes 1
**Scottish Cup (9):** Bailey 4, Grant 2, Bain 1, Black 1, Leask 1
**CIS Cup (0):**
**Bell's League Cup (5):** Sturrock 2, Grant 1, Leask 1,own goal 1
**Honours – Second Division:** Champions – 1982-83, 1989-90. **C Division:** Champions – 1953-54.

---

## CELTIC                                          PREMIER LEAGUE

**Ground:** Celtic Park, Glasgow G40 3RE (0141) 556 2611
**Ground capacity:** 60,506 (all seated). **Colours:** Green and white hooped shirts, white shorts.
**Manager:** Martin O'Neill.
**League Appearances:** Agathe D 26(1); Berkovic E 2(2); Boyd T 21(9); Burchill M (2); Crainey S (2); Douglas R 22; Fotheringham M 1(1); Gould J 15; Healy C 4(7); Johnson T 9(7); Kharine D 1; Lambert P 27; Larsson H 37; Lennon N 17; Mahe S 7(3); Maloney S 1(3); McNamara J 18(12); Mjallby J 30(5); Moravcik L 16(11); Petrov S 27(1); Petta B 20; Riseth V (1); Smith J 2(5); Stubbs A 7(4); Sutton C 24; Tebily O 2(2); Thompson A 29(1); Valgaeren J 35; Vega R 18.
**Goals – League (90):** Larsson 35 (2 pens), Sutton 11, Moravcik 9, Petrov 6, Johnson 5, Mjallby 4, Thompson 4, Agathe 3, Valgaeren 3, McNamara 2, Vega 2, Berkovic 1, Burchill 1, Lambert 1, Lennon 1, Smith 1, Stubbs 1
**Scottish Cup (17):** Larsson 9 (3 pens), McNamara 3, Vega 2, Moravcik 1, Valgaeren 1, own goal 1
**CIS Cup (15):** Larsson 5, Johnson 2 (1 pen) Sutton 2, Creaney 1, Healy 1, McNamara 1, Moravcik 1, Smith 1, Thompson 1
**Honours – Division I:** Champions – 1892-93, 1893-94, 1895-96, 1897-98, 1904-05, 1905-06, 1906-07, 1907-08, 1908-09, 1909-10, 1913-14, 1914-15, 1915-16, 1916-17, 1918-19, 1921-22, 1925-26, 1935-36, 1937-38, 1953-54, 1965-66, 1966-67, 1967-68, 1968-69, 1969-70, 1970-71, 1971-72, 1972-73, 1973-74. **Premier Division:** Champions – 1976-77, 1978-79, 1980-81, 1981-82, 1985-86, 1987-88, 1997-98, 2000-01. **Scottish Cup winners** 1892, 1899, 1900, 1904, 1907, 1908, 1911, 1912, 1914, 1923, 1925, 1927, 1931, 1933, 1937, 1951, 1954, 1965, 1967, 1969, 1971, 1972, 1974, 1975, 1977, 1980, 1985, 1988, 1989, 1995, 2001. **League Cup winners** 1957, 1958, 1966, 1967, 1968, 1969, 1970, 1975, 1983, 1998, 2000, 2001. **European Cup winners** 1967.

---

## CLYDE                                                        DIV. 1

**Ground:** Broadwood Stadium, Cumbernauld G68 9NE (01236) 451511
**Ground capacity:** 8200. **Colours:** White shirts with red and black trim, black shorts.
**Manager:** Allan Maitland.

**League Appearances:** Aitken C 7(11); Bingham C 10(5); Boniface F 8; Cannie P 4(11); Convery S 18(2); Cranmer C 16(4); Crawford B 11(7); Dunn D 11(7); Grant A 9(4); Greer G 27(3); Halliwell B 34; Hanley D 2(1); Hay P 2(1); Henderson N 3(2); Henry J 7(4); Hinds L 4(3); Kane A 25(8); Keogh P 28; McAulay S 2(2); McClay A 3(2); McCusker R 4(6); McFarlane N 7; McLaughlin M 20; McPherson C 1(2); Millen A 13; Mitchell J 25(1); Murray D 29(2); Proudlock A 4; Ross J 34; Sellars B 5(3); Smith B 23(2).
**Goals – League** (44): Kane 7, Convery 5 (1 pen), Crawford 5 (1 pen), Keogh 5, Proudlock 4, Hinds 3, McLaughlin 3, Aitken 2, Boniface 2, Cannie 2 (1 pen), Mitchell 2, Ross 2, Henry 1, Millen 1
**Scottish Cup** (1): McLaughlin 1
**CIS Cup** (6): Kane 2, Grant 1, McLaughlin 1, Proudlock 1, Ross 1
**Bell's League Cup** (1): Cannie 1
**Honours – Division II:** Champions – 1904-05, 1951-52, 1956-57, 1961-62, 1972-73.
**Second Division:** Champions – 1977-78, 1981-82, 1992-93, 1999-2000. **Scottish Cup winners** 1939, 1955, 1958.

---

# CLYDEBANK                                      DIV. 2

**Ground:** Sharing with Morton – Cappielow Park, Greenock (01475) 723571
**Ground capacity:** 14,891. **Colours:** Red and white stripes, black shorts.
**Manager:** To be appointed.
**League Appearances:** Bossy F 14; Brannigan K 34; Brown P (1); Burke A 15; Callaghan S 1(1); Campbell J 6; Conway C (1); Coyne T 10(5); Creaney G 3; Fal L 3; Farrell D 1; Farrell G 20(2); Ferguson P 26(2); Glancy M 17(4); Gow A (3); Hamilton B 14(1); Hernandez F 1; Hutchison S 2; Jacquel R 2; Johnson G 4; Kaak A 1(1); McCormick S 1(2); McKelvie D 8(9); McKinnon R 31; McKinstrey J 25(5); McQuilter R 3; McVey W 12(6); Milne D 3; Mooney G 2(1); Murdoch S 16(3); Murray S 17(12); Paton E 21(6); Racon A 2(2); Rodden P (1); Smith G 16(1); Taborda E 4; Walker J 16(10); Welsh B 7; Wishart F 12(2); Wylie D 28.
**Goals – League** (42): Burke 8, Paton 7 (3 pens), Coyne 4 (1 pen), Glancy 3, McKelvie 3, Brannigan 2, Fal 2, Hamilton 2, McKinstrey 2, Murray 2, Smith 2, Jacquel 1, Kaak 1, Murdoch 1, Walker 1, Welsh 1
**Scottish Cup** (0):
**CIS Cup** (0):
**Bell's League Cup** (3): Coyne 1, Jacquel 1, McCormick 1
**Honours – Second Division:** Champions – 1975-76.

---

# COWDENBEATH                                    DIV. 2

**Ground:** Central Park, Cowdenbeath KY4 9EY (01383) 610166
**Ground capacity:** 5268. **Colours:** Royal blue stripes with red trim, white shorts.
**Manager:** Gary Kirk.
**League Appearances:** Allan J 6(9); Barnes D (1); Boyle J 33; Bradley M 33(1); Brown G 21(12); Burns J 22(12); Carnie G 1; Courts T 23(2); Crabbe G (1); Gilfillan F (3); Hunter M 7(3); Juskowiak R 2(4); King T 20; Lakie J 2(1); Lawrence A 27(5); Martin J 36; McCulloch K 10; McDonald I (4); McDowell M 23(8); McMillan C 3; Mitchell W 3; Neeson C 11(2); Ramsay S 1; Simmons S 2(1); Smith A 18; Welsh B 3; White D 35; Winter C 34; Wright K 20(12).
**Goals – League** (58): McDowell 10, Bradley 8 (1 pen), Wright 7, Burns 6, Winter 6,

King 5, Brown 4, Allan 3, White D 3, Lawrence 2, Boyle 1 (pen), Courts 1, Smith 1, own goal 1
**Scottish Cup** (3): Bradley 2 (1 pen), Winter 1
**CIS Cup** (4): Allan 1, Burns 1, McDowell 1, Wright 1
**Bell's League Cup** (3): Brown 1, Juskowiak 1, McDowell 1
**Honours – Division II:** Champions – 1913-14, 1914-15, 1938-39.

---

# DUMBARTON                                        DIV. 3

**Ground:** Strathclyde Homes Stadium, Dumbarton G82 1JJ.
**Ground capacity:** 2050. **Colours:** Yellow shirts and shorts with black facing.
**Manager:** Tom Carson.
**League Appearances:** Bonar S 23(6); Brittain C 22(6); Brown Alan 1; Brown Andy 31; Bruce J 29; Dempsey G (1); Dickie M 29(1); Dillon J 20(5); Flannery P 30(1); Gentile C 2(4); Grace A 12(2); Hillcoat J 27; Jack S 25(3); King T 9; Lynes C 8; McCann K 23(4); McCormick S 1(2); McGinty B (1); Melvin M (17); O'Neil M 15; Ritchie J 1(2); Robertson J 27(6); Robinson R 4(1); Smith C 4(9); Stewart D 32; Wight J 9(1); Wilson S 1; Wilson W 11.
**Goals – League** (46): Flannery 17 (4 pens), Andy Brown 9, Dillon 3, Bruce 2, King 2, Lynes 2, Robertson 2 (1 pen), Stewart 2, Bonar 1, Brittain 1, Grace 1, McCann 1, O'Neill 1 (pen), Smith 1, own goal 1
**Scottish Cup** (2): Flannery 1, Robertson 1
**CIS Cup** (0):
**Bell's League Cup** (4): Flannery 3, Andy Brown 1
**Honours – Division I:** Champions – 1890-91 (Shared), 1891-92. **Division II:** Champions – 1910-11, 1971-72. **Second Division:** Champions – 1991-92. **Scottish Cup winners** 1883.

---

# DUNDEE                                 PREMIER LEAGUE

**Ground:** Dens Park, Dundee DD3 7JY (01382) 889966
**Ground capacity:** 11,760 (all seated). **Colours:** Navy shirts with white piping, white shorts with navy piping.
**Manager:** Ivano Bonetti.
**League Appearances:** Artero J 32(3); Billio P 8; Bonetti I 15(3); Caballero F 12(3); Caniggia C 20(1); Carranza A 15(7); Coyne C 16(2); Douglas R 11; Falconer W 8(6); Garrido A 8(2); Khizanishvili Z 5(1); Langfield J 8(1); Marrocco M 24; McSkimming S 7(5); Milne S 5(16); Nemsadze G 33(2); Rae G 31(1); Robertson H 2(1); Robertson M 2(2); Roccati M 19; Romano A 14(2); Russo M 4; Sara J 25(6); Smith B 36; Tweed S 32; Vargiu M (1); Wilkie L 5(4); Yates M 6(6); del Rio W 7(2).
**Goals – League** (51): Sara 14 (2 pens), Caniggia 7, Caballero 6 (1 pen), Milne 4, Rae 4, Artero 3, Carranza 3 (1 pen), Nemsadze 3, Bonetti 2, Billio 1, Falconer 1, Tweed 1, own goals 2
**Scottish Cup** (3): Sara 2, Caniggia 1
**CIS Cup** (3): Caballero 2, Wilkie 1
**Honours – Division I:** Champions – 1961-62. **First Division:** Champions – 1978-79, 1991-92, 1997-98. **Division II:** Champions – 1946-47. **Scottish Cup winners** 1910. **League Cup winners** 1952, 1953, 1974. **B&Q (Centenary) Cup winners** 1991.

# DUNDEE UNITED                    PREMIER LEAGUE

**Ground:** Tannadice Park, Dundee DD3 7JW (01382) 833166
**Ground capacity:** 14,223. **Colours:** Tangerine shirts, black shorts.
**Manager:** Alex Smith.
**League Appearances:** Aljofree H 24(2); Atangana M 8(3); Brady D (1); Buchan J 33(2); Combe A 23; Davidson H 6(5); De Vos J 33; Easton C 27(6); Fernandez J 6; Fuentes G 3; Fullarton J 3(2); Gallacher P 15; Galoppo M 2; Griffin D 18; Hamilton J 14(6); Hannah D 20(4); Heaney N 7(5); Lauchlan J 23; Leoni S 5(1); Licina J 5(2); Lilley D 18; Marcora C (1); Mathie A 3(1); McConalogue S 3(8); McCracken D 6(3); McCunnie J 15; McDonald K (1); McQuillan J 12(3); Miller C 24; Naveda A 7(6); O'Connor S 1(1); Partridge D 17(2); Paterson J 5(1); Ramirez F (1); Robinson P 2(4); Smith A 1(2); Tchami A 3; Thompson S 18(13); Venetis A 3(11); Winters D (5); Wright S 5.
**Goals – League** (38): Lilley 6, Easton 5 (1 pen), Miller 5 (3 pens), Thompson 4, Aljofree 2, Hamilton 2, Hannah 2, Naveda 2, Buchan 1, Davidson 1, Griffin 1, Lauchlan 1, McConalogue 1, McCracken 1, O'Connor 1, Paterson 1, Venetis 1, own goal 1
**Scottish Cup** (6): Lauchlan 2, Easton 1, Hannah 1, Lilley 1 Miller 1
**CIS Cup** (3): McConalogue 3
**Honours – Premier Division:** Champions – 1982-83. **Division II:** Champions – 1924-25, 1928-29. **Scottish Cup winners** 1994. **League Cup winners** 1980, 1981.

---

# DUNFERMLINE ATHLETIC     PREMIER LEAGUE

**Ground:** East End Park, Dunfermline KY12 7RB (01383) 724295
**Ground capacity:** 12,500. **Colours:** Black and white striped shirts, white shorts with black piping.
**Manager:** Jim Calderwood.
**League Appearances:** Boyle S 1(6); Bullen L 14(10); Coyle O 2(4); Crawford S 37; Dair J 25(8); Danilevicius T 3; Dijkhuizen M 2(7); Doesburg M 21(6); Ferguson J 28; Fotheringham G 2; Graham D 3(1); Hampshire S 11(8); Mason G 8(2); Matthaei R 11(6); May E 4(3); McGarty M 1(3); McGroarty C 19(3); Mendes J 7(6); Moss D 18(8); Nicholson B 36; Nish C (3); Petrie S 8(2); Reid B 1(1); Rossi Y 11; Ruitenbeek M 36; Skerla A 34; Skinner J 34(3); Templeman C (1); Thomson S 2; Thomson S 34; Tod A 5(3).
**Goals – League** (34): Crawford 9 (3 pens), Moss 6, Dair 5, Bullen 4, Nicholson 3, Hampshire 2, Boyle 1, Dijkhuizen 1, McGroarty 1, Rossi 1, Thomson SM 1
**Scottish Cup** (6): Thomson SM 2, Dijkhuizen 1, Moss 1, Nicholson 1, Skerla 1
**CIS Cup** (4): Boyle 1, Moss 1, Nicholson 1, Thomson SM 1
**Honours – First Division:** Champions – 1988-89, 1995-96. **Division II:** Champions – 1925-26. **Second Division:** Champions – 1985-86. **Scottish Cup winners** 1961, 1968.

---

# EAST FIFE                                    DIV. 3

**Ground:** Bayview Park, Methil, Fife KY8 3RW (01333) 426323
**Ground capacity:** 2000 (all seated). **Colours:** Amber shirts with black trim, black shorts.
**Manager:** Dave Clarke.

**League Appearances:** Agostini D 19; Allison J 19; Beith G 15; Bottiglieri E 11(2); Devine C 6(12); Ferguson S 7(4); Gallagher J 22(6); Gibb R 16(6); Hunter M 8(7); Kerrigan S 32(2); Lofting A 1(6); Logan R 1(3); Mackay S 27(2); Magee K 8; Mair L 13; McCloy B 29(2); McCulloch W 14; McKinnon R 4; McManus P 6(8); McWilliams D 2; Moffat B 22(6); Mortimer P 28(4); Munro K 16(3); Nairn J 4(1); O'Neill M 3(1); Reid A (2); Shannon R 4; Sharp R 22(2); Simpson P 2(4); Stewart A 22; Tinley G (2); Wilson W 11(3); Wood D 1; Wright D 1.
**Goals – League** (49): Kerrigan 8, Mackay 7, Ferguson 6, Moffat 6, Mortimer 5, Gallagher 2 (2 pens), Mair 2, Allison 1, Beith 1, Devine 1 (pen), Gibb 1, Hunter 1, McManus 1, Magee 1, Sharp 1, Simpson 1, Wilson 1, Wright 1, own goals 2
**Scottish Cup** (5): Ferguson 3, Moffat 2
**CIS Cup** (1): Moffat 1
**Bell's League Cup** (0):
**Honours – Division II:** Champions – 1947-48. **Scottish Cup winners** 1938. **League Cup winners** 1948, 1950, 1954.

---

# EAST STIRLINGSHIRE                                    DIV. 3

**Ground:** Firs Park, Falkirk FK2 7AY (01324) 623583
**Ground capacity:** 1880. **Colours:** Black and white stripes, black shorts.
**Manager:** Brian Ross.
**League Appearances:** Allison C 8(6); Butter J 36; Carlow R 4(6); Clarke J 8; Ferguson B 15(5); Gordon K 21(3); Hall M 26(2); Higgins G 4(8); Hislop S 36; Lindsay P 4(2); Lorimer D 9; Lynes C 9(7); McAuley S 6(1); McDonald I 20; McGhee G 13(2); McKechnie G 23(4); McKenzie C 2(5); McPherson D 13(10); McWilliams D 2; Quinn C 14(1); Russell G 35; Scott A 13(3); Spence J (1); Stewart S 29(4); Todd D 30(1); Tortolano J 10(1); Wilson J (1); Wood D 6.
**Goals – League** (37): Hislop 16 (3 pens), McKechnie 11, Ferguson 2, Stewart 2, Higgins 1, Lindsay 1, Lorimer 1, Lynes 1, McPherson 1, Wood 1
**Scottish Cup** (1): Hislop 1
**CIS Cup** (2): Gordon 1, McKechnie 1
**Bell's League Cup** (11): Hislop 3 (1 pen), Lynes 2, McKechnie 2, Ferguson 1, Gordon 1, Todd D 1, own goal 1
**Honours – Division II:** Champions – 1931-32. **C Division:** Champions – 1947-48.

---

# ELGIN CITY                                            DIV. 3

**Ground:** Borough Briggs, Elgin IV30 1AP (01343) 551114
**Ground capacity:** 5000 (478 seated). **Colours:** Black and white vertical stripes, black shorts.
**Manager:** Alex Caldwell.
**League Appearances:** Cameron S 1(3); Campbell C 21(4); Clinton S 15(4); Craig D 13; Craig R 1; Duncan R 6; Edwards S 18(5); Ellis S 5(7); Furphy W 17; Green M (1); Green R 23(8); Hind D 8; Irvine D 3(3); MacDonald J 36; Mackay S 4(1); Maguire P (2); McMullan M 6(1); Milne CD 26(1); Milne CR 29(1); Morris A 4(3); Morrison M 28; Munro G 8; Noble S (1); O'Brien L 2(2); Peters S 4; Pirie M 34; Rae M 2; Ross D 27; Russell G 6(2); Shanks L 1(1); Slythe M 5(7); Tully C 15; Whyte N 28(5).
**Goals – League** (29): Milne CR 6 (1 pen), Ross 6 (1 pen), Clinton 3, Green R 3, Morrison 3, Edwards 2, Slythe 2, Campbell 1, Craig D 1, Hind 1, own goal 1
**Scottish Cup** (0):
**CIS Cup** (0):
**Bell's League Cup** (2): Green R 2

# FALKIRK                                                    DIV. 1

**Ground:** Brockville Park, Falkirk FK1 5AX (01324) 624121
**Ground capacity:** 9706. **Colours:** Navy blue shirts, white shorts.
**Manager:** Alex Totten.
**League Appearances:** Avdiu K (1); Burke A 6(5); Christie K 25; Craig S 22(5); Denham G 24(1); Deuchar K 4(8); Henry J 27(1); Hogarth M 36; Hutchison G 34(2); Kerr M 30(2); Lawrie A 36; McAllister K 14(14); McDonald C (1); McMahon D 3; McQuilken J 34; McStay G 7(3); Morris I 4(12); Nicholls D 32(1); Pearson C 1(4); Rennie S 27(1); Roberts M 23(3); Seaton A 4(5); Waddell R 3(2).
**Goals – League** (57): Hutchison 11, Roberts 9 (5 pens), Nicholls 8 (1 pen), Henry 6, Craig 5, McAllister 5 (1 pen), Lawrie 4, Christie 2 (1 pen), Kerr 2, Pearson 2, Morris 1, Waddell 1, own goal 1
**Scottish Cup** (0):
**CIS Cup** (4): McAllister 1, McMahon 1, Nicholls 1, Roberts 1
**Bell's League Cup** (1): Hutchison 1
**Honours – Division II:** Champions – 1935-36, 1969-70, 1974-75. **First Division:** Champions – 1990-91, 1993-94. **Second Division:** Champions – 1979-80. **Scottish Cup winners** 1913, 1957. **League Challenge Cup winners** 1998.

# FORFAR ATHLETIC                                            DIV. 2

**Ground:** Station Park, Forfar, Angus (01307) 463576
**Ground capacity:** 4640. **Colours:** Sky blue shirts with navy piping, navy shorts.
**Manager:** Neil Cooper.
**League Appearances:** Beaton D 25(2); Bowman D 23; Brand R 7(5); Cargill A 19(5); Christie S 14(13); Craig D 7(2); Dolan J 5; Donaldson E 28(2); Duncan R 16; Farnan C 23(5); Farrell G 1(1); Ferguson I 24(3); Ferrie N 1(1); Garden S 31; Good I 12; Horn R 30; Keogh L 13; McCheyne G 7(3); McGraw M 4(1); McPhee G 9(5); Moffat J 4; Morris R 11; Rattray A 23(2); Sellars B 21(2); Sinclair D (2); Stewart W 16(12); Stirling J 6(2); Taylor S 4(3); Tully C 9; Winters D 3.
**Goals – League** (48): Stewart 9, Ferguson I 8 (2 pens), Sellars 5, Beaton 4, Donaldson 3, Keogh 3, Winters 3, Bowman 2, Cargill 2, Christie 2, Brand 1, Horn 1, McPhee 1, Morris 1, Sinclair 1, own goals 2
**Scottish Cup** (0):
**CIS Cup** (1): Taylor 1
**Bell's League Cup** (1): McPhee 1
**Honours – Second Division:** Champions – 1983-84. **Third Division:** Champions – 1994-95.

# HAMILTON ACADEMICAL                                        DIV. 2

**Ground:** New Douglas Park, Cadzow Avenue, Hamilton ML3 0FT (01698) 286103
**Ground capacity:** 14,538. **Colours:** Red and white hooped shirts, white shorts.
**Manager:** Ally Dawson
**League Appearances:** Bonnar M 33(1); Callaghan S 29; Clark G 12(8); Davidson W 15(4); Downs R 4(5); Eadie A 11(12); Gaughan P 36; Grant D 5; Hillcoat C 7(3); Hogg K 8(2); Kelly R 7(6); Kerr D 17; Lurinsky A (5); Lynn G 6; MacFarlane

I 33; MacLaren R 11(1); Martin M 13(5); McFarlane D 30(4); Moore M 27(4); Nelson M 23(2); Oliver N 5; Potter G 3(2); Prytz R 9; Renicks S 7(2); Russell A 22(2); Sherry J 20; Thomson S (1); Vaugh B 3(5).
**Goals – League** (75): McFarlane D 24, Moore 12 (1 pen), Callaghan 9 (5 pens), Russell 6, Nelson 5, Eadie 3, Kerr 3, Bonnar 2, Clark 2, Prytz 2 (1 pen), Gaughan 1, MacFarlane I 1, MacLaren 1, Martin 1, Sherry 1, own goals 2
**Scottish Cup** (0):
**CIS Cup** (1): Russell 1
**Bell's League Cup** (0):
**Honours – First Division:** Champions – 1985-86, 1987-88. **Divison II:** Champions – 1903-04. **Division III:** Champions – 2000-01. **B&Q Cup winners** 1992, 1993.

---

## HEART OF MIDLOTHIAN                    PREMIER LEAGUE

**Ground:** Tynecastle Park, Gorgie Road, Edinburgh EH11 2NL (0131) 200 7200
**Ground capacity:** 18,000. **Colours:** Maroon shirts, white shorts.
**Head Coach:** Craig Levein.
**League Appearances:** Adam S 5(1); Boyack S 9(3); Cameron C 37; Durie G 12(4); Floegel T 22(3); Fulton S 23(1); Goldie D 1; Jackson D 6(4); James K 4; Juanjo 23(14); Kaczan P (1); Kirk A 27(4); Locke G 7(6); Makel L 10(3); McAnespie K 3(2); McCann A 10; McKenna K 7(1); McKenzie R 1; McSwegan G 13(13); Milne K 3(4); Murray I 22(3); Naysmith G 9; Neilson R 16(2); Niemi A 37; O'Neil K (6); Petric G 19; Pressley S 36; Severin S 26(3); Simmons S (3); Simpson F 3(3); Tomaschek R 22(6); Wales G 2(5); Webster A 3(1).
**League** (56): Cameron 12 (2 pens), Kirk 12, McSwegan 6, Adam 5, Juanjo 4, Severin 4, Tomaschek 4, Durie 3, Flögel 1, Fulton 1, James 1, O'Neil 1, Wales 1, own goal 1
**Scottish Cup** (4): Juanjo 2, McSwegan 1, Tomaschek 1
**CIS Cup** (3): Cameron 3 (2 pens), Naysmith 1
**Honours – Division I:** Champions – 1894-95, 1896-97, 1957-58, 1959-60. **First Division:** Champions – 1979-80. **Scottish Cup winners** 1891, 1896, 1901, 1906, 1956, 1998. **League Cup winners** 1955, 1959, 1960, 1963.

---

## HIBERNIAN                              PREMIER LEAGUE

**Ground:** Easter Road Stadium, Edinburgh EH7 5QG (0131) 661 2159
**Ground capacity:** 17,500. **Colours:** Green shirts with white sleeves and collar, white shorts.
**Manager:** Alex McLeish.
**League Appearances:** Agathe D 5; Andrews L 4(7); Arpinion F 6(1); Bannerman S (2); Brebner G 5(6); Colgan N 37; Dempsie M 1; Fenwick P 31; Franks M 1(1); Jack M 37; Latapy R 31(2); Laursen U 29; Lehmann D 9(21); Libbra M 7(3); Lovell S 30(1); McIntosh M 4; McManus T 3(14); Murray I 11(10); O'Connor G (1); O'Neil J 33; Paatelainen M 32(4); Sar-Temsoury H (1); Sauzee F 33; Smith G 37; Smith T 8; Zitelli D 24(7).
**Goals – League** (57): Paatelainen 11, Zitelli 10, Latapy 7 (3 pens), Lovell 5, Agathe 4, Libbra 4, O'Neil 4, Laursen 2, Lehmann 2, McManus 2, Murray 2, Sauzee 2, Fenwick 1, own goal 1
**Scottish Cup** (13): O'Neil 3, Lehmann 2, McManus 2, Sauzee 2, Jack 1, Laursen 1, Paatelainen 1, Zitelli 1

**CIS Cup** (5): Latapy 3, Lehmann 1, McManus 1
**Honours – Division I:** Champions – 1902-03, 1947-48, 1950-51, 1951-52. **First Division:** Champions – 1980-81, 1998-99. **Division II:** Champions – 1893-94, 1894-95, 1932-33. **Scottish Cup winners** 1887, 1902. **League Cup winners** 1973, 1992.

## INVERNESS CALEDONIAN THISTLE                    DIV. 1

**Ground:** Caledonian Stadium, East Longman, Inverness IV1 1FF (01463) 222880
**Ground capacity:** 6500. **Colours:** Blue shirts with white trim, blue shorts.
**Manager:** Steven W.Paterson.
**League Appearances:** Bagan D 29(5); Bavidge M 23(7); Byers K 4(9); Calder J 28; Christie C 31(4); Fridge L 8; Golabek S 16; Graham D (2); Hastings R 21; MacDonald N 1(4); Mann R 33; McBain R 30(3); McCaffrey S 31; Munro G 4; Robson B 13(12); Sheerin P 33; Stewart G 1(1); Stewart I 4(2); Teasdale M 17(8); Tokely R 25(5); Wyness D 28(3); Xausa D 16(6).
**Goals – League** (71): Wyness 24, Sheerin 11 (3 pens), Bagan 8, Xausa 7, Bavidge 5, McBain 3, Teasdale 3, Christie 2, Mann 2, Robson 2, Stewart 2, McDonald 1, Tokely 1
**Scottish Cup** (6): Xausa 2, Mann 1, Robson 1, Sheerin 1, Wyness 1
**CIS Cup** (3): Mann 1, Stewart 1, Xausa 1
**Bell's League Cup** (4): Bavidge 2, Stewart 2
**Honours – Third Division:** Champions – 1996-97.

## KILMARNOCK                    PREMIER LEAGUE

**Ground:** Rugby Park, Kilmarnock KA1 2DP (01563) 525184
**Ground capacity:** 18,128. **Colours:** Blue and white striped shirts, blue shorts.
**Manager:** Bobby Williamson.
**League Appearances:** Baker M 14; Boyd K (1); Calderon A 7; Canero P 16(12); Canning M (1); Cocard C 16(17); Dargo C 16(9); Davidson S 2; Di Giacomo P 2(7); Dindeleux F 35; Durrant I 12(2); Fowler J 3(11); Hay G 27(4); Hessey S 6; Holt G 19; Innes C 23(1); MacPherson A 32; Mahood A 33(1); Marshall G 31; McCoist A 11(7); McGowne K 20; McLaren A 30(2); Meldrum C 7(1); Mitchell A 25(1); Reilly M 11(3); Sanjuan J 3; Vareille J 2(7); Wright P 15(10).
**Goals – League** (44): Wright 8 (2 pen), Dargo 6, McLaren 6 (1 pen), Cocard 4, Holt 3, Mahood 3, Dindeleux 2, Hay 2, Mitchell 2, Baker 1, Canero 1, Fowler 1, McCoist 1, McGowne 1, MacPherson 1, own goals 2
**Scottish Cup** (4): Hay 1, McGowne 1, Mitchell 1, Wright 1
**CIS Cup** (6): Dargo 2, McLaren 2, Canero 1, McCoist 1
**Honours – Division I:** Champions – 1964-65. **Division II:** Champions – 1897-98, 1898-99. **Scottish Cup winners** 1920, 1929, 1997.

## LIVINGSTON                    PREMIER LEAGUE

**Ground:** Almondvale Stadium, Livingston EH54 7DN (01506) 417 000
**Ground capacity:** 10,004. **Colours:** Gold shirts with black and white trim, black shorts with gold and white trim.
**Manager:** Jim Leishman.
**League Appearances:** Alexander N 26; Anderson J 30; Andrews M 13; Bingham D

33; Brinquin P 11; Britton G 3(9); Broto F 5(1); Burns A 20(4); Coughlan G 21; Crabbe S 17(11); Deas P 19(5); Dolan J 6(2); Fernandez D 6(2); Fleming D 24(4); Hagen D 8(12); Hart M 16(6); Jackson D 8(1); Keith M 7(4); Madsen J 1(1); McCaldon I 5(1); McCormick M (5); McCulloch M 35; McEwan D (1); McManus A 11(1); McPhee B 7(16); Ormiston D (1); Smith G (2); Sweeney S 1; Tosh S 24; Wilson B 34(1); Xausa D 6(3).

**Goals – League** (72): Bingham 14 (5 pens), Wilson B 13 (3 pens), Burns 7, McCulloch 5, Britton 4, Crabbe 4, Anderson 3, Fernandez 3, Fleming 3, Keith 3, Xausa 3, Coughlan 2, McPhee 2, Andrews 1, Deas 1, Hagan 1, Jackson 1, McCormick 1, Tosh 1

**Scottish Cup** (8): Anderson 2, Bingham 2, Wilson B 2, Britton 1, Crabbe 1

**CIS Cup** (4): Bingham 2, Hagan 2

**Bell's League Cup** (12): Britton 4, Anderson 2, Bingham 2 (1 pen), Crabbe 1, Keith 1, McCormick 1, Wilson B 1

**Honours – First Division:** Champions – 2000-01. **Second Division:** Champions – 1986-87, 1998-99. **Third Division:** Champions – 1995-96.

---

# MONTROSE                                                           DIV. 3

**Ground:** Links Park, Montrose DD10 8QD (01674) 673200
**Ground capacity:** 4338. **Colours:** Royal blue shirts and shorts.
**Manager:** Kevin Drinkell.
**League Appearances:** Black M 4; Byers K 2; Catto P 8(1); Christie G 23; Craib M 35; Craig D 14; Dailly G 5(5); Ferguson S 23(2); Fox R 3(1); Gilfillan F 2(2); Harrison T 24(3); Hutcheon A 14(4); Joy I 24(1); Laidlaw S 7; Lowe B 11(4); Mailer C 28(4); Marwick S 19(1); McGlynn G 33; McIlravey P 7(5); McKellar J 17(6); McKenzie M 22(11); McWilliam R 3(10); Mitchell J 12(18); Muirhead D 22; Niddrie K 1; O'Driscoll J 8(2); Ogboke C 1(5); Robertson S 8; Scott W 1; Shand M (1); Sneddon S 2; Thompson B 3; Young J 8; Zahana-Oni L 2.

**Goals – League** (31): Mitchell 7, McKenzie 6 (2 pens), Hutcheon 4, Laidlaw 3, Joy 2, Mailer 2, Craig 1, Ferguson 1, Harrison 1, McIlravey 1, Marwick 1, O'Driscoll 1, own goal 1

**Scottish Cup** (4): McKenzie 2, Harrison 1, Mitchell 1

**CIS Cup** (1): Dailly 1

**Bell's League Cup** (0):

**Honours – Second Division:** Champions – 1984-85.

---

# MORTON                                                            DIV. 2

**Ground:** Cappielow Park, Greenock (01475) 723571
**Ground capacity:** 14,891. **Colours:** Royal blue and white shirts, white shorts.
**Manager:** To be appointed.
**League Appearances:** Aitken S 27(4); Anderson D 29(1); Beattie D 1; Boswell M 9; Boukraa K 11(7); Broadfield G (3); Brownrigg A 1; Carlin A 20; Curran H 21; Davies D 20(2); Easton S 1; James K 9; Kerr B 5(6); Macdonald S 24(2); Matheson R 27(5); Maxwell A 1(1); McConalogue S 4; McDonald K 2; McDonald P 23(5); McGregor D 15(2); Medou Otye P 10; Millen A 15(1); Murie D 27(3); Naylor M 4(4); Patterson S 11; Raeside R 33; Redmond G 2(6); Robb R 5; Tweedie G 11(10); Webster S 6(1); Whalen S 21(2); Wingate D 1.

**Goals – League** (34): Matheson 9, Whalen 7 (1 pen), Aitken 3, Anderson 3, McDonald P 3, James 2, Boukraa 1, Curran 1, Kerr 1, Murie 1, Raeside 1, Redmond 1, own goal 1

**Scottish Cup** (1): Matheson 1
**CIS Cup** (1): Anderson 1
**Bell's League Cup** (6): Matheson 2, Whalen 2, Boukraa 1, Kerr 1
**Honours – First Division:** Champions – 1977-78, 1983-84, 1986-87. **Division II:** Champions – 1949-50, 1963-64, 1966-67. **Second Division:** Champions – 1994-95. **Scottish Cup winners** 1922.

## MOTHERWELL                                    PREMIER LEAGUE

**Ground:** Fir Park, Motherwell ML1 2QN (01698) 333333
**Ground capacity:** 13,742. **Colours:** Amber shirts with claret trim, white shorts.
**Manager:** Billy Davies.
**League Appearances:** Adams D 17(9); Brannan G 23; Chiba S 7; Connolly J 2; Corrigan M 31(4); Davies J 2; Elliott S 20(13); Goodman D 6(12); Goram A 22; Hammell S 32(2); Harvey P 10(1); Kemble B 23; Lasley K 6(6); Leitch S 23(3); McClen J 1(2); McCulloch L 26; McFadden J 1(5); McMillan S 25; Nicholas S 5(13); Okoli J 6; Oueifio A 14(3); Pearson S 3(3); Ramsay D 3(8); Spencer J 20(2); Strong G 31(1); Townsley D 22(8); Twaddle K 20(5); Wood M 3(5); Woods S 14.
**Goals – League** (42): Elliott 10, McCulloch 8, Brannan 6 (3 pens), Townsley 6, Adams 3, Spencer 2, Twaddle 2, Goodman 1, Lasley 1, Nicholas 1, Strong 1, own goal 1
**Scottish Cup** (2): McCulloch 1, Spencer 1
**CIS Cup** (3): Harvey 1, McCulloch 1, Strong 1
**Honours – Division I:** Champions – 1931-32. **First Division:** Champions – 1981-82, 1984-85. **Division II:** Champions – 1953-54, 1968-69. **Scottish Cup winners** 1952, 1991. **League Cup winners** 1951.

## PARTICK THISTLE                                          DIV. 1

**Ground:** Firhill Park, Glasgow G20 7AL (0141) 579 1971
**Ground capacity:** 14,538. **Colours:** Red and yellow hooped shirts, black shorts.
**Manager:** John Lambie.
**League Appearances:** Archibald A 34; Arthur K 34; Bottiglieri E 2; Brown M 2; Cameron I 3(10); Collins D 12; Craigan S 35; Docherty S 12; Dunn R (3); Elliot B 4(2); Hamilton B 12(4); Hardie M 27(3); Howie W 2(10); Legat G 1; Lennon D 33; Lindau P 29(2); Lyle D 1(12); McCallum D 18(8); McGrillen P 11(9); McKeown D 6(3); McLean S 32(1); McNally M 22; McWilliams D 2(1); Moore A 12(7); Shaw G 4(9); Smith J 30(1); Stewart A 12(10); Stirling J 4.
**Goals – League** (66): McLean 16 (2 pens), Hardie 14, Lindau 10, Lennon 6, McGrillen 5, Elliot 3, Shaw 3, Archibald 2, Smith 2, Collins 1, Creagan 1, McCallum 1, McNally 1, Moore 1
**Scottish Cup** (3): Hardie 2, Collins 1
**CIS Cup** (1): McLean 1
**Bell's League Cup** (0):
**Honours – First Division:** Champions – 1975-76. **Division II:** Champions – 1896-97, 1899-1900, 1970-71. **Second Division:** Champions 2000-01. **Scottish Cup winners** 1921. **League Cup winners** 1972.

## PETERHEAD                                                      DIV. 3

**Ground:** Balmoor Stadium, Peterhead AB42 1EU (01779) 478256
**Ground capacity:** 3250 (1000 seated). **Colours:** Blue and white shirts, white shorts.
**Manager:** Ian Wilson.
**League Appearances:** Bett B 4(2); Brown S 6(2); Buchanan R 1(1); Clark G 2; Clark P (1); Clark S 24(5); Cooper C 16(7); Craig D 7(1); De Barros M 4(8); Duffy J 11; Gibson A 16(10); Herd W 25(1); Huggon R 3(5); Johnston M 30(5); Keddie R (2); King S 35; Livingstone R 25(4); Murray I 11(5); O'Connor G 4; Paterson S 8(2); Pirie J 35; Simpson M 31; Smith D 17(11); Smith G 4(2); Stewart I 22(2); Tindal K 25(2); Watson C 3(8); Yeats C 27(5).
**Goals – League** (46): Yeats 11 (1 pen), Johnston 8, Stewart 8, Cooper 5 (2 pens), Smith D 5, Bett 1, Gibson 1, Herd 1, O'Connor 1, Paterson 1, Simpson 1, Smith G 1, own goals 2
**Scottish Cup** (11): Johnston 2, Cooper 1, Herd 1, King 1, Livingstone 1, Simpson 1, Smith D 1, Stewart 1, Tindal 1, own goal 1
**CIS Cup** (2): Cooper 2 (2 pens)
**Bell's League Cup** (1): Clark G 1

## QUEEN OF THE SOUTH                                             DIV. 2

**Ground:** Palmerston Park, Dumfries DG2 9BA (01387) 254853
**Ground capacity:** 8352. **Colours:** Royal blue shirts, white shorts.
**Manager:** John Connolly.
**League Appearances:** Aitken A 35; Angell M 4(1); Armstrong G 1(1); Atkinson P 29; Atkinson R 3(1); Boyle D 4(3); Caldwell B 5(5); Campbell J 8; Connell G 16; Creaney G (1); Davidson S 9; Gibson W (1); Greacan S 3; Hawke W 29(3); Hodge A 7(1); Hogg A 2(6); Hughes M 3(5); King S 6; Kinnaird P 5(1); Martin A 7; Mathieson D 25; McKeown D 16(2); McQuilter R 24; Milne D (1); Muir D 7(11); Nelson A 4(3); Nixon P 12(7); O'Neil J 17(1); Paterson G 3; Patterson D 7(2); Pickering S 20(7); Preen S 4; Scott C 3; Skinner S 1(5); Suddick J 9(2); Sunderland J 26(5); Walklate S 6(1); Weatherson P 31(3); Weir M 4(1); Young K 1(2).
**Goals – League** (52): Weatherson 16 (2 pens), O'Neil 10 (4 pens), Caldwell 3, Hawke 3, Atkinson P 2, Connell 2, Martin 2, Muir 2, Aitken 1, Angell 1, Armstrong 1, Hogg 1, King 1, Preen 1, Suddick 1, Sunderland 1, own goals 4
**Scottish Cup** (4): Weatherson 3, Hawke 1
**CIS Cup** (3): Hawke 1, Hodge 1, Weatherson 1
**Bell's League Cup** (1): Atkinson P 1
**Honours – Division II:** Champions – 1950-51.

## QUEEN'S PARK                                                   DIV. 3

**Ground:** Hampden Park, Glasgow G42 9BA (0141) 632 1275
**Ground capacity:** 52,000. **Colours:** Black and white hooped shirts, white shorts.
**Coach:** John McCormack.
**League Appearances:** Borland P 16(2); Brown J 12(7); Bruce G 7; Canning S 16(2); Carroll F 13(15); Caven R 21(3); Christie F (2); Clarke R (4); Collins N 2(3); Connaghan D 33; Connell G 12(1); Corr B 12; Cunningham J 11; Duncan G 16(1); Ferry D 28(1); Finlayson K 32; Fisher C (3); Flannigan C 3(2); Gallagher M 26(2);

Jackson R 5(7); Kwick-Ajet W (2); MacFarlane N 8; Marshall S 31; Martin H 2(3); Martin P (1); Martin W 5(6); Miller G 26(7); Orr S 12(11); Scobie R 4(9); Sinclair R 17(3); Smith A 4; Stewart C 13; Travers M 9(1).
**Goals – League** (28): Gallagher 7, Finlayson 4, Caven 3 (3 pens), Borland 2, Carroll 2, Marshall 2, Orr 2 (1 pen), Brown 1, Canning 1, Miller 1, Travers 1, own goals 2
**Scottish Cup** (0):
**CIS Cup** (2): Brown 1, Gallagher 1
**Bell's League Cup** (3): Gallagher 2, Finlayson 1
**Honours – Division II:** Champions – 1922-23. **B Division:** Champions – 1955-56.
**Second Division:** Champions – 1980-81. **Third Division:** Champions – 1999-2000.
**Scottish Cup winners** 1874, 1875, 1876, 1880, 1881, 1882, 1884, 1886, 1890, 1893.

---

# RAITH ROVERS                                        DIV. 1

**Ground:** Stark's Park, Pratt Street, Kirkcaldy KY1 1SA (01592) 263514
**Ground capacity:** 10,104 (all seated). **Colours:** Navy blue shirts, white shorts.
**Manager:** Peter Hetherston.
**League Appearances:** Agnew P (1); Alfonsolobez M 5(1); Andrews M 3(1); Bayne G 8; Black K 27(3); Browne P 32; Burns A 7; Capin S 7; Clark A 14(12); Coyle C 3; Creaney G 1(5); Dempsie M 2; Dennis S 21; Ellis L 24(4); Gaughan K 3; Hamilton S 15(3); Hampshire P 15(3); Hetherston B 13(6); Inglis J 12; Javary J 1; Jones M 8; Kelly P 7; Mballa I 12(19); McCulloch G 24; McEwan C 1(1); McInally D (2); McKinnon R 3; Monin S 11; Nanou W 4(3); Nicol K 17(5); Niven D (1); Opinel S 6(1); Shields D 1(6); Smith A 8; Stein J 33(2); Tosh P 19(10); Tosh S 7; Van De Kamp G 22.
**Goals – League** (41): Tosh P 9 (1 pen), Mballa 8, Stein 6, Burns 4, Jones 4, Andrews 3, Bayne 1, Creaney 1, Ellis 1, McKinnon 1, Nicol 1, Shields 1, Smith 1
**Scottish Cup** (0):
**CIS Cup** (4): Burns 2 (1 pen), Stein 1, Tosh P 1
**Bell's League Cup** (0):
**Honours – First Division:** Champions – 1992-93, 1994-95. **Division II:** Champions – 1907-08, 1909-10 (Shared); 1937-38, 1948-49. **League Cup winners** 1995.

---

# RANGERS                                    PREMIER LEAGUE

**Ground:** Ibrox Stadium, Glasgow G51 2XD (0870) 600 1972
**Ground capacity:** 50,444. **Colours:** Royal blue shirts with white trim and red panels, white shorts with blue trim.
**Manager:** Dick Advocaat.
**League Appearances:** Adamczuk D 1(2); Albertz J 20(4); Amoruso L 29; Brown M 3; Carson S 1(1); Christiansen J 3; Dodds W 16(14); Ferguson B 30; Fernandes F (4); Flo T 18(1); Gayle M 4; Hughes S (1); Johnston A 9(4); Kanchelskis A 3(4); Kauppila J 1(3); Klos S 32; Konterman B 36(1); Lovenkrands P 1(7); Malcolm R 3(3); McCann N 16(5); Miller K 12(15); Mols M 10(3); Moore C 5; Negri M 1; Numan A 22; Porrini S 12; Reyna C 16(2); Ricksen F 26(1); Ross M (1); Tugay 17(9); Van Bronckhorst G 10(1); Vidmar T 11(4); Wallace R 14(1); Wilson S 19(1); de Boer R 17.
**Goals – League** (76): Flo 11, Albertz 10 (2 pens), Dodds 9 (2 pens), Miller 8, de Boer 6, Mols 5, Wallace 5, Konterman 3, McCann 3, Tugay 3, Amoruso 2, Ferguson 2, Reyna 2, Van Bronckhorst 2, Fernandes 1, Kanchelskis 1, Malcolm 1, Ricksen 1, Vidmar 1

**Scottish Cup** (5): Flo 2, Ferguson 1, Johnston 1, Miller 1
**CIS Cup** (7): Albertz 1, Amoruso 1, Dodds 1, Ferguson 1, Miller 1, Van Bronckhorst 1, Wallace 1
**Honours – Division I: Champions –** 1890-91 (Shared), 1898-99, 1899-1900, 1900-01, 1901-02, 1910-11, 1911-12, 1912-13, 1917-18, 1919-20, 1920-21, 1922-23, 1923-24, 1924-25, 1926-27, 1927-28, 1928-29, 1929-30, 1930-31, 1932-33, 1933-34, 1934-35, 1936-37, 1938-39, 1946-47, 1948-49, 1949-50, 1952-53, 1955-56, 1956-57, 1958-59, 1960-61, 1962-63, 1963-64, 1974-75. **Premier Division: Champions –** 1975-76, 1977-78, 1986-87, 1988-89, 1989-90, 1990-91, 1991-92, 1992-93, 1993-94, 1994-95, 1995-96, 1996-97. **Premier League: Champions –** 1998-99, 1999-2000. **Scottish Cup winners** 1894, 1897, 1898, 1903, 1928, 1930, 1932, 1934, 1935, 1936, 1948, 1949, 1950, 1953, 1960, 1962, 1963, 1964, 1966, 1973, 1976, 1978, 1979, 1981, 1992, 1993, 1996, 1999, 2000. **League Cup winners** 1947, 1949, 1961, 1962, 1964, 1965, 1971, 1976, 1978, 1979, 1982, 1984, 1985, 1987, 1988, 1989, 1991, 1993, 1994, 1997, 1999. **European Cup-Winners' Cup winners** 1972.

## ROSS COUNTY                                                    DIV. 1

**Ground:** Victoria Park, Dingwall IV15 9QW (01349) 860860
**Ground capacity:** 5500 (2700 seated). **Colours:** Dark blue shirts, white shorts.
**Manager:** Neale Cooper.
**League Appearances:** Bone A 28(1); Boukraa K 14; Campbell C (1); Canning M 3(3); Cowie D 1; Coyle O 5; Cunnington E 22(2); Dlugonski B (1); Escalon F 10(4); Ferguson S 27(6); Fraser J 13(12); Gilbert K 11(2); Hamilton G 6; Henderson D 21(3); Holmes D 17(12); Irvine B 25(2); King S (1); Kinnaird P 5(4); Mackay D 23(4); Mackay S 2(1); Maxwell I 32; McCormick M 14(3); McQuade J 17(8); Millar M 12; Miller S (1); O'Neill J (3); Perry M 20; Prest M 3(5); Robertson H 16; Ross D (1); Shaw G 3(2); Smith A 3; Taggart C 13(1); Walker J 30; Zahani-Oni L (6).
**Goals – League** (48): Bone 14 (1 pen), Henderson 6, Holmes 6, Ferguson S 5, Prest 3, Coyle 2, Irvine 2, Taggart 2, Canning 1, McCormick 1, McQuade 1, Maxwell 1, Perry 1, Robertson 1, Shaw 1 (1 pen), own goal 1
**Scottish Cup** (4): Bone 2, Cunnington 1, Henderson 1
**CIS Cup** (2): Holmes 1, Shaw 1
**Bell's League Cup** (2): Bone 1, Henderson 1
**Honours – Third Division:** Champions – 1998-99.

## ST JOHNSTONE                                     PREMIER LEAGUE

**Ground:** McDiarmid Park, Crieff Road, Perth PH1 2SJ (01738) 459090
**Ground capacity:** 10,673. **Colours:** Royal blue shirts with white trim, white shorts.
**Manager:** Sandy Clark.
**League Appearances:** Bollan G 28; Connolly P 15(6); Crozier B 3(1); Dasovic N 35(1); Dods D 26(3); Evers S 5(1); Ferry M (1); Forsyth R 9(2); Fotheringham M (2); Frail S 6; Hartley P 16(7); Jones G 9; Kane P 27(1); Kernaghan A 17(1); Lauchlan M (1); Lovenkrands T 16(7); Lowndes N 2(8); Main A 38; Malcolm S (1); McBride J 20(6); McClune D 5; McCluskey S 18(1); McCulloch M 13(9); O'Neill M 7(3); Parker K 30(7); Russell C 6(8); Sylla M 34; Weir J 33.
**Goals – League** (40): Parker 9 (2 pens), Sylla 6, Connolly 4, Jones 3 (1 pen), Lovenkrands 3, McBride 3, Hartley 2, Lowndes 2, Bollan 1, Dods 1, Kane 1 (pen), Kernaghan 1, McClune 1, McCluskey 1, Russell 1, Weir 1

**Scottish Cup** (2): Lowndes 1, Russell 1
**CIS Cup** (3): Bollan 1, Dasovic 1, Hartley 1
**Honours – First Division:** Champions – 1982-83, 1989-90, 1996-97. **Division II:** Champions – 1923-24, 1959-60, 1962-63.

---

# ST MIRREN                                                    DIV. 1

---

**Ground:** St Mirren Park, Paisley PA3 2EJ (0141) 889 2558, 840 1337
**Ground capacity:** 10,866 (all seated). **Colours:** Black and white striped shirts, black shorts.
**Manager:** Tom Hendrie.
**League Appearances:** Baltacha S 17(3); Bowman G 12(5); Brown T 7(5); Dagnogo M 2(3); Drew C 1(1); Fenton G 26; Gillies R 34(2); Kerr C 12(2); Mackenzie S 22(6); McCaldon I 4(1); McGarry S 17(16); McGowan J 23; McKnight P (4); McLaughlin B 29; McPhee S 6(1); Murray H 22(1); Nicolson I 21(7); Paeslack J 9(6); Quitongo J 12(11); Renfurm M 8(8); Robinson R (2); Ross I 4; Roy L 28; Rudden P 10(4); Scrimgour D 6(1); Sharp L 4(2); Turner T 32; Walker S 30; Yardley M 20(13).
**Goals – League** (32): Gillies 10 (2 pens), McGarry 4, Yardley 4, McGowan 3, Fenton 2, Quitongo 2, Walker 2, Dagnogo 1, Paeslack 1, Renfurm 1, Rudden 1, own goal 1
**Scottish Cup** (1): Quitongo 1
**CIS Cup** (8): Brown 2, Walker 2, Gillies 1, McGarry 1, Murray 1, Paeslack 1
**Honours – First Division:** Champions – 1976-77, 1999-2000. **Division II:** Champions – 1967-68. **Scottish Cup winners** 1926, 1959, 1987.

---

# STENHOUSEMUIR                                               DIV. 2

---

**Ground:** Ochilview Park, Stenhousemuir FK5 5QL (01324) 562992
**Ground capacity:** 3520. **Colours:** Maroon shirts with silver trim, white shorts.
**Manager:** Brian Fairley.
**League Appearances:** Abbott G 5(5); Blaikie A 3(7); Cormack P 19(2); Davidson G 27; Donald B 26(2); Duncan G 16(5); English I 28(5); Fallon S 3; Ferguson P 9(4); Fisher J 11(3); Gibson J 6; Gibson L 2(7); Gow G 34; Graham T 15(1); Henderson N 14(9); Henry J 3; Jackson C 10(3); Lorimer D (3); McAneny P 19(1); McColligan B 11(1); McGurk R 2; McKinnon C 19(3); McLauchlan M 2(3); Menelaws D 11(14); Mensing S 15; Miller S 30(1); Mooney M 9(5); Murphy S (1); Pittman S 3; Sandison J 15; Smith G 1(2); Storrar A 20(5); Wood D 8(1).
**Goals – League** (45): English 18, Miller 8 (1 pen), McKinnon 5, Blaikie 2, Menelaws 2, Cormack 1, Davidson 1, Gibson 1, Henderson 1, Lorimer 1, McAneny 1, McColligan 1, Mensing 1 (pen), Mooney 1 (pen), Wood 1
**Scottish Cup** (1): Menelaws 1
**CIS Cup** (2): McKinnon 1, McLauchlan 1
**Bell's League Cup** (2): Gibson 1, Menelaws 1
**Honours – League Challenge Cup:** Winners – 1996.

---

# STIRLING ALBION                                             DIV. 3

---

**Ground:** Forthbank Stadium, Springkerse Industrial Estate, Stirling FK7 7UJ (01786) 450399
**Ground capacity:** 3808. **Colours:** Red and white halves.

**Manager:** Ray Stewart.
**League Appearances:** Aitken A 3(7); Bailey L 7(2); Bennett N 21; Devine S 7(1); Donald G 33(1); Feroz C 23(7); Gardner J 11(8); Gaughan K 26; Graham A 17(1); Hay P 12; Hunter G 4(1); Joy I (2); Kelly G 11(10); King C 16; Love G 17(1); Martin C 14(1); McAulay I 23(2); McCallion K 6(8); McGraw M (3); McKinnon R 1; McLellan K (1); McStea A 10; Millar J 28(4); Milne K 27; Munro G (3); O'Neill M (3); Reid C 36; Reilly S 2; Stuart W (6); Templeman C 20(1); Whiteford A 10; Williams A 11(18).
**Goals – League** (34): Feroz 5, Graham 5, Donald 4, Millar 4, Williams 4, Templeman 3, Gardner 2, King 2, Bennett 1, Gaughan 1, McAulay 1 (1 pen), McCallion 1, Martin 1
**Scottish Cup** (7): Graham 3 (1 pen), Templeman 2, Donald 1, Williams 1
**CIS Cup** (0):
**Bell's League Cup** (2): McAulay 1, O'Neill 1
**Honours – Division II:** Champions – 1952-53, 1957-58, 1960-61, 1964-65. **Second Division:** Champions – 1976-77, 1990-91, 1995-96.

---

# STRANRAER                                                    DIV. 2

**Ground:** Stair Park, Stranraer DG9 8BS (01776) 703271
**Ground capacity:** 6100. **Colours:** Blue shirts, white shorts.
**Manager:** Billy McLaren.
**League Appearances:** Blaikie A 2(5); Blair P 18(3); Bryce T 6(9); Edgar S (2); Farrell D 13; George D 32; Geraghty M 13(10); Grace A 10(2); Harty I 35; Hodge A 8; Hughes M (2); Jenkins A 11(4); Johnstone D 23; Knox K 34; Macdonald W 29; McCormick S 1(1); McDonald G 15(1); McGeown M 28; McGowan N 7; McLauchlan M 5(5); McMillan A 1(2); McQuilter R 1; O'Neill S 8(1); Paterson A 11; Rae D 8(8); Stewart P (3); Stirling J 7; Walker P 27(4); Weir M 8(4); Wright F 35.
**Goals – League** (51): Harty 13, Walker 12, George 4, Jenkins 4, Geraghty 3, Knox 3, Farrell 2, Macdonald W 2, Stirling 2, Wright 2, Blaikie 1, Blair 1, McGowan 1, Rae 1
**Scottish Cup** (3): Harty 2 (1 pen), Walker 1
**CIS Cup** (0):
**Bell's League Cup** (9): Harty 4, Geraghty 2, Rae 1, Walker 1, Wright 1
**Honours – Second Division:** Champions – 1993-94, 1997-98. **League Challenge Cup winners** 1997.

# SCOTTISH LEAGUE HONOURS

*On goal average (ratio)/difference. †Held jointly after indecisive play-off.
‡Won on deciding match. ††Held jointly. ¶Two points deducted for
fielding ineligible player. Competition suspended 1940–45 during war;
Regional Leagues operating.
‡‡Two points deducted for registration irregularities.

## PREMIER LEAGUE

Maximum points: 108

|         | First   | Pts | Second  | Pts | Third       | Pts |
|---------|---------|-----|---------|-----|-------------|-----|
| 1998–99 | Rangers | 77  | Celtic  | 71  | St Johnstone | 57 |
| 1999–00 | Rangers | 90  | Celtic  | 69  | Hearts      | 54  |
| 2000–01 | Celtic  | 97  | Rangers | 82  | Hibernian   | 66  |

## PREMIER DIVISION

Maximum points: 72

|         | First    | Pts | Second   | Pts | Third     | Pts |
|---------|----------|-----|----------|-----|-----------|-----|
| 1975–76 | Rangers  | 54  | Celtic   | 48  | Hibernian | 43  |
| 1976–77 | Celtic   | 55  | Rangers  | 46  | Aberdeen  | 43  |
| 1977–78 | Rangers  | 55  | Aberdeen | 53  | Dundee U  | 40  |
| 1978–79 | Celtic   | 48  | Rangers  | 45  | Dundee U  | 44  |
| 1979–80 | Aberdeen | 48  | Celtic   | 47  | St Mirren | 42  |
| 1980–81 | Celtic   | 56  | Aberdeen | 49  | Rangers*  | 44  |
| 1981–82 | Celtic   | 55  | Aberdeen | 53  | Rangers   | 43  |
| 1982–83 | Dundee U | 56  | Celtic*  | 55  | Aberdeen  | 55  |
| 1983–84 | Aberdeen | 57  | Celtic   | 50  | Dundee U  | 47  |
| 1984–85 | Aberdeen | 59  | Celtic   | 52  | Dundee U  | 47  |
| 1985–86 | Celtic*  | 50  | Hearts   | 50  | Dundee U  | 47  |

Maximum points: 88

|         | First   | Pts | Second | Pts | Third    | Pts |
|---------|---------|-----|--------|-----|----------|-----|
| 1986–87 | Rangers | 69  | Celtic | 63  | Dundee U | 60  |
| 1987–88 | Celtic  | 72  | Hearts | 62  | Rangers  | 60  |

Maximum points: 72

|         | First   | Pts | Second    | Pts | Third   | Pts |
|---------|---------|-----|-----------|-----|---------|-----|
| 1988–89 | Rangers | 56  | Aberdeen  | 50  | Celtic  | 46  |
| 1989–90 | Rangers | 51  | Aberdeen* | 44  | Hearts  | 44  |
| 1990–91 | Rangers | 55  | Aberdeen  | 53  | Celtic* | 41  |

Maximum points: 88

|         | First   | Pts | Second   | Pts | Third     | Pts |
|---------|---------|-----|----------|-----|-----------|-----|
| 1991–92 | Rangers | 72  | Hearts   | 63  | Celtic    | 62  |
| 1992–93 | Rangers | 73  | Aberdeen | 64  | Celtic    | 60  |
| 1993–94 | Rangers | 58  | Aberdeen | 55  | Motherwell | 54 |

Maximum points: 108

|         | First   | Pts | Second    | Pts | Third     | Pts |
|---------|---------|-----|-----------|-----|-----------|-----|
| 1994–95 | Rangers | 69  | Motherwell | 54 | Hibernian | 53  |
| 1995–96 | Rangers | 87  | Celtic    | 83  | Aberdeen* | 55  |
| 1996–97 | Rangers | 80  | Celtic    | 75  | Dundee U  | 60  |
| 1997–98 | Celtic  | 74  | Rangers   | 72  | Hearts    | 67  |

## DIVISION 1

Maximum points: 52

|         | First     | Pts | Second     | Pts | Third    | Pts |
|---------|-----------|-----|------------|-----|----------|-----|
| 1975–76 | Partick T | 41  | Kilmarnock | 35  | Montrose | 30  |

Maximum points: 78

|         | First        | Pts | Second      | Pts | Third       | Pts |
|---------|--------------|-----|-------------|-----|-------------|-----|
| 1976–77 | St Mirren    | 62  | Clydebank   | 58  | Dundee      | 51  |
| 1977–78 | Morton*      | 58  | Hearts      | 58  | Dundee      | 57  |
| 1978–79 | Dundee       | 55  | Kilmarnock* | 54  | Clydebank   | 54  |
| 1979–80 | Hearts       | 53  | Airdrieonians | 51 | Ayr U*      | 44  |
| 1980–81 | Hibernian    | 57  | Dundee      | 52  | St Johnstone | 51 |
| 1981–82 | Motherwell   | 61  | Kilmarnock  | 51  | Hearts      | 50  |
| 1982–83 | St Johnstone | 55  | Hearts      | 54  | Clydebank   | 50  |
| 1983–84 | Morton       | 54  | Dumbarton   | 51  | Partick T   | 46  |
| 1984–85 | Motherwell   | 50  | Clydebank   | 48  | Falkirk     | 45  |
| 1985–86 | Hamilton A   | 56  | Falkirk     | 45  | Kilmarnock  | 44  |

209

|  |  |  | *Maximum points: 88* |  |  |  |
|---|---|---|---|---|---|---|
| 1986–87 | Morton | 57 | Dunfermline Ath | 56 | Dumbarton | 53 |
| 1987–88 | Hamilton A | 56 | Meadowbank T | 52 | Clydebank | 49 |
|  |  |  | *Maximum points: 78* |  |  |  |
| 1988–89 | Dunfermline Ath | 54 | Falkirk | 52 | Clydebank | 48 |
| 1989–90 | St Johnstone | 58 | Airdrieonians | 54 | Clydebank | 44 |
| 1990–91 | Falkirk | 54 | Airdrieonians | 53 | Dundee | 52 |
|  |  |  | *Maximum points: 88* |  |  |  |
| 1991–92 | Dundee | 58 | Partick T* | 57 | Hamilton A | 57 |
| 1992–93 | Raith R | 65 | Kilmarnock | 54 | Dunfermline Ath | 52 |
| 1993–94 | Falkirk | 66 | Dunfermline Ath | 65 | Airdrieonians | 54 |
|  |  |  | *Maximum points: 108* |  |  |  |
| 1994–95 | Raith R | 69 | Dunfermline Ath* | 68 | Dundee | 68 |
| 1995–96 | Dunfermline Ath | 71 | Dundee U* | 67 | Morton | 67 |
| 1996–97 | St Johnstone | 80 | Airdrieonians | 60 | Dundee* | 58 |
| 1997–98 | Dundee | 70 | Falkirk | 65 | Raith R* | 60 |
| 1998–99 | Hibernian | 89 | Falkirk | 66 | Ayr U | 62 |
| 1999–00 | St Mirren | 76 | Dunfermline Ath | 71 | Falkirk | 68 |
| 2000–01 | Livingston | 76 | Ayr U | 69 | Falkirk | 56 |

## DIVISION 2

|  |  |  | *Maximum points: 52* |  |  |  |
|---|---|---|---|---|---|---|
| 1975–76 | Clydebank* | 40 | Raith R | 40 | Alloa | 35 |
|  |  |  | *Maximum points: 78* |  |  |  |
| 1976–77 | Stirling A | 55 | Alloa | 51 | Dunfermline Ath | 50 |
| 1977–78 | Clyde* | 53 | Raith R | 53 | Dunfermline Ath | 48 |
| 1978–79 | Berwick R | 54 | Dunfermline Ath | 52 | Falkirk | 50 |
| 1979–80 | Falkirk | 50 | East Stirling | 49 | Forfar Ath | 46 |
| 1980–81 | Queen's Park | 50 | Queen of the S | 46 | Cowdenbeath | 45 |
| 1981–82 | Clyde | 59 | Alloa* | 50 | Arbroath | 50 |
| 1982–83 | Brechin C | 55 | Meadowbank T | 54 | Arbroath | 49 |
| 1983–84 | Forfar Ath | 63 | East Fife | 47 | Berwick R | 43 |
| 1984–85 | Montrose | 53 | Alloa | 50 | Dunfermline Ath | 49 |
| 1985–86 | Dunfermline Ath | 57 | Queen of the S | 55 | Meadowbank T | 49 |
| 1986–87 | Meadowbank T | 55 | Raith R* | 52 | Stirling A* | 52 |
| 1987–88 | Ayr U | 61 | St Johnstone | 59 | Queen's Park | 51 |
| 1988–89 | Albion R | 50 | Alloa | 45 | Brechin C | 43 |
| 1989–90 | Brechin C | 49 | Kilmarnock | 48 | Stirling A | 47 |
| 1990–91 | Stirling A | 54 | Montrose | 46 | Cowdenbeath | 45 |
| 1991–92 | Dumbarton | 52 | Cowdenbeath | 51 | Alloa | 50 |
| 1992–93 | Clyde | 54 | Brechin C* | 53 | Stranraer | 53 |
| 1993–94 | Stranraer | 56 | Berwick R | 48 | Stenhousemuir* | 47 |
|  |  |  | *Maximum points: 108* |  |  |  |
| 1994–95 | Morton | 64 | Dumbarton | 60 | Stirling A | 58 |
| 1995–96 | Stirling A | 81 | East Fife | 67 | Berwick R | 60 |
| 1996–97 | Ayr U | 77 | Hamilton A | 74 | Livingston | 64 |
| 1997–98 | Stranraer | 61 | Clydebank | 60 | Livingston | 59 |
| 1998–99 | Livingston | 77 | Inverness CT | 72 | Clyde | 53 |
| 1999–00 | Clyde | 65 | Alloa | 64 | Ross County | 62 |
| 2000–01 | Partick T | 75 | Arbroath | 58 | Berwick R* | 54 |

## DIVISION 3

|  |  |  | *Maximum points: 108* |  |  |  |
|---|---|---|---|---|---|---|
| 1994–95 | Forfar Ath | 80 | Montrose | 67 | Ross Co | 60 |
| 1995–96 | Livingston | 72 | Brechin C | 63 | Caledonian T | 57 |
| 1996–97 | Inverness CT | 76 | Forfar Ath* | 67 | Ross Co | 67 |
| 1997–98 | Alloa | 76 | Arbroath | 68 | Ross Co* | 67 |
| 1998–99 | Ross Co | 77 | Stenhousemuir | 64 | Brechin C | 59 |
| 1999–00 | Queen's Park | 69 | Berwick R | 66 | Forfar Ath | 61 |
| 2000–01 | Hamilton A* | 76 | Cowdenbeath | 76 | Brechin C | 72 |

*Maximum points: a* 36; *b* 44; *c* 40; *d* 52; *e* 60; *f* 68; *g* 76; *h* 84.

| | First | Pts | Second | Pts | Third | Pts |
|---|---|---|---|---|---|---|
| 1890–91a | Dumbarton†† | 29 | Rangers†† | 29 | Celtic | 21 |
| 1891–92b | Dumbarton | 37 | Celtic | 35 | Hearts | 34 |
| 1892–93a | Celtic | 29 | Rangers | 28 | St Mirren | 20 |
| 1893–94a | Celtic | 29 | Hearts | 26 | St Bernard's | 23 |
| 1894–95a | Hearts | 31 | Celtic | 26 | Rangers | 22 |
| 1895–96a | Celtic | 30 | Rangers | 26 | Hibernian | 24 |
| 1896–97a | Hearts | 28 | Hibernian | 26 | Rangers | 25 |
| 1897–98a | Celtic | 33 | Rangers | 29 | Hibernian | 22 |
| 1898–99a | Rangers | 36 | Hearts | 26 | Celtic | 24 |
| 1899– | | | | | | |
| 1900a | Rangers | 32 | Celtic | 25 | Hibernian | 24 |
| 1900–01c | Rangers | 35 | Celtic | 29 | Hibernian | 25 |
| 1901–02a | Rangers | 28 | Celtic | 26 | Hearts | 22 |
| 1902–03b | Hibernian | 37 | Dundee | 31 | Rangers | 29 |
| 1903–04d | Third Lanark | 43 | Hearts | 39 | Celtic* | 38 |
| 1904–05d | Celtic‡ | 41 | Rangers | 41 | Third Lanark | 35 |
| 1905–06e | Celtic | 49 | Hearts | 43 | Airdrieonians | 38 |
| 1906–07f | Celtic | 55 | Dundee | 48 | Rangers | 45 |
| 1907–08f | Celtic | 55 | Falkirk | 51 | Rangers | 50 |
| 1908–09f | Celtic | 51 | Dundee | 50 | Clyde | 48 |
| 1909–10f | Celtic | 54 | Falkirk | 52 | Rangers | 46 |
| 1910–11f | Rangers | 52 | Aberdeen | 48 | Falkirk | 44 |
| 1911–12f | Rangers | 51 | Celtic | 45 | Clyde | 42 |
| 1912–13f | Rangers | 53 | Celtic | 49 | Hearts* | 41 |
| 1913–14g | Celtic | 65 | Rangers | 59 | Hearts* | 54 |
| 1914–15g | Celtic | 65 | Hearts | 61 | Rangers | 50 |
| 1915–16g | Celtic | 67 | Rangers | 56 | Morton | 51 |
| 1916–17g | Celtic | 64 | Morton | 54 | Rangers | 53 |
| 1917–18f | Rangers | 56 | Celtic | 55 | Kilmarnock* | 43 |
| 1918–19f | Celtic | 58 | Rangers | 57 | Morton | 47 |
| 1919–20h | Rangers | 71 | Celtic | 68 | Motherwell | 57 |
| 1920–21h | Rangers | 76 | Celtic | 66 | Hearts | 50 |
| 1921–22h | Celtic | 67 | Rangers | 66 | Raith R | 51 |
| 1922–23g | Rangers | 55 | Airdrieonians | 50 | Celtic | 46 |
| 1923–24g | Rangers | 59 | Airdrieonians | 50 | Celtic | 46 |
| 1924–25g | Rangers | 60 | Airdrieonians | 57 | Hibernian | 52 |
| 1925–26g | Celtic | 58 | Airdrieonians* | 50 | Hearts | 50 |
| 1926–27g | Rangers | 56 | Motherwell | 51 | Celtic | 49 |
| 1927–28g | Rangers | 60 | Celtic* | 55 | Motherwell | 55 |
| 1928–29g | Rangers | 67 | Celtic | 51 | Motherwell | 50 |
| 1929–30g | Rangers | 60 | Motherwell | 55 | Aberdeen | 53 |
| 1930–31g | Rangers | 60 | Celtic | 58 | Motherwell | 56 |
| 1931–32g | Motherwell | 66 | Rangers | 61 | Celtic | 48 |
| 1932–33g | Rangers | 62 | Motherwell | 59 | Hearts | 50 |
| 1933–34g | Rangers | 66 | Motherwell | 62 | Celtic | 47 |
| 1934–35g | Rangers | 55 | Celtic | 52 | Hearts | 50 |
| 1935–36g | Celtic | 66 | Rangers* | 61 | Aberdeen | 61 |
| 1936–37g | Rangers | 61 | Aberdeen | 54 | Celtic | 52 |
| 1937–38g | Celtic | 61 | Hearts | 58 | Rangers | 49 |
| 1938–39g | Rangers | 59 | Celtic | 48 | Aberdeen | 46 |
| 1946–47e | Rangers | 46 | Hibernian | 44 | Aberdeen | 39 |
| 1947–48e | Hibernian | 48 | Rangers | 46 | Partick T | 36 |
| 1948–49e | Rangers | 46 | Dundee | 45 | Hibernian | 39 |
| 1949–50e | Rangers | 50 | Hibernian | 49 | Hearts | 43 |

| 1950–51e | Hibernian | 48 | Rangers* | 38 | Dundee | 38 |
| 1951–52e | Hibernian | 45 | Rangers | 41 | East Fife | 37 |
| 1952–53e | Rangers* | 43 | Hibernian | 43 | East Fife | 39 |
| 1953–54e | Celtic | 43 | Hearts | 38 | Partick T | 35 |
| 1954–55e | Aberdeen | 49 | Celtic | 46 | Rangers | 41 |
| 1955–56f | Rangers | 52 | Aberdeen | 46 | Hearts* | 45 |
| 1956–57f | Rangers | 55 | Hearts | 53 | Kilmarnock | 42 |
| 1957–58f | Hearts | 62 | Rangers | 49 | Celtic | 46 |
| 1958–59f | Rangers | 50 | Hearts | 48 | Motherwell | 44 |
| 1959–60f | Hearts | 54 | Kilmarnock | 50 | Rangers* | 42 |
| 1960–61f | Rangers | 51 | Kilmarnock | 50 | Third Lanark | 42 |
| 1961–62f | Dundee | 54 | Rangers | 51 | Celtic | 46 |
| 1962–63f | Rangers | 57 | Kilmarnock | 48 | Partick T | 46 |
| 1963–64f | Rangers | 55 | Kilmarnock | 49 | Celtic* | 47 |
| 1964–65f | Kilmarnock* | 50 | Hearts | 50 | Dunfermline Ath | 49 |
| 1965–66f | Celtic | 57 | Rangers | 55 | Kilmarnock | 45 |
| 1966–67f | Celtic | 58 | Rangers | 55 | Clyde | 46 |
| 1967–68f | Celtic | 63 | Rangers | 61 | Hibernian | 45 |
| 1968–69f | Celtic | 54 | Rangers | 49 | DunfermlineAth | 45 |
| 1969–70f | Celtic | 57 | Rangers | 45 | Hibernian | 44 |
| 1970–71f | Celtic | 56 | Aberdeen | 54 | St Johnstone | 44 |
| 1971–72f | Celtic | 60 | Aberdeen | 50 | Rangers | 44 |
| 1972–73f | Celtic | 57 | Rangers | 56 | Hibernian | 45 |
| 1973–74f | Celtic | 53 | Hibernian | 49 | Rangers | 48 |
| 1974–75f | Rangers | 56 | Hibernian | 49 | Celtic | 45 |

## DIVISION 2 to 1974–75

*Maximum points: a 76; b 72; c 68; d 52; e 60; f 36; g 44.*

| 1893–94f | Hibernian | 29 | Cowlairs | 27 | Clyde | 24 |
| 1894–95f | Hibernian | 30 | Motherwell | 22 | Port Glasgow | 20 |
| 1895–96f | Abercorn | 27 | Leith Ath | 23 | Renton | 20 |
| 1896–97f | Partick T | 31 | Leith Ath | 27 | Kilmarnock* | 21 |
| 1897–98f | Kilmarnock | 29 | Port Glasgow | 25 | Morton | 22 |
| 1898–99f | Kilmarnock | 32 | Leith Ath | 27 | Port Glasgow | 25 |
| 1899– | | | | | | |
| 1900f | Partick T | 29 | Morton | 28 | Port Glasgow | 20 |
| 1900–01f | St Bernard's | 25 | Airdrieonians | 23 | Abercorn | 21 |
| 1901–02g | Port Glasgow | 32 | Partick T | 31 | Motherwell | 26 |
| 1902–03g | Airdrieonians | 35 | Motherwell | 28 | Ayr U* | 27 |
| 1903–04g | Hamilton A | 37 | Clyde | 29 | Ayr U | 28 |
| 1904–05g | Clyde | 32 | Falkirk | 28 | Hamilton A | 27 |
| 1905–06g | Leith Ath | 34 | Clyde | 31 | Albion R | 27 |
| 1906–07g | St Bernard's | 32 | Vale of Leven* | 27 | Arthurlie | 27 |
| 1907–08g | Raith R | 30 | Dumbarton | ‡‡27 | Ayr U | 27 |
| 1908–09g | Abercorn | 31 | Raith R* | 28 | Vale of Leven | 28 |
| 1909–10g | Leith Ath‡ | 33 | Raith R | 33 | St Bernard's | 27 |
| 1910–11g | Dumbarton | 31 | Ayr U | 27 | Albion R | 25 |
| 1911–12g | Ayr U | 35 | Abercorn | 30 | Dumbarton | 27 |
| 1912–13d | Ayr U | 34 | Dunfermline Ath | 33 | East Stirling | 32 |
| 1913–14g | Cowdenbeath | 31 | Albion R | 27 | Dunfermline Ath* | 26 |
| 1914–15d | Cowdenbeath* | 37 | St Bernard's* | 37 | Leith Ath | 37 |
| 1921–22a | Alloa | 60 | Cowdenbeath | 47 | Armadale | 45 |
| 1922–23a | Queen's Park | 57 | Clydebank ¶ | 50 | St Johnstone ¶ | 45 |
| 1923–24a | St Johnstone | 56 | Cowdenbeath | 55 | Bathgate | 44 |
| 1924–25a | Dundee U | 50 | Clydebank | 48 | Clyde | 47 |
| 1925–26a | Dunfermline Ath | 59 | Clyde | 53 | Ayr U | 52 |

| | | | | | |
|---|---|---|---|---|---|
| 1926–27a Bo'ness | 56 | Raith R | 49 | Clydebank | 45 |
| 1927–28a Ayr U | 54 | Third Lanark | 45 | King's Park | 44 |
| 1928–29b Dundee U | 51 | Morton | 50 | Arbroath | 47 |
| 1929–30a Leith Ath* | 57 | East Fife | 57 | Albion R | 54 |
| 1930–31a Third Lanark | 61 | Dundee U | 47 | Dunfermline Ath | 47 |
| 1931–32a East Stirling* | 55 | St Johnstone | 55 | Raith R* | 46 |
| 1932–33c Hibernian | 54 | Queen of the S | 49 | Dunfermline Ath | 47 |
| 1933–34c Albion R | 45 | Dunfermline Ath* | 44 | Arbroath | 44 |
| 1934–35c Third Lanark | 52 | Arbroath | 50 | St Bernard's | 47 |
| 1935–36c Falkirk | 59 | St Mirren | 52 | Morton | 48 |
| 1936–37c Ayr U | 54 | Morton | 51 | St Bernard's | 48 |
| 1937–38c Raith R | 59 | Albion R | 48 | Airdrieonians | 47 |
| 1938–39c Cowdenbeath | 60 | Alloa* | 48 | East Fife | 48 |
| 1946–47d Dundee | 45 | Airdrieonians | 42 | East Fife | 31 |
| 1947–48e East Fife | 53 | Albion R | 42 | Hamilton A | 40 |
| 1948–49e Raith R* | 42 | Stirling A | 42 | Airdrieonians* | 41 |
| 1949–50e Morton | 47 | Airdrieonians | 44 | Dunfermline Ath* | 36 |
| 1950–51e Queen of the S* | 45 | Stirling A | 45 | Ayr U* | 36 |
| 1951–52e Clyde | 44 | Falkirk | 43 | Ayr U | 39 |
| 1952–53e Stirling A | 44 | Hamilton A | 43 | Queen's Park | 37 |
| 1953–54e Motherwell | 45 | Kilmarnock | 42 | Third Lanark* | 36 |
| 1954–55e Airdrieonians | 46 | Dunfermline Ath | 42 | Hamilton A | 39 |
| 1955–56b Queen's Park | 54 | Ayr U | 51 | St Johnstone | 49 |
| 1956–57b Clyde | 64 | Third Lanark | 51 | Cowdenbeath | 45 |
| 1957–58b Stirling A | 55 | Dunfermline Ath | 53 | Arbroath | 47 |
| 1958–59b Ayr U | 60 | Arbroath | 51 | Stenhousemuir | 46 |
| 1959–60b St Johnstone | 53 | Dundee U | 50 | Queen of the S | 49 |
| 1960–61b Stirling A | 55 | Falkirk | 54 | Stenhousemuir | 50 |
| 1961–62b Clyde | 54 | Queen of the S | 53 | Morton | 44 |
| 1962–63b St Johnstone | 55 | East Stirling | 49 | Morton | 48 |
| 1963–64b Morton | 67 | Clyde | 53 | Arbroath | 46 |
| 1964–65b Stirling A | 59 | Hamilton A | 50 | Queen of the S | 45 |
| 1965–66b Ayr U | 53 | Airdrieonians | 50 | Queen of the S | 47 |
| 1966–67a Morton | 69 | Raith R | 58 | Arbroath | 57 |
| 1967–68b St Mirren | 62 | Arbroath | 53 | East Fife | 49 |
| 1968–69b Motherwell | 64 | Ayr U | 53 | East Fife* | 48 |
| 1969–70b Falkirk | 56 | Cowdenbeath | 55 | Queen of the S | 50 |
| 1970–71b Partick T | 56 | East Fife | 51 | Arbroath | 46 |
| 1971–72b Dumbarton* | 52 | Arbroath | 52 | Stirling A | 50 |
| 1972–73b Clyde | 56 | Dumfermline Ath | 52 | Raith R* | 47 |
| 1973–74b Airdrieonians | 60 | Kilmarnock | 58 | Hamilton A | 55 |
| 1974–75a Falkirk | 54 | Queen of the S* | 53 | Montrose | 53 |

Elected to Division 1: 1894 Clyde; 1895 Hibernian; 1896 Abercorn; 1897 Partick T;
1899 Kilmarnock; 1900 Morton and Partick T; 1902 Port Glasgow and Partick T;
1903 Airdrieonians and Motherwell; 1905 Falkirk and Aberdeen; 1906 Clyde and
Hamilton A; 1910 Raith R; 1913 Ayr U and Dumbarton.

# RELEGATED CLUBS

**From Premier League**

1998–99 Dunfermline Ath *(No relegation 1999–2000)*
2000–01 St Mirren

**From Premier Division**

1974–75 *No relegation due to League reorganisation*
1975–76 Dundee, St Johnstone
1976–77 Hearts, Kilmarnock
1977–78 Ayr U, Clydebank
1978–79 Hearts, Motherwell
1979–80 Dundee, Hibernian
1980–81 Kilmarnock, Hearts
1981–82 Partick T, Airdrieonians
1982–83 Morton, Kilmarnock
1983–84 St Johnstone, Motherwell
1984–85 Dumbarton, Morton
1985–86 *No relegation due to League reorganization*
1986–87 Clydebank, Hamilton A
1987–88 Falkirk, Dunfermline Ath, Morton
1988–89 Hamilton A
1989–90 Dundee
1990–91 None
1991–92 St Mirren, Dunfermline Ath
1992–93 Falkirk, Airdrieonians
1993–94 *See footnote*
1994–95 Dundee U
1995–96 Partick T, Falkirk
1996–97 Raith R
1997–98 Hibernian

**From Division 1**

1974–75 *No relegation due to League reorganisation*
1975–76 Dunfermline Ath, Clyde
1976–77 Raith R, Falkirk
1977–78 Alloa Ath, East Fife
1978–79 Montrose, Queen of the S
1979–80 Arbroath, Clyde
1980–81 Stirling A, Berwick R
1981–82 East Stirling, Queen of the S
1982–83 Dunfermline Ath, Queen's Park
1983–84 Raith R, Alloa
1984–85 Meadowbank T, St Johnstone
1985–86 Ayr U, Alloa

1986–87 Brechin C, Montrose
1987–88 East Fife, Dumbarton

1988–89 Kilmarnock, Queen of the S
1989–90 Albion R, Alloa
1990–91 Clyde, Brechin C
1991–92 Montrose, Forfar Ath
1992–93 Meadowbank T, Cowdenbeath
1993–94 *See footnote*
1994–95 Ayr U, Stranraer
1995–96 Hamilton A, Dumbarton
1996–97 Clydebank, East Fife
1997–98 Partick T, Stirling A
1998–99 Hamilton A, Stranraer
1999–00 Clydebank
2000–01 Morton, Alloa

**Relegated from Division 2**

1994–95 Meadowbank T, Brechin C
1995–96 Forfar Ath, Montrose
1996–97 Dumbarton, Berwick R
1997–98 Stenhousemuir, Brechin C
1998–99 East Fife, Forfar Ath
1999–00 Hamilton A**
2000–01 Queen's Park, Stirling A

**Relegated from Division 1 1973–74**

1921–22 *Queen's Park, Dumbarton, Clydebank
1922–23 Albion R, Alloa Ath
1923–24 Clyde, Clydebank
1924–25 Third Lanark, Ayr U
1925–26 Raith R, Clydebank
1926–27 Morton, Dundee U

1927–28 Dunfermline Ath, Bo'ness
1928–29 Third Lanark, Raith R
1929–30 St Johnstone, Dundee U
1930–31 Hibernian, East Fife
1931–32 Dundee U, Leith Ath
1932–33 Morton, East Stirling
1933–34 Third Lanark, Cowdenbeath

214

1934–35 St Mirren, Falkirk
1935–36 Airdrieonians, Ayr U
1936–37 Dunfermline Ath, Albion R
1937–38 Dundee, Morton
1938–39 Queen's Park, Raith R
1946–47 Kilmarnock, Hamilton A
1947–48 Airdrieonians, Queen's Park
1948–49 Morton, Albion R
1949–50 Queen of the S, Stirling A
1950–51 Clyde, Falkirk
1951–52 Morton, Stirling A
1952–53 Motherwell, Third Lanark
1953–54 Airdrieonians, Hamilton A
1954–55 *No clubs relegated*
1955–56 Stirling A, Clyde
1956–57 Dunfermline Ath, Ayr U
1957–58 East Fife, Queen's Park

1958–59 Queen of the S, Falkirk
1959–60 Arbroath, Stirling A
1960–61 Ayr U, Clyde
1961–62 St Johnstone, Stirling A
1962–63 Clyde, Raith R
1963–64 Queen of the S, East Stirling
1964–65 Airdrieonians, Third Lanark
1965–66 Morton, Hamilton A
1966–67 St Mirren, Ayr U
1967–68 Motherwell, Stirling A
1968–69 Falkirk, Arbroath
1969–70 Raith R, Partick T
1970–71 St Mirren, Cowdenbeath
1971–72 Clyde, Dunfermline Ath
1972–73 Kilmarnock, Airdrieonians
1973–74 East Fife, Falkirk

*Season 1921–22 – only 1 club promoted, 3 clubs relegated.

**15 pts deducted for failing to field a team.*

**Scottish League championship wins:** Rangers 49, Celtic 37, Aberdeen 4, Hearts 4, Hibernian 4, Dumbarton 2, Dundee 1, Dundee U 1, Kilmarnock 1, Motherwell 1, Third Lanark 1.

*The Scottish Football League was reconstructed into three divisions at the end of the 1974–75 season, so the usual relegation statistics do not apply. Further reorganization took place at the end of the 1985–86 season. From 1986–87, the Premier and First Division had 12 teams each. The Second Division remained at 14. From 1988–89, the Premier Division reverted to 10 teams, and the First Division to 14 teams but in 1991–92 the Premier and First Division reverted to 12. At the end of the 1997–98 season, the top nine clubs in Premier Division broke away from the Scottish League to form a new competition, the Scottish Premier League, with the club promoted from Division One. At the end of the 1999–2000 season two teams were added to the Scottish League. There was no relegation from the Premier League but two promoted from the First Division and three from each of the Second and Third Divisions. One team was relegated from the First Division and one from the Second Division, leaving 12 teams in each division.*

# PAST SCOTTISH LEAGUE CUP FINALS

|  | | | | |
|---|---|---|---|---|
| 1946–47 | Rangers | 4 | Aberdeen | 0 |
| 1947–48 | East Fife | 0 4 | Falkirk | 0* 1 |
| 1948–49 | Rangers | 2 | Raith Rovers | 0 |
| 1949–50 | East Fife | 3 | Dunfermline | 0 |
| 1950–51 | Motherwell | 3 | Hibernian | 0 |
| 1951–52 | Dundee | 3 | Rangers | 2 |
| 1952–53 | Dundee | 2 | Kilmarnock | 0 |
| 1953–54 | East Fife | 3 | Partick Thistle | 2 |
| 1954–55 | Hearts | 4 | Motherwell | 2 |
| 1955–56 | Aberdeen | 2 | St Mirren | 1 |
| 1956–57 | Celtic | 0 3 | Partick Thistle | 0 0 |
| 1957–58 | Celtic | 7 | Rangers | 1 |
| 1958–59 | Hearts | 5 | Partick Thistle | 1 |
| 1959–60 | Hearts | 2 | Third Lanark | 1 |
| 1960–61 | Rangers | 2 | Kilmarnock | 0 |
| 1961–62 | Rangers | 1 3 | Hearts | 1 1 |
| 1962–63 | Hearts | 1 | Kilmarnock | 0 |
| 1963–64 | Rangers | 5 | Morton | 0 |
| 1964–65 | Rangers | 2 | Celtic | 1 |
| 1965–66 | Celtic | 2 | Rangers | 1 |
| 1966–67 | Celtic | 1 | Rangers | 0 |
| 1967–68 | Celtic | 5 | Dundee | 3 |
| 1968–69 | Celtic | 6 | Hibernian | 2 |
| 1969–70 | Celtic | 1 | St Johnstone | 0 |
| 1970–71 | Rangers | 1 | Celtic | 0 |
| 1971–72 | Partick Thistle | 4 | Celtic | 1 |
| 1972–73 | Hibernian | 2 | Celtic | 1 |
| 1973–74 | Dundee | 1 | Celtic | 0 |
| 1974–75 | Celtic | 6 | Hibernian | 3 |
| 1975–76 | Rangers | 1 | Celtic | 0 |
| 1976–77 | Aberdeen | 2 | Celtic | 1 |
| 1977–78 | Rangers | 2 | Celtic | 1* |
| 1978–79 | Rangers | 2 | Aberdeen | 1 |
| 1979–80 | Aberdeen | 0 0 | Dundee U | 0* 3 |
| 1980–81 | Dundee | 0 | Dundee U | 3 |
| 1981–82 | Rangers | 2 | Dundee U | 1 |
| 1982–83 | Celtic | 2 | Rangers | 1 |
| 1983–84 | Rangers | 3 | Celtic | 2 |
| 1984–85 | Rangers | 1 | Dundee U | 0 |
| 1985–86 | Aberdeen | 3 | Hibernian | 0 |
| 1986–87 | Rangers | 2 | Celtic | 1 |
| 1987–88 | Rangers† | 3 | Aberdeen | 3* |
| 1988–89 | Aberdeen | 2 | Rangers | 3* |
| 1989–90 | Aberdeen | 2 | Rangers | 1 |
| 1990–91 | Rangers | 2 | Celtic | 1 |
| 1991–92 | Hibernian | 2 | Dunfermline Ath | 0 |
| 1992–93 | Rangers | 2 | Aberdeen | 1* |
| 1993–94 | Rangers | 2 | Hibernian | 1 |
| 1994–95 | Raith R† | 2 | Celtic | 2* |
| 1995–96 | Aberdeen | 2 | Dundee | 0 |
| 1996–97 | Rangers | 4 | Hearts | 3 |
| 1997–98 | Celtic | 3 | Dundee U | 0 |
| 1998–99 | Rangers | 2 | St Johnstone | 1 |
| 1999–2000 | Celtic | 2 | Aberdeen | 0 |

†Won on penalties  *After extra time

# CIS SCOTTISH LEAGUE CUP 2000–2001

## FIRST ROUND

| | | | |
|---|---|---|---|
| Arbroath | (0) 2 | Brechin C | (0) 0 |
| Clyde | (2) 5 | Morton | (0) 1 |
| Clydebank | (0) 0 | Alloa Ath | (0) 2 |
| Cowdenbeath | (2) 3 | Elgin C | (0) 0 |
| Dumbarton | (0) 0 | Ayr U | (0) 0 |
| *(aet; Dumbarton won 5-4 on penalties.)* | | | |
| East Fife | (0) 1 | Raith R | (0) 2 |
| East Stirling | (0) 2 | Hamilton A | (0) 1 |
| Montrose | (0) 1 | Berwick R | (0) 0 |
| Partick T | (0) 1 | Airdrieonians | (1) 2 |
| *(aet)* | | | |
| Peterhead | (0) 2 | Inverness CT | (2) 3 |
| Queen of the S | (1) 2 | Forfar Ath | (0) 1 |
| Queen's Park | (1) 2 | Stranraer | (0) 0 |
| Ross Co | (0) 1 | Albion R | (0) 0 |
| Stirling Albion | (0) 0 | Stenhousemuir | (0) 1 |

## SECOND ROUND

| | | | |
|---|---|---|---|
| Alloa Ath | (0) 0 | Dundee U | (2) 3 |
| Clyde | (0) 1 | Kilmarnock | (0) 2 |
| *(aet)* | | | |
| Dumbarton | (0) 0 | Livingston | (4) 4 |
| Dundee | (1) 3 | Montrose | (0) 0 |
| Dunfermline Ath | (0) 1 | East Stirling | (0) 0 |
| Falkirk | (3) 3 | Queen of the S | (0) 1 |
| Inverness CT | (0) 0 | Airdrieonians | (0) 2 |
| Queen's Park | (0) 0 | Motherwell | (1) 3 |
| Raith R | (0) 2 | Arbroath | (1) 1 |
| Ross Co | (0) 1 | St Mirren | (0) 3 |
| *(aet)* | | | |
| St Johnstone | (3) 3 | Cowdenbeath | (0) 1 |
| Stenhousemuir | (1) 1 | Hibernian | (1) 2 |

## THIRD ROUND

| | | | |
|---|---|---|---|
| Celtic | (2) 4 | Raith R | (0) 0 |
| Dundee U | (0) 0 | Airdrieonians | (0) 0 |
| *(aet; Dundee U won 4-3 on penalties.)* | | | |
| Dunfermline Ath | (1) 2 | Motherwell | (0) 0 |
| Falkirk | (0) 1 | Hibernian | (0) 2 |
| *(aet)* | | | |
| St Johnstone | (0) 0 | Kilmarnock | (0) 1 |
| St Mirren | (0) 3 | Dundee | (0) 0 |
| Livingston | (0) 0 | Hearts | (1) 2 |
| Rangers | (1) 4 | Aberdeen | (0) 2 |

## QUARTER-FINALS

| | | | |
|---|---|---|---|
| Hearts | (1) 2 | Celtic | (1) 5 |
| *(aet)* | | | |
| Kilmarnock | (0) 2 | Hibernian | (1) 1 |
| Rangers | (2) 2 | Dundee U | (0) 0 |
| St Mirren | (2) 2 | Dunfermline Ath | (1) 1 |

## SEMI-FINALS

| | | | |
|---|---|---|---|
| Celtic | (2) 3 | Rangers | (1) 1 |
| Kilmarnock | (1) 3 | St Mirren | (0) 0 |

## FINAL

| | | | |
|---|---|---|---|
| Celtic | (0) 3 | Kilmarnock | (0) 0 |

# BELL'S CHALLENGE CUP 2000–2001

**FIRST ROUND**

| | | | |
|---|---|---|---|
| Airdrieonians | (0) 2 | Queen of the S | (0) 1 |
| *(aet)* | | | |
| Albion R | (0) 0 | Clydebank | (1) 1 |
| Alloa | (2) 2 | Inverness CT | (0) 3 |
| Brechin C | (2) 3 | Ayr U | (0) 1 |
| Cowdenbeath | (1) 2 | Falkirk | (1) 1 |
| *(aet)* | | | |
| East Stirling | (1) 3 | East Fife | (0) 0 |
| Elgin C | (0) 2 | Dumbarton | (1) 4 |
| Forfar Ath | (0) 1 | Peterhead | (1) 1 |
| *(aet; Peterhead won 4-2 on penalties.)* | | | |
| Partick T | (0) 0 | Livingston | (0) 2 |
| Queen's Park | (2) 2 | Montrose | (0) 0 |
| Raith R | (0) 0 | Morton | (3) 4 |
| Ross Co | (1) 2 | Clyde | (0) 1 |
| Stirling Albion | (1) 2 | Arbroath | (1) 3 |
| Stranraer | (2) 4 | Berwick R | (0) 2 |

**SECOND ROUND**

| | | | |
|---|---|---|---|
| Arbroath | (0) 2 | Dumbarton | (0) 0 |
| Brechin C | (1) 1 | Queen's Park | (1) 1 |
| *(aet; Brechin C won 4-2 on penalties.)* | | | |
| Clydebank | (1) 1 | Peterhead | (0) 0 |
| Cowdenbeath | (0) 1 | Stenhousemuir | (0) 2 |
| East Stirling | (0) 3 | Morton | (1) 2 |
| Hamilton A | (0) 0 | Airdrieonians | (0) 1 |
| *(aet)* | | | |
| Inverness CT | (0) 1 | Stranraer | (1) 2 |
| Ross Co | (0) 0 | Livingston | (0) 3 |

**QUARTER-FINALS**

| | | | |
|---|---|---|---|
| Airdrieonians | (0) 1 | Clydebank | (0) 1 |
| *(aet; Airdrieonians won 4-3 on penalties.)* | | | |
| East Stirling | (2) 4 | Stenhousemuir | (0) 0 |
| Livingston | (0) 3 | Brechin C | (1) 1 |
| Stranraer | (3) 3 | Arbroath | (1) 2 |

**SEMI-FINALS**

| | | | |
|---|---|---|---|
| Livingston | (2) 2 | East Stirling | (1) 1 |
| Stranraer | (2) 2 | Airdrieonians | (2) 4 |
| *(aet)* | | | |

**FINAL**

| | | | |
|---|---|---|---|
| Airdrieonians | (1) 2 | Livingston | (1) 2 |
| *(aet; Airdrieonians won 4-3 on penalties.)* | | | |

# SCOTTISH CUP 2000–2001

### FIRST ROUND

| | | | |
|---|---|---|---|
| Albion R | (1) 1 | East Fife | (0) 1 |
| Brechin C | (1) 3 | Forfar Ath | (0) 0 |
| Dumbarton | (1) 1 | East Stirling | (0) 1 |
| Edinburgh C | (0) 0 | Buckie T | (1) 1 |
| Montrose | (0) 0 | Arbroath | (0) 1 |

*(SFA ordered game to be replayed as Arbroath fielded ineligible player.)*

| | | | |
|---|---|---|---|
| Montrose | (0) 0 | Arbroath | (0) 0 |
| Queen of the S | (2) 2 | Clydebank | (0) 0 |
| Stenhousemuir | (0) 1 | Berwick R | (3) 4 |
| Whitehill Welfare | (0) 0 | Peterhead | (0) 0 |

### FIRST ROUND REPLAYS

| | | | |
|---|---|---|---|
| Arbroath | (1) 1 | Montrose | (1) 2 |
| East Fife | (0) 2 | Albion R | (0) 0 |
| East Stirling | (0) 0 | Dumbarton | (0) 1 |
| Peterhead | (1) 3 | Whitehill Welfare | (0) 0 |

### SECOND ROUND

| | | | |
|---|---|---|---|
| Berwick R | (2) 3 | Cowdenbeath | (0) 3 |
| Buckie T | (0) 2 | Hamilton A | (0) 0 |
| Coldstream | (0) 2 | Brechin C | (3) 6 |
| East Fife | (1) 1 | Queen's Park | (0) 0 |
| Elgin C | (0) 0 | Queen of the S | (1) 1 |
| Montrose | (0) 1 | Keith | (0) 1 |
| Partick T | (0) 3 | Deveronvale | (0) 0 |
| Peterhead | (0) 3 | Cove R | (0) 0 |
| Spartans | (1) 1 | Stirling Albion | (1) 3 |
| Stranraer | (0) 2 | Dumbarton | (0) 0 |

### SECOND ROUND REPLAYS

| | | | |
|---|---|---|---|
| Cowdenbeath | (0) 0 | Berwick R | (0) 1 |
| Keith | (0) 0 | Montrose | (0) 1 |
| *(aet)* | | | |

### THIRD ROUND

| | | | |
|---|---|---|---|
| Alloa Ath | (0) 0 | Aberdeen | (1) 3 |
| Berwick R | (0) 0 | Hearts | (0) 0 |
| Dundee | (0) 0 | Falkirk | (0) 0 |
| East Fife | (1) 1 | Livingston | (2) 4 |
| Hibernian | (3) 6 | Clyde | (0) 1 |
| Inverness CT | (0) 4 | Ayr U | (3) 3 |
| Kilmarnock | (1) 1 | Partick T | (0) 0 |
| Montrose | (0) 0 | Dundee U | (2) 2 |
| Peterhead | (1) 4 | Morton | (1) 1 |
| Queen of the S | (1) 1 | Airdrieonians | (1) 3 |
| Rangers | (2) 2 | Brechin C | (0) 0 |
| Ross Co | (1) 2 | Buckie T | (0) 1 |
| St Johnstone | (0) 0 | Dunfermline Ath | (0) 0 |
| St Mirren | (0) 1 | Motherwell | (1) 2 |
| Stirling Albion | (0) 2 | Raith R | (0) 0 |
| Stranraer | (0) 1 | Celtic | (1) 4 |

## THIRD ROUND REPLAYS

| | | | |
|---|---|---|---|
| Falkirk | (0) 0 | Dundee | (0) 2 |
| Dunfermline Ath | (0) 3 | St Johnstone | (2) 2 |
| Hearts | (0) 2 | Berwick R | (1) 1 |

## FOURTH ROUND

| | | | |
|---|---|---|---|
| Dunfermline Ath | (0) 2 | Celtic | (0) 2 |
| Hearts | (0) 1 | Dundee | (1) 1 |
| Inverness CT | (0) 1 | Kilmarnock | (0) 1 |
| Livingston | (0) 0 | Aberdeen | (0) 0 |
| Motherwell | (0) 0 | Dundee U | (2) 2 |
| Peterhead | (0) 0 | Airdrieonians | (0) 0 |

*(Peterhead were awarded a walk-over as Airdrieonians could not produce a team.)*

| | | | |
|---|---|---|---|
| Ross Co | (1) 2 | Rangers | (2) 3 |
| Stirling Albion | (1) 2 | Hibernian | (2) 3 |

## FOURTH ROUND REPLAYS

| | | | |
|---|---|---|---|
| Aberdeen | (0) 0 | Livingston | (0) 1 |
| Celtic | (1) 4 | Dunfermline Ath | (1) 1 |
| Dundee | (0) 0 | Hearts | (0) 1 |
| Kilmarnock | (0) 2 | Inverness CT | (0) 1 |

## QUARTER-FINALS

| | | | |
|---|---|---|---|
| Celtic | (1) 1 | Hearts | (0) 0 |
| Dundee U | (0) 1 | Rangers | (0) 0 |
| Kilmarnock | (0) 0 | Hibernian | (0) 1 |
| Livingston | (2) 3 | Peterhead | (1) 1 |

## SEMI-FINALS

| | | | |
|---|---|---|---|
| Celtic | (1) 3 | Dundee U | (0) 1 |
| Hibernian | (1) 3 | Livingston | (0) 0 |

## FINAL

| | | | |
|---|---|---|---|
| Celtic | (1) 3 | Hibernian | (0) 0 |

# PAST SCOTTISH CUP FINALS

|  | | | | |
|------|------|------|------|------|
| 1874 | Queen's Park | 2 | Clydesdale | 0 |
| 1875 | Queen's Park | 3 | Renton | 0 |
| 1876 | Queen's Park | 1 2 | Third Lanark | 1 0 |
| 1877 | Vale of Leven | 0 1 3 | Rangers | 0 1 2 |
| 1878 | Vale of Leven | 1 | Third Lanark | 0 |
| 1879 | Vale of Leven | 1 | Rangers | 1 |

*Vale of Leven awarded cup, Rangers did not appear for replay*

| | | | | |
|------|------|------|------|------|
| 1880 | Queen's Park | 3 | Thornlibank | 0 |
| 1881 | Queen's Park | 2 3 | Dumbarton | 1 1 |

*Replayed because of protest*

| | | | | |
|------|------|------|------|------|
| 1882 | Queen's Park | 2 4 | Dumbarton | 2 1 |
| 1883 | Dumbarton | 2 2 | Vale of Leven | 2 1 |

*1884 Queen's Park awarded cup when Vale of Leven did not appear for the final*

| | | | | |
|------|------|------|------|------|
| 1885 | Renton | 0 3 | Vale of Leven | 0 1 |
| 1886 | Queen's Park | 3 | Renton | 1 |
| 1887 | Hibernian | 2 | Dumbarton | 1 |
| 1888 | Renton | 6 | Cambuslang | 1 |
| 1889 | Third Lanark | 3 2 | Celtic | 0 1 |

*Replayed because of protest*

| | | | | |
|------|------|------|------|------|
| 1890 | Queen's Park | 1 2 | Vale of Leven | 1 1 |
| 1891 | Hearts | 1 | Dumbarton | 0 |
| 1892 | Celtic | 1 5 | Queen's Park | 0 1 |

*Replayed because of protest*

| | | | | |
|------|------|------|------|------|
| 1893 | Queen's Park | 2 | Celtic | 1 |
| 1894 | Rangers | 3 | Celtic | 1 |
| 1895 | St Bernards | 3 | Renton | 1 |
| 1896 | Hearts | 3 | Hibernian | 1 |
| 1897 | Rangers | 5 | Dumbarton | 1 |
| 1898 | Rangers | 2 | Kilmarnock | 0 |
| 1899 | Celtic | 2 | Rangers | 0 |
| 1900 | Celtic | 4 | Queen's Park | 3 |
| 1901 | Hearts | 4 | Celtic | 3 |
| 1902 | Hibernian | 1 | Celtic | 0 |
| 1903 | Rangers | 1 0 2 | Hearts | 1 0 0 |
| 1904 | Celtic | 3 | Rangers | 2 |
| 1905 | Third Lanark | 0 3 | Rangers | 0 1 |
| 1906 | Hearts | 1 | Third Lanark | 0 |
| 1907 | Celtic | 3 | Hearts | 0 |
| 1908 | Celtic | 5 | St Mirren | 1 |

*1909 After two drawn games between Celtic and Rangers, 2.2, 1.1, there was a riot and the cup was withheld*

| | | | | |
|------|------|------|------|------|
| 1910 | Dundee | 2 0 2 | Clyde | 2 0 1 |
| 1911 | Celtic | 0 2 | Hamilton Acad | 0 0 |
| 1912 | Celtic | 2 | Clyde | 0 |
| 1913 | Falkirk | 2 | Raith R | 0 |
| 1914 | Celtic | 0 4 | Hibernian | 0 1 |
| 1920 | Kilmarnock | 3 | Albion R | 2 |
| 1921 | Partick Th | 1 | Rangers | 0 |
| 1922 | Morton | 1 | Rangers | 0 |
| 1923 | Celtic | 1 | Hibernian | 0 |
| 1924 | Airdrieonians | 2 | Hibernian | 0 |
| 1925 | Celtic | 2 | Dundee | 1 |
| 1926 | St Mirren | 2 | Celtic | 0 |
| 1927 | Celtic | 3 | East Fife | 1 |
| 1928 | Rangers | 4 | Celtic | 0 |
| 1929 | Kilmarnock | 2 | Rangers | 0 |
| 1930 | Rangers | 0 2 | Partick Th | 0 1 |
| 1931 | Celtic | 2 4 | Motherwell | 2 2 |
| 1932 | Rangers | 1 3 | Kilmarnock | 1 0 |
| 1933 | Celtic | 1 | Motherwell | 0 |

|  | | | | |
|------|------|------|------|------|
| 1934 | Rangers | 5 | St Mirren | 0 |
| 1935 | Rangers | 2 | Hamilton Acad | 1 |
| 1936 | Rangers | 1 | Third Lanark | 0 |
| 1937 | Celtic | 2 | Aberdeen | 1 |
| 1938 | East Fife | 1 4 | Kilmarnock | 1 2 |
| 1939 | Clyde | 4 | Motherwell | 0 |
| 1947 | Aberdeen | 2 | Hibernian | 1 |
| 1948 | Rangers | 1 1 | Morton | 1 0 |
| 1949 | Rangers | 4 | Clyde | 1 |
| 1950 | Rangers | 3 | East Fife | 0 |
| 1951 | Celtic | 1 | Motherwell | 0 |
| 1952 | Motherwell | 4 | Dundee | 0 |
| 1953 | Rangers | 1 1 | Aberdeen | 1 0 |
| 1954 | Celtic | 2 | Aberdeen | 1 |
| 1955 | Clyde | 1 1 | Celtic | 1 0 |
| 1956 | Hearts | 3 | Celtic | 1 |
| 1957 | Falkirk | 1 2 | Kilmarnock | 1 1 |
| 1958 | Clyde | 1 | Hibernian | 0 |
| 1959 | St Mirren | 3 | Aberdeen | 1 |
| 1960 | Rangers | 2 | Kilmarnock | 0 |
| 1961 | Dunfermline Ath | 0 2 | Celtic | 0 0 |
| 1962 | Rangers | 2 | St Mirren | 0 |
| 1963 | Rangers | 1 3 | Celtic | 1 0 |
| 1964 | Rangers | 3 | Dundee | 1 |
| 1965 | Celtic | 3 | Dunfermline Ath | 2 |
| 1966 | Rangers | 0 1 | Celtic | 0 0 |
| 1967 | Celtic | 2 | Aberdeen | 0 |
| 1968 | Dunfermline Ath | 3 | Hearts | 1 |
| 1969 | Celtic | 4 | Rangers | 0 |
| 1970 | Aberdeen | 3 | Celtic | 1 |
| 1971 | Celtic | 1 2 | Rangers | 1 1 |
| 1972 | Celtic | 6 | Hibernian | 1 |
| 1973 | Rangers | 3 | Celtic | 2 |
| 1974 | Celtic | 3 | Dundee U | 0 |
| 1975 | Celtic | 3 | Airdrieonians | 1 |
| 1976 | Rangers | 3 | Hearts | 1 |
| 1977 | Celtic | 1 | Rangers | 0 |
| 1978 | Rangers | 2 | Aberdeen | 1 |
| 1979 | Rangers | 0 0 3 | Hibernian | 0 0 2 |
| 1980 | Celtic | 1 | Rangers | 0 |
| 1981 | Rangers | 0 4 | Dundee U | 0 1 |
| 1982 | Aberdeen | 4 | Rangers | 1 (aet) |
| 1983 | Aberdeen | 1 | Rangers | 0 (aet) |
| 1984 | Aberdeen | 2 | Celtic | 1 (aet) |
| 1985 | Celtic | 2 | Dundee U | 1 |
| 1986 | Aberdeen | 3 | Hearts | 0 |
| 1987 | St Mirren | 1 | Dundee U | 0 (aet) |
| 1988 | Celtic | 2 | Dundee U | 1 |
| 1989 | Celtic | 1 | Rangers | 0 |
| 1990 | Aberdeen† | 0 | Celtic | 0 |
| 1991 | Motherwell | 4 | Dundee U | 3 (aet) |
| 1992 | Rangers | 2 | Airdrieonians | 1 |
| 1993 | Rangers | 2 | Aberdeen | 1 |
| 1994 | Dundee U | 1 | Rangers | 0 |
| 1995 | Celtic | 1 | Airdrieonians | 0 |
| 1996 | Rangers | 5 | Hearts | 1 |
| 1997 | Kilmarnock | 1 | Falkirk | 0 |
| 1998 | Hearts | 2 | Rangers | 1 |
| 1999 | Rangers | 1 | Celtic | 0 |
| 2000 | Rangers | 4 | Aberdeen | 0 |

*†won on penalties*

# WELSH FOOTBALL 2000–2001

**LEAGUE OF WALES**

|  | | Home | | Goals | | Away | | Goals | | | |
|---|---|---|---|---|---|---|---|---|---|---|---|
|  | P | W | D | L | F | A | W | D | L | F | A | GD Pts |

|  | P | W | D | L | F | A | W | D | L | F | A | GD | Pts |
|---|---|---|---|---|---|---|---|---|---|---|---|---|---|
| Barry Town | 34 | 14 | 2 | 1 | 54 | 11 | 10 | 3 | 4 | 30 | 19 | 54 | 77 |
| Cwmbran Town | 34 | 13 | 2 | 2 | 38 | 16 | 11 | 0 | 6 | 33 | 18 | 37 | 74 |
| Carmarthen Town | 34 | 10 | 3 | 4 | 39 | 18 | 7 | 4 | 6 | 29 | 21 | 29 | 58 |
| Newtown | 34 | 10 | 0 | 7 | 30 | 22 | 8 | 4 | 5 | 18 | 15 | 11 | 58 |
| Caersws | 34 | 7 | 5 | 5 | 35 | 19 | 9 | 4 | 4 | 37 | 20 | 33 | 57 |
| Aberystwyth Town | 34 | 9 | 6 | 2 | 41 | 16 | 6 | 4 | 7 | 23 | 26 | 22 | 55 |
| Rhyl | 34 | 10 | 2 | 5 | 45 | 26 | 6 | 4 | 7 | 29 | 26 | 22 | 54 |
| Total Network Solutions | 34 | 8 | 5 | 4 | 29 | 23 | 7 | 4 | 6 | 35 | 24 | 17 | 54 |
| Connah's Quay Nomads | 34 | 7 | 3 | 7 | 20 | 18 | 7 | 5 | 5 | 25 | 29 | −2 | 50 |
| Haverfordwest County | 34 | 6 | 3 | 8 | 24 | 31 | 8 | 4 | 5 | 32 | 24 | 1 | 49 |
| Afan Lido | 34 | 9 | 5 | 3 | 28 | 16 | 4 | 3 | 10 | 14 | 21 | 5 | 47 |
| Rhayader Town | 34 | 6 | 4 | 7 | 23 | 24 | 4 | 6 | 7 | 31 | 41 | −11 | 40 |
| Flexsys Cefn Druids | 34 | 8 | 1 | 8 | 38 | 37 | 3 | 4 | 10 | 22 | 33 | −10 | 38 |
| Bangor City | 34 | 5 | 3 | 9 | 28 | 37 | 5 | 4 | 8 | 28 | 47 | −28 | 37 |
| Oswestry Town | 34 | 4 | 5 | 8 | 19 | 28 | 6 | 1 | 10 | 21 | 46 | −34 | 36 |
| Port Talbot Athletic | 34 | 4 | 3 | 10 | 19 | 40 | 6 | 2 | 9 | 30 | 37 | −28 | 35 |
| Llanelli | 34 | 8 | 1 | 8 | 38 | 33 | 1 | 1 | 15 | 19 | 64 | −40 | 29 |
| UWIC Inter Cardiff | 34 | 2 | 4 | 11 | 18 | 49 | 1 | 0 | 16 | 8 | 55 | −78 | 13 |

# NORTHERN IRISH FOOTBALL 2000–2001

**IFL SMIRNOFF**

| Premiership | P | W | D | L | F | A | GD | Pts |
|---|---|---|---|---|---|---|---|---|
| Linfield | 36 | 22 | 9 | 5 | 75 | 31 | 44 | 75 |
| Glenavon | 36 | 18 | 8 | 10 | 56 | 42 | 14 | 62 |
| Glentoran | 36 | 15 | 12 | 9 | 52 | 37 | 15 | 57 |
| Coleraine | 36 | 14 | 11 | 11 | 48 | 44 | 4 | 53 |
| Cliftonville | 36 | 12 | 11 | 13 | 53 | 57 | −4 | 47 |
| Newry Town | 36 | 12 | 8 | 16 | 42 | 55 | −13 | 44 |
| Omagh Town | 36 | 11 | 10 | 15 | 48 | 54 | −6 | 43 |
| Portadown | 36 | 10 | 11 | 15 | 48 | 60 | −12 | 41 |
| Crusaders | 36 | 8 | 11 | 17 | 44 | 59 | −15 | 35 |
| Ballymena United | 36 | 9 | 7 | 20 | 41 | 68 | −27 | 34 |

*Relegated – Ballymena United.*

**Promotion and Relegation Play-Offs**
**First Leg:** Lisburn Distillery 2 Crusaders 1 (*at New Grosvenor Stadium*)
**Second Leg:** Crusaders 3 Lisburn Distillery 1
(*aggregate 4-3*)

# LEAGUE OF WALES—RESULTS 2000–2001

| | Aberystwyth Town | Afan Lido | Bangor City | Barry Town | Caersws | Carmarthen Town | Connah's Quay Nomads | Cwmbran Town | Flexsys Cefn Druids | Haverfordwest County | Llanelli | Newtown | Oswestry Town | Port Talbot Athletic | Rhayader Town | Rhyl | Total Network Solutions | UWIC Inter Cardiff |
|---|---|---|---|---|---|---|---|---|---|---|---|---|---|---|---|---|---|---|
| Aberystwyth Town | — | 1-1 | 0-2 | 3-2 | 2-2 | 2-2 | 1-1 | 2-0 | 3-0 | 0-2 | 6-0 | 3-0 | 6-0 | 1-0 | 2-2 | 2-2 | 2-0 | 5-0 |
| Afan Lido | 4-3 | — | 3-1 | 1-0 | 3-1 | 2-0 | 1-0 | 3-0 | 2-3 | 0-0 | 1-0 | 1-0 | 1-0 | 2-0 | 3-0 | 0-2 | 2-2 | 1-0 |
| Bangor City | 1-1 | 3-1 | — | 2-3 | 3-2 | 4-0 | 1-1 | 5-2 | 2-3 | 0-1 | 1-6 | 3-2 | 2-2 | 2-2 | 0-4 | 1-2 | 1-1 | 3-0 |
| Barry Town | 4-0 | 2-3 | 2-3 | — | 3-3 | 2-2 | 2-2 | 3-0 | 1-4 | 2-1 | 1-0 | 3-2 | 0-0 | 2-0 | 2-1 | 6-1 | 2-2 | 8-0 |
| Caersws | 1-1 | 2-2 | 3-3 | 3-3 | — | 0-0 | 2-1 | 1-0 | 1-2 | 2-3 | 7-1 | 0-2 | 6-0 | 2-0 | 2-2 | 0-0 | 0-1 | 6-1 |
| Carmarthen Town | 1-1 | 2-0 | 4-0 | 0-0 | 0-0 | — | 3-0 | 1-0 | 2-0 | 0-4 | 4-0 | 0-0 | 1-0 | 1-1 | 5-0 | 0-2 | 1-2 | 9-1 |
| Connah's Quay Nomads | 1-2 | 2-2 | 1-1 | 2-2 | 2-1 | 3-0 | — | 1-0 | 2-0 | 0-0 | 5-1 | 0-1 | 0-2 | 1-3 | 4-2 | 1-2 | 2-2 | 2-0 |
| Cwmbran Town | 1-0 | 3-0 | 5-2 | 3-0 | 1-0 | 1-0 | 1-0 | — | 2-1 | 0-2 | 2-1 | 0-3 | 0-1 | 2-0 | 4-2 | 2-1 | 2-1 | 2-0 |
| Flexsys Cefn Druids | 4-1 | 2-3 | 2-3 | 1-4 | 1-2 | 2-0 | 2-0 | 2-1 | — | 3-3 | 1-0 | 0-1 | 3-2 | 0-2 | 3-2 | 1-2 | 2-1 | 3-1 |
| Haverfordwest County | 1-3 | 0-1 | 0-1 | 2-1 | 2-3 | 0-4 | 0-0 | 0-2 | 3-3 | — | 3-3 | 0-2 | 2-1 | 1-2 | 0-4 | 3-3 | 4-1 | 3-0 |
| Llanelli | 2-4 | 3-3 | 1-6 | 1-0 | 7-1 | 4-0 | 5-1 | 2-1 | 1-0 | 3-3 | — | 0-3 | 1-0 | 4-1 | 5-1 | 1-0 | 2-0 | 3-1 |
| Newtown | 1-2 | 1-0 | 3-2 | 3-2 | 0-2 | 0-0 | 0-1 | 0-3 | 0-1 | 0-2 | 4-1 | — | 1-0 | 2-3 | 1-2 | 0-3 | 0-1 | 1-0 |
| Oswestry Town | 1-2 | 1-0 | 2-2 | 0-0 | 6-0 | 1-0 | 0-2 | 3-7 | 2-0 | 2-1 | 11-0 | 1-0 | — | 1-2 | 2-3 | 0-3 | 3-3 | 3-0 |
| Port Talbot Athletic | 0-2 | 2-0 | 2-2 | 2-0 | 2-0 | 1-1 | 1-3 | 1-3 | 0-2 | 1-2 | 4-1 | 2-3 | 1-2 | — | 1-2 | 0-6 | 0-2 | 2-1 |
| Rhayader Town | 0-0 | 2-4 | 2-4 | 0-1 | 2-1 | 5-0 | 5-0 | 4-2 | 1-3 | 1-2 | 5-2 | 1-2 | 2-2 | 2-1 | — | 2-1 | 0-0 | 2-0 |
| Rhyl | 1-0 | 0-2 | 1-2 | 6-1 | 0-0 | 0-2 | 1-2 | 2-1 | 1-2 | 3-3 | 1-0 | 0-3 | 0-3 | 1-2 | 1-6 | — | 2-0 | 2-1 |
| Total Network Solutions | 1-0 | 1-1 | 1-1 | 2-2 | 0-1 | 2-0 | 3-4 | 2-1 | 1-6 | 4-1 | 3-3 | 0-1 | 1-6 | 1-3 | 0-0 | 2-0 | — | 1-2 |
| UWIC Inter Cardiff | 2-1 | 0-5 | 1-2 | 2-1 | 1-2 | 1-4 | 1-0 | 3-3 | 0-3 | 1-4 | 1-2 | 1-0 | 3-0 | 1-3 | 3-0 | 2-2 | 0-3 | — |

# EUROPEAN REVIEW 2000–2001

Liverpool completed their treble-shot of cups with a thrilling 5-4 extra-time victory over Spain's Alaves. Their opponents from the Basque region were celebrating only their 80th year of existence. Ten years ago they were still a Third Division club. In 1996–97 they forced their way out of the Second Division and finished 16th in the First Division in 1998-99. The following season they were sixth and qualified for Europe for the first time in their history.

The final was Liverpool's 13th match in the UEFA Cup and began with a 1-0 win in Bucharest against Romania's Rapid. Though the Reds were held goalless at Anfield, they progressed to the second round against Slovan Liberec. Again only a goal separated the two teams after Liverpool took this slender advantage from Mersyside, but made it a double by winning 3-2 away.

Greece's Olympiakos provided third round opposition and Liverpool did well to draw 2-2 away before moving to a 2-0 win at Anfield in the second leg. Round four showed the Merseyside team's improvement and produced a 2-0 win over Roma in Italy. Alas came the first wobble in the return match as Liverpool hung on despite losing 1-0, with the visitors missing a glorious chance of pushing the tie to extra time in the dying seconds.

Composure restored, Liverpool drew 0-0 away to Porto in the quarter-final and then won 2-0 at Anfield. A classic semi-final saw the successful rearguard action in Barcelona finish goalless and a Gary McAllister penalty divided the teams in the second leg to give Liverpool a further crack at a European trophy.

There had appeared to be equal hopes of English involvement in the latter stages of the European Champions League. Arsenal, Leeds United and Manchester United all reached the second stage. Though the draw for the quarter-finals kept the trio apart, there was disappointment from the games played.

They began badly with Manchester United losing 1-0 at Old Trafford to Bayern Munich, the Germans clearly determined to avenge the final defeat suffered two years earlier. The following day Arsenal took a slender 2-1 lead over Valencia, but Leeds gave arguably their finest European performance in establishing a 3-0 lead over the other Spanish team La Coruna.

Leeds clung on in the second leg which they lost 2-0, but Arsenal were beaten 1-0 and went out on the away goals rule. A day later Manchester United faced the uphill task of having to go to Munich and win by more than one goal. They did fight back after being two goals down in the first half, but lost 2-1 at the final whistle.

Valencia, having put the skids under Arsenal, did the same to Leeds. After holding the Yorkshire club to a goalless draw at Elland Road, they won the return comprehensively enough 3-0 to end English interest in the competition.

Bayern and Valencia were unable to settle their differences in the final without the aid of penalties. In a largely disappointing match in Milan's San Siro, the only shots in the entire affair which counted were from the penalty spot. Mendieta put Valencia ahead after three minutes, Scholl missed one for the Germans only for Effenberg to level the scores again from a penalty six minutes after the restart. After extra time in which Valencia seemed to have settled for the lottery of a shoot-out, Bayern won 5-4 on penalties.

UEFA in its bulletin admitted the close season is a term which has almost lost its meaning since only three and a half weeks elapse between the Champions League final and the start of the Intertoto Cup. This competition is the back door into the UEFA Cup, while that tournament can as we know lead to a place in the Champions League.

Nowhere is there a sign of fewer matches being played under the banner of UEFA. The only pressures are on domestic football to curtail league games to take in the extra fixtures on the continent. Understandably since only a few clubs can participate in European competitions, there is no general rush to cut the number of clubs in leagues. Meanwhile the top players are the ones who suffer from too many matches.

Neither is there any let-up in the transfer fees leading clubs are prepared to pay for players. Italy's Lazio have led the field in this respect, having spent some £250 million in the nine years since Sergio Cragnotti became President. But the British record was broken in April when Manchester United signed Ruud van Nistelrooy for a fee of £19 million. It seems that the Bosman ruling has had little effect on this area of finance and legislation to deal with the free movement of players has some way to go before being finalised.

# EUROPEAN CUP 2000–2001

**FIRST QUALIFYING ROUND, FIRST LEG**

| | | | |
|---|---|---|---|
| Birkirkara | (1) 1 | KR Reykjavik | (0) 2 |
| F91 Dudelange | (0) 0 | Levski Sofia | (2) 4 |
| Haka | (0) 1 | Linfield | (0) 0 |
| KI | (0) 0 | Red Star Belgrade | (1) 3 |
| Shirak | (1) 1 | BATE Borisov | (1) 1 |
| Skonto Riga | (0) 2 | Shamkir | (0) 1 |
| Sloga | (0) 0 | Shelbourne | (0) 1 |
| SK Tirana | (2) 2 | Zimbru Chisinau | (2) 3 |
| TNS | (0) 2 | Levadia | (0) 2 |
| Zalgiris Kaunas | (3) 4 | Brotnjo | (0) 0 |

**FIRST QUALIFYING ROUND, SECOND LEG**

| | | | |
|---|---|---|---|
| BATE Borisov | (1) 2 | Shirak | (0) 1 |
| Brotnjo | (3) 3 | Zalgiris Kaunas | (0) 0 |
| KR Reykjavik | (2) 4 | Birkirkara | (0) 1 |
| Levadia | (1) 4 | TNS | (0) 0 |
| Levski Sofia | (1) 2 | F91 Dudelange | (0) 0 |
| Linfield | (1) 2 | Haka | (0) 1 |
| Red Star Belgrade | (2) 2 | KI | (0) 0 |
| Shamkir | (1) 4 | Skonto Riga | (1) 1 |
| Shelbourne | (0) 1 | Sloga | (0) 1 |
| Zimbru Chisinau | (2) 3 | SK Tirana | (2) 2 |

**SECOND QUALIFYING ROUND, FIRST LEG**

| | | | |
|---|---|---|---|
| Anderlecht | (3) 4 | Anorthosis | (1) 2 |
| Besiktas | (0) 1 | Levski Sofia | (0) 0 |
| Brondby | (1) 3 | KR Reykjavik | (1) 1 |
| Dinamo Bucharest | (2) 3 | Polonia | (2) 4 |
| Hajduk Split | (0) 0 | Dunaferr | (0) 2 |
| Haka | (0) 0 | Inter Bratislava | (0) 0 |
| Helsingborg | (0) 0 | BATE Borisov | (0) 0 |
| Rangers | (1) 4 | Zalgiris Kaunas | (1) 1 |
| Red Star Belgrade | (3) 4 | Torpedo Kutaisi | (0) 0 |
| Shakhtjor Donetsk | (2) 4 | Levadia | (0) 1 |
| Shelbourne | (0) 1 | Rosenborg | (2) 3 |
| Slavia Prague | (1) 1 | Shamkir | (0) 0 |
| Sturm Graz | (1) 3 | Hapoel Tel Aviv | (0) 0 |
| Zimbru Chisinau | (0) 2 | Maribor | (0) 0 |

**SECOND QUALIFYING ROUND, SECOND LEG**

| | | | |
|---|---|---|---|
| Anorthosis | (0) 0 | Anderlecht | (0) 0 |
| BATE Borisov | (0) 0 | Helsingborg | (2) 3 |
| Dunaferr | (1) 2 | Hajduk Split | (2) 2 |
| Hapoel Tel Aviv | (0) 1 | Sturm Graz | (0) 2 |
| Inter Bratislava | (0) 1 | Haka | (0) 0 |
| KR Reykjavik | (0) 0 | Brondby | (0) 0 |
| Levadia | (0) 1 | Shakhtjor Donetsk | (2) 5 |
| Levski Sofia | (0) 1 | Besiktas | (1) 1 |
| Maribor | (1) 1 | Zimbru Chisinau | (0) 0 |
| Polonia | (0) 3 | Dinamo Bucharest | (1) 1 |
| Rosenborg | (0) 1 | Shelbourne | (0) 1 |
| Shamkir | (0) 1 | Slavia Prague | (1) 4 |
| Torpedo Kutaisi | (1) 2 | Red Star Belgrade | (0) 0 |
| Zalgiris Kaunas | (0) 0 | Rangers | (0) 0 |

## THIRD QUALIFYING ROUND, FIRST LEG

| | | | |
|---|---|---|---|
| Anderlecht | (1) 1 | Porto | (0) 0 |
| Besiktas | (1) 3 | Lokomotiv Moscow | (0) 0 |
| Brondby | (0) 0 | Hamburg | (0) 2 |
| Dunaferr | (0) 2 | Rosenborg | (0) 2 |
| Helsingborg | (0) 1 | Internazionale | (0) 0 |
| Herfolge | (0) 0 | Rangers | (2) 3 |
| Inter Bratislava | (0) 1 | Lyon | (0) 2 |
| Dynamo Kiev | (0) 0 | Red Star Belgrade | (0) 0 |
| Leeds United | (1) 2 | 1860 Munich | (0) 1 |
| AC Milan | (1) 3 | Dynamo Zagreb | (1) 1 |
| Polonia | (1) 2 | Panathinaikos | (2) 2 |
| St Gallen | (1) 1 | Galatasaray | (1) 2 |
| Shakhtjor Donetsk | (0) 0 | Slavia Prague | (0) 1 |
| Sturm Graz | (1) 2 | Feyenoord | (1) 1 |
| Tirol Innsbruck | (0) 0 | Valencia | (0) 0 |
| Zimbru Chisinau | (0) 0 | Sparta Prague | (0) 1 |

## THIRD QUALIFYING ROUND, SECOND LEG

| | | | |
|---|---|---|---|
| Dynamo Zagreb | (0) 0 | AC Milan | (2) 3 |
| Feyenoord | (0) 1 | Sturm Graz | (0) 1 |
| Galatasaray | (2) 2 | St Gallen | (1) 2 |
| Hamburg | (0) 0 | Brondby | (0) 0 |
| Internazionale | (0) 0 | Helsingborg | (0) 0 |
| Lokomotiv Moscow | (0) 1 | Besiktas | (1) 3 |
| Lyon | (0) 2 | Inter Bratislava | (1) 1 |
| 1860 Munich | (0) 0 | Leeds United | (0) 1 |
| Panathinaikos | (1) 2 | Polonia | (0) 1 |
| Porto | (0) 0 | Anderlecht | (0) 0 |
| Rangers | (0) 3 | Herfolge | (0) 0 |
| Red Star Belgrade | (1) 1 | Dynamo Kiev | (1) 1 |
| Rosenborg | (1) 2 | Dunaferr | (1) 1 |
| Slavia Prague | (0) 0 | Shakhtjor Donetsk | (0) 2 |
| Sparta Prague | (0) 1 | Zimbru Chisinau | (0) 0 |
| Valencia | (2) 4 | Tirol Innsbruck | (0) 1 |

## CHAMPIONS LEAGUE

### GROUP A

| | | | |
|---|---|---|---|
| Spartak Moscow | (0) 2 | Leverkusen | (0) 0 |
| Sporting Lisbon | (2) 2 | Real Madrid | (0) 2 |
| Leverkusen | (0) 3 | Sporting Lisbon | (1) 2 |
| Real Madrid | (0) 1 | Spartak Moscow | (0) 0 |
| Spartak Moscow | (1) 3 | Sporting Lisbon | (1) 1 |
| Leverkusen | (2) 2 | Real Madrid | (1) 3 |
| Real Madrid | (2) 5 | Leverkusen | (1) 3 |
| Sporting Lisbon | (0) 0 | Spartak Moscow | (1) 3 |
| Leverkusen | (0) 1 | Spartak Moscow | (0) 0 |
| Real Madrid | (2) 4 | Sporting Lisbon | (0) 0 |
| Spartak Moscow | (0) 1 | Real Madrid | (0) 0 |
| Sporting Lisbon | (0) 0 | Leverkusen | (0) 0 |

| Final table | P | W | D | L | F | A | Pts |
|---|---|---|---|---|---|---|---|
| Real Madrid | 6 | 4 | 1 | 1 | 15 | 8 | 13 |
| Spartak Moscow | 6 | 4 | 0 | 2 | 9 | 3 | 12 |
| Leverkusen | 6 | 2 | 1 | 3 | 9 | 12 | 7 |
| Sporting Lisbon | 6 | 0 | 2 | 4 | 5 | 15 | 2 |

### GROUP B

| | | | |
|---|---|---|---|
| Shakhtjor Donetsk | (0) 0 | Lazio | (1) 3 |

| | | | |
|---|---|---|---|
| Sparta Prague | (0) 0 | Arsenal | (1) 1 |
| Arsenal | (1) 3 | Shakhtjor Donetsk | (2) 2 |
| Lazio | (1) 3 | Sparta Prague | (0) 0 |
| Arsenal | (1) 2 | Lazio | (0) 0 |
| Sparta Prague | (0) 3 | Shakhtjor Donetsk | (0) 2 |
| Lazio | (1) 1 | Arsenal | (0) 1 |
| Shakhtjor Donetsk | (1) 2 | Sparta Prague | (1) 1 |
| Arsenal | (3) 4 | Sparta Prague | (1) 2 |
| Lazio | (0) 5 | Shakhtjor Donetsk | (1) 1 |
| Shakhtjor Donetsk | (1) 3 | Arsenal | (0) 0 |
| Sparta Prague | (0) 0 | Lazio | (1) 1 |

| **Final table** | P | W | D | L | F | A | Pts |
|---|---|---|---|---|---|---|---|
| Arsenal | 6 | 4 | 1 | 1 | 11 | 8 | 13 |
| Lazio | 6 | 4 | 1 | 1 | 13 | 4 | 13 |
| Shakhtjor Donetsk | 6 | 2 | 0 | 4 | 10 | 15 | 6 |
| Sparta Prague | 6 | 1 | 0 | 5 | 6 | 13 | 3 |

## GROUP C

| | | | |
|---|---|---|---|
| Lyon | (2) 3 | Heerenveen | (1) 1 |
| Valencia | (2) 2 | Olympiakos | (0) 1 |
| Heerenveen | (0) 0 | Valencia | (1) 1 |
| Olympiakos | (2) 2 | Lyon | (0) 1 |
| Valencia | (0) 1 | Lyon | (0) 0 |
| Heerenveen | (0) 1 | Olympiakos | (0) 0 |
| Lyon | (0) 1 | Valencia | (1) 2 |
| Heerenveen | (0) 0 | Lyon | (0) 2 |
| Olympiakos | (0) 1 | Valencia | (0) 0 |
| Lyon | (1) 1 | Olympiakos | (0) 0 |
| Valencia | (1) 1 | Heerenveen | (1) 1 |

| **Final table** | P | W | D | L | F | A | Pts |
|---|---|---|---|---|---|---|---|
| Valencia | 6 | 4 | 1 | 1 | 7 | 4 | 13 |
| Lyon | 6 | 3 | 0 | 3 | 8 | 6 | 9 |
| Olympiakos | 6 | 3 | 0 | 3 | 6 | 5 | 9 |
| Heerenveen | 6 | 1 | 1 | 4 | 3 | 9 | 4 |

## GROUP D

| | | | |
|---|---|---|---|
| Galatasaray | (2) 3 | Monaco | (0) 2 |
| Rangers | (3) 5 | Sturm Graz | (0) 0 |
| Monaco | (0) 0 | Rangers | (1) 1 |
| Sturm Graz | (1) 3 | Galatasaray | (0) 0 |
| Galatasaray | (0) 3 | Rangers | (0) 2 |
| Monaco | (3) 5 | Sturm Graz | (0) 0 |
| Rangers | (0) 0 | Galatasaray | (0) 0 |
| Sturm Graz | (1) 2 | Monaco | (0) 0 |
| Monaco | (4) 4 | Galatasaray | (1) 2 |
| Sturm Graz | (1) 2 | Rangers | (0) 0 |
| Galatasaray | (1) 2 | Sturm Graz | (0) 2 |
| Rangers | (1) 2 | Monaco | (1) 2 |

| **Final table** | P | W | D | L | F | A | Pts |
|---|---|---|---|---|---|---|---|
| Sturm Graz | 6 | 3 | 1 | 2 | 9 | 12 | 10 |
| Galatasaray | 6 | 2 | 2 | 2 | 10 | 13 | 8 |
| Rangers | 6 | 2 | 2 | 2 | 10 | 7 | 8 |
| Monaco | 6 | 2 | 1 | 3 | 13 | 10 | 7 |

## GROUP E

| | | | |
|---|---|---|---|
| Hamburg | (1) 4 | Juventus | (2) 4 |
| Panathinaikos | (1) 1 | La Coruna | (0) 1 |

| Juventus | (1) 2 | Panathinaikos | (1) 1 |
| La Coruna | (1) 2 | Hamburg | (0) 1 |
| Hamburg | (0) 0 | Panathinaikos | (1) 1 |
| Juventus | (0) 0 | La Coruna | (0) 0 |
| La Coruna | (1) 1 | Juventus | (1) 1 |
| Panathinaikos | (0) 0 | Hamburg | (0) 0 |
| La Coruna | (0) 1 | Panathinaikos | (0) 0 |
| Juventus | (0) 1 | Hamburg | (1) 3 |
| Hamburg | (1) 1 | La Coruna | (0) 1 |
| Panathinaikos | (1) 3 | Juventus | (1) 1 |

| Final table | P | W | D | L | F | A | Pts |
|---|---|---|---|---|---|---|---|
| La Coruna | 6 | 2 | 4 | 0 | 6 | 4 | 10 |
| Panathinaikos | 6 | 2 | 2 | 2 | 6 | 5 | 8 |
| Hamburg | 6 | 1 | 3 | 2 | 9 | 6 | 6 |
| Juventus | 6 | 1 | 3 | 2 | 9 | 12 | 6 |

## GROUP F

| Helsingborg | (0) 1 | Bayern Munich | (1) 3 |
| Rosenborg | (1) 3 | Paris St Germain | (1) 1 |
| Bayern Munich | (0) 3 | Rosenborg | (1) 1 |
| Paris St Germain | (1) 4 | Helsingborg | (1) 1 |
| Paris St Germain | (0) 1 | Bayern Munich | (0) 0 |
| Rosenborg | (2) 6 | Helsingborg | (0) 1 |
| Bayern Munich | (1) 2 | Paris St Germain | (0) 0 |
| Helsingborg | (1) 2 | Rosenborg | (0) 0 |
| Bayern Munich | (0) 0 | Helsingborg | (0) 0 |
| Paris St Germain | (4) 7 | Rosenborg | (2) 2 |
| Helsingborg | (0) 1 | Paris St Germain | (1) 1 |
| Rosenborg | (1) 1 | Bayern Munich | (0) 1 |

| Final table | P | W | D | L | F | A | Pts |
|---|---|---|---|---|---|---|---|
| Bayern Munich | 6 | 3 | 2 | 1 | 9 | 4 | 11 |
| Paris St Germain | 6 | 3 | 1 | 2 | 14 | 9 | 10 |
| Rosenborg | 6 | 2 | 1 | 3 | 13 | 15 | 7 |
| Helsingborg | 6 | 1 | 2 | 3 | 6 | 14 | 5 |

## GROUP G

| Manchester United | (3) 5 | Anderlecht | (0) 1 |
| PSV Eindhoven | (1) 2 | Dynamo Kiev | (1) 1 |
| Anderlecht | (0) 1 | PSV Eindhoven | (0) 0 |
| Dynamo Kiev | (0) 0 | Manchester United | (0) 0 |
| Dynamo Kiev | (0) 4 | Anderlecht | (0) 0 |
| PSV Eindhoven | (2) 3 | Manchester United | (1) 1 |
| Anderlecht | (4) 4 | Dynamo Kiev | (1) 2 |
| Manchester United | (1) 3 | PSV Eindhoven | (1) 1 |
| Anderlecht | (2) 2 | Manchester United | (1) 1 |
| Dynamo Kiev | (0) 0 | PSV Eindhoven | (1) 1 |
| Manchester United | (1) 1 | Dynamo Kiev | (0) 0 |
| PSV Eindhoven | (1) 2 | Anderlecht | (2) 3 |

| Final table | P | W | D | L | F | A | Pts |
|---|---|---|---|---|---|---|---|
| Anderlecht | 6 | 4 | 0 | 2 | 11 | 14 | 12 |
| Manchester United | 6 | 3 | 1 | 2 | 11 | 7 | 10 |
| PSV Eindhoven | 6 | 3 | 0 | 3 | 9 | 9 | 9 |
| Dynamo Kiev | 6 | 1 | 1 | 4 | 7 | 8 | 4 |

## GROUP H

| Barcelona | (2) 4 | Leeds United | (0) 0 |
| AC Milan | (3) 4 | Besiktas | (1) 1 |
| Besiktas | (1) 3 | Barcelona | (0) 0 |

| Leeds United | (0) 1 | AC Milan | (0) 0 |
| Barcelona | (0) 0 | AC Milan | (1) 2 |
| Leeds United | (3) 6 | Besiktas | (0) 0 |
| Besiktas | (0) 0 | Leeds United | (0) 0 |
| AC Milan | (3) 3 | Barcelona | (2) 3 |
| Besiktas | (0) 0 | AC Milan | (2) 2 |
| Leeds United | (1) 1 | Barcelona | (0) 1 |
| Barcelona | (2) 5 | Besiktas | (0) 0 |
| AC Milan | (0) 1 | Leeds United | (1) 1 |

| Final table | P | W | D | L | F | A | Pts |
|---|---|---|---|---|---|---|---|
| AC Milan | 6 | 3 | 2 | 1 | 12 | 6 | 11 |
| Leeds United | 6 | 2 | 3 | 1 | 9 | 6 | 9 |
| Barcelona | 6 | 2 | 2 | 2 | 13 | 9 | 8 |
| Besiktas | 6 | 1 | 1 | 4 | 4 | 17 | 4 |

## SECOND STAGE

### GROUP A

| Manchester United | (0) 3 | Panathinaikos | (0) 1 |
| Valencia | (1) 2 | Sturm Graz | (0) 0 |
| Panathinaikos | (0) 0 | Valencia | (0) 0 |
| Sturm Graz | (0) 0 | Manchester United | (1) 2 |
| Sturm Graz | (0) 2 | Panathinaikos | (0) 0 |
| Valencia | (0) 0 | Manchester United | (0) 0 |
| Manchester United | (1) 1 | Valencia | (0) 1 |
| Panathinaikos | (0) 1 | Sturm Graz | (2) 2 |
| Panathinaikos | (1) 1 | Manchester United | (0) 1 |
| Sturm Graz | (0) 0 | Valencia | (1) 5 |
| Manchester United | (2) 3 | Sturm Graz | (0) 0 |
| Valencia | (1) 2 | Panathinaikos | (1) 1 |

| Final table | P | W | D | L | F | A | Pts |
|---|---|---|---|---|---|---|---|
| Valencia | 6 | 3 | 3 | 0 | 10 | 2 | 12 |
| Manchester United | 6 | 3 | 3 | 0 | 10 | 3 | 12 |
| Sturm Graz | 6 | 2 | 0 | 4 | 4 | 13 | 6 |
| Panathinaikos | 6 | 0 | 2 | 4 | 4 | 10 | 2 |

### GROUP B

| AC Milan | (0) 2 | Galatasaray | (2) 2 |
| Paris St Germain | (1) 1 | La Coruna | (0) 3 |
| La Coruna | (0) 0 | AC Milan | (1) 1 |
| Galatasaray | (0) 1 | Paris St Germain | (0) 0 |
| Galatasaray | (1) 1 | La Coruna | (0) 0 |
| AC Milan | (1) 1 | Paris St Germain | (1) 1 |
| La Coruna | (1) 2 | Galatasaray | (0) 0 |
| Paris St Germain | (0) 1 | AC Milan | (0) 1 |
| Galatasaray | (1) 2 | AC Milan | (0) 0 |
| La Coruna | (0) 4 | Paris St Germain | (2) 3 |
| AC Milan | (0) 1 | La Coruna | (0) 1 |
| Paris St Germain | (2) 2 | Galatasaray | (0) 0 |

| Final table | P | W | D | L | F | A | Pts |
|---|---|---|---|---|---|---|---|
| La Coruna | 6 | 3 | 1 | 2 | 10 | 7 | 10 |
| Galatasaray | 6 | 3 | 1 | 2 | 6 | 6 | 10 |
| AC Milan | 6 | 1 | 4 | 1 | 6 | 7 | 7 |
| Paris St Germain | 6 | 1 | 2 | 3 | 8 | 10 | 5 |

### GROUP C

| Bayern Munich | (0) 1 | Lyon | (0) 0 |
| Spartak Moscow | (1) 4 | Arsenal | (1) 1 |

| Arsenal | (1) 2 | Bayern Munich | (0) 2 |
| Lyon | (3) 3 | Spartak Moscow | (0) 0 |
| Bayern Munich | (0) 1 | Spartak Moscow | (0) 0 |
| Lyon | (0) 0 | Arsenal | (0) 1 |
| Arsenal | (1) 1 | Lyon | (0) 1 |
| Spartak Moscow | (0) 0 | Bayern Munich | (1) 3 |
| Arsenal | (0) 1 | Spartak Moscow | (0) 0 |
| Lyon | (2) 3 | Bayern Munich | (0) 0 |
| Bayern Munich | (1) 1 | Arsenal | (0) 0 |
| Spartak Moscow | (1) 1 | Lyon | (0) 1 |

| Final table | P | W | D | L | F | A | Pts |
|---|---|---|---|---|---|---|---|
| Bayern Munich | 6 | 4 | 1 | 1 | 8 | 5 | 13 |
| Arsenal | 6 | 2 | 2 | 2 | 6 | 8 | 8 |
| Lyon | 6 | 2 | 2 | 2 | 8 | 4 | 8 |
| Spartak Moscow | 6 | 1 | 1 | 4 | 5 | 10 | 4 |

**GROUP D**

| Anderlecht | (0) 1 | Lazio | (0) 0 |
| Leeds United | (0) 0 | Real Madrid | (0) 2 |
| Lazio | (0) 0 | Leeds United | (0) 1 |
| Real Madrid | (3) 4 | Anderlecht | (0) 1 |
| Leeds United | (0) 2 | Anderlecht | (0) 1 |
| Real Madrid | (1) 3 | Lazio | (1) 2 |
| Anderlecht | (0) 1 | Leeds United | (3) 4 |
| Lazio | (1) 2 | Real Madrid | (1) 2 |
| Lazio | (1) 2 | Anderlecht | (0) 1 |
| Real Madrid | (2) 3 | Leeds United | (1) 2 |
| Anderlecht | (0) 2 | Real Madrid | (0) 0 |
| Leeds United | (2) 3 | Lazio | (2) 3 |

| Final table | P | W | D | L | F | A | Pts |
|---|---|---|---|---|---|---|---|
| Real Madrid | 6 | 4 | 1 | 1 | 14 | 9 | 13 |
| Leeds United | 6 | 3 | 1 | 2 | 12 | 10 | 10 |
| Anderlecht | 6 | 2 | 0 | 4 | 7 | 12 | 6 |
| Lazio | 6 | 1 | 2 | 3 | 9 | 11 | 5 |

**QUARTER-FINALS, FIRST LEG**

| Arsenal | (0) 2 | Valencia | (1) 1 |
| Galatasaray | (0) 3 | Real Madrid | (2) 2 |
| Leeds United | (1) 3 | La Coruna | (0) 0 |
| Manchester United | (0) 0 | Bayern Munich | (0) 1 |

**QUARTER-FINALS, SECOND LEG**

| Bayern Munich | (2) 2 | Manchester United | (0) 1 |
| La Coruna | (1) 2 | Leeds United | (0) 0 |
| Real Madrid | (3) 3 | Galatasaray | (0) 0 |
| Valencia | (0) 1 | Arsenal | (0) 0 |

**SEMI-FINALS, FIRST LEG**

| Leeds United | (0) 0 | Valencia | (0) 0 |
| Real Madrid | (0) 0 | Bayern Munich | (0) 1 |

**SEMI-FINALS, SECOND LEG**

| Bayern Munich | (2) 2 | Real Madrid | (1) 1 |
| Valencia | (1) 3 | Leeds United | (0) 0 |

**FINAL**

| Bayern Munich | (0) 1 | Valencia | (1) 1 |

*(aet; Bayern Munich won 5-4 on penalties.)*

# INTER-TOTO CUP 2000–2001

**FIRST ROUND**
Cwmbran v Otaci 0-1, 0-1
Araks v Olomouc 1-2, 0-1
Dynamo Tbilisi v Standard Liege 2-2, 1-1
Dnepr v Silkeborg 2-1, 2-1
Trencin v Dinaburg 0-3, 0-1
Pelister v Hobscheid 3-1, 1-0
Floriana v Stabaek 1-1, 0-2
Glenavon v Belupo 1-1, 0-3
HB Torshavn v Tatabanya 0-4, 0-3
Cibalia v Obilic 3-1, 1-1
Trans v Ceahlaul 2-5, 2-4
Kocaeli v Atlantas 0-1, 1-0
*Atlantas won 5-3 on penalties.*
LASK v Hapoel Petah Tikva 3-0, 1-1
Leiftur v Lucerne 2-2, 4-4
MyPa v Neuchatel Xamax 1-2, 3-3
Nea v Vllaznia 4-1, 2-1
Primorje v Westerlo 5-0, 6-0
UCD v Velbazhd 3-3, 0-0
Vastra Frolunda v Zrinjski 1-0, 1-2
Lubin v Vllash 4-0, 3-1

**SECOND ROUND**
Perugia v Standard Liege 1-2, 1-1
Sedan v Leiftur 3-0, 3-2
Dinaburg v Aalborg 0-0, 0-1
Otaci v Salzburg 2-6, 1-1
Velbazhd v Olomouc 2-0, 0-8
Zenit v Primorje 3-0, 3-1
Atlantas v Bradford City 1-3, 1-4
Chmel v Dnepr 6-2, 2-0
Pelister v Vastra Frolunda 3-1, 0-0
LASK v Pribram 1-1, 2-3

**Atlantas (1) 1** *(Lukosevicius 26 (pen))*          3174
**Bradford City (2) 3** *(Rankin 9, Windass 38, Blake 74 (pen))*
*Bradford City:* Davison; Todd, Jacobs, Myers, Westwood, Bower, Kerr, Blake, Windass, Rankin, Whalley.

**Bradford City (2) 4** *(Mills 12, 36, Blake 70 (pen), Grant 85)*
**Atlantas (0) 1** *(Karalius 90)*          10,012
*Bradford City:* Clarke; Todd, Jacobs (Myers 75), McCall, Wetherall, O'Brien, Windass, Blake, Mills (Rankin 83), Saunders (Grant 70), Whalley.

**Bradford City (0) 2** *(Windass 50, 73 (pen))*
**RKC (0) 0**          8343
*Bradford City:* Clarke (Davison 46); Nolan, Myers, McCall, Wetherall, Atherton, Windass, Whalley (Hopkin 67), Mills, Saunders, Sharpe (Grant 80).

**RKC (0) 0**
**Bradford City (0) 1** *(Mills 81)*          3700
*Bradford City:* Walsh; Halle, Nolan, O'Brien, Wetherall (Westwood 85), Atherton, Hopkin (Lawrence 75), Windass (Blake 85), Mills, Whalley, Sharpe.

**Pribram (0) 0**
**Aston Villa (0) 0**          7852
*Aston Villa:* James; Delaney, Wright, Barry, Ehiogu, Samuel, Taylor, Boateng, Dublin, Merson, Stone (Vassell 71).

Tatabanya v Cibalia 3-2, 0-0
Nea v FK Austria 1-0, 0-3
Neuchatel Xamax v Stuttgart 1-6, 1-4
Mallorca v Ceahlaul 2-1, 1-3
Stabaek v Auxerre 0-2, 0-3
Lubin v Belupo 1-1, 0-0

**THIRD ROUND**
Aalborg v Udinese 0-2, 2-1
Bradford City v RKC 2-0, 1-0
Celta Vigo v Pelister 3-0, 2-1
Sedan v Wolfsburg 0-0, 1-2
Ceahlaul v FK Austria 2-2, 0-3
Pribram v Aston Villa 0-0, 1-3
Rostelmash v Auxerre 0-2, 1-3
Zenit v Tatabanya 2-1, 2-1
Chmel v Kalamata 5-0, 3-0
Belupo v Olomouc 1-1, 0-2
Standard Liege v Salzburg 3-1, 1-1
Lens v Stuttgart 2-1, 0-1

**SEMI-FINALS**
Auxerre v Wolfsburg 1-1, 2-1
Celta Vigo v Aston Villa 1-0, 2-1
Zenit v Bradford City 1-0, 3-0
FK Austria v Udinese 0-1, 0-2
Olomouc v Chmel 3-1, 1-0
Stuttgart v Standard Liege 1-1, 1-0

**FINALS**
Auxerre v Stuttgart 0-2, 1-1
Celta Vigo v Zenit 2-1, 2-2
Olomouc v Udinese 2-2, 2-4

*Stuttgart, Celta Vigo and Udinese qualified for the UEFA Cup.*

**Aston Villa (1) 3** *(Dublin 8, Taylor 56, Nilis 61)*
**Pribram (1) 1** *(Kulic 21)*          8200
*Aston Villa:* James; Barry, Wright, Southgate, Ehiogu, Taylor, Stone, Boateng (Hendrie 56), Dublin (Vassell 65), Nilis (Joachim 75), Merson.

**Zenit (1) 1** *(Tarasov 16)*
**Bradford City (0) 0**          18,500
*Bradford City:* Davison; Nolan, Myers, McCall, Atherton, O'Brien, Hopkin (Whalley 85), Windass, Mills, Saunders, Sharpe.

**Bradford City (0) 0**          9572
**Zenit (0) 3** *(Ugarov 68, Gorovoy 75, Tarasov 85)*
*Bradford City:* Clarke; Halle, Nolan, McCall, Atherton, O'Brien, Hopkin, Windass, Mills, Blake (Beagrie 73), Whalley (Lawrence 82).

**Celta Vigo (0) 1** *(McCarthy 89)*
**Aston Villa (0) 0**          9550
*Aston Villa:* James; Stone, Wright, Barry, Samuel, Taylor, Thompson, Boateng, Dublin, Hendrie, Nilis (Vassell 19) (Joachim 90).

**Aston Villa (1) 1** *(Barry 45 (pen))*
**Celta Vigo (1) 2** *(McCarthy 11, 58)*          11,909
*Aston Villa:* James; Stone (Thompson 48), Wright, Southgate, Barry, Samuel (Hendrie 33), Taylor, Boateng, Joachim (Cooke 74), Walker, Merson.

# UEFA CUP 2000–2001

## QUALIFYING ROUND, FIRST LEG

| | | | |
|---|---|---|---|
| AB Copenhagen | (2) 8 | B36 Torshavn | (0) 0 |
| Aberdeen | (0) 1 | Bohemians | (0) 2 |
| AIK Stockholm | (1) 1 | Gomel | (0) 0 |
| Amica | (1) 3 | Vaduz | (0) 0 |
| Ararat Erevan | (0) 2 | Kosice | (1) 3 |
| Bangor City | (0) 0 | Halmstad | (3) 7 |
| Boavista | (2) 2 | Barry Town | (0) 0 |
| Coleraine | (0) 1 | Orgryte | (1) 2 |
| Constelacio | (0) 0 | Rayo Vallecano | (6) 10 |
| Constructorul | (1) 2 | CSKA Sofia | (2) 3 |
| Ekranas | (0) 0 | Lierse | (2) 3 |
| FC Brugge | (1) 4 | Flora Tallinn | (1) 1 |
| Folgore | (0) 1 | Basle | (3) 5 |
| GI Gotu | (0) 0 | Norrkoping | (0) 2 |
| Glentoran | (0) 0 | Lillestrom | (2) 3 |
| HJK Helsinki | (2) 4 | Grevenmacher | (0) 1 |
| IA Akranes | (0) 0 | Gent | (0) 3 |
| IBV | (0) 0 | Hearts | (0) 2 |
| Jeunesse Esch | (0) 0 | Celtic | (1) 4 |
| Kapaz | (0) 0 | Antalya | (1) 2 |
| Lausanne | (0) 1 | Cork City | (0) 0 |
| Metalurgs | (0) 1 | Brann | (1) 1 |
| MTK Budapest | (1) 1 | Jokerit | (0) 0 |
| Napredak | (4) 5 | Tulevik | (0) 1 |
| Neftchi | (1) 1 | Gorica | (0) 0 |
| Omonia | (0) 0 | Neftochimik | (0) 0 |
| Petra Drnovice | (0) 3 | Buducnost | (0) 0 |
| Rapid Bucharest | (2) 3 | Mika | (0) 0 |
| Rapid Vienna | (0) 2 | Teuta | (0) 0 |
| Rijeka | (1) 3 | Valletta | (1) 2 |
| Serif | (0) 0 | Olimpija | (0) 0 |
| Slavia Mozyr | (0) 1 | Maccabi Haifa | (0) 1 |
| Sliema Wanderers | (1) 2 | Partizan Belgrade | (1) 1 |
| Slovan Bratislava | (1) 2 | Lokomotiv Tbilisi | (0) 0 |
| Tomori | (0) 2 | Apoel | (3) 3 |
| Uni Craiova | (1) 1 | Pobeda | (0) 1 |
| Ventspils | (2) 2 | Vasas | (0) 1 |
| Vorskla | (1) 2 | Rabotnicki | (0) 0 |
| WIT | (0) 0 | Beitar Jerusalem | (1) 3 |
| Zalgiris | (1) 2 | Ruch | (1) 1 |
| Zeljeznicar | (0) 0 | Wisla | (0) 0 |

## QUALIFYING ROUND, SECOND LEG

| | | | |
|---|---|---|---|
| Antalya | (1) 5 | Kapaz | (0) 0 |
| Apoel | (2) 2 | Tomori | (0) 0 |
| B36 Torshavn | (0) 0 | AB Copenhagen | (0) 1 |
| Barry Town | (0) 0 | Boavista | (1) 3 |
| Basle | (5) 7 | Folgore | (0) 0 |
| Beitar Jerusalem | (0) 1 | WIT | (0) 1 |
| Bohemians | (0) 0 | Aberdeen | (0) 1 |
| Brann | (0) 1 | Metalurgs | (0) 0 |
| Buducnost | (0) 0 | Petra Drnovice | (0) 1 |
| Celtic | (4) 7 | Jeunesse Esch | (0) 0 |
| Cork City | (0) 0 | Lausanne | (0) 1 |
| CSKA Sofia | (5) 8 | Constructorul | (0) 0 |

233

| | | | |
|---|---|---|---|
| Flora Tallin | (0) 0 | FC Brugge | (1) 2 |
| Gent | (1) 3 | IA Akranes | (2) 2 |
| Gomel | (0) 0 | AIK Stockholm | (0) 2 |
| Gorica | (1) 3 | Neftchi | (0) 1 |
| Grevenmacher | (0) 2 | HJK Helsinki | (0) 0 |
| Halmstad | (3) 4 | Bangor City | (0) 0 |
| Hearts | (3) 3 | IBV | (0) 0 |
| Jokerit | (0) 2 | MTK Budapest | (1) 4 |
| Kosice | (0) 1 | Ararat Erevan | (0) 1 |
| Lierse | (1) 4 | Ekranas | (0) 0 |
| Lillestrom | (0) 1 | Glentoran | (0) 0 |
| Lokomotiv Tbilisi | (0) 0 | Slovan Bratislava | (1) 2 |
| Maccabi Haifa | (0) 0 | Slavia Mozyr | (0) 0 |
| Mika | (0) 1 | Rapid Bucharest | (0) 0 |
| Neftochimik | (2) 2 | Omonia | (1) 1 |
| Norrkoping | (1) 2 | GI Gotu | (0) 1 |
| Olimpija | (1) 3 | Serif | (0) 0 |
| Orgryte | (1) 1 | Coleraine | (0) 0 |
| Partizan Belgrade | (3) 4 | Sliema Wanderers | (0) 1 |
| Pobeda | (0) 1 | Uni Craiova | (0) 0 |
| Rabotnicki | (0) 0 | Vorskla | (1) 2 |
| Rayo Vallecano | (2) 6 | Constelacio | (0) 0 |
| Ruch | (4) 6 | Zalgiris | (0) 0 |
| Teuta | (0) 0 | Rapid Vienna | (2) 4 |
| Tulevik | (1) 1 | Napredak | (1) 1 |
| Vaduz | (2) 3 | Amica | (2) 3 |
| Valletta | (0) 4 | Rijeka | (1) 5 |
| Vasas | (1) 3 | Ventspils | (1) 1 |
| Wisla | (1) 3 | Zeljeznicar | (1) 1 |

## FIRST ROUND, FIRST LEG

| | | | |
|---|---|---|---|
| AIK Stockholm | (0) 0 | Herfolge | (1) 1 |
| Alaves | (0) 0 | Gaziantep | (0) 0 |
| Antalya | (1) 2 | Werder Bremen | (0) 0 |
| Basle | (1) 3 | Brann | (0) 2 |
| Bohemians | (0) 1 | Kaiserslautern | (0) 3 |
| Brondby | (1) 1 | Osijek | (1) 2 |
| Celta Vigo | (0) 0 | Rijeka | (0) 0 |
| Celtic | (2) 2 | HJK Helsinki | (0) 0 |
| Chelsea | (1) 1 | St Gallen | (0) 0 |
| CSKA Moscow | (0) 0 | Viborg | (0) 0 |
| CSKA Sofia | (1) 1 | MTK Budapest | (0) 2 |
| Dunaferr | (0) 0 | Feyenoord | (0) 1 |
| FC Brugge | (1) 2 | Apoel | (0) 1 |
| Gent | (0) 0 | Ajax | (2) 6 |
| Gorica | (1) 1 | Roma | (3) 4 |
| Gueugnon | (0) 0 | Iraklis | (0) 0 |
| Halmstad | (1) 2 | Benfica | (1) 1 |
| Kosice | (0) 2 | Graz | (0) 3 |
| Krivbas | (0) 0 | Nantes | (0) 1 |
| Lausanne | (1) 3 | Torpedo Moscow | (2) 2 |
| Leicester City | (1) 1 | Red Star Belgrade | (1) 1 |
| Lierse | (0) 0 | Bordeaux | (0) 0 |
| Lillestrom | (2) 3 | Dynamo Moscow | (1) 1 |
| Lokomotiv Moscow | (2) 4 | Neftochimik | (1) 2 |
| Molde | (0) 0 | Rayo Vallecano | (1) 1 |
| Napredak | (0) 0 | Ofi Crete | (0) 0 |
| Norrkoping | (1) 2 | Slovan Liberec | (0) 2 |
| Olimpija | (2) 2 | Espanyol | (1) 1 |

| | | | |
|---|---|---|---|
| PAOK Salonika | (1) 3 | Beitar Jerusalem | (1) 1 |
| Partizan Belgrade | (1) 1 | Porto | (0) 1 |
| Petra Drnovice | (0) 0 | 1860 Munich | (0) 0 |
| Pobeda | (0) 0 | Parma | (1) 2 |
| Polonia | (0) 0 | Udinese | (0) 1 |
| Rapid Bucharest | (0) 0 | Liverpool | (1) 1 |
| Rapid Vienna | (2) 3 | Orgryte | (0) 0 |
| Roda | (0) 0 | Inter Bratislava | (1) 2 |
| Ruch | (0) 0 | Internazionale | (0) 3 |
| Slavia Prague | (1) 3 | AB Copenhagen | (0) 0 |
| Slovan Bratislava | (0) 0 | Dynamo Zagreb | (1) 3 |
| Stuttgart | (1) 1 | Hearts | (0) 0 |
| Tirol Innsbruck | (2) 3 | Fiorentina | (0) 1 |
| Vasas | (0) 2 | AEK Athens | (0) 2 |
| Vitesse | (1) 3 | Maccabi Haifa | (0) 0 |
| Vladikavkaz | (0) 0 | Amica | (1) 3 |
| Vorskla | (1) 1 | Boavista | (0) 2 |
| Zaragoza | (1) 4 | Wisla | (1) 1 |
| Zimbru Chisinau | (1) 1 | Hertha Berlin | (1) 2 |
| Zurich | (0) 1 | Genk | (0) 2 |

## FIRST ROUND, SECOND LEG

| | | | |
|---|---|---|---|
| AB Copenhagen | (0) 0 | Slavia Prague | (0) 2 |
| AEK Athens | (2) 2 | Vasas | (0) 0 |
| Ajax | (1) 3 | Gent | (0) 0 |
| Amica | (1) 2 | Vladikavkaz | (0) 0 |
| Apoel | (0) 0 | FC Brugge | (1) 1 |
| Beitar Jerusalem | (1) 3 | PAOK Salonika | (2) 3 |
| Benfica | (1) 2 | Halmstad | (1) 2 |
| Boavista | (2) 2 | Vorskla | (0) 1 |
| Bordeaux | (1) 5 | Lierse | (0) 1 |
| Brann | (4) 4 | Basle | (1) 4 |
| Dynamo Moscow | (2) 2 | Lillestrom | (0) 1 |
| Dynamo Zagreb | (0) 1 | Slovan Bratislava | (1) 1 |
| Espanyol | (2) 2 | Olimpija | (0) 0 |
| Feyenoord | (1) 3 | Dunaferr | (0) 1 |
| Fiorentina | (1) 2 | Tirol Innsbruck | (1) 2 |
| Gaziantep | (2) 3 | Alaves | (1) 4 |
| Genk | (1) 2 | Zurich | (0) 0 |
| Graz | (0) 0 | Kosice | (0) 0 |
| Hearts | (1) 3 | Stuttgart | (1) 2 |
| Herfolge | (0) 1 | AIK Stockholm | (0) 1 |
| Hertha Berlin | (2) 2 | Zimbru Chisinau | (0) 0 |
| HJK Helsinki | (1) 2 | Celtic | (0) 1 |
| Inter Bratislava | (2) 2 | Roda | (0) 1 |
| Internazionale | (2) 4 | Ruch | (0) 1 |
| Iraklis | (0) 1 | Gueugnon | (0) 0 |
| Kaiserslautern | (0) 0 | Bohemians | (1) 1 |
| Liverpool | (0) 0 | Rapid Bucharest | (0) 0 |
| Maccabi Haifa | (0) 2 | Vitesse | (0) 1 |
| MTK Budapest | (0) 0 | CSKA Sofia | (0) 1 |
| 1860 Munich | (0) 1 | Petra Drnovice | (0) 0 |
| Nantes | (3) 5 | Krivbas | (0) 0 |
| Neftochimik | (0) 0 | Lokomotiv Moscow | (0) 0 |
| Ofi Crete | (5) 6 | Napredak | (0) 0 |
| Orgryte | (0) 1 | Rapid Vienna | (1) 1 |
| Osijek | (0) 0 | Brondby | (0) 0 |
| Parma | (1) 4 | Pobeda | (0) 0 |
| Porto | (0) 1 | Partizan Belgrade | (0) 0 |

| | | | |
|---|---|---|---|
| Rayo Vallecano | (1) 1 | Molde | (0) 1 |
| Red Star Belgrade | (1) 3 | Leicester City | (1) 1 |
| Rijeka | (0) 0 | Celta Vigo | (0) 1 |
| Roma | (5) 7 | Gorica | (0) 0 |
| Slovan Liberec | (0) 2 | Norrkoping | (0) 1 |
| St Gallen | (2) 2 | Chelsea | (0) 0 |
| Torpedo Moscow | (0) 0 | Lausanne | (1) 2 |
| Udinese | (1) 2 | Polonia | (0) 0 |
| Viborg | (0) 1 | CSKA Moscow | (0) 0 |
| Werder Bremen | (2) 6 | Antalya | (0) 0 |
| Wisla | (0) 4 | Zaragoza | (1) 1 |

## SECOND ROUND, FIRST LEG

| | | | |
|---|---|---|---|
| AEK Athens | (0) 5 | Herfolge | (0) 0 |
| Basle | (0) 1 | Feyenoord | (0) 2 |
| Boavista | (0) 0 | Roma | (0) 1 |
| Bordeaux | (1) 1 | Celtic | (1) 1 |
| FC Brugge | (0) 2 | St Gallen | (1) 1 |
| Espanyol | (4) 4 | Graz | (0) 0 |
| Halmstad | (2) 3 | 1860 Munich | (2) 2 |
| Hertha Berlin | (1) 3 | Amica | (0) 1 |
| Internazionale | (0) 0 | Vitesse | (0) 0 |
| Iraklis | (0) 1 | Kaiserslautern | (2) 3 |
| Lausanne | (1) 1 | Ajax | (0) 0 |
| Lillestrom | (0) 1 | Alaves | (2) 3 |
| Liverpool | (0) 1 | Slovan Liberec | (0) 0 |
| Lokomotiv Moscow | (1) 1 | Inter Bratislava | (0) 0 |
| Nantes | (0) 2 | MTK Budapest | (1) 1 |
| Ofi Crete | (1) 2 | Slavia Prague | (1) 2 |
| Osijek | (1) 2 | Rapid Vienna | (1) 1 |
| Parma | (0) 2 | Dinamo Zagreb | (0) 0 |
| Rayo Vallecano | (1) 1 | Viborg | (0) 0 |
| Red Star Belgrade | (0) 1 | Celta Vigo | (0) 0 |
| Tirol Innsbruck | (0) 1 | Stuttgart | (0) 0 |
| Udinese | (0) 1 | PAOK Salonika | (0) 0 |
| Werder Bremen | (2) 4 | Genk | (1) 1 |
| Wisla | (0) 0 | Porto | (0) 0 |

## SECOND ROUND, SECOND LEG

| | | | |
|---|---|---|---|
| Ajax | (1) 2 | Lausanne | (1) 2 |
| Alaves | (1) 2 | Lillestrom | (1) 2 |
| Amica | (0) 1 | Hertha Berlin | (0) 1 |
| Celta Vigo | (1) 5 | Red Star Belgrade | (2) 3 |
| Celtic | (0) 1 | Bordeaux | (0) 2 |
| Dinamo Zagreb | (1) 1 | Parma | (0) 0 |
| Feyenoord | (1) 1 | Basle | (0) 0 |
| Genk | (1) 2 | Werder Bremen | (3) 5 |
| Graz | (0) 1 | Espanyol | (0) 0 |
| Herfolge | (1) 2 | AEK Athens | (1) 1 |
| Inter Bratislava | (0) 1 | Lokomotiv Moscow | (1) 2 |
| 1860 Munich | (2) 3 | Halmstad | (1) 1 |
| Kaiserslautern | (2) 2 | Iraklis | (0) 3 |
| MTK Budapest | (0) 0 | Nantes | (0) 1 |
| PAOK Salonika | (0) 3 | Udinese | (0) 0 |
| Porto | (1) 3 | Wisla | (0) 0 |
| Rapid Vienna | (0) 0 | Osijek | (1) 2 |
| Roma | (1) 1 | Boavista | (0) 1 |
| St Gallen | (1) 1 | FC Brugge | (0) 1 |

| | | | |
|---|---|---|---|
| Slavia Prague | (0) 4 | Ofi Crete | (0) 1 |
| Slovan Liberec | (1) 2 | Liverpool | (1) 3 |
| Stuttgart | (3) 3 | Tirol Innsbruck | (0) 1 |
| Viborg | (1) 2 | Rayo Vallecano | (0) 1 |
| Vitesse | (1) 1 | Internazionale | (0) 1 |

## THIRD ROUND, FIRST LEG

| | | | |
|---|---|---|---|
| Alaves | (0) 1 | Rosenborg | (0) 1 |
| Bordeaux | (2) 4 | Werder Bremen | (1) 1 |
| FC Brugge | (0) 0 | Barcelona | (2) 2 |
| Espanyol | (0) 0 | Porto | (0) 2 |
| Feyenoord | (2) 2 | Stuttgart | (1) 2 |
| Hertha Berlin | (0) 0 | Internazionale | (0) 0 |
| Leverkusen | (2) 4 | AEK Athens | (1) 4 |
| Lokomotiv Moscow | (0) 0 | Rayo Vallecano | (0) 0 |
| Nantes | (2) 4 | Lausanne | (1) 3 |
| Olympiakos | (0) 2 | Liverpool | (1) 2 |
| Osijek | (1) 2 | Slavia Prague | (0) 0 |
| Parma | (2) 2 | 1860 Munich | (0) 2 |
| PSV Eindhoven | (3) 3 | PAOK Salonika | (0) 0 |
| Rangers | (0) 1 | Kaiserslautern | (0) 0 |
| Roma | (1) 1 | Hamburg | (0) 0 |
| Shakhtjor Donetsk | (0) 0 | Celta Vigo | (0) 0 |

## THIRD ROUND, SECOND LEG

| | | | |
|---|---|---|---|
| AEK Athens | (1) 2 | Leverkusen | (0) 0 |
| Barcelona | (1) 1 | FC Brugge | (1) 1 |
| Celta Vigo | (1) 1 | Shakhtjor Donetsk | (0) 0 |
| Hamburg | (0) 0 | Roma | (1) 3 |
| Internazionale | (1) 2 | Hertha Berlin | (0) 1 |
| 1860 Munich | (0) 0 | Parma | (0) 2 |
| Kaiserslautern | (1) 3 | Rangers | (0) 0 |
| Lausanne | (0) 1 | Nantes | (1) 3 |
| Liverpool | (1) 2 | Olympiakos | (0) 0 |
| PAOK Salonika | (0) 0 | PSV Eindhoven | (1) 1 |
| Porto | (0) 0 | Espanyol | (0) 0 |
| Rayo Vallecano | (0) 2 | Lokomotiv Moscow | (0) 0 |
| Rosenborg | (0) 1 | Alaves | (2) 3 |
| Slavia Prague | (2) 5 | Osijek | (1) 1 |
| Stuttgart | (1) 2 | Feyenoord | (0) 1 |
| Werder Bremen | (0) 0 | Bordeaux | (0) 0 |

## FOURTH ROUND, FIRST LEG

| | | | |
|---|---|---|---|
| AEK Athens | (0) 0 | Barcelona | (1) 1 |
| Alaves | (1) 3 | Internazionale | (1) 3 |
| Porto | (1) 3 | Nantes | (1) 1 |
| PSV Eindhoven | (1) 2 | Parma | (0) 1 |
| Rayo Vallecano | (1) 4 | Bordeaux | (1) 1 |
| Roma | (0) 0 | Liverpool | (0) 2 |
| Slavia Prague | (0) 0 | Kaiserslautern | (0) 0 |
| Stuttgart | (0) 0 | Celta Vigo | (0) 0 |

## FOURTH ROUND, SECOND LEG

| | | | |
|---|---|---|---|
| Barcelona | (2) 5 | AEK Athens | (0) 0 |
| Bordeaux | (1) 1 | Rayo Vallecano | (1) 2 |
| Celta Vigo | (1) 2 | Stuttgart | (1) 1 |

| Internazionale | (0) 0 | Alaves | (0) 2 |
| Kaiserslautern | (0) 1 | Slavia Prague | (0) 0 |
| Liverpool | (0) 0 | Roma | (0) 1 |
| Nantes | (0) 2 | Porto | (1) 1 |
| Parma | (0) 3 | PSV Eindhoven | (2) 2 |

## QUARTER-FINALS, FIRST LEG

| Alaves | (1) 3 | Rayo Vallecano | (0) 0 |
| Barcelona | (1) 2 | Celta Vigo | (0) 1 |
| Kaiserslautern | (1) 1 | PSV Eindhoven | (0) 0 |
| Porto | (0) 0 | Liverpool | (0) 0 |

## QUARTER-FINALS, SECOND LEG

| Celta Vigo | (1) 3 | Barcelona | (2) 2 |
| Liverpool | (2) 2 | Porto | (0) 0 |
| PSV Eindhoven | (0) 0 | Kaiserslautern | (0) 1 |
| Rayo Vallecano | (1) 2 | Alaves | (1) 1 |

## SEMI-FINALS, FIRST LEG

| Alaves | (3) 5 | Kaiserslautern | (0) 1 |
| Barcelona | (0) 0 | Liverpool | (0) 0 |

## SEMI-FINALS, SECOND LEG

| Kaiserslautern | (1) 1 | Alaves | (1) 4 |
| Liverpool | (1) 1 | Barcelona | (0) 0 |

## FINAL

### Liverpool (3) 5, Alaves (1) 4

(in Dortmund 16 May 2001, 65,000)

*Liverpool:* Westerveld; Babbel, Carragher, Hamann, Henchoz (Smicer 56), Hyypia, Gerrard, McAllister, Heskey (Fowler 65), Owen (Berger 79), Murphy.
*Scorers:* Babbel 4, Gerrard 16, McAllister 41 (pen), Fowler 73, Geli 117 (og).
*Alaves:* Herrera; Eggen (Alonso 23), Karmona, Tellez, Contra, Tomic, Desio, Astudillo (Magno 46), Geli, Cruyff, Javi Moreno (Pablo 65).
*Scorers:* Alonso 27, Javi Moreno 48, 51, Cruyff 89.
*Referee:* Veissiere (France).
*(aet; Liverpool won in sudden death.)*

# PAST EUROPEAN CUP FINALS

| Year | Winner | Score | Runner-up | Score |
|---|---|---|---|---|
| 1956 | Real Madrid | 4 | Stade de Rheims | 3 |
| 1957 | Real Madrid | 2 | Fiorentina | 0 |
| 1958 | Real Madrid | 3 | AC Milan | 2* |
| 1959 | Real Madrid | 2 | Stade de Rheims | 0 |
| 1960 | Real Madrid | 7 | Eintracht Frankfurt | 3 |
| 1961 | Benfica | 3 | Barcelona | 2 |
| 1962 | Benfica | 5 | Real Madrid | 3 |
| 1963 | AC Milan | 2 | Benfica | 1 |
| 1964 | Internazionale | 3 | Real Madrid | 1 |
| 1965 | Internazionale | 1 | SL Benfica | 0 |
| 1966 | Real Madrid | 2 | Partizan Belgrade | 1 |
| 1967 | Celtic | 2 | Internazionale | 1 |
| 1968 | Manchester U | 4 | Benfica | 1* |
| 1969 | AC Milan | 4 | Ajax | 1 |
| 1970 | Feyenoord | 2 | Celtic | 1* |
| 1971 | Ajax | 2 | Panathinaikos | 0 |
| 1972 | Ajax | 2 | Internazionale | 0 |
| 1973 | Ajax | 1 | Juventus | 0 |
| 1974 | Bayern Munich | 1 4 | Atletico Madrid | 1 0 |
| 1975 | Bayern Munich | 2 | Leeds U | 0 |
| 1976 | Bayern Munich | 1 | St Etienne | 0 |
| 1977 | Liverpool | 3 | Borussia Moenchengladbach | 1 |
| 1978 | Liverpool | 1 | FC Brugge | 0 |
| 1979 | Nottingham F | 1 | Malmö | 0 |
| 1980 | Nottingham F | 1 | Hamburg | 0 |
| 1981 | Liverpool | 1 | Real Madrid | 0 |
| 1982 | Aston Villa | 1 | Bayern Munich | 0 |
| 1983 | Hamburg | 1 | Juventus | 0 |
| 1984 | Liverpool† | 1 | Roma | 1 |
| 1985 | Juventus | 1 | Liverpool | 0 |
| 1986 | Steaua Bucharest† | 0 | Barcelona | 0 |
| 1987 | Porto | 2 | Bayern Munich | 1 |
| 1988 | PSV Eindhoven† | 0 | Benfica | 0 |
| 1989 | AC Milan | 4 | Steaua Bucharest | 0 |
| 1990 | AC Milan | 1 | Benfica | 0 |
| 1991 | Red Star Belgrade† | 0 | Marseille | 0 |
| 1992 | Barcelona | 1 | Sampdoria | 0 |
| 1993 | Marseille | 1 | AC Milan | 0 |

*(Marseille subsequently stripped of title)*

| Year | Winner | Score | Runner-up | Score |
|---|---|---|---|---|
| 1994 | AC Milan | 4 | Barcelona | 0 |
| 1995 | Ajax | 1 | AC Milan | 0 |
| 1996 | Juventus† | 1 | Ajax | 1 |
| 1997 | Borussia Dortmund | 3 | Juventus | 1 |
| 1998 | Real Madrid | 1 | Juventus | 0 |
| 1999 | Manchester U | 2 | Bayern Munich | 1 |
| 2000 | Real Madrid | 3 | Valencia | 0 |
| 2001 | Bayern Munich† | 1 | Valencia | 1 |

# PAST EUROPEAN CUP-WINNERS FINALS

| Year | Winner | Score | Runner-up | Score |
|---|---|---|---|---|
| 1961 | Fiorentina | 4 | Rangers | 1‡ |
| 1962 | Atletico Madrid | 1 3 | Fiorentina | 1 0 |
| 1963 | Tottenham H | 5 | Atletico Madrid | 1 |
| 1964 | Sporting Lisbon | 3 1 | MTK Budapest | 3* 0 |
| 1965 | West Ham U | 2 | Munich 1860 | 0 |
| 1966 | Borussia Dortmund | 2 | Liverpool | 1* |
| 1967 | Bayern Munich | 1 | Rangers | 0* |

| Year | Winner | Score | Runner-up | Score |
|---|---|---|---|---|
| 1968 | AC Milan | 2 | Hamburg | 0 |
| 1969 | Slovan Bratislava | 3 | Barcelona | 2 |
| 1970 | Manchester C | 2 | Gornik Zabrze | 1 |
| 1971 | Chelsea | 1 2 | Real Madrid | 1* 1* |
| 1972 | Rangers | 3 | Dynamo Moscow | 2 |
| 1973 | AC Milan | 1 | Leeds U | 0 |
| 1974 | Magdeburg | 2 | AC Milan | 0 |
| 1975 | Dynamo Kiev | 3 | Ferencvaros | 0 |
| 1976 | Anderlecht | 4 | West Ham U | 2 |
| 1977 | Hamburg | 2 | Anderlecht | 0 |
| 1978 | Anderlecht | 4 | Austria Vienna | 0 |
| 1979 | Barcelona | 4 | Fortuna Dusseldorf | 3* |
| 1980 | Valencia† | 0 | Arsenal | 0 |
| 1981 | Dynamo Tbilisi | 2 | Carl Zeiss Jena | 1 |
| 1982 | Barcelona | 2 | Standard Liege | 1 |
| 1983 | Aberdeen | 2 | Real Madrid | 1* |
| 1984 | Juventus | 2 | Porto | 1 |
| 1985 | Everton | 3 | Rapid Vienna | 1 |
| 1986 | Dynamo Kiev | 3 | Atletico Madrid | 0 |
| 1987 | Ajax | 1 | Lokomotiv Leipzig | 0 |
| 1988 | Mechelen | 1 | Ajax | 0 |
| 1989 | Barcelona | 2 | Sampdoria | 0 |
| 1990 | Sampdoria | 2 | Anderlecht | 0 |
| 1991 | Manchester U | 2 | Barcelona | 1 |
| 1992 | Werder Bremen | 2 | Monaco | 0 |
| 1993 | Parma | 3 | Antwerp | 1 |
| 1994 | Arsenal | 1 | Parma | 0 |
| 1995 | Real Zaragoza | 2 | Arsenal | 1* |
| 1996 | Paris St Germain | 1 | Rapid Vienna | 0 |
| 1997 | Barcelona | 1 | Paris St Germain | 0 |
| 1998 | Chelsea | 1 | Stuttgart | 0 |
| 1999 | Lazio | 2 | Mallorca | 1 |

## PAST FAIRS CUP FINALS

| Year | Winner | Score | Runner-up | Score |
|---|---|---|---|---|
| 1958 | Barcelona | 8 | London | 2‡ |
| 1960 | Barcelona | 4 | Birmingham C | 1‡ |
| 1961 | Roma | 4 | Birmingham C | 2‡ |
| 1962 | Valencia | 7 | Barcelona | 3‡ |
| 1963 | Valencia | 4 | Dynamo Zagreb | 1‡ |
| 1964 | Real Zaragoza | 2 | Valencia | 1 |
| 1965 | Ferencvaros | 1 | Juventus | 0 |
| 1966 | Barcelona | 4 | Real Zaragoza | 3‡ |
| 1967 | Dynamo Zagreb | 2 | Leeds U | 0‡ |
| 1968 | Leeds U | 1 | Ferencvaros | 0‡ |
| 1969 | Newcastle U | 6 | Ujpest Dozsa | 2‡ |
| 1970 | Arsenal | 4 | Anderlecht | 3‡ |
| 1971 | Leeds U** | 3 | Juventus | 3‡ |

## PAST UEFA CUP FINALS

| Year | Winner | Score | Runner-up | Score |
|---|---|---|---|---|
| 1972 | Tottenham H | 2 1 | Wolverhampton W | 1 1 |
| 1973 | Liverpool | 3 0 | Borussia Moenchengladbach | 0 2 |
| 1974 | Feyenoord | 2 0 | Tottenham H | 2 0 |
| 1975 | Borussia Moenchengladbach | 0 5 | Twente Enschede | 0 1 |
| 1976 | Liverpool | 3 1 | FC Brugge | 2 1 |
| 1977 | Juventus** | 1 1 | Athletic Bilbao | 0 2 |
| 1978 | PSV Eindhoven | 0 3 | SEC Bastia | 0 0 |
| 1979 | Borussia Moenchengladbach | 1 1 | Red Star Belgrade | 1 0 |
| 1980 | Borussia Moenchengladbach | 3 0 | Eintracht Frankfurt** | 2 1 |

| 1981 | Ipswich T | 3 2 | AZ 67 Alkmaar | 0 4 |
|---|---|---|---|---|
| 1982 | IFK Gothenburg | 1 3 | SV Hamburg | 0 0 |
| 1983 | Anderlecht | 1 1 | Benfica | 0 1 |
| 1984 | Tottenham H† | 1 1 | RSC Anderlecht | 1 1 |
| 1985 | Real Madrid | 3 0 | Videoton | 0 1 |
| 1986 | Real Madrid | 5 0 | Cologne | 1 2 |
| 1987 | IFK Gothenburg | 1 1 | Dundee U | 0 1 |
| 1988 | Bayer Leverkusen† | 0 3 | Espanol | 0 3 |
| 1989 | Napoli | 2 3 | Stuttgart | 1 3 |
| 1990 | Juventus | 3 0 | Fiorentina | 1 0 |
| 1991 | Internazionale | 2 0 | AS Roma | 0 1 |
| 1992 | Ajax** | 0 2 | Torino | 0 2 |
| 1993 | Juventus | 3 3 | Borussia Dortmund | 1 0 |
| 1994 | Internazionale | 1 0 | Salzburg | 0 1 |
| 1995 | Parma | 1 1 | Juventus | 0 1 |
| 1996 | Bayern Munich | 2 3 | Bordeaux | 0 1 |
| 1997 | Schalke*† | 1 0 | Internazionale | 0 1 |
| 1998 | Internazionale | 3 | Lazio | 0 |
| 1999 | Parma | 3 | Marseille | 0 |
| 2000 | Galatasaray† | 0 | Arsenal | 0 |
| 2001 | Liverpool§ | 5 | Alaves | 4 |

* After extra time ** Won on away goals † Won on penalties ‡ Aggregate score
§ Won on sudden death.

# EUROPEAN DRAWS 2001–2002

**EUROPEAN CUP**
**FIRST QUALIFYING ROUND**
1. Levski Sofia v Zeljeznicar
2. Linfield v Kutaisi
3. KR v Vllaznia
4. Jugo v Kaunas
5. VB v Slavia Mozyr
6. Bohemians v Levadia
7. Barry Town v Shamkir
8. Valletta v Haka
9. Dudelange v Skonto Riga
10. Araks v Serif

**SECOND QUALIFYING ROUND**
Anderlecht v Winners of 10
Shakhtjor Donetsk v Lugano
Dunaferr or Ferencvaros v Hajduk Split
Winners of 6 v Halmstad
Winners of 2 v FC Copenhagen
Omonia v Red Star Belgrade
Winners of 8 v Maccabi Haifa
Winners of 1 v Brann
Galatasaray v Winners of 3
Porto v Winners of 7
Steaua v Winners of 4
Winners of 9 v Wisla
Winners of 5 v Inter Bratislava
Maribor v Glasgow Rangers

**UEFA CUP**
**QUALIFYING ROUND**
Cosmos v Rapid Vienna
Pelister v St Gallen
Dinamo Bucharest v Dynamo Tirana
Olimpija v Baku
Midtjylland v Glentoran
Trans v Elfsborg

FC Brugge v IA Akranes
GI Gotu v Obilic
Brasov v Mika
Viking v Brotnjo
CSKA Kiev v Jokerit
Vardar v Standard Liege
HJK Helsinki v Ventspils
Cwmbran Town v Slovan Bratislava
Maritimo v Sarajevo
Pogon v Fylkir
Dynamo Zagreb v Flora
Glenavon v Kilmarnock
AEL v SK Tirana
Hapoel Tel Aviv v Ararat Erevan
Etzella v Legia
Zimbru Chisinau v Gaziantep
Dinaburg v Osijek
Neftchi v Gorica
HB v Graz
Atlantas v Rapid Bucharest
Pouchov v Sliema Wanderers
Longford Town v Litets
Brondby v Shelbourne
Santa Coloma v Partizan Belgrade
Maccabi Tel Aviv v Zalgiris
Shakhter v CSKA Sofia
MyPa v Helsingborg
Dynamo Tbilisi v BATE Borisov
Debrecen v Otaci
Polonia v TNS
Lokomotiv Tbilisi v Birkirkara
Grevenmacher v AEK Athens
Ruzomberok v Belshina
Olympiakos Nicosia v Dunaferr,
   Ferencvaros or Hajduk Split
Vaduz v Varteks

# PAST EUROPEAN CHAMPIONSHIP FINALS

| Year | Winners | | Runners-up | | Venue | Attendance |
|------|---------|---|------------|---|-------|------------|
| 1960 | USSR | 2 | Yugoslavia | 1 | Paris | 17,966 |
| 1964 | Spain | 2 | USSR | 1 | Madrid | 120,000 |
| 1968 | Italy | 2 | Yugoslavia | 2 | Rome | 60,000 |
| | After 1-1 draw | | | | | 75,000 |
| 1972 | West Germany | 3 | USSR | 0 | Brussels | 43,437 |
| 1976 | Czechoslovakia | 2 | West Germany | 2 | Belgrade | 45,000 |
| | *(Czechoslovakia won on penalties)* | | | | | |
| 1980 | West Germany | 2 | Belgium | 1 | Rome | 47,864 |
| 1984 | France | 2 | Spain | 0 | Paris | 48,000 |
| 1988 | Holland | 2 | USSR | 0 | Munich | 72,308 |
| 1992 | Denmark | 2 | Germany | 0 | Gothenburg | 37,800 |
| 1996 | Germany | 2 | Czech Republic | 1 | Wembley | 73,611 |
| | *(Germany won on sudden death)* | | | | | |
| 2000 | France | 2 | Italy | 1 | Rotterdam | 50,000 |
| | *(France won on sudden death)* | | | | | |

# PAST WORLD CUP FINALS

| Year | Winners | | Runners-up | | Venue | Att. | Referee |
|------|---------|---|------------|---|-------|------|---------|
| 1930 | Uruguay | 4 | Argentina | 2 | Montevideo | 90,000 | Langenus (B) |
| 1934 | Italy | 2 | Czechoslovakia | 1 | Rome | 50,000 | Eklind (Se) |
| | *(after extra time)* | | | | | | |
| 1938 | Italy | 4 | Hungary | 2 | Paris | 45,000 | Capdeville (F) |
| 1950 | Uruguay | 2 | Brazil | 1 | Rio de Janeiro | 199,854 | Reader (E) |
| 1954 | West Germany | 3 | Hungary | 2 | Berne | 60,000 | Ling (E) |
| 1958 | Brazil | 5 | Sweden | 2 | Stockholm | 49,737 | Guigue (F) |
| 1962 | Brazil | 3 | Czechoslovakia | 1 | Santiago | 68,679 | Latychev (USSR) |
| 1966 | England | 4 | West Germany | 2 | Wembley | 93,802 | Dienst (Sw) |
| | *(after extra time)* | | | | | | |
| 1970 | Brazil | 4 | Italy | 1 | Mexico City | 107,412 | Glockner (EG) |
| 1974 | West Germany | 2 | Holland | 1 | Munich | 77,833 | Taylor (E) |
| 1978 | Argentina | 3 | Holland | 1 | Buenos Aires | 77,000 | Gonella (I) |
| | *(after extra time)* | | | | | | |
| 1982 | Italy | 3 | West Germany | 1 | Madrid | 90,080 | Coelho (Br) |
| 1986 | Argentina | 3 | West Germany | 2 | Mexico City | 114,580 | Filho (Br) |
| 1990 | West Germany | 1 | Argentina | 0 | Rome | 73,603 | Codesal (Mex) |
| 1994 | Brazil | 0 | Italy | 0 | Los Angeles | 94,194 | Puhl (H) |
| | *(Brazil won 3-2 on penalties aet)* | | | | | | |
| 1998 | France | 3 | Brazil | 0 | St-Denis | 75,000 | Belqola (Mor) |

# FIFA WORLD CUP 2002 RESULTS & FIXTURES

## EUROPE

(Members 51, Entries 51)

Fourteen or fifteen teams qualify including France as world champions and play-offs between UEFA and Asia.

### GROUP 1

**Zurich, 2 September 2000, 14,500**

**Switzerland (0) 0**
**Russia (0) 1** *(Bestchastnykh 74)*

*Switzerland:* Pascolo; Lubamba, Henchoz, Muller P, Mazarelli (Buhlmann 72), Cantaluppi (Wicky 64), Vogel, Sforza, Comisetti, Rey, Yakin H (N'Kufo 64).
*Russia:* Nigmatullin; Khlestov, Chugainov, Smertin, Gusev (Alenichev 52), Drozdov, Onopko, Karpin, Titov (Panov 46) (Semak 88), Mostovoi, Bestchastnykh.
*Referee:* Nielsen (Denmark).

**Toftir, 3 September 2000, 3200**

**Faeroes (0) 2** *(Arge 87, Hansen O 90)*
**Slovenia (1) 2** *(Udovic 25, Osterc 86)*

*Faeroes:* Mikkelsen; Hansen H, Johannesen O, Hansen JK, Morkore A, Joensen S, Petersen (Joensen J 78), Johnsson, Hansen O, Arge, Jonsson T (Morkore K 57).
*Slovenia:* Simeunovic; Bulajic, Vugdalic, Milinovic, Novak, Karic, Ceh, Pavlin, Zahovic, Rudonja (Zlogar 89), Udovic (Osterc 71).
*Referee:* Vuorela (Finland).

**Luxembourg, 3 September 2000, 3305**

**Luxembourg (0) 0**
**Yugoslavia (2) 2** *(Milosevic 4, Jokanovic 26)*

*Luxembourg:* Besic; Vanek, Schauls, Funck, Strasser, Deville L, Saibene, Alverdi (Theis 84), Holtz (Ferron 89), Schneider, Zaritski (Huss 62).
*Yugoslavia:* Cicovic; Mirkovic, Dudic (Sakic 62), Jokanovic, Bunjevcevic, Djordjevic, Lazetic, Stankovic D (Ilic 73), Drulovic, Mijatovic (Kovacevic 70), Milosevic.
*Referee:* Smolik (Belarus).

**Luxembourg, 7 October 2000, 1788**

**Luxembourg (0) 1** *(Strasser 46)*
**Slovenia (2) 2** *(Zahovic 39, Milinovic 41)*

*Luxembourg:* Besic; Vanek, Schauls, Funck, Strasser (Posing 88), Saibene, Peters, Holtz, Schneider, Cardoni (Zaritski 80), Huss (Braun 73).
*Slovenia:* Dabanovic; Milinovic, Vugdalic, Karic, Knavs, Novak, Ceh, Siljak (Udovic 80), Zahovic, Pavlin (Pavlovic 67), Acimovic.
*Referee:* Benes (Czech Republic).

**Zurich, 7 October 2000, 9500**

**Switzerland (4) 5** *(Zwyssig 26, Fournier 35, Turkyilmaz 43 (pen), 45 (pen), 53 (pen))*
**Faeroes (1) 1** *(Petersen 4)*

*Switzerland:* Zuberbuhler; Lubamba (Wicky 66), Henchoz, Zwyssig, Fournier, Sesa, Vogel (Celestini 66), Sforza, Comisetti, Chapuisat, Turkyilmaz (Cantaluppi 76).
*Faeroes:* Mikkelsen; Morkore A, Johannesen O, Hansen JK, Hansen H, Petersen (Jacobsen 63), Joensen S (Joensen J 63), Johnsson, Hansen O, Hansen JB, Arge.
*Referee:* Kapitanis (Cyprus).

**Moscow, 11 October 2000, 12,000**

**Russia (1) 3** *(Buznikin 19, Khokhlov 57, Titov 90)*

**Luxembourg (0) 0**

*Russia:* Nigmatullin; Khlestov, Khokhlov, Smertin, Tetradze, Buznikin, Onopko, Karpin, Titov, Mostovoi, Bestchastnykh.
*Luxembourg:* Gillet; Funck (Ferron 86), Schauls, Vanek, Strasser, Saibene, Peters, Holtz, Schneider (Posing 77), Cardoni, Huss (Zaritsky 61).
*Referee:* Ferry (Northern Ireland).

**Ljubljana, 11 October 2000, 7000**

**Slovenia (1) 2** *(Siljak 44, Acimovic 78)*

**Switzerland (1) 2** *(Turkyilmaz 20, 66)*

*Slovenia:* Dabanovic; Milinovic, Vugdalic, Knavs, Novak, Ceh, Pavlin (Acimovic 69), Karic, Udovic (Tavcar 46), Zahovic, Siljak (Osterc 59).
*Switzerland:* Zuberbuhler; Zellweger, Mazzarelli, Zwyssig, Fournier (Magnin 64) (Muller P 72), Wicky (Cantaluppi 46), Comisetti, Vogel, Chapuisat, Sforza, Turkyilmaz.
*Referee:* Durkin (England).

**Luxembourg, 24 March 2001, 2380**

**Luxembourg (0) 0**

**Faeroes (0) 2** *(Jacobsen C 75, Morkore K 82)*

*Luxembourg:* Besic; Deville L, Schauls, Posing, Strasser, Saibene, Peters (Huss 46), Holtz, Zaritski, Cardoni, Schneider (Braun 77).
*Faeroes:* Mikkelsen; Johannesen O, Hansen JB, Borg (Olsen 84), Hansen HF, Hansen O, Benjaminsen (Jacobsen R 73), Johnsson J, Morkore K, Jonsson T (Jacobsen C 20), Petersen.
*Referee:* Hanacsek (Hungary).

**Moscow, 24 March 2001, 35,000**

**Russia (1) 1** *(Khlestov 8)*

**Slovenia (1) 1** *(Knavs 22)*

*Russia:* Nigmatullin; Khlestov, Nikiforov, Kovtun, Tetradze, Karpin, Smertin (Bestchastnykh 46), Onopko, Alenichev (Semak 66), Titov, Buznikin.
*Slovenia:* Simeunovic; Gajser, Milinovic, Knavs, Bulajic, Novak, Ceh, Pavlin, Rudonja (Pavlovic 88), Zahovic, Osterc (Cimerotic 66).
*Referee:* Dallas (Scotland).

**Belgrade, 24 March 2001, 36,000**

**Yugoslavia (0) 1** *(Mihajlovic 68)*

**Switzerland (0) 1** *(Chapuisat 84)*

*Yugoslavia:* Kocic; Duljaj, Djukic, Mihajlovic, Obradovic, Lazetic (Stefanovic 78), Jugovic, Stankovic D (Ivic 56), Djordjevic (Kovacevic 64), Kezman, Milosevic.
*Switzerland:* Pascolo; Zellweger, Henchoz, Muller P, Quentin, Lombardo (Buhlmann 72), Vogel, Fournier, Lonfat, Yakin H (Frei 58), Chapuisat (Vega 86).
*Referee:* Nilsson (Sweden).

**Moscow, 28 March 2001, 10,500**

**Russia (1) 1** *(Mostovoi 19)*

**Faeroes (0) 0**

*Russia:* Nigmatullin; Tetradze (Alenichev 46), Nikiforov, Kovtun, Karpin, Gusev (Drozdov 46), Onopko, Khokhlov, Mostovoi, Titov, Buznikin (Bestchastnykh 67).
*Faeroes:* Mikkelsen; Johannesen O, Thorsteinsson, Borg, Hansen BH, Hansen HF, Benjaminsen, Johnsson J, Morkore K (Joensen 75), Jacobsen C, Petersen.
*Referee:* Irvine (Republic of Ireland).

**Ljubljana, 28 March 2001, 10,000**

**Slovenia (0) 1** *(Zahovic 90)*

**Yugoslavia (1) 1** *(Milosevic 32)*

*Slovenia:* Simeunovic; Gajser (Acimovic 37), Vugdalic, Bulajic, Knavs, Novak, Ceh, Osterc (Cimerotic 46), Pavlin (Pavlovic 62), Zahovic, Rudonja.

*Yugoslavia:* Kocic; Obradovic, Djukic, Mihajlovic, Krstajic, Stefanovic, Jokanovic (Duljaja 68), Lazetic, Djordjevic, Milosevic (Ivic 79), Kezman (Drulic 57).
*Referee:* Jol (Holland).

**Zurich, 28 March 2001, 8600**

**Switzerland (2) 5** *(Frei 9, 31, 90, Lonfat 64, Chapuisat 72)*

**Luxembourg (0) 0**

*Switzerland:* Pascolo; Zellweger, Henchoz, Muller P, Quentin, Lonfat (Buhlmann 74), Vogel, Fournier, Lombardo (Muller S 86), Frei, Chapuisat (Yakin H 79).
*Luxembourg:* Besic; Schauls, Saibene, Deville L, Peters (Reimer 77), Cardoni, Strasser, Posing, Holtz, Schneider (Schaak 53), Huss (Zaritski 68).
*Referee:* Larsen (Denmark).

**Belgrade, 25 April 2001, 48,000**

**Yugoslavia (0) 0**

**Russia (0) 1** *(Bestchastnykh 72)*

*Yugoslavia:* Ilic; Dudic, Djukic, Bunjevcevic, Krstajic (Stefanovic 84), Jokanovic, Mihajlovic, Lazetic, Tomic, Drulic (Stankovic 73), Kezman (Djordjevic 63).
*Russia:* Nigmatullin; Tugaynov, Onopko, Drozdov (Tetradze 47), Kovtun, Alenichev, Mostovoi, Khokhlov, Gusev (Semak 87), Titov, Fedkov (Bestchastnykh 46).
*Referee:* Plautz (Austria).

**Toftir, 2 June 2001, 4000**

**Faeroes (0) 0**

**Switzerland (0) 1** *(Frei 81)*

*Faeroes:* Mikkelsen; Hansen HF, Johannesen O, Hansen JB, Borg, Benjaminsen, Petersen J (Petersen H 87), Johnsson, Hansen O, Arge (Jacobsen J 78), Jacobsen C.
*Switzerland:* Pascolo; Zellweger, Henchoz, Muller P, Quentin, Wicky, Vogel, Sforza (Lonfat 69), Lombardo, Sesa (N'Kufo 58), Frei (Magnin 87).
*Referee:* McDonald (Scotland).

**Moscow, 2 June 2001, 70,000**

**Russia (1) 1** *(Kovtun 25)*

**Yugoslavia (1) 1** *(Mijatovic 38)*

*Russia:* Nigmatullin; Smertin, Chugainov, Onopko, Kovtun, Karpin, Titov, Mostovoi, Khokhlov, Alenichev, Bestchastnykh (Buznikin 71).
*Yugoslavia:* Radakovic; Obradovic, Djukic, Mihajlovic, Djorovic, Mirkovic (Bunjevcevic 85), Lazetic (Drulovic 71), Dmitrovic, Tomic, Mijatovic (Kezman 65), Milosevic.
*Referee:* Fandel (Germany).

**Ljubljana, 2 June 2001, 5000**

**Slovenia (1) 2** *(Zahovic 35, 65 (pen))*

**Luxembourg (0) 0**

*Slovenia:* Simeunovic; Galic, Milinovic, Knavs, Novak, Ceh, Pavlin, Cimerotic (Osterc 80), Karic (Rudonja 46), Zahovic, Acimovic (Pavlovic 62).
*Luxembourg:* Gillet; Deville L, Schauls, Theis, Strasser, Saibene, Peters, Holtz, Huss, Cardoni (Braun 82), Schneider.
*Referee:* Brugger (Austria).

**Toftir, 6 June 2001, 4371**

**Faeroes (0) 0**

**Yugoslavia (2) 6** *(Stankovic D 20, 55, Kezman 29, 87, 90, Milosevic 68)*

*Faeroes:* Mikkelsen; Hansen HF, Benjaminsen, Hansen JB, Borg, Hansen O, Joensen S (Jacobsen R 88), Johnsson (Morkore A 75), Jacobsen C (Petersen H 75), Arge, Petersen J.
*Yugoslavia:* Radakovic; Mirkovic (Bunjevcevic 46), Mihajlovic, Djorovic, Dmitrovic, Lazetic (Obradovic 46), Stankovic D, Drulovic (Ilic 74), Mijatovic, Milosevic, Kezman.
*Referee:* Jara (Czech Republic).

**Luxembourg, 6 June 2001, 2200**

**Luxembourg (0) 1** *(Schneider 48)*

**Russia (1) 2** *(Alenichev 16, Semak 76)*

*Luxembourg:* Gillet; Schauls, Deville L, Theis, Strasser, Peters (Reiter 89), Saibene, Holtz, Cardoni, Schneider (Braun 83), Huss (Christophe 64).
*Russia:* Nigmatullin; Smertin (Popov 52), Nikiforov, Onopko, Kovtun, Karpin, Titov, Mostovoi, Khokhlov, Alenichev (Semak 61), Bestchastnykh (Fedkov 66).
*Referee:* Skjervold (Norway).

**Basle, 6 June 2001, 26,000**

**Switzerland (0) 0**

**Slovenia (0) 1** *(Cimerotic 83)*

*Switzerland:* Pascolo; Zellweger, Henchoz, Muller P, Quentin, Wicky (Lonfat 66), Vogel, Fournier, Lombardo (Sforza 56), N'Kufo, Frei (Sesa 79).
*Slovenia:* Simeunovic; Galic, Milinovic, Knavs, Novak, Ceh, Pavlin, Rudonja, Karic (Cimerotic 32), Zahovic, Osterc (Acimovic 46).
*Referee:* Granat (Poland).

| Group 1 Table | P | W | D | L | F | A | Pts |
|---|---|---|---|---|---|---|---|
| Russia | 7 | 5 | 2 | 0 | 10 | 3 | 17 |
| Slovenia | 7 | 3 | 4 | 0 | 11 | 7 | 13 |
| Switzerland | 7 | 3 | 2 | 2 | 14 | 6 | 11 |
| Yugoslavia | 6 | 2 | 3 | 1 | 11 | 4 | 9 |
| Faeroes | 6 | 1 | 1 | 4 | 5 | 15 | 4 |
| Luxembourg | 7 | 0 | 0 | 7 | 2 | 18 | 0 |

## GROUP 2

**Tallinn, 16 August 2000, 1695**

**Estonia (0) 1** *(Reim 64 (pen))*

**Andorra (0) 0**

*Estonia:* Tohver; Allas, Lemsalu, Stepanovs, Rooba U, Piiroja (Jurisson 73), Reim, Alonen (Anniste 67), Terehov, Oper, Zelinski (Ustritski 87).
*Andorra:* Koldo; Alvarez F (Forla 71), Jonas, Garcia T, Lima I, Escura, Sonejee, Gonzalez E (Pujol 74), Manolo, Ruiz, Sanchez J.
*Referee:* Arsic (Yugoslavia).

**La Vella, 2 September 2000, 1000**

**Andorra (1) 2** *(Gonzalez E 45, Lima I 51)*

**Cyprus (1) 3** *(Constantinou M 25 (pen), 90, Agathocleous 77)*

*Andorra:* Koldo; Ramirez, Garcia T, Jonas, Sonejee, Lima I, Gonzalez E (Lucendo 89), Escura, Ruiz, Jimenez, Sanchez J.
*Cyprus:* Panayiotou N; Theodotou, Charalambous Z (Agathocleous 54), Ioannou D, Charalambous M, Ioakim, Engomitis, Aristocleous (Yiasonmi 71), Christodolou M, Okkas (Kotsonis 85), Constantinou M.
*Referee:* Yarmenchuk (Ukraine).

**Amsterdam, 2 September 2000, 50,000**

**Holland (0) 2** *(Talan 71, Van Bronckhorst 84)*

**Republic of Ireland (1) 2** *(Robbie Keane 21, McAteer 65)*

*Holland:* Van der Sar; Reiziger (Seedorf 46), Konterman (Talan 66), Frank de Boer, Van Bronckhorst, Witschge (Bruggnik 59), Ronald de Boer, Bosvelt, Cocu, Bouma, Kluivert.
*Republic of Ireland:* Kelly A; Carr, Harte, Dunne, Breen, Roy Keane, McAteer (Kelly G 75), Kinsella, Quinn (Connolly 71), Robbie Keane, Kilbane (Staunton 79).
*Referee:* Michel (Slovakia).

**Tallinn, 3 September 2000, 4700**

**Estonia (0) 0**

**Portugal (1) 3** *(Rui Costa 15, Figo 49, Sa Pinto 57)*

*Estonia:* Poom; Allas, Stepanovs, Lemsalu, Rooba U, Jurisson (Haavistu 71), Alonen (Anniste 36), Reim, Terehov, Zelinski (Viikmae 67), Oper.

*Portugal:* Quim; Nelson (Costinho 64), Fernando Couto, Jorge Costa, Rui Jorge, Figo, Rui Costa, Paulo Sousa, Simao (Vidigal 71), Sa Pinto, Joao Pinto (Pauleta 74).
*Referee:* Agius (Malta).

**La Vella, 7 October 2000, 800**

**Andorra (0) 1** *(Ruiz 90 (pen))*
**Estonia (0) 2** *(Reim 54, Oper 65)*

*Andorra:* Koldo; Ramirez, Garcia T, Jonas, Lima T, Lima I, Gonzalez E, Sonejee (Lucendo 60), Sanchez J, Jimenez (Soria 83), Ruiz.
*Estonia:* Poom; Allas, Rooba U, Lemsalu, Stepanovs, Viikmae (Haavistu 80), Terehov, Oper, Kristal (Anniste 58), Reim, Zelinski (Ustritski 46).
*Referee:* Koren (Israel).

**Nicosia, 7 October 2000, 12,000**

**Cyprus (0) 0**
**Holland (0) 4** *(Seedorf 69, 78, Overmars 81, Kluivert 90)*

*Cyprus:* Panayiotou N; Theodotou, Charalambous C, Ioannou D, Charalambous M (Poyiatzis 62), Pounas (Dziouref 80), Melanarkitis, Spoljaric, Ioakim, Malekkos (Okkas 77), Agathocleous.
*Holland:* Van der Sar; Bosvelt (Van Bommel 75), Reiziger, Frank de Boer, Van Bronckhorst, Cocu, Talan (Seedorf 58), Davids, Kluivert, Ronald de Boer (Bouma 80), Overmars.
*Referee:* Cesari (Italy).

**Lisbon, 7 October 2000, 65,000**

**Portugal (0) 1** *(Conceicao 57)*
**Republic of Ireland (0) 1** *(Holland 72)*

*Portugal:* Quim; Beto, Fernando Couto, Jorge Costa, Dimas (Capucho 88), Conceicao, Rui Costa, Vidigal, Figo, Sa Pinto (Pauleta 76), Joao Pinto (Simao 76).
*Republic of Ireland:* Kelly A; Carr, Harte, Dunne, Breen, Roy Keane, McAteer (Duff 69), Kinsella, Quinn (Holland 46), Robbie Keane (Finnan 83), Kilbane.
*Referee:* Ouzounov (Bulgaria).

**Rotterdam, 11 October 2000, 48,000**

**Holland (0) 0**
**Portugal (2) 2** *(Conceicao 11, Pauleta 44)*

*Holland:* Van der Sar; Melchiot, Frank de Boer, Cocu, Reiziger, Van Bommel (Bosvelt 72), Overmars (Talan 46), Davids, Kluivert (Vennegoor of Hesselink 65), Seedorf, Bouma.
*Portugal:* Quim; Jorge Costa, Dimas, Secretario, Fernando Couto, Vidigal (Fernando Meira 90), Figo, Bino, Pauleta (Simao 90), Rui Costa (Sa Pinto 87), Conceicao.
*Referee:* Poll (England).

**Dublin, 11 October 2000, 34,562**

**Republic of Ireland (1) 2** *(Kinsella 25, Dunne 50)*
**Estonia (0) 0**

*Republic of Ireland:* Kelly A; Carr, Harte, Dunne, Breen, Roy Keane, McAteer (Duff 46), Kinsella, Quinn, Robbie Keane (Foley 87), Kilbane (Finnan 87).
*Estonia:* Poom; Allas, Stepanovs, Lemsalu, Saviauk, Viikmae (Haavistu 68), Reim, Anniste, Terehov, Oper, Zelinski (Ustritski 68).
*Referee:* Hauge (Norway).

**Nicosia, 15 November 2000, 8000**

**Cyprus (3) 5** *(Okkas 10, 18, Agathocleous 42, Christodoulou M 74, Spoljaric 90 (pen))*
**Andorra (0) 0**

*Cyprus:* Panayiotou N; Konnafis, Charalambous Z, Ioannou D (Nicolaou 82), Charalambous M, Pounas, Ioakim, Spoljaric, Okkas, Agathocleous (Neophytou 74), Constantinou M (Christodoulou M 46).
*Andorra:* Koldo; Garcia T, Bernaus, Alonso, Sonejee, Lima I (Jonas 88), Gonzalez E (Ramirez 59), Sanchez J, Lucendo, Jimenez, Ruiz (Escura 78).
*Referee:* Johansson (Sweden).

**Madeira, 28 February 2001, 12,000**

**Portugal (2) 3** *(Figo 1, 48, Pauleta 36)*

**Andorra (0) 0**

*Portugal:* Quim; Xavier, Rui Jorge, Fernando Couto (Capucho 46), Beto, Paulo Bento (Joao Pinto 63), Rui Costa, Conceicao, Figo, Nuno Gomes (Tomas 75), Pauleta.
*Andorra:* Koldo; Pol, Ramirez, Jonas, Lucendo (Soria 89), Txema, Gonzalez E (Escura 61), Sonejee, Ruiz, Dernaus, Sanchez J (Garcia 89).
*Referee:* Allaerts (Belgium).

**Barcelona, 24 March 2001, 1000**

**Andorra (0) 0**

**Holland (2) 5** *(Kluivert 9, Hasselbaink 36, Van Hooijdonk 60, 71, Van Bommel 85)*

*Andorra:* Sanchez A; Pol, Jonas, Sonejee, Lima I, Ramirez, Emiliano (Escura 85), Txema, Lucendo (Jimenez 64), Ruiz (Fernandez 90), Sanchez J.
*Holland:* Van der Sar; Bosvelt, Stam (Bouma 72), Frank de Boer, Cocu, Van Bommel, Davids (Paauwe 46), Zenden, Hasselbaink, Kluivert (Van Hooijdonk 58), Overmars.
*Referee:* Trivkovic (Croatia).

**Nicosia, 24 March 2001, 13,000**

**Cyprus (0) 0**

**Republic of Ireland (2) 4** *(Roy Keane 32, 89, Harte 42 (pen), Kelly 81)*

*Cyprus:* Panayiotou N; Melanarkitis (Filippou 56), Konnafis, Charalambous M, Christodolou M, Theodotou, Pounnas (Malekkos 43), Ioachim, Spoljaric, Constantinou M, Okkas (Agathocleous 75).
*Republic of Ireland:* Given; Kelly G, Harte, Roy Keane, Breen, Cunningham, McAteer (Holland 78), Kinsella, Connolly, Robbie Keane (Doherty 89), Kilbane (Duff 82).
*Referee:* De Bleeckere (Belgium).

**Barcelona, 28 March 2001, 5000**

**Andorra (0) 0**

**Republic of Ireland (1) 3** *(Harte 33 (pen), Kilbane 76, Holland 80)*

*Andorra:* Sanchez A; Pol, Jonas (Soria 90), Lima T, Lucendo, Lima I, Sonejee, Txema, Sanchez J (Jimenez 87), Emiliano (Escura 80), Ruiz.
*Republic of Ireland:* Given; Kelly G, Harte, Roy Keane, Breen, Cunningham, Holland, Kilbane (Finnan 84), Connolly (Doherty 25), Robbie Keane, Duff.
*Referee:* Ishchenko (Ukraine).

**Limassol, 28 March 2001, 5000**

**Cyprus (0) 2** *(Constantinou M 48, Okkas 66)*

**Estonia (0) 2** *(Kristal 77, Piiroja 79)*

*Cyprus:* Panayiotou N; Ioachim, Germanou, Charalambous M, Theodotou, Kunnafis, Agathocleous (Christodolou M 63), Engomitis (Melanarkitis 69), Malekkos (Spoljaric 46), Okkas, Constantinou M.
*Estonia:* Kaalma; Rooba M, Stepanov, Piiroja, Rooba U, Novikov (Alonen 81), Reim, Kristal, Haavistu (Terehov 54), Zelinski (Viikmae 59), Oper.
*Referee:* Mikulski (Poland).

**Oporto, 28 March 2001, 45,000**

**Portugal (0) 2** *(Pauleta 83, Figo 90 (pen))*

**Holland (1) 2** *(Hasselbaink 17 (pen), Kluivert 47)*

*Portugal:* Quim; Secretario, Litos, Fernando Couto, Rui Jorge, Da Costa, Paulo Bento (Chapucho 32), Conceicao (Nuno Gomes 57), Figo, Rui Costa, Pauleta.
*Holland:* Van der Sar; Reiziger, Frank de Boer, Stam, Cocu, Zenden (Makaay 72), Davids, Van Bommel (Bosvelt 68), Overmars, Kluivert, Hasselbaink (Van Hooijdonk 80).
*Referee:* Meier (Switzerland).

**Eindhoven, 25 April 2001, 30,000**

**Holland (3) 4** *(Hasselbaink 29, Overmars 35, Kluivert 44, Van Nistelrooy 82)*

**Cyprus (0) 0**

*Holland:* Van der Sar; Melchiot, Hofland, Frank de Boer, Cocu, Zenden, Seedorf (Van Nistelrooy 71), Van Bommel, Overmars (Sikora 83), Kluivert, Hasselbaink (Van Hooijdonk 71).
*Cyprus:* Morphis; Konnafis, Filippou, Charalambous, Germanou, Melanarkitis, Engomitis (Kaiafas 89), Christodolou M (Yiasoumi 76), Satsias, Okkas (Agathocleous 84), Constantinou M.
*Referee:* Baskakov (Russia).

**Dublin, 25 April 2001, 34,000**

**Republic of Ireland (2) 3** *(Kilbane 34, Kinsella 36, Breen 76)*

**Andorra (1) 1** *(Lima I 32)*

*Republic of Ireland:* Given; Kelly G, Harte, Breen (Staunton 84), Dunne, Holland, Kennedy (Carr 66), Kinsella (Finnan 79), Connolly, Doherty, Kilbane.
*Andorra:* Sanchez A; Escura, Lima I, Lima A, Jonas, Txema, Emiliano (Soria 86), Ruiz, Oscar, Jimenez (Pujol 81), Sanchez J (Fernandez 90).
*Referee:* Jakobsson (Iceland).

**Tallinn, 2 June 2001, 9500**

**Estonia (0) 2** *(Oper 65, Zelinski 78)*

**Holland (0) 4** *(Frank de Boer 68, Van Nistelrooy 82, 90, Kluivert 89)*

*Estonia:* Kaalma; Saviauk, Stepanovs, Piiroja, Rooba U, Viikmae (Zelinski 29), Reim, Haavistu (Rahn 70), Novikov, Kristal, Oper.
*Holland:* Van der Sar; Reiziger, Melchiot, Frank de Boer, Cocu, Paauwe (Landzaat 60), Zenden, Makaay (Van Hooijdonk 69), Hasselbaink (Van Nistelrooy 60), Kluivert, Overmars.
*Referee:* Richards (Wales).

**Dublin, 2 June 2001, 34,000**

**Republic of Ireland (0) 1** *(Roy Keane 65)*

**Portugal (0) 1** *(Figo 79)*

*Republic of Ireland:* Given; Carr, Harte, Kelly G, Dunne, Staunton, Kinsella (Doherty 79), Roy Keane, Quinn (Holland 75), Robbie Keane (Duff 60), Kilbane.
*Portugal:* Ricardo; Frechaut, Litos (Boa Morte 87), Jorge Costa, Rui Jorge (Joao Pinto 74), Beto, Petit, Barbosa (Capucho 71), Figo, Rui Costa, Pauleta.
*Referee:* Fisker (Denmark).

**Tallinn, 6 June 2001, 9000**

**Estonia (0) 0**

**Republic of Ireland (2) 2** *(Dunne 9, Holland 39)*

*Estonia:* Kaalma; Saviauk, Stepanovs, Piiroja, Rooba U (Allas 69), Reim, Novikov (Ustritski 72), Haavistu (Terehov 49), Kristal, Oper, Zelinski.
*Republic of Ireland:* Given; Carr, Harte, Kelly G, Dunne, Staunton, Kinsella, Holland, Quinn (Doherty 37), Kilbane, Duff (O'Brien 89).
*Referee:* Mircea (Romania).

**Lisbon, 6 June 2001, 35,000**

**Portugal (1) 6** *(Pauleta 36, 71, Barbosa 55, 59, Joao Pinto 76, 81)*

**Cyprus (0) 0**

*Portugal:* Ricardo; Frechaut, Jorge Costa (Nuno Gomes 82), Beto, Rui Jorge, Petit (Paulo Bento 87), Rui Costa, Barbosa (Sa Pinto 72), Capucho, Pauleta, Joao Pinto.
*Cyprus:* Morphis; Theodotou, Filippou, Charalambous, Ioakim, Satsias, Engomitis (Yiasoumi 69), Christodoulou M (Melanarkitis 61), Germanou, Okkas (Stavrou 83), Constantinou M.
*Referee:* Farina (Italy).

| Group 2 Table | P | W | D | L | F | A | Pts |
|---|---|---|---|---|---|---|---|
| Republic of Ireland | 8 | 5 | 3 | 0 | 18 | 5 | 18 |
| Portugal | 7 | 4 | 3 | 0 | 18 | 5 | 15 |
| Holland | 7 | 4 | 2 | 1 | 21 | 8 | 14 |
| Estonia | 7 | 2 | 1 | 4 | 8 | 14 | 7 |
| Cyprus | 7 | 2 | 1 | 4 | 10 | 22 | 7 |
| Andorra | 8 | 0 | 0 | 8 | 4 | 25 | 0 |

**GROUP 3**

**Sofia, 2 September 2000, 15,000**

**Bulgaria (0) 0**

**Czech Republic (0) 1** *(Poborsky 73 (pen))*

*Bulgaria:* Zdravkov; Peev, Markov, Ivanov B, Kirilov (Topuzakov 76), Petrov S, Todorov (Ivanov G 63), Stoyanov, Yovov (Petrov M 33), Balakov, Iliev.
*Czech Republic:* Srnicek; Repka, Rada, Nedved, Fukal, Horvath (Rosicky 77), Tyce, Poborsky, Koller (Lokvenc 63), Smicer (Vicek 90), Bejbl.
*Referee:* Marin (Spain).

**Reykjavik, 2 September 2000, 7072**

**Iceland (1) 1** *(Sverrisson E 12)*

**Denmark (1) 2** *(Tomasson 26, Bisgaard 49)*

*Iceland:* Arason; Helgason A (Gunnarsson B 29), Hreidarsson, Marteinsson, Kolvidsson, Kristinsson R, Gudmundsson (Helguson 70), Sverrisson E, Gudjohnsen E, Gudjonsson T (Sigurdsson I 70), Dadason.
*Denmark:* Schmeichel; Goldbaek (Nielsen A 76), Henriksen, Gravesen, Heintze, Helveg, Steen-Nielsen, Rommedahl (Michaelsen 81), Tomasson, Bisgaard (Jensen C 70), Sand.
*Referee:* Bre (France).

**Belfast, 2 September 2000, 8227**

**Northern Ireland (0) 1** *(Gray 70)*

**Malta (0) 0**

*Northern Ireland:* Carroll; Nolan, Hughes, Murdock, Taggart, Horlock, Johnson, Magilton, Healy, Elliott (Gray 61), Lomas.
*Malta:* Barry; Dimech, Debono, Said, Carabott, Sylla (Brincat 46), Thuma, Camilleri (Veselji 78), Chetcuti, Busuttil, Mallia (Turner 58).
*Referee:* Bezubiak (Russia).

**Sofia, 7 October 2000, 4000**

**Bulgaria (1) 3** *(Ivanov G 39, 65, Todorov 90)*

**Malta (0) 0**

*Bulgaria:* Zdravkov; Markov, Pazjin, Petrov S, Hristov, Stoyanov (Petkov M 59), Ivanov G (Todorov 88), Balakov, Iliev (Petkov I 70), Peev, Petrov M.
*Malta:* Barry; Carabott, Chetcuti, Said, Debono, Dimech (Holland 67), Busuttil (Mallia 60), Giglio, Nwoko, Brincat (Agius 75), Zahra.
*Referee:* Caljia (Bosnia).

**Teplice, 7 October 2000, 9843**

**Czech Republic (3) 4** *(Koller 17, 41, Nedved 44, 90)*

**Iceland (0) 0**

*Czech Republic:* Srnicek; Repka, Rada, Nedved, Fukal, Horvath (Rosicky 79), Tyce, Poborsky (Latal 68), Koller (Lokvenc 75), Sionko, Bejbl.
*Iceland:* Kristinsson B; Helgason A, Hreidarsson, Marteinsson (Gudmundsson T 46), Kolvidsson, Kristinsson R (Gretarsson 85), Jonsson S, Sverrisson E, Gudjohnsen E, Helguson, Dadason (Gudjonsson T 46).
*Referee:* Vassaros (Greece).

**Belfast, 7 October 2000, 11,823**

**Northern Ireland (1) 1** *(Healy 38)*

**Denmark (0) 1** *(Rommedahl 60)*

*Northern Ireland:* Carroll; Lomas, Hughes, Murdock, Taggart, Horlock, Magilton, Jeff Whitley (Mulryne 72), Healy, Elliott (Gray 84), Lennon.
*Denmark:* Schmeichel; Helveg, Henriksen, Gravesen, Heintze, Steen-Nielsen, Tofting, Rommedahl, Tomasson, Sand (Jensen C 82), Gronkjaer (Bisgaard 63).
*Referee:* Pereira (Portugal).

**Copenhagen, 11 October 2000, 39,847**

**Denmark (0) 1** *(Sand 73)*
**Bulgaria (0) 1** *(Berbatov 82)*
*Denmark:* Schmeichel; Helveg, Henriksen, Gravesen, Heintze, Rommedahl, Tofting, Steen-Nielsen (Jensen C 46), Gronkjaer (Mikaelsen 55), Tomasson (Nielsen A 79), Sand.
*Bulgaria:* Zdravkov; Kishishev, Petkov M (Todorov 77), Kirilov, Pazjin, Petrov S, Hristov (Peev 68), Ivanov B, Balakov, Ivanov G (Berbatov 64), Petrov M.
*Referee:* Sarvan (Turkey).

**Reykjavik, 11 October 2000, 5415**

**Iceland (0) 1** *(Gudjonsson T 89)*
**Northern Ireland (0) 0**
*Iceland:* Kristinsson B; Helgason A, Hreidarsson, Sverrisson E, Vidarsson, Helguson, Gunnarsson, Kristinsson R (Gretarsson 46), Gudjonsson T, Gudjohnsen E, Dadason (Sigurdsson H 64).
*Northern Ireland:* Carroll; Lomas, Hughes, Murdock, Taggart (Williams 46), Horlock, Lennon, Johnson, Healy, Magilton, Elliott (Gray 82).
*Referee:* Merk (Germany).

**Valletta, 11 October 2000, 4000**

**Malta (0) 0**
**Czech Republic (0) 0**
*Malta:* Muscat; Said, Chetcuti (Camilleri 61), Spiteri, Debono, Agius, Busuttil, Giglio (Turner 75), Brincat (Theuma 63), Nwoko, Zahra.
*Czech Republic:* Srnicek; Fukal (Latal 46), Rada, Repka, Tyce, Poborsky, Nedved, Bejbl, Horvath (Vicek 65), Koller, Sionko (Lokvenc 82).
*Referee:* Siric (Croatia).

**Sofia, 24 March 2001, 20,000**

**Bulgaria (1) 2** *(Chamokov 36, Berbatov 78)*
**Iceland (1) 1** *(Hreidarsson 24)*
*Bulgaria:* Zdravkov; Kishishev (Pejev 63), Pazjin, Chomakov, Markov, Kirilov (Todorov 77), Petkov M, Balakov, Hristov, Ivanov G (Berbatov 63), Petrov M.
*Iceland:* Arason; Sigurdsson, Hreidarsson, Vidarsson, Gunnarsson, Kristinsson R, Helguson, Sverrisson, Gudjonsson T (Gretarsson 59), Gudjohnsen E (Highorsson 61), Dadason.
*Referee:* Riley (England).

**Valletta, 24 March 2001, 2500**

**Malta (0) 0**
**Denmark (1) 5** *(Sand 8, 65, 80, Heintze 50, Jensen C 76)*
*Malta:* Muscat; Turner (Okoh 46), Carabott, Dimech (Holland 65), Zahra, Debono, Giglio (Camilleri 65), Busuttil, Saliba, Nwoko, Brincat.
*Denmark:* Sorensen; Tofting, Henriksen, Laursen, Heintze, Helveg (Goldbaek 68), Gravesen (Steen-Nielsen 63), Gronkjaer, Rommedahl, Sand, Jorgensen (Jensen C 75).
*Referee:* McCurry (Scotland).

**Belfast, 24 March 2001, 10,368**

**Northern Ireland (0) 0**
**Czech Republic (0) 1** *(Nedved 11)*
*Northern Ireland:* Carroll; Griffin, Hughes A, Elliott (Gray 78), Williams, Murdock, Gillespie, Lennon, Healy (Ferguson 78), Magilton, Hughes M.
*Czech Republic:* Srnicek; Fukal, Votava, Ujfalusi, Tyce, Poborsky, Bejbl, Rosicky (Jarosik 81), Nedved, Smicer (Nemec 90), Koller (Lokvenc 73).
*Referee:* Gonzalez (Spain).

**Sofia, 28 March 2001, 20,000**

**Bulgaria (2) 4** *(Balakov 10, Petrov M 17, 78, Chomakov 72)*
**Northern Ireland (1) 3** *(Williams 14, Healy 83, 90 (pen))*
*Bulgaria:* Zdravkov; Kishishev, Petkov M (Stoilov 58), Markov, Chomakov, Pazjin, Ivanov B, Hristov (Petrov S 67), Berbatov (Ivanov G 81), Balakov, Petrov M.
*Northern Ireland:* Carroll; Griffin, Nolan (McCarthy 90), Elliott, Williams, Murdock, Gillespie (Johnson 85), Lennon (Kennedy 85), Healy, Magilton, Hughes M.
*Referee:* Hrinak (Slovakia).

**Prague, 28 March 2001, 16,354**

**Czech Republic (0) 0**

**Denmark (0) 0**

*Czech Republic:* Srnicek; Fukal, Votava, Ujfalusi, Poborsky, Rosicky (Jarosik 86), Bejbl, Nedved, Nemec, Smicer (Kuka 67), Koller (Lokvenc 89).

*Denmark:* Sorensen; Helveg, Henriksen, Laursen, Heintze (Nygaard 88), Rommedahl (Jensen C 78), Tofting, Gravesen, Gronkjaer (Jorgensen 46), Tomasson, Sand.

*Referee:* Barber (England).

**Valletta, 25 April 2001, 1500**

**Malta (1) 1** *(Mifsud 14)*

**Iceland (2) 4** *(Gudmundsson 42, Sigurdsson 45, Gudjohnsen 83, Gudjonsson T 90)*

*Malta:* Muscat; Debono, Said, Carabott, Spiteri, Giglio (Theuma 63), Busuttil, Mifsud, Zahra (Mallia 70), Nwoko, Brincat (Turner 56).

*Iceland:* Arason; Vidarsson, Sverrisson (Marteinsson 67), Hreidarsson, Kristinsson R, Gudmundsson, Gretarsson, Gunnarsson, Sigurdsson, Gudjohnsen, Sigthorsson (Gudjonsson T 80).

*Referee:* Zotta (Romania).

**Copenhagen, 2 June 2001, 41,669**

**Denmark (1) 2** *(Sand 6, Tomasson 82)*

**Czech Republic (1) 1** *(Tyce 40)*

*Denmark:* Sorensen; Helveg, Henriksen, Laursen, Heintze, Tofting, Tomasson, Steen-Nielsen (Jensen C 58), Rommedahl (Gronkjaer 74), Sand, Jorgensen (Nielsen A 87).

*Czech Republic:* Srnicek; Johana, Ujfalusi, Votava, Tyce (Rada 60), Poborsky (Kuka 85), Nedved, Galasek, Berger, Lokvenc (Koller 68), Smicer.

*Referee:* Merk (Germany).

**Reykjavik, 2 June 2001, 3554**

**Iceland (2) 3** *(Gudmundsson 7, Dadason 38, Gudjohnsen E 68)*

**Malta (0) 0**

*Iceland:* Arason; Helgason, Vidarsson, Gretarsson, Gunnarsson, Kristinsson R (Kolvidsson 74), Gudmundsson, Sverrisson E (Marteinsson 74), Gudjohnsen E, Sigurdsson, Dadason (Helguson 74).

*Malta:* Muscat; Said, Turner, Spiteri, Theuma, Dimech, Agius, Ciglio (Suda 74), Mifsud, Brincat (Camilleri 46), Mallia (Nwoko 69).

*Referee:* Lajuks (Latvia).

**Belfast, 2 June 2001, 7663**

**Northern Ireland (0) 0**

**Bulgaria (0) 1** *(Ivanov G 52)*

*Northern Ireland:* Taylor; Nolan (Quinn 86), Griffin, Murdock, Hughes A, Lennon (Mulryne 79), Gillespie, Johnson, Healy, Elliott (Ferguson 79), Hughes M.

*Bulgaria:* Zdravkov; Ivanov B, Markov, Pazjin, Kishishev (Peev 23), Hristov (Stoilov 87), Petrov M (Kirilov 77), Balakov, Chomokov, Petkov M, Ivanov G.

*Referee:* Busacca (Switzerland).

**Teplice, 6 June 2001, 14,850**

**Czech Republic (1) 3** *(Kuka 40, 88, Baros 90)*

**Northern Ireland (1) 1** *(Mulryne 45)*

*Czech Republic:* Srnicek; Repka, Votava (Bejbl 46), Tyce, Poborsky (Lokvenc 83), Nedved, Galasek, Rosicky, Berger, Koller (Baros 65), Kuka.

*Northern Ireland:* Taylor; Nolan, Hughes A, Murdock, Williams, Griffin, Johnson (Ferguson 76), Mulryne (Kennedy 81), Healy, Elliott (Quinn 65), Hughes M.

*Referee:* Sundell (Sweden).

**Copenhagen, 6 June 2001, 38,499**

**Denmark (1) 2** *(Sand 43, 83)*

**Malta (1) 1** *(Mallia 8)*

*Denmark:* Sorensen; Helveg, Henriksen, Heintze, Tofting (Nielsen A 75), Tomasson (Nygaard 68), Gravesen, Jensen C, Rommedahl (Gronkjaer 55), Sand, Jorgensen.

*Malta:* Barry; Debono, Said, Theuma, Camilleri, Turner, Brincat (Holland 73), Mallia (Nwoko 65), Dimech, Agius (Okoh 78), Mifsud.
*Referee:* Shmolik (Belarus).

**Reykjavik, 6 June 2001, 4316**

**Iceland (1) 1** *(Dadason 43)*

**Bulgaria (0) 1** *(Berbatov 81)*

*Iceland:* Arason; Helgason, Vidarsson, Gretarsson, Gunnarsson, Kristinsson R, Hreidarsson, Sverrisson E, Gudjohnsen E, Sigurdsson, Dadason (Helguson 46).
*Bulgaria:* Zdravkov; Pazjin (Petrov S 54), Markov, Ivanov B, Stoilov, Chomakov (Petrov M 65), Balakov (Todorov 73), Kirilov, Peev, Ivanov G, Berbatov.
*Referee:* Gallagher (England).

| Group 3 Table | P | W | D | L | F | A | Pts |
|---|---|---|---|---|---|---|---|
| Denmark | 7 | 4 | 3 | 0 | 13 | 5 | 15 |
| Czech Republic | 7 | 4 | 2 | 1 | 10 | 3 | 14 |
| Bulgaria | 7 | 4 | 2 | 1 | 12 | 7 | 14 |
| Iceland | 7 | 3 | 1 | 3 | 11 | 10 | 10 |
| Northern Ireland | 7 | 1 | 1 | 5 | 6 | 11 | 4 |
| Malta | 7 | 0 | 1 | 6 | 2 | 18 | 1 |

## GROUP 4

**Baku, 2 September 2000, 20,000**

**Azerbaijan (0) 0**

**Sweden (1) 1** *(Svensson A 10)*

*Azerbaijan:* Kramarenko; Kuliyev E, Agayev, Akhmedov, Yadullayev, Kuliyev S, Mamedov R (Aliev 86), Tagizade, Musayev (Kurbanov 65), Vasilyev, Kvaratshelia.
*Sweden:* Hedman; Nilsson R, Andersson P, Bjorklund, Mellberg, Mjallby, Alexandersson, Svensson A (Mild 75), Ljungberg, Andersson K, Larsson.
*Referee:* Luinge (Holland).

**Istanbul, 2 September 2000, 22,000**

**Turkey (1) 2** *(Okan 45, Emre 70)*

**Moldova (0) 0**

*Turkey:* Rustu; Umit D, Ogun, Fatih, Emre, Bulent K, Okan (Tayfur 60), Suat (Tayfun 65), Hakan Sukur, Cenk (Umit K 84), Unsal.
*Moldova:* Dinov; Kovalenko, Sosnovski, Testimitanu, Rebeja, Stroenco, Curtianu (Sischin 46), Oprea (Tanurkov 77), Catansus, Epureanu (Stratulat 34), Rogaciov.
*Referee:* Benko (Austria).

**Bratislava, 3 September 2000, 4011**

**Slovakia (1) 2** *(Lazarevski 3 (og), Demo 74)*

**Macedonia (0) 0**

*Slovakia:* Konig; Dzurik, Karhan, Timko, Leitner, Balis, Kratochvil, Moravcik (Nemeth P 46), Ujlaky (Demo 46), Jancula (Meszaros 76), Nemeth S.
*Macedonia:* Filevski; Veselinovski, Stojanoski (Lazarevski 64), Sedloski, Nikolovski, Stavrevski, Serafimovski, Micevski (Gerasimovski 69), Hristov, Ciric (Bekiri 77), Savevski.
*Referee:* Hamer (Luxembourg).

**Skopje, 6 October 2000, 4000**

**Macedonia (2) 3** *(Hristov 35, 42, Bekiri 75)*

**Azerbaijan (0) 0**

*Macedonia:* Filevski; Lazarevski (Veselinovski 70), Stavrevski, Sedloski, Nikolovski (Gerasimovski 20), Serafimovski, Sainovski, Micevski, Hristov, Sakiri, Bekiri (Miserdovski 80).
*Azerbaijan:* Kramarenko; Asadov, Yadullayev, Akhmedov, Agayev, Kuliyev E (Garaselia 55), Kurbanov, Tagizade, Musayev, Vasiliev, Rzayev (Loesjki 80).
*Referee:* Fisker (Denmark).

**Chisinau, 7 October 2000, 5000**

**Moldova (0) 0**

**Slovakia (0) 1** *(Nemeth S 79)*

*Moldova:* Dinov; Kovalenko, Catinsus, Testimitanu, Rebeja, Stroenco, Curtianu, Sischin (Rogaciov 60), Sosnovski (Epureanu 82), Gaidamasciuc (Stratulat 72), Clescenco.
*Slovakia:* Konig; Dzurik, Sobona, Sucanchak, Karhan, Demo (Nemeth P 74), Valachovic, Leitner, Pinte, Nemeth S (Prohaszka 88), Moravcik (Meszaros 53).
*Referee:* Stuchlik (Austria).

**Gothenburg, 7 October 2000, 42,152**

**Sweden (0) 1** *(Larsson 68)*

**Turkey (0) 1** *(Tayfur 90 (pen))*

*Sweden:* Hedman; Nilsson R, Andersson P, Bjorklund, Alexandersson (Corneliusson 55), Jonsson (Svensson A 63), Mjallby, Ljungberg, Mild, Andersson K, Larsson (Osmanovski 90).
*Turkey:* Rustu; Ogun, Fatih, Bulent K, Arif, Ergun (Abdullah 80), Suat (Tayfur 64), Hakan Sukur, Nihat, Izzet (Hasan Sas 75), Unsal.
*Referee:* Krug (Germany).

**Baku, 11 October 2000, 40,000**

**Azerbaijan (0) 0**

**Turkey (0) 1** *(Hakan Sukur 72)*

*Azerbaijan:* Kramarenko; Agayev, Yadullayev, Akhmedov, Lichkin (Mamedov 85), Kuliyev S, Kurbanov, Tagizade (Kambarov 72), Musayev (Charimov 58), Vasiliev, Kuliyev E.
*Turkey:* Rustu; Nihat (Fatih 46), Ogun, Bulent K, Alpay, Arif (Tayfur 90), Ergun, Suat, Hakan Sukur, Izzet (Hasan Sas 62), Unsal.
*Referee:* Snoddy (Northern Ireland).

**Chisinau, 11 October 2000, 4000**

**Moldova (0) 0**

**Macedonia (0) 0**

*Moldova:* Khmaruk; Stratulat, Catinsus, Testimitanu, Rebeja (Epureanu 46), Stroenco, Curtianu (Borets 65), Sischin (Rogaciov 56), Sosnovski, Gaidamasciuc, Clescenco.
*Macedonia:* Filevski; Stavrevski, Lazarevski, Sedloski, Gerasimovski, Serafimovski (Veselinovski 70), Sainovski (Karanfilovski 76), Micevski, Hristov, Ciric (Miserdovski 85), Sakiri.
*Referee:* Ibanez (Spain).

**Bratislava, 11 October 2000, 11,227**

**Slovakia (0) 0**

**Sweden (0) 0**

*Slovakia:* Konig; Dzurik, Sobona, Timko, Karhan, Sucanchak, Balis, Leitner, Meszaros (Prohaszka 86), Nemeth S, Moravcik (Gresko 58).
*Sweden:* Hedman; Nilsson R, Andersson P, Bjorklund, Mellberg, Mjallby, Svensson A (Osmanovski 70), Jonsson (Mild 47), Ljungberg, Andersson K (Andersson D 82), Larsson.
*Referee:* Dallas (Scotland).

**Baku, 24 March 2001, 20,000**

**Azerbaijan (0) 0**

**Moldova (0) 0**

*Azerbaijan:* Kramarenko; Agayev, Akhmedov, Kuliyev E (Getman 68), Yadullayev, Niftalijev (Ismailov 46), Kuliyev K, Tagizade, Rzayev, Lichkin (Kuliyev R 80), Vasiliev.
*Moldova:* Khmaruk; Kovalenko, Rebeja, Testimitanu (Romanenco 13), Sosnovschi, Catinsus, Epureanu, Gaidamasciuc, Sischin, Rogaciov (Oprea 46), Clescenco (Pogreban 61).
*Referee:* Stark (Germany).

**Gothenburg, 24 March 2001, 22,106**

**Sweden (1) 1** *(Svensson A 43)*

**Macedonia (0) 0**

*Sweden:* Hedman; Mellberg, Andersson P, Matovac, Corneliusson, Linderoth (Andersson D 64), Schwarz (Selakovic 80), Svensson A (Mild 66), Ljungberg, Osmanovski, Larsson.

*Macedonia:* Milosevski; Mitrevski, Stavrevski, Sedloski, Zdravevski (Krstev 68), Veselinovski, Serafimovski, Micevski, Lazarevski, Sakiri, Bekiri (Sainoski 82).
*Referee:* Wegereef (Holland).

**Istanbul, 24 March 2001, 23,000**

**Turkey (0) 1** *(Hakan Sukur 53 (pen))*

**Slovakia (0) 1** *(Tomaschek 68)*

*Turkey:* Rustu; Bulent K, Ogun, Fatih, Alpay, Okan (Arif 77) (Tayfun 83), Umit, Emre (Ergun 1), Abdullah, Hakan Sukur, Sas.
*Slovakia:* Konig; Karhan, Valachovic, Varga, Dzurik, Dimo (Nemeth P 89), Labant, Tomaschek, Gresko, Nemeth S, Pinte.
*Referee:* Wojcik (Poland).

**Chisinau, 28 March 2001, 8000**

**Macedonia (1) 1** *(Micevski 20)*

**Turkey (0) 2** *(Mitrevski 68 (og), Umit D 69)*

*Macedonia:* Milosevski; Stavrevski, Zdravevski (Krstev 82), Sedloski, Mitrevski, Serafimovski (Georgievski 75), Micevski (Krsevski 75), Hristov, Bekiri, Sakiri, Lazarevski.
*Turkey:* Rustu; Fatih, Alpay, Tayfur, Okan (Tayfun 82), Umit D, Ogun (Umit O 37), Ergun (Ozer 59), Abdullah, Hakan Sukur, Sas.
*Referee:* Colombo (France).

**Skopje, 28 March 2001, 7000**

**Moldova (0) 0**

**Sweden (0) 2** *(Allback 89, 90)*

*Moldova:* Romanenko; Kovalenco, Rebeja, Catinsus, Sosnovski, Gaidamasciuc, Rogaciov (Pogreban 67), Oprea (Berco 72), Cebotari (Lungu 55), Sischin, Clescenco.
*Sweden:* Hedman; Mellberg, Andersson P, Matovac, Corneliusson, Selakovic (Andersson D 55), Schwarz, Mild (Jonson 44), Ljungberg, Larsson, Svensson A (Allback 78).
*Referee:* Duhamel (France).

**Trnava, 28 March 2001, 10,000**

**Slovakia (2) 3** *(Nemeth S 1, 10, Meszaros 57)*

**Azerbaijan (1) 1** *(Vasiliev 3 (pen))*

*Slovakia:* Konig; Varga, Karhan, Meszaros, Tomaschek, Labant, Pinte, Dzurik (Ujlaky 64), Demo (Jancula 78), Gresko, Nemeth S (Valachovic 68).
*Azerbaijan:* Kramarenko; Agayev, Yadullayev, Akhmedov, Kulyev E, Kulyev K, Kurbanov, Aliev I, Niftalijev, Vasiliev (Musayev 82), Lichkin (Aliev S 46).
*Referee:* Kapitanis (Cyprus).

**Skopje, 2 June 2001, 3000**

**Macedonia (1) 2** *(Sakiri 20 (pen), Krstev M 65)*

**Moldova (1) 2** *(Pogreban 10, Barbaros 72)*

*Macedonia:* Zekir; Stavrevski, Stojanov, Guzelov, Nikolovski (Trajanov 46), Jovanovski Z, Serafimovski (Jovanovski G 70), Krstev M, Krstev S, Sakiri, Bekiri (Nacevski 46).
*Moldova:* Romanenko; Kovalenko, Rebeja, Testimitanu (Osipenco 65), Sosnovski, Stroenco, Sischin (Barbaros 70), Catinsus, Pogreban (Epureanu 46), Gaidamasciuc, Clescenco.
*Referee:* Van Hulten (Holland).

**Stockholm, 2 June 2001, 34,327**

**Sweden (1) 2** *(Allback 45, 51)*

**Slovakia (0) 0**

*Sweden:* Hedman; Mellberg, Andersson P, Saarenpaa, Lucic, Alexandersson (Jonson 73), Linderoth (Svensson A 90), Svensson M, Allback (Andersson D 88), Larsson, Ljungberg.
*Slovakia:* Konig; Karhan, Timko, Varga, Dzurik, Tomaschek, Demo (Janocko 58), Nemeth S (Vittek 58), Gresko (Babnik 82), Labant, Pinte.
*Referee:* Aranda (Spain).

**Istanbul, 2 June 2001, 25,000**

**Turkey (3) 3** *(Tayfun 2, Oktay 29, Hakan Sukur 33)*
**Azerbaijan (0) 0**

*Turkey:* Rustu; Umit D, Alpay, Bulent K, Abdullah, Tayfun, Okan, Tugay, Emre (Ergun 80), Hakan Sukur, Oktay (Sas 37).
*Azerbaijan:* Gasanadze; Yunusov, Mamedov A (Niftalijev 68), Akhmedov, Mamedov R, Berbanov, Kuliyev K, Tagizade (Kuliyev R 80), Rzayev (Oruov 50), Kurbanov, Mardanov.
*Referee:* Roca (Spain).

**Baku, 6 June 2001, 20,000**

**Azerbaijan (1) 2** *(Vasiliev 26, Tagizade 55)*
**Slovakia (0) 0**

*Azerbaijan:* Gasanzade; Yemosov, Akhmedov, Mamedov R, Niftalijev, Kurbanov M, Yadullayev, Tagizade (Kuliyev R 82), Kurbanov G (Ismailov 89), Getman, Vasiliev (Rzayev 75).
*Slovakia:* Konig; Dzurik, Vittek (Bencik 69), Varga, Karhan, Tomaschek, Janocko, Nemeth S, Labant, Gresko, Pinte (Babnic 62).
*Referee:* Vollquartz (Denmark).

**Gothenburg, 6 June 2001, 30,233**

**Sweden (1) 6** *(Larsson 38 (pen), 58, 68 (pen), 79 (pen), Alexandersson 74, Allback 77)*
**Moldova (0) 0**

*Sweden:* Hedman; Mellberg, Andersson P, Saarenpaa (Andersson C 34), Lucic, Alexandersson, Linderoth, Magnus Svensson (Mathias Svensson 83), Svensson A (Andersson D 71), Allback, Larsson.
*Moldova:* Romanenko; Kovalenko, Stroenco, Rebeja (Osipenco 63), Catinsus, Gaidamasciuc, Epureanu, Testimitanu, Oprea, Pogreban (Barburos 46), Clescenco (Sischin 78).
*Referee:* Dunn (England).

**Bursa, 6 June 2001, 20,000**

**Turkey (1) 3** *(Alpay 43, 58, 70)*
**Macedonia (2) 3** *(Sakiri 7, Serafimovski 20, Nikolovski 62)*

*Turkey:* Rustu; Umit O, Bulent K, Alpay, Abdullah, Tayfun (Fatih 84), Okan (Basturk 69), Tugay, Emre, Hakan Sukur, Oktay (Ozer 46).
*Macedonia:* Filevski; Stavrevski, Nikolovski, Mitreveski, Stojanov, Serafimovski (Trajanov 72), Krstev M, Guzelov, Sakiri, Nacevski (Lazarevski 48), Bekiri (Pandev 66).
*Referee:* Rodomonti (Italy).

| Group 4 Table | P | W | D | L | F | A | Pts |
|---|---|---|---|---|---|---|---|
| Sweden | 7 | 5 | 2 | 0 | 13 | 1 | 17 |
| Turkey | 7 | 4 | 3 | 0 | 13 | 6 | 15 |
| Slovakia | 7 | 3 | 2 | 2 | 7 | 6 | 11 |
| Macedonia | 7 | 1 | 3 | 3 | 9 | 10 | 6 |
| Azerbaijan | 7 | 1 | 1 | 5 | 3 | 11 | 4 |
| Moldova | 7 | 0 | 3 | 4 | 2 | 13 | 3 |

## GROUP 5

**Minsk, 2 September 2000, 35,000**

**Belarus (1) 2** *(Khatskevich 40, Belkevich 56)*
**Wales (0) 1** *(Speed 89)*

*Belarus:* Tumilovich; Lukhvich, Yakhimovic, Shtanyuk, Gurenko, Khatskevich, Yaskovich (Shuneiko 71), Orlovski (Skripchenko 85), Vasilyuk, Romashchenko M (Ryndyuk 28), Belkevich.
*Wales:* Jones P; Page, Roberts G, Savage, Coleman, Melville, Robinson, Speed, Bellamy, Roberts I (Blake 73), Giggs.
*Referee:* Trentalange (Italy).

**Oslo, 2 September 2000, 19,201**

**Norway (0) 0**

**Armenia (0) 0**

*Norway:* Olsen F; Bergdolmo, Hoftun, Berg, Riseth (Basma 49), Mykland, Leonhardsen, Iversen, Flo T (Helstad 85), Solskjaer, Skammelsrud (Strand 70).
*Armenia:* Berezovski; Soukiassian, Hovsepian, Khodgoyan, Vardanian, Khachatrian, Art Petrossian (Minasian 90), Voskanian, Dokhoyan, Shahgeldian (Demirchian 65), Movsissian (Karamian 85).
*Referee:* Young (Scotland).

**Kiev, 2 September 2000, 50,000**

**Ukraine (1) 1** *(Shevchenko 13)*

**Poland (2) 3** *(Olisadebe 3, 33, Kaluzny 57)*

*Ukraine:* Kernozenko; Luzhny, Tymoshchuk (Zubov 46), Golovko, Vashchuk, Dmitrulin, Gusin, Popov (Kossovski V 75), Vorobei (Yashkin 61), Shevchenko, Rebrov.
*Poland:* Dudek; Klos (Hajto 85), Zielinski, Michal Zewlakow, Waldoch, Kozminski (Krzynowek 89), Czereszewski, Iwan, Juskowiak (Gilewicz 70), Kaluzny, Olisadebe.
*Referee:* Aranda (Spain).

**Erevan, 7 October 2000, 14,000**

**Armenia (2) 2** *(Art Petrossian 17, 44)*

**Ukraine (1) 3** *(Shevchenko 45, 59, Gusin 55)*

*Armenia:* Berezovski; Soukiassian, Khodgoyan (Arm Karamian 63), Hovsepian, Vardanian, Khachatrian, Art Petrossian, Voskanian, Dokhoyan, Shahgeldian (Akopian 77), Movsissian (Art Karamian 63).
*Ukraine:* Shovkovskyi; Luzhny, Nesmachni, Golovko, Vashchuk, Dmitrulin, Shevchenko, Gusin, Vorobei (Mikhailenko 67), Tymoshchuk (Yashkin 46), Rebrov.
*Referee:* Larsen (Denmark).

**Lodz, 7 October 2000, 7000**

**Poland (1) 3** *(Kaluzny 24, 62, 73)*

**Belarus (1) 1** *(Ryndyuk 37)*

*Poland:* Dudek; Klos, Zielinksi, Michal Zewlakow, Waldoch, Krzynowek, Swierczewski P, Karwan (Iwan 81), Juskowiak (Kryszalowicz 46), Kaluzny, Olisadebe.
*Belarus:* Varivonchik; Yakhimovic, Ostrovski, Lukhvich, Shtanyuk, Gurenko, Baranov (Lavrik 74), Belkevich, Romashchenko, Vasilyuk (Ryndyuk 30), Skripchenko (Orlovski 68).
*Referee:* Frisk (Sweden).

**Cardiff, 7 October 2000, 51,000**

**Wales (0) 1** *(Blake 60)*

**Norway (0) 1** *(Helstad 80)*

*Wales:* Jones P; Delaney, Savage, Page, Coleman, Melville, Robinson, Speed, Hartson (Roberts I 86), Blake, Giggs.
*Norway:* Olsen F; Basma, Bjornebye, Leonhardsen, Berg, Johnsen, Bakke (Helstad 78), Mykland, Iversen (Flo T 59), Solskjaer, Strand.
*Referee:* Strampe (Germany).

**Minsk, 11 October 2000, 20,000**

**Belarus (2) 2** *(Khatskevich 23, Ryndyuk 34)*

**Armenia (0) 1** *(Khodgoyan 50)*

*Belarus:* Tumilovich; Yakhimovic, Ostrovski, Lukhvich, Lavrik, Gurenko, Khatskevich, Belkevich, Romashchenko (Skripchenko 89), Vasilyuk (Shumeiko 60), Ryndyuk.
*Armenia:* Abramian; Soukiassian, Khodgoyan (Art Karamian 61), Hovsepian, Vardanian, Khachatrian, Art Petrossian (Arm Karamian 85), Voskanian, Dokhoyan, Shakhgeldian, Movsissian.
*Referee:* Corpodean (Romania).

**Oslo, 11 October 2000, 23,612**

**Norway (0) 0**

**Ukraine (0) 1** *(Shevchenko 49)*

*Norway:* Olsen F; Basma, Johnsen, Berg, Bergdolmo, Bakke (Helstad 75), Mykland, Iversen, Solskjaer, Leonhardsen (Flo T 54), Strand.
*Ukraine:* Shovkovskyi; Luzhny (Federov 80), Nesmachni, Golovko, Vashchuk, Dmitrulin, Shevchenko, Gusin, Vorobei, Popov (Yashkin 50), Rebrov.
*Referee:* Meier (Switzerland).

**Warsaw, 11 October 2000, 14,000**

**Poland (0) 0**

**Wales (0) 0**

*Poland:* Dudek; Klos, Zielinski, Waldoch, Michal Zewlakow, Karwan, Kaluzny, Czereszewski, Krzynowek (Rzasa 70), Gilewicz (Kryszalowicz 56), Juskowiak (Olisadebe 75).
*Wales:* Jones P; Delaney, Savage, Page, Coleman, Melville, Robinson, Speed, Hartson (Jones N 75), Blake, Giggs.
*Referee:* Cortez (Portugal).

**Erevan, 24 March 2001, 12,000**

**Armenia (1) 2** *(Minasian 32, Movsissian 71)*

**Wales (1) 2** *(Hartson 41, 48)*

*Armenia:* Abramian; Vardanian, Hovsepian, Khodgoyan (Art Karamian 58), Sargsyan, Art Petrossian, Voskanian (Hakobian 70), Dokhoyan, Minasian (Demirchian 39), Shakhgeldian, Movsissian.
*Wales:* Jones P; Delaney, Legg, Melville, Page, Pembridge (Jones M 46), Saunders (Robinson C 70), Speed, Bellamy, Hartson (Roberts I 79), Robinson J.
*Referee:* Kasnaferis (Greece).

**Oslo, 24 March 2001, 15,077**

**Norway (0) 2** *(Carew 58, Solskjaer 66)*

**Poland (2) 3** *(Olisadebe 23, 29, Karwan 80)*

*Norway:* Myhre; Bergdolmo, Berg, Lundekvam, Stensaas (Flo T 84), Winsnes, Larsen T, Tessem, Solskjaer, Carew, Helstad (Iversen 60).
*Poland:* Matysek (Dudek 64); Klos, Hajto, Zielinski, Michal Zewlakow, Iwan (Karwan 64), Kaluzny, Swierzcewski P (Zdebel 88), Kozminski, Kryszalowicz, Olisadebe.
*Referee:* Dougal (Scotland).

**Kiev, 24 March 2001, 75,000**

**Ukraine (0) 0**

**Belarus (0) 0**

*Ukraine:* Shovkovsky; Luzhny, Golovko, Vashchuk, Nesmachni, Popov (Vorobei 61), Dmitrulin (Tymoshchuk 78), Cardash, Yashkin, Shevchenko, Rebrov.
*Belarus:* Tumilovich; Shuneiko, Ostrovski, Shtanyuk, Yaskovich, Gurenko, Khatskevich, Belkevich, Vasilyuk, Milevski, Romashchenko (Lavrik 73).
*Referee:* Marin (Spain).

**Minsk, 28 March 2001, 39,000**

**Belarus (1) 2** *(Khatskevich 19, Vasilyuk 90)*

**Norway (0) 1** *(Solskjaer 68)*

*Belarus:* Tumilovich; Shumeiko, Yakhimovic, Shtanyuk, Lukhvich, Gurenko, Khatskevich, Belkevich, Vasilyuk, Milevski (Lavrik 46), Romashchenko.
*Norway:* Myhre; Riseth, Berg, Eggen, Bergdolmo, Tessem (Stensaas 87), Larsen, Winsnes, Solskjaer, Carew, Iversen S (Flo T 46).
*Referee:* Vassaras (Greece).

**Warsaw, 28 March 2001, 11,000**

**Poland (2) 4** *(Michal Zewlakow 15 (pen), Olisadebe 41, Marcin Zewlakow 81, Karwan 88)*
**Armenia (0) 0**

*Poland:* Dudec; Klos, Zielinski, Hajto, Michal Zewlakow (Krzynowek 76), Swierczewski P, Iwan (Karwan 67), Kaluzny, Kozminsky, Kryszalowicz (Marcin Zewlakow 79), Olisadebe.
*Armenia:* Abramian; Mkrchian, Demirchian, Hovsepian, Vardanian, Khachatrian, Art Petrossian, Voskanian (Art Karamian 66), Dokhoyan, Shakhgeldian (Arm Karamian 73), Movsissian.
*Referee:* Poulat (France).

**Cardiff, 28 March 2001, 46,750**

**Wales (1) 1** *(Hartson 12)*
**Ukraine (0) 1** *(Shevchenko 52)*

*Wales:* Jones P; Delaney, Barnard, Melville, Page, Jones M (Davies 55), Robinson C, Speed, Bellamy, Hartson (Saunders 70), Giggs.
*Ukraine:* Shovkovskyi; Luzhny, Golovko, Vashchuk, Nesmachni, Tymoshchuk, Popov (Melashchenko 70), Yashkin, Rebrov (Kardash 46), Vorobei, Shevchenko.
*Referee:* Romain (Belgium).

**Erevan, 2 June 2001, 10,000**

**Armenia (0) 0**
**Belarus (0) 0**

*Armenia:* Abramian; Soukiassian, Khodgoyan, Demirchian (Dokhoyan A 65), Vardanian A, Khachatrian, Art Petrossian, Minasian (Art Karamian 36), Sarkissian, Arm Karamian (Gevorgian 69), Dokhoyan K.
*Belarus:* Tumilovic; Yakhimovic, Ostrovski, Lukavic, Shtanyuk (Kulchi 84), Gurenko, Khatskevich, Belkevich, Shuneiko (Romashchenko 80), Vasilyuk, Milevski (Yaskovich 72).
*Referee:* Guenov (Bulgaria).

**Kiev, 2 June 2001, 42,000**

**Ukraine (0) 0**
**Norway (0) 0**

*Ukraine:* Shovkovskyi; Starostyak, Golovko, Vashchuk, Dmitrulin, Parfionov, Tymoshchuk, Zoubov, Vorobei (Spivak 68), Shevchenko, Yashkin (Rebrov 46).
*Norway:* Myhre; Basma, Hoftun, Berg, Riseth, Rudi, Leonhardsen, Andersen T, Bakke, Strand (Helstad 78), Carew.
*Referee:* Maric (Croatia).

**Cardiff, 2 June 2001, 48,500**

**Wales (1) 1** *(Blake 13)*
**Poland (1) 2** *(Olisadebe 32, Kryszalowicz 72)*

*Wales:* Jones P; Page (Jenkins 84), Barnard (Jones M 79), Melville, Symons, Pembridge, Savage, Speed, Hartson, Blake, Giggs.
*Poland:* Dudec; Klos, Bak J, Hajto, Michal Zewlakow, Iwan, Zdebel (Krynowek 62), Bak A, Kozminski, Juskowiak (Kryszalowicz 54), Olisadebe (Marcin Zewlakow 90).
*Referee:* Ersoy (Turkey).

**Erevan, 6 June 2001, 10,000**

**Armenia (1) 1** *(Art Petrossian 11)*
**Poland (1) 1** *(Kaluzny 4)*

*Armenia:* Abramian; Soukiassian, Khodgoyan, Hovsepian, Vardanian (Demirchian 41), Khachatrian, Art Petrossian, Dokhoyan A (Okopian 33) (Gevorgian 66), Dokhoyan K, Sarkissian, Art Karamian.
*Poland:* Dudec; Kukielka, Hajto, Bak J, Michal Zewlakow, Swierczewski P, Bak A, Kaluzny (Krzynowek 36), Kozminsky (Zdebel 84), Juskowiak (Marcin Zewlakow 64), Kryszalowicz.
*Referee:* Romain (Belgium).

**Oslo, 6 June 2001, 17,164**

**Norway (0) 1** *(Carew 80)*

**Belarus (1) 1** *(Belkevich 23)*

*Norway:* Myhre; Basma (Aas 90), Hoftun, Berg, Riseth, Johnsen F, Leonhardsen, Andersen T, Bakke (Rudi 69), Strand (Nevland 69), Carew.

*Belarus:* Tumilovic; Yakhimovic, Ostrovski (Tarlovski 85), Lukavic, Shtanyuk, Gurenko, Khatskevich, Belkevich, Shuneiko, Vasilyuk (Khomutovsky 81), Milevski (Yaskovich 50).

*Referee:* Radoman (Yugoslavia).

**Kiev, 6 June 2001, 33,000**

**Ukraine (1) 1** *(Zoubov 44)*

**Wales (0) 1** *(Pembridge 74)*

*Ukraine:* Shovkovskyi (Levytsky 90); Starostiak (Luzhny 46), Golovko, Vashchuk, Dmitrulin (Nesmachni 46), Parfionov, Tymoshchuk, Zoubov, Vorobei, Shevchenko, Rebrov.

*Wales:* Jones P; Delaney (Jenkins 38), Barnard, Page, Melville, Pembridge, Davies, Speed, Hartson, Blake (Koumas 73), Giggs.

*Referee:* Gomes (Portugal).

| Group 5 Table | P | W | D | L | F | A | Pts |
|---|---|---|---|---|---|---|---|
| Poland | 7 | 5 | 2 | 0 | 16 | 6 | 17 |
| Belarus | 7 | 3 | 3 | 1 | 8 | 7 | 12 |
| Ukraine | 7 | 2 | 4 | 1 | 7 | 7 | 10 |
| Wales | 7 | 0 | 5 | 2 | 7 | 9 | 5 |
| Norway | 7 | 0 | 4 | 3 | 5 | 8 | 4 |
| Armenia | 7 | 0 | 4 | 3 | 6 | 12 | 4 |

## GROUP 6

**Brussels, 2 September 2000, 40,000**

**Belgium (0) 0**

**Croatia (0) 0**

*Belgium:* De Vlieger; Deflandre, Valgaeren, Van Meir, Van Kerckhoven, Vanderhaeghe, Wilmots, Goor (Henrikx 88), Mpenza E (Mpenza M 74), Strupar (Peeters 60), Verheyen.

*Croatia:* Pletikosa; Kovac R, Jarni, Soldo, Stimac, Simic, Vugrinec (Biscan 46), Jurcic, Suker, Kovac N, Balaban (Tudor 90).

*Referee:* Levnikov (Russia).

**Riga, 2 September 2000, 9500**

**Latvia (0) 0**

**Scotland (0) 1** *(McCann 89)*

*Latvia:* Kolinko; Laizans, Lobanyov, Stepanovs, Blagonadezhdin, Bleidelis, Ivanov, Astafjevs, Rubins, Pahars, Stolcers.

*Scotland:* Sullivan; Boyd, Davidson (Naysmith 46), Weir (Cameron 46), Hendry, Dailly, Ferguson B, Elliott, Dodds (Holt 90), Hutchison, McCann.

*Referee:* Schluchter (Switzerland).

**Riga, 7 October 2000, 9000**

**Latvia (0) 0**

**Belgium (2) 4** *(Wilmots 5, Peeters 13, Cavens 82, Verheyen 90)*

*Latvia:* Kolinko; Stepanovs, Laizans, Lobanyov (Zemlinsky 75), Blagonadezhdin (Polyakov 63), Astafjevs, Bleidelis, Ivanov, Pahars, Rubins, Stolcers (Peltsis 68).

*Belgium:* De Vlieger; Deflandre, Valgaeren, Van Meir, Van Kerckhoven, Vanderhaeghe, Wilmots (Goossens 88), Goor, Peeters (Cavens 80), Walem (Boffin 85), Verheyen.

*Referee:* Irvine (Northern Ireland).

**Serravalle, 7 October 2000, 4377**

**San Marino (0) 0**

**Scotland (0) 2** *(Elliott 71, Hutchison 73)*

*San Marino:* Gasperoni F; Gennari, Gobbi, Matteoni (Valentini V 74), Bacciocchi S, Marani, Gasperoni B, Zonzini (Della Valle 80), Manzaroli, Muccioli R, Montagna (De Luigi 60).

*Scotland:* Sullivan; McNamara, Naysmith, Elliott, Hendry, Dailly (Weir 36), Cameron, Gallacher (Dickov 65), Dodds, Hutchison, McCann (Johnston 46).

*Referee:* Orrason (Iceland).

**Zagreb, 11 October 2000, 30,000**

**Croatia (1) 1** *(Boksic 16)*
**Scotland (1) 1** *(Gallacher 24)*
*Croatia:* Pavalovic; Kovac R, Stimac, Simic D, Saric, Kovac N, Soldo (Biscan 46), Jarni (Zivkovic 46), Prosinecki, Balaban, Boksic (Vugrinec 75).
*Scotland:* Sullivan; Boyd, Naysmith, Elliott, Hendry, Weir, Cameron, Burley, Gallacher, Hutchison, Johnston (Dickov 46) (Holt 90).
*Referee:* Veissiere (France).

**Serravalle, 15 November 2000, 537**

**San Marino (0) 0**
**Latvia (1) 1** *(Yeliseyev 9)*
*San Marino:* Gasperoni F; Gennari, Marani, Valentini V, Matteoni, Bacciocchi, Muccioli, Zonzoni (Selva R 84), Montagna (De Luigi 78), Manzaroli (Bugli 74), Selva A.
*Latvia:* Kolinko; Stepanovs, Laizans, Zemlinsky, Blagonadezhdin, Bleidelis, Troitsky, Astafjevs, Pahars, Rubins (Verpakovsky 66), Yeliseyev (Ivanov 84).
*Referee:* Cheferin (Slovakia).

**Brussels, 28 February 2001, 40,104**

**Belgium (3) 10** *(Vanderhaeghe 10, 50, Mpenza E 13, Goor 26, 60, Baseggio 64, Wilmots 72, Peeters 76, 84, 88)*
**San Marino (0) 1** *(Selva 90)*
*Belgium:* De Vlieger; Deflandre (Crasson 67), Van Meir, Van Buyton, Dheedene, Englebert (Peeters 59), Vanderhaeghe, Baseggio (Vermant 75), Goor, Mpenza E, Wilmots.
*San Marino:* Gasperoni F; Gennari, Gobbi, Della Balda, Marani, Matteoni, Muccioli, Selva, Valentini, Zonzini (Vannucci 78), De Luigi (Bugli 87).
*Referee:* Kaldma (Estonia).

**Osijek, 24 March 2001, 18,000**

**Croatia (3) 4** *(Balaban 8, 43, 45, Vugrinec 89)*
**Latvia (0) 1** *(Stolcers 60)*
*Croatia:* Pletikosa; Simic D, Tudor, Kovac (Vranjes 77), Jarni, Zivkovic, Stanic (Citanovic 46), Prosinecki (Bjelica 63), Balaban, Suker, Vugrinec.
*Latvia:* Kolinko; Troitsky, Stepanovs, Zemlinsky, Blagonadezhdin, Bleidelis (Verpakovsky 39), Astafjevs, Laizans, Rubins (Rimkus 73), Pahars, Yeliseyev (Stolcers 54).
*Referee:* Ingvarsson (Sweden).

**Glasgow, 24 March 2001, 37,480**

**Scotland (2) 2** *(Dodds 1, 28 (pen))*
**Belgium (0) 2** *(Wilmots 58, Van Buyten 90)*
*Scotland:* Sullivan; Weir, Boyd, Elliott, Hendry, Ferguson B, Burley, Lambert, Dodds (Gallacher 88), Hutchison, Matteo.
*Belgium:* De Vlieger (Vermant 79); Mpenza M, Wilmots, Goor, Vanderhaege, Baseggio, Hendrikx (Peeters 46), Dheedene, De Boeck, Valgaeren (Van Buyten 57), Deflandre.
*Referee:* Nielsen (Denmark).

**Glasgow, 28 March 2001, 27,313**

**Scotland (3) 4** *(Hendry 22, 33, Dodds 34, Cameron 65)*
**San Marino (0) 0**
*Scotland:* Sullivan; Johnston, Matteo (Gallacher 64), Elliott (Boyd 46), Hendry, Weir, Burley, Lambert, Dodds, Hutchison, Cameron (Gemmill 82).
*San Marino:* Gasperoni F; Della Balda (Albani 90), Marani, Gobbi, Matteoni, Bacciocchi, Manzaroli (Selva R 80), Zonzini, Muccioli, Vannucci (Bugli 69), Selva A.
*Referee:* Kari (Finland).

**Riga, 25 April 2001, 4000**

**Latvia (1) 1** *(Pahars 1)*
**San Marino (0) 1** *(Albani 59)*
*Latvia:* Kolinko; Astafjevs, Stepanovs, Zemlinsky, Kolesnichenko (Mikholap 46), Ivanov (Zakreshevski 77), Blagonadezhdin, Rubins, Rimkus (Yeliseyev 66), Pahars, Stolcers.
*San Marino:* Gasperoni F; Albani, Vannucci, Della Balda, Matteoni, Bugli (Selva R 80), Bacciocchi, Muccioli, Zonzini, Manzaroli (Nanni 90), Selva A (Montagna P 83).
*Referee:* Nalbandian (Albania).

**Brussels, 2 June 2001, 30,000**

**Belgium (2) 3** *(Wilmots 2, Mpenza E 12, Zemlinsky 49 (og))*

**Latvia (0) 1** *(Pahars 51)*

*Belgium:* De Vlieger; Crasson, Valgaeren, Van Meir, Van der Heyden, Simons, Wilmots (Vermant 83), Goor (Boffin 68), Mpenza E (Sonck 78), Walem, Verheyen.
*Latvia:* Kolinko; Stepanovs, Astafjevs (Stolcers 67), Zemlinsky, Laizans, Blagonadezhdin (Zakreshevsky 68), Ivanov, Bleidelis, Pahars (Mikholap 71), Rubins, Isakov.
*Referee:* Dobrinov (Bulgaria).

**Varazdin, 2 June 2001, 15,000**

**Croatia (2) 4** *(Vlaovic 3, Balaban 29, Suker 54 (pen), Vugrinec 61)*

**San Marino (0) 0**

*Croatia:* Pletikosa; Saric, Tudor, Simic D, Jarni, Kovac R, Kovac N (Agic 64), Prosinecki, Vugrinec (Vucko 76), Vlaovic, Balaban (Suker 46).
*San Marino:* Gasperoni F; Albani, Della Balda, Matteoni (Manzaroli 26), Bacciocchi, Marani, Gennari, Vannucci, Gasperoni B (Ugolini 86), Zonzini (Selva R 76), Selva A.
*Referee:* Timofejev (Estonia).

**Riga, 6 June 2001, 5000**

**Latvia (0) 0**

**Croatia (1) 1** *(Balaban 40)*

*Latvia:* Kolinko; Stepanovs, Astafjevs (Mikholap 71), Zemlinsky, Laizans, Blagonadezhdin, Zakreshevsky, Bleidelis (Dobretsov 88), Isakov, Rubins (Verpakovsky 61), Stolcers.
*Croatia:* Pletikosa; Saric, Jarni, Tomas, Tudor, Simic D, Rapaic (Vugrinec 75), Prosinecki, Suker, Kovac (Agic 90), Balaban (Vlaovic 65).
*Referee:* McDermott (Republic of Ireland).

**Serraville, 6 June 2001, 1000**

**San Marino (1) 1** *(Selva A 11)*

**Belgium (1) 4** *(Wilmots 10, 89 (pen), Verheyen 60, Sonck 68)*

*San Marino:* Gasperoni F; Albani (Selva R 69), Della Balda, Bacciocchi, Marani, Gennari, Muccioli, Vannucci, Zonzini (Ugolini 82), Selva A, Gasperoni B (Bugli 74).
*Belgium:* De Vlieger; Deflandre, Van Meir, Valgaeren, Van Kerckhoven (Boffin 79), Verheyen, Vanderhaeghe, Walem, Goor (Vermant 75), Peeters (Sonck 52), Wilmots.
*Referee:* Yakov (Israel).

| Group 6 Table | P | W | D | L | F | A | Pts |
|---|---|---|---|---|---|---|---|
| Belgium | 6 | 4 | 2 | 0 | 23 | 5 | 14 |
| Croatia | 5 | 3 | 2 | 0 | 10 | 2 | 11 |
| Scotland | 5 | 3 | 2 | 0 | 10 | 3 | 11 |
| Latvia | 7 | 1 | 1 | 5 | 4 | 14 | 4 |
| San Marino | 7 | 0 | 1 | 6 | 3 | 26 | 1 |

## GROUP 7

**Sarajevo, 2 September 2000, 35,000**

**Bosnia (1) 1** *(Baljic 41)*

**Spain (1) 2** *(Gerard 39, Etxeberria 72)*

*Bosnia:* Guso; Akrapovic, Hujdurovic, Mujcin (Topic 79), Varesanovic, Hibic, Bolic, Sabic (Muratovic 86), Barbarez, Salihamidzic, Baljic.
*Spain:* Casillas; Manuel Pablo, Sergi, Paco, Abelardo, Mendieta, Helguera, Gerard (Guerrero 85), Urzaiz (Celades 70), Raul, Munitis (Etxeberria 58).
*Referee:* Fandel (Germany).

**Ramat Gan, 3 September 2000, 14,000**

**Israel (1) 2** *(Mizrahi A 1, Balili 79)*

**Liechtenstein (0) 0**

*Israel:* Davidovich; Talkar (Benayoun 66), Shelach, Gershon, Harazi A, Keissi, Berkovic (Zohar 82), Tal (Balili 77), Nimny, Mizrahi A, Banin.
*Liechtenstein:* Jehle; Ospelt, Zech, Hasler D, Frick C (Gigon 76), Martin Stocklasa (Hanselmann 85), Michael Stocklasa (Burgmeier 85), Hefti, Telser, Frick M, Beck T.
*Referee:* O'Hanlon (Republic of Ireland).

262

**Vaduz, 7 October 2000, 3500**

**Liechtenstein (0) 0**

**Austria (1) 1** *(Flogel 20)*

*Liechtenstein:* Jehle; Ospelt, Hasler D, Telser, Martin Stocklasa, Hanselmann, Hefti, Michael Stocklasa (Nigg 74), Gigon, Beck T, Frick M.
*Austria:* Wohlfahrt; Hiden, Baur, Stranzi, Schopp (Hortnagl 67), Kuhbauer, Herzog, Flogel, Kirchler, Brunmayr (Kitzbichler 46), Mayrleb.
*Referee:* Rowbotham (Scotland).

**Madrid, 7 October 2000, 80,000**

**Spain (1) 2** *(Gerard 22, Hierro 53)*

**Israel (0) 0**

*Spain:* Casillas; Hierro, Manuel Pablo, Abelardo, Sergi, Helguera, Gerard (Baraja 31), Mendieta, Munitis, Raul (Guerrero 85), Urzaiz (Catanha 75).
*Israel:* Davidovich; Alfon, Talkar, Shelach, Benado, Keissi, Tal, Nimny (Benayoun 65), Badir (Berkovic 75), Revivo, Mizrahi A.
*Referee:* Colombo (France).

**Vienna, 11 October 2000, 48,000**

**Austria (1) 1** *(Baur 21)*

**Spain (1) 1** *(Baraja 27)*

*Austria:* Wohlfahrt; Hatz, Baur, Hiden, Stranzi (Hortnagl 46), Flogel, Cerny, Kuhbauer (Schopp 75), Mayrleb, Herzog, Kocijan (Kirchler 54).
*Spain:* Casillas; Hierro, Abelardo, Sergi, Baraja, Helguera, Mendieta, Urzaiz (Catanha 60), Raul (Guerrero 88), Victor Sanchez (Rufete 46), Luis Enrique.
*Referee:* Ivanov (Russia).

**Tel Aviv, 11 October 2000, 30,000**

**Israel (1) 3** *(Berkovic 12, Abuksis 62, Katan 76)*

**Bosnia (0) 1** *(Akrapovic 48)*

*Israel:* Davidovich; Benado, Talkar, Shelach, Gershon, Keissi (Ben-Dayan 86), Tal, Revivo, Abuksis, Berkovic (Benayoun 60), Mizrahi A (Katan 73).
*Bosnia:* Guso; Akrapovic, Music, Hujdurovic (Krupinac 79), Varesanovic, Hibic, Bolic, Demirovich (Juldic 73), Barbarez, Salihamidzic, Baljic.
*Referee:* Jol (Holland).

**Sarajevo, 24 March 2001, 25,000**

**Bosnia (1) 1** *(Barbarez 42)*

**Austria (0) 1** *(Baur 61)*

*Bosnia:* Piplica; Varesanovic, Hujdorovic, Hibic, Rizvic (Hota 70), Sabic, Akrapovic, Barbarez, Music, Bolic, Baljic (Topic 83).
*Austria:* Wohlfahrt; Baur, Hiden, Neukirchner (Prilasnig 54), Cerny (Schopp 46), Kuhbauer, Stranzl, Herzog (Haas 71), Flogel, Vastic, Mayrleb.
*Referee:* Ovrebo (Norway).

**Alicante, 24 March 2001, 29,900**

**Spain (2) 5** *(Helguera 20, Mendieta 36, 81, Hierro 54 (pen), Raul 68)*

**Liechtenstein (0) 0**

*Spain:* Casillas; Manuel Pablo, Hierro, Nadal, Romero, Mendieta, Guardiola (Sergio 82), Helguera (Baraja 67), Raul, Moreno, Munitis (Etxeberria 39).
*Liechtenstein:* Jehle; Ospelt, Zech, Hefti, Hasler D, Gigon, Beck (Buchel 88), Martin Stocklasa (Gerster 90), Telser, Michael Stocklasa, Frick M.
*Referee:* Ceferin (Slovakia).

**Vienna, 28 March 2001, 21,000**

**Austria (2) 2** *(Baur 9, Herzog 41 (pen))*

**Israel (1) 1** *(Baur 6 (og))*

*Austria:* Wohlfahrt; Baur, Hiden, Prilasnig, Schopp, Kuhbauer, Herzog (Kitzbichler 90), Stranzl, Flogel, Vastic (Hortnagl 57), Mayrleb (Haas 63).
*Israel:* Davidovich; Benado (Mizrahi A 57), Talkar, Shelach (Brumer 46), Gershon, Banin (Tal 72), Keisi, Nimni, Berkovic, Zeituni, Benayoun.
*Referee:* Trentalange (Italy).

**Vaduz, 28 March 2001, 3400**

**Liechtenstein (0) 0**
**Bosnia (1) 3** *(Barbarez 10, 72, Hota 89)*

*Liechtenstein:* Jehle; Ospelt, Hefti, Zech, Martin Stocklasa, Hasler D, Beck (Nigg 73), Telser M (Buchel 46), Michael Stocklasa (Rither 90), Gigon, Frick M.
*Bosnia:* Piplica; Varesanovic, Hujdurovic, Hibic, Music, Salihamidzic, Akrapovic, Sabic (Rivzic 90), Barbarez, Bolic (Topic 63), Baljic (Hota 81).
*Referee:* Sipailo (Latvia).

**Innsbruck, 25 April 2001, 13,000**

**Austria (1) 2** *(Glieder 43, Flogel 75)*
**Liechtenstein (0) 0**

*Austria:* Manninger; Prilasnig, Baur, Hiden, Kitzbichler (Ibertsberger 75), Kirchler, Flogel, Herzog (Wallner 89), Hortnagel, Vastic (Weissenberger 61), Glieder.
*Liechtenstein:* Jehle; Ospelt (Buchel 66), Hefti, Ritter, Zech, Beck T (D'Elia 52), Hasler, Telser, Martin Stocklasa, Gigon, Frick (Michael Stocklasa 81).
*Referee:* Malcolm (Northern Ireland).

**Vaduz, 2 June 2001, 1500**

**Liechtenstein (0) 0**
**Israel (3) 3** *(Revivo 2, Tal 6, Nimni 17)*

*Liechtenstein:* Jehle; Ospelt J, Ritter, Zech, Martin Stocklasa, Michael Stocklasa, Beck T (Gerster 85), Buchel (Beck M 71), Telser, Gigon, Hasler D (D'Elia 65).
*Israel:* Davidovich; Ben-Dayan (Badir 65), Talkar, Benado, Gershon, Keisi, Zeituni, Revivo (Mizrahi A 74), Nimni, Berkovic (Banayoun 65), Tal.
*Referee:* Isaksen (Faeroes).

**Oviedo, 2 June 2001, 27,000**

**Spain (1) 4** *(Hierro 26, Javi Moreno 75, Raul 88, Diego Tristan 90)*
**Bosnia (1) 1** *(Beslija 41)*

*Spain:* Canizares; Manuel Pablo, Hierro, Nadal, Juanfran, Mendieta (Munitis 55), Guardiola, Helguera (Valeron 46), Luis Enrique (Javi Moreno 75), Raul, Diego Tristan.
*Bosnia:* Piplica; Hujdurovic, Varesanovic, Hibic, Beslija, Akrapovic, Mujcin, Barbarez, Music (Hota 70), Baljic, Bolic (Demirovic 82).
*Referee:* Olsen (Norway).

**Tel Aviv, 6 June 2001, 25,000**

**Israel (1) 1** *(Revivo 4)*
**Spain (0) 1** *(Raul 63)*

*Israel:* Davidovich (Awat 46); Brumer G, Talkar, Benado, Gershon, Keisi, Zeituni, Berkovic (Benayoun 87), Tal, Nimni, Revivo (Banin 70).
*Spain:* Canizares; Manuel Pablo, Hierro, Nadal, Sergi, Valeron (Helguera 76), Guardiola (Diego Tristan 60), Baraja, Luis Enrique (Puyol 83), Javi Moreno, Raul.
*Referee:* Frisk (Sweden).

| Group 7 Table | P | W | D | L | F | A | Pts |
|---|---|---|---|---|---|---|---|
| Spain | 6 | 4 | 2 | 0 | 15 | 4 | 14 |
| Austria | 5 | 3 | 2 | 0 | 7 | 3 | 11 |
| Israel | 6 | 3 | 1 | 2 | 10 | 6 | 10 |
| Bosnia | 5 | 1 | 1 | 3 | 7 | 10 | 4 |
| Liechtenstein | 6 | 0 | 0 | 6 | 0 | 16 | 0 |

## GROUP 8

**Budapest, 3 September 2000, 57,000**

**Hungary (1) 2** *(Horvath 29, 78)*
**Italy (1) 2** *(Inzaghi F 26, 35)*

*Hungary:* Kiraly; Korsos G, Sebok V, Matyus (Peto 46), Feher C, Halmai, Hamar (Lendvai 89), Illes, Lisztes, Horvath, Tokoli (Dombi 75).
*Italy:* Toldo; Cannavaro, Nesta, Iuliano, Zambrotta, Albertini, Maldini, Fiore (Gattuso 80), Totti, Inzaghi F, Del Piero (Delvecchio 73).
*Referee:* Barber (England).

**Bucharest, 3 September 2000, 4500**

**Romania (0) 1** *(Ganea 89)*

**Lithuania (0) 0**

*Romania:* Stelea; Ciobotariu (Mutu 49), Filipescu, Belodedici, Contra (Petre 58), Petrescu, Munteanu C, Munteanu D, Chivu, Moldovan (Ganea 67), Vladoiu.

*Lithuania:* Padimanskas; Kanchelskis, Gleveckas, Skerla, Zvrigzdauskas, Zutautas, Danilevicius, Semberas, Preiksaitis (Butkus 46), Maciulevicius (Mikalajunas 46), Fomenka (Radzius 80).

*Referee:* Norman (Sweden).

**Milan, 7 October 2000, 54,297**

**Italy (3) 3** *(Inzaghi F 13, Delvecchio 17, Totti 42)*

**Romania (0) 0**

*Italy:* Toldo; Cannavaro, Nesta, Maldini, Di Livio, Albertini, Fiore (Pancaro 55), Coco, Totti, Inzaghi F (Del Piero 81), Delvecchio (Gattuso 71).

*Romania:* Stelea; Petrescu (Contra 46), Belodedici, Filipescu, Chivu, Rosu, Galca, Lupescu, Munteanu D (Munteanu C 62), Moldovan (Mutu 58), Ganea.

*Referee:* Wegereef (Holland).

**Vilnius, 7 October 2000, 5000**

**Lithuania (0) 0**

**Georgia (2) 4** *(Ketsbaia 18, 33, Kinkladze 46, Arveladze A 84)*

*Lithuania:* Padimanskas; Skerla, Gleveckas, Graziunas (Maciulevicius 39), Zutautas, Butkus, Zemberas, Ivanauskas (Morinas 46), Fomenka (Zvinglas 55), Danilevicius, Jankauskas.

*Georgia:* Gvaramadze; Silagadze, Kobiashvili, Rekhviashvili, Khizanishvili, Kaladze, Nemsadze, Kavelashvili, Ketsbaia (Menteshashvili 67), Kinkladze (Jamarauli 70), Demetradze (Arveladze A 56).

*Referee:* Wojcik (Poland).

**Ancona, 11 October 2000, 26,000**

**Italy (0) 2** *(Del Piero 47 (pen), 88 (pen))*

**Georgia (0) 0**

*Italy:* Toldo; Cannavaro, Nesta, Bertotto, Di Livio, Albertini, Fiore (Pancaro 76), Coco, Totti (Montella 83), Delvecchio (Gattuso 52), Del Piero.

*Georgia:* Gvaramadze; Silagadze, Kobiashvili, Rekhviashvili, Khizanishvili, Kaladze, Nemsadze, Kavelashvili, Ketsbaia (Menteshashvili 68), Kinkladze (Jamarauli 61), Arveladze A (Demetradze 61).

*Referee:* Nilsson (Sweden).

**Vilnius, 11 October 2000, 2000**

**Lithuania (0) 1** *(Butkus 71)*

**Hungary (2) 6** *(Illes 24, Feher M 36, 62, 72, Horvath 66, Lisztes 84 (pen))*

*Lithuania:* Padimanskas; Skerla, Gleveckas, Radzius, Kanchelskis (Graziunas 69), Butkus, Semberas, Ivanauskas, Preiksaitis, Morinas (Danilevicius 83), Jankauskas.

*Hungary:* Kiraly; Korsos G (Bodnar 84), Feher C (Juhar 78), Matyus (Dombi 73), Sebok V, Peto, Feher M, Lisztes, Horvath, Illes, Hamar.

*Referee:* Erdemir (Turkey).

**Budapest, 24 March 2001, 20,000**

**Hungary (0) 1** *(Sebok V 70 (pen))*

**Lithuania (0) 1** *(Razanauskas 74)*

*Hungary:* Kiraly; Feher C, Sebok V, Korsos G, Juhar, Miriuta, Dardai, Illes, Hamar (Egressy 46), Horvath, Feher M (Dombi 64).

*Lithuania:* Stauce; Skarbalius, Dedura (Dziaukstas 35), Gleveckas, Zvirgzdauskas, Razanauskas (Joksas 89), Zutautas, Poskus, Morinas, Semberas, Mikalajunas.

*Referee:* Melnischuk (Ukraine).

**Bucharest, 24 March 2001, 24,500**

**Romania (0) 0**

**Italy (2) 2** *(Inzaghi F 29, 32)*

*Romania:* Stelea; Rodai (Serban 71), Filipescu, Prodan, Contra, Codrea, Galca (Munteanu C 59), Munteanu D, Moldovan (Ganea 78), Niculae, Ilie A.
*Italy:* Buffon; Cannavaro, Nesta, Maldini, Zambrotta, Tommasi, Fiore (Tacchinardi 62), Albertini, Pancaro, Inzaghi F (Montella 86), Del Piero.
*Referee:* Fandel (Germany).

**Tbilisi, 28 March 2001, 27,000**

**Georgia (0) 0**

**Romania (0) 2** *(Munteanu D 68, Contra 81)*

*Georgia:* Gvaramadze; Silagadze, Rekhviashvili (Lashvili 73), Kobiashvili, Khizanishvili, Nemsadze, Kaladze, Kavelashvili (Dzhavashia 52), Ketsbaia (Kemoklidze 62), Arveladze S, Kinkladze.
*Romania:* Stelea; Contra, Filipescu, Prodan, Radoi (Galca 58), Munteanu C, Codrea, Chivu, Munteanu D, Moldovan (Stoica 82), Ilie A (Niculae 21).
*Referee:* Pedersen (Norway).

**Trieste, 28 March 2001, 14,800**

**Italy (1) 4** *(Inzaghi F 17, 63, Del Piero 49, 79)*

**Lithuania (0) 0**

*Italy:* Buffon; Cannavaro, Nesta, Maldini, Zambrotta, Tomassi, Tacchinardi, Coco, Totti (Fiore 75), Inzaghi F (Montella 69), Del Piero (Di Livio 83).
*Lithuania:* Stauce; Zvrigzdauskas, Skarbalius, Joksas, Dziaukstas, Razanauskas (Danilevicius 50), Zutautas, Semberas, Morinas, Poskus (Stankevicius 77), Mikalajunas (Jankauskas 65).
*Referee:* Shmolik (Belarus).

**Tbilisi, 2 June 2001, 28,000**

**Georgia (0) 1** *(Gakhokidze 80)*

**Italy (1) 2** *(Delvecchio 45, Totti 66)*

*Georgia:* Zoidze; Silagadze, Abramidze, Kaladze, Kobiashvili, Khizanishvili (Gakhokidze 79), Nemsadze (Arveladze S 80), Rekhviashvili, Menteshashvili (Arveladze A 60), Ketsbaia, Kavelashvili.
*Italy:* Buffon; Cannavaro, Nesta (Materazzi 74), Maldini, Zambrotta, Tommasi, Tacchinardi, Pancaro, Totti, Delvecchio (Montella 79), Del Piero (Di Livio 58).
*Referee:* Iturralde (Spain).

**Bucharest, 2 June 2001, 22,000**

**Romania (1) 2** *(Niculae 4, 54)*

**Hungary (0) 0**

*Romania:* Stelea; Contra, Radoi (Prodan 64), Ciobotariu, Chivu, Munteanu D, Codrea, Ilie A (Munteanu C 75), Dumitru, Moldovan (Ganea 72), Niculae.
*Hungary:* Kiraly; Feher C, Korsos G, Sebok V, Matyus, Peto, Lisztes, Sowunmi (Kabat 73), Dardai, Horvath (Korsos A 46), Hamar (Dombi 41).
*Referee:* Poulat (France).

**Budapest, 6 June 2001, 10,000**

**Hungary (2) 4** *(Matyus 40, Sebok V 45 (pen), Korsos A 55, 62)*

**Georgia (0) 1** *(Kobiashvili 77)*

*Hungary:* Kiraly; Korsos G, Sebok V, Peto, Matyus, Lisztes (Lendvai 80), Halmai (Dardai 70), Illes, Korsos A (Dombi 77), Horvath, Kabat.
*Georgia:* Zoidze; Abramidze, Kaladze (Todua 67), Arveladze A, Kobiashvili, Nemsadze (Kemoklidze 67), Rekhviashvili, Khizanishvili, Ketsbaia, Arveladze S, Kavelashvili (Kinkladze 53).
*Referee:* Strampe (Germany).

**Kaunas, 6 June 2001, 7000**
**Lithuania (0) 1** *(Fomenko 87)*
**Romania (1) 2** *(Ilie A 31, Moldovan 49)*
*Lithuania:* Stauce; Zvirgzdauskas, Dedura, Skarbalius, Graziunas, Morinas (Fomenko 46), Zutautas, Mikalajunas, Semberas, Razanauskas (Butkis 73), Poskus.
*Romania:* Stelea; Contra (Ganea 54), Radoi, Filipescu, Chivu, Dumutru, Niculae, Kodrea, Munteanu D, Moldovan (Prodan 57), Ilie A (Mutu 63).
*Referee:* Stredak (Slovakia).

| Group 8 Table | P | W | D | L | F | A | Pts |
|---|---|---|---|---|---|---|---|
| Italy | 6 | 5 | 1 | 0 | 15 | 3 | 16 |
| Romania | 6 | 4 | 0 | 2 | 7 | 6 | 12 |
| Hungary | 5 | 2 | 2 | 1 | 13 | 7 | 8 |
| Georgia | 5 | 1 | 0 | 4 | 6 | 10 | 3 |
| Lithuania | 6 | 0 | 1 | 5 | 3 | 18 | 1 |

## GROUP 9

**Helsinki, 2 September 2000, 10,770**
**Finland (1) 2** *(Litmanen 45, Riihilahti 67)*
**Albania (0) 1** *(Murati 63)*
*Finland:* Jaaskelainen; Saarinen, Turpeinen, Hyypia, Tihinen, Nurmela (Johansson 57), Koppinen (Riihilahti 46), Valakari, Forssell (Ylonen 77), Litmanen, Kolkka.
*Albania:* Strakosha; Lala, Cipi, Xhumba, Vata R, Murati (Bushi 76), Haxhi, Muka (Skela 46), Kola, Rraklli, Tare.
*Referee:* Timmink (Holland).

**Hamburg, 2 September 2000, 48,500**
**Germany (1) 2** *(Deisler 17, Ouzounidis 75 (og))*
**Greece (0) 0**
*Germany:* Kahn; Rehmer, Nowotny, Heinrich (Linke 46), Deisler, Ramelow, Ballack, Bode, Scholl, Jancker, Zickler (Rink 71).
*Greece:* Eleftheropoulos; Ouzounidis, Goumas, Amanatidis, Georgatos, Poursanidis (Choutos 66), Mavrogenidis (Patsatzoglou 23), Tsartas, Zagorakis, Limberopoulos, Georgiadis (Lakis 76).
*Referee:* Nieto (Spain).

**Wembley, 7 October 2000, 76,377**
**England (0) 0**
**Germany (1) 1** *(Hamann 14)*
*England:* Seaman; Neville G (Dyer 46), Le Saux (Barry 77), Southgate, Keown, Adams, Beckham (Parlour 82), Barmby, Andy Cole, Owen, Scholes.
*Germany:* Kahn; Rehmer, Nowotny, Linke, Deisler, Ramelow, Hamann, Ballack, Bode (Ziege 86), Scholl, Bierhoff.
*Referee:* Braschi (Italy).

**Athens, 7 October 2000, 14,800**
**Greece (0) 1** *(Limberopoulos 59)*
**Finland (0) 0**
*Greece:* Nikopolidis; Georgatos (Venetidis 72), Patsatzoglou, Amanatidis, Ouzounidis, Karagounis (Lakis 76), Zagorakis, Basinas, Limberopoulos, Georgiadis, Choutos (Antzas 83).
*Finland:* Niemi; Reini, Helin, Hyypia, Tihinen, Nurmela, Jarkko (Kottila 81), Valakari, Johansson (Kuqi 64), Litmanen, Kolkka (Forssell 46).
*Referee:* Collina (Italy).

**Tirana, 11 October 2000, 11,000**
**Albania (0) 2** *(Bushi 50, Fakaj 90)*
**Greece (0) 0**
*Albania:* Strakosha; Muka, Cipi, Xhumba (Fakaj 75), Vata R, Vata F (Basha 78), Skela, Kola, Haxhi, Bushi, Tare (Bogdani 86).
*Greece:* Nikopolidis; Bassinas, Venetidis (Kyparissis 72), Patsatzoglou, Ouzounidis, Zagorakis (Lakis 70), Georgiadis, Karagounis, Choutos, Limberopoulos, Zikos (Poursanidis 70).
*Referee:* Pedersen (Norway).

**Helsinki, 11 October 2000, 36,210**

**Finland (0) 0**

**England (0) 0**

*Finland:* Niemi; Helin (Reini 36), Tihinen, Hyypia, Saarinen (Salli 66), Nurmela, Wiss, Valakari, Johansson, Litmanen, Forssell (Kuqi 76).
*England:* Seaman; Neville P, Barry (Brown 69), Southgate, Keown, Wise, Parlour, Scholes, Andy Cole, Sheringham (McManaman 69), Heskey.
*Referee:* Sars (France).

**Liverpool, 24 March 2001, 44,262**

**England (1) 2** *(Owen 43, Beckham 50)*

**Finland (1) 1** *(Neville G 26 (og))*

*England:* Seaman; Neville G, Powell, Ferdinand R, Campbell, Scholes, Beckham, Gerrard, Andy Cole (Fowler 82), Owen (Butt 90), McManaman (Heskey 72).
*Finland:* Niemi; Pasanen, Hyypia, Tihinen, Ylonen (Helin 89), Wiss, Nurmela (Forssell 63), Riihilahti, Litmanen, Kolka (Kuqi 63), Johansson.
*Referee:* Ivanov (Russia).

**Leverkusen, 24 March 2001, 22,500**

**Germany (0) 2** *(Deisler 50, Klose 88)*

**Albania (0) 1** *(Kola 65)*

*Germany:* Kahn; Nowotny, Worns, Jeremies, Ramelow, Deisler, Hamann (Rehmer 46), Bode, Neuville (Klose 73), Bierhoff (Jancker 46), Scholl.
*Albania:* Strakosha; Cipi, Vata R, Lala, Xhumba, Vata F (Skela 79), Hasi (Fakaj 86), Kola, Murati, Tare, Bushi (Rraklli 67).
*Referee:* Cesari (Italy).

**Tirana, 28 March 2001, 18,000**

**Albania (0) 1** *(Rraklli 90)*

**England (0) 3** *(Owen 73, Scholes 85, Andy Cole 90)*

*Albania:* Strakosha; Cipi, Fakaj, Lala, Xhumba, Hasi, Vata F (Rraklli 88), Kola (Beqaj 82), Bellai (Skela 90), Tare, Bushi.
*England:* Seaman; Neville G, Ashley Cole, Ferdinand R, Campbell (Brown 29), Butt, Beckham, Scholes, Andy Cole, Owen (Sheringham 84), McManaman (Heskey 46).
*Referee:* Hamer (Luxembourg).

**Athens, 28 March 2001, 53,000**

**Greece (2) 2** *(Haristeas 21, Georgiadis 44)*

**Germany (2) 4** *(Rehmer 6, Ballack 25 (pen), Klose 82, Bode 90)*

*Greece:* Eleftheropoulos; Patsatzoglou, Kostoulas (Mavrogenidis 35), Goumas, Basinas, Karagounis (Niniadis 75), Zagorakis, Georgiadis, Haristeas (Alexandris 84), Liberopoulos, Georgatos.
*Germany:* Kahn; Worns, Nowotny, Heinrich, Rehmer, Jeremies (Ramelow 90), Deisler, Ballack, Ziege, Jancker (Bode 78), Neuville (Klose 67).
*Referee:* Pereira (Portugal).

**Helsinki, 2 June 2001, 35,774**

**Finland (2) 2** *(Forssell 28, 43)*

**Germany (0) 2** *(Ballack 68 (pen), Jancker 72)*

*Finland:* Niemi; Pasanen, Nylund, Hyypia, Tihinen, Nurmela (Johansson 71), Riihilati (Gronlund 80), Litmanen, Rantanen, Forssell, Kolka (Kuqi 85).
*Germany:* Kahn; Rehmer, Nowotny, Linke, Asamoah, Ramelow, Ballack, Bode (Ziege 69), Ricken, Neuville (Klose 62), Jancker (Bierhoff 83).
*Referee:* Jol (Holland).

**Iraklion, 2 June 2001, 4000**

**Greece (1) 1** *(Mahlas 72)*

**Albania (0) 0**

*Greece:* Nikopolidis; Patsatzoglou, Dabizas, Venetidis, Zagorakis, Goumas, Ouzounidis, Georgiadis (Basinas 85), Karagounis, Alexandris (Charisteas 62), Liberopoulos (Mahlas 46).

*Albania:* Strakosha; Cipi, Vata R, Lala, Xhumba, Hasi, Haxhi (Skela 76), Bushi, Vata F, Murati, Tare (Bogdani 71).
*Referee:* Levnikov (Russia).

**Tirana, 6 June 2001, 18,000**

**Albania (0) 0**
**Germany (1) 2** *(Rehmer 28, Ballack 68)*

*Albania:* Strakosha; Vata R, Cipi, Xhumba (Bellai 46), Lala, Vata F, Murati, Hasi (Skela 61), Haxhi (Muka 81), Bushi, Tare.
*Germany:* Kahn; Rehmer, Nowotny, Linke, Asamoah (Ricken 70), Ramelow, Ballack, Ziege, Deisler (Baumann 84), Jancker, Neuville (Zickler 46).
*Referee:* Veissiere (France).

**Athens, 6 June 2001, 46,000**

**Greece (0) 0**
**England (0) 2** *(Scholes 64, Beckham 87)*

*Greece:* Nikopolidis; Goumas, Ouzounidis, Dabizas, Mavrogenidis (Giannakopoulos 70), Basinas, Zagorakis, Fyssas, Karagounis (Limberopoulos 24), Mahlas (Alexandris 64), Vryzas.
*England:* Seaman; Neville P, Ashley Cole, Gerrard, Keown, Ferdinand, Beckham, Scholes (Butt 88), Fowler (Smith 79), Owen, Heskey (McManaman 74).
*Referee:* Pedersen (Norway).

| Group 9 Table | P | W | D | L | F | A | Pts |
|---|---|---|---|---|---|---|---|
| Germany | 6 | 5 | 1 | 0 | 13 | 5 | 16 |
| England | 5 | 3 | 1 | 1 | 7 | 3 | 10 |
| Greece | 6 | 2 | 0 | 4 | 4 | 10 | 6 |
| Finland | 5 | 1 | 2 | 2 | 5 | 6 | 5 |
| Albania | 6 | 1 | 0 | 5 | 5 | 10 | 3 |

# SOUTH AMERICA

(Members 10, Entries 10)

Four or five teams qualify including play-offs with Oceania.

**Bogota, 28 March 2000, 42,493**

**Colombia (0) 0**
**Brazil (0) 0**

*Colombia:* Cordoba O; Bermudez, Cordoba I, Yepes, Martinez, Viveros, Dinas, Rincon, Oviedo (Moreno 74), Angel, Ricard (Maturana 60).
*Brazil:* Dida; Evanilson, Aldair, Antonio Carlos, Roberto Carlos, Emerson, Ze Roberto, Vampeta, Alex (Ricardinho 46), Elber (Ronaldinho Gaucho 68), Jardel (Edilson 46).
*Referee:* Mendez (Uruguay).

**Buenos Aires, 29 March 2000, 50,000**

**Argentina (2) 4** *(Batistuta 9, Veron 33, 71 (pen), Lopez C 88)*
**Chile (1) 1** *(Tello 29)*

*Argentina:* Bonano; Pochettino, Roberto Ayala, Samuel, Zanetti, Simeone, Kily Gonzalez, Veron, Ortega (Sensini 85), Batistuta (Crespo 89), Lopez C (Lopez G 89).
*Chile:* Ramirez; Maldonado, Reyes, Margas, Contreras, Ormazabal (Aros 83), Acuna, Tello, Pizarro (Sierra 70), Zamorano, Salas.
*Referee:* Moreno (Ecuador).

**Quito, 29 March 2000, 50,000**

**Ecuador (1) 2** *(Delgado 17, Aguinaga 51)*
**Venezuela (0) 0**

*Ecuador:* Cevallos; De La Cruz, Jacome, Montano, Cagua (Ayovi 49), Blandon, Tenorio (Chala 73), Aguinaga, Obregon, Graziani (Porozo 38), Delgado.
*Venezuela:* Dudamel; Alvarez, Villafraz (Mea Vitali 62), Becerra, Rey, Urdaneta, Rojas (Arango 55), Bidoglio, Jesus Vera, Casseres, Garcia (Ochoa 55).
*Referee:* Gamboa (Chile).

**Lima, 29 March 2000, 45,000**

**Peru (0) 2** *(Solano 55 (pen), Palacios 60)*
**Paraguay (0) 0**

*Peru:* Ibanez; Soto J, Rebosio, Pajuelo, Percy Olivares (Huaman 72), Jayo, Palacios, Del Solar, Solano, Pizarro (Ciurlizza 81), Zuniga (Holsen 59).
*Paraguay:* Chilavert; Arce, Ayala, Gamarra, Caniza, Enciso (Struway 68), Paredes (Gavilan 74), Acuna, Jorge Campos, Santa Cruz, Cardozo (Gonzales 68).
*Referee:* Elizondo (Argentina).

**Montevideo, 29 March 2000, 55,000**

**Uruguay (1) 1** *(Pablo Garcia 26)*
**Bolivia (0) 0**

*Uruguay:* Carini; Mendez, Diego Lopez, Montero, Rodriguez, Coelho, Pablo Garcia, O'Neill, Cedres (Olivera 58), Alonso (Zalayeta 76), Recoba (Poyet 89).
*Bolivia:* Fernandez; Rivera, Pena, Oscar Sanchez, Sandy (Rimba 75), Ivan Castillo, Cristaldo, Justiniano, Erwin Sanchez, Gutierrez (Suarez 59), Moreno (Botero 70).
*Referee:* Pereira (Argentina).

**La Paz, 26 April 2000, 20,000**

**Bolivia (1) 1** *(Sanchez 16)*
**Colombia (1) 1** *(Castillo 32)*

*Bolivia:* Fernandez; Ribeiro, Pena, Sandy (Rimba 33), Ivan Castillo, Cristaldo, Soria, Gutierrez (Galindo 63), Sanchez, Antelo (Suarez 46), Moreno.
*Colombia:* Cordoba O; Cordoba I, Bermudez, Yepes, Viveros, Martinez (Cardona 79), Dinas, Oviedo (Ortegon 82), Rincon, Ricard (Angel 74), Castillo.
*Referee:* Arana (Peru).

**Sao Paulo, 26 April 2000, 65,000**

**Brazil (2) 3** *(Rivaldo 18, 51, Antonio Carlos 42)*
**Ecuador (1) 2** *(Aguinaga 12, De La Cruz 76)*

*Brazil:* Dida; Cafu, Antonio Carlos, Aldair, Roberto Carlos (Athirson 68), Cesar Sampaio, Vampeta, Rivaldo, Ze Roberto (Alex 68), Amoroso, Edilson.
*Ecuador:* Cevallos; De La Cruz, Poroso, Capurro, Hurtado I, Tenorio, Obregon, Aguinaga (Ayovi 40) (Kaviedes 88), Blandon, Delgado, Graziani (Hurtado E 66).
*Referee:* Cervantes (Colombia).

**Santiago, 26 April 2000, 45,000**

**Chile (1) 1** *(Margas 42)*
**Peru (1) 1** *(Jayo 38)*

*Chile:* Tapia N; Vargas, Reyes, Margas, Maldonado (Nunez C 70), Acuna, Rojas (Nunez R 70), Pizarro (Sierra 58), Tello, Zamorano, Salas.
*Peru:* Ibanez; Soto, Rebosio, Pajuelo, Olivares, Jayo, Soria (Zuniga 58), Del Solar, Palacios, Solano, Pizarro.
*Referee:* Rojas (Paraguay).

**Asuncion, 26 April 2000, 15,000**

**Paraguay (1) 1** *(Ayala 35)*
**Uruguay (0) 0**

*Paraguay:* Chilavert; Espinola, Gamarra, Ayala, Caniza, Quintana (Gonzalez 59), Paredes, Struway, Acuna (Enciso 68), Santa Cruz, Baez (Benitez 82).
*Uruguay:* Carini; Mendez, Ramos, Lembo, Tabare Silva (Guigou 67), Coelho, Pablo Garcia, De Los Santos, Poyet (Olivera 63), Recoba, Dario Silva (Alvez 75).
*Referee:* Sanchez (Argentina).

**Maracaibo, 26 April 2000, 27,000**

**Venezuela (0) 0**
**Argentina (2) 4** *(Ayala 7, Ortega 23, 76, Crespo 88)*

*Venezuela:* Dudamel; Rojas, Rey, Villafraz (Luzardo 46), Gonzalez, Mea, Bidoglio, Urdaneta, Vera, Juan Garcia (Martinez 70), Castellin.

*Argentina:* Bonano; Ayala, Samuel, Sensini, Kily Gonzalez, Zanetti, Simeone, Veron, Ortega (Gallardo 78), Lopez C (Lopez G 68), Crespo.
*Referee:* Amarilla (Paraguay).

**Ascunion, 3 June 2000, 22,000**

**Paraguay (2) 3** *(Toledo 11, Brizuela 43, 64)*
**Ecuador (0) 1** *(Graziani 87)*

*Paraguay:* Chilavert; Caniza, Gamarra, Ayala, Toledo, Paredes, Struway (Enciso 82), Quintana, Acuna, Brizuela (Gonzalez 76), Baez (Benitez 66).
*Ecuador:* Ceballos; De La Cruz, Poroso (Kaviedes 66), Montano, Capurro, Blandon, Hurtado I, Tenorio (Chala 46), Aguinaga, Juarez, Delgado (Graziani 61).
*Referee:* Gallesio (Uruguay).

**Montevideo, 3 June 2000, 60,000**

**Uruguay (2) 2** *(Dario Silva 35, Montero 41)*
**Chile (1) 1** *(Zamorano 39 (pen))*

*Uruguay:* Carini; Mendez, Montero, Lembo, Rodriguez, Pablo Garcia, Guigou, O'Neill, Olivera, Recoba (Giacomazzi 89), Dario Silva (Alonso 81).
*Chile:* Tapia N; Rojas, Vargas, Reyes, Olarra (Rozental 68), Galdames, Estay (Nunez C 87), Vallaseca, Tello, Zamorano, Salas.
*Referee:* Troxler (Paraguay).

**Buenos Aires, 4 June 2000, 50,669**

**Argentina (0) 1** *(Lopez G 83)*
**Bolivia (0) 0**

*Argentina:* Bonano; Sensini, Ayala, Samuel, Zanetti (Lopez G 71), Simeone, Kily Gonzalez, Veron, Ortega (Aimar 83), Batistuta, Lopez C (Almeyda 88).
*Bolivia:* Fernandez; Carballo, Pena, Sandy, Ivan Castillo, Ribera, Baldivieso, Cristaldo, Etcheverry (Galindo 78), Suarez (Garcia 65), Botero (Coimbra 83).
*Referee:* Rezende (Brazil).

**Bogota, 4 June 2000, 22,000**

**Colombia (2) 3** *(Viveros 27, Cordoba I 42 (pen), Valenciano 88)*
**Venezuela (0) 0**

*Colombia:* Cordoba O; Martinez, Cordoba I, Ortegon, Bedoya, Rincon, Bolano, Oviedo (Candelo 70), Viveros (Dinas 77), Angel, Castillo (Valenciano 81).
*Venezuela:* Dudamel; Filosa, Gonzalez, Alvarado, Echenausi, Arango, Vera (Farias 55), Mea, Bidoglio (De Ornelas 67), Castellin (Savarese 52), Moran.
*Referee:* Godoi (Brazil).

**Lima, 4 June 2000, 45,000**

**Peru (0) 0**
**Brazil (1) 1** *(Antonio Carlos 35)*

*Peru:* Miranda; Soto, Pajuelo, Olivares, Rebosio, Palacios, Del Solar, Jayo (Searrano 49), Zuniga, Holsen (Ciurlizza 46), Huaman (Maldonado 46).
*Brazil:* Dida; Cafu, Roberto Carlos, Aldair, Antonio Carlos, Cesar Sampaio, Alex (Denilson 65), Emerson, Edmundo, Rivaldo (Vampeta 90), Franca (Ze Roberto 77).
*Referee:* Giminez (Argentina).

**Rio, 28 June 2000, 47,715**

**Brazil (0) 1** *(Rivaldo 85 (pen))*
**Uruguay (1) 1** *(Dario Silva 6)*

*Brazil:* Dida; Cafu, Antonio Carlos, Aldair, Roberto Carlos, Emerson, Vampeta (Ze Roberto 70), Rivaldo, Ronaldinho (Guilherme 46), Franca, Savio (Alex 46).
*Uruguay:* Carini; Tais, Lembo, Montero, Rodriguez, Garcia, O'Neill (Giacomazzi 82), Recoba (Coelho 59), Olivera, Dario Silva, Guigou.
*Referee:* Acosta (Colombia).

271

**Santiago, 28 June 2000, 60,000**

**Chile (2) 3** *(Caniza 18 (og), Salas 35, Zamorano 78 (pen))*

**Paraguay (0) 1** *(Cardoso 71)*

*Chile:* Tapia N; Fuentes, Rojas, Reyes, Villarroel, Maldonado, Tello, Estay, Nunez (Pizarro 68), Zamorano, Salas.
*Paraguay:* Chilavert; Caniza, Zelaya, Ayala, Toledo, Quintana, Struway (Gonzalez 46), Paredes, Acuna (Gabilan 37), Santa Cruz (Cardoso 76), Brizuela.
*Referee:* Martin (Argentina).

**Bogota, 28 June 2000, 50,000**

**Colombia (1) 1** *(Oviedo 27)*

**Argentina (2) 3** *(Batistuta 24, 45, Crespo 75)*

*Colombia:* Cordoba O; Cordoba I, Bermudez, Yepes, Bolano, Oviedo, Rincon, Dinas (Grisales 51) (Candelo 85), Viveros, Angel, Castillo (Valenciano 58).
*Argentina:* Bonano; Sensini, Ayala, Samuel, Zanetti, Veron (Lopez G 70), Kily Gonzalez, Ortega (Sorin 86), Simeone, Lopez C, Batistuta (Crespo 70).
*Referee:* Larrionda (Uruguay).

**San Cristobal, 28 June 2000, 7000**

**Venezuela (2) 4** *(Vitali 23, Moran 38, Savaresse 61, Tortolero 67 (pen))*

**Bolivia (0) 2** *(Moreno 49, Baldivieso 59)*

*Venezuela:* Angelucci; Gimenez, Gonzalez, Alvarado, Martinez, Urdaneta (Echenausi 90), Farias, Tortolero, Vitali, Moran, Savaresse (Galan 72).
*Bolivia:* Fernandez; Ribera, Etcheverry (Galindo 80), Pena, Sandy, Ivan Castillo, Cristaldo, Sanchez, Baldivieso, Suarez (Garcia 73), Botero (Moreno 46).
*Referee:* Zambrano (Ecuador).

**Quito, 29 June 2000, 45,000**

**Ecuador (1) 2** *(Chala 16, Hurtado E 51)*

**Peru (0) 1** *(Pajuelo 76)*

*Ecuador:* Cevallos; De La Cruz, Hurtado I, Poroso, Ayovi, Abregon, Blandon, Chala, Aguinaga (Burbano 70), Delgado (Graziani 70), Hurtado E (Kaviedes 74).
*Peru:* Ibanez; Soto, Rebosio, Pajuelo, Olivares (Zuniga 75), Solano, Del Solar, Jayo (Ciurlizza 75), Serrano (Soria 20), Palacios, Pizarro.
*Referee:* Simon (Brazil).

**Asuncion, 18 July 2000, 36,000**

**Paraguay (1) 2** *(Paredes 6, Campos 84)*

**Brazil (0) 1** *(Rivaldo 75)*

*Paraguay:* Chilavert; Sarabia, Ayala, Gamarra, Caniza, Gavilan (Quintana 72), Enciso, Acuna, Paredes (Campos 63), Cardozo, Santa Cruz (Avalos 79).
*Brazil:* Dida; Cafu, Roque Junior, Edmilson, Roberto Carlos, Cesar Sampaio, Flavio Conceicao, Rivaldo, Ze Roberto (Marques 70), Djalminha (Vampeta 60), Franca (Guilherme 46).
*Referee:* Larrionda (Uruguay).

**Montevideo, 18 July 2000, 62,000**

**Uruguay (1) 3** *(Olivera 29, 89, Rodriguez 52)*

**Venezuela (1) 1** *(Noriega 23)*

*Uruguay:* Carini; Tais, Lembo, Montero (Ramos 81), Rodriguez, O'Neill, Garcia, Olivera, Guigou, Recoba, Dario Silva.
*Venezuela:* Angelucci; Jimenez, Gonzalez, Alvarado, Martinez, Urdaneta, Farias (Vera 63), Tortolero, Vitali, Savarese (Perez 73), Noriega (Alvarez 63).
*Referee:* Ortube (Bolivia).

**Buenos Aires, 19 July 2000, 50,000**

**Argentina (1) 2** *(Crespo 23, Lopez C 50)*

**Ecuador (0) 0**

*Argentina:* Bonano; Ayala, Sensini, Samuel, Zanetti, Simeone, Kily Gonzalez (Sorin 76), Veron, Ortega, Crespo (Aimar 76), Lopez C.

*Ecuador:* Cevallos; De La Cruz, Hurtado I, Poroso, Ayovi, Tenorio E, Blandon, Obregon, Aguinaga (Chala 88), Hurtado E, Delgado (Graziani 73).
*Referee:* Bello (Uruguay).

**La Paz, 19 July 2000, 35,000**

**Bolivia (0) 1** *(Suarez 84)*

**Chile (0) 0**

*Bolivia:* Soria; Ribeiro, Pena, Sandy, Carballo (Rimba 38), Galindo (Colque 65), Garcia, Calustro, Baldivieso, Botero (Gutierrez 55), Suarez.
*Chile:* Tapia N; Villarroel, Reyes, Fuentes, Rojas R, Maldonado, Cornejo, Tello, Estay (Tapia H 69), Zamorano (Navia 84), Rozental (Pizarro 69).
*Referee:* Toro (Colombia).

**Lima, 19 July 2000, 45,000**

**Peru (0) 0**

**Colombia (0) 1** *(Angel 48)*

*Peru:* Vegas; Jorge Soto (Carlos Flores 57), Rebosio, Pajuela, Olivares, Jayo, Solano, Del Solar, Palacios, Pizarro, Zuniga (Lobaton 57).
*Colombia:* Cordoba O; Martinez, Cordoba I, Yepes, Bolano, Candelo (Hernandez 66), Viveros, Luis Garcia (Dinas 77), Bedoya, Angel, Valenciano (Restrepo 46).
*Referee:* Sanchez (Chile).

**Quito, 25 July 2000, 43,000**

**Ecuador (0) 0**

**Colombia (0) 0**

*Ecuador:* Cevallos; De La Cruz, Hurtado I, Poroso, Ayovi, Obregon, Chala (Herrera 68), Aguinaga, Hurtado Ed, Graziani (Delgado 68), Hurtado E (Juarez 76).
*Colombia:* Cordoba O; Martinez, Cordoba I, Yepes, Bolano, Candelo (Hurtado 46), Viveros, Luis Garcia, Bedoya, Moreno (Restrepo 46), Preciado (Dinas 78).
*Referee:* Aquino (Paraguay).

**San Cristobal, 25 July 2000, 23,000**

**Venezuela (0) 0**

**Chile (0) 2** *(Tapia H 69, Zamorano 90)*

*Venezuela:* Angelucci; Alvarez, Alvarado, Ornella, Martinez, Vitali (Urango 72), Farias, Tortolero, Urdaneta, Moran, Savarese (Perez 85).
*Chile:* Tapia N; Fuentes, Rojas R, Margas, Rojas F, Maldonado, Tello, Estay (Cornejo 72), Sierra (Pizarro 65), Zamorano, Rozental (Tapia H 46).
*Referee:* Baldassi (Argentina).

**Sao Paulo, 26 July 2000, 80,000**

**Brazil (2) 3** *(Alex 4, Vampeta 44, 50)*

**Argentina (1) 1** *(Almeyda 45)*

*Brazil:* Dida; Evanilson, Antonio Carlos, Roque Junior, Roberto Carlos, Emerson, Vampeta, Ze Roberto (Marques 60), Alex (Cesar Sampaio 75), Ronaldinho, Rivaldo.
*Argentina:* Bonano; Sensini, Ayala, Samuel, Zanetti (Almeyda 39), Simeone, Veron, Kily Gonzalez (Sorin 73), Ortega (Lopez G 73), Crespo, Lopez C.
*Referee:* Mendez (Uruguay).

**Montevideo, 26 July 2000, 60,000**

**Uruguay (0) 0**

**Peru (0) 0**

*Uruguay:* Carini; Tais, Lembo, Montero, Rodriguez, O'Neill, Garcia, Olivera, Guigou (Zalayeta 56), Recoba (Coelho 69), Magallanes.
*Peru:* Vegas; Jorge Soto, Rebosio, Pajuelo, Olivares, Serrano (Torres 81), Jayo, Ciurlizza, Solano, Palacios, Pizarro.
*Referee:* Godoi (Brazil).

273

**La Paz, 27 July 2000, 40,000**

**Bolivia (0) 0**

**Paraguay (0) 0**

*Bolivia:* Soria; Ribeiro, Pena, Sandy, Rimba (Paz Garcia 38), Calustro (Cardenas 71), Garcia, Colque, Baldivieso, Botero (Gutierrez 52), Suarez.
*Paraguay:* Chilavert; Caballero, Ayala, Gamarra, Da Silva, Esteche, Enciso, Acuna (Ortiz 85), Paredes (Struway 55), Gonzalez (Benitez 58), Cardozo.
*Referee:* Almeida (Brazil).

**Santiago, 15 August 2000, 65,000**

**Chile (2) 3** *(Estay 26, Zamorano 43, Salas 75)*

**Brazil (0) 0**

*Chile:* Tapia N; Fuentes, Rojas R, Reyes, Villaseca (Pizarro 13), Rojas F, Galdames, Tello, Estay, Salas (Villarroel 80), Zamorano (Tapia H 87).
*Brazil:* Dida; Evanilson, Edmilson, Antonio Carlos, Roberto Carlos, Assuncao (Djalminha 46), Emerson, Alex (Marques 61), Ricardinho, Rivaldo, Amoroso (Luizao 46).
*Referee:* Gonzalez (Paraguay).

**Bogota, 15 August 2000, 32,000**

**Colombia (0) 1** *(Castillo 72)*

**Uruguay (0) 0**

*Colombia:* Cordoba O; Martinez, Cordoba I, Yepes, Bedoya, Luis Garcia (Morantes 64), Bolano, Oviedo, Aristizabal (Dinas 88), Angel, Castillo (Bezerra 90).
*Uruguay:* Carini; Mendez, Lembo, Sorondo, Rodriguez, O'Neill, Garcia, Guigou (Giacomazzi 56), Olivera, Otero (Ruben Da Silva 51), Dario Silva (Magallanes 85).
*Referee:* Gimenez (Argentina).

**Buenos Aires, 16 August 2000, 55,000**

**Argentina (0) 1** *(Aimar 67)*

**Paraguay (0) 1** *(Acuna 61)*

*Argentina:* Bonano; Sensini, Ayala, Samuel, Veron, Simeone (Vivas 71), Kily Gonzalez (Sorin 46), Aimar, Ortega, Crespo, Lopez C (Saviola 75).
*Paraguay:* Tavarelli; Sarabia, Ayala, Gamarra, Caniza, Esteche, Struway (Quintana 78), Enciso, Acuna, Santa Cruz (Campos 55), Cardozo (Benitez 85).
*Referee:* Pereira (Brazil).

**Quito, 16 August 2000, 25,000**

**Ecuador (1) 2** *(Delgado 17, 59)*

**Bolivia (0) 0**

*Ecuador:* Ibarra; De La Cruz, Hurtado I, Poroso, Ayovi (Reascos 46), Obregon, Chala, Aguinaga, Ed Hurtado, Graziani (Juarez 62), Delgado.
*Bolivia:* Soria; Paz, Ribera, Sandy, Arana, Garcia, Calustro (Vaca 76), Castillo S, Galindo, Baldivieso (Coimbra 46), Suarez.
*Referee:* Solorzano (Venezuela).

**Lima, 16 August 2000, 40,000**

**Peru (0) 1** *(Palacios 70)*

**Venezuela (0) 0**

*Peru:* Ibanez; Jorge Soto, Jose Soto, Pajuelo (Marengo 40), Soria, Solano (Maldonado 67), Jayo, Palacios, Del Solar, Pizarro, Zuniga.
*Venezuela:* Angelucci; Jimenez, Alvarado, Gonzalez, Martinez, Vitali (De Ornelas 82), Farias, Tortolero, Urdaneta, Moran, Savarese (Caceres 71).
*Referee:* Moreno (Ecuador).

**Santiago, 2 September 2000, 60,000**

**Chile (0) 0**

**Colombia (0) 1** *(Castillo 66)*

*Chile:* Tapia N; Fuentes, Rojas R (Contreras 30), Reyes, Rojas F, Galdames, Tello, Estay (Cornejo 63), Sierra (Valencia 63), Zamorano, Salas.

*Colombia:* Cordoba O; Martinez, Cordoba I, Yepes, Mazziri, Luis Garcia (Viveros 46), Bolano, Grisales, Aristizabal, Castillo (Dinas 86), Angel.
*Referee:* Gallesio (Uruguay).

**Asuncion, 2 September 2000, 40,000**

**Paraguay (3) 3** *(Gonzalez 30, Cardozo 35, Paredes 44)*
**Venezuela (0) 0**

*Paraguay:* Chilavert; Gamarra (Gonzalez 21), Sarabia, Arce, Ayala, Caniza, Acuna, Enciso, Paredes, Santa Cruz (Caceres 87), Cardozo (Campos 77).
*Venezuela:* Angelucci; Jimenez, Alvarado, Gonzalez (Rey 46), Martinez, Vitali (Garcia 55), Tortolero (Paez 67), Farias, Urdaneta, De Ornelas, Moran.
*Referee:* Arandia (Bolivia).

**Rio de Janeiro, 3 September 2000, 55,000**

**Brazil (1) 5** *(Romario 11 (pen), 78, 81, Rivaldo 46, Marques 88)*
**Bolivia (0) 0**

*Brazil:* Rogerio; Cafu, Antonio Carlos, Emerson Carvalho, Junior (Athirson 64), Vampeta, Flavio Conceicao, Alex (Juninho 59), Rivaldo, Ronaldinho (Marques 80), Romario.
*Bolivia:* Soria; Ribeiro, Sanchez O, Paz Garcia (Gutierrez 73), Sandy, Garcia, Baldivieso, Alvarez, Cristaldo, Etcheverry, Moreno (Lider Paz 28).
*Referee:* Aros (Chile).

**Lima, 3 September 2000, 45,000**

**Peru (0) 1** *(Samuel 69 (og))*
**Argentina (2) 2** *(Crespo 25, Veron 38)*

*Peru:* Vegas; Solano, Pajuelo, Jose Soto, Olivares (Zuniga 78), Pereda, Jayo, Del Solar (Tempone 46), Palacios, Mendoza, Pizarro.
*Argentina:* Bonano; Sensini, Ayala, Samuel, Veron, Simeone (Vivas 80), Sorin, Aimar, Ortega (Husain 73), Crespo, Lopez C (Lopez G 84).
*Referee:* Ruiz (Colombia).

**Montevideo, 3 September 2000, 60,000**

**Uruguay (2) 4** *(Magallanes 14, Dario Silva 37, Olivera 55, Cedras 87)*
**Ecuador (0) 0**

*Uruguay:* Carini; Tais, Lembo, Rodriguez, Mendez, Garcia (Fleurquin 68), Cedras, Olivera, Guigou, Dario Silva (Recoba 73), Magallanes (Abreu 63).
*Ecuador:* Cevallos; De La Cruz, Poroso, Hurtado I, Capurro, Tenorio (Burbano 56), Obregon, Chala (Candelario 46), Aguinaga, Juarez, Graziani.
*Referee:* Jimenez (Colombia).

**Bogota, 7 October 2000, 46,000**

**Colombia (0) 0**
**Paraguay (1) 2** *(Santa Cruz 4, Chilavert 90)*

*Colombia:* Cordoba O; Cordoba I, Yepes, Mazziri (Grisales 46), Martinez, Dinas, Bolano, Oviedo (Morantes 59), Aristizabal, Bonilla (Castro 67), Angel.
*Paraguay:* Chilavert; Arce, Sarabia, Ayala, Da Silva, Struway, Quintana (Alvarengo 66), Paredes, Acuna, Santa Cruz (Yegros 66) (Esteche 90), Cardozo.
*Referee:* Gallesio (Uruguay).

**Buenos Aires, 8 October 2000, 60,000**

**Argentina (2) 2** *(Gallardo 28, Batistuta 42)*
**Uruguay (0) 1** *(Magallanes 48)*

*Argentina:* Burgos; Vivas, Ayala, Samuel, Sorin, Simeone, Husain, Gallardo (Delgado 80), Kily Gonzalez, Lopez C (Lopez G 73), Batistuta.
*Uruguay:* Carini; Garcia, Tais, Lembo, Rodriguez, Sorondo, Cedres (Regueiro 65), Olivera, Guigou, Recoba (Abreu 70), Magallanes (Alonso 87).
*Referee:* Rezende (Brazil).

**La Paz, 8 October 2000, 25,000**

**Bolivia (1) 1** *(Suarez 4)*

**Peru (0) 0**

*Bolivia:* Soria; Ribeiro, Sanchez O, Pena, Paz Garcia, Colque, Calustro, Garcia, Vaca (Gutierrez 66), Lider Paz (Moreno 46), Suarez (Galindo 80).
*Peru:* Ibanez; Zeballos, Rebosio, Pajuelo, Soria, Jayo, Solano (Carmona 46), Bernales, Palacios, Pizarro (Lobaton 57), Zuniga (Alba 57).
*Referee:* Guevara (Ecuador).

**Quito, 8 October 2000, 45,000**

**Ecuador (0) 1** *(Delgado 76)*

**Chile (0) 0**

*Ecuador:* Cevallos; De La Cruz, Espinoza, Hurtado I, Guerron, Obregon, Tenorio (Fernandez 63), Aguinaga, Chala (Sanchez 59), Kaviedes (Ordonez 76), Delgado.
*Chile:* Tapia N; Alvarez, Contreras, Vargas, Olarra, Pizarro (Valencia 85), Maldonado, Tello, Estay (Rozental 78), Navia (Nunez 46), Zamorano.
*Referee:* Rendon (Colombia).

**San Cristobal, 8 October 2000, 20,000**

**Venezuela (0) 0**

**Brazil (5) 6** *(Euller 21, Paulista 29, Romario 31, 36 (pen), 39, 64)*

*Venezuela:* Angelucci; Gonzalez, Martinez, Rey, Alvarado, Farias, De Ornelas, Jimenez, Echenausi (Arango 46), Moran (Paz 66), Garcia (Savarese 77).
*Brazil:* Rogerio; Cafu, Antonio Carlos, Cleber, Silvinho, Donizete, Vampeta, Juninho (Ze Roberto 66), Paulista (Ricardinho 81), Euller (Marquez 70), Romario.
*Referee:* Aquino (Paraguay).

**La Paz, 15 November 2000, 29,112**

**Bolivia (0) 0**

**Uruguay (0) 0**

*Bolivia:* Soria; Sanchez O, Sandy, Paz Garcia (Vaca 80), Ribeiro, Calustro, Garcia, Sanchez E, Colque, Menacho, Suarez (Lider Paz 66).
*Uruguay:* Carini; Varela, Lembo, Sorondo, Rodriguez, Garcia, Romero, Coelho (Callejas 64), Regueiro, Magallanes (Dario Silva 56), Franco (Cedres 76).
*Referee:* Elizondo (Argentina).

**Sao Paulo, 15 November 2000, 56,213**

**Brazil (0) 1** *(Roque Junior 90)*

**Colombia (0) 0**

*Brazil:* Rogerio; Cafu, Lucio, Roque Junior, Junior, Cesar Sampaio, Vampeta (Permanbucano 71), Rivaldo, Paulista, Franca (Adriano 79), Edmundo (Marques 67).
*Colombia:* Calero; Martinez, Dinas, Yepes, Bedoya, Bolano, Serna, Viveros, Aristizabal, Angel (Bonilla 67), Castillo.
*Referee:* Larrionda (Uruguay).

**Santiago, 15 November 2000, 56,529**

**Chile (0) 0**

**Argentina (1) 2** *(Ortega 26, Husain 90)*

*Chile:* Tapia N; Reyes, Rojas R, Contreras (Navia 79), Galdames, Maldonado (Villarroel 74), Rojas F, Pizarro, Estay (Valencia 64), Salas, Zamorano.
*Argentina:* Burgos (Bonano 74); Vivas, Ayala, Samuel, Almeyda, Husain, Sorin, Veron (Aimar 52), Kily Gonzalez, Cruz (Berizzo 84), Ortega.
*Referee:* Amarilla (Paraguay).

**Asuncion, 15 November 2000, 30,000**

**Paraguay (3) 5** *(Santa Cruz 15, Del Solar 25 (og), Cardozo 44, Paredes 65, Chilavert 84 (pen))*

**Peru (0) 1** *(Garcia 78)*

*Paraguay:* Chilavert; Arce, Sarabia, Ayala, Caniza, Paredes, Enciso, Acuna, Cardozo (Brizuela 76), Alvarenga (Campos 86), Santa Cruz (Ferreira 70).

*Peru:* Ibanez; Zevallos (Garcia 60), Pajuelo (Velasquez 16), Rebosio, Soria, Bernales, Del Solar, Pereda (Lobaton 46), Palacios, Muchotrigo, Alva.
*Referee:* Gimenez (Argentina).

**Maracaibo, 15 November 2000, 11,000**

**Venezuela (0) 1** *(Arango 65)*

**Ecuador (2) 2** *(Kaviedes 4, Sanchez 21)*

*Venezuela:* Angelucci; De Ornelas, Alvarado, Gonzalez, Vallenilla (Perez J 86), Vitali (Luzardo 46), Farias, Urdaneta, Arango, Castellin (Perez G 64), Garcia.
*Ecuador:* Ceballos; De La Cruz, Poroso, Hurtado I, Guerron, Burbano, Chala, Mendez (Zamora 72), Sanchez, Kaviedes (Fernandez 67), Delgado.
*Referee:* Betancourt (Peru).

**Bogota, 27 March 2001, 45,000**

**Colombia (0) 2** *(Angel 53, 73 (pen))*

**Bolivia (0) 0**

*Colombia:* Cordoba O; Gonzalez, Dinas, Yepes, Bedoya, Serna, Grisales, Aristizabal (Viveros 46), Asprilla, Bonilla (Ferreira 46), Angel (Quintana 84).
*Bolivia:* Fernandez; Ribeiro, Pena, Sandy, Arana, Colque, Justiniano, Rojas, Vaca, Coimbra (Lider Paz 79), Cardenas (Suarez 57).
*Referee:* Souza (Brazil).

**Lima, 27 March 2001, 45,000**

**Peru (0) 3** *(Maestri 54, Mendoza 73, Pizarro 81)*

**Chile (0) 1** *(Navia 62)*

*Peru:* Miranda; Solano, Rebosio, Pajuela, Olivares (Hidalgo 42), Jayo, Palacios, Del Solar (Maestri 46), Muchotrigo (Ciurlizza 75), Mendoza, Pizarro.
*Chile:* Tapia N; Vargas, Rojas, Ramirez, Ponce, Parraguez (Mirosevic 25) (Reyes 65), Maldonado, Osorio, Tello (Tapia H 46), Zamorano, Navia.
*Referee:* Sanchez (Argentina).

**Buenos Aires, 28 March 2001, 32,000**

**Argentina (2) 5** *(Crespo 13, Sorin 31, Veron 51, Gallardo 60, Samuel 85)*

**Venezuela (0) 0**

*Argentina:* Burgos; Vivas, Pochettino, Samuel, Sorin (Zanetti 61), Simeone, Veron, Ortega (Lopez G 70), Kily Gonzalez, Gallardo (Lopez C 76), Crespo.
*Venezuela:* Dudamel; Alvarado, Rey, Vallenilla (Perez R 86), De Ornelas (Perez G 51), Urdaneta, Vera J (Vitali 74), Vera L, Rojas (Martinez 65), Noriega, Paez.
*Referee:* Zamora (Peru).

**Quito, 28 March 2001, 40,800**

**Ecuador (0) 1** *(Delgado 49)*

**Brazil (0) 0**

*Ecuador:* Cevallos; De La Cruz, Hurtado I, Poroso, Gueron, Tenorio (Sanchez W 69), Burbano, Mendes, Aguinaga, Kaviedes (Obregon 90), Delgado.
*Brazil:* Rogerio; Belletti, Lucio, Roque Junior, Silvinho (Cesar 59), Emerson, Vampeta, Paulista, Rivaldo (Luizao 64), Ronaldinho (Euller 46), Romario.
*Referee:* Rizo (Mexico).

**Montevideo, 28 March 2001, 60,000**

**Uruguay (0) 0**

**Paraguay (0) 1** *(Alvarenga 64)*

*Uruguay:* Carini; Varela, Sorondo, Montero, Rodriguez, De Los Santos, Fleurquin (O'Neill 69), Olivera, Guigou (Pandiani 49), Dario Silva (Zalayeta 76), Recoba.
*Paraguay:* Chilavert; Ayala, Gamarra, Sarabia, Quintana (Alvarenga 46), Struway, Paredes, Acuna, Caniza, Caceres (Cuevas 83), Cardozo (Esteche 88).
*Referee:* Aranda (Spain).

277

**Santiago, 24 April 2001, 51,000**

**Chile (0) 0**

**Uruguay (1) 1** *(Diaz 12 (og))*

*Chile:* Vargas S; Diaz (Valdes 57), Reyes, Contreras, Tello, Maldonado, Galdames, Osorio (Gomez 74), Estay, Tapia H (Nunez 46), Zamorano.
*Uruguay:* Carini; Mendez, Lembo, Sorondo, Rodriguez, Garcia, Guigou, Olivera (Regueiro 84), Magallanes, Recoba (Romero 72), Dario Silva (Varela 76).
*Referee:* Elizondo (Argentina).

**Quito, 24 April 2001, 40,000**

**Ecuador (1) 2** *(Delgado 45, 54)*

**Paraguay (1) 1** *(Cardozo 26)*

*Ecuador:* Cevallos; De la Cruz, Hurtado I, Poroso, Guerron, Burbano (Espinoza 46), Chala (Sanchez 68), Aguinaga (Mendez 46), Tenorio, Kaviedes, Delgado.
*Paraguay:* Tavarelli; Espinola, Gamarra, Ayala, Da Silva (Quintana 73), Esteche, Struway, Paredes, Alvarenga (Gonzalez 62), Quevas (Brizuela 46), Cardozo.
*Referee:* Sanchez (Argentina).

**San Cristobal, 24 April 2001, 35,000**

**Venezuela (1) 2** *(Rondon 22, Arango 81)*

**Colombia (0) 2** *(Bedoya 83, Bonilla 88)*

*Venezuela:* Dudamel; Valenilla, Vitali RM, Rey, Rojas J, Vera L, Arango, Vitali MM (De Ornelas 61), Urdaneta (Paez 70), Savarese (Vera J 55), Rondon.
*Colombia:* Calera; Martinez, Bermudez, Dinas, Bedoya, Grisales, Viveros (Quintana 70), Bolano (Gonzalez 61), Restrepo (Ferreira 46), Bonilla, Angel.
*Referee:* Alvaredo (Chile).

**La Paz, 25 April 2001, 35,000**

**Bolivia (1) 3** *(Lider Paz 41, Colque 55, Botero 81)*

**Argentina (1) 3** *(Crespo 44, 89, Sorin 90)*

*Bolivia:* Fernandez; Ribeiro, Pena, Garcia, Sandy, Colque, Justiniano, Baldivieso, Vaca (Rojas R 59), Lider Paz (Cardenas 74), Botero.
*Argentina:* Burgos; Vivas, Ayala, Samuel, Zanetti (Ortega 62), Simeone, Veron, Sorin, Aimar (Gallardo 57), Crespo, Lopez G (Lopez C 46).
*Referee:* Ruiz (Colombia).

**Sao Paolo, 25 April 2001, 40,000**

**Brazil (0) 1** *(Romario 66)*

**Peru (0) 1** *(Pajuelo 79)*

*Brazil:* Rogerio; Alessandro, Edmilson, Lucio, Cesar, Leomar, Vampeta (Washington 80), Ricardinho (Mineiro 77), Marcelinho Carioca (Paulista 46), Ewerthon, Romario.
*Peru:* Miranda; Rebosio, Pajuelo, Hidalgo, Solano, Jayo, Ciurlizza, Muchotrigo (Mendoza 46), Palacios, Olivares (Tempone 75), Maestri (Pizarro 46).
*Referee:* Al-Zaid (Saudi Arabia).

**Asuncion, 2 June 2001, 45,000**

**Paraguay (0) 1** *(Paredes 90)*

**Chile (0) 0**

*Paraguay:* Chilavert; Arce, Sarabia, Ayala, Caniza, Quintana (Amarilla 77), Paredes, Acuna, Alvarenga, Santa Cruz (Cuevas 66), Brizuela (Julio Gonzalez 46).
*Chile:* Vargas S; Reyes, Vargas J, Contreras, Pozo, Osorio, Villaseca, Perez (Valenzuela 78), Tello, Montecinos, Navia (Neira 63).
*Referee:* Badilla (Costa Rica).

**Lima, 2 June 2001, 60,000**

**Peru (1) 1** *(Pizarro 2)*

**Ecuador (1) 2** *(Mendez 12, Delgado 90)*

*Peru:* Miranda; Pajuelo, Rebosio, Olivares (Hidalgo 62), Solano, Jayo, Palacios, Ciurlizza, Mendoza (Muchotrigo 74), Pizarro, Maestri (Roberto Silva 46).
*Ecuador:* Cevallos; De la Cruz, Hurtado I, Espinosa, Guerron, Obregon (Guagua 71), Tenorio E, Chala (Aguinaga 86), Mendez, Delgado, Kaviedes (Fernandez 81).
*Referee:* Marrufo (Mexico).

278

**Buenos Aires, 3 June 2001, 40,000**

**Argentina (3) 3** *(Kily Gonzalez 23, Lopez C 35, Crespo 38)*

**Colombia (0) 0**

*Argentina:* Cavallero; Vivas, Ayala, Pochettino, Simeone, Zanetti, Veron (Gallardo 84), Zorin, Kily Gonzalez, Lopez C (Aimar 82), Crespo (Delgado 48).
*Colombia:* Cordoba O; Martinez, Dinas, Yepes, Bedoya, Serna, Rincon, Viveros (Gonzalez 46), Asprilla F (Ferreira 46), Castillo, Angel (Murillo 77).
*Referee:* Sanchez (Chile).

**La Paz, 3 June 2001, 20,000**

**Bolivia (3) 5** *(Baldivieso 32, 68, Botero 35, 51, Justiniano 38)*

**Venezuela (0) 0**

*Bolivia:* Arias; Raldes, Pena J, Paz Garcia, Ribeiro (Rojas R 85), Justiniano, Baldivieso (Pena D 90), Calustro, Colque, Lider Paz (Cardenas 73), Botero.
*Venezuela:* Sanhouse; Valenilla, Rey, Vitali RM, Martinez, Vera, Vitali MM, Arango (Casseres 67), Gonzalez (Alvarado 54), Paez (Jimenez 42), Rondon.
*Referee:* Carpio (Ecuador).

**Montevideo, 1 July 2001, 62,000**

**Uruguay (1) 1** *(Magallanes 32 (pen))*

**Brazil (0) 0**

*Uruguay:* Carini; Mendez, Montero, Sorondo, Guigou, De Los Santos, Garcia, Romero, Recoba (Lembo 76), Dario Silva (Reguero 62), Magallanes.
*Brazil:* Marcos; Cris, Antonio Carlos (Jardel 76), Roque Junior, Cafu, Emerson, Rivaldo, Paulista, Roberto Carlos, Elber (Euller 60), Romario.
*Referee:* Dallas (Scotland)

| Table | P | W | D | L | F | A | Pts |
|---|---|---|---|---|---|---|---|
| Argentina | 13 | 10 | 2 | 1 | 33 | 11 | 32 |
| Paraguay | 13 | 8 | 2 | 3 | 21 | 11 | 26 |
| Ecuador | 13 | 8 | 1 | 4 | 17 | 16 | 25 |
| Brazil | 13 | 6 | 3 | 4 | 22 | 12 | 21 |
| Uruguay | 13 | 6 | 3 | 4 | 14 | 8 | 21 |
| Colombia | 13 | 5 | 4 | 4 | 12 | 12 | 19 |
| Bolivia | 13 | 3 | 4 | 6 | 13 | 19 | 13 |
| Peru | 13 | 3 | 3 | 7 | 12 | 17 | 12 |
| Chile | 13 | 3 | 1 | 9 | 12 | 18 | 10 |
| Venezuela | 13 | 1 | 1 | 11 | 8 | 40 | 4 |

## OCEANIA (Members 11, Entries 10)

Either one or no team qualifies, play-offs with South America.

**Group 1:** Australia, Tonga, Fiji, American Samoa, Samoa.

Samoa 0, Tonga 1; Fiji 13, American Samoa 0; Tonga 0, Australia 22; American Samoa 0, Samoa 8; Samoa 1, Fiji 6; Australia 31, American Samoa 0; Fiji 0, Australia 2; American Samoa 0, Tonga 5; Australia 11, Samoa 0; Tonga 1, Fiji 8.

**Group 2:** New Zealand, Tahiti, Solomon Islands, Vanuatu, Cook Islands.

Vanuatu 1, Tahiti 6; Solomon Islands 9, Cook Islands 1; Tahiti 0, New Zealand 5; Cook Islands 1, Vanuatu 8; Vanuatu 2, Soloman Islands 7; New Zealand 2, Cook Islands 0; Soloman Islands 1, New Zealand 5; Cook Islands 0, Tahiti 6; New Zealand 7, Vanuatu 0; Tahiti 2, Soloman Islands 0.

**Final Round, First Leg:** New Zealand 0, Australia 2.

**Final Round, Second Leg:** Australia 4, New Zealand 1.

## ASIA (Members 44, Entries 42)

Four or five teams qualify, including hosts South Korea and Japan plus play-offs with UEFA.

**Group 1:** Laos, Oman, Philippines, Syria.

Oman 12, Laos 0; Syria 12, Philippines 0; Philippines 1, Syria 5; Laos 0, Oman 7; Oman 7, Philippines 0; Syria 11, Laos 0; Philippines 0, Oman 2; Laos 0, Syria 9; Syria 3, Oman 3; Laos 2, Philippines 0; Oman 2, Syria 0; Philippines 1, Laos 1.

**Group 2:** Guam, Iran, Tajikistan.
Iran 19, Guam 0; Tajikistan 16, Guam 0; Iran 2, Tajikistan 0.
*(all ties played in Iran)*
**Group 3:** Hong Kong, Malaysia, Palestine, Qatar.
Qatar 5, Malaysia 1; Hong Kong 1, Palestine 1; Palestine 1, Qatar 2; Malaysia 2, Hong Kong 0; Palestine 1, Malaysia 0; Qatar 2, Hong Kong 0; Palestine 1, Hong Kong 0; Malaysia 0, Qatar 0; Qatar 2, Palestine 1; Hong Kong 2, Malaysia 1; Hong Kong 0, Qatar 3; Malaysia 4, Palestine 3.
**Group 4:** Bahrain, Kuwait, Kyrgyzstan, Singapore.
Bahrain 1, Kuwait 2; Singapore 0, Kyrgyzstan 1; Bahrain 1, Kyrgyzstan 0; Kuwait 1, Singapore 1; Kyrgyzstan 0, Kuwait 3; Singapore 1, Bahrain 2; Kyrgyzstan 1, Bahrain 2; Singapore 0, Kuwait 1; Kuwait 2, Kyrgyzstan 0; Bahrain 2, Singapore 0; Kyrgyzstan 1, Singapore 1; Kuwait 0, Bahrain 1.
**Group 5:** Lebanon, Pakistan, Sri Lanka, Thailand.
Thailand 4, Sri Lanka 2; Lebanon 6, Pakistan 0; Thailand 3, Pakistan 0; Lebanon 4, Sri Lanka 0; Pakistan 3, Sri Lanka 1; Lebanon 1, Thailand 2; Pakistan 1, Lebanon 8; Sri Lanka 0, Thailand 0; Sri Lanka 0, Lebanon 5; Pakistan 0, Thailand 6; Sri Lanka 3, Pakistan 1; Thailand 1, Lebanon 2.
**Group 6:** Iraq, Kazakhstan, Macao, Nepal.
Nepal 0, Kazakhstan 6; Iraq 8, Macao 0; Kazakhstan 3, Macao 0; Nepal 1, Iraq 9; Nepal 4, Macao 3; Kazakhstan 1, Iraq 1; Kazakhstan 4, Nepal 0; Macao 0, Iraq 5; Macao 0, Kazakhstan 5; Iraq 4, Nepal 2; Macao 1, Nepal 6; Iraq 1, Kazakhstan 1.
**Group 7:** Uzbekistan, Jordan, Turkmenistan, Taiwan.
Turkmenistan 2, Jordan 0; Uzbekistan 7, Taiwan 0; Taiwan 0, Jordan 2; Uzbekistan 1, Turkmenistan 0; Taiwan 0, Turkmenistan 5; Uzbekistan 2, Jordan 2; Jordan 6, Taiwan 0; Turkmenistan 2, Uzbekistan 5; Taiwan 0, Uzbekistan 4; Jordan 1, Turkmenistan 2; Turkmenistan 1, Taiwan 0; Jordan 1, Uzbekistan 1.
**Group 8:** Brunei, India, UAE, Yemen.
Brunei 0, Yemen 5; India 1, UAE 0; Brunei 0, UAE 12; India 1, Yemen 1; UAE 1, India 0; Yemen 1, Brunei 0; Yemen 3, India 3; UAE 4, Brunei 0; Yemen 2, UAE 1; Brunei 0, India 1; UAE 3, Yemen 2; India 3, Brunei 0.
**Group 9:** Cambodia, China, Indonesia, Maldives.
Maldives 6, Cambodia 0; Indonesia 5, Maldives 0; Cambodia 1, Maldives 1; China 10, Maldives 1; Indonesia 6, Cambodia 0; Maldives 0, China 1; Cambodia 0, Indonesia 2; China 4, Maldives 0, Indonesia 2; China 5, Indonesia 1; China 3, Cambodia 1; Indonesia 0, China 2.

**Group 10:** Bangladesh, Mongolia, Saudi Arabia, Vietnam.
Vietnam 0, Bangladesh 0; Saudi Arabia 6, Mongolia 0; Mongolia 0, Vietnam 1; Bangladesh 0, Saudi Arabia 3; Mongolia 0, Bangladesh 3; Saudi Arabia 5, Vietnam 0; Mongolia 0, Saudi Arabia 6; Bangladesh 0, Vietnam 4; Mongolia 0, Saudi Arabia 6, Bangladesh 0; Bangladesh 2, Mongolia 2; Vietnam 0, Saudi Arabia 4.
**Second Round**
**Group A:** Saudi Arabia, Bahrain, Iraq, Thailand, Iran.
**Group B:** UAE, Uzbekistan, Qatar, Oman, China.

# CONCACAF

(Members 35, Entries 35)
Three teams qualify

*Caribbean Zone*
**First Round**
**Group 1:** Barbados 2, Grenada 2; Grenada 2, Barbados 3; Cuba 4, Cayman Islands 0; Cayman Islands 0, Cuba 0; St Lucia 1, Surinam 0; Surinam 1, St Lucia 0 (Surinam won 3-1 on penalties); Aruba 4, Puerto Rico 2; Puerto Rico 2, Aruba 2.
**Group 2:** St Vincent & Grenadines 9, US Virgin Islands 0; US Virgin Islands 1, St Vincent & Grenadines 5; British Virgin Islands 1, Bermuda 5; Bermuda 9, British Virgin Islands 0; St Kitts & Nevis 8, Turks & Caicos Islands 0; Turks & Caicos Islands 0, St Kitts & Nevis 6; Guyana suspended, Antigua and Barbuda w.o.
**Group 3:** Trinidad & Tobago 5, Netherlands Antilles 0; Netherlands Antilles 1, Trinidad & Tobago 1; Anguilla 1, Bahamas 3; Bahamas 2, Anguilla 1; Dominican Republic 3, Montserrat 0; Montserrat 1, Dominican Republic 3; Haiti 4, Dominica 0; Dominica 1, Haiti 3.

*Caribbean Zone*
**Second Round**
**Group 1:** Cuba 1, Surinam 0; Surinam 0, Cuba 0; Aruba 1, Barbados 3; Barbados 4, Aruba 0.
**Group 2:** St Vincent & Grenadines 1, St Kitts & Nevis 0; St Kitts & Nevis 1, St Vincent & the Grenadines 0; Antigua & Barbuda 1, Bermuda 0; Bermuda 1, Antigua & Barbuda 1.
**Group 3:** Trinidad & Tobago 3, Dominican Republic 0; Dominican Republic 0, Trinidad & Tobago 1; Haiti 9, Bahamas 0; Bahamas 0, Haiti 4.
*Caribbean Zone Finals*
**Group 1:** Cuba 1, Barbados 1, Barbados 0, Cuba 1 *(Barbados won 5-4 on penalties).*
**Group 2:** Antigua & Barbuda 2, St Vincent & the Grenadines 1; St Vincent & the Grenadines 4, Antigua & Barbuda 0.
**Group 3:** Trinidad & Tobago 3, Haiti 1; Haiti 1, Trinidad & Tobago 1.

*Central American Zone*
**Group A:** El Salvador 5, Belize 0; Belize 1, Guatemala 2; Guatemala 0, El Salvador 1; Belize 1, El Salvador 3; El Salvador 1, Guatemala 1; Guatemala 0, Belize 0.
**Group B:** Honduras 3, Nicaragua 0; Nicaragua 0, Panama 2; Panama 1, Honduras 0; Nicaragua 0, Honduras 1; Honduras 3, Panama 1; Panama 4, Nicaragua 0

*Inter zone round*
**Group 1:** Cuba 0, Canada 1; Canada 0, Cuba 0.
**Group 2:** Antigua & Barbuda 0, Guatemala 1; Guatemala 8, Antigua & Barbuda 1.
**Group 3:** Honduras 4, Haiti 0; Haiti 1, Honduras 3.

*Semi-Final Round*
Costa Rica, Jamaica, Mexico and USA qualified.

**Group C:** Canada, Mexico, Panama, Trinidad & Tobago.
Canada 0, Trinidad & Tobago 2; Panama 0, Mexico 1; Panama 0, Canada 0; Trinidad & Tobago 1, Mexico 0; Mexico 2, Canada 0; Trinidad & Tobago 6, Panama 0; Mexico 7, Panama 1; Trinidad & Tobago 4, Canada 0; Mexico 7, Trinidad & Tobago 0; Canada 1, Panama 0; Canada 0, Mexico 0; Panama 0, Trinidad & Tobago 1.
**Group D:** El Salvador, Honduras, Jamaica, St Vincent & the Grenadines.
El Salvador 2, Honduras 5; St Vincent & the Grenadines 0, Jamaica 1; El Salvador 7, St Vincent & the Grenadines 1; Jamaica 3, Honduras 1; Honduras 6, St Vincent & the Grenadines 0; Jamaica 1, El Salvador 0; Honduras 5, El Salvador 0; Jamaica 2, St Vincent & the Grenadines 0; Honduras 1, Jamaica 0; St Vincent & the Grenadines 1, El Salvador 2; St Vincent & the Grenadines 0, Honduras 7; El Salvador 2, Jamaica 0.
**Group E:** Barbados, Costa Rica, Guatemala, USA.
Barbados 0, Costa Rica 1; Guatemala 1, USA 1; Guatemala 2, Barbados 0; Costa Rica 2, USA 1; Costa Rica 2, Guatemala 1; USA 7, Barbados 0; Costa Rica 3, Barbados 0; USA 1, Guatemala 0; Barbados 1, Guatemala 3; USA 0, Costa Rica 0; Barbados 0, USA 4; Guatemala 2, Costa Rica 1.
**Play-Off:** Costa Rica 5, Guatemala 0.

**Final Round:** Costa Rica, Honduras, Jamaica, Mexico, Trinidad & Tobago, USA.
USA 2, Mexico 0; Jamaica 1, Trinidad & Tobago 0; Costa Rica 2, Honduras 2; Mexico 4, Jamaica 0; Costa Rica 3, Trinidad & Tobago 0; Honduras 1, USA 2; Jamaica 1, Honduras 1; Trinidad & Tobago 1, Mexico 1; USA 1, Costa Rica 0; Mexico 1, Costa Rica 2; Trinidad & Tobago 2, Honduras 4; Jamaica 0, USA 0; USA 2, Trinidad &

Tobago 0; Honduras 3, Mexico 1; Costa Rica 2, Jamaica 1; Trinidad & Tobago 1, Jamaica 2; Mexico 1, USA 0; Honduras 2, Costa Rica 3.

# AFRICA
(Members 52, Entries 50)
Five teams qualify

**First Round**
**Group A:** Mauritania 1, Tunisia 2; Tunisia 3, Mauritania 0; Guinea Bissau 0, Togo 0; Togo 3, Guinea Bissau 0; Benin 1, Senegal 1; Senegal 1, Benin 0; Cape Verde Islands 0, Algeria 0; Algeria 2, Cape Verde Islands 0; Gambia 0, Morocco 1; Morocco 2, Gambia 0.
**Group B:** Botswana 0, Zambia 1; Zambia 1, Botswana 0; Madagascar 0, Gabon 0; Gabon 1, Madagascar 0; Lesotho 0, South Africa 2; South Africa 1, Lesotho 0; Sudan 1, Mozambique 0; Mozambique 2, Sudan 1; Swaziland 0, Angola 1; Angola 7, Swaziland 1.
**Group C:** Sao Tome e Principe 2, Sierra Leone 0; Sierra Leone 4, Sao Tome e Principe 0; Central African Republic 0, Zimbabwe 1; Zimbabwe 3, Central African Republic 1; Equatorial Guinea 1, Congo 3; Congo 2, Equatorial Guinea 1; Libya 3, Mali 0; Mali 1, Libya 1; Rwanda 2, Ivory Coast 2; Ivory Coast 2, Rwanda 0.
**Group D:** Djibouti 1, Congo DR 1; Congo DR 9, Djibouti 1; Seychelles 1, Namibia 1; Namibia 3, Seychelles 0; Eritrea 0, Nigeria 0; Nigeria 4, Eritrea 0; Mauritius 0, Egypt 2; Egypt 4, Mauritius 2; Somalia 0, Cameroon 3; Cameroon 3, Somalia 0.
**Group E:** Malawi 2, Kenya 0; Kenya v Malawi abandoned 0-0 after 88 minutes; result stands; Tanzania 0, Ghana 1; Ghana 3, Tanzania 2; Uganda 4, Guinea 4; Guinea 3, Uganda 0; Chad 0, Liberia 1; Liberia 0, Chad 0; Ethiopia 0, Burkina Faso 1; Burkina Faso 3, Ethiopia 0.

**Second Round**
**Group A:** Angola, Cameroon, Libya, Togo, Zambia.
Angola 0, Zambia 1; Libya 0, Cameroon 3; Zambia 2, Togo 0; Cameroon 3, Angola 0; Angola 3, Libya 1; Togo 0, Cameroon 2; Libya 3, Togo 3; Cameroon 1, Zambia 0; Zambia 2, Libya 0; Togo 1, Angola 1; Zambia 1, Angola 1; Cameroon 1, Libya 0; Togo 3, Zambia 2; Angola 2, Cameroon 0; Libya 1, Angola 1; Cameroon 2, Togo 0.
**Group B:** Ghana, Liberia, Nigeria, Sierra Leone, Sudan.
Nigeria 2, Sierra Leone 0; Sudan 2, Liberia 0; Ghana 5, Sierra Leone 0; Liberia 2, Nigeria 1; Nigeria 3, Sudan 0; Ghana 1, Liberia 3; Sudan 1, Ghana 0; Liberia 1, Sierra Leone 0; Sierra Leone 0, Sudan 2; Ghana 0, Nigeria 0; Sierra Leone 1, Nigeria 0; Liberia 2, Sudan 0; Sierra Leone 1, Ghana 1; Nigeria 2, Liberia 0; Sudan 0, Nigeria 4; Liberia 1, Ghana 2.

**Group C:** Algeria, Egypt, Morocco, Namibia, Senegal.
Algeria 1, Senegal 1; Namibia 0, Morocco 0; Morocco 2, Algeria 1; Senegal 0, Egypt 0; Algeria 1, Namibia 0; Egypt 0, Morocco 0; Namibia 1, Egypt 1; Morocco 0, Senegal 0; Senegal 4, Namibia 0; Egypt 5, Algeria 2; Senegal 3, Algeria 0; Morocco 3, Namibia 0; Algeria 1, Morocco 2; Egypt 1, Senegal 0; Morocco 1, Egypt 0; Namibia 0, Algeria 4.
**Group D:** Congo, Congo DR, Ivory Coast, Madagascar, Tunisia.
Ivory Coast 2, Tunisia 2; Madagascar 3, Congo DR 0; Tunisia 1, Madagascar 0; Congo DR 2, Congo 0; Congo 1, Tunisia 2; Madagascar 1, Ivory Coast 3; Tunisia 6, Congo DR 0; Congo DR 1, Ivory Coast 2;

Congo DR 1, Madagascar 0; Ivory Coast 2, Congo 0; Congo 2, Madagascar 0; Madagascar 0, Tunisia 2; Congo 1, Congo DR 1; Tunisia 1, Ivory Coast 1; Tunisia 6, Cogo 0; Ivory Coast 6, Madagascar 0.
**Group E:** Burkina Faso, Guinea\*, Malawi, South Africa, Zimbabwe.
Malawi 1, Burkina Faso 1; Guinea 3, Zimbabwe 0; Burkina Faso 2, Guinea 3; Zimbabwe 0, South Africa 2 (abandoned 82 minutes; result stands); South Africa 1, Burkina Faso 0; Guinea 1, Malawi 1; Burkina Faso 1, Zimbabwe 2; Malawi 1, South Africa 2; Zimbabwe 2, Malawi 0; Burkina Faso 4, Malawi 2; South Africa 2, Zimbabwe 1; Burkina Faso 1, South Africa 1.
\**Guinea subsequently suspended.*

# REMAINING FIXTURES

### EUROPE

**Group 1**
01.09.01 Faeroes v Luxembourg
01.09.01 Switzerland v Yugoslavia
01.09.01 Slovenia v Russia
05.09.01 Yugoslavia v Slovenia
05.09.01 Faeroes v Russia
05.09.01 Luxembourg v Switzerland
06.10.01 Russia v Switzerland
06.10.01 Slovenia v Faeroes
06.10.01 Yugoslavia v Luxembourg

**Group 2**
15.08.01 Estonia v Cyprus
01.09.01 Republic of Ireland v Holland
01.09.01 Andorra v Portugal
05.09.01 Holland v Estonia
05.09.01 Cyprus v Portugal
06.10.01 Republic of Ireland v Cyprus
06.10.01 Holland v Andorra
06.10.01 Portugal v Estonia

**Group 3**
01.09.01 Denmark v Northern Ireland
01.09.01 Malta v Bulgaria
01.09.01 Iceland v Czech Republic

05.09.01 Northern Ireland v Iceland
05.09.01 Czech Republic v Malta
05.09.01 Bulgaria v Denmark
06.10.01 Czech Republic v Bulgaria
06.10.01 Malta v Northern Ireland
06.10.01 Denmark v Iceland

**Group 4**
01.09.01 Moldova v Azerbaijan
01.09.01 Slovakia v Turkey
01.09.01 Macedonia v Sweden
05.09.01 Turkey v Sweden
05.09.01 Azerbaijan v Macedonia
05.09.01 Slovakia v Moldova
07.10.01 Sweden v Azerbaijan
07.10.01 Moldova v Turkey
07.10.01 Macedonia v Slovakia

**Group 5**
01.09.01 Wales v Armenia
01.09.01 Belarus v Ukraine
01.09.01 Poland v Norway
04.09.01 Norway v Wales
04.09.01 Belarus v Poland
04.09.01 Ukraine v Armenia
06.10.01 Armenia v Norway
06.10.01 Poland v Ukraine

06.10.01 Wales v Belarus

**Group 6**
01.09.01 Scotland v Croatia
05.09.01 Belgium v Scotland
05.09.01 San Marino v Croatia
06.10.01 Scotland v Latvia
06.10.01 Croatia v Belgium

**Group 7**
01.09.01 Spain v Austria
01.09.01 Bosnia v Israel
05.09.01 Liechtenstein v Spain
05.09.01 Austria v Bosnia
07.10.01 Bosnia v Liechtenstein
07.10.01 Israel v Austria

**Group 8**
01.09.01 Lithuania v Italy
01.09.01 Georgia v Hungary
05.09.01 Georgia v Lithuania
05.09.01 Hungary v Romania
06.10.01 Romania v Georgia
06.10.01 Italy v Hungary

**Group 9**
01.09.01 Albania v Finland
01.09.01 Germany v England
05.09.01 Finland v Greece
05.09.01 England v Albania
06.10.01 Germany v Finland
06.10.01 England v Greece

### SOUTH AMERICA

14.08.01 Venezuela v Uruguay
14.08.01 Chile v Bolivia
15.08.01 Colombia v Peru
15.08.01 Brazil v Paraguay
15.08.01 Ecuador v Argentina
04.09.01 Peru v Uruguay
04.09.01 Chile v Venezuela
05.09.01 Argentina v Brazil
05.09.01 Colombia v Ecuador

05.09.01 Paraguay v Bolivia
06.10.01 Venezuela v Peru
06.10.01 Brazil v Chile
06.10.01 Paraguay v Argentina
06.10.01 Bolivia v Ecuador
06.10.01 Uruguay v Colombia
07.11.01 Venezuela v Paraguay
07.11.01 Colombia v Chile
07.11.01 Ecuador v Uruguay

07.11.01 Argentina v Peru
07.11.01 Bolivia v Brazil
14.11.01 Chile v Ecuador
14.11.01 Peru v Bolivia
14.11.01 Uruguay v Argentina
14.11.01 Paraguay v Colombia
14.11.01 Brazil v Venezuela

# WORLD CLUB CHAMPIONSHIP

Played annually up to 1974 and intermittently since then between the winners of the European Cup and the winners of the South American Champions Cup — known as the Copa Libertadores. In 1980 the winners were decided by one match arranged in Tokyo in February 1981 and the venue has been the same since. AC Milan replaced Marseille who had been stripped of their European Cup title in 1993.

1960    Real Madrid beat Penarol 0-0, 5-1
1961    Penarol beat Benfica 0-1, 5-0, 2-1
1962    Santos beat Benfica 3-2, 5-2
1963    Santos beat AC Milan 2-4, 4-2, 1-0
1964    Inter-Milan beat Independiente 0-1, 2-0, 1-0
1965    Inter-Milan beat Independiente 3-0, 0-0
1966    Penarol beat Real Madrid 2-0, 2-0
1967    Racing Club beat Celtic 0-1, 2-1, 1-0
1968    Estudiantes beat Manchester United 1-0, 1-1
1969    AC Milan beat Estudiantes 3-0, 1-2
1970    Feyenoord beat Estudiantes 2-2, 1-0
1971    Nacional beat Panathinaikos* 1-1, 2-1
1972    Ajax beat Independiente 1-1, 3-0
1973    Independiente beat Juventus* 1-0
1974    Atlético Madrid* beat Independiente 0-1, 2-0
1975    Independiente and Bayern Munich could not agree dates; no matches.
1976    Bayern Munich beat Cruzeiro 2-0, 0-0
1977    Boca Juniors beat Borussia Moenchengladbach* 2-2, 3-0
1978    Not contested
1979    Olimpia beat Malmö* 1-0, 2-1
1980    Nacional beat Nottingham Forest 1-0
1981    Flamengo beat Liverpool 3-0
1982    Penarol beat Aston Villa 2-0
1983    Gremio Porto Alegre beat SV Hamburg 2-1
1984    Independiente beat Liverpool 1-0
1985    Juventus beat Argentinos Juniors 4-2 on penalties after a 2-2 draw
1986    River Plate beat Steaua Bucharest 1-0
1987    FC Porto beat Penarol 2-1 after extra time
1988    Nacional (Uru) beat PSV Eindhoven 7-6 on penalties after 1-1 draw
1989    AC Milan beat Atletico Nacional (Col) 1-0 after extra time
1990    AC Milan beat Olimpia 3-0
1991    Red Star Belgrade beat Colo Colo 3-0
1992    Sao Paulo beat Barcelona 2-1
1993    Sao Paulo beat AC Milan 3-2
1994    Velez Sarsfield beat AC Milan 2-0
1995    Ajax beat Gremio Porto Alegre 4-3 on penalties after 0-0 draw
1996    Juventus beat River Plate 1-0
1997    Borussia Dortmund beat Cruzeiro 2-0
1998    Real Madrid beat Vasco da Gama 2-1
1999    Manchester U beat Palmeiras 1-0

*European Cup runners-up; winners declined to take part.

## 2000

**28 November, Tokyo**

**Boca Juniors (2) 2** *(Palermo 3, 6)*

**Real Madrid (1) 1** *(Roberto Carlos 11)*                                    51,000

*Boca Juniors:* Cordoba; Bermudez, Matellan, Serna, Traverso, Ibarra, Basualdo, Battaglia (Burdisso 88), Delgardo (Schelotto 85), Palermo, Riquelme.
*Real Madrid:* Casillas; McManaman (Savio 66), Geremi, Karanka, Hierro, Roberto Carlos, Figo, Makelele (Mientes 75), Raul, Guti, Helguera.
*Referee:* Acosta (Colombia).

# EUROPEAN SUPER CUP

Played annually between the winners of the European Champions' Cup and the European Cup-Winners' Cup. AC Milan replaced Marseille in 1993–94.

**Previous Matches**
1972  Ajax beat Rangers 3-1, 3-2
1973  Ajax beat AC Milan 0-1, 6-0
1974  Not contested
1975  Dynamo Kiev beat Bayern Munich 1-0, 2-0
1976  Anderlecht beat Bayern Munich 4-1, 1-2
1977  Liverpool beat Hamburg 1-1, 6-0
1978  Anderlecht beat Liverpool 3-1, 1-2
1979  Nottingham F beat Barcelona 1-0, 1-1
1980  Valencia beat Nottingham F 1-0, 1-2
1981  Not contested
1982  Aston Villa beat Barcelona 0-1, 3-0
1983  Aberdeen beat Hamburg 0-0, 2-0
1984  Juventus beat Liverpool 2-0
1985  Juventus v Everton not contested due to UEFA ban on English clubs
1986  Steaua Bucharest beat Dynamo Kiev 1-0
1987  FC Porto beat Ajax 1-0, 1-0
1988  KV Mechelen beat PSV Eindhoven 3-0, 0-1
1989  AC Milan beat Barcelona 1-1, 1-0
1990  AC Milan beat Sampdoria 1-1, 2-0
1991  Manchester U beat Red Star Belgrade 1-0
1992  Barcelona beat Werder Bremen 1-1, 2-1
1993  Parma beat AC Milan 0-1, 2-0
1994  AC Milan beat Arsenal 0-0, 2-0
1995  Ajax beat Zaragoza 1-1, 4-0
1996  Juventus beat Paris St Germain 6-1, 3-1
1997  Barcelona beat Borussia Dortmund 2-0, 1-1
1998  Chelsea beat Real Madrid 1-0
1999  Lazio beat Manchester U 1-0

## 2000

### 25 August, Monaco

**Galatasaray (1) 2** *(Jardel 40 (pen), 102)*

**Real Madrid (0) 1** *(Raul 78 (pen))*                                    14,000
*Galatasaray:* Taffarel; Capone (Fatih 85), Unsal, Emre, Popescu, Bulent K, Okan (Hasan Sas 81), Suat, Jardel, Hagi (Bulent A 72), Umit.
*Real Madrid:* Casillas; Geremi, Helguera, Roberto Carlos, Celades (Michel Salgado 100), Campo (Conceicao 66), Guti (Munitis 53), Figo, Raul, Savio, Makelele.
*(aet; Galatasaray won on sudden death.)*
*Referee:* Benko (Austria).

# SOUTH AMERICAN CHAMPIONSHIP

*(Copa America)*

| | | | | | |
|---|---|---|---|---|---|
| 1916 | Uruguay | 1937 | Argentina | 1959 | Uruguay |
| 1917 | Uruguay | 1939 | Peru | 1963 | Bolivia |
| 1919 | Brazil | 1941 | Argentina | 1967 | Uruguay |
| 1920 | Uruguay | 1942 | Uruguay | 1975 | Peru |
| 1921 | Argentina | 1945 | Argentina | 1979 | Paraguay |
| 1922 | Brazil | 1946 | Argentina | 1983 | Uruguay |
| 1923 | Uruguay | 1947 | Argentina | 1987 | Uruguay |
| 1924 | Uruguay | 1949 | Brazil | 1989 | Brazil |
| 1925 | Argentina | 1953 | Paraguay | 1991 | Argentina |
| 1926 | Uruguay | 1955 | Argentina | 1993 | Argentina |
| 1927 | Argentina | 1956 | Uruguay | 1995 | Uruguay |
| 1929 | Argentina | 1957 | Argentina | 1997 | Brazil |
| 1935 | Uruguay | 1959 | Argentina | 1999 | Brazil |

# SOUTH AMERICAN CUP

*(Copa Libertadores)*

| | | | |
|---|---|---|---|
| 1960 | Penarol (Uruguay) | 1981 | Flamengo (Brazil) |
| 1961 | Penarol | 1982 | Penarol |
| 1962 | Santos (Brazil) | 1983 | Gremio Porto Alegre (Brazil) |
| 1963 | Santos | 1984 | Independiente |
| 1964 | Independiente (Argentina) | 1985 | Argentinos Juniors (Argentina) |
| 1965 | Independiente | 1986 | River Plate (Argentina) |
| 1966 | Penarol | 1987 | Penarol |
| 1967 | Racing Club (Argentina) | 1988 | Nacional (Uruguay) |
| 1968 | Estudiantes (Argentina) | 1989 | Nacional (Colombia) |
| 1969 | Estudiantes | 1990 | Olimpia |
| 1970 | Estudiantes | 1991 | Colo Colo (Chile) |
| 1971 | Nacional (Uruguay) | 1992 | São Paulo (Brazil) |
| 1972 | Independiente | 1993 | São Paulo |
| 1973 | Independiente | 1994 | Velez Sarsfield (Argentina) |
| 1974 | Independiente | 1995 | Gremio Porto Alegre |
| 1975 | Independiente | 1996 | River Plate |
| 1976 | Cruzeiro (Brazil) | 1997 | Cruzeiro |
| 1977 | Boca Juniors (Argentina) | 1998 | Vasco da Gama |
| 1978 | Boca Juniors | 1999 | Palmeiras |
| 1979 | Olimpia (Paraguay) | 2000 | Boca Juniors |
| 1980 | Nacional | 2001 | Boca Juniors |

# OTHER BRITISH AND IRISH INTERNATIONAL MATCHES 2000–2001

**Stade de France, 2 September 2000, 70,000**

**France (0) 1** *(Petit 64)*

**England (0) 1** *(Owen 86)*

*France:* Lama; Thuram (Candela 80), Lizarazu, Deschamps (Vieira 59), Blanc (Leboeuf 59), Desailly, Djorkaeff, Anelka (Wiltord 46), Zidane (Pires 64), Henry (Trezeguet 73), Petit.
*England:* Seaman; Anderton (Dyer 69), Barry, Campbell, Keown, Adams (Southgate 46), Beckham, Barmby (McManaman 83), Andy Cole, Scholes (Owen 79), Wise.
*Referee:* Roca (Spain).

**Turin, 15 November 2000, 22,000**

**Italy (0) 1** *(Gattuso 57)*

**England (0) 0**

*Italy:* Buffon; Di Livio (Di Biagio 52), Maldini (Bertotto 74), Cannavaro (Adani 66), Nesta, Albertini (Zenoni 52), Gattuso, Coco, Inzaghi F (Del Piero 72), Delvecchio (Inzaghi S 61), Fiore.
*England:* James; Parlour (Anderton 78), Barry (Johnson 72), Neville G, Ferdinand, Southgate, Beckham, Butt (Carragher 25), Dyer (Fowler 80), Barmby, Heskey (Phillips 72).
*Referee:* Puhl (Hungary).

**Villa Park, 28 February 2001, 42,129**

**England (1) 3** *(Barmby 38, Heskey 53, Ehiogu 70)*

**Spain (0) 0**

*England:* James (Martyn 46); Neville P (Neville G 77), Powell (Ball 46), Butt (McCann 46), Campbell, Ferdinand (Ehiogu 46), Beckham (Heskey 46), Scholes (Lampard 46), Andy Cole, Owen, Barmby.
*Spain:* Casillas (Canizares 64); Pablo, Romero, Guardiola (Baraja 80), Abelardo (Sanchez 64), Unal, Helguera (Paco 80), Mendieta, Raul (Etxeberria J 80), Luis Enrique (Sergi 64), Urzaiz (Javi Moreno 46).
*Referee:* Vassaras (Greece).

**Pride Park, 25 May 2001, 33,597**

**England (3) 4** *(Scholes 3, Fowler 14, Beckham 29, Sheringham 74)*

**Mexico (0) 0**

*England:* Martyn (James 46); Neville P, Ashley Cole (Powell 46), Gerrard (Carrick 46), Keown (Southgate 46), Ferdinand (Carragher 46), Beckham (Cole J 46), Scholes (Butt 46), Fowler (Sheringham 54), Owen (Smith 46), Heskey (Mills 66).
*Mexico:* Sanchez; Beltran (Davino 46), Suarez, Oteo, Chavez (Pardo 46), Ruiz V (Osomo 58), Rodriguez (Perez 82), Coyote (Rangel 77), Ruiz M, de Nigris, Abundis.
*Referee:* Batista (Portugal).

**Hampden Park, 15 November 2000, 30,985**

**Scotland (0) 0**

**Australia (1) 2** *(Emerton 12, Zdrilic 66)*

*Scotland:* Gould; Boyd, Matteo, O'Neil B (Hendry 57), Dailly, Weir (Elliott 46), Burley (Dickov 63), Ferguson B, Dodds, Hutchison, Cameron (McCann 46).
*Australia:* Schwarzer; Muscat, Lazaridis, Popovic, Murphy, Okon, Emerton, Skoko (Wehrman 73), Agostino (Sterjovski 46), Zdrilic (Zane 90), Tiatto (Burns 67).
*Referee:* Garibian (France).

**Bydgoszcz, 25 April 2001 20,000**

**Poland (0) 1** *(Kaluzny 49)*

**Scotland (0) 1** *(Booth 69 (pen))*

*Poland:* Dudek; Klos, Michal Zewlakow (Mieciel 64), Iwan, Kozminski (Kaluzny 46), Waldoch, Zielinski, Zdebel (Swierczewski 59), Hajto (Krzynuwek 46), Krysalowicz (Zurawski 75), Marcin Zewlakow.
*Scotland:* Sullivan; Nicholson, O'Neil J (Gemmill 74), Dailly, Boyd, Davidson (Weir 73), Miller C (Caldwell 56), Rae, Dodds (Crawford 46), Booth (Miller K 80), Cameron (McLaren 46).
*Referee:* Roca (Spain).

**Belfast, 16 August 2000, 6095**

**Northern Ireland (1) 1** *(Healy 45)*

**Yugoslavia (0) 2** *(Kezman 63, Mijatovic 78)*

*Northern Ireland:* Taylor; Nolan, Hughes A, Murdock (Griffin 81), Williams, Horlock (Gillespie 72), Johnson, Mulryne (Quinn 68), Healy, Jeff Whitley, Magilton.
*Yugoslavia:* Cicovic; Grujic (Obradovic 71), Bunjevcevic, Sakic, Dudic, Stankovic, Lazertic, Grozdic (Ilic 67), Djordevic, Milosevic (Kezman 55), Mijatovic.
*Referee:* Young (Scotland).

**Belfast, 28 February 2001, 7502**

**Northern Ireland (0) 0**

**Norway (3) 4** *(Helstad 20, 49, Carew 30, Stensaas 37)*

*Northern Ireland:* Taylor; McCarthy (Johnson 62), Kennedy (Griffin 46), Murdock, Taggart (Williams 46), Hughes A, Lennon (Elliott 46), Ferguson (Gray 69), Healy (Kirk 69), Jeff Whitley (Sonner 66), Magilton.
*Norway:* Myhre; Bergdolmo, Stensaas, Berg (Eggen 36), Lundekvam, Bakke (Aarsheim 78), Tessem, Larsen, Solskjaer (Berre 79), Carew (Johnsen F 62), Helstad (Andersen T 78).
*Referee:* Clark (Scotland).

**Dublin, 15 November 2000, 22,368**

**Republic of Ireland (1) 3** *(Finnan 14, Kilbane 84, Staunton 90)*

**Finland (0) 0**

*Republic of Ireland:* Given; Kelly G (McAteer 46), Harte (Staunton 46), Finnan, Breen, Dunne, Kinsella, Holland, Robbie Keane (Connolly 90), Foley (Carsley 46), Kilbane.
*Finland:* Jaaskelainen; Nylund, Pasanen (Nurmela 78), Tihinen, Saarinen, Johansson (Kuqi 46), Tainio (Kuivasto 66), Riihilahti, Kolkka (Kottila 85), Litmanen, Forssell (Gronlund 46).
*Referee:* Durkin (England).

# ENGLAND UNDER-21 TEAMS 2000–2001

**31 Aug**

**England (4) 6** *(Young 18, Ashley Cole 37, Jeffers 44, Dunn 45, Greening 61, Smith 90)*

**Georgia (1) 1** *(Tskitishvili 30)*      5103

*England:* Robinson; Newton (Stockdale 79), Ashley Cole (Smith T 74), Bramble (Wright 46), Young (Carlisle 46), Dunn (Prutton 46), Greening (Campbell 63), Jeffers (Chadwick 63), Vassell (Thirlwell 74), Cole J (Parker 74), Carrick (Hargreaves 63).

**6 Oct**

**England (1) 1** *(Bramble 45)*

**Germany (0) 1** *(Ernst 88)*      30,155

*England:* Robinson; Wright, Ashley Cole, Bramble, Brown, Dunn (Vernazza 83), Parker (Prutton 41), Vassell (Carlisle 66), Smith A, Greening, Carrick.

**10 Oct**

**Finland (1) 2** *(Sjolund 15, 76)*

**England (1) 2** *(Dunn 31, Smith A 48)*      1426

*England:* Robinson; Roche, Ashley Cole, Bramble (Carlisle 46), Terry, Dunn (Parker 90), Prutton, Vassell (Christie 87), Smith A, Greening, Carrick.

**14 Nov**

**Italy (0) 0**

**England (0) 0**

*Abandoned 11 minutes; fog.*
*England:* Weaver; Griffin, Ashley Cole, Upson, King, Dunn, Chadwick, Hargreaves, Vassell, Greening, Carrick.

**27 Feb**

**England (0) 0**

**Spain (2) 4** *(Gonzalez 14, 21, Colsa 64, Xisco 86)*      13,761

*England:* Robinson; Griffin (Thelwell 59), Bridge, Barry (Riggott 46), Terry (Upson 46), Dunn (King 46), Chadwick (Greening 46), Hargreaves (Prutton 71), Christie (Ameobi 46), Smith A, Wilson.

**23 Mar**

**England (1) 4** *(Vassell 28, Terry 75, Ameobi 82, 90)*

**Finland (0) 0**      17,176

*England:* Weaver; Young, Barry, King (Riggott 46), Terry, Davis, Chadwick, Vassell, Christie (Ameobi 71), Johnson (Wilson 61), Greening.

**27 Mar**

**Albania (0) 0**

**England (0) 1** *(Greening 69 (pen))*      2000

*England:* Weaver; Young, Barry, Riggott (Bramble 25), Terry, Davis, Chadwick, Vassell, Christie (Ameobi 59), Wilson (Parker 59), Greening.

**24 May**

**England (0) 3** *(Christie 49, Defoe 74, Bothroyd 85)*

**Mexico (0) 0**      10,000

*England:* Kirkland (Bywater 46); Young (Wright 46), Naylor (Upson 46), Bramble (Riggott 46), Terry (Taylor 46), Dunn (Wilson 46), Prutton (Cadamarteri 87), Defoe (Bothroyd 76), Christie (Benjamin 63), Ameobi (Pennant 46), Davis (Vernazza 78).

**5 June**

**Greece (2) 3** *(Papadopoulos 27, Vakouftsis 42, Terry 60 (og))*

**England (0) 1** *(Carrick 85)*      1500

*England:* Bywater; Young, Naylor, Upson, Terry, Dunn, Defoe (Pennant 46), Cole J, Christie (Ameobi 72), Davis (Prutton 74), Carrick.

**As at July 2001** *(Season of first cap given)*

## ENGLAND

A'Court, A. (5) 1957/8 Liverpool
Adams, T. A. (66) 1986/7 Arsenal
Allen, C. (5) 1983/4 QPR, Tottenham H
Allen, R. (5) 1951/2 WBA
Allen, T. (3) 1959/60 Stoke C
Anderson, S. (2) 1961/2 Sunderland
Anderson, V. (30) 1978/9 Nottingham F, Arsenal, Manchester U
Anderton, D. R. (29) 1993/4 Tottenham H
Angus, J. (1) 1960/1 Burnley
Armfield, J. (43) 1958/9 Blackpool
Armstrong, D. (3) 1979/80 Middlesbrough, Southampton
Armstrong, K. (1) 1954/5 Chelsea
Astall, G. (2) 1955/6 Birmingham C
Astle, J. (5) 1968/9 WBA
Aston, J. (17) 1948/9 Manchester U
Atyeo, J. (6) 1955/6 Bristol C

Bailey, G. R. (2) 1984/5 Manchester U
Bailey, M. (2) 1963/4 Charlton
Baily, E. (9) 1949/50 Tottenham H
Baker, J. (8) 1959/60 Hibernian, Arsenal
Ball, A. (72) 1964/5 Blackpool, Everton, Arsenal
Ball, M. J. (1) 2000/01 Everton
Banks, G. (73) 1962/3 Leicester C, Stoke C
Banks, T. (6) 1957/8 Bolton W
Bardsley, D. (2) 1992/3 QPR
Barham, M. (2) 1982/3 Norwich C
Barlow, R. (1) 1954/5 WBA
Barmby, N. J. (19) 1994/5 Tottenham H, Middlesbrough, Everton, Liverpool
Barnes, J. (79) 1982/3 Watford, Liverpool
Barnes, P. (22) 1977/8 Manchester C, WBA, Leeds U
Barrass, M. (3) 1951/2 Bolton W
Barrett, E. D. (3) 1990/1 Oldham Ath, Aston Villa
Barry, G. (6) 1999/00 Aston Villa
Barton, W. D. (3) 1994/5 Wimbledon, Blackburn R
Batty, D. (42) 1990/1 Leeds U, Blackburn R, Newcastle U, Leeds U
Baynham, R. (3) 1955/6 Luton T
Beardsley, P. A. (59) 1985/6 Newcastle U, Liverpool, Newcastle U
Beasant, D. J. (2) 1989/90 Chelsea

Beattie, T. K. (9) 1974/5 Ipswich T
Beckham, D. R. J. (42) 1996/7 Manchester U
Bell, C. (48) 1967/8 Manchester C
Bentley, R. (12) 1948/9 Chelsea
Berry, J. (4) 1952/3 Manchester U
Birtles, G. (3) 1979/80 Nottingham F, Manchester U
Blissett, L. (14) 1982/3 Watford, AC Milan
Blockley, J. (1) 1972/3 Arsenal
Blunstone, F. (5) 1954/5 Chelsea
Bonetti, P. (7) 1965/6 Chelsea
Bould, S. A. (2) 1993/4 Arsenal
Bowles, S. (5) 1973/4 QPR
Boyer, P. (1) 1975/6 Norwich C
Brabrook, P. (3) 1957/8 Chelsea
Bracewell, P. W. (3) 1984/5 Everton
Bradford, G. (1) 1955/6 Bristol R
Bradley, W. (3) 1958/9 Manchester U
Bridges, B. (4) 1964/5 Chelsea
Broadbent, P. (7) 1957/8 Wolverhampton W
Broadis, I. (14) 1951/2 Manchester C, Newcastle U
Brooking, T. (47) 1973/4 West Ham U
Brooks, J. (3) 1956/7 Tottenham H
Brown, A. (1) 1970/1 WBA
Brown, K. (1) 1959/60 West Ham U
Brown, W. M. (3) 1998/9 Manchester U
Bull, S. G. (13) 1988/9 Wolverhampton W
Butcher, T. (77) 1979/80 Ipswich T, Rangers
Butt, N. (14) 1996/7 Manchester U
Byrne, G. (2) 1962/3 Liverpool
Byrne, J. (11) 1961/2 Crystal P, West Ham U
Byrne, R. (33) 1953/4 Manchester U

Callaghan, I. (4) 1965/6 Liverpool
Campbell, S. (40) 1995/6 Tottenham H
Carragher, J. L. (3) 1998/9 Liverpool
Carrick, M. (1) 2000/01 West Ham U
Carter, H. (7) 1946/7 Derby Co
Chamberlain, M. (8) 1982/3 Stoke C
Channon, M. (46) 1972/3 Southampton, Manchester C
Charles, G. A. (2) 1990/1 Nottingham F
Charlton, J. (35) 1964/5 Leeds U
Charlton, R. (106) 1957/8 Manchester U
Charnley, R. (1) 1961/2 Blackpool
Cherry, T. (27) 1975/6 Leeds U
Chilton, A. (2) 1950/1 Manchester U

Chivers, M. (24) 1970/1 Tottenham H
Clamp, E. (4) 1957/8 Wolverhampton W
Clapton, D. (1) 1958/9 Arsenal
Clarke, A. (19) 1969/70 Leeds U
Clarke, H. (1) 1953/4 Tottenham H
Clayton, R. (35) 1955/6 Blackburn R
Clemence, R (61) 1972/3 Liverpool, Tottenham H
Clement, D. (5) 1975/6 QPR
Clough, B. (2) 1959/60 Middlesbrough
Clough, N. H. (14) 1988/9 Nottingham F
Coates, R. (4) 1969/70 Burnley, Tottenham H
Cockburn, H. (13) 1946/7 Manchester U
Cohen, G. (37) 1963/4 Fulham
Cole, Andy (13) 1994/5 Manchester U
Cole, Ashley (3) 2000/01 Arsenal
Cole, J. J. (1) 2000/01 West Ham U
Collymore, S. V. (3) 1994/5 Nottingham F
Compton, L. (2) 1950/1 Arsenal
Connelly J. (20) 1959/60 Burnley, Manchester U
Cooper, C. T. (2) 1994/5 Nottingham F
Cooper, T. (20) 1968/9 Leeds U
Coppell, S. (42) 1977/8 Manchester U
Corrigan J. (9) 1975/6 Manchester C
Cottee, A. R. (7) 1986/7 West Ham U, Everton
Cowans, G. (10) 1982/3 Aston Villa, Bari, Aston Villa
Crawford, R. (2) 1961/2 Ipswich T
Crowe, C. (1) 1962/3 Wolverhampton W
Cunningham, L. (6) 1978/9 WBA, Real Madrid
Curle, K. (3) 1991/2 Manchester C
Currie, A. (17) 1971/2 Sheffield U, Leeds U
Daley, A. M. (7) 1991/2 Aston Villa
Davenport, P. (1) 1984/5 Nottingham F
Deane, B. C. (3) 1990/1 Sheffield U
Deeley, N. (2) 1958/9 Wolverhampton W
Devonshire, A. (8) 1979/80 West Ham U
Dickinson, J. (48) 1948/9 Portsmouth
Ditchburn, E. (6) 1948/9 Tottenham H
Dixon, K. M. (8) 1984/5 Chelsea
Dixon, L. M. (22) 1989/90 Arsenal
Dobson, M. (5) 1973/4 Burnley, Everton
Dorigo, A. R. (15) 1989/90 Chelsea, Leeds U
Douglas, B. (36) 1957/8 Blackburn R
Doyle, M. (5) 1975/6 Manchester C
Dublin, D. (4) 1997/8 Coventry C, Aston Villa

Duxbury, M. (10) 1983/4 Manchester U
Dyer, K. C. (8) 1999/00 Newcastle U

Eastham, G. (19) 1962/3 Arsenal
Eckersley, W. (17) 1949/50 Blackburn R
Edwards, D. (18) 1954/5 Manchester U
Ehiogu, U. (2) 1995/6 Aston Villa, Middlesbrough
Ellerington, W. (2) 1948/9 Southampton
Elliott, W. H. (5) 1951/2 Burnley

Fantham, J. (1) 1961/2 Sheffield W
Fashanu, J. (2) 1988/9 Wimbledon
Fenwick, T. (20) 1983/4 QPR, Tottenham H
Ferdinand, L. (17) 1992/3 QPR, Newcastle U, Tottenham H
Ferdinand, R. G. (15) 1997/8 West Ham U, Leeds U
Finney, T. (76) 1946/7 Preston NE
Flowers, R. (49) 1954/5 Wolverhampton W
Flowers, T. (11) 1992/3 Southampton, Blackburn R
Foster, S. (3) 1981/2 Brighton
Foulkes, W. (1) 1954/5 Manchester U
Fowler, R. B. (18) 1995/6 Liverpool
Francis, G. (12) 1974/5 QPR
Francis, T. (52) 1976/7 Birmingham C, Nottingham F, Manchester C, Sampdoria
Franklin, N. (27) 1946/7 Stoke C
Froggatt, J. (13) 1949/50 Portsmouth
Froggatt, R. (4) 1952/3 Sheffield W

Garrett, T. (3) 1951/2 Blackpool
Gascoigne, P. J. (57) 1988/9 Tottenham H, Lazio, Rangers, Middlesbrough
Gates, E. (2) 1980/1 Ipswich T
George, F. C. (1) 1976/7 Derby Co
Gerrard, S. G. (5) 1999/00 Liverpool
Gidman, J. (1) 1976/7 Aston Villa
Gillard, I. (3) 1974/5 QPR
Goddard, P. (1) 1981/2 West Ham U
Grainger, C. (7) 1955/6 Sheffield U, Sunderland
Gray, A. A. (1) 1991/2 Crystal P
Gray, M. (3) 1998/9 Sunderland
Greaves, J. (57) 1958/9 Chelsea, Tottenham H
Greenhoff, B. (18) 1975/6 Manchester U
Gregory, J. (6) 1982/3 QPR
Guppy, S. (1) 1999/00 Leicester C

Hagan, J. (1) 1948/9 Sheffield U
Haines, J. (1) 1948/9 WBA
Hall, J. (17) 1955/6 Birmingham C

**Hancocks, J.** (3) 1948/9 Wolverhampton W
**Hardwick, G.** (13) 1946/7 Middlesbrough
**Harford, M. G.** (2) 1987/8 Luton T
**Harris, G.** (1) 1965/6 Burnley
**Harris, P.** (2) 1949/50 Portsmouth
**Harvey, C.** (1) 1970/1 Everton
**Hassall, H.** (5) 1950/1 Huddersfield T, Bolton W
**Hateley, M.** (32) 1983/4 Portsmouth, AC Milan, Monaco, Rangers
**Haynes, J.** (56) 1954/5 Fulham
**Hector, K.** (2) 1973/4 Derby Co
**Hellawell, M.** (2) 1962/3 Birmingham C
**Hendrie, L. A.** (1) 1998/9 Aston Villa
**Henry, R.** (1) 1962/3 Tottenham H
**Heskey, E. W.** (16) 1998/9 Leicester C, Liverpool
**Hill, F.** (2) 1962/3 Bolton W
**Hill, G.** (6) 1975/6 Manchester U
**Hill, R.** (3) 1982/3 Luton T
**Hinchcliffe, A. G.** (7) 1996/7 Everton, Sheffield W
**Hinton A.** (3) 1962/3 Wolverhampton W, Nottingham F
**Hirst, D. E.** (3) 1990/1 Sheffield W
**Hitchens, G.** (7) 1960/1 Aston Villa, Internazionale
**Hoddle, G.** (53) 1979/80 Tottenham H, Monaco
**Hodge, S. B.** (24) 1985/6 Aston Villa, Tottenham H, Nottingham F
**Hodgkinson, A.** (5) 1956/7 Sheffield U
**Holden, D.** (5) 1958/9 Bolton W
**Holliday, E.** (3) 1959/60 Middlesbrough
**Hollins, J.** (1) 1966/7 Chelsea
**Hopkinson, E.** (14) 1957/8 Bolton W
**Howe, D.** (23) 1957/8 WBA
**Howe, J.** (3) 1947/8 Derby Co
**Howey, S. N.** (4) 1994/5 Newcastle U
**Hudson, A.** (2) 1974/5 Stoke C
**Hughes, E.** (62) 1969/70 Liverpool, Wolverhampton W
**Hughes, L.** (3) 1949/50 Liverpool
**Hunt, R.** (34) 1961/2 Liverpool
**Hunt, S.** (2) 1983/4 WBA
**Hunter, N.** (28) 1965/6 Leeds U
**Hurst, G.** (49) 1965/6 West Ham U

**Ince, P.** (53) 1992/3 Manchester U, Internazionale, Liverpool, Middlesbrough

**James, D. B.** (4) 1996/7 Liverpool, Aston Villa
**Jezzard, B.** (2) 1953/4 Fulham
**Johnson, D.** (8) 1974/5 Ipswich T, Liverpool
**Johnson, S.A.M.** (1) 2000/01 Derby Co

**Johnston, H.** (10) 1946/7 Blackpool
**Jones, M.** (3) 1964/5 Sheffield U, Leeds U
**Jones, R.** (8) 1991/2 Liverpool
**Jones, W. H.** (2) 1949/50 Liverpool

**Kay, A.** (1) 1962/3 Everton
**Keegan, K.** (63) 1972/3 Liverpool, SV Hamburg, Southampton
**Kennedy, A.** (2) 1983/4 Liverpool
**Kennedy, R.** (17) 1975/6 Liverpool
**Keown, M. R.** (38) 1991/2 Everton, Arsenal
**Kevan, D.** (14) 1956/7 WBA
**Kidd, B.** (2) 1969/70 Manchester U
**Knowles, C.** (4) 1967/8 Tottenham H

**Labone, B.** (26) 1962/3 Everton
**Lampard, F. J.** (2) 1999/00 West Ham U
**Lampard, F. R. G.** (2) 1972/3 West Ham U
**Langley, J.** (3) 1957/8 Fulham
**Langton, R.** (11) 1946/7 Blackburn R, Preston NE, Bolton W
**Latchford, R.** (12) 1977/8 Everton
**Lawler, C.** (4) 1970/1 Liverpool
**Lawton, T.** (15) 1946/7 Chelsea, Notts Co
**Lee, F.** (27) 1968/9 Manchester C
**Lee, J.** (1) 1950/1 Derby C
**Lee, R. M.** (21) 1994/5 Newcastle U
**Lee, S.** (14) 1982/3 Liverpool
**Le Saux, G. P.** (36) 1993/4 Blackburn R, Chelsea
**Le Tissier, M. P.** (8) 1993/4 Southampton
**Lindsay, A.** (4) 1973/4 Liverpool
**Lineker, G.** (80) 1983/4 Leicester C, Everton, Barcelona, Tottenham H
**Little, B.** (1) 1974/5 Aston Villa
**Lloyd, L.** (4) 1970/1 Liverpool, Nottingham F
**Lofthouse, N.** (33) 1950/1 Bolton W
**Lowe, E.** (3) 1946/7 Aston Villa

**Mabbutt, G.** (16) 1982/3 Tottenham H
**Macdonald, M.** (14) 1971/2 Newcastle U, Arsenal
**Madeley, P.** (24) 1970/1 Leeds U
**Mannion, W.** (26) 1946/7 Middlesbrough
**Mariner, P.** (35) 1976/7 Ipswich T, Arsenal
**Marsh, R.** (9) 1971/2 QPR, Manchester C
**Martin, A.** (17) 1980/1 West Ham U
**Martyn, A. N.** (16) 1991/2 Crystal P, Leeds U
**Marwood, B.** (1) 1988/9 Arsenal
**Matthews, R.** (5) 1955/6 Coventry C

**Matthews, S.** (37) 1946/7 Stoke C, Blackpool
**McCann, G. P.** (1) 2000/01 Sunderland
**McDermott, T.** (25) 1977/8 Liverpool
**McDonald, C.** (8) 1957/8 Burnley
**McFarland, R.** (28) 1970/1 Derby C
**McGarry, W.** (4) 1953/4 Huddersfield T
**McGuinness, W.** (2) 1958/9 Manchester U
**McMahon, S.** (17) 1987/8 Liverpool
**McManaman, S.** (34) 1994/5 Liverpool, Real Madrid
**McNab, R.** (4) 1968/9 Arsenal
**McNeil, M.** (9) 1960/1 Middlesbrough
**Meadows, J.** (1) 1954/5 Manchester C
**Medley, L.** 1950/1 Tottenham H
**Melia, J.** (2) 1962/3 Liverpool
**Merrick, G.** (23) 1951/2 Birmingham C
**Merson, P. C.** (21) 1991/2 Arsenal, Middlesbrough, Aston Villa
**Metcalfe, V.** (2) 1950/1 Huddersfield T
**Milburn, J.** (13) 1948/9 Newcastle U
**Miller, B.** (1) 1960/1 Burnley
**Mills, D. J.** (1) 2000/01 Leeds U
**Mills, M.** (42) 1972/3 Ipswich T
**Milne, G.** (14) 1962/3 Liverpool
**Milton, C. A.** (1) 1951/2 Arsenal
**Moore, R.** (108) 1961/2 West Ham U
**Morley, A.** (6) 1981/2 Aston Villa
**Morris, J.** (3) 1948/9 Derby Co
**Mortensen, S.** (25) 1946/7 Blackpool
**Mozley, B.** (3) 1949/50 Derby Co
**Mullen, J.** (12) 1946/7 Wolverhampton W
**Mullery, A.** (35) 1964/5 Tottenham H

**Neal, P.** (50) 1975/6 Liverpool
**Neville, G. A.** (44) 1994/5 Manchester U
**Neville, P. J.** (33) 1995/6 Manchester U
**Newton, K.** (27) 1965/6 Blackburn R, Everton
**Nicholls, J.** (2) 1953/4 WBA
**Nicholson, W.** (1) 1950/1 Tottenham H
**Nish, D.** (5) 1972/3 Derby Co
**Norman, M.** (23) 1961/2 Tottenham H

**O'Grady, M.** (2) 1962/3 Huddersfield T, Leeds U
**Osgood, P.** (4) 1969/70 Chelsea
**Osman, R.** (11) 1979/80 Ipswich T
**Owen, M. J.** (29) 1997/8 Liverpool
**Owen, S.** (3) 1953/4 Luton T

**Paine, T.** (19) 1962/3 Southampton
**Pallister, G.** (22) 1987/8 Middlesbrough, Manchester U
**Palmer, C. L.** (18) 1991/2 Sheffield W
**Parker, P. A.** (19) 1988/9 QPR, Manchester U
**Parkes, P.** (1) 1973/4 QPR

**Parlour, R.** (10) 1998/9 Arsenal
**Parry, R.** (2) 1959/60 Bolton W
**Peacock, A.** (6) 1961/2 Middlesbrough, Leeds U
**Pearce, S.** (78) 1986/7 Nottingham F, West Ham U
**Pearson, Stan** (8) 1947/8 Manchester U
**Pearson, Stuart** (15) 1975/6 Manchester U
**Pegg, D.** (1) 1956/7 Manchester U
**Pejic, M.** (4) 1973/4 Stoke C
**Perry, W.** (3) 1955/6 Blackpool
**Perryman, S.** (1) 1981/2 Tottenham H
**Peters, M.** (67) 1965/6 West Ham U, Tottenham H
**Phelan, M. C.** (1) 1989/90 Manchester U
**Phillips, K.** (6) 1998/9 Sunderland
**Phillips, L.** (3) 1951/2 Portsmouth
**Pickering, F.** (3) 1963/4 Everton
**Pickering, N.** (1) 1982/3 Sunderland
**Pilkington, B.** (1) 1954/5 Burnley
**Platt, D.** (62) 1989/90 Aston Villa, Bari, Juventus, Sampdoria, Arsenal
**Pointer, R.** (3) 1961/2 Burnley
**Powell, C.G.** (3) 2000/01 Charlton Ath
**Pye, J.** (1) 1949/50 Wolverhampton W

**Quixall, A.** (5) 1953/4 Sheffield W

**Radford, J.** (2) 1968/9 Arsenal
**Ramsey, A.** (32) 1948/9 Southampton, Tottenham H
**Reaney, P.** (3) 1968/9 Leeds U
**Redknapp, J. F.** (17) 1995/6 Liverpool
**Reeves, K.** (2) 1979/80 Norwich C
**Regis, C.** (5) 1981/2 WBA, Coventry C
**Reid, P.** (13) 1984/5 Everton
**Revie, D.** (6) 1954/5 Manchester C
**Richards, J.** (1) 1972/3 Wolverhampton W
**Richardson, K.** (1) 1993/4 Aston Villa
**Rickaby, S.** (1) 1953/4 WBA
**Rimmer, J.** (1) 1975/6 Arsenal
**Ripley, S. E.** (2) 1993/4 Blackburn R
**Rix, G.** (17) 1980/1 Arsenal
**Robb, G.** (1) 1953/4 Tottenham H
**Roberts, G.** (6) 1982/3 Tottenham H
**Robson, B.** (90) 1979/80 WBA, Manchester U
**Robson, R.** (20) 1957/8 WBA
**Rocastle, D.** (14) 1988/9 Arsenal
**Rowley, J.** (6) 1948/9 Manchester U
**Royle, J.** (6) 1970/1 Everton, Manchester C
**Ruddock, N.** (1) 1994/5 Liverpool

**Sadler, D.** (4) 1967/8 Manchester U
**Salako, J. A.** (5) 1990/1 Crystal P
**Sansom, K.** (86) 1978/9 Crystal P, Arsenal

Scales, J. R. (3) 1994/5 Liverpool
Scholes, P. (35) 1996/7 Manchester U
Scott, L. (17) 1946/7 Arsenal
Seaman, D. A. (65) 1988/9 QPR, Arsenal
Sewell, J. (6) 1951/2 Sheffield W
Shackleton, L. (5) 1948/9 Sunderland
Sharpe, L. S. (8) 1990/1 Manchester U
Shaw, G. (5) 1958/9 Sheffield U
Shearer, A. (63) 1991/2 Southampton, Blackburn R, Newcastle U
Shellito, K. (1) 1962/3 Chelsea
Sheringham, E. (41) 1992/3 Tottenham H, Manchester U
Sherwood, T. A. (3) 1998/9 Tottenham H
Shilton, P. (125) 1970/1 Leicester C, Stoke C, Nottingham F, Southampton, Derby Co
Shimwell, E. (1) 1948/9 Blackpool
Sillett, P. (3) 1954/5 Chelsea
Sinton, A. (12) 1991/2 QPR, Sheffield W
Slater, W. (12) 1954/5 Wolverhampton W
Smith, A. (2) 2000/01 Leeds U
Smith, A. M. (13) 1988/9 Arsenal
Smith, L. (6) 1950/1 Arsenal
Smith, R. (15) 1960/1 Tottenham H
Smith, Tom (1) 1970/1 Liverpool
Smith, Trevor (2) 1959/60 Birmingham C
Southgate, G. (42) 1995/6 Aston Villa
Spink, N. (1) 1982/3 Aston Villa
Springett, R. (33) 1959/60 Sheffield W
Staniforth, R. (8) 1953/4 Huddersfield T
Statham, D. (3) 1982/3 WBA
Stein, B. (1) 1983/4 Luton T
Stepney, A. (1) 1967/8 Manchester U
Sterland, M. (1) 1988/9 Sheffield W
Steven, T. M. (36) 1984/5 Everton, Rangers, Marseille
Stevens, G. A. (7) 1984/5 Tottenham H
Stevens, M. G. (46) 1984/5 Everton, Rangers
Stewart, P. A. (3) 1991/2 Tottenham H
Stiles, N. (28) 1964/5 Manchester U
Stone, S. B. (9) 1995/6 Nottingham F
Storey-Moore, I. (1) 1969/70 Nottingham F
Storey, P. (19) 1970/1 Arsenal
Streten, B. (1) 1949/50 Luton T
Summerbee, M. (8) 1967/8 Manchester C
Sunderland, A. (1) 1979/80 Arsenal
Sutton, C. R. (1) 1997/8 Blackburn R
Swan, P. (19) 1959/60 Sheffield W
Swift, F. (19) 1946/7 Manchester C

Talbot, B. (6) 1976/7 Ipswich T
Tambling, R. (3) 1962/3 Chelsea
Taylor, E. (1) 1953/4 Blackpool
Taylor, J. (2) 1950/1 Fulham
Taylor, P. H. (3) 1947/8 Liverpool
Taylor, P. J. (4) 1975/6 Crystal P
Taylor, T. (19) 1952/3 Manchester U
Temple, D. (1) 1964/5 Everton
Thomas, Danny (2) 1982/3 Coventry C
Thomas, Dave (8) 1974/5 QPR
Thomas, G. R. (9) 1990/1 Crystal P
Thomas, M. L. (2) 1988/9 Arsenal
Thompson, P. (16) 1963/4 Liverpool
Thompson, P. B. (42) 1975/6 Liverpool
Thompson, T. (2) 1951/2 Aston Villa, Preston NE
Thomson, R. (8) 1963/4 Wolverhampton W
Todd, C. (27) 1971/2 Derby Co
Towers, T. (3) 1975/6 Sunderland
Tueart, D. (6) 1974/5 Manchester C

Ufton, D. (1) 1953/4 Charlton Ath
Unsworth, D. G. (1) 1994/5 Everton

Venables, T. (2) 1964/5 Chelsea
Venison, B. (2) 1994/5 Newcastle U
Viljoen, C. (2) 1974/5 Ipswich T
Viollet, D. (2) 1959/60 Manchester U

Waddle, C. R. (62) 1984/5 Newcastle U, Tottenham H, Marseille
Waiters, A. (5) 1963/4 Blackpool
Walker, D. S. (59) 1988/9 Nottingham F, Sampdoria, Sheffield W
Walker, I. M. (3) 1995/6 Tottenham H
Wallace, D. L. (1) 1985/6 Southampton
Walsh, P. (5) 1982/3 Luton T
Walters, K. M. (1) 1990/1 Rangers
Ward, P. (1) 1979/80 Brighton
Ward, T. (2) 1947/8 Derby C
Watson, D. (12) 1983/4 Norwich C, Everton
Watson D. V. (65) 1973/4 Sunderland, Manchester C, Southampton, Werder Bremen, Southampton, Stoke C
Watson, W. (4) 1949/50 Sunderland
Webb, N. (26) 1987/8 Nottingham F, Manchester U
Weller, K. (4) 1973/4 Leicester C
West, G. (3) 1968/9 Everton
Wheeler, J. (1) 1954/5 Bolton W
White, D. (1) 1992/3 Manchester C
Whitworth, S. (7) 1974/5 Leicester C
Whymark, T. (1) 1977/8 Ipswich T
Wignall, F. (2) 1964/5 Nottingham F
Wilcox, J. M. (3) 1995/6 Blackburn R, Leeds U
Wilkins, R. (84) 1975/6 Chelsea, Manchester U, AC Milan

**Williams, B.** (24) 1948/9 Wolverhampton W

**Williams, S.** (6) 1982/3 Southampton

**Willis, A.** (1) 1951/2 Tottenham H

**Wilshaw, D.** (12) 1953/4 Wolverhampton W

**Wilson, R.** (63) 1959/60 Huddersfield T, Everton

**Winterburn, N.** (2) 1989/90 Arsenal

**Wise, D. F.** (21) 1990/1 Chelsea

**Withe, P.** (11) 1980/1 Aston Villa

**Wood, R.** (3) 1954/5 Manchester U

**Woodcock, A.** (42) 1977/8 Nottingham F, FC Cologne, Arsenal

**Woodgate, J. S.** (1) 1998/9 Leeds U

**Woods, C. C. E.** (43) 1984/5 Norwich C, Rangers, Sheffield W

**Worthington, F.** (8) 1973/4 Leicester C

**Wright, I. E.** (33) 1990/1 Crystal P, Arsenal, West Ham U

**Wright M.** (45) 1983/4 Southampton, Derby C, Liverpool

**Wright R. I.** (1) 1999/00 Ipswich T

**Wright, T.** (11) 1967/8 Everton

**Wright, W.** (105) 1946/7 Wolverhampton W

**Young, G.** (1) 1964/5 Sheffield W

# NORTHERN IRELAND

**Aherne, T.** (4) 1946/7 Belfast Celtic, Luton T

**Anderson, T.** (22) 1972/3 Manchester U, Swindon T, Peterborough U

**Armstrong, G.** (63) 1976/7 Tottenham H, Watford, Real Mallorca, WBA, Chesterfield

**Barr, H.** (3) 1961/2 Linfield, Coventry C

**Best, G.** (37) 1963/4 Manchester U, Fulham

**Bingham, W.** (56) 1950/1 Sunderland, Luton T, Everton, Port Vale

**Black, K.** (30) 1987/8 Luton T, Nottingham F

**Blair, R.** (5) 1974/5 Oldham Ath

**Blanchflower, D.** (54) 1949/50 Barnsley, Aston Villa, Tottenham H

**Blanchflower, J.** (12) 1953/4 Manchester U

**Bowler, G.** (3) 1949/50 Hull C

**Braithwaite, R.** (10) 1961/2 Linfield, Middlesbrough

**Brennan, R.** (5) 1948/9 Luton T, Birmingham C, Fulham

**Briggs, R.** (2) 1961/2 Manchester U, Swansea

**Brotherston, N.** (27) 1979/80 Blackburn R

**Bruce, W.** (2) 1960/1 Glentoran

**Campbell, A.** (2) 1962/3 Crusaders

**Campbell, D. A.** (10) 1985/6 Nottingham F, Charlton Ath

**Campbell, J.** (2) 1950/1 Fulham

**Campbell, R. M.** (2) 1981/2 Bradford C

**Campbell, W.** (6) 1967/8 Dundee

**Carey, J.** (7) 1946/7 Manchester U

**Carroll, R. E.** (9) 1996/7 Wigan Ath

**Casey, T.** (12) 1954/5 Newcastle U, Portsmouth

**Caskey, A.** (7) 1978/9 Derby C, Tulsa Roughnecks

**Cassidy, T.** (24) 1970/1 Newcastle U, Burnley

**Caughey, M.** (2) 1985/6 Linfield

**Clarke, C. J.** (38) 1985/6 Bournemouth, Southampton, Portsmouth

**Cleary, J.** (5) 1981/2 Glentoran

**Clements, D.** (48) 1964/5 Coventry C, Sheffield W, Everton, New York Cosmos

**Cochrane, D.** (10) 1946/7 Leeds U

**Cochrane, T.** (26) 1975/6 Coleraine, Burnley, Middlesbrough, Gillingham

**Coote, A.** (6) 1998/9 Norwich C

**Cowan, J.** (1) 1969/70 Newcastle U

**Coyle, F.** (4) 1955/6 Coleraine, Nottingham F

**Coyle, L.** (1) 1988/9 Derry C

**Coyle, R.** (5) 1972/3 Sheffield W

**Craig, D.** (25) 1966/7 Newcastle U

**Crossan, E.** (3) 1949/50 Blackburn R

**Crossan, J.** (23) 1959/60 Sparta Rotterdam, Sunderland, Manchester C, Middlesbrough

**Cunningham, W.** (30) 1950/1 St Mirren, Leicester C, Dunfermline Ath

**Cush, W.** (26) 1950/1 Glentoran, Leeds U, Portadown

**D'Arcy, S.** (5) 1951/2 Chelsea, Brentford

**Davison, A. J.** (3) 1995/6 Bolton W, Bradford C, Grimsby T

**Dennison, R.** (18) 1987/8 Wolverhampton W

**Devine, J.** (1) 1989/90 Glentoran

**Dickson, D.** (4) 1969/70 Coleraine

**Dickson, T.** (1) 1956/7 Linfield

**Dickson, W.** (12) 1950/1 Chelsea, Arsenal

**Doherty, L.** (2) 1984/5 Linfield

**Doherty, P.** (6) 1946/7 Derby Co, Huddersfield T, Doncaster R

**Donaghy, M.** (91) 1979/80 Luton T, Manchester U, Chelsea

**Dougan, D.** (43) 1957/8 Portsmouth, Blackburn R, Aston Villa, Leicester C, Wolverhampton W

**Douglas, J. P.** (1) 1946/7 Belfast Celtic

**Dowd, H.** (3) 1972/3 Glentoran, Sheffield W

**Dowie, I.** (59) 1989/90 Luton T, Southampton, Crystal P, West Ham, QPR

**Dunlop, G.** (4) 1984/5 Linfield

**Eglington, T.** (6) 1946/7 Everton

**Elder, A.** (40) 1959/60 Burnley, Stoke C

**Elliott, S.** (8) 2000/01 Motherwell

**Farrell, P.** (7) 1946/7 Everton

**Feeney, J.** (2) 1946/7 Linfield, Swansea C

**Feeney, W.** (1) 1975/6 Glentoran

**Ferguson, G.** (5) 1998/9 Linfield

**Ferguson, W.** (2) 1965/6 Linfield

**Ferris, R.** (3) 1949/50 Birmingham C

**Fettis, A.** (25) 1991/2 Hull C, Nottingham F, Blackburn R

**Finney, T.** (14) 1974/5 Sunderland, Cambridge U

**Fleming, J. G.** (31) 1986/7 Nottingham F, Manchester C, Barnsley

**Forde, T.** (4) 1958/9 Ards

**Gallogly, C.** (2) 1950/1 Huddersfield T

**Garton, R.** (1) 1968/9 Oxford U

**Gillespie, K. R.** (36) 1994/5 Manchester U, Newcastle U, Blackburn R

**Gorman, W.** (4) 1946/7 Brentford

**Graham, W.** (14) 1950/1 Doncaster R

**Gray, P.** (26) 1992/3 Luton T, Sunderland, Nancy, Luton T, Burnley, Oxford U

**Gregg, H.** (25) 1953/4 Doncaster R, Manchester U

**Griffin, D. J.** (18) 1995/6 St Johnstone, Dundee U

**Hamill, R.** (1) 1998/9 Glentoran

**Hamilton, B.** (50) 1968/9 Linfield, Ipswich T, Everton, Millwall, Swindon T

**Hamilton, W.** (41) 1977/8 QPR, Burnley, Oxford U

**Harkin, T.** (5) 1967/8 Southport, Shrewsbury T

**Harvey, M.** (34) 1960/1 Sunderland

**Hatton, S.** (2) 1962/3 Linfield

**Healy, D. J.** (12) 1999/00 Manchester U, Preston NE

**Healy, P. J.** (4) 1981/2 Coleraine, Glentoran

**Hegan, D.** (7) 1969/70 WBA, Wolverhampton W

**Hill, C. F.** (27) 1989/90 Sheffield U, Leicester C, Trelleborg, Northampton T

**Hill, J.** (7) 1958/9 Norwich C, Everton

**Hinton, E.** (7) 1946/7 Fulham, Millwall

**Horlock, K.** (25) 1994/5 Swindon T, Manchester C

**Hughes, A. W.** (20) 1997/8 Newcastle U

**Hughes, M. E.** (58) 1991/2 Manchester C, Strasbourg, West Ham U, Wimbledon

**Hughes, P.** (3) 1986/7 Bury

**Hughes, W.** (1) 1950/1 Bolton W

**Humphries, W.** (14) 1961/2 Ards, Coventry C, Swansea T

**Hunter, A.** (53) 1969/70 Blackburn R, Ipswich T

**Hunter, B. V.** (15) 1994/5 Wrexham, Reading

**Irvine, R.** (8) 1961/2 Linfield, Stoke C

**Irvine, W.** (23) 1962/3 Burnley, Preston NE, Brighton & HA

**Jackson, T.** (35) 1968/9 Everton, Nottingham F, Manchester U

**Jamison, A.** (1) 1975/6 Glentoran

**Jenkins, I.** (6) 1996/7 Chester C, Dundee U

**Jennings, P.** (119) 1963/4 Watford, Tottenham H, Arsenal, Tottenham H, Everton, Tottenham H

**Johnson, D. M.** (12) 1998/9 Blackburn R

**Johnston, W.** (1) 1961/2 Glentoran, Oldham Ath

**Jones, J.** (3) 1955/6 Glenavon

**Keane, T.** (1) 1948/9 Swansea T

**Kee, P. V.** (9) 1989/90 Oxford U, Ards

**Keith, R.** (23) 1957/8 Newcastle U

**Kelly, H.** (4) 1949/50 Fulham, Southampton

**Kelly, P.** (1) 1949/50 Barnsley

**Kennedy, P. H.** (9) 1998/9 Watford

**Kirk, A.** (2) 1999/00 Heart of Midlothian

**Lawther, I.** (4) 1959/60 Sunderland, Blackburn R

**Lennon, N. F.** (39) 1993/4 Crewe Alexandra, Leicester C, Celtic

**Lockhart, N.** (8) 1946/7 Linfield, Coventry C, Aston Villa

**Lomas, S. M.** (38) 1993/4 Manchester C, West Ham U

**Lutton, B.** (6) 1969/70 Wolverhampton W, West Ham U

**Magill, E.** (26) 1961/2 Arsenal, Brighton & HA

**Magilton, J.** (47) 1990/1 Oxford U, Southampton, Sheffield W, Ipswich T

**Martin, C.** (6) 1946/7 Glentoran, Leeds U, Aston Villa

**McAdams, W.** (15) 1953/4 Manchester C, Bolton W, Leeds U

**McAlinden, J.** (2) 1946/7 Portsmouth, Southend U

**McBride, S.** (4) 1990/1 Glenavon

**McCabe, J.** (6) 1948/9 Leeds U

**McCarthy, J. D.** (18) 1995/6 Port Vale, Birmingham C

**McCavana, T.** (3) 1954/5 Coleraine

**McCleary, J. W.** (1) 1954/5 Cliftonville

**McClelland, J.** (6) 1960/1 Arsenal, Fulham

**McClelland, J.** (53) 1979/80 Mansfield T, Rangers, Watford, Leeds U

**McCourt, F.** (6) 1951/2 Manchester C

**McCoy, R.** (1) 1986/7 Coleraine

**McCreery, D.** (67) 1975/6 Manchester U, QPR, Tulsa Roughnecks, Newcastle U, Heart of Midlothian

**McCrory, S.** (1) 1957/8 Southend U

**McCullough, W.** (10) 1960/1 Arsenal, Millwall

**McCurdy, C.** (1) 1979/80 Linfield

**McDonald, A.** (52) 1985/6 QPR

**McElhinney, G.** (6) 1983/4 Bolton W

**McFaul, I.** (6) 1966/7 Linfield, Newcastle U

**McGarry, J. K.** (3) 1950/1 Cliftonville

**McGaughey, M.** (1) 1984/5 Linfield

**McGibbon, P. C. G.** (7) 1994/5 Manchester U, Wigan Ath

**McGrath, R.** (21) 1973/4 Tottenham H, Manchester U

**McIlroy, J.** (55) 1951/2 Burnley, Stoke C

**McIlroy, S. B.** (88) 1971/2 Manchester U, Stoke C, Manchester C

**McKeag, W.** (2) 1967/8 Glentoran

**McKenna, J.** (7) 1949/50 Huddersfield T

**McKenzie, R.** (1) 1966/7 Airdrieonians

**McKinney, W.** (1) 1965/6 Falkirk

**McKnight, A.** (10) 1987/8 Celtic, West Ham U

**McLaughlin, J.** (12) 1961/2 Shrewsbury T, Swansea T

**McMahon, G. J.** (17) 1994/5 Tottenham H, Stoke C

**McMichael, A.** (39) 1949/50 Newcastle U

**McMillan, S.** (2) 1962/3 Manchester U

**McMordie, E.** (21) 1968/9 Middlesbrough

**McMorran, E.** (15) 1946/7 Belfast Celtic, Barnsley, Doncaster R

**McNally, B. A.** (5) 1985/6 Shrewsbury T

**McParland, P.** (34) 1953/4 Aston Villa, Wolverhampton W

**McVeigh, P.** (1) 1998/9 Tottenham H

**Montgomery, F. J.** (1) 1954/5 Coleraine

**Moore, C.** (1) 1948/9 Glentoran

**Moreland, V.** (6) 1978/9 Derby Co

**Morgan, S.** (18) 1971/2 Port Vale, Aston Villa, Brighton & HA, Sparta Rotterdam

**Morrow, S. J.** (39) 1989/90 Arsenal, QPR

**Mullan, G.** (4) 1982/3 Glentoran

**Mulryne, P. P.** (12) 1996/7 Manchester U, Norwich C

**Murdock, C. J.** (12) 1999/00 Preston NE

**Napier, R.** (1) 1965/6 Bolton W

**Neill, T.** (59) 1960/1 Arsenal, Hull C

**Nelson, S.** (51) 1969/70 Arsenal, Brighton & HA

**Nicholl, C.** (51) 1974/5 Aston Villa, Southampton, Grimsby T

**Nicholl, J. M.** (73) 1975/6 Manchester U, Toronto Blizzard, Sunderland, Rangers, WBA

**Nicholson, J.** (41) 1960/1 Manchester U, Huddersfield T

**Nolan, I. R.** (17) 1996/7 Sheffield W, Bradford C

**O'Boyle, G.** (13) 1993/4 Dunfermline Ath, St Johnstone

**O'Doherty, A.** (2) 1969/70 Coleraine

**O'Driscoll, J.** (3) 1948/9 Swansea T

**O'Kane, L.** (20) 1969/70 Nottingham F

**O'Neill, C.** (3) 1988/9 Motherwell

**O'Neill, H. M.** (64) 1971/2 Distillery, Nottingham F, Norwich C, Manchester C, Norwich C, Notts Co

**O'Neill, J.** (1) 1961/2 Sunderland

**O'Neill, J.** (39) 1979/80 Leicester C

**O'Neill, M. A.** (31) 1987/8 Newcastle U, Dundee U, Hibernian, Coventry C

**Parke, J.** (13) 1963/4 Linfield, Hibernian, Sunderland

**Patterson, D. J.** (17) 1993/4 Crystal P, Luton T, Dundee U

**Peacock, R.** (31) 1951/2 Celtic, Coleraine

**Penney, S.** (17) 1984/5 Brighton & HA

**Platt, J. A.** (23) 1975/6 Middlesbrough, Ballymena U, Coleraine

Quinn, J. M. (46) 1984/5 Blackburn R,
  Leicester, Bradford C, West Ham U,
  Bournemouth, Reading
Quinn, S. J. (24) 1995/6 Blackpool,
  WBA

Rafferty, P. (1) 1979/80 Linfield
Ramsey, P. (14) 1983/4 Leicester C
Rice, P. (49) 1968/9 Arsenal
Robinson, S. (5) 1996/7 Bournemouth
Rogan, A. (18) 1987/8 Celtic,
  Sunderland, Millwall
Ross, E. (1) 1968/9 Newcastle U
Rowland, K. (19) 1994/5 West Ham U
Russell, A. (1) 1946/7 Linfield
Ryan, R. (1) 1949/50 WBA

Sanchez, L. P. (3) 1986/7 Wimbledon
Scott, J. (2) 1957/8 Grimsby T
Scott, P. (10) 1974/5 Everton, York C,
  Aldershot
Sharkey, P. (1) 1975/6 Ipswich T
Shields, J. (1) 1956/7 Southampton
Simpson, W. (12) 1950/1 Rangers
Sloan, D. (2) 1968/9 Oxford
Sloan, T. (3) 1978/9 Manchester U
Sloan, W. (1) 1946/7 Arsenal
Smyth, S. (9) 1947/8 Wolverhampton
  W, Stoke C
Smyth, W. (4) 1948/9 Distillery
Sonner, D. J. (7) 1997/8 Ipswich T,
  Sheffield W, Birmingham C
Spence, D. (29) 1974/5 Bury,
  Blackpool, Southend U
Stevenson, A. (3) 1946/7 Everton
Stewart, A. (7) 1966/7 Glentoran,
  Derby
Stewart, D. (1) 1977/8 Hull C
Stewart, I. (31) 1981/2 QPR, Newcastle
  U

Stewart, T. (1) 1960/1 Linfield

Taggart, G. P. (50) 1989/90 Barnsley,
  Bolton W, Leicester C
Taylor, M. S. (15) 1998/9 Fulham
Todd, S. (11) 1965/6 Burnley, Sheffield
  W
Trainor, D. (1) 1966/7 Crusaders
Tully, C. (10) 1948/9 Celtic

Uprichard, N. (18) 1951/2 Swindon T,
  Portsmouth

Vernon, J. (17) 1946/7 Belfast Celtic,
  WBA

Walker, J. (1) 1954/5 Doncaster R
Walsh, D. (9) 1946/7 WBA
Walsh, W. (5) 1947/8 Manchester C
Watson, P. (1) 1970/1 Distillery
Welsh, S. (4) 1965/6 Carlisle U
Whiteside, N. (38) 1981/2 Manchester
  U, Everton
Whitley, Jeff (7) 1996/7 Manchester C
Whitley, Jim (3) 1997/8 Manchester C
Williams, M. S. (17) 1998/9
  Chesterfield, Watford
Williams, P. (1) 1990/1 WBA
Wilson, D. J. (24) 1986/7 Brighton &
  HA, Luton, Sheffield W
Wilson, K. J. (42) 1986/7 Ipswich T,
  Chelsea, Notts C, Walsall
Wilson, S. (12) 1961/2 Glenavon,
  Falkirk, Dundee
Wood, T. J. (1) 1995/6 Walsall
Worthington, N. (66) 1983/4 Sheffield
  W, Leeds U, Stoke C
Wright, T. J. (31) 1988/9 Newcastle U,
  Nottingham F, Manchester C

## SCOTLAND

Aird, J. (4) 1953/4 Burnley
Aitken, G. G. (8) 1948/9 East Fife,
  Sunderland
Aitken, R. (57) 1979/80 Celtic,
  Newcastle U, St Mirren
Albiston, A. (14) 1981/2 Manchester U
Allan, T. (2) 1973/4 Dundee
Anderson, J. (1) 1953/4 Leicester C
Archibald, S. (27) 1979/80 Aberdeen,
  Tottenham H, Barcelona
Auld, B. (3) 1958/9 Celtic

Baird, H. (1) 1955/6 Airdrieonians
Baird, S. (7) 1956/7 Rangers
Bannon, E. (11) 1979/80 Dundee U
Bauld, W. (3) 1949/50 Heart of
  Midlothian

Baxter, J. (34) 1960/1 Rangers,
  Sunderland
Bell, W. (2) 1965/6 Leeds U
Bernard, P. R. (2) 1994/5 Oldham Ath
Bett, J. (25) 1981/2 Rangers, Lokeren,
  Aberdeen
Black, E. (2) 1987/8 Metz
Black, I. (1) 1947/8 Southampton
Blacklaw, A. (3) 1962/3 Burnley
Blackley, J. (7) 1973/4 Hibernian
Blair, J. (1) 1946/7 Blackpool
Blyth, J. (2) 1977/8 Coventry C
Bone, J. (2) 1971/2 Norwich C
Booth, S. (18) 1992/3 Aberdeen,
  Borussia Dortmund, Twente
Bowman, D. (6) 1991/2 Dundee U

Boyd, T. (71) 1990/1 Motherwell, Chelsea, Celtic
Brand, R. (8) 1960/1 Rangers
Brazil, A. (13) 1979/80 Ipswich T, Tottenham H
Bremner, D. (1) 1975/6 Hibernian
Bremner, W. (54) 1964/5 Leeds U
Brennan, F. (7) 1946/7 Newcastle U
Brogan, J. (4) 1970/1 Celtic
Brown, A. (14) 1949/50 East Fife, Blackpool
Brown, H. (3) 1946/7 Partick Thistle
Brown, J. (1) 1974/5 Sheffield U
Brown, R. (3) 1946/7 Rangers
Brown, W. (28) 1957/8 Dundee, Tottenham H
Brownlie, J. (7) 1970/1 Hibernian
Buchan, M. (34) 1971/2 Aberdeen, Manchester U
Buckley, P. (3) 1953/4 Aberdeen
Burchill, M. J. (6) 1999/00 Celtic
Burley, C. W. (42) 1994/5 Chelsea, Celtic, Derby Co
Burley, G. (11) 1978/9 Ipswich T
Burns, F. (1) 1969/70 Manchester U
Burns, K. (20) 1973/4 Birmingham C, Nottingham F
Burns, T. (8) 1980/1 Celtic

Calderwood, C. (36) 1994/5 Tottenham H, Aston Villa
Caldow, E. (40) 1956/7 Rangers
Caldwell, S. (1) 2000/01 Newcastle U
Callaghan, W. (2) 1969/70 Dunfermline
Cameron, C. (11) 1998/9 Heart of Midlothian
Campbell, R. (5) 1946/7 Falkirk, Chelsea
Campbell, W. (5) 1946/7 Morton
Carr, W. (6) 1969/70 Coventry C
Chalmers, S. (5) 1964/5 Celtic
Clark, J. (4) 1965/6 Celtic
Clark, R. (17) 1967/8 Aberdeen
Clarke, S. (6) 1987/8 Chelsea
Collins, J. (58) 1987/8 Hibernian, Celtic, Monaco, Everton
Collins, R. (31) 1950/1 Celtic, Everton, Leeds U
Colquhoun, E. (9) 1971/2 Sheffield U
Colquhoun, J. (1) 1987/8 Heart of Midlothian
Combe, R. (3) 1947/8 Hibernian
Conn, A. (1) 1955/6 Heart of Midlothian
Conn, A. (2) 1974/5 Tottenham H
Connachan, E. (2) 1961/2 Dunfermline Ath
Connelly, G. (2) 1973/4 Celtic
Connolly, J. (1) 1972/3 Everton

Connor, R. (4) 1985/6 Dundee, Aberdeen
Cooke, C. (16) 1965/6 Dundee, Chelsea
Cooper, D. (22) 1979/80 Rangers, Motherwell
Cormack, P. (9) 1965/6 Hibernian, Nottingham F
Cowan, J. (25) 1947/8 Morton, Motherwell
Cowie, D. (20) 1952/3 Dundee
Cox, C. (1) 1947/8 Heart of Midlothian
Cox, S. (24) 1947/8 Rangers
Craig, J. (1) 1976/7 Celtic
Craig, J. P. (1) 1967/8 Celtic
Craig, T. (1) 1975/6 Newcastle U
Crawford, S. (2) 1994/5 Raith R, Dunfermline Ath
Crerand, P. (16) 1960/1 Celtic, Manchester U
Cropley, A. (2) 1971/2 Hibernian
Cruickshank, J. (6) 1963/4 Heart of Midlothian
Cullen, M. (1) 1955/6 Luton T
Cumming, J. (9) 1954/5 Heart of Midlothian
Cunningham, W. (8) 1953/4 Preston NE
Curran, H. (5) 1969/70 Wolverhampton W

Dailly, C. (27) 1996/7 Derby Co, Blackburn R, West Ham U
Dalglish, K. (102) 1971/2 Celtic, Liverpool
Davidson, C. I. (14) 1998/9 Blackburn R, Leicester C
Davidson, J. (8) 1953/4 Partick Thistle
Dawson, A. (5) 1979/80 Rangers
Deans, D. (2) 1974/5 Celtic
Delaney, J. (4) 1946/7 Manchester U
Dick, J. (1) 1958/9 West Ham U
Dickov, P. (3) 2000/01 Mancheser C
Dickson, W. (5) 1969/70 Kilmarnock
Docherty, T. (25) 1951/2 Preston NE, Arsenal
Dodds, D. (2) 1983/4 Dundee U
Dodds, W. (24) 1996/7 Aberdeen, Dundee U, Rangers
Donachie, W. (35) 1971/2 Manchester C
Donnelly, S. (10) 1996/7 Celtic
Dougall, C. (1) 1946/7 Birmingham C
Dougan, R. (1) 1949/50 Heart of Midlothian
Doyle, J. (1) 1975/6 Ayr U
Duncan, A. (6) 1974/5 Hibernian
Duncan, D. (3) 1947/8 East Fife
Duncanson, J. (1) 1946/7 Rangers
Durie, G. S. (43) 1987/8 Chelsea, Tottenham H, Rangers

**Durrant, I.** (20) 1987/8 Rangers, Kilmarnock

**Elliott, M. S.** (15) 1997/8 Leicester C
**Evans, A.** (4) 1981/2 Aston Villa
**Evans, R.** (48) 1948/9 Celtic, Chelsea
**Ewing, T.** (2) 1957/8 Partick Thistle

**Farm, G.** (10) 1952/3 Blackpool
**Ferguson, B.** (10) 1998/9 Rangers
**Ferguson, Derek** (2) 1987/8 Rangers
**Ferguson, Duncan** (7) 1991/2 Dundee U, Everton
**Ferguson, I.** (9) 1988/9 Rangers
**Ferguson, R.** (7) 1965/6 Kilmarnock
**Fernie, W.** (12) 1953/4 Celtic
**Flavell, R.** (2) 1946/7 Airdrieonians
**Fleck, R.** (4) 1989/90 Norwich C
**Fleming, C.** (1) 1953/4 East Fife
**Forbes, A.** (14) 1946/7 Sheffield U, Arsenal
**Ford, D.** (3) 1973/4 Heart of Midlothian
**Forrest, J.** (1) 1957/8 Motherwell
**Forrest, J.** (5) 1965/6 Rangers, Aberdeen
**Forsyth, A.** (10) 1971/2 Partick Thistle, Manchester U
**Forsyth, C.** (4) 1963/4 Kilmarnock
**Forsyth, T.** (22) 1970/1 Motherwell, Rangers
**Fraser, D.** (2) 1967/8 WBA
**Fraser, W.** (2) 1954/5 Sunderland

**Gabriel, J.** (2) 1960/1 Everton
**Gallacher, K. W.** (53) 1987/8 Dundee U, Coventry C, Blackburn R, Newcastle U
**Galloway, M.** (1) 1991/2 Celtic
**Gardiner, W.** (1) 1957/8 Motherwell
**Gemmell, T.** (2) 1954/5 St Mirren
**Gemmell, T.** (18) 1965/6 Celtic
**Gemmill, A.** (43) 1970/1 Derby Co, Nottingham F, Birmingham C
**Gemmill, S.** (17) 1994/5 Nottingham F, Everton
**Gibson, D.** (7) 1962/3 Leicester C
**Gillespie, G. T.** (13) 1987/8 Liverpool, Celtic
**Gilzean, A.** (22) 1963/4 Dundee, Tottenham H
**Glass, S.** (1) 1998/9 Newcastle U
**Glavin, R.** (1) 1976/7 Celtic
**Glen, A.** (2) 1955/6 Aberdeen
**Goram, A. L.** (43) 1985/6 Oldham Ath, Hibernian, Rangers
**Gough, C. R.** (61) 1982/3 Dundee U, Tottenham H, Rangers
**Gould, J.** (2) 1999/00 Celtic
**Govan, J.** (6) 1947/8 Hibernian
**Graham, A.** (10) 1977/8 Leeds U

**Graham, G.** (12) 1971/2 Arsenal, Manchester U
**Grant, J.** (2) 1958/9 Hibernian
**Grant, P.** (2) 1988/9 Celtic
**Gray, A.** (20) 1975/6 Aston Villa, Wolverhampton W, Everton
**Gray, E.** (12) 1968/9 Leeds U
**Gray F.** (32) 1975/6 Leeds U, Nottingham F, Leeds U
**Green, A.** (6) 1970/1 Blackpool, Newcastle U
**Greig, J.** (44) 1963/4 Rangers
**Gunn, B.** (6) 1989/90 Norwich C

**Haddock, H.** (6) 1954/5 Clyde
**Haffey, F.** (2) 1959/60 Celtic
**Hamilton, A.** (24) 1961/2 Dundee
**Hamilton, G.** (5) 1946/7 Aberdeen
**Hamilton, W.** (1) 1964/5 Hibernian
**Hansen, A.** (26) 1978/9 Liverpool
**Hansen J.** (2) 1971/2 Partick Thistle
**Harper, J.** (4) 1972/3 Aberdeen
**Hartford, A.** (50) 1971/2 WBA, Manchester C, Everton, Manchester C
**Harvey, D.** (16) 1972/3 Leeds U
**Haughney, M.** (1) 1953/4 Celtic
**Hay, D.** (27) 1969/70 Celtic
**Hegarty, P.** (8) 1978/9 Dundee U
**Henderson, J.** (7) 1952/3 Portsmouth, Arsenal
**Henderson, W.** (29) 1962/3 Rangers
**Hendry, E. C. J.** (51) 1992/3 Blackburn R, Rangers, Coventry C, Bolton W
**Herd, D.** (5) 1958/9 Arsenal
**Herd, G.** (5) 1957/8 Clyde
**Herriot, J.** (8) 1968/9 Birmingham C
**Hewie, J.** (19) 1955/6 Charlton Ath
**Holt, D. D.** (5) 1962/3 Heart of Midlothian
**Holt, G. J.** (2) 2000/01 Kilmarnock
**Holton, J.** (15) 1972/3 Manchester U
**Hope, R.** (2) 1967/8 WBA
**Hopkin, D.** (7) 1996/7 Crystal P, Leeds U
**Houliston, W.** (3) 1948/9 Queen of the South
**Houston, S.** (1) 1975/6 Manchester U
**Howie, H.** (1) 1948/9 Hibernian
**Hughes, J.** (8) 1964/5 Celtic
**Hughes, W.** (1) 1974/5 Sunderland
**Humphries, W.** (1) 1951/2 Motherwell
**Hunter, A.** (4) 1971/2 Kilmarnock, Celtic
**Hunter, W.** (3) 1959/60 Motherwell
**Husband, J.** (1) 1946/7 Partick Thistle
**Hutchison, D.** (16) 1998/9 Everton, Sunderland
**Hutchison, T.** (17) 1973/4 Coventry C

**Imlach, S.** (4) 1957/8 Nottingham F
**Irvine, B.** (9) 1990/1 Aberdeen

**Jackson, C.** (8) 1974/5 Rangers
**Jackson, D.** (28) 1994/5 Hibernian, Celtic
**Jardine, A.** (38) 1970/1 Rangers
**Jarvie, A.** (3) 1970/1 Airdrieonians
**Jess, E.** (18) 1992/3 Aberdeen, Coventry C, Aberdeen
**Johnston, A.** (12) 1998/9 Sunderland, Rangers
**Johnston, M.** (38) 1983/4 Watford, Celtic, Nantes, Rangers
**Johnston, W.** (22) 1965/6 Rangers, WBA
**Johnstone, D.** (14) 1972/3 Rangers
**Johnstone, J.** (23) 1964/5 Celtic
**Johnstone, L.** (2) 1947/8 Clyde
**Johnstone, R.** (17) 1950/1 Hibernian, Manchester C
**Jordan, J.** (52) 1972/3 Leeds U, Manchester U, AC Milan

**Kelly, H.** (1) 1951/2 Blackpool
**Kelly, J.** (2) 1948/9 Barnsley
**Kennedy, J.** (6) 1963/4 Celtic
**Kennedy, S.** (8) 1977/8 Aberdeen
**Kennedy, S.** (5) 1974/5 Rangers
**Kerr, A.** (2) 1954/5 Partick Thistle

**Lambert, P.** (26) 1994/5 Motherwell, Borussia Dortmund, Celtic
**Law, D.** (55) 1958/9 Huddersfield T, Manchester C, Torino, Manchester U, Manchester C
**Lawrence, T.** (3) 1962/3 Liverpool
**Leggat, G.** (18) 1955/6 Aberdeen, Fulham
**Leighton, J.** (91) 1982/3 Aberdeen, Manchester U, Hibernian, Aberdeen
**Lennox, R.** (10) 1966/7 Celtic
**Leslie, L.** (5) 1960/1 Airdrieonians
**Levein, C.** (16) 1989/90 Heart of Midlothian
**Liddell, W.** (28) 1946/7 Liverpool
**Linwood, A.** (1) 1949/50 Clyde
**Little, A.** (1) 1952/3 Rangers
**Logie, J.** (1) 1952/3 Arsenal
**Long, H.** (1) 1946/7 Clyde
**Lorimer, P.** (21) 1969/70 Leeds U

**Macari, L.** (24) 1971/2 Celtic, Manchester U
**Macaulay, A.** (7) 1946/7 Brentford, Arsenal
**MacDougall, E.** (7) 1974/5 Norwich C
**Mackay, D.** (22) 1956/7 Heart of Midlothian, Tottenham H

**Mackay, G.** (4) 1987/8 Heart of Midlothian
**Malpas, M.** (55) 1983/4 Dundee U
**Marshall, G.** (1) 1991/2 Celtic
**Martin, B.** (2) 1994/5 Motherwell
**Martin, F.** (6) 1953/4 Aberdeen
**Martin, N.** (3) 1964/5 Hibernian, Sunderland
**Martis, J.** (1) 1960/1 Motherwell
**Mason, J.** (7) 1948/9 Third Lanark
**Masson, D.** (17) 1975/6 QPR, Derby C
**Mathers, D.** (1) 1953/4 Partick Thistle
**Matteo, D.** (3) 2000/01 Leeds U
**McAllister, B.** (3) 1996/7 Wimbledon
**McAllister, G.** (57) 1989/90 Leicester C, Leeds U, Coventry C
**McAvennie, F.** (5) 1985/6 West Ham U, Celtic
**McBride, J.** (2) 1966/7 Celtic
**McCall, S. M.** (40) 1989/90 Everton, Rangers
**McCalliog, J.** (5) 1966/7 Sheffield W, Wolverhampton W
**McCann, N. D.** (11) 1998/9 Heart of Midlothian, Rangers
**McCann, R.** (5) 1958/9 Motherwell
**McClair, B.** (30) 1986/7 Celtic, Manchester U
**McCloy, P.** (4) 1972/3 Rangers
**McCoist, A.** (61) 1985/6 Rangers, Kilmarnock
**McColl, I.** (14) 1949/50 Rangers
**McCreadie, E.** (23) 1964/5 Chelsea
**MacDonald, A.** (1) 1975/6 Rangers
**MacDonald, J.** (2) 1955/6 Sunderland
**McFarlane, W.** (1) 1946/7 Heart of Midlothian
**McGarr, E.** (2) 1969/70 Aberdeen
**McGarvey, F.** (7) 1978/9 Liverpool, Celtic
**McGhee, M.** (4) 1982/3 Aberdeen
**McGinlay, J.** (13) 1993/4 Bolton W
**McGrain, D.** (62) 1972/3 Celtic
**McGrory, J.** (3) 1964/5 Kilmarnock
**McInally, A.** (8) 1988/9 Aston Villa, Bayern Munich
**McInally, J.** (10) 1986/7 Dundee U
**McKay, D.** (14) 1958/9 Celtic
**McKean, R.** (1) 1975/6 Rangers
**McKenzie, J.** (9) 1953/4 Partick Thistle
**McKimmie, S.** (40) 1988/9 Aberdeen
**McKinlay, T.** (22) 1995/6 Celtic
**McKinlay, W.** (29) 1993/4 Dundee U, Blackburn R
**McKinnon, R.** (28) 1965/6 Rangers
**McKinnon, R.** (3) 1993/4 Motherwell
**McLaren, A.** (4) 1946/7 Preston NE
**McLaren, A.** (24) 1991/2 Heart of Midlothian, Rangers
**McLaren, A.** (1) 2000/01 Kilmarnock

McLean, G. (1) 1967/8 Dundee
McLean, T. (6) 1968/9 Kilmarnock
McLeish, A. (77) 1979/80 Aberdeen
McLeod, J. (4) 1960/1 Hibernian
MacLeod, M. (20) 1984/5 Celtic, Borussia Dortmund, Hibernian
McLintock, F. (9) 1962/3 Leicester C, Arsenal
McMillan, I. (6) 1951/2 Airdrieonians, Rangers
McNamara, J. (11) 1996/7 Celtic
McNaught, W. (5) 1950/1 Raith R
McNeill, W. (29) 1960/1 Celtic
McPhail, J. (5) 1949/50 Celtic
McPherson, D. (27) 1988/9 Heart of Midlothian, Rangers
McQueen, G. (30) 1973/4 Leeds U, Manchester U
McStay, P. (76) 1983/4 Celtic
McSwegan, G. (2) 1999/00 Heart of Midlothian
Millar, J. (2) 1962/3 Rangers
Miller, C. (1) 2000/01 Dundee U
Miller, K. (1) 2000/01 Rangers
Miller, W. (6) 1946/7 Celtic
Miller, W. (65) 1974/5 Aberdeen
Mitchell, R. (2) 1950/1 Newcastle U
Mochan, N. (3) 1953/4 Celtic
Moir, W. (1) 1949/50 Bolton W
Moncur, R. (16) 1967/8 Newcastle U
Morgan, W. (21) 1967/8 Burnley, Manchester U
Morris, H. (1) 1949/50 East Fife
Mudie, J. (17) 1956/7 Blackpool
Mulhall, G. (3) 1959/60 Aberdeen, Sunderland
Munro, F. (9) 1970/1 Wolverhampton W
Munro, I. (7) 1978/9 St Mirren
Murdoch, R. (12) 1965/6 Celtic
Murray, J. (5) 1957/8 Heart of Midlothian
Murray, S. (1) 1971/2 Aberdeen

Narey, D. (35) 1976/7 Dundee U
Naysmith, G. A. (4) 1999/00 Heart of Midlothian
Nevin, P. K. F. (28) 1985/6 Chelsea, Everton, Tranmere R
Nicholas, C. (20) 1982/3 Celtic, Arsenal, Aberdeen
Nicholson, B. (1) 2000/01 Dunfermline Ath
Nicol, S. (27) 1984/5 Liverpool

O'Donnell, P. (1) 1993/4 Motherwell
O'Hare, J. (13) 1969/70 Derby Co
O'Neil, B. (6) 1995/6 Celtic, Wolfsburg, Derby Co
O'Neil, J. (1) 2000/01 Hibernian

Ormond, W. (6) 1953/4 Hibernian
Orr, T. (2) 1951/2 Morton

Parker, A. (15) 1954/5 Falkirk
Parlane, D. (12) 1972/3 Rangers
Paton, A. (2) 1951/2 Motherwell
Pearson, T. (2) 1946/7 Newcastle U
Penman, A. (1) 1965/6 Dundee
Pettigrew, W. (5) 1975/6 Motherwell
Plenderleith, J. (1) 1960/1 Manchester C
Pressley, S. J. (2) 1999/00 Heart of Midlothian
Provan, D. (5) 1963/4 Rangers
Provan, D. (10) 1979/80 Celtic

Quinn, P. (4) 1960/1 Motherwell

Rae, G. (1) 2000/01 Dundee
Redpath, W. (9) 1948/9 Motherwell
Reilly, L. (38) 1948/9 Hibernian
Ring, T. (12) 1952/3 Clydebank
Rioch, B. (24) 1974/5 Derby Co, Everton, Derby Co
Ritchie, P. S. (6) 1998/9 Heart of Midlothian, Bolton W
Robb, D. (5) 1970/1 Aberdeen
Robertson, A. (5) 1954/5 Clyde
Robertson, D. (3) 1991/2 Rangers
Robertson, H. (1) 1961/2 Dundee
Robertson, J. (16) 1990/1 Heart of Midlothian
Robertson, J. G. (1) 1964/5 Tottenham H
Robertson, J. N. (28) 1977/8 Nottingham F, Derby Co
Robinson, B. (4) 1973/4 Dundee
Rough, A. (53) 1975/6 Partick Thistle, Hibernian
Rougvie, D. (1) 1983/4 Aberdeen
Rutherford, E. (1) 1947/8 Rangers

St John, I. (21) 1958/9 Motherwell, Liverpool
Schaedler, E. (1) 1973/4 Hibernian
Scott, A. (16) 1956/7 Rangers, Everton
Scott, J. (1) 1965/6 Hibernian
Scott, J. (2) 1970/1 Dundee
Scoular, J. (9) 1950/1 Portsmouth
Sharp, G. M. (12) 1984/5 Everton
Shaw, D. (8) 1946/7 Hibernian
Shaw, J. (4) 1946/7 Rangers
Shearer, D. (7) 1993/4 Aberdeen
Shearer, R. (4) 1960/1 Rangers
Simpson, N. (4) 1982/3 Aberdeen
Simpson, R. (5) 1966/7 Celtic
Sinclair, J. (1) 1965/6 Leicester C
Smith, D. (2) 1965/6 Aberdeen, Rangers
Smith, E. (2) 1958/9 Celtic

**Smith, G.** (18) 1946/7 Hibernian
**Smith, H. G.** (3) 1987/8 Heart of
Midlothian
**Smith, J.** (4) 1967/8 Aberdeen,
Newcastle U
**Souness, G.** (54) 1974/5 Middlesbrough,
Liverpool, Sampdoria
**Speedie, D. R.** (10) 1984/5 Chelsea,
Coventry C
**Spencer, J.** (14) 1994/5 Chelsea, QPR
**Stanton, P.** (16) 1965/6 Hibernian
**Steel, W.** (30) 1946/7 Morton, Derby C,
Dundee
**Stein, C.** (21) 1968/9 Rangers, Coventry
C
**Stephen, J.** (2) 1946/7 Bradford C
**Stewart, D.** (1) 1977/8 Leeds U
**Stewart, J.** (2) 1976/7 Kilmarnock,
Middlesbrough
**Stewart, R.** (10) 1980/1 West Ham U
**Strachan, G.** (50) 1979/80 Aberdeen,
Manchester U, Leeds U
**Sturrock, P.** (20) 1980/1 Dundee U
**Sullivan, N.** (22) 1996/7 Wimbledon,
Tottenham H

**Telfer, P. N.** (1) 1999/00 Coventry C
**Telfer, W.** (1) 1953/4 St Mirren
**Thomson, W.** (7) 1979/80 St Mirren
**Thornton, W.** (7) 1946/7 Rangers
**Toner, W.** (2) 1958/9 Kilmarnock
**Turnbull, E.** (8) 1947/8 Hibernian

**Ure, I.** (11) 1961/2 Dundee, Arsenal

**Waddell, W.** (17) 1946/7 Rangers
**Walker, A.** (3) 1987/8 Celtic
**Walker, J. N.** (2) 1992/3 Heart of
Midlothian, Partick Thistle

**Wallace, L. A.** (3) 1977/8 Coventry C
**Wallace, W. S. B.** (7) 1964/5 Heart of
Midlothian, Celtic
**Wardhaugh, J.** (2) 1954/5 Heart of
Midlothian
**Wark, J.** (29) 1978/9 Ipswich T,
Liverpool
**Watson, J.** (2) 1947/8 Motherwell,
Huddersfield T
**Watson, R.** (1) 1970/1 Motherwell
**Weir, A.** (6) 1958/9 Motherwell
**Weir, D. G.** (27) 1996/7 Heart of
Midlothian, Everton
**Weir, P.** (6) 1979/80 St Mirren,
Aberdeen
**White, J.** (22) 1958/9 Falkirk,
Tottenham H
**Whyte, D.** (12) 1987/8 Celtic,
Middlesbrough, Aberdeen
**Wilson, A.** (1) 1953/4 Portsmouth
**Wilson, D.** (22) 1960/1 Rangers
**Wilson, I. A.** (5) 1986/7 Leicester C,
Everton
**Wilson, P.** (1) 1974/5 Celtic
**Wilson, R.** (2) 1971/2 Arsenal
**Winters, R.** (1) 1998/9 Aberdeen
**Wood, G.** (4) 1978/9 Everton, Arsenal
**Woodburn, W.** (24) 1946/7 Rangers
**Wright, K.** (1) 1991/2 Hibernian
**Wright, S.** (2) 1992/3 Aberdeen
**Wright, T.** (3) 1952/3 Sunderland

**Yeats, R.** (2) 1964/5 Liverpool
**Yorston, H.** (1) 1954/5 Aberdeen
**Young, A.** (9) 1959/60 Heart of
Midlothian, Everton
**Young, G.** (53) 1946/7 Rangers
**Younger, T.** (24) 1954/5 Hibernian,
Liverpool

## WALES

**Aizlewood, M.** (39) 1985/6 Charlton
Ath, Leeds U, Bradford C, Bristol C,
Cardiff C
**Allchurch, I.** (68) 1950/1 Swansea T,
Newcastle U, Cardiff C, Swansea T
**Allchurch, L.** (11) 1954/5 Swansea T,
Sheffield U
**Allen, B.** (2) 1950/1 Coventry C
**Allen, M.** (14) 1985/6 Watford,
Norwich C, Millwall, Newcastle U

**Baker, C.** (7) 1957/8 Cardiff C
**Baker, W.** (1) 1947/8 Cardiff C
**Barnard, D. S.** (15) 1997/8 Barnsley
**Barnes, W.** (22) 1947/8 Arsenal
**Bellamy, C. D.** (12) 1997/8 Norwich C,
Coventry C

**Berry, G.** (5) 1978/9 Wolverhampton
W, Stoke C
**Blackmore, C. G.** (39) 1984/5
Manchester U, Middlesbrough
**Blake, N.** (20) 1993/4 Sheffield U,
Bolton W, Blackburn R
**Bodin, P. J.** (23) 1989/90 Swindon T,
Crystal P, Swindon T
**Bowen, D.** (19) 1954/5 Arsenal
**Bowen, J. P.** (2) 1993/4 Swansea C,
Birmingham C
**Bowen, M. R.** (41) 1985/6 Tottenham
H, Norwich C, West Ham U
**Boyle, T.** (2) 1980/1 Crystal P
**Browning, M. T.** (5) 1995/6 Bristol R,
Huddersfield T
**Burgess, R.** (32) 1946/7 Tottenham H

302

**Burton, O.** (9) 1962/3 Norwich C, Newcastle U

**Cartwright, L.** (7) 1973/4 Coventry C, Wrexham
**Charles, J.** (38) 1949/50 Leeds U, Juventus, Leeds U, Cardiff C
**Charles, J. M.** (19) 1980/1 Swansea C, QPR, Oxford U
**Charles, M.** (31) 1954/5 Swansea T, Arsenal, Cardiff C
**Clarke, R.** (22) 1948/9 Manchester C
**Coleman, C.** (31) 1991/2 Crystal P, Blackburn R, Fulham
**Cornforth, J. M.** (2) 1994/5 Swansea C
**Coyne, D.** (1) 1995/6 Tranmere R
**Crossley, M. G.** (3) 1996/7 Nottingham F
**Crowe, V.** (16) 1958/9 Aston Villa
**Curtis, A.** (35) 1975/6 Swansea C, Southampton, Cardiff C

**Daniel, R.** (21) 1950/1 Arsenal, Sunderland
**Davies, A.** (13) 1982/3 Manchester U, Newcastle U, Swansea C, Bradford C
**Davies, D.** (52) 1974/5 Everton, Wrexham, Swansea C
**Davies, G.** (16) 1979/80 Fulham, Chelsea, Manchester C
**Davies, R. Wyn** (34) 1963/4 Bolton W, Newcastle U, Manchester C, Manchester U, Blackpool
**Davies, Reg** (6) 1952/3 Newcastle U
**Davies, Ron** (29) 1963/4 Norwich C, Southampton, Portsmouth
**Davies, S.** (2) 2000/01 Tottenham H
**Davies, S. I.** (1) 1995/6 Manchester U
**Davis, C.** (1) 1971/2 Charlton Ath
**Davis, G.** (4) 1977/8 Wrexham
**Deacy, N.** (11) 1976/7 PSV Eindhoven, Beringen
**Delaney, M. A.** (9) 1999/00 Aston Villa
**Derrett, S.** (4) 1968/9 Cardiff C
**Dibble, A.** (3) 1985/6 Luton T, Manchester C
**Durban, A.** (27) 1965/6 Derby C
**Dwyer, P.** (10) 1977/8 Cardiff C

**Edwards. C. N. H.** (1) 1995/6 Swansea C
**Edwards, G.** (12) 1946/7 Birmingham C, Cardiff C
**Edwards, I.** (4) 1977/8 Chester
**Edwards, R. W.** (4) 1997/8 Bristol C
**Edwards, T.** (2) 1956/7 Charlton Ath
**Emanuel, J.** (2) 1972/3 Bristol C
**England, M.** (44) 1961/2 Blackburn R, Tottenham H

**Evans, B.** (7) 1971/2 Swansea C, Hereford U
**Evans, I.** (13) 1975/6 Crystal P
**Evans, R.** (1) 1963/4 Swansea T

**Felgate, D.** (1) 1983/4 Lincoln C
**Flynn, B.** (66) 1974/5 Burnley, Leeds U, Burnley
**Ford, T.** (38) 1946/7 Swansea T, Aston Villa, Sunderland, Cardiff C
**Foulkes, W.** (11) 1951/2 Newcastle U
**Freestone, R.** (1) 1999/00 Swansea C

**Giggs, R. J.** (32) 1991/2 Manchester U
**Giles, D.** (12) 1979/80 Swansea C, Crystal P
**Godfrey, B.** (3) 1963/4 Preston NE
**Goss, J.** (9) 1990/1 Norwich C
**Green, C.** (15) 1964/5 Birmingham C
**Green, R. M.** (2) 1997/8 Wolverhampton W
**Griffiths, A.** (17) 1970/1 Wrexham
**Griffiths, H.** (1) 1952/3 Swansea T
**Griffiths, M.** (11) 1946/7 Leicester C

**Hall, G. D.** (9) 1987/8 Chelsea
**Harrington, A.** (11) 1955/6 Cardiff C
**Harris, C.** (24) 1975/6 Leeds U
**Harris, W.** (6) 1953/4 Middlesbrough
**Hartson, J.** (24) 1994/5 Arsenal, West Ham U, Wimbledon, Coventry C
**Haworth, S. O.** (5) 1996/7 Cardiff C, Coventry C
**Hennessey, T.** (39) 1961/2 Birmingham C, Nottingham F, Derby Co
**Hewitt, R.** (5) 1957/8 Cardiff C
**Hill, M.** (2) 1971/2 Ipswich T
**Hockey, T.** (9) 1971/2 Sheffield U, Norwich C, Aston Villa
**Hodges, G.** (18) 1983/4 Wimbledon, Newcastle U, Watford, Sheffield U
**Holden, A.** (1) 1983/4 Chester C
**Hole, B.** (30) 1962/3 Cardiff C, Blackburn R, Aston Villa, Swansea T
**Hollins, D.** (11) 1961/2 Newcastle U
**Hopkins, J.** (16) 1982/3 Fulham, Crystal P
**Hopkins, M.** (34) 1955/6 Tottenham H
**Horne, B.** (59) 1987/8 Portsmouth, Southampton, Everton, Birmingham C
**Howells, R.** (2) 1953/4 Cardiff C
**Hughes, C. M.** (8) 1991/2 Luton T, Wimbledon
**Hughes, I.** (4) 1950/1 Luton T
**Hughes, L. M.** (72) 1983/4 Manchester U, Barcelona, Manchester U, Chelsea, Southampton
**Hughes, W.** (3) 1946/7 Birmingham C
**Hughes, W. A.** (5) 1948/9 Blackburn R

**Humphreys, J.** (1) 1946/7 Everton

**Jackett, K.** (31) 1982/3 Watford
**James, G.** (9) 1965/6 Blackpool
**James, L.** (54) 1971/2 Burnley, Derby C, QPR, Burnley, Swansea C, Sunderland
**James, R. M.** (47) 1978/9 Swansea C, Stoke C, QPR, Leicester C, Swansea C
**Jarvis, A.** (3) 1966/7 Hull C
**Jenkins, S. R.** (14) 1995/6 Swansea C, Huddersfield T
**Johnson, A. J.** (7) 1998/9 Nottingham F
**Johnson, M.** (1) 1963/4 Swansea T
**Jones, A.** (6) 1986/7 Port Vale, Charlton Ath
**Jones, Barrie** (15) 1962/3 Swansea T, Plymouth Argyle, Cardiff C
**Jones, Bryn** (4) 1946/7 Arsenal
**Jones, C.** (59) 1953/4 Swansea T, Tottenham H, Fulham
**Jones, D.** (8) 1975/6 Norwich C
**Jones, E.** (4) 1947/8 Swansea T, Tottenham H
**Jones, J.** (72) 1975/6 Liverpool, Wrexham, Chelsea, Huddersfield T
**Jones, K.** (1) 1949/50 Aston Villa
**Jones, M. G.** (8) 1999/00 Leeds U, Leicester C
**Jones, P. L.** (2) 1996/7 Liverpool, Tranmere R
**Jones, P. S.** (21) 1996/7 Stockport Co, Southampton
**Jones, R.** (1) 1993/4 Sheffield W
**Jones, T. G.** (13) 1946/7 Everton
**Jones, V. P.** (9) 1994/5 Wimbledon
**Jones, W.** (1) 1970/1 Bristol C

**Kelsey, J.** (41) 1953/4 Arsenal
**King, J.** (1) 1954/5 Swansea T
**Kinsey, N.** (7) 1950/1 Norwich C, Birmingham C
**Knill, A. R.** (1) 1988/9 Swansea C
**Koumas, J.** (1) 2000/01 Tranmere R
**Krzywicki, R.** 1969/70 WBA, Huddersfield T

**Lambert, R.** (5) 1946/7 Liverpool
**Law, B. J.** (1) 1989/90 QPR
**Lea, C.** (2) 1964/5 Ipswich T
**Leek, K.** (13) 1960/1 Leicester C, Newcastle U, Birmingham C
**Legg, A.** (6) 1995/6 Birmingham C, Cardiff C
**Lever, A.** (1) 1952/3 Leicester C
**Lewis, D.** (1) 1982/3 Swansea C
**Llewellyn, C. M.** (2) 1997/8 Norwich C
**Lloyd, B.** (3) 1975/6 Wrexham
**Lovell, S.** (6) 1981/2 Crystal P, Millwall

**Lowndes, S.** (10) 1982/3 Newport Co, Millwall, Barnsley
**Lowrie, G.** (4) 1947/8 Coventry C, Newcastle U
**Lucas, M.** (4) 1961/2 Leyton Orient
**Lucas, W.** (7) 1948/9 Swansea T

**Maguire, G. T.** (7) 1989/90 Portsmouth
**Mahoney, J.** (51) 1967/8 Stoke C, Middlesbrough, Swansea C
**Mardon, P. J.** (1) 1995/6 WBA
**Marriott, A.** (5) 1995/6 Wrexham
**Marustik, C.** (6) 1981/2 Swansea C
**Medwin, T.** (30) 1952/3 Swansea T, Tottenham H
**Melville, A. K.** (46) 1989/90 Swansea C, Oxford U, Sunderland, Fulham
**Mielczarek, R.** (1) 1970/1 Rotherham U
**Millington, A.** (21) 1962/3 WBA, Crystal P, Peterborough U, Swansea C
**Moore, G.** (21) 1959/60 Cardiff C, Chelsea, Manchester U, Northampton T, Charlton Ath
**Morris, W.** (5) 1946/7 Burnley

**Nardiello, D.** (2) 1977/8 Coventry C
**Neilson, A. B.** (5) 1991/2 Newcastle U, Southampton
**Nicholas, P.** (73) 1978/9 Crystal P, Arsenal, Crystal P, Luton T, Aberdeen, Chelsea, Watford
**Niedzwiecki, E. A.** (2) 1984/5 Chelsea
**Nogan, L. M.** (2) 1991/2 Watford, Reading
**Nurse, E. A.** (2) 1984/5 Chelsea
**Norman, A. J.** (5) 1985/6 Hull C
**Nurse, M.** (12) 1959/60 Swansea T, Middlesbrough

**O'Sullivan, P.** (3) 1972/3 Brighton & HA
**Oster, J. M.** (4) 1997/8 Everton, Sunderland

**Page, M.** (28) 1970/1 Birmingham C
**Page, R. J.** (20) 1996/7 Watford
**Palmer, D.** (3) 1956/7 Swansea T
**Parry, J.** (1) 1950/1 Swansea T
**Pascoe, C.** (10) 1983/4 Swansea C, Sunderland
**Paul, R.** (33) 1948/9 Swansea T, Manchester C
**Pembridge, M. A.** (39) 1991/2 Luton T, Derby C, Sheffield W, Benfica, Everton
**Perry, J.** (1) 1993/4 Cardiff C
**Phillips, D.** (62) 1983/4 Plymouth Argyle, Manchester C, Coventry C, Norwich C, Nottingham F

**Phillips, J.** (4) 1972/3 Chelsea
**Phillips, L.** (58) 1970/1 Cardff C, Aston Villa, Swansea C, Charlton Ath
**Pontin, K.** (2) 1979/80 Cardiff C
**Powell, A.** (8) 1946/7 Leeds U, Everton, Birmingham C
**Powell, D.** (11) 1967/8 Wrexham, Sheffield U
**Powell, I.** (8) 1946/7 QPR, Aston Villa
**Price, P.** (25) 1979/80 Luton T, Tottenham H
**Pring, K.** (3) 1965/6 Rotherham U
**Pritchard, H. K.** (1) 1984/5 Bristol C

**Rankmore, F.** (l) 1965/6 Peterborough U
**Ratcliffe, K.** (59) 1980/1 Everton, Cardiff C
**Ready, K.** (5) 1996/7 QPR
**Reece, G.** (29) 1965/6 Sheffield U, Cardiff C
**Reed, W.** (2) 1954/5 Ipswich T
**Rees, A.** (1) 1983/4 Birmingham C
**Rees, J. M.** (1) 1991/2 Luton T
**Rees, R.** (39) 1964/5 Coventry C, WBA, Nottingham F
**Rees, W.** (4) 1948/9 Cardiff C, Tottenham H
**Richards, S.** (1) 1946/7 Cardiff C
**Roberts, A. M.** (2) 1992/3 QPR
**Roberts, D.** (17) 1972/3 Oxford U, Hull C
**Roberts, G. W.** (4) 1999/00 Tranmere R
**Roberts, I. W.** (13) 1989/90 Watford, Huddersfield T, Leicester C, Norwich C
**Roberts, J. G.** (22) 1970/1 Arsenal, Birmingham C
**Roberts, J. H.** (1) 1948/9 Bolton W
**Roberts, N. W.** (1) 1999/00 Wrexham
**Roberts, P.** (4) 1973/4 Portsmouth
**Robinson, C. P.** (4) 1999/00 Wolverhampton W
**Robinson, J. R. C.** (26) 1995/6 Charlton Ath
**Rodrigues, P.** (40) 1964/5 Cardiff C, Leicester C, Sheffield W
**Rouse, V.** (1) 1958/9 Crystal P
**Rowley, T.** (1) 1958/9 Tranmere R
**Rush, I.** (73) 1979/80 Liverpool, Juventus, Liverpool

**Saunders, D.** (75) 1985/6 Brighton & HA, Oxford U, Derby C, Liverpool, Aston Villa, Galatasaray, Nottingham F, Sheffield U, Benfica, Bradford C
**Savage, R. W.** (20) 1995/6 Crewe Alexandra, Leicester C
**Sayer, P.** (7) 1976/7 Cardiff C

**Scrine, F.** (2) 1949/50 Swansea T
**Sear, C.** (1) 1962/3 Manchester C
**Sherwood, A.** (41) 1946/7 Cardiff C, Newport C
**Shortt, W.** (12) 1946/7 Plymouth Argyle
**Showers, D.** (2) 1974/5 Cardiff C
**Sidlow, C.** (7) 1946/7 Liverpool
**Slatter, N.** (22) 1982/3 Bristol R, Oxford U
**Smallman, D.** (7) 1973/4 Wrexham, Everton
**Southall, N.** (92) 1981/2 Everton
**Speed, G. A.** (65) 1989/90 Leeds U, Everton, Newcastle U
**Sprake, G.** (37) 1963/4 Leeds U, Birmingham C
**Stansfield, F.** (1) 1948/9 Cardiff C
**Stevenson, B.** (15) 1977/8 Leeds U, Birmingham C
**Stevenson, N.** (4) 1981/2 Swansea C
**Stitfall, R.** (2) 1952/3 Cardiff C
**Sullivan, D.** (17) 1952/3 Cardiff C
**Symons, C. J.** (33) 1991/2 Portsmouth, Manchester C, Fulham

**Tapscott, D.** (14) 1953/4 Arsenal, Cardiff C
**Taylor, G. K.** (8) 1995/6 Crystal P, Sheffield U
**Thomas, D.** (2) 1956/7 Swansea T
**Thomas, M.** (51) 1976/7 Wrexham, Manchester U, Everton, Brighton & HA, Stoke C, Chelsea, WBA
**Thomas, M. R.** (1) 1986/7 Newcastle U
**Thomas, R.** (50) 1966/7 Swindon T, Derby C, Cardiff C
**Thomas, S.** (4) 1947/8 Fulham
**Toshack, J.** (40) 1968/9 Cardiff C, Liverpool, Swansea C
**Trollope, P. J.** (5) 1996/7 Derby Co, Fulham

**Van Den Hauwe, P. W. R.** (13) 1984/5 Everton
**Vaughan, N.** (10) 1982/3 Newport Co, Cardiff C
**Vearncombe, G.** (2) 1957/8 Cardiff C
**Vernon, R.** (32) 1956/7 Blackburn R, Everton, Stoke C
**Villars, A.** (3) 1973/4 Cardiff C

**Walley, T.** (1) 1970/1 Watford
**Walsh, I.** (18) 1979/80 Crystal P, Swansea C
**Ward, D.** (2) 1958/9 Bristol R, Cardiff C
**Ward, D.** (1) 1999/00 Notts Co
**Webster, C.** (4) 1956/7 Manchester U
**Weston, R. D.** (1) 1999/00 Arsenal

Williams, A. (12) 1993/4 Reading, Wolverhampton W
Williams, A. P. (2) 1997/8 Southampton
Williams, D. G. 1987/8 13, Derby Co, Ipswich T
Williams, D. M. (5) 1985/6 Norwich C
Williams, G. (1) 1950/1 Cardiff C
Williams, G. E. (26) 1959/60 WBA
Williams, G. G. (5) 1960/1 Swansea T
Williams, H. (4) 1948/9 Newport Co, Leeds U
Williams, Herbert (3) 1964/5 Swansea T

Williams, S. (43) 1953/4 WBA, Southampton
Witcomb, D. (3) 1946/7 WBA, Sheffield W
Woosnam, P. (17) 1958/9 Leyton Orient, West Ham U, Aston Villa

Yorath, T. (59) 1969/70 Leeds U, Coventry C, Tottenham H, Vancouver Whitecaps
Young, E. (21) 1989/90 Wimbledon, Crystal P, Wolverhampton W

## EIRE

Aherne, T. (16) 1945/6 Belfast Celtic, Luton T
Aldridge, J. W. (69) 1985/6 Oxford U, Liverpool, Real Sociedad, Tranmere R
Ambrose, P. (5) 1954/5 Shamrock R
Anderson, J. (16) 1979/80 Preston NE, Newcastle U

Babb, P. (34) 1993/4 Coventry C, Liverpool
Bailham, E. (1) 1963/4 Shamrock R
Barber, E. (2) 1965/6 Shelbourne, Birmingham C
Beglin, J. (15) 1983/4 Liverpool
Bonner, P. (80) 1980/1 Celtic
Braddish, S. (1) 1977/8 Dundalk
Brady, T. R. (6) 1963/4 QPR
Brady, W. L. (72) 1974/5 Arsenal, Juventus, Sampdoria, Internazionale, Ascoli, West Ham U
Branagan, K. G. (1) 1996/7 Bolton W
Breen, G. (38) 1995/6 Birmingham C, Coventry C
Breen, T. (3) 1946/7 Shamrock R
Brennan, F. (1) 1964/5 Drumcondra
Brennan, S. A. (19) 1964/5 Manchester U, Waterford
Browne, W. (3) 1963/4 Bohemians
Buckley, L. (2) 1983/4 Shamrock R, Waregem
Burke, F. (1) 1951/2 Cork Ath
Butler, P. J. (1) 1999/00 Sunderland
Byrne, A. B. (14) 1969/70 Southampton
Byrne, J. (23) 1984/5 QPR, Le Havre, Brighton & HA, Sunderland, Millwall
Byrne, P. (8) 1983/4 Shamrock R

Campbell, A. (3) 1984/5 Santander
Campbell, N. (11) 1970/1 St Patrick's Ath, Fortuna Cologne
Cantwell, N. (36) 1953/4 West Ham U, Manchester U

Carey, B. P. (3) 1991/2 Manchester U, Leicester C
Carey, J. J. (21) 1945/6 Manchester U
Carolan, J. (2) 1959/60 Manchester U
Carr, S. (18) 1998/9 Tottenham H
Carroll, B. (2) 1948/9 Shelbourne
Carroll, T. R. (17) 1967/8 Ipswich T, Birmingham C
Carsley, L. K. (16) 1997/8 Derby Co, Blackburn R
Cascarino, A. G. (88) 1985/6 Gillingham, Millwall, Aston Villa, Celtic, Chelsea, Marseille, Nancy
Chandler, J. (2) 1979/80 Leeds U
Clarke, J. (1) 1977/8 Drogheda U
Clarke, K. (2) 1947/8 Drumcondra
Clarke, M. (1) 1949/50 Shamrock R
Clinton, T. J. (3) 1950/1 Everton
Coad, P. (11) 1946/7 Shamrock R
Coffey, T. (1) 1949/50 Drumcondra
Colfer, M. D. (2) 1949/50 Shelbourne
Conmy, O. M. (5) 1964/5 Peterborough U
Connolly, D. J. (27) 1995/6 Watford, Feyenoord, Wolverhampton W, Excelsior
Conroy, G. A. (27) 1969/70 Stoke C
Conway, J. P. (20) 1966/7 Fulham, Manchester C
Corr, P. J. (4) 1948/9 Everton
Courtney, E. (1) 1945/6 Cork U
Coyle, O. (1) 1993/4 Bolton W
Coyne, T. (22) 1991/2 Celtic, Tranmere R, Motherwell
Cummins, G. P. (19) 1953/4 Luton T
Cuneen, T. (1) 1950/1 Limerick
Cunningham, K. (33) 1995/6 Wimbledon
Curtis, D. P. (17) 1956/7 Shelbourne, Bristol C, Ipswich T, Exeter C
Cusack, S. (1) 1952/3 Limerick

Daish, L. S. (5) 1991/2 Cambridge U, Coventry C

**Daly, G. A.** (48) 1972/3 Manchester U, Derby C, Coventry C, Birmingham C, Shrewsbury T

**Daly, M.** (2) 1977/8 Wolverhampton W

**Daly, P.** (1) 1949/50 Shamrock R

**Delap, R. J.** (6) 1997/8 Derby Co

**De Mange, K. J. P. P.** (2) 1986/7 Liverpool, Hull C

**Deacy, E.** (4) 1981/2 Aston Villa

**Dempsey, J. T.** (19) 1966/7 Fulham, Chelsea

**Dennehy, J.** (11) 1971/2 Cork Hibernian, Nottingham F, Walsall

**Desmond, P.** (4) 1949/50 Middlesbrough

**Devine, J.** (12) 1979/80 Arsenal, Norwich C

**Doherty, G. M. T.** (8) 1999/00 Luton T, Tottenham H

**Donovan, D. C.** (5) 1954/5 Everton

**Donovan, T. C.** (1) 1979/80 Aston Villa

**Doyle, C.** (1) 1958/9 Shelbourne

**Duff, D. A.** (20) 1997/8 Blackburn R

**Duffy, B.** (1) 1949/50 Shamrock R

**Dunne, A. P.** (33) 1961/2 Manchester U, Bolton W

**Dunne, J. C.** (1) 1970/1 Fulham

**Dunne, P. A.** (5) 1964/5 Manchester U

**Dunne, R. P.** (10) 1999/00 Everton, Manchester C

**Dunne, S.** (15) 1952/3 Luton T

**Dunne, T.** (3) 1955/6 St Patrick's Ath

**Dunning, P.** (2) 1970/1 Shelbourne

**Dunphy, E. M.** (23) 1965/6 York C, Millwall

**Dwyer, N. M.** (14) 1959/60 West Ham U, Swansea T

**Eccles, P.** (1) 1985/6 Shamrock R

**Eglington, T. J.** (24) 1945/6 Shamrock R, Everton

**Evans, M. J.** (1) 1997/8 Southampton

**Fagan, E.** (1) 1972/3 Shamrock R

**Fagan, F.** (8) 1954/5 Manchester C, Derby C

**Fairclough, M.** (2) 1981/2 Dundalk

**Fallon, S.** (8) 1950/1 Celtic

**Farrell, P. D.** (28) 1945/6 Shamrock R, Everton

**Farrelly, G.** (6) 1995/6 Aston Villa, Everton, Bolton W

**Finnan, S.** (7) 1999/00 Fulham

**Finucane, A.** (11) 1966/7 Limerick

**Fitzgerald, F. J.** (2) 1954/5 Waterford

**Fitzgerald, P. J.** (5) 1960/1 Leeds U, Chester

**Fitzpatrick, K.** (1) 1969/70 Limerick

**Fitzsimons, A. G.** (26) 1949/50 Middlesbrough, Lincoln C

**Fleming, C.** (10) 1995/6 Middlesbrough

**Fogarty, A.** (11) 1959/60 Sunderland, Hartlepool U

**Foley, D. J.** (6) 1999/00 Watford

**Foley, T. C.** (9) 1963/4 Northampton T

**Fullam, J.** (1960/1 Preston NE, Shamrock R

**Gallagher, C.** (2) 1966/7 Celtic

**Gallagher, M.** (1) 1953/4 Hibernian

**Galvin, A.** (29) 1982/3 Tottenham H, Sheffield W

**Gannon, E.** (14) 1948/9 Notts Co, Sheffield W, Shelbourne K

**Gannon, M.** (1) 1971/2 Shelbourne

**Gavin, J. T.** (7) 1949/50 Norwich C, Tottenham H, Norwich C

**Gibbons, A.** (4) 1951/2 St Patrick's Ath

**Gilbert, R.** (1) 1965/6 Shamrock R

**Giles, C.** (1) 1950/1 Doncaster R

**Giles, M. J.** (59) 1959/60 Manchester U, Leeds U, WBA, Shamrock R

**Given, S. J. J.** (31) 1995/6 Blackburn R, Newcastle U

**Givens, D. J.** (56) 1968/9 Manchester U, Luton T, QPR, Birmingham C, Neuchatel Xamax

**Glynn, D.** (2) 1951/2 Drumcondra

**Godwin, T. F.** (13) 1948/9 Shamrock R, Leicester C, Bournemouth

**Goodman, J.** (4) 1996/7 Wimbledon

**Gorman, W. C.** (2) 1946/7 Brentford

**Grealish, A.** (44) 1975/6 Orient, Luton T, Brighton & HA, WBA

**Gregg, E.** (8) 1977/8 Bohemians

**Grimes, A. A.** (17) 1977/8 Manchester U, Coventry C, Luton T

**Hale, A.** (13) 1961/2 Aston Villa, Doncaster R, Waterford

**Hamilton, T.** (2) 1958/9 Shamrock R

**Hand, E. K.** (20) 1968/9 Portsmouth

**Harte, I. P.** (31) 1995/6 Leeds U

**Hartnett, J. B.** (2) 1948/9 Middlesbrough

**Haverty, J.** (32) 1955/6 Arsenal, Blackburn R, Millwall, Celtic, Bristol R, Shelbourne

**Hayes, A. W. P.** (1) 1978/9 Southampton

**Hayes, W. E.** (2) 1946/7 Huddersfield T

**Hayes, W. J.** (1) 1948/9 Limerick

**Healey, R.** (2) 1976/7 Cardiff C

**Heighway, S. D.** (34) 1970/1 Liverpool, Minnesota Kicks

**Henderson, B.** (2) 1947/8 Drumcondra

**Hennessy, J.** (5) 1955/6 Shelbourne, St Patrick's Ath

**Herrick, J.** (3) 1971/2 Cork Hibernians, Shamrock R

307

Higgins, J. (1) 1950/1 Birmingham C
Holland, M. R. (11) 1999/00 Ipswich T
Holmes, J. 1970/1 Coventry C,
Tottenham H, Vancouver Whitecaps
Houghton, R. J. (73) 1985/6 Oxford U,
Liverpool, Aston Villa, Crystal P,
Reading
Howlett, G. (1) 1983/4 Brighton & HA
Hughton, C. (53) 1979/80 Tottenham
H, West Ham U
Hurley, C. J. (40) 1956/7 Millwall,
Sunderland, Bolton W

Irwin, D. J. (56) 1990/1 Manchester U

Kavanagh, G. A. (3) 1997/8 Stoke C
Keane, R. D. (25) 1997/8
Wolverhampton W, Coventry C,
Internazionale
Keane, R. M. (52) 1990/1 Nottingham
F, Manchester U
Keane, T. R. (4) 1948/9 Swansea T
Kearin, M. (1) 1971/2 Shamrock R
Kearns, F. T. (1) 1953/4 West Ham U
Kearns, M. (18) 1969/70 Oxford U,
Walsall, Wolverhampton W
Kelly, A. T. (33) 1992/3 Sheffield U,
Blackburn R
Kelly, D. T. (26) 1987/8 Walsall, West
Ham U, Leicester C, Newcastle U,
Wolverhampton W, Sunderland,
Tranmere R
Kelly, G. (38) 1993/4 Leeds U
Kelly J A. (48) 1956/7 Drumcondra,
Preston NE
Kelly, J. P. V. (5) 1960/1
Wolverhampton W
Kelly, M. J. (4) 1987/8 Portsmouth
Kelly, N. (1) 1953/4 Nottingham F
Kenna, J. J. (27) 1994/5 Blackburn R
Kennedy, M. (31) 1995/6 Liverpool,
Wimbledon, Manchester C
Kennedy, M. F. (2) 1985/6 Portsmouth
Keogh, J. (1) 1965/6 Shamrock R
Keogh, S. (1) 1958/9 Shamrock R
Kernaghan, A. N. (22) 1992/3
Middlesbrough, Manchester C
Kiely, D. L. (4) 1999/00 Charlton Ath
Kiernan, F. W. (5) 1950/1 Shamrock R,
Southampton
Kilbane, K. D. (25) 1997/8 WBA,
Sunderland
Kinnear, J. P. (26) 1966/7 Tottenham
H, Brighton & HA
Kinsella, M. A. (24) 1997/8 Charlton Ath

Langan, D. (25) 1977/8 Derby Co,
Birmingham C, Oxford U
Lawler, J. F. (8) 1952/3 Fulham
Lawlor, J. C. (3) 1948/9 Drumcondra,
Doncaster R
Lawlor, M. (5) 1970/1 Shamrock R
Lawrenson, M. (39) 1976/7 Preston NE,
Brighton & HA, Liverpool
Leech, M. (8) 1968/9 Shamrock R
Lowry, D. (1) 1961/2 St Patrick's Ath

McAlinden, J. (2) 1945/6 Portsmouth
McAteer, J. W. (40) 1993/4 Bolton W,
Liverpool, Blackburn R
McCann, J. (1) 1956/7 Shamrock R
McCarthy, M. (57) 1983/4 Manchester
C, Celtic, Lyon, Millwall
McConville, T. (6) 1971/2 Dundalk,
Waterford
McDonagh, J. (24) 1980/1 Everton,
Bolton W, Notts C
McDonagh, Joe (3) 1983/4 Shamrock R
McEvoy, M. A. (17) 1960/1 Blackburn R
McGee, P. (15) 1977/8 QPR, Preston
NE
McGoldrick, E. J. (15) 1991/2 Crystal P,
Arsenal
McGowan, D. (3) 1948/9 West Ham U
McGowan, J. (1) 1946/7 Cork U
McGrath, M. (22) 1957/8 Blackburn R,
Bradford Park Avenue
McGrath, P. (83) 1984/5 Manchester U,
Aston Villa, Derby C
Macken, A. (1) 1976/7 Derby Co
Mackey, G. (3) 1956/7 Shamrock R
McLoughlin, A. F. (42) 1989/90
Swindon T, Southampton,
Portsmouth
McMillan, W. (2) 1945/6 Belfast Celtic
McNally, J. B. (3) 1958/9 Luton T
McPhail, S. (3) 1999/00 Leeds U
Mahon, A. J. (2) 1999/00 Tranmere R
Malone, G. (1) 1948/9 Shelbourne
Mancini, T. J. (5) 1973/4 QPR, Arsenal
Martin, C. J. (30) 1945/6 Glentoran,
Leeds U, Aston Villa
Martin, M. P. (51) 1971/2 Bohemians,
Manchester U, WBA, Newcastle U
Maybury, A. (2) 1997/8 Leeds U
Meagan, M. K. (17) 1960/1 Everton,
Huddersfield T, Drogheda
Milligan, M. J. (1) 1991/2 Oldham Ath
Mooney, J. (2) 1964/5 Shamrock R
Moore, A. (8) 1995/6 Middlesbrough
Moran, K. (70) 1979/80 Manchester U,
Sporting Gijon, Blackburn R
Moroney, T. (12) 1947/8 West Ham U
Morris, C. B. (35) 1987/8 Celtic,
Middlesbrough
Moulson, G. B. (3) 1947/8 Lincoln C
Mucklan, C. (1) 1977/8 Drogheda
Mulligan, P. M. (50) 1968/9 Shamrock
R, Chelsea, Crystal P, WBA,
Shamrock R

308

**Munroe, L.** (1) 1953/4 Shamrock R
**Murphy, A.** (1) 1955/6 Clyde
**Murphy, B.** (1) 1985/6 Bohemians
**Murphy, J.** (1) 1979/80 Crystal P
**Murray, T.** (1) 1949/50 Dundalk

**Newman, W.** (1) 1968/9 Shelbourne
**Nolan, R.** (10) 1956/7 Shamrock R

**O'Brien, A. J.** (1) 2000/01 Newcastle U
**O'Brien, F.** (4) 1979/80 Philadelphia
Fury
**O'Brien, L.** (16) 1985/6 Shamrock R,
Manchester U, Newcastle U,
Tranmere R
**O'Brien, R.** (4) 1975/6 Notts Co
**O'Byrne, L. B.** (1) 1948/9 Shamrock R
**O'Callaghan, B. R.** (6) 1978/9 Stoke C
**O'Callaghan, K.** (20) 1980/1 Ipswich T,
Portsmouth
**O'Connell, A.** (2) 1966/7 Dundalk,
Bohemians
**O'Connor, T.** (4) 1949/50 Shamrock R
**O'Connor, T.** (7) 1967/8 Fulham,
Dundalk, Bohemians
**O'Driscoll, J. F.** (3) 1948/9 Swansea T
**O'Driscoll, S.** (3) 1981/2 Fulham
**O'Farrell, F.** (9) 1951/2 West Ham U,
Preston NE
**O'Flanagan, K. P.** (3) 1946/7 Arsenal
**O'Flanagan, M.** (1) 1946/7 Bohemians
**O'Hanlon, K. G.** (1) 1987/8 Rotherham
U
**O'Keefe, E.** (5) 1980/1 Everton, Port
Vale
**O'Leary, D.** (68) 1976/7 Arsenal
**O'Leary, P.** (7) 1979/80 Shamrock R
**O'Neill, F. S.** (20) 1961/2 Shamrock R
**O'Neill, J.** (17) 1951/2 Everton
**O'Neill, J.** (1) 1960/1 Preston NE
**O'Neill, K. P.** (13) 1995/6 Norwich C,
Middlesbrough
**O'Regan, K.** (4) 1983/4 Brighton & HA
**O'Reilly, J.** (2) 1945/6 Cork U

**Peyton, G.** (33) 1976/7 Fulham,
Bournemouth, Everton
**Peyton, N.** (6) 1956/7 Shamrock R,
Leeds U
**Phelan, T.** (42) 1991/2 Wimbledon,
Manchester C, Chelsea, Everton,
Fulham

**Quinn, B. S.** (4) 1999/00 Coventry C
**Quinn, N. J.** (84) 1985/6 Arsenal,
Manchester C, Sunderland

**Richardson, D. J.** (3) 1971/2 Shamrock
R, Gillingham
**Ringstead, A.** (20) 1950/1 Sheffield U

**Robinson, M.** (23) 1980/1 Brighton &
HA, Liverpool, QPR
**Roche, P. J.** (8) 1971/2 Shelbourne,
Manchester U
**Rogers, E.** (19) 1967/8 Blackburn R,
Charlton Ath
**Ryan, G.** (16) 1977/8 Derby Co,
Brighton & HA
**Ryan, R. A.** (16) 1949/50 WBA, Derby C

**Savage, D. P. T.** (5) 1995/6 Millwall
**Saward, P.** (18) 1953/4 Millwall, Aston
Villa, Huddersfield T
**Scannell, T.** (1) 1953/4 Southend U
**Scully, P. J.** (1) 1988/9 Arsenal
**Sheedy, K.** (45) 1983/4 Everton,
Newcastle U
**Sheridan, J. J.** (34) 1987/8 Leeds U,
Sheffield W
**Slaven, B.** (7) 1989/90 Middlesbrough
**Sloan, J. W.** (2) 1945/6 Arsenal
**Smyth, M.** (1) 1968/9 Shamrock R
**Stapleton, F.** (70) 1976/7 Arsenal,
Manchester U, Ajax, Derby Co, Le
Havre, Blackburn R
**Staunton, S.** (89) 1988/9 Liverpool,
Aston Villa, Liverpool, Aston Villa
**Stevenson, A. E.** (6) 1946/7 Everton
**Strahan, F.** (5) 1963/4 Shelbourne
**Swan, M. M. G.** (1) 1959/60 Drumcondra
**Synott, N.** (3) 1977/8 Shamrock R

**Thomas, P.** (2) 1973/4 Waterford
**Tsend, A. D.** (70) 1988/9 Norwich C,
Chelsea, Aston Villa, Middlesbrough
**Traynor, T. J.** (8) 1953/4 Southampton
**Treacy, R. C. P.** (42) 1965/6 WBA,
Charlton Ath, Swindon T, Preston
NE, WBA, Shamrock R
**Tuohy, L.** (8) 1955/6 Shamrock R,
Newcastle U, Shamrock R
**Turner, P.** (2) 1962/3 Celtic

**Vernon, J.** (2) 1945/6 Belfast Celtic

**Waddock, G.** (20) 1979/80 QPR,
Millwall
**Walsh, D. J.** (20) 1945/6 WBA, Aston
Villa
**Walsh, J.** (1) 1981/2 Limerick
**Walsh, M.** (21) 1975/6 Blackpool,
Everton, QPR, Porto
**Walsh, M.** (4) 1981/2 Everton, Norwich
C
**Walsh, W.** (9) 1946/7 Manchester C
**Waters, J.** (2) 1976/7 Grimsby T
**Whelan, R.** (2) 1963/4 St Patrick's Ath
**Whelan, R.** (53) 1980/1 Liverpool,
Southend U
**Whelan, W.** (4) 1955/6 Manchester U
**Whittaker, R.** (1) 1958/9 Chelsea

# BRITISH ISLES INTERNATIONAL GOALSCORERS SINCE 1946

## ENGLAND

| Name | Goals | Name | Goals | Name | Goals |
|---|---|---|---|---|---|
| A'Court, A. | 1 | Eastham, G. | 2 | Lee, S. | 2 |
| Adams, T.A. | 5 | Edwards, D. | 5 | Le Saux, G.P. | 1 |
| Allen, R. | 2 | Ehiogu, U. | 1 | Lineker, G. | 48 |
| Anderson, V. | 2 | Elliott, W.H. | 3 | Lofthouse, N. | 30 |
| Anderton, D.R. | 7 | | | | |
| Astall, G. | 1 | Ferdinand, L. | 5 | Mabbutt, G. | 1 |
| Atyeo, P.J.W. | 5 | Finney, T. | 30 | McDermott, T. | 3 |
| | | Flowers, R. | 10 | Macdonald, M. | 6 |
| Baily, E.F. | 5 | Fowler, R.B. | 4 | McManaman, S. | 3 |
| Baker, J.H. | 3 | Francis, G.C.J. | 3 | Mannion, W.J. | 11 |
| Ball, A.J. | 8 | Francis, T. | 12 | Mariner, P. | 13 |
| Barnes, J. | 11 | Froggatt, J. | 2 | Marsh, R.W. | 1 |
| Barnes, P.S. | 4 | Froggatt, R. | 2 | Matthews, S. | 3 |
| Barmby, N.J. | 4 | | | Medley, L.D. | 1 |
| Beardsley, P.A. | 9 | Gascoigne, P.J. | 10 | Melia, J. | 1 |
| Beattie, J.K. | 1 | Goddard, P. | 1 | Merson, P.C. | 3 |
| Beckham, D.R.J. | 4 | Grainger, C. | 3 | Milburn, J.E.T. | 10 |
| Bell, C. | 9 | Greaves, J. | 44 | Moore, R.F. | 2 |
| Bentley, R.T.F. | 9 | | | Morris, J. | 3 |
| Blissett, L. | 3 | Haines, J.T.W. | 2 | Mortensen, S.H. | 23 |
| Bowles, S. | 1 | Hancocks, J. | 2 | Mullen, J. | 6 |
| Bradford, G.R.W. | 1 | Hassall, H.W. | 4 | Mullery, A.P. | 1 |
| Bradley, W. | 2 | Hateley, M. | 9 | | |
| Bridges, B.J. | 1 | Haynes, J.N. | 18 | Neal, P.G. | 5 |
| Broadbent, P.F. | 2 | Heskey, E.W. | 2 | Nicholls, J. | 1 |
| Broadis, I.A. | 8 | Hirst, D.E. | 1 | Nicholson, W.E. | 1 |
| Brooking, T.D. | 5 | Hitchens, G.A. | 5 | | |
| Brooks, J. | 2 | Hoddle, G. | 8 | O'Grady, M. | 3 |
| Bull, S.G. | 4 | Hughes, E.W. | 1 | Owen, M.J. | 10 |
| Butcher, T. | 3 | Hunt, R. | 18 | Own goals | 23 |
| Byrne, J.J. | 8 | Hunter, N. | 2 | | |
| | | Hurst, G.C. | 24 | Paine, T.L. | 7 |
| Carter, H.S. | 5 | | | Palmer, C.L. | 1 |
| Chamberlain, M. | 1 | Ince P.E.C. | 2 | Parry, R.A. | 1 |
| Channon, M.R. | 21 | | | Peacock, A. | 3 |
| Charlton, J. | 6 | Johnson, D.E. | 6 | Pearce, S. | 5 |
| Charlton, R. | 49 | | | Pearson, J.S. | 5 |
| Chivers, M. | 13 | Kay, A.H. | 1 | Pearson, S.C. | 5 |
| Clarke, A.J. | 10 | Keegan, J.K. | 21 | Perry, W. | 2 |
| Cole, A. | 1 | Kennedy, R. | 3 | Peters, M. | 20 |
| Connelly, J.M. | 7 | Keown, M.R. | 2 | Pickering, F. | 5 |
| Coppell, S.J. | 7 | Kevan, D.T. | 8 | Platt, D. | 27 |
| Cowans, G. | 2 | Kidd, B. | 1 | Pointer, R. | 2 |
| Crawford, R. | 1 | | | | |
| Currie, A.W. | 3 | Langton, R. | 1 | Ramsay, A.E. | 3 |
| | | Latchford, R.D. | 5 | Redknapp, J.F. | 1 |
| Dixon, L.M. | 1 | Lawler, C. | 1 | Revie, D.G. | 4 |
| Dixon, K.M. | 4 | Lawton, T. | 16 | Robson, B. | 26 |
| Douglas, B. | 11 | Lee, F. | 10 | Robson, R. | 4 |
| | | Lee, J. | 1 | Rowley, J.F. | 6 |
| | | Lee, R.M. | 2 | Royle, J. | 2 |

Williams, G.E. 1
Williams, G.G. 1
Woosnam, A.P. 3

Yorath, T.C. 2
Young, E. 1

# NORTHERN IRELAND

Anderson, T. 4
Armstrong, G. 12

Barr, H.H. 1
Best, G. 9
Bingham, W.L. 10
Black, K. 1
Blanchflower, D. 2
Blanchflower, J. 1
Brennan, R.A. 1
Brotherston, N. 3

Campbell, W.G. 1
Casey, T. 2
Caskey, W. 1
Cassidy, T. 1
Clarke, C.J. 13
Clements, D. 2
Cochrane, T. 1
Crossan, E. 1
Crossan, J.A. 10
Cush, W.W. 5

D'Arcy, S.D. 1
Doherty, I. 1
Doherty, P.D. 2
Dougan, A.D. 8
Dowie, I. 12

Elder, A.R. 1

Ferguson, W. 1
Ferris, R.O. 1
Finney, T. 2

Gillespie, K.R. 1
Gray, P. 6
Griffin, D.J. 1

Hamilton, B. 4
Hamilton, W. 5
Harkin, J.T. 2
Harvey, M. 3
Healy, D.J. 7
Hill, C.F. 1

Humphries, W. 1
Hughes, M.E. 4
Hunter, A. 1
Hunter, B.V. 1

Irvine, W.J. 8

Johnston, W.C. 1
Jones, J. 1

Lennon, N.F. 2
Lockhart, N. 3
Lomas, S.M. 2

Magilton, J. 5
McAdams, W.J. 7
McClelland, J. 1
McCrory, S. 1
McCurdy, C. 1
McDonald, A. 3
McGarry, J.K. 1
McGrath, R.C. 4
McIlroy, J. 10
McIlroy, S.B. 5
McLaughlin, J.C. 6
McMahon, G.J. 2
McMordie, A.S. 3
McMorran, E.J. 4
McParland, P.J. 10
Moreland, V. 1
Morgan, S. 3
Morrow, S.J. 1
Mulryne, P.P. 2

Neill, W.J.T. 2
Nelson, S. 1
Nicholl, C.J. 3
Nicholl, J.M. 1
Nicholson, J.J. 6

O'Boyle, G. 1
O'Kane, W.J. 1
O'Neill, J. 2
O'Neill, M.A. 4
O'Neill, M.H. 8
Own goals 5

Patterson, D.J. 1
Peacock, R. 2
Penney, S. 2

Quinn, J.M. 12
Quinn, S.J. 3

Rowland, K. 1

Simpson, W.J. 5
Smyth, S. 5
Spence, D.W. 3
Stewart, I. 2

Taggart, G.P. 7
Tully, C.P. 3

Walker, J. 1
Walsh, D.J. 5
Welsh, E. 1
Whiteside, N. 9
Whitley, Jeff 1
Williams, M.S. 1
Wilson, D.J. 1
Wilson, K.J. 6
Wilson, S.J. 7

# EIRE

Aldridge, J. 19
Ambrose, P. 1
Anderson, J. 1

Brady, L. 9
Breen, G. 5
Byrne, J. *(QPR)* 4

Cantwell, J. 14
Carey, J. 3
Carroll, T. 1
Cascarino, A. 19
Coad, P. 3
Connolly, D.J. 7
Conroy, T. 2
Conway, J. 3
Coyne, T. 6
Cummings, G. 5
Curtis, D. 8

Daly, G. 13
Dempsey, J. 1
Dennehy, M. 2
Duffy, B. 1
Dunne, R.P. 3

Eglinton, T. 2

Fagan, F. 5
Fallon, S. 2
Farrell, P. 3
Finnan, S. 1
Fitzgerald, J. 1
Fitzgerald, P. 2
Fitzsimons, A. 7
Fogarty, A. 3

|  | |  | |  | |
|---|---|---|---|---|---|
| Foley, D. | 2 | Kernaghan, A. | 1 | O'Neill, K.P. | 4 |
| Fullam, J. | 1 | Kilbane, K.D. | 3 | O'Reilly, J. | 1 |
| | | Kinsella, M.A. | 2 | Own goals | 8 |
| Galvin, A. | 1 | | | | |
| Gavin, J. | 2 | Lawrenson, M. | 5 | Quinn, N. | 20 |
| Giles, J. | 5 | Leech, M. | 2 | | |
| Givens, D. | 19 | | | Ringstead, A. | 7 |
| Glynn, D. | 1 | McAteer, J.W. | 2 | Robinson, M. | 4 |
| Grealish, T. | 8 | McCann, J. | 1 | Rogers, E. | 5 |
| Grimes, A.A. | 1 | McCarthy, M. | 2 | Ryan, G. | 1 |
| | | McEvoy, A. | 6 | Ryan, R. | 3 |
| Hale, A. | 2 | McGee, P. | 4 | | |
| Hand, E. | 2 | McGrath, P. | 8 | Sheedy, K. | 9 |
| Harte, I.P. | 5 | McLoughlin, A. | 2 | Sheridan, J. | 5 |
| Haverty, J. | 3 | McPhail, S. | 1 | Slaven, B. | 1 |
| Holland, M.R. | 3 | Mancini, T. | 1 | Sloan, W. | 1 |
| Holmes, J. | 1 | Martin, C. | 6 | Stapleton, F. | 20 |
| Houghton, R. | 6 | Martin, M. | 4 | Staunton, S. | 8 |
| Hughton, C. | 1 | Mooney, J. | 1 | Strahan, F. | 1 |
| Hurley, C. | 2 | Moran, K. | 6 | | |
| | | Moroney, T. | 1 | Townsend, A.D. | 7 |
| Irwin, D. | 4 | Mulligan, P. | 1 | Treacy, R. | 5 |
| | | | | Tuohy, L. | 4 |
| Kavanagh, G.A. | 1 | O'Callaghan, K. | 1 | | |
| Keane, R.D. | 7 | O'Connor, T. | 2 | Waddock, G. | 3 |
| Keane, R.M. | 8 | O'Farrell, F. | 2 | Walsh, D. | 5 |
| Kelly, D. | 9 | O'Keefe, E. | 1 | Walsh, M. | 3 |
| Kelly, G. | 2 | O'Leary, D.A. | 1 | Waters, J. | 1 |
| Kennedy, M. | 3 | O'Neill, F. | 1 | Whelan, R. | 3 |

# UEFA UNDER-21 CHAMPIONSHIP 2000–2002

## GROUP 1
Switzerland 3, Russia 1
Luxembourg 0, Yugoslavia 3
Luxembourg 1, Slovenia 5
Slovenia 0, Switzerland 0
Russia 2, Luxembourg 0
Yugoslavia 3, Switzerland 3
Russia 0, Slovenia 0
Slovenia 1, Yugoslavia 2
Switzerland 6, Luxembourg 0
Yugoslavia 2, Russia 2
Slovenia 1, Luxembourg 0
Russia 2, Yugoslavia 0
Switzerland 2, Slovenia 1
Luxembourg 0, Russia 10

## GROUP 2
Holland 2, Republic of Ireland 0
Estonia 2, Portugal 3
Portugal 3, Republic of Ireland 1
Cyprus 0, Holland 1
Holland 1, Portugal 1
Republic of Ireland 1, Estonia 0
Cyprus 0, Republic of Ireland 1
Cyprus 3, Estonia 1
Portugal 3, Holland 0
Holland 4, Cyprus 2
Estonia 0, Holland 5
Republic of Ireland 0, Portugal 1
Estonia 0, Republic of Ireland 3
Portugal 7, Cyprus 0

## GROUP 3
Bulgaria 1, Czech Republic 0
Iceland 0, Denmark 0
N Ireland 3, Malta 0
Czech Republic 2, Iceland 1
N Ireland 0, Denmark 3
Bulgaria 2, Malta 0
Iceland 2, N Ireland 5
Malta 0, Czech Republic 1
Denmark 2, Bulgaria 2
Bulgaria 1, Iceland 0
Malta 1, Denmark 0
N Ireland 0, Czech Republic 2

Bulgaria 2, N Ireland 0
Czech Republic 3, Denmark 0
Malta 1, Iceland 1
Iceland 3, Malta 0
Denmark 3, Czech Republic 4
N Ireland 1, Bulgaria 1
Denmark 3, Malta 0
Iceland 3, Bulgaria 2
Czech Republic 4, N Ireland 0

## GROUP 4
Turkey 1, Moldova 0
Azerbaijan 0, Sweden 5
Slovakia 2, Macedonia 0
Sweden 0, Turkey 0
Macedonia 1, Azerbaijan 2
Moldova 0, Slovakia 3
Slovakia 1, Sweden 1
Moldova 3, Macedonia 0
Azerbaijan 1, Turkey 2
Sweden 2, Macedonia 0
Turkey 0, Slovakia 1
Azerbaijan 0, Moldova 1
Macedonia 1, Turkey 4
Slovakia 5, Azerbaijan 0
Moldova 0, Sweden 2
Sweden 4, Slovakia 0
Turkey 3, Azerbaijan 0
Macedonia 2, Moldova 0
Azerbaijan 0, Slovakia 0
Sweden 3, Moldova 0
Turkey 2, Macedonia 0

## GROUP 5
Belarus 4, Wales 1
Norway 5, Armenia 1
Ukraine 2, Poland 2
Armenia 1, Ukraine 2
Poland 0, Belarus 4
Wales 0, Norway 2
Belarus 5, Armenia 0
Poland 2, Wales 1
Norway 3, Ukraine 1
Armenia 1, Wales 0
Ukraine 1, Belarus 0
Norway 1, Poland 2
Belarus 1, Norway 0
Poland 1, Armenia 1
Wales 0, Ukraine 3
Armenia 1, Belarus 0
Ukraine 1, Norway 3
Wales 0, Poland 4
Armenia 2, Poland 0
Ukraine 1, Wales 0

Norway 5, Belarus 1

## GROUP 6
Latvia 1, Scotland 3
Belgium 2, Croatia 1
Latvia 0, Belgium 2
Croatia 3, Scotland 1
Croatia 2, Latvia 1
Scotland 0, Belgium 1
Belgium 3, Latvia 0
Latvia 1, Croatia 1

## GROUP 7
France 3, Israel 0
Bosnia 0, Spain 2
France 2, Austria 1
Spain 1, Israel 0
Austria 2, Spain 1
Israel 2, Bosnia 1
Bosnia 0, France 1
Israel 3, France 4
Bosnia 0, Austria 0
Spain 1, France 1
Austria 0, Israel 2
Austria 1, France 1
Spain 5, Bosnia 1
Israel 0, Spain 1

## GROUP 8
Romania 3, Lithuania 0
Hungary 0, Italy 3
Lithuania 2, Georgia 1
Italy 1, Romania 1
Lithuania 0, Hungary 1
Italy 3, Georgia 2
Hungary 4, Lithuania 1
Romania 0, Italy 1
Georgia 0, Romania 3
Italy 1, Lithuania 0
Romania 1, Hungary 0
Georgia 0, Italy 2
Lithuania 0, Romania 1
Hungary 2, Georgia 1

## GROUP 9
Finland 3, Albania 0
Germany 2, Greece 1
Greece 3, Finland 1
England 1, Germany 1
Albania 0, Greece 1
Finland 2, England 2
Germany 8, Albania 0
England 4, Finland 0
Albania 0, England 1
Greece 2, Germany 0
Finland 1, Germany 3
Greece 0, Albania 0
Greece 3, England 1

# OLYMPIC FOOTBALL

**Previous winners**

| | | | | | |
|---|---|---|---|---|---|
| 1896 | Athens* | 1. Denmark | 1960 | Rome | 1. Yugoslavia |
| | | 2. Greece | | | 2. Denmark |
| 1900 | Paris* | 1. England | | | 3. Hungary |
| | | 2. France | 1964 | Tokyo | 1. Hungary |
| 1904 | St Louis** | 1. Canada | | | 2. Czechoslovakia |
| | | 2. USA | | | 3. East Germany |
| 1908 | London | 1. England | 1968 | Mexico City | 1. Hungary |
| | | 2. Denmark | | | 2. Bulgaria |
| | | 3. Holland | | | 3. Japan |
| 1912 | Stockholm | 1. England | 1972 | Munich | 1. Poland |
| | | 2. Denmark | | | 2. Hungary |
| | | 3. Holland | | | 3. East Germany/ USSR joint bronze |
| 1920 | Antwerp | 1. Belgium | | | |
| | | 2. Spain | 1976 | Montreal | 1. East Germany |
| | | 3. Holland | | | 2. Poland |
| 1924 | Paris | 1. Uruguay | | | 3. USSR |
| | | 2. Switzerland | 1980 | Moscow | 1. Czechoslovakia |
| | | 3. Sweden | | | 2. East Germany |
| 1928 | Amsterdam | 1. Uruguay | | | 3. USSR |
| | | 2. Argentina | 1984 | Los Angeles | 1. France |
| | | 3. Italy | | | 2. Brazil |
| 1932 | Los Angeles no competition | | | | 3. Yugoslavia |
| 1936 | Berlin | 1. Italy | 1988 | Seoul | 1. USSR |
| | | 2. Austria | | | 2. Brazil |
| | | 3. Norway | | | 3. West Germany |
| 1948 | London | 1. Sweden | 1992 | Barcelona | 1. Spain |
| | | 2. Yugoslavia | | | 2. Poland |
| | | 3. Denmark | | | 3. Ghana |
| 1952 | Helsinki | 1. Hungary | 1996 | Atlanta | 1. Nigeria |
| | | 2. Yugoslavia | | | 2. Argentina |
| | | 3. Sweden | | | 3. Brazil |
| 1956 | Melbourne | 1. USSR | 2000 | Sydney | 1. Cameroon |
| | | 2. Yugoslavia | | | 2. Spain |
| | | 3. Bulgaria | | | 3. Chile |

*No official tournament*
**No official tournament but gold medal later awarded by IOC*

# REPUBLIC OF IRELAND LEAGUE

|  | P | W | D | L | F | A | Pts |
|---|---|---|---|---|---|---|---|
| Bohemians | 33 | 18 | 8 | 7 | 66 | 35 | 62 |
| Shelbourne | 33 | 17 | 9 | 7 | 53 | 37 | 60 |
| Cork City | 33 | 15 | 11 | 7 | 36 | 29 | 56 |
| Bray Wanderers | 33 | 15 | 10 | 8 | 52 | 35 | 55 |
| St Patrick's Ath | 33 | 14 | 11 | 8 | 54 | 41 | 53 |
| Derry City | 33 | 12 | 9 | 12 | 31 | 28 | 45 |
| Shamrock Rovers | 33 | 10 | 12 | 11 | 50 | 47 | 42 |
| Longford Town | 33 | 12 | 6 | 15 | 40 | 47 | 42 |
| Galway United | 33 | 10 | 10 | 13 | 34 | 47 | 40 |
| UCD | 33 | 9 | 10 | 14 | 36 | 44 | 37 |
| Finn Harps | 33 | 8 | 12 | 13 | 36 | 46 | 36 |
| Kilkenny City | 33 | 1 | 6 | 26 | 14 | 66 | 9 |

# HIGHLAND LEAGUE

|  |  | Home | | | Away | | | Goals | | | |
|---|---|---|---|---|---|---|---|---|---|---|---|
|  | P | W | D | L | W | D | L | F | A | Pts | GD |
| Cove Rangers | 26 | 12 | 1 | 0 | 8 | 2 | 3 | 74 | 32 | 63 | 42 |
| Huntly | 26 | 11 | 0 | 2 | 8 | 2 | 3 | 61 | 28 | 59 | 33 |
| Buckie Thistle | 26 | 8 | 3 | 2 | 5 | 4 | 4 | 46 | 33 | 46 | 13 |
| Clachnacuddin | 26 | 9 | 2 | 2 | 4 | 3 | 6 | 47 | 34 | 44 | 13 |
| Keith | 26 | 8 | 3 | 2 | 3 | 6 | 4 | 54 | 43 | 42 | 11 |
| Deveronvale | 26 | 5 | 5 | 3 | 6 | 3 | 4 | 39 | 32 | 41 | 7 |
| Forres Mechanics | 26 | 7 | 2 | 4 | 3 | 8 | 2 | 44 | 39 | 40 | 5 |
| Fraserburgh | 26 | 6 | 3 | 4 | 6 | 0 | 7 | 47 | 38 | 39 | 9 |
| Nairn County | 26 | 5 | 4 | 4 | 3 | 3 | 7 | 44 | 58 | 31 | −14 |
| Wick Academy | 26 | 6 | 3 | 4 | 2 | 2 | 9 | 39 | 43 | 29 | −4 |
| Rothes | 26 | 4 | 3 | 6 | 2 | 2 | 9 | 30 | 45 | 23 | −15 |
| Lossiemouth | 26 | 4 | 4 | 5 | 2 | 0 | 11 | 27 | 60 | 22 | −33 |
| Brora Rangers | 26 | 4 | 3 | 6 | 0 | 0 | 13 | 41 | 78 | 15 | −37 |
| Fort William | 26 | 3 | 2 | 8 | 0 | 3 | 10 | 27 | 57 | 14 | −30 |

# NATIONWIDE FOOTBALL CONFERENCE 2000–2001

| | | Home | | | Goals | | Away | | | Goals | | |
|---|---|---|---|---|---|---|---|---|---|---|---|---|
| | P | W | D | L | F | A | W | D | L | F | A | Pts |
| Rushden & Diamonds | 42 | 14 | 6 | 1 | 41 | 13 | 11 | 5 | 5 | 37 | 23 | 86 |
| Yeovil Town | 42 | 14 | 3 | 4 | 41 | 17 | 10 | 5 | 6 | 32 | 33 | 80 |
| Dagenham & Redbridge | 42 | 13 | 4 | 4 | 39 | 19 | 10 | 4 | 7 | 32 | 35 | 77 |
| Southport | 42 | 9 | 5 | 7 | 33 | 24 | 11 | 4 | 6 | 25 | 22 | 69 |
| Leigh RMI | 42 | 11 | 5 | 5 | 38 | 24 | 8 | 6 | 7 | 25 | 33 | 68 |
| Telford United | 42 | 13 | 1 | 7 | 33 | 23 | 6 | 7 | 8 | 18 | 28 | 65 |
| Stevenage Borough | 42 | 8 | 7 | 6 | 36 | 33 | 7 | 11 | 3 | 35 | 28 | 63 |
| Chester City | 42 | 9 | 8 | 4 | 29 | 19 | 7 | 6 | 8 | 20 | 24 | 62 |
| Doncaster Rovers | 42 | 11 | 5 | 5 | 28 | 17 | 4 | 8 | 9 | 19 | 26 | 58 |
| Scarborough | 42 | 7 | 9 | 5 | 29 | 25 | 7 | 7 | 7 | 27 | 29 | 58 |
| Hereford United | 42 | 6 | 12 | 3 | 27 | 19 | 8 | 3 | 10 | 33 | 27 | 57 |
| Boston United | 42 | 10 | 7 | 4 | 43 | 28 | 3 | 10 | 8 | 31 | 35 | 56 |
| Nuneaton Borough | 42 | 9 | 5 | 7 | 35 | 26 | 4 | 10 | 7 | 25 | 34 | 54 |
| Woking | 42 | 5 | 10 | 6 | 30 | 30 | 8 | 5 | 8 | 22 | 27 | 54 |
| Dover Athletic | 42 | 9 | 6 | 6 | 32 | 22 | 5 | 5 | 11 | 22 | 34 | 53 |
| Forest Green Rovers | 42 | 6 | 9 | 6 | 28 | 28 | 5 | 6 | 10 | 15 | 26 | 48 |
| Northwich Victoria | 42 | 8 | 7 | 6 | 31 | 24 | 3 | 6 | 12 | 18 | 43 | 46 |
| Hayes | 42 | 5 | 6 | 10 | 22 | 31 | 7 | 4 | 10 | 22 | 40 | 46 |
| Morecambe | 42 | 8 | 5 | 8 | 35 | 29 | 3 | 7 | 11 | 29 | 37 | 45 |
| Kettering Town | 42 | 5 | 5 | 11 | 23 | 31 | 6 | 5 | 10 | 23 | 31 | 43 |
| Kingstonian | 42 | 3 | 5 | 13 | 19 | 40 | 5 | 5 | 11 | 28 | 33 | 34 |
| Hednesford Town | 42 | 2 | 6 | 13 | 24 | 38 | 3 | 7 | 11 | 22 | 48 | 28 |

**Leading Goalscorers 2000–2001**

| Conf. | | | NVCT | FAC | UT |
|---|---|---|---|---|---|
| 24 | Duane Darby (Rushden & Diamonds) | + | – | – | 3 |
| 19 | Steve Jones (Leigh RMI) | + | 1 | 1 | – |
| 18 | Warren Patmore (Yeovil Town) | + | 1 | 3 | – |
| 18 | Justin Jackson (Rushden & Diamonds) | + | – | 1 | 1 |
| 15 | Darran Hay (Stevenage Borough) | + | – | – | 1 |
| 14 | Rob Elmes (Hereford United) | + | – | – | 4 |
| 13 | Alex Meechan (Forest Green Rovers) | + | – | – | 5 |
| 13 | Ken Charlery (Boston United) | + | – | 3 | 1 |
| 13 | Marc McGregor (Nuneaton Borough) | + | 2 | 1 | – |
| 13 | Ian Arnold (Southport) | + | – | 1 | 1 |
| 13 | Dave Ridings (Leigh RMI) | + | 1 | – | – |
| 13 | Simon Parke (Southport) | + | – | – | – |
| 13 | Charlie Griffin (Woking) | + | – | – | – |
| 12 | Mark Beesley (Chester City) | + | 3 | 1 | 1 |
| 12 | Tony Black (Leigh RMI) | + | 1 | 3 | 1 |
| 12 | Darren Collins (Kettering Town) | + | – | 2 | – |
| 12 | Gary Paterson (Doncaster Rovers) | + | – | 1 | – |
| 12 | Jeff Vansittart (Dover Athletic) | + | – | – | – |
| 11 | Neil Illman (Stevenage Borough) | + | 2 | – | 4 |
| 11 | Rocky Baptiste (Hayes) | + | – | – | – |
| 11 | Dale Watkins (Kettering Town) | + | – | – | – |
| 11 | Jon Brady (Rushden & Diamonds) | + | – | – | – |

NVCT: National Variety Club Trophy; FAC: FA Cup; UT: Umbro Trophy.

# NATIONWIDE FOOTBALL CONFERENCE RESULTS 2000–2001

| Home \ Away | Boston United | Chester City | Dagenham & Redbridge | Doncaster Rovers | Dover Athletic | Forest Green Rovers | Hayes | Hednesford Town | Hereford United | Kettering Town | Kingstonian | Leigh RMI | Morecambe | Northwich Victoria | Nuneaton Borough | Rushden & Diamonds | Scarborough | Southport | Stevenage Borough | Telford United | Woking | Yeovil Town |
|---|---|---|---|---|---|---|---|---|---|---|---|---|---|---|---|---|---|---|---|---|---|---|
| Boston United | — | 2-1 | 1-1 | 3-1 | 3-2 | 2-2 | 0-0 | 1-2 | 0-3 | 2-0 | 0-3 | 2-0 | 0-0 | 2-2 | 1-1 | 2-4 | 1-1 | 0-3 | 0-0 | 4-2 | 2-1 | 2-2 |
| Chester City | 0-0 | — | 3-0 | 1-0 | 1-0 | 0-2 | 2-2 | 4-0 | 1-0 | 2-3 | 4-0 | 2-0 | 4-1 | 1-3 | 2-0 | 0-0 | 1-3 | 1-1 | 1-1 | 1-0 | 1-1 | 1-1 |
| Dagenham & Redbridge | 5-1 | 2-1 | — | 0-1 | 1-0 | 1-0 | 1-2 | 0-1 | 2-1 | 1-5 | 2-3 | 2-4 | 0-2 | 4-1 | 0-2 | 1-1 | 4-4 | 1-1 | 2-1 | 1-0 | 1-0 | 1-2 |
| Doncaster Rovers | 4-2 | 2-1 | 0-0 | — | 3-1 | 1-0 | 0-0 | 1-1 | 1-1 | 3-2 | 4-0 | 1-0 | 2-1 | 1-1 | 6-1 | 2-0 | 3-1 | 1-1 | 1-0 | 0-0 | 1-2 | 2-0 |
| Dover Athletic | 1-1 | 1-1 | 1-1 | 4-2 | — | 2-1 | 3-1 | 1-0 | 0-2 | 3-1 | 1-2 | 1-1 | 1-2 | 0-3 | 1-1 | 5-1 | 0-0 | 4-1 | 1-0 | 2-1 | 0-1 | 2-0 |
| Forest Green Rovers | 0-3 | 1-2 | 1-0 | 1-1 | 1-0 | — | 1-2 | 0-1 | 4-1 | 2-2 | 0-2 | 1-2 | 2-4 | 0-3 | 2-0 | 2-0 | 0-0 | 2-0 | 1-1 | 1-3 | 0-0 | 1-1 |
| Hayes | 3-0 | 1-2 | 2-0 | 4-1 | 3-3 | 2-0 | — | 0-0 | 2-0 | 2-0 | 4-0 | 3-4 | 4-0 | 4-0 | 3-2 | 1-3 | 1-0 | 1-2 | 4-1 | 2-0 | 2-0 | 0-1 |
| Hednesford Town | 1-1 | 0-1 | 2-0 | 0-0 | 2-0 | 5-1 | 2-4 | — | 0-0 | 2-0 | 5-1 | 5-1 | 2-0 | 1-0 | 2-1 | 1-1 | 1-1 | 1-1 | 4-0 | 1-1 | 6-1 | 3-4 |
| Hereford United | 2-3 | 0-3 | 1-0 | 2-1 | 1-0 | 0-1 | 1-0 | 1-1 | — | 2-4 | 1-1 | 2-0 | 1-0 | 0-3 | 0-1 | 0-2 | 0-2 | 1-0 | 1-0 | 2-1 | 2-1 | 5-3 |
| Kettering Town | 3-1 | 0-0 | 3-0 | 2-1 | 2-3 | 1-3 | 0-1 | 2-5 | 2-0 | — | 1-1 | 2-1 | 3-2 | 0-1 | 0-0 | 3-1 | 1-2 | 1-0 | 3-2 | 2-1 | 5-1 | 4-3 |
| Kingstonian | 3-1 | 2-1 | 1-2 | 3-0 | 0-1 | 2-5 | 2-1 | 2-1 | 1-0 | 2-1 | — | 3-2 | 2-1 | 0-0 | 3-2 | 1-2 | 3-1 | 1-3 | 0-2 | 1-2 | 2-0 | 2-1 |
| Leigh RMI | 6-1 | 1-1 | 1-2 | 1-1 | 1-1 | 3-0 | 4-4 | 2-2 | 0-1 | 1-1 | 2-1 | — | 1-1 | 0-2 | 1-0 | 1-2 | 1-0 | 1-0 | 1-2 | 4-0 | 0-0 | 0-1 |
| Morecambe | 3-2 | 0-2 | 3-1 | 3-1 | 1-1 | 1-0 | 1-0 | 2-2 | 2-2 | 1-1 | 1-0 | 1-5 | — | 4-1 | 1-1 | 1-1 | 0-0 | 1-1 | 0-1 | 3-2 | 2-1 | 2-1 |
| Northwich Victoria | 1-0 | 1-1 | 1-1 | 2-3 | 2-0 | 4-0 | 4-0 | 3-0 | 3-1 | 3-0 | 3-0 | 1-1 | 3-0 | — | 4-0 | 1-1 | 2-2 | 2-0 | 7-1 | 1-0 | 1-0 | 1-1 |
| Nuneaton Borough | 0-0 | 0-2 | 2-1 | 1-2 | 3-1 | 3-0 | 1-1 | 2-2 | 2-2 | 1-0 | 6-2 | 1-2 | 1-2 | 2-1 | — | 2-1 | 0-3 | 0-0 | 1-1 | 1-1 | 1-1 | 4-1 |
| Rushden & Diamonds | 1-2 | 1-0 | 1-4 | 1-2 | 1-2 | 4-4 | 1-3 | 1-1 | 0-3 | 1-0 | 2-4 | 3-1 | 3-1 | 2-0 | 0-2 | — | 1-1 | 4-1 | 3-1 | 0-2 | 1-0 | 1-1 |
| Scarborough | 0-1 | 3-0 | 1-0 | 1-3 | 1-0 | 2-1 | 2-2 | 4-1 | 3-0 | 4-4 | 2-2 | 1-0 | 1-1 | 0-1 | 0-2 | 0-2 | — | 2-3 | 1-1 | 1-0 | 3-2 | 2-2 |
| Southport | 0-1 | 1-2 | 1-2 | 2-3 | 1-1 | 2-1 | 4-0 | 0-2 | 3-1 | 2-0 | 1-3 | 0-2 | 3-1 | 2-0 | 1-3 | 3-1 | 0-0 | — | 4-0 | 2-0 | 1-0 | 1-0 |
| Stevenage Borough | 0-0 | 1-1 | 1-0 | 0-1 | 3-0 | 1-1 | 1-1 | 2-1 | 2-1 | 1-2 | 3-2 | 2-2 | 1-3 | 1-0 | 2-4 | 3-1 | 3-2 | 3-2 | — | 0-0 | 2-2 | 1-2 |
| Telford United | 2-0 | 0-3 | 0-0 | 1-0 | 1-3 | 0-0 | 0-1 | 1-1 | 2-0 | 0-1 | 1-0 | 2-2 | 2-1 | 3-1 | 5-3 | 3-0 | 3-0 | 3-1 | 5-3 | — | 0-3 | 2-1 |
| Woking | 1-0 | 3-1 | 1-2 | 0-1 | 0-0 | 1-1 | 1-2 | 1-2 | 0-1 | 0-3 | 3-0 | 4-0 | 1-1 | 3-2 | 1-2 | 0-2 | 3-0 | 0-3 | 3-1 | 1-0 | — | 1-0 |
| Yeovil Town | 2-2 | 0-0 | 2-1 | 3-3 | 1-0 | 2-2 | 1-1 | 4-1 | 1-1 | 4-3 | 2-1 | 0-1 | 2-1 | 1-1 | 2-0 | 0-2 | 3-1 | 1-0 | 3-4 | 5-3 | 0-0 | — |

# DR MARTENS LEAGUE 2000–2001

**Premier Division**

| | P | W | D | L | F | A | GD | Pts |
|---|---|---|---|---|---|---|---|---|
| Margate | 42 | 28 | 7 | 7 | 75 | 27 | 48 | 91 |
| Burton Albion | 42 | 25 | 13 | 4 | 76 | 36 | 40 | 88 |
| King's Lynn | 42 | 18 | 11 | 13 | 67 | 58 | 9 | 65 |
| Welling United | 42 | 17 | 13 | 12 | 59 | 55 | 4 | 64 |
| Weymouth | 42 | 17 | 12 | 13 | 69 | 51 | 18 | 63 |
| Havant & Waterlooville | 42 | 18 | 9 | 15 | 66 | 54 | 12 | 63 |
| Stafford Rangers | 42 | 18 | 9 | 15 | 70 | 59 | 11 | 63 |
| Worcester City | 42 | 18 | 8 | 16 | 52 | 53 | −1 | 62 |
| Moor Green | 42 | 18 | 8 | 16 | 50 | 53 | −3 | 62 |
| Newport County | 42 | 17 | 10 | 15 | 70 | 61 | 9 | 61 |
| Crawley Town | 42 | 17 | 10 | 15 | 61 | 54 | 7 | 61 |
| Tamworth | 42 | 17 | 8 | 17 | 58 | 55 | 3 | 59 |
| Salisbury City | 42 | 17 | 8 | 17 | 64 | 69 | −5 | 59 |
| Ilkeston Town | 42 | 16 | 11 | 15 | 51 | 61 | −10 | 59 |
| Bath City* | 42 | 15 | 13 | 14 | 67 | 68 | −1 | 55 |
| Cambridge City | 42 | 13 | 11 | 18 | 56 | 59 | −3 | 50 |
| Folkestone Invicta | 42 | 14 | 6 | 22 | 49 | 74 | −25 | 48 |
| Merthyr Tydfil | 42 | 11 | 13 | 18 | 49 | 62 | −13 | 46 |
| Clevedon Town | 42 | 11 | 7 | 24 | 61 | 74 | −13 | 40 |
| Fisher Athletic Lon* | 42 | 12 | 6 | 24 | 51 | 85 | −34 | 39 |
| Dorchester Town | 42 | 10 | 8 | 24 | 40 | 71 | −31 | 38 |
| Halesowen Town | 42 | 8 | 13 | 21 | 47 | 69 | −22 | 37 |

(*Bath City & Fisher Athletic London, 3 points deducted – ineligible player)

**Leading Goalscorers 2000–2001**
**(League and Cup)**

**Premier Division**

| | |
|---|---|
| Philip Collins (Margate) | 31 |
| Gary Shepherd (Newport County) | 26 |
| Mark Owen (Worcester City) | 22 |
| Darren Rowbotham (Weymouth) | 19 |
| Warren Haughton (Tamworth) | 18 |
| Lyndon Rowland (King's Lynn) | 18 |
| Paul Sales (Salisbury City) | 18 |
| Scott Dundas (Stafford Rangers) | 17 |
| Andrew Mainwaring (Clevedon Town) | 17 |
| Martin Paul (Bath City) | 17 |
| Mark Hallam (Tamworth) | 16 |
| Paul Chambers (Folkestone Invicta) | 15 |
| Mark Hynes (Crawley Town) | 15 |
| Darren Stride (Burton Albion) | 15 |
| Kevin Wilkin (Cambridge City) | 15 |
| Robert Gould (Ilkeston Town) | 14 |
| David Leworthy (Havant & Waterlooville) | 14 |
| John Palmer (King's Lynn) | 14 |
| Samuel Bowen (Halesowen Town) | 13 |
| David Laws (Weymouth) | 13 |
| Dean Wordsworth (Crawley Town) | 13 |
| Christian Moore (Burton Albion) | 12 |
| Mark Munday (Margate) | 12 |
| Joseph O'Connor (Stafford Rangers) | 12 |

# DR MARTENS PREMIER LEAGUE RESULTS 2000–2001

| | Bath City | Burton Albion | Cambridge City | Clevedon Town | Crawley Town | Dorchester Town | Fisher Athletic | Folkestone Invicta | Halesowen Town | Havant & Waterlooville | Ilkeston Town | King's Lynn | Margate | Merthyr Tydfil | Moor Green | Newport County | Salisbury City | Stafford Rangers | Tamworth | Welling United | Weymouth | Worcester City |
|---|---|---|---|---|---|---|---|---|---|---|---|---|---|---|---|---|---|---|---|---|---|---|
| Bath City | — | 3-1 | 0-0 | 1-0 | 2-1 | 0-1 | 2-1 | 4-3 | 4-0 | 4-3 | 1-0 | 2-2 | 1-2 | 1-0 | 3-1 | 2-0 | 1-0 | 0-0 | 2-3 | 0-2 | 3-2 | 3-2 |
| Burton Albion | 3-1 | — | 2-2 | 1-2 | 2-1 | 1-3 | 0-4 | 0-2 | 0-2 | 4-0 | 1-0 | 1-2 | 2-0 | 1-0 | 2-1 | 2-1 | 5-0 | 1-0 | 3-1 | 0-0 | 1-0 | 1-0 |
| Cambridge City | 2-0 | 1-1 | — | 1-0 | 1-2 | 3-0 | 3-0 | 1-2 | 3-0 | 1-0 | 1-0 | 1-0 | 1-2 | 2-2 | 1-2 | 5-6 | 1-2 | 1-1 | 2-1 | 4-1 | 2-2 | 2-3 |
| Clevedon Town | 0-1 | 1-2 | 3-0 | — | 1-2 | 8-1 | 0-1 | 4-1 | 1-4 | 1-0 | 2-3 | 1-0 | 0-2 | 2-1 | 1-2 | 2-3 | 5-1 | 2-2 | 0-2 | 4-1 | 2-1 | 0-1 |
| Crawley Town | 1-2 | 2-2 | 1-2 | 1-0 | — | 4-3 | 1-0 | 1-2 | 3-0 | 1-0 | 1-1 | 3-0 | 0-0 | 2-2 | 1-2 | 1-2 | 1-2 | 2-2 | 0-2 | 2-1 | 2-1 | 0-1 |
| Dorchester Town | 4-3 | 1-3 | 1-0 | 1-0 | 2-2 | — | 3-2 | 1-2 | 0-3 | 0-3 | 2-3 | 1-0 | 3-0 | 4-0 | 0-3 | 0-3 | 1-2 | 2-3 | 0-2 | 1-1 | 2-3 | 1-2 |
| Fisher Athletic | 1-0 | 0-4 | 0-2 | 1-2 | 2-1 | 1-2 | — | 2-1 | 0-3 | 0-1 | 1-3 | 2-1 | 1-0 | 2-1 | 3-0 | 3-1 | 1-2 | 2-2 | 1-1 | 1-1 | 2-0 | 1-2 |
| Folkestone Invicta | 0-2 | 0-2 | 4-3 | 3-2 | 3-2 | — | 4-4 | 2-1 | 2-2 | 4-0 | 0-4 | 2-3 | 1-0 | 1-0 | 0-0 | 1-3 | 3-0 | 0-1 | 1-0 | 0-2 | 1-3 | 1-2 |
| Halesowen Town | 2-0 | 2-1 | 3-0 | 1-0 | 1-1 | 1-0 | 2-1 | — | 0-4 | 0-2 | 0-0 | 0-0 | 2-3 | 2-1 | 0-0 | 1-3 | 3-0 | 2-1 | 3-2 | 2-0 | 3-0 | 1-2 |
| Havant & Waterlooville | 2-0 | 1-1 | 4-2 | 0-0 | 1-1 | 2-1 | 3-2 | 4-4 | 0-0 | — | 2-1 | 1-1 | 1-1 | 1-0 | 0-0 | 3-0 | 2-1 | 0-1 | 3-2 | 0-1 | 5-1 | 1-0 |
| Ilkeston Town | 3-0 | 1-1 | 3-0 | 3-1 | 1-1 | 2-1 | 0-1 | 2-2 | 2-1 | 2-1 | — | 2-0 | 1-0 | 2-0 | 0-1 | 0-0 | 2-1 | 3-2 | 0-0 | 0-0 | 1-6 | 2-4 |
| King's Lynn | 1-1 | 1-1 | 0-2 | 1-1 | 0-4 | 0-1 | 0-1 | 2-2 | 2-1 | 1-1 | 2-2 | — | 3-1 | 0-1 | 0-1 | 2-3 | 1-1 | 1-3 | 3-1 | 0-1 | 3-0 | 1-2 |
| Margate | 2-0 | 0-4 | 2-1 | 2-0 | 5-0 | 1-0 | 0-1 | 0-0 | 0-2 | 2-0 | 4-0 | 3-1 | — | 1-1 | 2-0 | 0-0 | 2-1 | 0-2 | 1-0 | 1-0 | 3-0 | 1-0 |
| Merthyr Tydfil | 3-3 | 3-1 | 2-1 | 2-0 | 3-2 | 1-0 | 0-1 | 2-1 | 0-0 | 2-1 | 2-1 | 3-1 | 1-1 | — | 2-0 | 0-0 | 2-1 | 3-2 | 6-0 | 0-1 | 0-1 | 0-1 |
| Moor Green | 3-0 | 1-5 | 2-2 | 3-1 | 3-1 | 3-2 | 3-2 | 2-2 | 0-2 | 4-4 | 4-0 | 2-1 | 0-4 | 3-2 | — | 2-0 | 1-0 | 1-2 | 1-0 | 5-0 | 3-0 | 4-1 |
| Newport County | 3-2 | 1-1 | 2-1 | 1-0 | 2-1 | 3-1 | 2-2 | 5-0 | 0-0 | 2-1 | 2-1 | 1-3 | 0-1 | 1-1 | 2-0 | — | 1-0 | 1-2 | 0-1 | 1-1 | 0-1 | 1-0 |
| Salisbury City | 4-4 | 3-0 | 3-0 | 3-0 | 3-1 | 1-2 | 0-0 | 0-2 | 2-0 | 2-2 | 4-2 | 0-2 | 2-1 | 2-2 | 3-1 | 4-0 | — | 4-1 | 1-0 | 1-1 | 0-1 | 2-0 |
| Stafford Rangers | 6-2 | 1-1 | 0-0 | 5-2 | 1-2 | 5-0 | 3-0 | 3-0 | 1-1 | 2-2 | 0-1 | 3-0 | 0-0 | 0-2 | 2-0 | 1-0 | 0-2 | — | 4-2 | 2-1 | 3-2 | 0-4 |
| Tamworth | 3-1 | 2-3 | 0-0 | 0-2 | 0-2 | 2-0 | 3-0 | 1-1 | 4-1 | 3-2 | 0-0 | 3-1 | 1-0 | 2-2 | 3-1 | 1-0 | 4-1 | 1-2 | — | 5-2 | 3-2 | 1-2 |
| Welling United | 1-0 | 1-1 | 2-3 | 2-3 | 1-1 | 3-0 | 4-0 | 1-1 | 1-1 | 1-2 | 4-1 | 1-4 | 1-0 | 1-0 | 0-1 | 1-0 | 2-1 | 1-1 | 4-0 | — | 3-2 | 2-0 |
| Weymouth | 1-0 | 1-1 | 1-1 | 1-1 | 2-0 | 1-1 | 3-0 | 1-1 | 1-1 | 4-1 | 4-1 | 1-1 | 1-0 | 1-1 | 5-1 | 0-0 | 3-1 | 0-2 | 4-0 | 2-1 | — | 4-1 |
| Worcester City | 0-0 | 1-1 | 2-0 | 3-3 | 2-0 | 1-2 | 1-2 | 4-1 | 2-0 | 1-0 | 1-0 | 0-1 | 0-1 | 1-1 | 1-0 | 0-1 | 0-1 | 2-4 | 1-0 | 1-2 | 0-0 | — |

# UNIBOND LEAGUE 2000–2001

| Premier Division | | Home | | | Goals | | Away | | | Goals | | |
|---|---|---|---|---|---|---|---|---|---|---|---|---|
| | P | W | D | L | F | A | W | D | L | F | A | Pts |
| Stalybridge Celtic | 44 | 19 | 1 | 2 | 57 | 15 | 12 | 8 | 2 | 39 | 17 | 102 |
| Emley | 44 | 16 | 5 | 1 | 44 | 19 | 15 | 3 | 4 | 43 | 23 | 101 |
| Bishop Auckland | 44 | 15 | 2 | 5 | 45 | 24 | 11 | 5 | 6 | 43 | 29 | 85 |
| Lancaster City | 44 | 15 | 4 | 3 | 48 | 27 | 9 | 5 | 8 | 36 | 33 | 81 |
| Worksop Town | 44 | 10 | 8 | 4 | 60 | 30 | 10 | 5 | 7 | 42 | 30 | 73 |
| Barrow | 44 | 14 | 3 | 5 | 49 | 26 | 7 | 6 | 9 | 34 | 37 | 72 |
| Altrincham | 44 | 13 | 4 | 5 | 45 | 24 | 7 | 6 | 9 | 35 | 34 | 70 |
| Gainsborough Trinity | 44 | 13 | 6 | 3 | 35 | 19 | 4 | 8 | 10 | 24 | 37 | 65 |
| Accrington Stanley | 44 | 12 | 4 | 6 | 44 | 34 | 6 | 6 | 10 | 28 | 33 | 64 |
| Hucknall Town | 44 | 11 | 4 | 7 | 34 | 30 | 6 | 8 | 8 | 23 | 33 | 63 |
| Gateshead | 44 | 9 | 7 | 6 | 39 | 26 | 7 | 5 | 10 | 29 | 35 | 60 |
| Bamber Bridge | 44 | 9 | 3 | 10 | 34 | 31 | 8 | 5 | 9 | 29 | 34 | 59 |
| Runcorn | 44 | 12 | 5 | 5 | 35 | 27 | 3 | 5 | 14 | 21 | 43 | 55 |
| Blyth Spartans | 44 | 10 | 6 | 6 | 28 | 17 | 5 | 3 | 14 | 33 | 47 | 54 |
| Burscough | 44 | 8 | 6 | 8 | 32 | 27 | 6 | 4 | 12 | 27 | 41 | 52 |
| Hyde United | 44 | 9 | 8 | 5 | 48 | 36 | 4 | 4 | 14 | 24 | 43 | 51 |
| Whitby Town | 44 | 4 | 8 | 10 | 27 | 35 | 9 | 3 | 10 | 33 | 41 | 50 |
| Marine | 44 | 8 | 7 | 7 | 30 | 31 | 4 | 6 | 12 | 32 | 47 | 49 |
| Colwyn Bay | 44 | 9 | 6 | 7 | 42 | 45 | 3 | 4 | 15 | 26 | 57 | 46 |
| Frickley Athletic | 44 | 6 | 8 | 8 | 31 | 34 | 4 | 7 | 11 | 19 | 45 | 45 |
| Droylsden | 44 | 7 | 3 | 12 | 29 | 40 | 6 | 3 | 13 | 21 | 40 | 45 |
| Leek Town | 44 | 8 | 5 | 9 | 26 | 30 | 4 | 3 | 15 | 19 | 40 | 44 |
| Spennymoor United* | 44 | 3 | 2 | 17 | 17 | 48 | 1 | 3 | 18 | 15 | 60 | 16 |

*1 point deducted for breach of rule*

## Leading Goalscorers

### (In order of League Goals)

### Premier Division

| Lge | Cup | Tot | |
|---|---|---|---|
| 29 | 14 | 43 | Chris Ward (Lancaster City) |
| 28 | 12 | 40 | Kirk Jackson (Worksop Town) |
| 24 | 9 | 33 | Nicky Peverill (Barrow) |
| 23 | 8 | 31 | Simeon Bambrook (Emley) |
| 22 | 10 | 32 | Simon Yeo (Hyde United) |
| 22 | 9 | 31 | Andy Shaw (Bishop Auckland) |
| 22 | 7 | 29 | Glen Robson (Blyth Spartans) |
| 22 | 7 | 29 | Andy Whittaker (Bamber Bridge) |
| 22 | 5 | 27 | Rod Thornley (Altrincham) |
| | | | (13 + 5 for Congleton Town) |

# UNIBOND LEAGUE—PREMIER DIVISION RESULTS 2000–2001

| | Accrington Stanley | Altrincham | Barrow | Bamber Bridge | Bishop Auckland | Blyth Spartans | Burscough | Colwyn Bay | Droylsden | Emley | Frickley Athletic | Gainsborough Trinity | Gateshead | Hucknall Town | Hyde United | Lancaster City | Leek Town | Marine | Runcorn | Spennymoor United | Stalybridge Celtic | Whitby Town | Worksop Town |
|---|---|---|---|---|---|---|---|---|---|---|---|---|---|---|---|---|---|---|---|---|---|---|---|
| Accrington Stanley | — | 2-1 | 3-0 | 1-3 | 3-1 | 3-3 | 2-0 | 2-2 | 3-0 | 3-1 | 0-2 | 1-1 | 0-0 | 1-2 | 4-1 | 1-2 | 2-1 | 3-2 | 2-1 | 1-0 | 1-4 | 0-2 | 3-4 |
| Altrincham | 5-2 | — | 2-3 | 3-1 | 0-2 | 2-2 | 1-1 | 2-1 | 0-1 | 1-2 | 3-1 | 1-0 | 0-2 | 1-3 | 4-1 | 4-1 | 1-0 | 1-0 | 4-1 | 2-3 | 0-0 | 3-1 | 1-2 |
| Barrow | 3-0 | 1-2 | — | 3-1 | 0-2 | 2-0 | 0-1 | 3-4 | 3-2 | 0-1 | 2-0 | 2-0 | 4-2 | 5-0 | 1-0 | 1-4 | 3-0 | 3-1 | 3-1 | 5-0 | 0-0 | 5-0 | 1-2 |
| Bamber Bridge | 2-2 | 1-2 | 1-4 | — | 1-2 | 0-3 | 1-0 | 1-2 | 0-3 | 3-1 | 0-1 | 0-0 | 1-3 | 1-0 | 1-0 | 3-2 | 2-0 | 1-1 | 2-3 | 1-1 | 0-0 | 2-3 | 2-1 |
| Bishop Auckland | 3-1 | 0-2 | 0-2 | 1-4 | — | 1-2 | 1-2 | 3-3 | 0-3 | 3-1 | 0-0 | 3-1 | 2-2 | 2-4 | 1-0 | 3-2 | 1-0 | 1-1 | 4-4 | 3-1 | 1-1 | 5-0 | 2-1 |
| Blyth Spartans | 3-3 | 3-1 | 2-0 | 2-0 | 1-2 | — | 4-1 | 1-2 | 1-0 | 4-2 | 2-5 | 4-1 | 2-1 | 3-1 | 6-2 | 1-1 | 0-4 | 3-5 | 2-0 | 1-0 | 1-1 | 0-2 | 2-1 |
| Burscough | 2-0 | 0-1 | 4-0 | 1-0 | 4-1 | 1-0 | — | 4-1 | 2-1 | 0-1 | 2-1 | 4-2 | 3-1 | 2-0 | 5-2 | 1-1 | 0-4 | 2-0 | 2-0 | 2-0 | 0-2 | 2-1 | 1-0 |
| Colwyn Bay | 2-2 | 1-1 | 3-4 | 3-2 | 5-2 | 1-0 | 1-0 | — | 4-1 | 6-2 | 4-2 | 1-1 | 1-1 | 1-2 | 2-4 | 2-4 | 1-0 | 2-1 | 1-0 | 2-1 | 3-3 | 1-1 | 3-2 |
| Droylsden | 3-0 | 3-0 | 2-1 | 2-1 | 0-1 | 1-0 | 3-2 | 2-1 | — | 1-1 | 1-3 | 1-2 | 0-2 | 3-3 | 1-0 | 0-2 | 3-1 | 1-0 | 3-0 | 1-3 | 0-3 | 0-2 | 5-3 |
| Emley | 3-1 | 0-2 | 1-3 | 1-3 | 0-1 | 0-4 | 1-3 | 0-2 | 1-3 | — | 1-3 | 1-0 | 0-2 | 3-3 | 1-2 | 2-3 | 0-1 | 1-0 | 1-3 | 3-0 | 1-7 | 4-0 | 1-5 |
| Frickley Athletic | 1-1 | 0-1 | 2-1 | 0-1 | 2-0 | 3-0 | 1-2 | 1-2 | 0-0 | 1-1 | — | 4-0 | 0-2 | 2-2 | 2-1 | 1-0 | 0-5 | 1-0 | 0-1 | 2-0 | 2-3 | 1-1 | 1-1 |
| Gainsborough Trinity | 1-1 | 2-0 | 1-0 | 2-1 | 3-1 | 1-0 | 1-1 | 3-3 | 1-1 | 4-0 | 1-0 | — | 2-2 | 5-0 | 3-0 | 1-0 | 0-3 | 2-2 | 1-4 | 3-1 | 2-1 | 1-3 | 0-0 |
| Gateshead | 1-2 | 1-0 | 0-2 | 2-4 | 0-1 | 2-0 | 1-0 | 1-2 | 1-1 | 2-0 | 2-2 | 0-2 | — | 1-2 | 2-0 | 5-1 | 1-2 | 1-2 | 1-4 | 1-2 | 0-1 | 1-1 | 1-3 |
| Hucknall Town | 5-0 | 0-2 | 1-3 | 5-0 | 2-1 | 1-0 | 2-1 | 1-1 | 0-0 | 0-0 | 5-1 | 4-1 | 2-1 | — | 5-1 | 3-0 | 2-1 | 4-1 | 2-1 | 2-2 | 2-1 | 3-2 | 1-3 |
| Hyde United | 4-1 | 2-0 | 1-0 | 1-0 | 0-0 | 2-1 | 2-4 | 3-1 | 2-1 | 2-1 | 2-1 | 3-0 | 1-1 | 3-0 | — | 1-4 | 2-0 | 2-0 | 3-0 | 3-1 | 1-2 | 4-0 | 0-3 |
| Lancaster City | 1-2 | 3-1 | 1-4 | 1-2 | 1-3 | 0-1 | 2-3 | 3-2 | 1-0 | 1-1 | 1-1 | 3-1 | 0-1 | 1-3 | 1-1 | — | 2-0 | 0-2 | 1-3 | 5-0 | 1-5 | 0-3 | 2-3 |
| Leek Town | 2-1 | 1-0 | 1-2 | 3-0 | 0-0 | 0-4 | 4-1 | 1-1 | 1-1 | 1-3 | 2-0 | 1-1 | 2-0 | 3-1 | 2-0 | 1-3 | — | 2-0 | 0-1 | 0-1 | 1-2 | 3-1 | 1-0 |
| Marine | 3-2 | 3-1 | 3-1 | 0-1 | 1-1 | 4-1 | 2-3 | 2-3 | 0-2 | 2-1 | 0-1 | 2-0 | 2-1 | 3-1 | 3-1 | 3-1 | 2-2 | — | 2-2 | 2-1 | 1-2 | 3-3 | 1-1 |
| Runcorn | 2-1 | 3-1 | 3-1 | 1-2 | 0-2 | 2-1 | 3-0 | 0-0 | 2-1 | 2-1 | 2-0 | 2-0 | 2-0 | 1-0 | 1-0 | 3-1 | 3-1 | 4-1 | — | 2-0 | 0-1 | 4-1 | 2-2 |
| Spennymoor United | 1-0 | 5-0 | 5-0 | 0-1 | 4-1 | 3-2 | 3-3 | 2-0 | 4-0 | 4-0 | 2-0 | 3-1 | 0-0 | 1-0 | 2-0 | 4-0 | 2-0 | 1-0 | 3-2 | — | 2-1 | 2-0 | 2-0 |
| Stalybridge Celtic | 1-4 | 0-0 | 0-0 | 1-1 | 1-7 | 2-3 | 0-0 | 2-2 | 1-2 | 0-3 | 2-1 | 2-1 | 0-3 | 2-1 | 0-3 | 0-1 | 2-1 | 2-1 | 1-0 | 3-3 | — | 2-1 | 0-1 |
| Whitby Town | 0-2 | 3-1 | 5-0 | 2-3 | 2-3 | 0-2 | 2-1 | 3-1 | 4-0 | 1-3 | 1-1 | 1-3 | 1-1 | 3-2 | 2-1 | 0-3 | 4-1 | 2-1 | 1-1 | 2-0 | 0-1 | — | 3-2 |
| Worksop Town | 0-2 | 1-1 | 1-2 | 2-1 | 2-1 | 1-0 | 2-2 | 3-2 | 5-3 | 1-5 | 1-1 | 0-0 | 1-3 | 1-3 | 0-3 | 2-3 | 0-3 | 2-0 | 1-0 | 0-1 | 2-1 | 3-2 | — |

# RYMAN FOOTBALL LEAGUE 2000–2001

## Premier Division

| | P | | | Home | | | | | Away | | | |
|---|---|---|---|---|---|---|---|---|---|---|---|---|
| | P | W | D | L | F | A | W | D | L | F | A | Pts |
| Farnborough Town | 42 | 14 | 5 | 2 | 43 | 13 | 17 | 1 | 3 | 43 | 14 | 99 |
| Canvey Island | 42 | 16 | 4 | 1 | 46 | 17 | 11 | 4 | 6 | 33 | 24 | 89 |
| Basingstoke Town | 42 | 13 | 6 | 2 | 40 | 19 | 9 | 7 | 5 | 33 | 21 | 79 |
| Aldershot Town | 41 | 15 | 4 | 1 | 41 | 11 | 6 | 7 | 8 | 32 | 28 | 74 |
| Chesham United | 42 | 13 | 3 | 5 | 42 | 22 | 9 | 3 | 9 | 36 | 30 | 72 |
| Gravesend & Northfleet | 42 | 12 | 3 | 6 | 32 | 21 | 10 | 2 | 9 | 31 | 25 | 71 |
| Heybridge Swifts | 42 | 11 | 7 | 3 | 47 | 29 | 7 | 6 | 8 | 27 | 31 | 67 |
| Billericay Town | 41 | 10 | 8 | 3 | 34 | 22 | 8 | 5 | 7 | 28 | 32 | 67 |
| Hampton & Richmond | 42 | 14 | 3 | 4 | 43 | 22 | 4 | 9 | 8 | 30 | 38 | 66 |
| Hitchin Town | 42 | 10 | 2 | 9 | 40 | 32 | 8 | 3 | 10 | 32 | 37 | 59 |
| Purfleet | 42 | 8 | 8 | 5 | 31 | 21 | 6 | 5 | 10 | 24 | 34 | 55 |
| Hendon | 40 | 9 | 2 | 9 | 32 | 28 | 7 | 4 | 9 | 30 | 34 | 54 |
| Sutton United | 41 | 7 | 6 | 7 | 40 | 35 | 7 | 5 | 9 | 34 | 35 | 53 |
| St Albans City | 42 | 7 | 2 | 12 | 25 | 33 | 8 | 3 | 10 | 25 | 36 | 50 |
| Grays Athletic | 42 | 9 | 6 | 6 | 32 | 28 | 5 | 2 | 14 | 17 | 40 | 50 |
| Maidenhead United | 42 | 10 | 1 | 10 | 28 | 27 | 5 | 1 | 15 | 19 | 36 | 47 |
| Croydon | 42 | 9 | 6 | 6 | 34 | 24 | 3 | 4 | 14 | 21 | 53 | 46 |
| Enfield | 42 | 9 | 5 | 7 | 31 | 32 | 3 | 4 | 14 | 17 | 42 | 45 |
| Harrow Borough | 41 | 6 | 4 | 11 | 32 | 48 | 4 | 7 | 9 | 30 | 43 | 41 |
| Slough Town | 42 | 8 | 4 | 9 | 26 | 29 | 2 | 5 | 14 | 14 | 33 | 39 |
| Carshalton Athletic | 42 | 9 | 3 | 9 | 26 | 36 | 1 | 3 | 17 | 14 | 49 | 36 |
| Dulwich Hamlet | 42 | 4 | 4 | 13 | 18 | 36 | 0 | 6 | 15 | 15 | 48 | 22 |

NB. The following games were not played:
Aldershot Town v Billericay Town, Hendon v Harrow Borough, Sutton United v Hendon.

## Leading Goalscorers

| Premier Division | | Lge | RLC | FMC |
|---|---|---|---|---|
| 29 | Gary Abbott (Aldershot Town) | 29 | | |
| 26 | Kris Lee (Heybridge Swifts) | 22 | 4 | |
| 26 | Simon Parker (Heybridge Swifts) | 22 | 4 | |
| 24 | Craig Maskell (Hampton & Richmond B) | 16 | 8 | |
| 23 | Danny Bolt (Sutton United) | 20 | | 3 |
| 23 | Tim Sills (Basingstoke Town) | 19 | 3 | 1 |
| | *(includes while at Staines Town)* | 7 | | 1 |
| 21 | Lenny Piper (Farnborough Town) | 19 | 2 | |

Lge: Ryman League; RLC: Ryman League Cup; FMC: Full Members Cup.

# RYMAN FOOTBALL LEAGUE—PREMIER DIVISION RESULTS 2000–2001

| | Aldershot Town | Basingstoke Town | Billericay Town | Canvey Island | Carshalton Athletic | Chesham United | Croydon | Dulwich Hamlet | Enfield | Farnborough Town | Gravesend & Northfleet | Grays Athletic | Hampton & Richmond | Harrow Borough | Hendon | Heybridge Swifts | Hitchin Town | Maidenhead United | Purfleet | Slough Town | St Albans City | Sutton United |
|---|---|---|---|---|---|---|---|---|---|---|---|---|---|---|---|---|---|---|---|---|---|---|
| Aldershot Town | — | 1-0 | NP | 1-0 | 4-0 | 1-0 | 4-0 | 1-0 | 2-1 | 1-1 | 4-0 | 6-0 | 2-2 | 3-0 | 1-1 | 1-1 | 2-0 | 2-1 | 3-0 | 1-0 | 2-3 | 1-1 |
| Basingstoke Town | 2-1 | — | 2-2 | 0-0 | 5-0 | 1-2 | 1-1 | 0-1 | 0-1 | 0-2 | 0-2 | 1-0 | 3-1 | 1-1 | 2-2 | 3-2 | 0-2 | 1-0 | 1-2 | 3-2 | 2-1 | 1-0 |
| Billericay Town | NP | 2-2 | — | 0-0 | 0-2 | 1-1 | 3-0 | 2-0 | 1-1 | 0-1 | 3-1 | 1-0 | 3-1 | 1-1 | 5-1 | 5-1 | 2-0 | 2-0 | 1-0 | 0-0 | 1-1 | 0-5 |
| Canvey Island | 1-0 | 2-0 | 2-1 | — | 2-1 | 1-4 | 4-1 | 1-0 | 1-0 | 1-4 | 2-1 | 1-0 | 3-1 | 0-1 | 1-2 | 2-1 | 1-1 | 1-0 | 2-3 | 0-1 | 3-1 | 6-2 |
| Carshalton Athletic | 0-3 | 0-0 | 0-0 | 3-2 | — | 3-2 | 5-0 | 2-1 | 1-0 | 0-5 | 1-1 | 3-1 | 0-2 | 4-2 | 0-5 | 1-2 | 0-5 | 2-1 | 5-0 | 0-1 | 1-1 | 0-3 |
| Chesham United | 2-2 | 2-2 | 0-4 | 2-1 | 3-1 | — | 3-2 | 2-2 | 0-3 | 2-2 | 1-2 | 3-1 | 1-1 | 1-0 | 1-0 | 2-3 | 1-2 | 1-1 | 5-0 | 4-1 | 0-2 | 0-3 |
| Croydon | 2-4 | 2-2 | 1-0 | 4-1 | 2-1 | 1-0 | — | 2-2 | 1-4 | 2-0 | 0-1 | 1-2 | 1-2 | 2-1 | 5-1 | 2-0 | 2-5 | 2-3 | 0-0 | 4-1 | 0-2 | 0-1 |
| Dulwich Hamlet | 0-2 | 0-1 | 3-1 | 1-0 | 0-3 | 1-4 | 1-4 | — | 1-1 | 0-3 | 3-1 | 1-2 | 2-0 | 2-4 | 0-2 | 0-3 | 0-2 | 2-3 | 1-1 | 4-1 | 0-2 | 2-1 |
| Enfield | 2-4 | 1-4 | 1-1 | 1-0 | 2-1 | 3-0 | 3-1 | 1-1 | — | 1-1 | 2-0 | 3-1 | 1-1 | 3-0 | 2-5 | 0-2 | 2-1 | 4-1 | 2-3 | 1-1 | 4-0 | 2-1 |
| Farnborough Town | 0-2 | 0-2 | 3-0 | 1-4 | 1-0 | 2-2 | 2-0 | 0-3 | 1-1 | — | 1-0 | 3-0 | 0-2 | 3-2 | 3-0 | 1-0 | 1-1 | 0-1 | 0-1 | 0-2 | 6-0 | 1-2 |
| Gravesend & Northfleet | 1-0 | 0-2 | 3-1 | 2-1 | 1-1 | 1-2 | 0-1 | 3-1 | 2-0 | 1-0 | — | 0-1 | 4-5 | 3-3 | NP | 1-4 | 1-4 | 0-2 | 1-3 | 2-0 | 2-2 | 2-2 |
| Grays Athletic | 1-0 | 1-0 | 1-0 | 1-0 | 3-1 | 3-1 | 1-2 | 1-2 | 3-0 | 0-1 | 0-1 | — | 0-0 | 0-0 | 0-1 | 2-0 | 1-2 | 2-0 | 2-1 | 2-0 | 0-0 | 1-0 |
| Hampton & Richmond | 2-2 | 3-1 | 3-1 | 1-0 | 0-3 | 1-1 | 1-1 | 1-2 | 1-1 | 3-4 | 3-4 | 0-1 | — | 4-5 | 3-2 | 0-2 | 1-1 | 2-2 | 0-0 | 5-0 | 1-2 | 2-2 |
| Harrow Borough | 3-0 | 1-1 | 2-1 | 1-1 | 1-1 | 2-0 | 0-1 | 0-1 | 2-1 | 3-1 | 3-1 | 3-3 | 1-3 | — | NP | 3-6 | 4-2 | 4-2 | 0-1 | 1-0 | 0-0 | 3-3 |
| Hendon | 2-1 | 1-2 | 5-0 | 2-1 | 1-0 | 1-0 | 0-1 | 2-0 | 2-0 | 2-1 | 0-6 | 0-1 | 4-5 | 2-4 | — | 1-4 | 0-0 | 2-1 | 0-1 | 3-0 | 0-1 | 2-1 |
| Heybridge Swifts | 2-5 | 3-2 | 2-1 | 2-1 | 1-2 | 2-3 | 0-3 | 0-2 | 0-1 | 1-2 | 0-0 | 1-4 | 3-2 | 1-1 | 1-4 | — | 1-3 | 0-2 | 1-1 | 2-0 | 2-2 | 2-1 |
| Hitchin Town | 2-5 | 0-2 | 3-0 | 1-2 | 0-5 | 1-2 | 2-0 | 2-1 | 2-5 | 1-1 | 3-2 | 2-4 | 2-4 | 2-4 | 0-0 | 1-3 | — | 0-1 | 0-1 | 3-0 | 1-3 | 2-1 |
| Maidenhead United | 3-0 | 3-2 | 2-1 | 0-1 | 3-0 | 1-2 | 1-2 | 3-1 | 1-2 | 0-2 | 3-6 | 2-0 | 3-2 | 4-6 | 3-0 | 1-3 | 0-1 | — | 0-2 | 3-0 | 0-0 | 2-1 |
| Purfleet | 2-2 | 0-1 | 1-0 | 0-1 | 1-2 | 2-1 | 1-2 | 3-0 | 0-2 | 2-4 | 1-3 | 3-1 | 2-2 | 4-2 | 0-1 | 1-1 | 0-1 | 1-2 | — | 0-2 | 1-0 | 3-0 |
| Slough Town | 0-1 | 3-2 | 0-1 | 1-0 | 2-0 | 2-0 | 3-0 | 1-2 | 3-0 | 2-0 | 2-0 | 1-2 | 5-0 | 1-0 | 3-0 | 1-1 | 2-0 | 1-0 | 3-2 | — | 1-3 | 2-1 |
| St Albans City | 0-3 | 0-3 | 2-3 | 0-1 | 0-1 | 2-3 | 1-2 | 2-1 | 0-1 | 0-1 | 5-0 | 2-3 | 2-2 | 1-0 | 1-3 | 3-0 | 0-3 | 3-1 | 1-0 | 1-0 | — | 4-2 |
| Sutton United | 1-1 | 2-0 | 1-4 | 0-1 | 3-1 | 0-3 | 2-1 | 7-1 | 2-3 | 1-4 | 2-2 | 2-3 | 2-2 | 3-3 | NP | 1-2 | 2-1 | 2-0 | 2-2 | 1-1 | 4-2 | — |

NP indicates match not played

# AVON LEAGUE

**Premier Division**

|  | P | W | D | L | F | A | GD | Pts |
|---|---|---|---|---|---|---|---|---|
| Tranmere R | 24 | 16 | 4 | 4 | 46 | 25 | 21 | 52 |
| Huddersfield T | 24 | 16 | 3 | 5 | 57 | 28 | 29 | 51 |
| Birmingham C | 24 | 10 | 3 | 11 | 30 | 29 | 7 | 39 |
| Burnley | 24 | 12 | 3 | 9 | 44 | 43 | 1 | 39 |
| WBA | 24 | 11 | 4 | 9 | 34 | 25 | 9 | 37 |
| Barnsley | 24 | 11 | 4 | 9 | 36 | 54 | −1 | 37 |
| Oldham Ath | 24 | 10 | 4 | 10 | 38 | 44 | −6 | 34 |
| Preston NE | 24 | 9 | 3 | 12 | 44 | 41 | 3 | 30 |
| Port Vale | 24 | 9 | 3 | 12 | 38 | 42 | −4 | 27 |
| Rotherham U | 24 | 6 | 8 | 10 | 25 | 34 | −9 | 26 |
| Bolton W | 24 | 7 | 4 | 13 | 25 | 44 | −19 | 25 |
| Wolverhampton W | 24 | 6 | 6 | 12 | 31 | 37 | −6 | 24 |
| Stockport Co | 24 | 4 | 5 | 15 | 26 | 51 | −25 | 17 |

**Division One**

|  | P | W | D | L | F | A | GD | Pts |
|---|---|---|---|---|---|---|---|---|
| Sheffield U | 22 | 13 | 2 | 7 | 34 | 20 | 14 | 41 |
| Wrexham | 22 | 12 | 2 | 8 | 41 | 32 | 9 | 38 |
| Walsall | 22 | 10 | 6 | 6 | 30 | 26 | 4 | 36 |
| Lincoln C | 22 | 10 | 3 | 9 | 42 | 43 | −1 | 33 |
| Stoke C | 22 | 9 | 5 | 8 | 35 | 32 | 3 | 32 |
| Scunthorpe U | 22 | 8 | 6 | 8 | 37 | 34 | 3 | 30 |
| Grimsby T | 22 | 8 | 6 | 8 | 31 | 30 | 1 | 30 |
| Blackpool | 22 | 8 | 5 | 9 | 32 | 41 | −9 | 29 |
| York C | 22 | 8 | 4 | 10 | 31 | 32 | −1 | 28 |
| Shrewsbury T | 22 | 8 | 3 | 11 | 35 | 40 | −5 | 27 |
| Darlington | 22 | 7 | 4 | 11 | 29 | 38 | −9 | 25 |
| Wigan Ath | 22 | 7 | 2 | 13 | 29 | 38 | −9 | 23 |

**Division Two**

|  | P | W | D | L | F | A | Pts |
|---|---|---|---|---|---|---|---|
| Bury | 20 | 14 | 3 | 3 | 51 | 21 | 45 |
| Doncaster R | 20 | 12 | 4 | 4 | 40 | 19 | 40 |
| Mansfield T | 20 | 11 | 3 | 6 | 40 | 27 | 36 |
| Notts Co | 20 | 9 | 6 | 5 | 42 | 32 | 33 |
| Hull C | 20 | 8 | 4 | 8 | 31 | 35 | 28 |
| Scarborough | 20 | 7 | 4 | 9 | 27 | 31 | 25 |
| Halifax T | 20 | 6 | 6 | 8 | 23 | 27 | 24 |
| Hartlepool U | 20 | 6 | 5 | 9 | 23 | 33 | 23 |
| Chesterfield | 20 | 6 | 4 | 10 | 22 | 33 | 22 |
| Macclesfield T | 20 | 5 | 4 | 11 | 18 | 31 | 19 |
| Rochdale | 20 | 4 | 1 | 15 | 17 | 45 | 13 |

# AVON INSURANCE COMBINATION

**Division One**

|  | P | W | D | L | F | A | GD | Pts |
|---|---|---|---|---|---|---|---|---|
| Fulham | 24 | 18 | 3 | 3 | 66 | 17 | 49 | 57 |
| Norwich C | 24 | 16 | 6 | 2 | 73 | 27 | 46 | 54 |
| Reading | 24 | 17 | 2 | 5 | 43 | 22 | 21 | 53 |
| QPR | 24 | 15 | 2 | 7 | 36 | 22 | 14 | 47 |
| Cambridge U | 24 | 13 | 4 | 7 | 37 | 30 | 7 | 43 |
| Millwall | 24 | 12 | 5 | 7 | 33 | 18 | 15 | 41 |
| Crystal Palace | 24 | 11 | 6 | 7 | 42 | 35 | 7 | 39 |
| Luton T | 24 | 9 | 9 | 6 | 27 | 21 | 6 | 36 |
| Brighton & HA | 24 | 10 | 6 | 8 | 45 | 40 | 5 | 36 |
| Gillingham | 24 | 10 | 6 | 8 | 32 | 32 | 0 | 36 |
| Portsmouth | 24 | 9 | 7 | 8 | 31 | 29 | 2 | 34 |
| Brentford | 24 | 8 | 10 | 6 | 28 | 33 | −5 | 34 |
| Oxford U | 24 | 9 | 5 | 10 | 37 | 40 | −3 | 32 |
| Swindon T | 24 | 8 | 7 | 9 | 33 | 31 | 2 | 31 |
| Peterborough U | 24 | 8 | 5 | 11 | 32 | 32 | 0 | 29 |
| Bristol R | 24 | 7 | 7 | 10 | 24 | 34 | −10 | 28 |
| Bristol C | 24 | 6 | 9 | 9 | 26 | 30 | −4 | 27 |
| Southend U | 24 | 7 | 6 | 11 | 36 | 42 | −6 | 27 |
| Barnet | 24 | 7 | 5 | 12 | 29 | 40 | −11 | 26 |
| Colchester U | 24 | 6 | 6 | 12 | 25 | 38 | −13 | 24 |
| Cheltenham T | 24 | 5 | 9 | 10 | 28 | 44 | −16 | 24 |
| AFC Bournemouth | 24 | 5 | 6 | 13 | 27 | 51 | −24 | 21 |
| Northampton T | 24 | 5 | 5 | 14 | 20 | 40 | −20 | 20 |
| Wycombe W | 24 | 4 | 5 | 15 | 21 | 55 | −34 | 17 |
| Leyton O | 24 | 2 | 5 | 17 | 22 | 50 | −28 | 11 |

This table assumes that the following 18 games did not take place, and are counted as 0-0 draws: Barnet v Colchester U, Barnet v Peterborough U, Brighton & HA v Barnet, Bristol R v Crystal Palace, Bristol R v Northampton T, Cheltenham T v Northampton T, Gillingham v Brighton & HA, Gillingham v Bristol R, Leyton O v Bristol C, Luton T v Brighton & HA, Luton T v Bristol R, Luton T v Cheltenham T, Northampton T v Luton T, Northampton T v Gillingham, Peterborough U v Luton T, Portsmouth v Crystal P (the two teams did however play a 2-2 draw in the League Cup before certain fixtures started counting for both competitions), Swindon T v Bristol C, Swindon T v Gillingham.

# FA ACADEMY UNDER-19 LEAGUE

| Group A | P | W | D | L | F | A | GD | Pts |
|---|---|---|---|---|---|---|---|---|
| Nottingham F | 28 | 16 | 9 | 3 | 67 | 34 | 33 | 57 |
| Derby Co | 28 | 14 | 8 | 6 | 38 | 24 | 14 | 50 |
| Middlesbrough | 28 | 13 | 7 | 8 | 46 | 33 | 13 | 46 |
| Sheffield W | 28 | 13 | 3 | 12 | 47 | 49 | -2 | 42 |
| Huddersfield T | 28 | 12 | 4 | 12 | 43 | 47 | -4 | 40 |
| Leicester C | 28 | 11 | 5 | 12 | 35 | 34 | 1 | 38 |
| Leeds U | 28 | 11 | 5 | 12 | 39 | 47 | -8 | 38 |
| Sunderland | 28 | 9 | 8 | 11 | 28 | 32 | -4 | 35 |
| Barnsley | 28 | 10 | 4 | 14 | 34 | 44 | -10 | 34 |
| Newcastle U | 28 | 5 | 6 | 17 | 32 | 54 | -22 | 21 |

| Group B | P | W | D | L | F | A | GD | Pts |
|---|---|---|---|---|---|---|---|---|
| Everton | 28 | 19 | 4 | 5 | 50 | 16 | 34 | 61 |
| Manchester C | 28 | 16 | 4 | 8 | 50 | 27 | 23 | 52 |
| Blackburn R | 28 | 13 | 9 | 6 | 46 | 34 | 12 | 48 |
| Crewe Alex | 28 | 15 | 3 | 10 | 56 | 46 | 10 | 48 |
| Manchester U | 28 | 13 | 5 | 10 | 43 | 32 | 11 | 44 |
| Liverpool | 28 | 12 | 5 | 11 | 47 | 35 | 12 | 41 |
| Wolves | 28 | 11 | 4 | 13 | 38 | 39 | -1 | 37 |
| Stoke C | 28 | 6 | 7 | 15 | 37 | 59 | -22 | 25 |
| Bolton W | 28 | 5 | 3 | 20 | 31 | 61 | -30 | 18 |
| Wrexham | 28 | 2 | 4 | 22 | 24 | 77 | -53 | 10 |

| Group C | P | W | D | L | F | A | GD | Pts |
|---|---|---|---|---|---|---|---|---|
| Arsenal | 28 | 21 | 4 | 3 | 75 | 24 | 51 | 67 |
| Watford | 28 | 19 | 3 | 6 | 53 | 22 | 31 | 60 |
| Aston Villa | 28 | 16 | 5 | 7 | 54 | 37 | 17 | 53 |
| Millwall | 28 | 14 | 7 | 7 | 51 | 37 | 14 | 49 |
| Birmingham C | 28 | 14 | 5 | 9 | 42 | 37 | 5 | 47 |
| Coventry C | 27 | 12 | 7 | 8 | 64 | 40 | 24 | 43 |
| Ipswich T | 28 | 9 | 6 | 13 | 40 | 52 | -12 | 33 |
| Norwich C | 28 | 6 | 7 | 15 | 30 | 54 | -24 | 25 |
| Charlton Ath | 28 | 5 | 7 | 16 | 36 | 69 | -33 | 22 |
| Peterborough U | 28 | 4 | 2 | 22 | 18 | 75 | -57 | 14 |

| Group D | P | W | D | L | F | A | GD | Pts |
|---|---|---|---|---|---|---|---|---|
| QPR | 28 | 16 | 7 | 5 | 47 | 27 | 20 | 55 |
| Chelsea | 28 | 12 | 8 | 8 | 57 | 36 | 21 | 44 |
| Tottenham H | 27 | 13 | 5 | 9 | 37 | 37 | 0 | 44 |
| Fulham | 27 | 10 | 8 | 9 | 39 | 42 | -3 | 38 |
| Wimbledon | 27 | 9 | 9 | 9 | 38 | 26 | 12 | 36 |
| West Ham U | 27 | 11 | 3 | 13 | 47 | 51 | -4 | 36 |
| Crystal Palace | 28 | 9 | 6 | 13 | 39 | 48 | -9 | 33 |
| Reading | 26 | 8 | 4 | 14 | 45 | 57 | -12 | 28 |
| Southampton | 28 | 7 | 5 | 16 | 52 | 65 | -13 | 26 |
| Bristol C | 27 | 6 | 3 | 18 | 36 | 71 | -35 | 21 |

## UNDER-19 PLAY-OFFS

**Semi-finals**
Nottingham F 2, Everton 0
QPR 1, Arsenal 1 (aet)
(QPR won 4-3 on penalties)

**Final (two legs)**
QPR 1, Nottingham F 0
Nottingham F 4 QPR 2 (aet)

# FA ACADEMY UNDER-17 LEAGUE

| Group A | P | W | D | L | F | A | GD | Pts |
|---|---|---|---|---|---|---|---|---|
| Derby Co | 24 | 20 | 2 | 2 | 68 | 28 | 40 | 62 |
| Middlesbrough | 24 | 13 | 7 | 4 | 50 | 23 | 27 | 46 |
| Blackburn R | 24 | 14 | 3 | 7 | 55 | 30 | 25 | 45 |
| Newcastle U | 24 | 14 | 1 | 9 | 64 | 43 | 21 | 43 |
| Leeds U | 24 | 8 | 7 | 9 | 36 | 44 | −8 | 31 |
| Nottingham F | 24 | 8 | 5 | 11 | 42 | 60 | −18 | 29 |
| Sunderland | 24 | 5 | 5 | 14 | 17 | 31 | −14 | 20 |
| Sheffield W | 24 | 3 | 3 | 18 | 29 | 75 | −46 | 12 |

| Group C | P | W | D | L | F | A | GD | Pts |
|---|---|---|---|---|---|---|---|---|
| Ipswich T | 24 | 14 | 4 | 6 | 51 | 29 | 22 | 46 |
| Tottenham H | 24 | 12 | 6 | 6 | 57 | 37 | 20 | 42 |
| Coventry C | 24 | 13 | 3 | 8 | 52 | 40 | 12 | 42 |
| Watford | 24 | 8 | 6 | 10 | 40 | 39 | 1 | 30 |
| Millwall | 24 | 7 | 6 | 11 | 42 | 51 | −9 | 27 |
| Charlton Ath | 24 | 6 | 5 | 13 | 31 | 60 | −29 | 23 |
| Birmingham C | 24 | 6 | 3 | 15 | 28 | 61 | −33 | 21 |
| QPR | 24 | 3 | 4 | 17 | 28 | 67 | −39 | 13 |

| Group B | P | W | D | L | F | A | GD | Pts |
|---|---|---|---|---|---|---|---|---|
| Manchester U | 24 | 13 | 6 | 5 | 50 | 36 | 14 | 45 |
| Aston Villa | 24 | 12 | 7 | 5 | 57 | 33 | 24 | 43 |
| Manchester C | 24 | 13 | 3 | 8 | 48 | 34 | 14 | 42 |
| Wolves | 24 | 10 | 4 | 10 | 36 | 44 | −8 | 34 |
| Liverpool | 24 | 7 | 10 | 7 | 45 | 41 | 4 | 31 |
| Everton | 24 | 7 | 6 | 11 | 42 | 42 | 0 | 27 |
| Bolton W | 24 | 7 | 2 | 15 | 30 | 44 | −14 | 23 |
| Crewe Alex | 24 | 6 | 4 | 14 | 23 | 49 | −26 | 22 |

| Group D | P | W | D | L | F | A | GD | Pts |
|---|---|---|---|---|---|---|---|---|
| West Ham U | 23 | 16 | 3 | 4 | 63 | 29 | 34 | 51 |
| Arsenal | 24 | 15 | 2 | 7 | 54 | 22 | 32 | 47 |
| Wimbledon | 22 | 12 | 1 | 9 | 28 | 19 | 9 | 37 |
| Southampton | 23 | 10 | 4 | 9 | 52 | 43 | 9 | 34 |
| Fulham | 23 | 10 | 4 | 9 | 49 | 48 | 1 | 34 |
| Crystal Palace | 23 | 9 | 6 | 8 | 40 | 46 | −6 | 33 |
| Reading | 22 | 6 | 1 | 15 | 20 | 51 | −31 | 19 |
| Bristol C | 24 | 4 | 5 | 15 | 33 | 61 | −28 | 17 |

## UNDER-17 PLAY-OFFS

| Group 1 | P | W | D | L | F | A | Pts |
|---|---|---|---|---|---|---|---|
| Derby Co | 3 | 2 | 1 | 0 | 9 | 3 | 7 |
| Manchester C | 3 | 1 | 2 | 0 | 7 | 5 | 5 |
| Bolton W | 3 | 1 | 0 | 2 | 4 | 6 | 3 |
| Leeds U | 3 | 0 | 1 | 2 | 3 | 9 | 1 |

| Group 5 | P | W | D | L | F | A | Pts |
|---|---|---|---|---|---|---|---|
| Ipswich T | 3 | 2 | 1 | 0 | 15 | 4 | 6 |
| Reading | 3 | 1 | 1 | 1 | 4 | 4 | 4 |
| Millwall | 3 | 1 | 1 | 1 | 2 | 8 | 4 |
| Wimbledon | 3 | 1 | 0 | 2 | 4 | 9 | 3 |

| Group 2 | P | W | D | L | F | A | Pts |
|---|---|---|---|---|---|---|---|
| Blackburn R | 3 | 2 | 1 | 0 | 8 | 4 | 7 |
| Manchester U | 3 | 1 | 2 | 0 | 3 | 2 | 5 |
| Liverpool | 3 | 1 | 0 | 2 | 5 | 6 | 3 |
| Sunderland | 3 | 0 | 1 | 2 | 1 | 5 | 1 |

| Group 6 | P | W | D | L | F | A | Pts |
|---|---|---|---|---|---|---|---|
| West Ham U | 3 | 2 | 0 | 1 | 12 | 4 | 6 |
| Coventry C | 3 | 1 | 2 | 0 | 6 | 5 | 5 |
| Birmingham C | 3 | 1 | 1 | 1 | 6 | 4 | 4 |
| Fulham | 3 | 0 | 1 | 2 | 2 | 13 | 1 |

| Group 3 | P | W | D | L | F | A | Pts |
|---|---|---|---|---|---|---|---|
| Middlesbrough | 3 | 3 | 0 | 0 | 8 | 1 | 9 |
| Nottingham F | 3 | 2 | 0 | 1 | 6 | 3 | 6 |
| Wolverhampton W | 3 | 1 | 0 | 2 | 2 | 6 | 3 |
| Crewe Alex | 3 | 0 | 0 | 3 | 0 | 6 | 0 |

| Group 7 | P | W | D | L | F | A | Pts |
|---|---|---|---|---|---|---|---|
| Tottenham H | 3 | 2 | 1 | 0 | 7 | 1 | 7 |
| Charlton Ath | 3 | 1 | 1 | 1 | 2 | 3 | 4 |
| Bristol C | 3 | 1 | 1 | 1 | 3 | 5 | 4 |
| Southampton | 3 | 0 | 1 | 2 | 1 | 4 | 1 |

| Group 4 | P | W | D | L | F | A | Pts |
|---|---|---|---|---|---|---|---|
| Newcastle U | 3 | 3 | 0 | 0 | 13 | 6 | 9 |
| Everton | 3 | 2 | 0 | 1 | 4 | 4 | 6 |
| Aston Villa | 3 | 0 | 1 | 2 | 6 | 8 | 1 |
| Sheffield W | 3 | 0 | 1 | 3 | 3 | 10 | 1 |

| Group 8 | P | W | D | L | F | A | Pts |
|---|---|---|---|---|---|---|---|
| Watford | 3 | 1 | 2 | 0 | 5 | 4 | 5 |
| QPR | 3 | 1 | 2 | 0 | 1 | 0 | 5 |
| Arsenal | 3 | 1 | 1 | 1 | 7 | 5 | 4 |
| Crystal Palace | 3 | 0 | 1 | 2 | 2 | 6 | 1 |

**Quarter-finals**
Blackburn R 1, Middlesbrough 2
Derby Co 1, Newcastle U 6
Ipswich T 3, Watford 1
West Ham U 2, Tottenham H 1

**Final (two legs)**
Ipswich T 5, Newcastle U 0
Newcastle U 2, Ipswich T 0

**Semi-finals**
Newcastle U 3, Middlesbrough 1
West Ham U 0 Ipswich T 2

# FA PREMIER RESERVE LEAGUES

## NORTH

### FINAL TABLE

| | P | W | D | L | F | A | W | D | L | F | A | GD | Pts |
|---|---|---|---|---|---|---|---|---|---|---|---|---|---|
| Everton | 22 | 7 | 1 | 3 | 14 | 9 | 7 | 1 | 3 | 21 | 13 | 13 | 44 |
| Sunderland | 22 | 6 | 4 | 1 | 20 | 9 | 6 | 2 | 3 | 18 | 12 | 17 | 42 |
| Leeds U | 22 | 6 | 2 | 3 | 19 | 7 | 5 | 2 | 4 | 21 | 17 | 16 | 37 |
| Blackburn R | 22 | 5 | 5 | 1 | 17 | 10 | 4 | 5 | 2 | 14 | 13 | 8 | 37 |
| Manchester U | 22 | 7 | 2 | 2 | 22 | 13 | 4 | 0 | 7 | 17 | 23 | 3 | 35 |
| Manchester C | 22 | 4 | 3 | 4 | 21 | 20 | 4 | 3 | 4 | 21 | 13 | 9 | 33 |
| Middlesbrough | 22 | 6 | 1 | 4 | 26 | 23 | 3 | 5 | 3 | 13 | 15 | 1 | 33 |
| Liverpool | 22 | 5 | 3 | 3 | 23 | 11 | 4 | 5 | 2 | 20 | 21 | 11 | 32 |
| Aston Villa | 22 | 4 | 2 | 5 | 16 | 18 | 4 | 4 | 3 | 17 | 16 | –1 | 30 |
| Newcastle U | 22 | 4 | 2 | 5 | 15 | 15 | 4 | 2 | 5 | 19 | 20 | –1 | 28 |
| Bradford C | 22 | 2 | 2 | 7 | 18 | 25 | 1 | 0 | 10 | 12 | 38 | –33 | 11 |
| Sheffield W | 22 | 1 | 1 | 9 | 16 | 42 | 0 | 2 | 9 | 9 | 26 | –43 | 6 |

**HIGHEST ATTENDANCE**  Sunderland v Manchester U  8060

**LEADING APPEARANCES**

| | |
|---|---|
| Hackworth (Leeds U) | 22 |
| Melaugh (Aston Villa) | 22 |
| O'Brien (Blackburn R) | 22 |
| Kerr (Bradford C) | 21 |
| Clegg M (Manchester U) | 21 |
| Djordjic (Manchester U) | 21 |
| Southern K (Everton) | 21 |
| McLeod (Everton) | 20 |
| Standing (Aston Villa) | 20 |
| Evans (Leeds U) | 20 |

**LEADING GOALSCORERS**

| | |
|---|---|
| Taylor (Manchester C) | 9 |
| Huckerby (Manchester C) | 9 |
| *Including 8 for Leeds U* | |
| Hackworth (Leeds U) | 9 |
| Jevons (Everton) | 7 |
| Moore (Aston Villa) | 7 |
| Fowler (Liverpool) | 6 |
| Grant (Bradford C) | 6 |
| Lua-Lua (Newcastle U) | 6 |
| Marinelli (Middlesbrough) | 6 |
| Kyle (Sunderland) | 6 |
| Chadwick (Everton) | 6 |
| Wilson (Manchester U) | 6 |
| Richards (Manchester U) | 6 |

## SOUTH

### FINAL TABLE

| | P | W | D | L | F | A | W | D | L | F | A | GD | Pts |
|---|---|---|---|---|---|---|---|---|---|---|---|---|---|
| Derby Co | 24 | 11 | 0 | 1 | 31 | 6 | 4 | 4 | 4 | 19 | 17 | 27 | 49 |
| Coventry C | 24 | 8 | 2 | 2 | 22 | 11 | 5 | 1 | 6 | 23 | 20 | 14 | 42 |
| Watford | 24 | 8 | 1 | 3 | 28 | 15 | 4 | 3 | 5 | 20 | 22 | 11 | 40 |
| Tottenham H | 24 | 6 | 4 | 2 | 19 | 6 | 5 | 1 | 6 | 13 | 30 | –4 | 38 |
| Chelsea | 24 | 6 | 4 | 2 | 20 | 19 | 5 | 2 | 5 | 13 | 21 | –7 | 37 |
| Ipswich T | 24 | 6 | 1 | 5 | 21 | 20 | 4 | 5 | 3 | 18 | 21 | –2 | 36 |
| Arsenal | 24 | 5 | 2 | 5 | 25 | 24 | 5 | 1 | 6 | 24 | 16 | 9 | 33 |
| Charlton Ath | 24 | 3 | 3 | 6 | 18 | 30 | 5 | 3 | 4 | 17 | 14 | –9 | 30 |
| Southampton | 24 | 4 | 3 | 5 | 27 | 20 | 4 | 1 | 7 | 13 | 20 | –1 | 28 |
| Leicester C | 24 | 2 | 4 | 6 | 17 | 18 | 5 | 3 | 4 | 20 | 26 | –7 | 28 |
| Nottingham F | 24 | 3 | 5 | 4 | 24 | 26 | 4 | 2 | 6 | 19 | 25 | –8 | 28 |
| Wimbledon | 24 | 5 | 3 | 4 | 17 | 14 | 2 | 3 | 7 | 17 | 30 | –10 | 27 |
| West Ham U | 24 | 2 | 2 | 8 | 15 | 22 | 3 | 3 | 6 | 15 | 21 | –13 | 20 |

**HIGHEST ATTENDANCE**  Leicester C v Chelsea  4731

**LEADING APPEARANCES**

| | |
|---|---|
| Bolder (Derby Co) | 24 |
| Nicholls (Ipswich T) | 24 |
| Miller (Ipswich T) | 23 |
| Gibbens (Southampton) | 23 |
| Abidallah (Ipswich T) | 23 |
| Osei-Kuffour (Arsenal) | 23 |
| Etherington (Tottenham H) | 22 |
| Hillier (Tottenham H) | 22 |
| Hunt (Derby Co) | 22 |
| Forde (Watford) | 22 |

**LEADING GOALSCORERS**

| | |
|---|---|
| Harewood (Nottingham F) | 14 |
| Osei-Kuffour (Arsenal) | 11 |
| Korsten (Tottenham H) | 11 |
| Smart (Watford) | 10 |
| Logan (Ipswich T) | 10 |
| Morris (Derby Co) | 9 |
| Benjamin (Leicester C) | 9 |
| Sturridge (Derby Co) | 8 |
| Forde (Watford) | 7 |
| Dudfield (Leicester C) | 7 |
| Caceres (Southampton) | 7 |

# FA UMBRO TROPHY 2000–2001

## FINAL (at Villa Park)

### 13 MAY

**Canvey Island (1) 1** *(Chenery 16)*
**Forest Green Rovers (0) 0**         10,007

*Canvey Island:* Harrison; Ward, Bodley, Chenery, Kennedy, Parmenter, Stimson (Tanner 84), Tilson, Duffy, Gregory, Vaughan (Jones 75).
*Forest Green Rovers:* Perrin; Lockwood, Cousins, Clark, Daley, Drysdale (Bennett F 46), Foster M, Slater, Burns, Foster A (Hunt 74), Meechan.
*Referee:* A. Wiley (Burntwood).


# FA CARLSBERG VASE 2000–2001

## FINAL (at Villa Park)

### 6 MAY

**Berkhamsted Town (0) 1** *(Lowe 73 (pen))*
**Taunton Town (2) 2** *(Fields 31, Laight 45)*         8439

*Berkhamsted Town:* O'Connor; Mullins, Nightingale, Aldridge, Coleman, Lowe, Yates, Brockett, Richardson, Smith B, Adebowale.
*Taunton Town:* Draper; Down, Chapman, Cann (Tallon), West, Hawkings, Fields (Groves), Kelly, Laight, Lynch (Hapgood), Bastow.
*Referee:* E. Wolstenholme (Lancs).


# THE AXA FA YOUTH CUP 2000–2001
(in association with *The Times*)

## FINAL First Leg

### 18 MAY

**Arsenal (2) 5** *(Aliadiere 13, 66, Thomas 14, Sidwell 56, Volz 72)*
**Blackburn Rovers (0) 0**

*Arsenal:* Holloway; Bailey, Svard, Garry, Nicolau, Volz, Sidwell, Ricketts (Santry 84), Thomas, Pennant (Itonga 80), Aliadiere (Brown 88).
*Blackburn Rovers:* Stone, Hockenhull, Woodhead, Cole, Blakeman, Watt, Danns, Morgan, Hevicon (Black 51) (Donnelly 80), Walters.
*Referee:* J. Winter (Stockton).

## FINAL Second Leg

### 22 MAY

**Blackburn Rovers (2) 3** *(Walters 13, Morgan 25, Danns 59)*
**Arsenal (1) 1** *(Chorley 45)*

*Blackburn Rovers:* Robinson; Stone, Hockenhull, Woodhead, Cole, Blakeman (Watt 85), Nelson, Donnelly, Morgan, Danns (Bell 89), Walters.
*Arsenal:* Holloway; Bailey, Svard, Chorley, Garry, Volz (Santry 87), Sidwell, Ricketts, Thomas, Aliadiere, Itonga (Brown 69).
*Referee:* J. Winter (Stockton).

# WOMEN'S NATIONAL DIVISION 2000–2001

|  | P | W | D | L | F | A | GD | Pts |
|---|---|---|---|---|---|---|---|---|
| Arsenal LFC | 18 | 17 | 1 | 0 | 88 | 9 | +79 | 52 |
| Doncaster Belles LFC | 18 | 15 | 0 | 3 | 58 | 13 | +45 | 45 |
| Charlton Athletic WFC | 18 | 10 | 5 | 3 | 43 | 11 | +32 | 35 |
| Everton LFC | 18 | 11 | 2 | 5 | 42 | 24 | +18 | 35 |
| Tranmere Rovers LFC | 18 | 9 | 1 | 8 | 42 | 39 | +3 | 28 |
| Barry Town LFC | 18 | 7 | 2 | 9 | 22 | 39 | −17 | 23 |
| Sunderland AFC Women | 18 | 5 | 1 | 12 | 29 | 50 | −21 | 16 |
| Southampton Saints LFC | 18 | 3 | 6 | 9 | 27 | 52 | −25 | 15 |
| Millwall Lionesses LFC | 18 | 3 | 2 | 13 | 17 | 55 | −38 | 11 |
| Liverpool LFC | 18 | 0 | 0 | 18 | 13 | 89 | −76 | 0 |

# FA WOMEN'S CUP 2000–2001

### FINAL (at Selhurst Park)

### 7 MAY

**Arsenal (0) 1** *(Banks 52)*
**Fulham (0) 0**                                                      13,824

*Arsenal:* Byrne; Pealling, Wheatley, Harwood, White, Stoney, Ludlow, Williams, Spacey (Maggs 82), Banks, Grant.
*Fulham:* Bowry; Gibbons, Jerray-Silver, Petersen, Phillip, Duncan (Mork 77), Chapman, McArthur (Rahman 81), Haugenes, Pettersen, Yankey.
*Referee:* T. Parkes (Birmingham).

# FA UMBRO SUNDAY CUP 2000–2001

**FINAL**
Hartlepool Lion Hillcarter v FC Houghton Centre                      3-2

# COUNTY YOUTH CUP

**FINAL**
Birmingham v Northamptonshire                                        0-3

# NATIONAL LIST OF REFEREES FOR SEASON 2001–2002

Alcock, P.E. (Paul) – (Kent)
Armstrong, P. (Paul) – (Berkshire)
Baines, S.J. (Steve) – (Chesterfield)
Barber, G.P. (Graham) – (Hertfordshire)
Barry, N.S. (Neale) – (N. Lincolnshire)
Bates, A. (Tony) – (Stoke-on-Trent)
Beeby, R.J. (Richard) – (Northampton)
Bennett, S.G. (Steve) – (Kent)
Brandwood, M.J. (John) – (Staffordshire)
Butler, A.N. (Alan) – (Notts)
Cable, L.E. (Lee) – (Woking)
Cain, G. (George) – (Merseyside)
Clattenburg, M. (Mark) – (Chester-le-Street)
Cooper, M.A. (Mark) – (Walsall)
Cowburn, M.G. (Mark) – (Blackpool)
Crick, D.R. (David) – (Surrey)
Curson, B. (Brian) – (Leicestershire)
Danson, P.S. (Paul) (Leicester)
Dean, M.L. (Mike) – (Wirral)
Dowd, P. (Phil) – (Stoke-on-Trent)
Dunn, S.W. (Steve) – (Bristol)
Durkin, P.A. (Paul) – (Dorset)
D'Urso, A.P. (Andy) – (Essex)
Elleray, D.R. (David) – (Harrow-on-the-Hill)
Fletcher, M. (Mick) – (Worcestershire)
Foy, C.J. (Chris) – (Merseyside)
Frankland, G.B. (Graham) – (Middlesbrough)
Furnandiz, R.D. (Roger) – (Doncaster)
Gallagher, D.J. (Dermot) – (Oxfordshire)
Hall, A.R. (Andy) – (Birmingham)
Halsey, M.R. (Mark) – (Welwyn Garden City)
Harris, R.J. (Rob) – (Isle of Wight)
Hegley, G.K. (Grant) – (Bishops Stortford)
Hill, K.D. (Keith) – (Hertfordshire)
Jones, M.J. (Michael) – (Chester)

Jones, P. (Peter) – (Loughborough)
Jones, T. (Trevor) – (Cumbria)
Jordan, W.M. (Bill) – (Hertfordshire)
Joslin, P.J. (Phil) – (Nottinghamshire)
Kaye, A. (Alan) – (Wakefield)
Knight, B. (Barry) – (Kent)
Laws, D. (David) – (Whitley Bay)
Laws, G. (Graham) – (Whitley Bay)
Leake, A.R. (Tony) – (Lancashire)
Mathieson, S.W. (Scott) – (Stockport)
Messias, M.D. (Matt) – (York)
Olivier, R.J. (Ray) – (Sutton Coldfield)
Parkes, T.A. (Trevor) – (Birmingham)
Pearson, R. (Roy) – (Durham)
Penton, C. (Clive) – (Sussex)
Pike, M.S. (Mike) – (Barrow-in-Furness)
Poll, G. (Graham) – (Hertfordshire)
Prosser, P.J. (Phil) – (Tewkesbury)
Pugh, D. (David) – (Merseyside)
Rejer, P. (Paul) – (Worcestershire)
Rennie, U.D. (Uriah) – (Sheffield)
Richards, P.R. (Phil) – (Lancashire)
Riley, M.A. (Mike) – (Leeds)
Robinson, J.P. (Paul) – (Hull)
Ross, J.J. (Joe) – (London)
Ryan, M. (Michael) – (Preston)
Salisbury, G. (Graham) – (Preston)
Stretton, F.G. (Frazer) – (Nottingham)
Styles, R. (Rob) – (Hampshire)
Taylor, P. (Paul) – (Hertfordshire)
Tomlin, S.G. (Steve) – (East Sussex)
Walton, P. (Peter) – (Northants)
Warren, M.R. (Mark) – (Walsall)
Webb, H.M. (Howard) – (Rotherham)
Webster, C.H. (Colin) – (Durham)
Wiley, A.G. (Alan) – (Burntwood)
Wilkes, C.R. (Clive) – (Gloucester)
Winter, J.T. (Jeff) – (Stockton-on-Tees)
Wolstenholme, E.K. (Eddie) – (Blackburn)

# USEFUL ADDRESSES

**The Football Association:** The Secretary, 25 Soho Square, London W1D 4FA. *0207 745 4545*

**Scotland:** The Secretary, Hampden Park, Glasgow G42 9AY. *0141 616 6000*

**Northern Ireland** (Irish FA): D. I. Bowen, 20 Windsor Avenue, Belfast BT9 6EG. *028 9066 9458*

**Wales:** A. Evans, 3 Westgate Street, Cardiff, South Glamorgan CF1 1DD. *029 2037 2325*

**Republic of Ireland** (FA of Ireland): B. O'Byrne, 80 Merrion Square South, Dublin 2. *00353-16766864*

**International Federation** (FIFA): M. Zen-Ruffinen, P. O. Box 85 8030 Zurich, Switzerland. *00 411 384 9595. Fax: 00 411 384 9696*

**Union of European Football Associations:** G. Aigner, Route de Geneve 46, Case Postal, CH-1260 Nyon, Switzerland. *0041 22 994 4444. Fax: 0041 22 994 4488*

**The Premier League:** The Secretary, 11 Connaught Place, London W2 2ET. *0207 298 1651*

**The Football League:** D Burns, The Football League, Unit 5, Edward VII Quay, Navigation Way, Preston, Lancashire PR2 2YF. *01772 325800. Fax 01772 325801*

**Scottish Premier League:** R. Mitchell, Hampden Park, Somerville Drive, Glasgow G42 9BA. *0141 646 6962*

**The Scottish League:** The Secretary, Hampden Park, Glasgow G42 9AY. *0141 616 6000*

**The Irish League:** H. Wallace, 96 University Street, Belfast BT7 1HE. *028 9024 2888*

**Football League of Ireland:** D Crowther, 80 Merrion Square, Dublin 2. *00353 167 65120*

**The Nationwide Football Conference:** J. A. Moules, Riverside House, 14b High Street, Crayford DA1 4HG. *01322 411021*

**Northern Premier:** R. D. Bayley, 22 Woburn Drive, Hale, Altrincham, Cheshire, WA15 8LZ. *0161-980 7007*

**Isthmian League:** N. Robinson, 226 Rye Lane, Peckham, SE15 4NL. *020 8409 1978. Fax 020 7639 5726*

**English Schools FA:** Ms A Pritchard, 1/2 Eastgate Street, Stafford ST16 2NN. *01785-51142*

**Southern League:** D. J. Strudwick, PO Box 90, Worcester WR3 8RX. *01905-757509.*

**National Federation of Football Supporters' Clubs:** Chairman: Ian D. Todd MBE, 8 Wyke Close, Wyke Gardens, Isleworth, Middlesex TW7 5PE. *020 8847 2905 (and fax). Mobile: 0961-558908.* National Secretary: Mark Agate, "The Stadium", 14 Coombe Close, Lordswood, Chatham, Kent ME5 8NU. *01634 319461 (and fax)*

**Professional Footballers' Association:** G. Taylor, 2 Oxford Court, Bishopsgate, Off Lower Mosley Street, Manchester M2 3WQ. *0161-236 0575*

**Referees' Association:** A. Smith, 1 Westhill Road, Coundon, Coventry CV6 2AD. *024 7660 1701*

**Women's Football Alliance:** The Football Association, 25 Soho Square, London W1D 4FA. *0207 745 4545*

**The Football Programme Directory:** David Stacey, 'The Beeches', 66 Southend Road, Wickford, Essex SS11 8EN. *01268 732041 (and fax)*

**England Football Supporters Association:** Publicity Officer, David Stacey, 66 Southend Road, Wickford, Essex SS11 8EN. *01268 732041 (and fax)*

**World Cup (1966) Association:** as above.

**The Football Foundation Ltd:** 25 Soho Square, London W1D 4FF. *0207 534 4210. Fax 0207 287 0459*

# ENGLISH LEAGUE FIXTURES 2001–2002

## Saturday, 11 August 2001

**Nationwide Football League Division 1**
Bradford v Barnsley
Gillingham v Preston
Grimsby v Crewe
Man City v Watford
Millwall v Norwich
Nottm Forest v Sheff Utd
Rotherham v Crystal Palace
Stockport v Coventry
Walsall v West Brom
Wimbledon v Birmingham
Wolverhampton v Portsmouth

**Nationwide Football League Division 2**
Blackpool v Reading
Cambridge Utd v Brighton
Cardiff v Wycombe
Chesterfield v Colchester
Huddersfield v Bournemouth
Northampton v Bristol City
Port Vale v Notts County
QPR v Stoke
Swindon v Peterborough
Tranmere v Bury
Wigan v Brentford
Wrexham v Oldham

**Nationwide Football League Division 3**
Bristol Rovers v Torquay
Carlisle v Luton
Cheltenham v Leyton Orient
Exeter v Hull
Hartlepool v Mansfield
Kidderminster v Scunthorpe
Lincoln City v Halifax
Macclesfield v Swansea
Oxford Utd v Rochdale
Plymouth v Shrewsbury
Southend v Darlington
York v Rushden & D'monds

## Sunday, 12 August 2001

**Nationwide Football League Division 1**
Sheff Wed v Burnley

## Thursday, 16 August 2001

**Nationwide Football League Division 3**
Rushden & D'monds v Lincoln City

## Saturday, 18 August 2001

**FA Barclaycard Premiership**
Charlton v Everton
Derby v Blackburn
Leeds v Southampton
Leicester v Bolton
Liverpool v West Ham
Middlesbrough v Arsenal
Sunderland v Ipswich
Tottenham v Aston Villa

**Nationwide Football League Division 1**
Barnsley v Nottm Forest
Burnley v Wimbledon
Crewe v Sheff Wed
Crystal Palace v Stockport
Norwich v Man City
Portsmouth v Bradford
Preston v Walsall
Sheff Utd v Gillingham
Watford v Rotherham
West Brom v Grimsby

**Nationwide Football League Division 2**
Bournemouth v Blackpool
Brentford v Port Vale
Brighton v Wigan
Bristol City v Swindon
Bury v QPR
Colchester v Tranmere
Notts County v Cambridge Utd
Oldham v Chesterfield
Peterborough v Cardiff
Reading v Huddersfield
Stoke v Northampton
Wycombe v Wrexham

**Nationwide Football League Division 3**
Darlington v Kidderminster
Halifax v Exeter
Hull v Plymouth
Leyton Orient v Carlisle
Luton v Cheltenham
Mansfield v Southend
Rochdale v Macclesfield
Scunthorpe v Bristol Rovers
Shrewsbury v Hartlepool
Swansea v Oxford Utd
Torquay v York

**Nationwide Football Conference**
Boston Utd v Margate
Chester v Woking
Dag & Red v Southport
Dover v Telford
Farnborough v Doncaster
Hereford v Barnet
Leigh RMI v Hayes
Morecambe v Nuneaton
Scarborough v Forest Green
Stevenage v Stalybridge
Yeovil v Northwich

**Sunday, 19 August 2001**

**FA Barclaycard Premiership**
Chelsea v Newcastle
Man Utd v Fulham

**Nationwide Football League Division 1**
Birmingham v Millwall
Coventry v Wolverhampton

**Monday, 20 August 2001**

**FA Barclaycard Premiership**
Everton v Tottenham

**Tuesday, 21 August 2001**

**FA Barclaycard Premiership**
Arsenal v Leeds
Bolton v Middlesbrough
Ipswich v Derby

**Nationwide Football Conference**
Barnet v Dover
Doncaster v Leigh RMI
Hayes v Stevenage
Margate v Dag & Red
Northwich v Scarborough
Nuneaton v Hereford
Southport v Chester
Stalybridge v Morecambe
Telford v Yeovil
Woking v Boston Utd

**Wednesday, 22 August 2001**

**FA Barclaycard Premiership**
Aston Villa v Charlton
Blackburn v Man Utd
Fulham v Sunderland
Newcastle v Leicester

**Nationwide Football Conference**
Forest Green v Farnborough

**Thursday, 23 August 2001**

**Nationwide Football League Division 1**
Rotherham v Sheff Utd

**Friday, 24 August 2001**

**Nationwide Football League Division 1**
Bradford v Coventry

**Saturday, 25 August 2001**

**FA Barclaycard Premiership**
Arsenal v Leicester
Blackburn v Tottenham
Everton v Middlesbrough
Fulham v Derby
Ipswich v Charlton
Southampton v Chelsea
West Ham v Leeds

**Nationwide Football League Division 1**
Gillingham v Barnsley
Grimsby v Preston
Man City v Crewe
Millwall v Burnley
Nottm Forest v Crystal Palace
Sheff Wed v West Brom
Stockport v Portsmouth
Walsall v Birmingham
Wimbledon v Norwich
Wolverhampton v Watford

**Nationwide Football League Division 2**
Blackpool v Wycombe
Cambridge Utd v Stoke
Cardiff v Bournemouth
Chesterfield v Brentford
Huddersfield v Bury
Northampton v Notts County
Port Vale v Peterborough
QPR v Reading
Swindon v Oldham
Tranmere v Brighton
Wigan v Bristol City
Wrexham v Colchester

**Nationwide Football League Division 3**
Bristol Rovers v Luton
Carlisle v Hull
Cheltenham v Mansfield
Exeter v Scunthorpe
Hartlepool v Darlington
Kidderminster v Torquay
Lincoln City v Swansea
Macclesfield v Rushden & D'monds
Oxford Utd v Shrewsbury
Plymouth v Rochdale
Southend v Halifax
York v Leyton Orient

**Nationwide Football Conference**
Barnet v Scarborough
Doncaster v Yeovil
Forest Green v Boston Utd
Hayes v Chester
Margate v Leigh RMI
Northwich v Stevenage
Nuneaton v Dover
Southport v Farnborough
Stalybridge v Hereford
Telford v Dag & Red
Woking v Morecambe

**Sunday, 26 August 2001**

**FA Barclaycard Premiership**
Aston Villa v Man Utd
Newcastle v Sunderland

**Monday, 27 August 2001**

**FA Barclaycard Premiership**
Bolton v Liverpool

**Nationwide Football League Division 1**
Barnsley v Rotherham
Birmingham v Stockport
Burnley v Man City
Coventry v Nottm Forest
Norwich v Sheff Wed
Portsmouth v Grimsby
Preston v Wimbledon
Sheff Utd v Wolverhampton
Watford v Walsall
West Brom v Gillingham

**Nationwide Football League Division 2**
Brentford v Cambridge Utd
Brighton v Blackpool
Bury v Swindon
Colchester v Port Vale
Notts County v Chesterfield
Peterborough v Huddersfield
Stoke v Tranmere
Wycombe v QPR

**Nationwide Football League Division 3**
Darlington v Bristol Rovers
Halifax v Oxford Utd
Hull v Kidderminster
Leyton Orient v Hartlepool
Luton v Southend
Mansfield v Macclesfield
Rochdale v Exeter
Rushden & D'monds v Plymouth
Scunthorpe v Lincoln City
Swansea v Cheltenham
Torquay v Carlisle

**Nationwide Football Conference**
Chester v Nuneaton
Dag & Red v Woking
Dover v Forest Green
Farnborough v Barnet
Hereford v Southport
Leigh RMI v Northwich
Morecambe v Telford
Scarborough v Margate
Stevenage v Doncaster
Yeovil v Hayes

**Tuesday, 28 August 2001**

**Nationwide Football League Division 1**
Crewe v Millwall
Crystal Palace v Bradford

**Nationwide Football League Division 2**
Bournemouth v Wigan
Bristol City v Cardiff
Oldham v Northampton
Reading v Wrexham

**Nationwide Football League Division 3**
Shrewsbury v York

**Wednesday, 29 August 2001**

**Nationwide Football Conference**
Boston Utd v Stalybridge

**Thursday, 30 August 2001**

**Nationwide Football League Division 2**
QPR v Bristol City

**Friday, 31 August 2001**

**Nationwide Football League Division 1**
Gillingham v Crystal Palace

**Nationwide Football League Division 2**
Cardiff v Brentford
Northampton v Brighton
Wrexham v Bury

**Saturday, 1 September 2001**

**Nationwide Football League Division 1**
Grimsby v Barnsley
Man City v Sheff Utd
Millwall v Watford
Nottm Forest v Birmingham
Rotherham v Coventry
Sheff Wed v Preston
Stockport v West Brom
Walsall v Norwich
Wimbledon v Portsmouth
Wolverhampton v Crewe

**Nationwide Football League Division 2**
Blackpool v Stoke
Cambridge Utd v Bournemouth
Chesterfield v Peterborough
Port Vale v Reading
Swindon v Colchester
Tranmere v Oldham
Wigan v Notts County

**Nationwide Football League Division 3**
Bristol Rovers v Shrewsbury
Carlisle v Rochdale
Cheltenham v Torquay
Exeter v Luton
Hartlepool v Hull
Kidderminster v Mansfield
Lincoln City v Darlington
Macclesfield v Scunthorpe
Oxford Utd v Rushden & D'monds
Plymouth v Swansea
Southend v Leyton Orient
York v Halifax

**Nationwide Football Conference**
Barnet v Chester
Doncaster v Dover
Forest Green v Dag & Red
Hayes v Morecambe
Margate v Hereford
Northwich v Boston Utd
Nuneaton v Yeovil
Southport v Stevenage
Stalybridge v Farnborough
Telford v Leigh RMI
Woking v Scarborough

**Sunday, 2 September 2001**

**Nationwide Football League Division 1**
Bradford v Burnley

**Nationwide Football League Division 2**
Huddersfield v Wycombe

**Monday, 3 September 2001**

**Nationwide Football Conference**
Dover v Hayes
Stevenage v Nuneaton

**Tuesday, 4 September 2001**

**Nationwide Football Conference**
Chester v Telford
Dag & Red v Barnet
Farnborough v Margate
Hereford v Forest Green
Leigh RMI v Southport
Morecambe v Northwich
Scarborough v Stalybridge

Yeovil v Woking

**Wednesday, 5 September 2001**

**Nationwide Football Conference**
Boston Utd v Doncaster

**Saturday, 8 September 2001**

**FA Barclaycard Premiership**
Chelsea v Arsenal
Derby v West Ham
Leeds v Bolton
Leicester v Ipswich
Liverpool v Aston Villa
Man Utd v Everton
Middlesbrough v Newcastle
Sunderland v Blackburn

**Nationwide Football League Division 1**
Barnsley v Stockport
Birmingham v Sheff Wed
Burnley v Rotherham
Coventry v Grimsby
Crewe v Walsall
Crystal Palace v Millwall
Norwich v Nottm Forest
Portsmouth v Gillingham
Preston v Wolverhampton
Sheff Utd v Bradford
West Brom v Man City

**Nationwide Football League Division 2**
Bournemouth v Swindon
Brentford v Tranmere
Brighton v QPR
Bristol City v Port Vale
Bury v Wigan
Colchester v Northampton
Notts County v Wrexham
Oldham v Blackpool
Peterborough v Cambridge Utd
Reading v Cardiff
Stoke v Huddersfield
Wycombe v Chesterfield

**Nationwide Football League Division 3**
Darlington v Carlisle
Halifax v Macclesfield
Hull v York
Leyton Orient v Bristol Rovers
Luton v Oxford Utd
Mansfield v Lincoln City
Rochdale v Kidderminster
Rushden & D'monds v Southend
Scunthorpe v Hartlepool
Shrewsbury v Cheltenham
Swansea v Exeter
Torquay v Plymouth

**Nationwide Football Conference**
Barnet v Southport
Boston Utd v Yeovil
Doncaster v Woking
Farnborough v Chester
Forest Green v Morecambe
Hereford v Dover
Leigh RMI v Stevenage
Margate v Telford
Northwich v Nuneaton
Scarborough v Hayes
Stalybridge v Dag & Red

**Sunday, 9 September 2001**

**FA Barclaycard Premiership**
Charlton v Fulham
Tottenham v Southampton

**Nationwide Football League Division 1**
Watford v Wimbledon

**Monday, 10 September 2001**

**Nationwide Football Conference**
Dover v Boston Utd
Stevenage v Scarborough

**Tuesday, 11 September 2001**

**Nationwide Football Conference**
Chester v Stalybridge
Dag & Red v Hereford
Hayes v Forest Green
Morecambe v Barnet
Nuneaton v Leigh RMI
Southport v Northwich
Telford v Doncaster
Woking v Margate
Yeovil v Farnborough

**Friday, 14 September 2001**

**Nationwide Football League Division 2**
Wrexham v Brighton

**Nationwide Football League Division 3**
Mansfield v Shrewsbury

**Saturday, 15 September 2001**

**FA Barclaycard Premiership**
Aston Villa v Sunderland
Bolton v Southampton
Derby v Leicester
Everton v Liverpool
Fulham v Arsenal
Middlesbrough v West Ham
Newcastle v Man Utd

**Nationwide Football League Division 1**
Barnsley v Crewe
Bradford v Gillingham
Burnley v Walsall
Grimsby v Nottm Forest
Man City v Birmingham
Portsmouth v Crystal Palace
Preston v Millwall
Rotherham v Norwich
Sheff Utd v Coventry
Watford v West Brom
Wimbledon v Sheff Wed
Wolverhampton v Stockport

**Nationwide Football League Division 2**
Bournemouth v Bury
Bristol City v Colchester
Cambridge Utd v Cardiff
Huddersfield v Blackpool
Northampton v Chesterfield
Notts County v Brentford
Oldham v Peterborough
QPR v Port Vale
Stoke v Reading
Swindon v Tranmere
Wycombe v Wigan

**Nationwide Football League Division 3**
Cheltenham v Carlisle
Exeter v Oxford Utd
Kidderminster v Plymouth
Leyton Orient v Rushden & D'monds
Lincoln City v Bristol Rovers
Macclesfield v Hull
Rochdale v Scunthorpe
Southend v Hartlepool
Swansea v Halifax
Torquay v Darlington
York v Luton

**Nationwide Football Conference**
Chester v Boston Utd
Dag & Red v Leigh RMI
Dover v Stalybridge
Hayes v Doncaster
Morecambe v Hereford
Nuneaton v Forest Green
Southport v Margate
Stevenage v Farnborough
Telford v Barnet
Woking v Northwich
Yeovil v Scarborough

**Sunday, 16 September 2001**

**FA Barclaycard Premiership**
Charlton v Leeds
Ipswich v Blackburn
Tottenham v Chelsea

**Monday, 17 September 2001**

**FA Barclaycard Premiership**
Leicester v Middlesbrough

**Nationwide Football League Division 1**
Nottm Forest v Rotherham

**Tuesday, 18 September 2001**

**FA Barclaycard Premiership**
Arsenal v Newcastle

**Nationwide Football League Division 1**
Birmingham v Burnley
Crewe v Wimbledon
Crystal Palace v Grimsby
Gillingham v Wolverhampton
Millwall v Barnsley
Norwich v Watford
Stockport v Sheff Utd
Walsall v Portsmouth
West Brom v Preston

**Nationwide Football League Division 2**
Blackpool v QPR
Brentford v Bristol City
Brighton v Stoke
Bury v Wycombe
Cardiff v Northampton
Chesterfield v Wrexham
Colchester v Oldham
Peterborough v Bournemouth
Port Vale v Swindon
Reading v Cambridge Utd
Tranmere v Notts County
Wigan v Huddersfield

**Nationwide Football League Division 3**
Bristol Rovers v Southend
Carlisle v York
Darlington v Leyton Orient
Exeter v Plymouth
Halifax v Mansfield
Hartlepool v Cheltenham
Hull v Rochdale
Luton v Lincoln City
Oxford Utd v Macclesfield
Rushden & D'monds v Torquay
Scunthorpe v Swansea
Shrewsbury v Kidderminster

**Nationwide Football Conference**
Barnet v Hayes
Doncaster v Nuneaton
Farnborough v Dover
Hereford v Yeovil
Leigh RMI v Chester
Margate v Stevenage
Northwich v Telford

Scarborough v Morecambe
Stalybridge v Southport

**Wednesday, 19 September 2001**

**FA Barclaycard Premiership**
Blackburn v Bolton
Chelsea v Charlton
Leeds v Everton
Liverpool v Fulham
Southampton v Ipswich
Sunderland v Tottenham
West Ham v Aston Villa

**Nationwide Football League Division 1**
Coventry v Man City
Sheff Wed v Bradford

**Nationwide Football Conference**
Boston Utd v Dag & Red
Forest Green v Woking

**Thursday, 20 September 2001**

**Nationwide Football League Division 1**
Nottm Forest v Bradford

**Friday, 21 September 2001**

**Nationwide Football League Division 1**
Walsall v Wolverhampton

**Nationwide Football League Division 2**
Tranmere v Wrexham

**Saturday, 22 September 2001**

**FA Barclaycard Premiership**
Arsenal v Bolton
Blackburn v Everton
Chelsea v Middlesbrough
Leicester v Fulham
Liverpool v Tottenham
Man Utd v Ipswich
Sunderland v Charlton

**Nationwide Football League Division 1**
Coventry v Portsmouth
Crewe v Watford
Crystal Palace v Barnsley
Gillingham v Rotherham
Millwall v Sheff Utd
Norwich v Burnley
Sheff Wed v Man City
Stockport v Grimsby
West Brom v Wimbledon

**Nationwide Football League Division 2**
Blackpool v Cambridge Utd
Brentford v Oldham

Brighton v Bournemouth
Bury v Stoke
Cardiff v Huddersfield
Chesterfield v Swindon
Colchester v Notts County
Peterborough v Bristol City
Port Vale v Northampton
Reading v Wycombe
Wigan v QPR

### Nationwide Football League Division 3
Bristol Rovers v York
Carlisle v Lincoln City
Darlington v Exeter
Halifax v Leyton Orient
Hartlepool v Kidderminster
Hull v Swansea
Luton v Torquay
Oxford Utd v Southend
Plymouth v Macclesfield
Rushden & D'monds v Cheltenham
Scunthorpe v Mansfield
Shrewsbury v Rochdale

### Nationwide Football Conference
Barnet v Northwich
Boston Utd v Hayes
Chester v Dag & Red
Doncaster v Morecambe
Dover v Yeovil
Forest Green v Southport
Hereford v Stevenage
Leigh RMI v Farnborough
Scarborough v Nuneaton
Stalybridge v Margate
Woking v Telford

## Sunday, 23 September 2001

### FA Barclaycard Premiership
Leeds v Derby
West Ham v Newcastle

### Nationwide Football League Division 1
Birmingham v Preston

## Monday, 24 September 2001

### FA Barclaycard Premiership
Southampton v Aston Villa

## Tuesday, 25 September 2001

### Nationwide Football League Division 1
Barnsley v Coventry
Bradford v Stockport
Burnley v Crewe
Grimsby v Gillingham
Portsmouth v West Brom
Rotherham v Sheff Wed

Sheff Utd v Crystal Palace
Wimbledon v Millwall
Wolverhampton v Nottm Forest

### Nationwide Football League Division 2
Bournemouth v Reading
Bristol City v Tranmere
Cambridge Utd v Wigan
Huddersfield v Chesterfield
Northampton v Blackpool
Notts County v Peterborough
Oldham v Bury
QPR v Cardiff
Swindon v Brentford
Wrexham v Port Vale
Wycombe v Brighton

### Nationwide Football League Division 3
Cheltenham v Bristol Rovers
Exeter v Rushden & D'monds
Kidderminster v Oxford Utd
Leyton Orient v Luton
Lincoln City v Hartlepool
Macclesfield v Darlington
Mansfield v Hull
Rochdale v Halifax
Southend v Carlisle
Swansea v Shrewsbury
Torquay v Scunthorpe
York v Plymouth

## Wednesday, 26 September 2001

### Nationwide Football League Division 1
Man City v Walsall
Preston v Norwich
Watford v Birmingham

### Nationwide Football League Division 2
Stoke v Colchester

## Friday, 28 September 2001

### Nationwide Football League Division 1
Barnsley v Portsmouth

### Nationwide Football League Division 3
Southend v Cheltenham

## Saturday, 29 September 2001

### FA Barclaycard Premiership
Aston Villa v Blackburn
Bolton v Sunderland
Charlton v Leicester
Derby v Arsenal
Everton v West Ham
Middlesbrough v Southampton
Tottenham v Man Utd

**Nationwide Football League Division 1**
Bradford v Grimsby
Crewe v Birmingham
Crystal Palace v Sheff Wed
Gillingham v Coventry
Man City v Wimbledon
Nottm Forest v Stockport
Rotherham v Wolverhampton
Sheff Utd v Norwich
Walsall v Millwall
West Brom v Burnley

**Nationwide Football League Division 2**
Blackpool v Wigan
Brentford v Colchester
Cambridge Utd v QPR
Cardiff v Brighton
Chesterfield v Tranmere
Huddersfield v Bristol City
Northampton v Swindon
Oldham v Notts County
Reading v Bury
Stoke v Bournemouth
Wrexham v Peterborough
Wycombe v Port Vale

**Nationwide Football League Division 3**
Bristol Rovers v Oxford Utd
Darlington v Rushden & D'monds
Exeter v Macclesfield
Hartlepool v Carlisle
Hull v Halifax
Kidderminster v Swansea
Leyton Orient v Torquay
Lincoln City v York
Plymouth v Luton
Rochdale v Mansfield
Scunthorpe v Shrewsbury

**Nationwide Football Conference**
Dag & Red v Scarborough
Farnborough v Boston Utd
Hayes v Hereford
Margate v Barnet
Morecambe v Dover
Northwich v Forest Green
Nuneaton v Woking
Southport v Doncaster
Stevenage v Chester
Telford v Stalybridge
Yeovil v Leigh RMI

**Sunday, 30 September 2001**

**FA Barclaycard Premiership**
Fulham v Chelsea
Ipswich v Leeds
Newcastle v Liverpool

**Nationwide Football League Division 1**
Watford v Preston

**Tuesday, 2 October 2001**

**Nationwide Football Conference**
Barnet v Yeovil
Dag & Red v Stevenage
Hereford v Farnborough
Margate v Hayes
Morecambe v Leigh RMI
Northwich v Doncaster
Nuneaton v Southport
Scarborough v Chester
Telford v Boston Utd
Woking v Dover

**Wednesday, 3 October 2001**

**Nationwide Football Conference**
Forest Green v Stalybridge

**Thursday, 4 October 2001**

**Nationwide Football League Division 2**
Tranmere v Blackpool

**Friday, 5 October 2001**

**Nationwide Football League Division 1**
Burnley v Watford
Grimsby v Rotherham
Portsmouth v Nottm Forest
Preston v Bradford
Stockport v Gillingham

**Nationwide Football League Division 2**
Bournemouth v Oldham
Brighton v Brentford
Port Vale v Cambridge Utd
Wigan v Stoke

**Nationwide Football League Division 3**
Halifax v Scunthorpe
Mansfield v Leyton Orient
Rushden & D'monds v Hartlepool
Shrewsbury v Hull
Torquay v Southend

**Saturday, 6 October 2001**

**Nationwide Football League Division 1**
Birmingham v West Brom
Coventry v Crystal Palace
Millwall v Man City
Wimbledon v Walsall
Wolverhampton v Barnsley

**Nationwide Football League Division 2**
Bristol City v Chesterfield
Colchester v Reading
Notts County v Wycombe

Swindon v Wrexham

**Nationwide Football League Division 3**
Carlisle v Bristol Rovers
Cheltenham v Lincoln City
Luton v Darlington
Oxford Utd v Plymouth
Swansea v Rochdale
York v Exeter

**Nationwide Football Conference**
Boston Utd v Scarborough
Chester v Margate
Doncaster v Forest Green
Dover v Northwich
Farnborough v Dag & Red
Hayes v Nuneaton
Leigh RMI v Hereford
Southport v Telford
Stalybridge v Barnet
Stevenage v Woking
Yeovil v Morecambe

**Sunday, 7 October 2001**

**Nationwide Football League Division 1**
Norwich v Crewe
Sheff Wed v Sheff Utd

**Nationwide Football League Division 2**
Bury v Cardiff
Peterborough v Northampton
QPR v Huddersfield

**Nationwide Football League Division 3**
Macclesfield v Kidderminster

**Monday, 8 October 2001**

**Nationwide Football Conference**
Dover v Dag & Red
Stevenage v Telford

**Tuesday, 9 October 2001**

**Nationwide Football Conference**
Chester v Hereford
Doncaster v Barnet
Farnborough v Nuneaton
Hayes v Woking
Leigh RMI v Forest Green
Southport v Scarborough
Stalybridge v Northwich
Yeovil v Margate

**Wednesday, 10 October 2001**

**Nationwide Football Conference**
Boston Utd v Morecambe

**Thursday, 11 October 2001**

**Nationwide Football League Division 1**
West Brom v Millwall

**Friday, 12 October 2001**

**Nationwide Football League Division 1**
Rotherham v Portsmouth

**Nationwide Football League Division 2**
Cardiff v Wigan

**Saturday, 13 October 2001**

**FA Barclaycard Premiership**
Bolton v Newcastle
Charlton v Middlesbrough
Chelsea v Leicester
Ipswich v Everton
Liverpool v Leeds
Southampton v Arsenal
Sunderland v Man Utd

**Nationwide Football League Division 1**
Barnsley v Birmingham
Bradford v Wolverhampton
Crewe v Preston
Crystal Palace v Wimbledon
Gillingham v Norwich
Man City v Stockport
Nottm Forest v Burnley
Sheff Utd v Grimsby
Watford v Sheff Wed

**Nationwide Football League Division 2**
Blackpool v Colchester
Brentford v Peterborough
Cambridge Utd v Bury
Chesterfield v Port Vale
Huddersfield v Brighton
Northampton v Tranmere
Oldham v Bristol City
Reading v Swindon
Stoke v Notts County
Wrexham v QPR
Wycombe v Bournemouth

**Nationwide Football League Division 3**
Bristol Rovers v Macclesfield
Darlington v Mansfield
Exeter v Carlisle
Hartlepool v York
Hull v Torquay
Kidderminster v Cheltenham
Leyton Orient v Shrewsbury
Lincoln City v Oxford Utd
Plymouth v Halifax
Rochdale v Rushden & D'monds
Scunthorpe v Luton

Southend v Swansea

**Nationwide Football Conference**
Barnet v Leigh RMI
Dag & Red v Yeovil
Forest Green v Stevenage
Hereford v Boston Utd
Margate v Doncaster
Morecambe v Chester
Northwich v Hayes
Nuneaton v Stalybridge
Scarborough v Dover
Telford v Farnborough
Woking v Southport

**Sunday, 14 October 2001**

**FA Barclaycard Premiership**
Aston Villa v Fulham
Blackburn v West Ham

**Monday, 15 October 2001**

**FA Barclaycard Premiership**
Tottenham v Derby

**Friday, 19 October 2001**

**Nationwide Football League Division 1**
Norwich v West Brom

**Saturday, 20 October 2001**

**FA Barclaycard Premiership**
Arsenal v Blackburn
Derby v Charlton
Everton v Aston Villa
Fulham v Ipswich
Leicester v Liverpool
Man Utd v Bolton
West Ham v Southampton

**Nationwide Football League Division 1**
Birmingham v Bradford
Burnley v Barnsley
Grimsby v Watford
Millwall v Nottm Forest
Portsmouth v Sheff Utd
Sheff Wed v Walsall
Stockport v Rotherham
Wimbledon v Gillingham
Wolverhampton v Crystal Palace

**Nationwide Football League Division 2**
Bournemouth v Brentford
Brighton v Oldham
Bristol City v Wycombe
Bury v Chesterfield
Colchester v Cambridge Utd
Notts County v Reading
Peterborough v Blackpool

Port Vale v Stoke
QPR v Northampton
Tranmere v Huddersfield
Wigan v Wrexham

**Nationwide Football League Division 3**
Carlisle v Kidderminster
Cheltenham v Exeter
Halifax v Bristol Rovers
Luton v Rochdale
Macclesfield v Lincoln City
Mansfield v Plymouth
Oxford Utd v Scunthorpe
Rushden & D'monds v Hull
Shrewsbury v Darlington
Swansea v Leyton Orient
Torquay v Hartlepool
York v Southend

**Nationwide Football Conference**
Barnet v Boston Utd
Chester v Doncaster
Dag & Red v Nuneaton
Farnborough v Hayes
Hereford v Scarborough
Leigh RMI v Woking
Margate v Northwich
Southport v Dover
Stalybridge v Yeovil
Stevenage v Morecambe
Telford v Forest Green

**Sunday, 21 October 2001**

**FA Barclaycard Premiership**
Leeds v Chelsea
Newcastle v Tottenham

**Nationwide Football League Division 1**
Coventry v Crewe
Preston v Man City

**Nationwide Football League Division 2**
Swindon v Cardiff

**Monday, 22 October 2001**

**FA Barclaycard Premiership**
Middlesbrough v Sunderland

**Tuesday, 23 October 2001**

**Nationwide Football League Division 1**
Birmingham v Gillingham
Burnley v Crystal Palace
Man City v Grimsby
Millwall v Bradford
Norwich v Portsmouth
Preston v Sheff Utd
Walsall v Rotherham

Watford v Nottm Forest
West Brom v Wolverhampton
Wimbledon v Coventry

**Nationwide Football League Division 2**
Brentford v Bury
Bristol City v Bournemouth
Chesterfield v Stoke
Colchester v Wycombe
Northampton v Huddersfield
Notts County v Brighton
Oldham v Reading
Peterborough v QPR
Port Vale v Cardiff
Swindon v Cambridge Utd
Tranmere v Wigan
Wrexham v Blackpool

**Nationwide Football League Division 3**
Exeter v Bristol Rovers
Halifax v Luton
Hull v Leyton Orient
Kidderminster v York
Macclesfield v Hartlepool
Mansfield v Torquay
Oxford Utd v Carlisle
Plymouth v Lincoln City
Rochdale v Cheltenham
Scunthorpe v Southend
Shrewsbury v Rushden & D'monds
Swansea v Darlington

**Wednesday, 24 October 2001**

**FA Barclaycard Premiership**
Southampton v Liverpool
West Ham v Chelsea

**Nationwide Football League Division 1**
Crewe v Stockport
Sheff Wed v Barnsley

**Friday, 26 October 2001**

**Nationwide Football League Division 1**
Grimsby v Birmingham

**Nationwide Football League Division 3**
Cheltenham v Scunthorpe

**Saturday, 27 October 2001**

**FA Barclaycard Premiership**
Aston Villa v Bolton
Charlton v Liverpool
Everton v Newcastle
Fulham v Southampton
Ipswich v West Ham
Man Utd v Leeds
Sunderland v Arsenal

Tottenham v Middlesbrough

**Nationwide Football League Division 1**
Barnsley v West Brom
Bradford v Watford
Coventry v Sheff Wed
Gillingham v Walsall
Portsmouth v Preston
Rotherham v Wimbledon
Sheff Utd v Crewe
Stockport v Millwall
Wolverhampton v Burnley

**Nationwide Football League Division 2**
Blackpool v Chesterfield
Bournemouth v Notts County
Brighton v Colchester
Bury v Peterborough
Cambridge Utd v Northampton
Cardiff v Tranmere
Huddersfield v Wrexham
QPR v Oldham
Reading v Brentford
Stoke v Bristol City
Wigan v Port Vale
Wycombe v Swindon

**Nationwide Football League Division 3**
Carlisle v Halifax
Darlington v Hull
Hartlepool v Oxford Utd
Leyton Orient v Rochdale
Lincoln City v Exeter
Luton v Swansea
Rushden & D'monds v Mansfield
Southend v Kidderminster
Torquay v Shrewsbury
York v Macclesfield

**Sunday, 28 October 2001**

**FA Barclaycard Premiership**
Derby v Chelsea

**Nationwide Football League Division 1**
Crystal Palace v Norwich
Nottm Forest v Man City

**Nationwide Football League Division 3**
Bristol Rovers v Plymouth

**Monday, 29 October 2001**

**FA Barclaycard Premiership**
Blackburn v Leicester

**Tuesday, 30 October 2001**

**Nationwide Football League Division 1**
Bradford v Wimbledon

Crystal Palace v West Brom
Gillingham v Burnley
Grimsby v Norwich
Portsmouth v Birmingham
Rotherham v Crewe
Sheff Utd v Watford
Stockport v Walsall
Wolverhampton v Millwall

## Wednesday, 31 October 2001

**Nationwide Football League Division 1**
Barnsley v Man City
Coventry v Preston
Nottm Forest v Sheff Wed

## Saturday, 3 November 2001

**FA Barclaycard Premiership**
Bolton v Everton
Leeds v Tottenham
Leicester v Sunderland
Middlesbrough v Derby
Newcastle v Aston Villa
Southampton v Blackburn
West Ham v Fulham

**Nationwide Football League Division 1**
Birmingham v Rotherham
Crewe v Bradford
Man City v Gillingham
Millwall v Coventry
Norwich v Wolverhampton
Preston v Stockport
Sheff Wed v Portsmouth
Walsall v Crystal Palace
Watford v Barnsley
Wimbledon v Grimsby

**Nationwide Football League Division 2**
Brentford v Blackpool
Bristol City v Brighton
Chesterfield v Cambridge Utd
Colchester v Bournemouth
Northampton v Reading
Notts County v QPR
Oldham v Huddersfield
Peterborough v Wigan
Port Vale v Bury
Swindon v Stoke
Tranmere v Wycombe

**Nationwide Football League Division 3**
Exeter v Southend
Halifax v Darlington
Hull v Cheltenham
Kidderminster v Bristol Rovers
Macclesfield v Carlisle
Mansfield v Luton
Oxford Utd v York

Plymouth v Hartlepool
Rochdale v Torquay
Scunthorpe v Leyton Orient
Shrewsbury v Lincoln City
Swansea v Rushden & D'monds

**Nationwide Football Conference**
Boston Utd v Southport
Doncaster v Stalybridge
Dover v Stevenage
Forest Green v Margate
Hayes v Telford
Morecambe v Dag & Red
Northwich v Farnborough
Nuneaton v Barnet
Scarborough v Leigh RMI
Woking v Hereford
Yeovil v Chester

## Sunday, 4 November 2001

**FA Barclaycard Premiership**
Arsenal v Charlton
Chelsea v Ipswich
Liverpool v Man Utd

**Nationwide Football League Division 1**
Burnley v Sheff Utd
West Brom v Nottm Forest

**Nationwide Football League Division 2**
Wrexham v Cardiff

## Friday, 9 November 2001

**Nationwide Football League Division 2**
Wigan v Colchester

## Saturday, 10 November 2001

**Nationwide Football League Division 1**
Birmingham v Crystal Palace
Burnley v Portsmouth
Crewe v Gillingham
Man City v Wolverhampton
Millwall v Rotherham
Norwich v Bradford
Preston v Barnsley
Sheff Wed v Grimsby
Walsall v Nottm Forest
Watford v Stockport
West Brom v Coventry
Wimbledon v Sheff Utd

**Nationwide Football League Division 2**
Blackpool v Swindon
Bournemouth v Wrexham
Brighton v Port Vale
Bury v Northampton
Cambridge Utd v Oldham

Cardiff v Chesterfield
Huddersfield v Notts County
QPR v Tranmere
Reading v Bristol City
Stoke v Brentford
Wycombe v Peterborough

**Nationwide Football League Division 3**
Bristol Rovers v Rochdale
Carlisle v Mansfield
Cheltenham v Plymouth
Darlington v Oxford Utd
Hartlepool v Exeter
Leyton Orient v Kidderminster
Lincoln City v Hull
Luton v Shrewsbury
Rushden & D'monds v Halifax
Southend v Macclesfield
Torquay v Swansea
York v Scunthorpe

**Nationwide Football Conference**
Barnet v Woking
Chester v Forest Green
Dag & Red v Northwich
Farnborough v Morecambe
Hereford v Doncaster
Leigh RMI v Dover
Margate v Nuneaton
Southport v Yeovil
Stalybridge v Hayes
Stevenage v Boston Utd
Telford v Scarborough

**Saturday, 17 November 2001**

**FA Barclaycard Premiership**
Aston Villa v Middlesbrough
Blackburn v Liverpool
Derby v Southampton
Everton v Chelsea
Fulham v Newcastle
Man Utd v Leicester
Sunderland v Leeds
Tottenham v Arsenal

**Nationwide Football League Division 1**
Barnsley v Wimbledon
Bradford v Walsall
Coventry v Burnley
Crystal Palace v Crewe
Gillingham v Watford
Grimsby v Millwall
Nottm Forest v Preston
Portsmouth v Man City
Rotherham v West Brom
Sheff Utd v Birmingham
Stockport v Norwich

**Sunday, 18 November 2001**

**FA Barclaycard Premiership**
Ipswich v Bolton

**Nationwide Football League Division 1**
Wolverhampton v Sheff Wed

**Monday, 19 November 2001**

**FA Barclaycard Premiership**
Charlton v West Ham

**Tuesday, 20 November 2001**

**Nationwide Football League Division 2**
Blackpool v Notts County
Bournemouth v Port Vale
Bury v Bristol City
Cambridge Utd v Wrexham
Cardiff v Colchester
Huddersfield v Brentford
QPR v Swindon
Reading v Tranmere
Wigan v Chesterfield
Wycombe v Northampton

**Nationwide Football League Division 3**
Bristol Rovers v Mansfield
Carlisle v Shrewsbury
Cheltenham v Macclesfield
Darlington v Rochdale
Hartlepool v Halifax
Leyton Orient v Oxford Utd
Lincoln City v Kidderminster
Luton v Hull
Rushden & D'monds v Scunthorpe
Southend v Plymouth
Torquay v Exeter
York v Swansea

**Wednesday, 21 November 2001**

**Nationwide Football League Division 2**
Brighton v Peterborough
Stoke v Oldham

**Friday, 23 November 2001**

**Nationwide Football League Division 3**
Mansfield v York
Swansea v Hartlepool

**Saturday, 24 November 2001**

**FA Barclaycard Premiership**
Bolton v Fulham
Chelsea v Blackburn
Leeds v Aston Villa
Leicester v Everton
Liverpool v Sunderland
Middlesbrough v Ipswich

Newcastle v Derby
Southampton v Charlton
West Ham v Tottenham

**Nationwide Football League Division 1**
Burnley v Grimsby
Crewe v Nottm Forest
Man City v Rotherham
Millwall v Gillingham
Norwich v Barnsley
Preston v Crystal Palace
Sheff Wed v Stockport
Walsall v Sheff Utd
Watford v Portsmouth
West Brom v Bradford
Wimbledon v Wolverhampton

**Nationwide Football League Division 2**
Brentford v QPR
Bristol City v Blackpool
Chesterfield v Bournemouth
Colchester v Bury
Northampton v Wigan
Notts County v Cardiff
Oldham v Wycombe
Peterborough v Reading
Port Vale v Huddersfield
Swindon v Brighton
Tranmere v Cambridge Utd
Wrexham v Stoke

**Nationwide Football League Division 3**
Exeter v Leyton Orient
Halifax v Torquay
Hull v Bristol Rovers
Kidderminster v Rushden & D'monds
Macclesfield v Luton
Oxford Utd v Cheltenham
Plymouth v Carlisle
Rochdale v Lincoln City
Scunthorpe v Darlington
Shrewsbury v Southend

**Nationwide Football Conference**
Boston Utd v Leigh RMI
Doncaster v Dag & Red
Dover v Chester
Forest Green v Barnet
Hayes v Southport
Morecambe v Margate
Northwich v Hereford
Nuneaton v Telford
Scarborough v Farnborough
Woking v Stalybridge
Yeovil v Stevenage

**Sunday, 25 November 2001**

**FA Barclaycard Premiership**
Arsenal v Man Utd

**Nationwide Football League Division 1**
Birmingham v Coventry

**Friday, 30 November 2001**

**Nationwide Football League Division 3**
Hartlepool v Rochdale

**Saturday, 1 December 2001**

**FA Barclaycard Premiership**
Aston Villa v Leicester
Blackburn v Middlesbrough
Charlton v Newcastle
Derby v Liverpool
Fulham v Leeds
Ipswich v Arsenal
Man Utd v Chelsea
Sunderland v West Ham
Tottenham v Bolton

**Nationwide Football League Division 1**
Barnsley v Sheff Wed
Bradford v Millwall
Coventry v Wimbledon
Crystal Palace v Burnley
Gillingham v Birmingham
Grimsby v Man City
Nottm Forest v Watford
Rotherham v Walsall
Sheff Utd v Preston
Stockport v Crewe

**Nationwide Football League Division 2**
Bournemouth v Tranmere
Bristol City v Notts County
Bury v Brighton
Cardiff v Oldham
Huddersfield v Cambridge Utd
Peterborough v Stoke
Port Vale v Blackpool
QPR v Colchester
Reading v Chesterfield
Wigan v Swindon
Wrexham v Northampton
Wycombe v Brentford

**Nationwide Football League Division 3**
Carlisle v Scunthorpe
Cheltenham v Halifax
Darlington v York
Hull v Oxford Utd
Kidderminster v Luton
Leyton Orient v Plymouth
Mansfield v Swansea
Rushden & D'monds v Bristol Rovers
Shrewsbury v Exeter
Southend v Lincoln City
Torquay v Macclesfield

**Nationwide Football Conference**
Barnet v Hereford
Doncaster v Farnborough
Forest Green v Scarborough
Hayes v Leigh RMI
Margate v Boston Utd
Northwich v Yeovil
Nuneaton v Morecambe
Southport v Dag & Red
Stalybridge v Stevenage
Telford v Dover
Woking v Chester

**Sunday, 2 December 2001**

**FA Barclaycard Premiership**
Everton v Southampton

**Nationwide Football League Division 1**
Portsmouth v Norwich
Wolverhampton v West Brom

**Saturday, 8 December 2001**

**FA Barclaycard Premiership**
Blackburn v Leeds
Charlton v Tottenham
Derby v Bolton
Fulham v Everton
Ipswich v Newcastle
Leicester v Southampton
Liverpool v Middlesbrough
Man Utd v West Ham
Sunderland v Chelsea

**Nationwide Football League Division 1**
Barnsley v Walsall
Birmingham v Norwich
Bradford v Rotherham
Crystal Palace v Man City
Grimsby v Wolverhampton
Nottm Forest v Gillingham
Portsmouth v Crewe
Preston v Burnley
Sheff Wed v Millwall
Stockport v Wimbledon
West Brom v Sheff Utd

**Sunday, 9 December 2001**

**FA Barclaycard Premiership**
Arsenal v Aston Villa

**Nationwide Football League Division 1**
Coventry v Watford

**Wednesday, 12 December 2001**

**FA Barclaycard Premiership**
Man Utd v Derby

**Friday, 14 December 2001**

**Nationwide Football League Division 2**
Brighton v Reading

**Saturday, 15 December 2001**

**FA Barclaycard Premiership**
Aston Villa v Ipswich
Bolton v Charlton
Chelsea v Liverpool
Everton v Derby
Leeds v Leicester
Middlesbrough v Man Utd
Newcastle v Blackburn
Southampton v Sunderland
Tottenham v Fulham
West Ham v Arsenal

**Nationwide Football League Division 1**
Burnley v Stockport
Crewe v West Brom
Gillingham v Sheff Wed
Millwall v Portsmouth
Norwich v Coventry
Rotherham v Preston
Sheff Utd v Barnsley
Walsall v Grimsby
Watford v Crystal Palace

**Nationwide Football League Division 2**
Blackpool v Cardiff
Brentford v Wrexham
Cambridge Utd v Bristol City
Chesterfield v QPR
Colchester v Peterborough
Northampton v Bournemouth
Notts County v Bury
Oldham v Wigan
Stoke v Wycombe
Swindon v Huddersfield
Tranmere v Port Vale

**Nationwide Football League Division 3**
Bristol Rovers v Hartlepool
Exeter v Kidderminster
Halifax v Shrewsbury
Lincoln City v Torquay
Luton v Rushden & D'monds
Macclesfield v Leyton Orient
Oxford Utd v Mansfield
Plymouth v Darlington
Rochdale v Southend
Scunthorpe v Hull
Swansea v Carlisle
York v Cheltenham

**Nationwide Football Conference**
Boston Utd v Woking
Chester v Southport

Dag & Red v Margate
Dover v Barnet
Farnborough v Forest Green
Hereford v Nuneaton
Leigh RMI v Doncaster
Morecambe v Stalybridge
Scarborough v Northwich
Stevenage v Hayes
Yeovil v Telford

## Sunday, 16 December 2001

**Nationwide Football League Division 1**
Man City v Bradford
Wimbledon v Nottm Forest
Wolverhampton v Birmingham

## Wednesday, 19 December 2001

**Nationwide Football League Division 2**
Stoke v Cardiff

## Friday, 21 December 2001

**Nationwide Football League Division 1**
Portsmouth v Stockport

**Nationwide Football League Division 2**
Brentford v Northampton
Brighton v Chesterfield
Notts County v Swindon
Oldham v Port Vale

**Nationwide Football League Division 3**
Hull v Southend
Mansfield v Exeter
Shrewsbury v Macclesfield

## Saturday, 22 December 2001

**FA Barclaycard Premiership**
Charlton v Blackburn
Chelsea v Bolton
Derby v Aston Villa
Leeds v Newcastle
Leicester v West Ham
Man Utd v Southampton
Middlesbrough v Fulham
Sunderland v Everton
Tottenham v Ipswich

**Nationwide Football League Division 1**
Barnsley v Gillingham
Birmingham v Walsall
Burnley v Millwall
Coventry v Bradford
Crewe v Man City
Crystal Palace v Nottm Forest
Norwich v Wimbledon
Preston v Grimsby
Sheff Utd v Rotherham

Watford v Wolverhampton
West Brom v Sheff Wed

**Nationwide Football League Division 2**
Bournemouth v QPR
Bristol City v Wrexham
Bury v Blackpool
Colchester v Huddersfield
Peterborough v Tranmere
Reading v Wigan
Wycombe v Cambridge Utd

**Nationwide Football League Division 3**
Darlington v Cheltenham
Halifax v Kidderminster
Leyton Orient v Lincoln City
Luton v Hartlepool
Rochdale v York
Rushden & D'monds v Carlisle
Scunthorpe v Plymouth
Swansea v Bristol Rovers
Torquay v Oxford Utd

## Sunday, 23 December 2001

**FA Barclaycard Premiership**
Liverpool v Arsenal

## Wednesday, 26 December 2001

**FA Barclaycard Premiership**
Arsenal v Chelsea
Aston Villa v Liverpool
Blackburn v Sunderland
Bolton v Leeds
Everton v Man Utd
Fulham v Charlton
Ipswich v Leicester
Newcastle v Middlesbrough
Southampton v Tottenham
West Ham v Derby

**Nationwide Football League Division 1**
Bradford v Sheff Utd
Gillingham v Portsmouth
Grimsby v Coventry
Man City v West Brom
Millwall v Crystal Palace
Nottm Forest v Norwich
Rotherham v Burnley
Sheff Wed v Birmingham
Stockport v Barnsley
Walsall v Crewe
Wimbledon v Watford
Wolverhampton v Preston

**Nationwide Football League Division 2**
Blackpool v Oldham
Cambridge Utd v Brentford
Cardiff v Reading

Chesterfield v Wycombe
Huddersfield v Peterborough
Northampton v Colchester
Port Vale v Bristol City
QPR v Brighton
Swindon v Bournemouth
Tranmere v Stoke
Wigan v Bury
Wrexham v Notts County

### Nationwide Football League Division 3
Bristol Rovers v Leyton Orient
Carlisle v Darlington
Cheltenham v Shrewsbury
Exeter v Swansea
Hartlepool v Scunthorpe
Kidderminster v Rochdale
Lincoln City v Mansfield
Macclesfield v Halifax
Oxford Utd v Luton
Plymouth v Torquay
Southend v Rushden & D'monds
York v Hull

### Nationwide Football Conference
Barnet v Stevenage
Doncaster v Scarborough
Forest Green v Yeovil
Hayes v Dag & Red
Margate v Dover
Northwich v Chester
Nuneaton v Boston Utd
Southport v Morecambe
Stalybridge v Leigh RMI
Telford v Hereford
Woking v Farnborough

### Saturday, 29 December 2001

### FA Barclaycard Premiership
Arsenal v Middlesbrough
Aston Villa v Tottenham
Blackburn v Derby
Bolton v Leicester
Everton v Charlton
Fulham v Man Utd
Ipswich v Sunderland
Newcastle v Chelsea
Southampton v Leeds
West Ham v Liverpool

### Nationwide Football League Division 1
Bradford v Crystal Palace
Gillingham v West Brom
Grimsby v Portsmouth
Man City v Burnley
Millwall v Crewe
Nottm Forest v Coventry
Rotherham v Barnsley
Sheff Wed v Norwich

Stockport v Birmingham
Walsall v Watford
Wimbledon v Preston
Wolverhampton v Sheff Utd

### Nationwide Football League Division 2
Blackpool v Brighton
Cambridge Utd v Peterborough
Cardiff v Bristol City
Chesterfield v Notts County
Huddersfield v Stoke
Northampton v Oldham
Port Vale v Colchester
QPR v Wycombe
Swindon v Bury
Tranmere v Brentford
Wigan v Bournemouth
Wrexham v Reading

### Nationwide Football League Division 3
Bristol Rovers v Darlington
Carlisle v Torquay
Cheltenham v Swansea
Exeter v Rochdale
Hartlepool v Leyton Orient
Kidderminster v Hull
Lincoln City v Scunthorpe
Macclesfield v Mansfield
Oxford Utd v Halifax
Plymouth v Rushden & D'monds
Southend v Luton
York v Shrewsbury

### Nationwide Football Conference
Boston Utd v Forest Green
Chester v Hayes
Dag & Red v Telford
Dover v Nuneaton
Farnborough v Southport
Hereford v Stalybridge
Leigh RMI v Margate
Morecambe v Woking
Scarborough v Barnet
Stevenage v Northwich
Yeovil v Doncaster

### Tuesday, 1 January 2002

### FA Barclaycard Premiership
Charlton v Ipswich
Chelsea v Southampton
Leeds v West Ham
Leicester v Arsenal
Liverpool v Bolton
Man Utd v Newcastle
Middlesbrough v Everton
Sunderland v Aston Villa
Tottenham v Blackburn

**Nationwide Football League Division 1**
Barnsley v Grimsby
Birmingham v Nottm Forest
Burnley v Bradford
Coventry v Rotherham
Crewe v Wolverhampton
Crystal Palace v Gillingham
Norwich v Walsall
Portsmouth v Wimbledon
Preston v Sheff Wed
Sheff Utd v Man City
Watford v Millwall
West Brom v Stockport

**Nationwide Football League Division 2**
Bournemouth v Cambridge Utd
Brentford v Cardiff
Brighton v Northampton
Bristol City v QPR
Bury v Wrexham
Colchester v Swindon
Notts County v Wigan
Oldham v Tranmere
Peterborough v Chesterfield
Reading v Port Vale
Stoke v Blackpool
Wycombe v Huddersfield

**Nationwide Football League Division 3**
Darlington v Lincoln City
Halifax v York
Hull v Hartlepool
Leyton Orient v Southend
Luton v Exeter
Mansfield v Kidderminster
Rochdale v Carlisle
Rushden & D'monds v Oxford Utd
Scunthorpe v Macclesfield
Shrewsbury v Bristol Rovers
Swansea v Plymouth
Torquay v Cheltenham

**Nationwide Football Conference**
Boston Utd v Nuneaton
Chester v Northwich
Dag & Red v Hayes
Dover v Margate
Farnborough v Woking
Hereford v Telford
Leigh RMI v Stalybridge
Morecambe v Southport
Scarborough v Doncaster
Stevenage v Barnet
Yeovil v Forest Green

**Wednesday, 2 January 2002**

**FA Barclaycard Premiership**
Derby v Fulham

**Saturday, 5 January 2002**

**Nationwide Football League Division 2**
Bournemouth v Cardiff
Brentford v Chesterfield
Brighton v Tranmere
Bristol City v Wigan
Bury v Huddersfield
Colchester v Wrexham
Notts County v Northampton
Oldham v Swindon
Peterborough v Port Vale
Reading v QPR
Stoke v Cambridge Utd
Wycombe v Blackpool

**Nationwide Football League Division 3**
Darlington v Hartlepool
Halifax v Southend
Hull v Carlisle
Leyton Orient v York
Luton v Bristol Rovers
Mansfield v Cheltenham
Rochdale v Plymouth
Rushden & D'monds v Macclesfield
Scunthorpe v Exeter
Shrewsbury v Oxford Utd
Swansea v Lincoln City
Torquay v Kidderminster

**Nationwide Football Conference**
Barnet v Dag & Red
Doncaster v Boston Utd
Forest Green v Hereford
Hayes v Dover
Margate v Farnborough
Northwich v Morecambe
Nuneaton v Stevenage
Southport v Leigh RMI
Stalybridge v Scarborough
Telford v Chester
Woking v Yeovil

**Saturday, 12 January 2002**

**FA Barclaycard Premiership**
Arsenal v Liverpool
Aston Villa v Derby
Blackburn v Charlton
Bolton v Chelsea
Everton v Sunderland
Fulham v Middlesbrough
Ipswich v Tottenham
Newcastle v Leeds
Southampton v Man Utd
West Ham v Leicester

**Nationwide Football League Division 1**
Bradford v Portsmouth
Gillingham v Sheff Utd

Grimsby v West Brom
Man City v Norwich
Millwall v Birmingham
Nottm Forest v Barnsley
Rotherham v Watford
Sheff Wed v Crewe
Stockport v Crystal Palace
Walsall v Preston
Wimbledon v Burnley
Wolverhampton v Coventry

**Nationwide Football League Division 2**
Blackpool v Bournemouth
Cambridge Utd v Notts County
Cardiff v Peterborough
Chesterfield v Oldham
Huddersfield v Reading
Port Vale v Brentford
QPR v Bury
Swindon v Bristol City
Tranmere v Colchester
Wigan v Brighton
Wrexham v Wycombe

**Nationwide Football League Division 3**
Bristol Rovers v Scunthorpe
Carlisle v Leyton Orient
Cheltenham v Luton
Exeter v Halifax
Hartlepool v Shrewsbury
Kidderminster v Darlington
Lincoln City v Rushden & D'monds
Macclesfield v Rochdale
Oxford Utd v Swansea
Plymouth v Hull
Southend v Mansfield
York v Torquay

**Sunday, 13 January 2002**

**Nationwide Football League Division 2**
Northampton v Stoke

**Saturday, 19 January 2002**

**FA Barclaycard Premiership**
Charlton v Aston Villa
Chelsea v West Ham
Derby v Ipswich
Leeds v Arsenal
Leicester v Newcastle
Liverpool v Southampton
Man Utd v Blackburn
Middlesbrough v Bolton
Sunderland v Fulham
Tottenham v Everton

**Nationwide Football League Division 1**
Barnsley v Bradford
Birmingham v Wimbledon

Burnley v Sheff Wed
Coventry v Stockport
Crewe v Grimsby
Crystal Palace v Rotherham
Norwich v Millwall
Portsmouth v Wolverhampton
Preston v Gillingham
Sheff Utd v Nottm Forest
Watford v Man City
West Brom v Walsall

**Nationwide Football League Division 2**
Bournemouth v Huddersfield
Brentford v Wigan
Brighton v Cambridge Utd
Bristol City v Northampton
Bury v Tranmere
Colchester v Chesterfield
Notts County v Port Vale
Oldham v Wrexham
Peterborough v Swindon
Reading v Blackpool
Stoke v QPR
Wycombe v Cardiff

**Nationwide Football League Division 3**
Darlington v Southend
Halifax v Lincoln City
Hull v Exeter
Leyton Orient v Cheltenham
Luton v Carlisle
Mansfield v Hartlepool
Rochdale v Oxford Utd
Rushden & D'monds v York
Scunthorpe v Kidderminster
Shrewsbury v Plymouth
Swansea v Macclesfield
Torquay v Bristol Rovers

**Nationwide Football Conference**
Boston Utd v Northwich
Chester v Barnet
Dag & Red v Forest Green
Dover v Doncaster
Farnborough v Stalybridge
Hereford v Margate
Leigh RMI v Telford
Morecambe v Hayes
Scarborough v Woking
Stevenage v Southport
Yeovil v Nuneaton

**Wednesday, 23 January 2002**

**Nationwide Football League Division 2**
Blackpool v Bury
Cambridge Utd v Wycombe
Cardiff v Stoke
Chesterfield v Brighton
Huddersfield v Colchester

Northampton v Brentford
Port Vale v Oldham
QPR v Bournemouth
Swindon v Notts County
Tranmere v Peterborough
Wigan v Reading
Wrexham v Bristol City

**Nationwide Football League Division 3**
Bristol Rovers v Swansea
Carlisle v Rushden & D'monds
Cheltenham v Darlington
Exeter v Mansfield
Hartlepool v Luton
Kidderminster v Halifax
Lincoln City v Leyton Orient
Macclesfield v Shrewsbury
Oxford Utd v Torquay
Plymouth v Scunthorpe
Southend v Hull
York v Rochdale

**Friday, 25 January 2002**

**Nationwide Football Conference**
Doncaster v Stevenage

**Saturday, 26 January 2002**

**Nationwide Football League Division 2**
Blackpool v Tranmere
Brentford v Brighton
Cambridge Utd v Port Vale
Cardiff v Bury
Chesterfield v Bristol City
Huddersfield v QPR
Northampton v Peterborough
Oldham v Bournemouth
Reading v Colchester
Stoke v Wigan
Wrexham v Swindon
Wycombe v Notts County

**Nationwide Football League Division 3**
Bristol Rovers v Carlisle
Darlington v Luton
Exeter v York
Hartlepool v Rushden & D'monds
Hull v Shrewsbury
Kidderminster v Macclesfield
Leyton Orient v Mansfield
Lincoln City v Cheltenham
Plymouth v Oxford Utd
Rochdale v Swansea
Scunthorpe v Halifax
Southend v Torquay

**Nationwide Football Conference**
Barnet v Farnborough
Forest Green v Dover

Hayes v Yeovil
Margate v Scarborough
Northwich v Leigh RMI
Nuneaton v Chester
Southport v Hereford
Stalybridge v Boston Utd
Telford v Morecambe
Woking v Dag & Red

**Tuesday, 29 January 2002**

**FA Barclaycard Premiership**
Bolton v Man Utd
Charlton v Derby
Ipswich v Fulham
Sunderland v Middlesbrough

**Nationwide Football League Division 1**
Barnsley v Wolverhampton
Bradford v Preston
Crewe v Norwich
Crystal Palace v Coventry
Gillingham v Stockport
Rotherham v Grimsby
Sheff Utd v Sheff Wed
Walsall v Wimbledon
Watford v Burnley
West Brom v Birmingham

**Wednesday, 30 January 2002**

**FA Barclaycard Premiership**
Aston Villa v Everton
Blackburn v Arsenal
Chelsea v Leeds
Liverpool v Leicester
Southampton v West Ham
Tottenham v Newcastle

**Nationwide Football League Division 1**
Man City v Millwall
Nottm Forest v Portsmouth

**Friday, 1 February 2002**

**Nationwide Football League Division 3**
Cheltenham v Southend

**Saturday, 2 February 2002**

**FA Barclaycard Premiership**
Arsenal v Southampton
Derby v Tottenham
Everton v Ipswich
Fulham v Aston Villa
Leeds v Liverpool
Leicester v Chelsea
Man Utd v Sunderland
Middlesbrough v Charlton
Newcastle v Bolton
West Ham v Blackburn

**Nationwide Football League Division 1**
Birmingham v Crewe
Burnley v West Brom
Coventry v Gillingham
Grimsby v Bradford
Millwall v Walsall
Norwich v Sheff Utd
Portsmouth v Barnsley
Preston v Watford
Sheff Wed v Crystal Palace
Stockport v Nottm Forest
Wimbledon v Man City
Wolverhampton v Rotherham

**Nationwide Football League Division 2**
Bournemouth v Stoke
Brighton v Cardiff
Bristol City v Huddersfield
Bury v Reading
Colchester v Brentford
Notts County v Oldham
Peterborough v Wrexham
Port Vale v Wycombe
QPR v Cambridge Utd
Swindon v Northampton
Tranmere v Chesterfield
Wigan v Blackpool

**Nationwide Football League Division 3**
Carlisle v Hartlepool
Halifax v Hull
Luton v Plymouth
Macclesfield v Exeter
Mansfield v Rochdale
Oxford Utd v Bristol Rovers
Rushden & D'monds v Darlington
Shrewsbury v Scunthorpe
Swansea v Kidderminster
Torquay v Leyton Orient
York v Lincoln City

**Nationwide Football Conference**
Boston Utd v Telford
Chester v Scarborough
Doncaster v Northwich
Dover v Woking
Farnborough v Hereford
Hayes v Margate
Leigh RMI v Morecambe
Southport v Nuneaton
Stalybridge v Forest Green
Stevenage v Dag & Red
Yeovil v Barnet

**Saturday, 9 February 2002**

**FA Barclaycard Premiership**
Aston Villa v Chelsea
Bolton v West Ham
Charlton v Man Utd

Derby v Sunderland
Everton v Arsenal
Fulham v Blackburn
Ipswich v Liverpool
Middlesbrough v Leeds
Newcastle v Southampton
Tottenham v Leicester

**Nationwide Football League Division 1**
Barnsley v Burnley
Bradford v Birmingham
Crewe v Coventry
Crystal Palace v Wolverhampton
Gillingham v Wimbledon
Man City v Preston
Nottm Forest v Millwall
Rotherham v Stockport
Sheff Utd v Portsmouth
Walsall v Sheff Wed
Watford v Grimsby
West Brom v Norwich

**Nationwide Football League Division 2**
Blackpool v Peterborough
Brentford v Bournemouth
Cambridge Utd v Colchester
Cardiff v Swindon
Chesterfield v Bury
Huddersfield v Tranmere
Northampton v QPR
Oldham v Brighton
Reading v Notts County
Stoke v Port Vale
Wrexham v Wigan
Wycombe v Bristol City

**Nationwide Football League Division 3**
Bristol Rovers v Halifax
Darlington v Shrewsbury
Exeter v Cheltenham
Hartlepool v Torquay
Hull v Rushden & D'monds
Kidderminster v Carlisle
Leyton Orient v Swansea
Lincoln City v Macclesfield
Plymouth v Mansfield
Rochdale v Luton
Scunthorpe v Oxford Utd
Southend v York

**Nationwide Football Conference**
Barnet v Stalybridge
Dag & Red v Farnborough
Forest Green v Doncaster
Hereford v Leigh RMI
Margate v Chester
Morecambe v Yeovil
Northwich v Dover
Nuneaton v Hayes

Scarborough v Boston Utd
Telford v Southport
Woking v Stevenage

**Friday, 15 February 2002**

**Nationwide Football League Division 3**
Swansea v Southend

**Saturday, 16 February 2002**

**Nationwide Football League Division 1**
Birmingham v Barnsley
Burnley v Nottm Forest
Coventry v Walsall
Grimsby v Sheff Utd
Millwall v West Brom
Norwich v Gillingham
Portsmouth v Rotherham
Preston v Crewe
Sheff Wed v Watford
Stockport v Man City
Wimbledon v Crystal Palace
Wolverhampton v Bradford

**Nationwide Football League Division 2**
Bournemouth v Wycombe
Brighton v Huddersfield
Bristol City v Oldham
Bury v Cambridge Utd
Colchester v Blackpool
Notts County v Stoke
Peterborough v Brentford
Port Vale v Chesterfield
QPR v Wrexham
Swindon v Reading
Tranmere v Northampton
Wigan v Cardiff

**Nationwide Football League Division 3**
Carlisle v Exeter
Cheltenham v Kidderminster
Halifax v Plymouth
Luton v Scunthorpe
Macclesfield v Bristol Rovers
Mansfield v Darlington
Oxford Utd v Lincoln City
Rushden & D'monds v Rochdale
Shrewsbury v Leyton Orient
Torquay v Hull
York v Hartlepool

**Nationwide Football Conference**
Boston Utd v Hereford
Chester v Morecambe
Doncaster v Margate
Dover v Scarborough
Farnborough v Telford
Hayes v Northwich
Leigh RMI v Barnet

Southport v Woking
Stalybridge v Nuneaton
Stevenage v Forest Green
Yeovil v Dag & Red

**Friday, 22 February 2002**

**Nationwide Football League Division 2**
Tranmere v Swindon

**Nationwide Football League Division 3**
Hull v Macclesfield

**Saturday, 23 February 2002**

**FA Barclaycard Premiership**
Arsenal v Fulham
Blackburn v Ipswich
Chelsea v Tottenham
Leeds v Charlton
Leicester v Derby
Liverpool v Everton
Man Utd v Aston Villa
Southampton v Bolton
Sunderland v Newcastle
West Ham v Middlesbrough

**Nationwide Football League Division 1**
Birmingham v Watford
Coventry v Barnsley
Crewe v Burnley
Crystal Palace v Sheff Utd
Gillingham v Bradford
Millwall v Wimbledon
Norwich v Preston
Nottm Forest v Grimsby
Sheff Wed v Rotherham
Stockport v Wolverhampton
Walsall v Man City
West Brom v Portsmouth

**Nationwide Football League Division 2**
Blackpool v Huddersfield
Brentford v Notts County
Brighton v Wrexham
Bury v Bournemouth
Cardiff v Cambridge Utd
Chesterfield v Northampton
Colchester v Bristol City
Peterborough v Oldham
Port Vale v QPR
Reading v Stoke
Wigan v Wycombe

**Nationwide Football League Division 3**
Bristol Rovers v Lincoln City
Carlisle v Cheltenham
Darlington v Torquay
Halifax v Swansea
Hartlepool v Southend

Luton v York
Oxford Utd v Exeter
Plymouth v Kidderminster
Rushden & D'monds v Leyton Orient
Scunthorpe v Rochdale
Shrewsbury v Mansfield

**Nationwide Football Conference**
Barnet v Doncaster
Dag & Red v Dover
Forest Green v Leigh RMI
Hereford v Chester
Margate v Yeovil
Morecambe v Boston Utd
Northwich v Stalybridge
Nuneaton v Farnborough
Scarborough v Southport
Telford v Stevenage
Woking v Hayes

**Tuesday, 26 February 2002**

**Nationwide Football League Division 1**
Barnsley v Crystal Palace
Bradford v Nottm Forest
Burnley v Birmingham
Grimsby v Stockport
Portsmouth v Coventry
Preston v West Brom
Rotherham v Gillingham
Sheff Utd v Millwall
Watford v Norwich
Wimbledon v Crewe
Wolverhampton v Walsall

**Nationwide Football League Division 2**
Bournemouth v Brighton
Bristol City v Peterborough
Cambridge Utd v Blackpool
Huddersfield v Cardiff
Northampton v Port Vale
Notts County v Colchester
Oldham v Brentford
QPR v Wigan
Swindon v Chesterfield
Wrexham v Tranmere
Wycombe v Reading

**Nationwide Football League Division 3**
Cheltenham v Hartlepool
Kidderminster v Shrewsbury
Leyton Orient v Darlington
Lincoln City v Luton
Macclesfield v Oxford Utd
Mansfield v Halifax
Plymouth v Exeter
Rochdale v Hull
Southend v Bristol Rovers
Swansea v Scunthorpe
Torquay v Rushden & D'monds

York v Carlisle

**Wednesday, 27 February 2002**

**Nationwide Football League Division 1**
Man City v Sheff Wed

**Nationwide Football League Division 2**
Stoke v Bury

**Friday, 1 March 2002**

**Nationwide Football League Division 3**
Swansea v Hull

**Saturday, 2 March 2002**

**FA Barclaycard Premiership**
Aston Villa v West Ham
Bolton v Blackburn
Charlton v Chelsea
Derby v Man Utd
Everton v Leeds
Fulham v Liverpool
Ipswich v Southampton
Middlesbrough v Leicester
Newcastle v Arsenal
Tottenham v Sunderland

**Nationwide Football League Division 1**
Barnsley v Millwall
Bradford v Sheff Wed
Burnley v Norwich
Grimsby v Crystal Palace
Man City v Coventry
Portsmouth v Walsall
Preston v Birmingham
Rotherham v Nottm Forest
Sheff Utd v Stockport
Watford v Crewe
Wimbledon v West Brom
Wolverhampton v Gillingham

**Nationwide Football League Division 2**
Bournemouth v Peterborough
Bristol City v Brentford
Cambridge Utd v Reading
Huddersfield v Wigan
Northampton v Cardiff
Notts County v Tranmere
Oldham v Colchester
QPR v Blackpool
Stoke v Brighton
Swindon v Port Vale
Wrexham v Chesterfield
Wycombe v Bury

**Nationwide Football League Division 3**
Cheltenham v Rushden & D'monds
Exeter v Darlington

Kidderminster v Hartlepool
Leyton Orient v Halifax
Lincoln City v Carlisle
Macclesfield v Plymouth
Mansfield v Scunthorpe
Rochdale v Shrewsbury
Southend v Oxford Utd
Torquay v Luton
York v Bristol Rovers

**Nationwide Football Conference**
Chester v Leigh RMI
Dag & Red v Boston Utd
Dover v Farnborough
Hayes v Barnet
Morecambe v Scarborough
Nuneaton v Doncaster
Southport v Stalybridge
Stevenage v Margate
Telford v Northwich
Woking v Forest Green
Yeovil v Hereford

**Tuesday, 5 March 2002**

**FA Barclaycard Premiership**
Arsenal v Derby
Leeds v Ipswich
Sunderland v Bolton

**Nationwide Football League Division 1**
Birmingham v Man City
Crewe v Barnsley
Crystal Palace v Portsmouth
Gillingham v Grimsby
Millwall v Preston
Norwich v Rotherham
Stockport v Bradford
Walsall v Burnley
West Brom v Watford

**Nationwide Football League Division 2**
Blackpool v Northampton
Brentford v Swindon
Brighton v Wycombe
Bury v Oldham
Cardiff v QPR
Chesterfield v Huddersfield
Colchester v Stoke
Peterborough v Notts County
Port Vale v Wrexham
Reading v Bournemouth
Tranmere v Bristol City
Wigan v Cambridge Utd

**Nationwide Football League Division 3**
Bristol Rovers v Cheltenham
Carlisle v Southend
Darlington v Macclesfield
Halifax v Rochdale

Hartlepool v Lincoln City
Hull v Mansfield
Luton v Leyton Orient
Oxford Utd v Kidderminster
Plymouth v York
Rushden & D'monds v Exeter
Scunthorpe v Torquay
Shrewsbury v Swansea

**Wednesday, 6 March 2002**

**FA Barclaycard Premiership**
Blackburn v Aston Villa
Chelsea v Fulham
Leicester v Charlton
Liverpool v Newcastle
Man Utd v Tottenham
Southampton v Middlesbrough
West Ham v Everton

**Nationwide Football League Division 1**
Coventry v Sheff Utd
Nottm Forest v Wolverhampton
Sheff Wed v Wimbledon

**Saturday, 9 March 2002**

**Nationwide Football League Division 1**
Barnsley v Sheff Utd
Birmingham v Wolverhampton
Bradford v Man City
Coventry v Norwich
Crystal Palace v Watford
Grimsby v Walsall
Nottm Forest v Wimbledon
Portsmouth v Millwall
Preston v Rotherham
Sheff Wed v Gillingham
Stockport v Burnley
West Brom v Crewe

**Nationwide Football League Division 2**
Bournemouth v Northampton
Bristol City v Cambridge Utd
Bury v Notts County
Cardiff v Blackpool
Huddersfield v Swindon
Peterborough v Colchester
Port Vale v Tranmere
QPR v Chesterfield
Reading v Brighton
Wigan v Oldham
Wrexham v Brentford
Wycombe v Stoke

**Nationwide Football League Division 3**
Carlisle v Swansea
Cheltenham v York
Darlington v Plymouth
Hartlepool v Bristol Rovers

Hull v Scunthorpe
Kidderminster v Exeter
Leyton Orient v Macclesfield
Mansfield v Oxford Utd
Rushden & D'monds v Luton
Shrewsbury v Halifax
Southend v Rochdale
Torquay v Lincoln City

**Nationwide Football Conference**
Barnet v Morecambe
Boston Utd v Dover
Doncaster v Telford
Farnborough v Yeovil
Forest Green v Hayes
Hereford v Dag & Red
Leigh RMI v Nuneaton
Margate v Woking
Northwich v Southport
Scarborough v Stevenage
Stalybridge v Chester

**Saturday, 16 March 2002**

**FA Barclaycard Premiership**
Aston Villa v Arsenal
Bolton v Derby
Chelsea v Sunderland
Everton v Fulham
Leeds v Blackburn
Middlesbrough v Liverpool
Newcastle v Ipswich
Southampton v Leicester
Tottenham v Charlton
West Ham v Man Utd

**Nationwide Football League Division 1**
Burnley v Preston
Crewe v Portsmouth
Gillingham v Nottm Forest
Man City v Crystal Palace
Millwall v Sheff Wed
Norwich v Birmingham
Rotherham v Bradford
Sheff Utd v West Brom
Walsall v Barnsley
Watford v Coventry
Wimbledon v Stockport
Wolverhampton v Grimsby

**Nationwide Football League Division 2**
Blackpool v Port Vale
Brentford v Wycombe
Brighton v Bury
Cambridge Utd v Huddersfield
Chesterfield v Reading
Colchester v QPR
Northampton v Wrexham
Notts County v Bristol City
Oldham v Cardiff

Stoke v Peterborough
Swindon v Wigan
Tranmere v Bournemouth

**Nationwide Football League Division 3**
Bristol Rovers v Rushden & D'monds
Exeter v Shrewsbury
Halifax v Cheltenham
Lincoln City v Southend
Luton v Kidderminster
Macclesfield v Torquay
Oxford Utd v Hull
Plymouth v Leyton Orient
Rochdale v Hartlepool
Scunthorpe v Carlisle
Swansea v Mansfield
York v Darlington

**Nationwide Football Conference**
Chester v Farnborough
Dag & Red v Stalybridge
Dover v Hereford
Hayes v Scarborough
Morecambe v Forest Green
Nuneaton v Northwich
Southport v Barnet
Stevenage v Leigh RMI
Telford v Margate
Woking v Doncaster
Yeovil v Boston Utd

**Friday, 22 March 2002**

**Nationwide Football League Division 2**
Cardiff v Wrexham

**Nationwide Football League Division 3**
Hartlepool v Macclesfield

**Nationwide Football Conference**
Doncaster v Hayes

**Saturday, 23 March 2002**

**FA Barclaycard Premiership**
Arsenal v West Ham
Blackburn v Newcastle
Charlton v Bolton
Derby v Everton
Fulham v Tottenham
Ipswich v Aston Villa
Leicester v Leeds
Liverpool v Chelsea
Man Utd v Middlesbrough
Sunderland v Southampton

**Nationwide Football League Division 1**
Barnsley v Watford
Bradford v Crewe
Coventry v Birmingham

Crystal Palace v Walsall
Gillingham v Millwall
Grimsby v Wimbledon
Nottm Forest v West Brom
Portsmouth v Sheff Wed
Rotherham v Man City
Sheff Utd v Burnley
Stockport v Preston
Wolverhampton v Norwich

**Nationwide Football League Division 2**
Blackpool v Brentford
Bournemouth v Bristol City
Brighton v Notts County
Bury v Port Vale
Cambridge Utd v Swindon
Huddersfield v Northampton
QPR v Peterborough
Reading v Oldham
Stoke v Chesterfield
Wigan v Tranmere
Wycombe v Colchester

**Nationwide Football League Division 3**
Bristol Rovers v Exeter
Carlisle v Oxford Utd
Cheltenham v Rochdale
Darlington v Swansea
Leyton Orient v Hull
Lincoln City v Plymouth
Luton v Halifax
Rushden & D'monds v Shrewsbury
Southend v Scunthorpe
Torquay v Mansfield
York v Kidderminster

**Nationwide Football Conference**
Barnet v Telford
Boston Utd v Chester
Farnborough v Stevenage
Forest Green v Nuneaton
Hereford v Morecambe
Leigh RMI v Dag & Red
Margate v Southport
Northwich v Woking
Scarborough v Yeovil
Stalybridge v Dover

**Friday, 29 March 2002**

**Nationwide Football League Division 1**
Watford v Bradford

**Nationwide Football League Division 2**
Northampton v Bury

**Nationwide Football League Division 3**
Halifax v Carlisle

**Saturday, 30 March 2002**

**FA Barclaycard Premiership**
Arsenal v Sunderland
Bolton v Aston Villa
Chelsea v Derby
Leeds v Man Utd
Leicester v Blackburn
Liverpool v Charlton
Middlesbrough v Tottenham
Newcastle v Everton
Southampton v Fulham
West Ham v Ipswich

**Nationwide Football League Division 1**
Birmingham v Grimsby
Burnley v Wolverhampton
Crewe v Sheff Utd
Man City v Nottm Forest
Millwall v Stockport
Norwich v Crystal Palace
Preston v Portsmouth
Sheff Wed v Coventry
Walsall v Gillingham
Watford v Bradford
West Brom v Barnsley
Wimbledon v Rotherham

**Nationwide Football League Division 2**
Brentford v Stoke
Bristol City v Reading
Chesterfield v Cardiff
Colchester v Brighton
Notts County v Bournemouth
Oldham v Cambridge Utd
Peterborough v Wycombe
Port Vale v Wigan
Swindon v Blackpool
Tranmere v QPR
Wrexham v Huddersfield

**Nationwide Football League Division 3**
Exeter v Lincoln City
Halifax v Carlisle
Hull v Darlington
Kidderminster v Southend
Macclesfield v York
Mansfield v Rushden & D'monds
Oxford Utd v Hartlepool
Plymouth v Bristol Rovers
Rochdale v Leyton Orient
Scunthorpe v Cheltenham
Shrewsbury v Torquay
Swansea v Luton

**Nationwide Football Conference**
Boston Utd v Barnet
Doncaster v Chester
Dover v Southport
Forest Green v Telford

Hayes v Farnborough
Morecambe v Stevenage
Northwich v Margate
Nuneaton v Dag & Red
Scarborough v Hereford
Woking v Leigh RMI
Yeovil v Stalybridge

## Monday, 1 April 2002

**FA Barclaycard Premiership**
Blackburn v Southampton
Charlton v Arsenal
Derby v Middlesbrough
Everton v Bolton
Fulham v West Ham
Ipswich v Chelsea
Man Utd v Liverpool
Sunderland v Leicester
Tottenham v Leeds

**Nationwide Football League Division 1**
Barnsley v Preston
Bradford v Norwich
Coventry v West Brom
Crystal Palace v Birmingham
Gillingham v Crewe
Grimsby v Sheff Wed
Nottm Forest v Walsall
Portsmouth v Burnley
Rotherham v Millwall
Sheff Utd v Wimbledon
Stockport v Watford
Wolverhampton v Man City

**Nationwide Football League Division 2**
Blackpool v Wrexham
Bournemouth v Colchester
Brighton v Bristol City
Bury v Brentford
Cardiff v Port Vale
Huddersfield v Oldham
QPR v Notts County
Reading v Northampton
Stoke v Swindon
Wigan v Peterborough
Wycombe v Tranmere

**Nationwide Football League Division 3**
Bristol Rovers v Kidderminster
Carlisle v Macclesfield
Cheltenham v Hull
Darlington v Halifax
Hartlepool v Plymouth
Leyton Orient v Scunthorpe
Lincoln City v Shrewsbury
Luton v Mansfield
Rushden & D'monds v Swansea
Southend v Exeter
Torquay v Rochdale

York v Oxford Utd

**Nationwide Football Conference**
Barnet v Nuneaton
Chester v Yeovil
Dag & Red v Morecambe
Farnborough v Northwich
Hereford v Woking
Leigh RMI v Scarborough
Margate v Forest Green
Southport v Boston Utd
Stalybridge v Doncaster
Stevenage v Dover
Telford v Hayes

## Tuesday, 2 April 2002

**FA Barclaycard Premiership**
Aston Villa v Newcastle

**Nationwide Football League Division 2**
Bournemouth v Colchester
Cambridge Utd v Chesterfield

## Saturday, 6 April 2002

**FA Barclaycard Premiership**
Arsenal v Tottenham
Bolton v Ipswich
Chelsea v Everton
Leeds v Sunderland
Leicester v Man Utd
Middlesbrough v Aston Villa
Newcastle v Fulham
Southampton v Derby
West Ham v Charlton

**Nationwide Football League Division 1**
Birmingham v Portsmouth
Burnley v Gillingham
Crewe v Crystal Palace
Man City v Barnsley
Millwall v Wolverhampton
Norwich v Grimsby
Preston v Coventry
Sheff Wed v Nottm Forest
Walsall v Stockport
Watford v Sheff Utd
West Brom v Rotherham
Wimbledon v Bradford

**Nationwide Football League Division 2**
Brentford v Huddersfield
Bristol City v Bury
Chesterfield v Wigan
Colchester v Cardiff
Northampton v Wycombe
Notts County v Blackpool
Oldham v Stoke
Peterborough v Brighton

Port Vale v Bournemouth
Swindon v QPR
Wrexham v Cambridge Utd

**Nationwide Football League Division 3**
Exeter v Torquay
Halifax v Hartlepool
Hull v Luton
Kidderminster v Lincoln City
Macclesfield v Cheltenham
Mansfield v Bristol Rovers
Oxford Utd v Leyton Orient
Plymouth v Southend
Rochdale v Darlington
Scunthorpe v Rushden & D'monds
Shrewsbury v Carlisle
Swansea v York

**Nationwide Football Conference**
Boston Utd v Stevenage
Doncaster v Hereford
Dover v Leigh RMI
Forest Green v Chester
Hayes v Stalybridge
Morecambe v Farnborough
Northwich v Dag & Red
Nuneaton v Margate
Scarborough v Telford
Woking v Barnet
Yeovil v Southport

**Sunday, 7 April 2002**

**FA Barclaycard Premiership**
Liverpool v Blackburn

**Nationwide Football League Division 2**
Tranmere v Reading

**Saturday, 13 April 2002**

**FA Barclaycard Premiership**
Aston Villa v Leeds
Blackburn v Chelsea
Charlton v Southampton
Derby v Newcastle
Everton v Leicester
Fulham v Bolton
Ipswich v Middlesbrough
Man Utd v Arsenal
Sunderland v Liverpool
Tottenham v West Ham

**Nationwide Football League Division 1**
Barnsley v Norwich
Bradford v West Brom
Coventry v Millwall
Crystal Palace v Preston
Gillingham v Man City
Grimsby v Burnley
Nottm Forest v Crewe

Portsmouth v Watford
Rotherham v Birmingham
Sheff Utd v Walsall
Stockport v Sheff Wed
Wolverhampton v Wimbledon

**Nationwide Football League Division 2**
Blackpool v Bristol City
Bournemouth v Chesterfield
Brighton v Swindon
Bury v Colchester
Cambridge Utd v Tranmere
Cardiff v Notts County
Huddersfield v Port Vale
QPR v Brentford
Reading v Peterborough
Stoke v Wrexham
Wigan v Northampton
Wycombe v Oldham

**Nationwide Football League Division 3**
Bristol Rovers v Hull
Carlisle v Plymouth
Cheltenham v Oxford Utd
Darlington v Scunthorpe
Hartlepool v Swansea
Leyton Orient v Exeter
Lincoln City v Rochdale
Luton v Macclesfield
Rushden & D'monds v Kidderminster
Southend v Shrewsbury
Torquay v Halifax
York v Mansfield

**Nationwide Football Conference**
Barnet v Forest Green
Chester v Dover
Dag & Red v Doncaster
Farnborough v Scarborough
Hereford v Northwich
Leigh RMI v Boston Utd
Margate v Morecambe
Southport v Hayes
Stalybridge v Woking
Stevenage v Yeovil
Telford v Nuneaton

**Saturday, 20 April 2002**

**FA Barclaycard Premiership**
Arsenal v Ipswich
Bolton v Tottenham
Chelsea v Man Utd
Leeds v Fulham
Leicester v Aston Villa
Liverpool v Derby
Middlesbrough v Blackburn
Newcastle v Charlton
Southampton v Everton
West Ham v Sunderland

**Nationwide Football League Division 2**
Brentford v Reading
Bristol City v Stoke
Chesterfield v Blackpool
Colchester v Wigan
Northampton v Cambridge Utd
Notts County v Huddersfield
Oldham v QPR
Peterborough v Bury
Port Vale v Brighton
Swindon v Wycombe
Tranmere v Cardiff
Wrexham v Bournemouth

**Nationwide Football League Division 3**
Exeter v Hartlepool
Halifax v Rushden & D'monds
Hull v Lincoln City
Kidderminster v Leyton Orient
Macclesfield v Southend
Mansfield v Carlisle
Oxford Utd v Darlington
Plymouth v Cheltenham
Rochdale v Bristol Rovers
Scunthorpe v York
Shrewsbury v Luton
Swansea v Torquay

**Nationwide Football Conference**
Barnet v Margate
Boston Utd v Farnborough
Chester v Stevenage
Doncaster v Southport
Dover v Morecambe
Forest Green v Northwich
Hereford v Hayes
Leigh RMI v Yeovil
Scarborough v Dag & Red
Stalybridge v Telford
Woking v Nuneaton

**Sunday, 21 April 2002**

**Nationwide Football League Division 1**
Birmingham v Sheff Utd
Burnley v Coventry
Crewe v Rotherham
Man City v Portsmouth
Millwall v Grimsby

Norwich v Stockport
Preston v Nottm Forest
Sheff Wed v Wolverhampton
Walsall v Bradford
Watford v Gillingham
West Brom v Crystal Palace
Wimbledon v Barnsley

**Saturday, 27 April 2002**

**FA Barclaycard Premiership**
Aston Villa v Southampton
Bolton v Arsenal
Charlton v Sunderland
Derby v Leeds
Everton v Blackburn
Fulham v Leicester
Ipswich v Man Utd
Middlesbrough v Chelsea
Newcastle v West Ham
Tottenham v Liverpool

**Nationwide Football Conference**
Dag & Red v Chester
Farnborough v Leigh RMI
Hayes v Boston Utd
Margate v Stalybridge
Morecambe v Doncaster
Northwich v Barnet
Nuneaton v Scarborough
Southport v Forest Green
Stevenage v Hereford
Telford v Woking
Yeovil v Dover

**Saturday, 11 May 2002**

**FA Barclaycard Premiership**
Arsenal v Everton
Blackburn v Fulham
Chelsea v Aston Villa
Leeds v Middlesbrough
Leicester v Tottenham
Liverpool v Ipswich
Man Utd v Charlton
Southampton v Newcastle
Sunderland v Derby
West Ham v Bolton

# OTHER FIXTURES — SEASON 2001–2002

**July 2001**

1 Sun   UEFA Intertoto Cup 2 (1)
9/10 Sat/Sun  UEFA Intertoto Cup 2 (2)
14/15 Sat/Sun  UEFA Intertoto Cup 3 (1)
21 Sat   UEFA Intertoto Cup 3 (2)
25 Wed   UEFA Intertoto Cup SF (1)
         UEFA Women's U18 Championship Final Round commences

**August 2001**

1 Wed   UEFA Intertoto Cup SF (2)
7 Tue   UEFA Intertoto Cup Final (1)
7/8 Tue/Wed  UEFA Champions League 3Q (1)
11 Sat   Football League commences
12 Sun   F.A. Charity Shield
14 Tue   U21 Friendly International – venue & ko tbc
15 Wed   Friendly International – England v Netherlands (at Tottenham Hotspur FC)
18 Sat   Premier League commences
         Football Conference commences
21 Tue   UEFA Intertoto Cup Final (2)
21/22 Tue/Wed  UEFA Champions League 3Q (2)
22 Wed   Worthington Cup 1
24 Fri   UEFA Super Cup
25 Sat   F.A. Cup sponsored by AXA EP
31 Fri   UEFA U21 Qualifier – Germany v England venue & ko tbc

**September 2001**

1 Sat   FIFA World Cup Qualifier – Germany v England (at Bayern Munich FC)
         F.A. Cup sponsored by AXA P
         AXA F.A. Youth Cup 1Q*

4 Tue   UEFA U21 Qualifier – England v Albania venue & ko tbc
5 Wed   FIFA World Cup Qualifier – (at Newcastle United FC) England v Albania
8 Sat   F.A. Carlsberg Vase 1Q
9 Sun   AXA F.A. Women's Cup 1Q
11/12 Tue/Wed  UEFA Champions League – Group Stage 1 – Match Day 1
         Worthington Cup 2
13 Thu   UEFA Cup 1 (1)
14 Fri   World U17 Championship commences – Trinidad & Tobago
15 Sat   F.A. Cup sponsored by AXA 1Q
18/19 Tue/Wed  UEFA Champions League – Group Stage 1 – Match Day 2
22 Sat   F.A. Carlsberg Vase 2Q
         AXA F.A. Youth Cup 2Q*
25/26 Tue/Wed  UEFA Champions League – Group Stage 1 – Match Day 3
27 Thu   UEFA Cup 1 (2)
29 Sat   F.A. Cup sponsored by AXA 2Q
30 Sun   World U17 Championship ends
         AXA F.A. Women's Cup 2Q

**October 2001**

5 Fri   UEFA U21 Qualifier – England v Greece venue & ko tbc
6 Sat   FIFA World Cup Qualifier – England v Greece (at Manchester United FC)
         AXA F.A. Youth Cup 3Q*
         F.A. County Youth Cup 1*
7 Sun   F.A. Umbro Sunday Cup 1
10 Wed   Worthington Cup 3
13 Sat   F.A. Cup sponsored by AXA 3Q

| 16/17 Tue/Wed | UEFA Champions League – Group Stage 1 – Match Day 4 |
| 18 Thu | UEFA CUP 2 (1) |
| 20 Sat | F.A. Carlsberg Vase 1P |
| 23/24 Tue/Wed | UEFA Champions League – Group Stage 1 – Match Day 5 |
| 27 Sat | F.A. Cup sponsored by AXA 4Q |
| | AXA F.A. Youth Cup 1P* |
| 28 Sun | AXA F.A. Women's Cup 3Q |
| 30/31 Tue/Wed | UEFA Champions League – Group Stage 1 – Match Day 6 |

## November 2001

| 1 Thu | UEFA Cup 2 (2) |
| 3 Sat | F.A. Umbro Trophy 1 |
| 4 Sun | F.A. Umbro Sunday Cup 2 |
| 10 Sat | F.A. Carlsberg Vase 2P |
| | AXA F.A. Youth Cup 2P* |
| | F.A. County Youth Cup 2* |
| 11 Sun | AXA F.A. Women's Cup 1P |
| 17 Sat | F.A. Cup sponsored by AXA 1P |
| 20/21 Tue/Wed | UEFA Champions League – Group Stage 2 – Match Day 7 |
| 22 Thu | UEFA Cup 3 (1) |
| 27 Tue | EU/SA Cup |
| 28 Wed | Worthington Cup 4 |

## December 2001

| 1 Sat | F.A. Umbro Trophy 2 |
| 2 Sun | F.A. Umbro Sunday Cup 3 |
| 4/5 Tue/Wed | UEFA Champions League – Group Stage 2 – Match Day 8 |
| 6 Thu | UEFA Cup 3 (2) |
| 8 Sat | F.A. Cup sponsored by AXA 2P |
| | F.A. Carlsberg Vase 3P |
| | AXA F.A. Youth Cup 3P* |
| 9 Sun | AXA F.A. Women's Cup 2P |
| 12 Wed | Worthington Cup 5 |
| 15 Sat | F.A. County Youth Cup 3* |
| 24 Mon | Christmas Eve |
| 25 Tue | Christmas Day |

| 26 Wed | Boxing Day |

## January 2002

| 1 Tue | New Year's Day |
| 5 Sat | F.A. Cup sponsored by AXA 3P |
| 6 Sun | AXA F.A. Women's Cup 3P |
| 9 Wed | Worthington Cup SF (1) |
| 12 Sat | F.A. Umbro Trophy 3 |
| 13 Sun | F.A. Umbro Sunday Cup 4 |
| 19 Sat | F.A. Carlsberg Vase 4P |
| | AXA F.A. Youth Cup 4P* |
| 23 Wed | Worthington Cup SF (2) |
| 26 Sat | F.A. Cup sponsored by AXA 4P |
| 27 Sun | AXA F.A. Women's Cup 4P |

## February 2002

| 2 Sat | F.A. Umbro Trophy 4 |
| 3 Sun | F.A. County Youth Cup 4* |
| 9 Sat | F.A. Umbro Sunday Cup 5 |
| 10 Sun | F.A. Carlsberg Vase 5P |
| 12/13 Tue/Wed | International Friendly dates |
| 16 Sat | F.A. Cup sponsored by AXA 5P |
| | AXA F.A. Youth Cup 5P* |
| 19/20 Tue/Wed | UEFA Champions League – Group Stage 2 – Match Day 9 |
| 21 Thu | UEFA Cup 4 (1) |
| 23 Sat | F.A. Umbro Trophy 5 |
| 24 Sun | Worthington Cup Final |
| 26/27 Tue/Wed | UEFA Champions League – Group Stage 2 – Match Day 10 |
| 28 Thu | UEFA Cup 4 (2) |

## March 2002

| 2 Sat | F.A. Carlsberg Vase 6P |
| 3 Sun | F.A. Umbro Sunday Cup SF |
| 9 Sat | F.A. Cup sponsored by AXA 6P |
| | AXA F.A. Youth Cup SF* |
| | F.A. County Youth Cup SF* |
| 10 Sun | AXA F.A. Women's Cup 6P |

12/13 Tue/Wed  UEFA Champions
                League –
                Group Stage 2 – Match Day
                11
14 Thu         UEFA Cup QF (1)
16 Sat         F.A. Umbro Trophy 6
19/20 Tue/Wed  UEFA Champions
                League –
                Group Stage 2 – Match Day
                12
21 Thu         UEFA Cup QF (2)
23 Sat         F.A. Carlsberg Vase SF (1)
26/27 Tue/Wed  International Friendly
                dates
29 Fri         Good Friday
30 Sat         F.A. Carlsberg Vase SF (2)
                AXA F.A. Youth Cup
                SF (1)*
31 Sun         Easter Sunday

**April 2002**
 1 Mon         Easter Monday
 2/3 Tue/Wed   UEFA Champions
                League – QF (1)
 4 Thu         UEFA Cup SF (1)
 6 Sat         F.A. Umbro Trophy SF (1)
 7 Sun         AXA F.A. Women's Cup SF
 9/10 Tue/Wed  UEFA Champions
                League – QF (2)
11 Thu         UEFA Cup SF (2)
13 Sat         F.A. Umbro Trophy SF (2)
                AXA F.A. Youth Cup
                SF (2)*
14 Sun         F.A. Cup sponsored by AXA
                SF
16/17 Tue/Wed  International Friendly
                dates

20 Sat         Football League finishes
23/24 Tue/Wed  UEFA Champions
                League – SF (1)
27 Sat         AXA F.A. Youth Cup Final
28 Sun         Football League Play-Off
                SF (1)
30/1 Tue/Wed   UEFA Champions
                League – SF (2)

**May 2002**
 1 Wed         Football League Play-Off
                SF (2)
 2 Thu         AXA F.A. Youth Cup Final
                (1) - tbc
 4 Sat
 6 Mon         Bank Holiday
                AXA F.A. Women's Cup
                Final – tbc
 7 Tue         AXA F.A. Youth Cup Final
                (2) – tbc
 8 Wed         UEFA Cup Final
10-12 Fri/Sun  Football League Play-Off
                Finals
15 Wed         UEFA Champions League
                Final
31 Fri         World Cup 2002 commences

**June 2002**
30 Sun         World Cup 2002 Final

To be confirmed:
F.A. Cup sponsored by AXA Final
F.A. Umbro Trophy Final
F.A. Carlsberg Vase Final
F.A. Umbro Sunday Cup Final

* = Closing date of Round